Hunting Wildlife in the Tropics and Subtropics

The hunting of wild animals for their meat has been a crucial activity in the evolution of humans. It continues to be an essential source of food and a generator of income for millions of Indigenous and rural communities worldwide. Conservationists rightly fear that excessive hunting of many animal species will cause their demise, as has already happened throughout the Anthropocene. Many species of large mammals and birds have been decimated or annihilated due to overhunting by humans. If such pressures continue, many other species will meet the same fate. Equally, if the use of wildlife resources is to continue by those who depend on it, sustainable practices must be implemented. These communities need to remain or become custodians of the wildlife resources within their lands, for their own well-being as well as for biodiversity in general. This title is also available via Open Access on Cambridge Core.

JULIA E. FA is Professor of Biodiversity and Human Development at Manchester Metropolitan University and Senior Research Associate at the Center for International Forestry Research (CIFOR), Indonesia. Her research embraces ecology, anthropology and development issues. She leads projects in Europe, Africa and Latin America.

STEPHAN M. FUNK is a passionate scientist leading the consultancy Nature Heritage, Jersey, to conserve biodiversity and natural heritage for our sustainable future. He is Head of Earth Sciences at Lemu, Chile. After training in ecology, genetics and biology, and environmental management, he has worked and lived around the world.

ROBERT NASI is the Director General of the Center for International Forestry Research (CIFOR), Indonesia. He has lived and travelled extensively in Africa, Asia and the Pacific, undertaking research in ecology and management of tropical forests.

ECOLOGY, BIODIVERSITY AND CONSERVATION

The world's biological diversity faces unprecedented threats. The urgent challenge facing the concerned biologist is to understand ecological processes well enough to maintain their functioning in the face of the pressures resulting from human population growth. Those concerned with the conservation of biodiversity and with restoration also need to be acquainted with the political, social, historical, economic and legal frameworks within which ecological and conservation practice must be developed. The new Ecology, Biodiversity and Conservation series will present balanced, comprehensive, up-to-date and critical reviews of selected topics within the sciences of ecology and conservation biology, both botanical and zoological, and both 'pure' and 'applied'. It is aimed at advanced final-year undergraduates, graduate students, researchers and university teachers, as well as ecologists and conservationists in industry, government and the voluntary sectors. The series encompasses a wide range of approaches and scales (spatial, temporal and taxonomic), including quantitative, theoretical, population, community, ecosystem, landscape, historical, experimental, behavioural and evolutionary studies. The emphasis is on science related to the real world of plants and animals rather than on purely theoretical abstractions and mathematical models. Books in this series will, wherever possible, consider issues from a broad perspective. Some books will challenge existing paradigms and present new ecological concepts, empirical or theoretical models, and testable hypotheses. Other books will explore new approaches and present syntheses on topics of ecological importance.

Ecology and Control of Introduced Plants
Judith H. Myers and Dawn Bazely

Invertebrate Conservation and Agricultural Ecosystems
T. R. New

Risks and Decisions for Conservation and Environmental Management
Mark Burgman

Hunting Wildlife in the Tropics and Subtropics

JULIA E. FA

Manchester Metropolitan University and Center for International Forestry Research, Indonesia

STEPHAN M. FUNK

Nature Heritage, Jersey

ROBERT NASI

Center for International Forestry Research, Indonesia

 CAMBRIDGE
UNIVERSITY PRESS

CAMBRIDGE
UNIVERSITY PRESS

University Printing House, Cambridge CB2 8BS, United Kingdom

One Liberty Plaza, 20th Floor, New York, NY 10006, USA

477 Williamstown Road, Port Melbourne, VIC 3207, Australia

314–321, 3rd Floor, Plot 3, Splendor Forum, Jasola District Centre, New Delhi – 110025, India

103 Penang Road, #05-06/07, Visioncrest Commercial, Singapore 238467

Cambridge University Press is part of the University of Cambridge.
It furthers the University's mission by disseminating knowledge in the pursuit of
education, learning, and research at the highest international levels of excellence.

www.cambridge.org
Information on this title: www.cambridge.org/9781107117570
DOI: 10.1017/9781316338704

© Julia E. Fa, Stephan M. Funk and Robert Nasi 2022

First published 2022

A catalogue record for this publication is available from the British Library.

Library of Congress Cataloging-in-Publication Data
Names: Fa, Julia E., 1954– author. | Funk, Stephan M., author. | Nasi, Robert, author.
Title: Hunting wildlife in the tropics and subtropics / Julia E. Fa, Manchester Metropolitan University and
    Center for International Forestry (CIFOR), Indonesia, Stephan M. Funk, Nature Heritage, Robert
    Nasi, Center for International Forestry Research (CIFOR), Indonesia.
Description: First edition. | Cambridge, United Kingdom ; New York, NY : Cambridge University Press,
    2022. | Series: Ecology, biodiversity and conservation | Includes bibliographical references and index.
Identifiers: LCCN 2022022804 (print) | LCCN 2022022805 (ebook) | ISBN 9781107117570 (hardback)
    | ISBN 9781107540347 (paperback) | ISBN 9781316338704 (epub)
Subjects: LCSH: Wildlife as food. | Wildlife conservation. | Wildlife resources. | BISAC: NATURE /
    Ecology
Classification: LCC SF84.6 .F35 2022 (print) | LCC SF84.6 (ebook) | DDC 333.95/416–dc23/eng/
    20220625
LC record available at https://lccn.loc.gov/2022022804
LC ebook record available at https://lccn.loc.gov/2022022805

ISBN 978-1-107-11757-0 Hardback
ISBN 978-1-107-54034-7 Paperback

Contents

Foreword

In *The Savage Mind*, Claude Lévi-Strauss contrasts nature ('the diversity of species') and culture ('the diversity of functions'), and their symmetry involves 'the assimilation of natural species on the cultural plane'. Much of that assimilation involves the hunting of wild animals. Hunting can be seen as mediating the relationship between nature and culture, both in traditional and in modern cultures, and it is not surprising that the topic of hunting attracts both attention and passion.

This book is about 'how' people hunt, but assumptions about 'why' we hunt influence the arguments about how to manage the way we hunt. For some people, hunting symbolizes the inhumanity of humans to the natural world. Hunting results in defaunation and the loss of bio-diversity, and it should be controlled. For others, hunting defines the relationship of people with their environment. Perhaps especially in the case of Indigenous and pre-industrial cultures, hunting seeks to establish an equilibrium, pushing back against the wilderness, assimilating nature and defining culture. In this case, hunting almost defines who we are. For some people, hunting can be seen as a necessity, allowing people to use wildlife resources for their sustenance and betterment. For still others, hunting is a right, and the wildlife species are theirs to harvest: hunting defines the self-sufficiency of rural populations. For these people, hunting should be protected and respected. Of course, hunting can be any or all of the above, but each informs different approaches to the way hunting could be managed in today's world.

It is this challenge to understand how to manage hunting that Julia E. Fa, Stephan M. Funk and Robert Nasi take on in this volume. The focus is on meat hunting for human consumption, which links the argument back into our prehistory and indeed to the very definition of what it means to be human. Raymond Dart in his descriptions of *Australopithecus africanus* in the 1920s argued that these hominids, some 3 million years ago, were hunters, and though the argument has gone back and forth, hunting and humanity were forever joined. Today, while few groups depend exclusively on wild meat, it remains a major source of protein and income to some 154 million households across Central and South America, sub-Saharan Africa, China, Southeast Asia and Indochina. Rural consumption of wild meat is an important part of household food and nutritional security. The trade is a source of rural income and feeds consumption in towns and cities.

The reason for worrying about how to manage hunting is that many species in many parts of the world are overexploited, leading to local extirpation and even extinction. A lot has changed through the course of human history. There are many more of us, and Julia Fa and her colleagues, focusing on the tropics and subtropics, exploring how population density, plus changes in hunting technology and group mobility, have influenced hunting pressure. In the transition to agriculture and urbanization, human diets have shifted onto farmed foods, but that has had concomitant effects on the extent of natural ecosystems and their resident wild species. In the remaining areas, hunting can be intense.

Hunting for food has been blamed for declines and loss of wild populations. Going back into prehistory, the extinction of large-bodied mammals and birds in the late Pleistocene was correlated with the arrival of humans in different parts of the world: to some, *prima facie* evidence of the impact of hunting. The higher extinction rates today as compared to background are blamed in part on hunting. Many studies have tracked the effect of hunting on wild populations: Numbers go down, the demographics of mortality and fecundity shift, population structure changes and populations can be extirpated or cease to function ecologically. Defaunation, a generalized loss of large-bodied animals in otherwise intact ecosystems, is a phenomenon of many hunted areas often described as 'the empty forest'.

On the other hand, wild meat is a vital resource for millions of people around the world. Especially in forested parts of the tropics, many rural people have little access to other sources of animal protein. In previous work, Julia Fa documented the staggering dependence of people on meat from wild species in the tropics. In the Congo basin, for example, the harvest of wild meat exceeds 2 million metric tonnes a year, equivalent to tens of millions of individual animals. Rural consumption of wild meat is an important part of household food and nutritional security, as well as providing an indispensable income stream for the rural poor as much of the meat is sold in town and city markets.

It is this tension between a limited and dwindling supply of wild populations and the constant demand for wild meat that provided the imperative to understand when and where hunting is sustainable. The twists and turns of the narrative around sustainability are explored in thoughtful detail by Julia Fa and her colleagues. Some of the original work in the field of hunting sustainability was done by anthropologists working with hunter-gatherer societies. The very existence over the long term of such societies that hunted for their food, and the integrity of the faunal communities where they lived, seemed to provide an argument that their hunting was sustainable. Cultural constraints such as food or hunting taboos seemed to provide the mechanisms for such societies to act to avoid overhunting. The phrase 'ecologically noble savage', coined by Kent Redford, raised the question of whether that was indeed the case, or whether the apparent long-term equilibrium of these traditional societies was an epiphenomenon resulting from a human population not involved in a market economy, living in the forest at low densities and able to move when wildlife resources were depleted. In an elegant set of studies, anthropologists examined the question by asking whether these traditional hunters were 'optimal foragers' – pragmatically harvesting the most from the forest that they could, as opposed to being 'natural conservationists' or 'prudent predators'. The answer was unequivocally that they were the former.

This understanding shifted the whole inquiry to one of seeking the ecological, social and economic conditions that promoted hunting sustainability. This volume provides a wonderfully complete examination of these questions. How does the production of meat from wild species vary with rainfall and primary productivity? How does harvest shift as wildlife populations are diminished? Does hunting technology, from traditional to modern firearms, influence harvest rates? How does poverty and proximity to wild areas influence the decision on where and how to hunt? How do hunters decide what to consume and what to sell? What influences markets for wild meat in urban settings?

Central to this endeavour was the need to measure sustainability, and this volume reviews the ebb and flow of arguments on sustainability metrics. The fundamental question is what is the balance between production and harvest. The challenge is always the paucity of information on characteristics of hunters and especially hunted populations. As metrics improved, the argument shifted from 'assessing' sustainability to 'achieving' it. Robert Nasi and his colleagues have led much of this transitional thinking, and the story of these efforts is compelling. Achieving sustainability increasingly sought to ensure that use of wild species was both equitable and ecologically sustainable, while respecting the rights of people depending on the resource.

Achieving sustainability of hunting thus often required devolving the authority and responsibility to local communities, strengthening wildlife management and governance while restricting the access of outsiders. At the same time, efforts to promulgate national laws and regulations governing the sale of wild meat were developed (though often not enforced). Without both stronger management and an appropriate legal framework, the increased commercialization of wild meat for urban markets might create a demand which could swamp out the sustenance and economic needs of rural people, and ravage the biodiversity on which they depend.

There is of course another reason to manage hunting and the trade of wild meat for human consumption. COVID-19 has emphasized the importance of newly emerging zoonotic diseases to the human condition. Julia Fa and her colleagues build a case that establishes how hunters and the wildlife trade are primary contributors to the emergence of zoonotic diseases. The transmission of such diseases is brought about by the direct contact of people and animals, and of recent zoonoses, the great majority originate in wildlife. In tropical ecosystems, especially when fragmented and degraded, hunters are often the first to make that contact, and they are vectors for viral spillovers that result. The wildlife trade disperses wild meat into increasingly larger and more urban markets where viral transmission to other species and to humans is enhanced.

COVID-19 and other zoonoses provide a new challenge to our uncertain relationship with nature, and Julia Fa and her co-authors thoughtfully navigate what this means for the management of hunting and trade. They note that calls for blanket bans on the sale and consumption of wild meat would penalize the rural people who depend on the trade for entrance into the cash economy. Perhaps enforcing existing laws, and halting the sale of wild species for human consumption in urban markets catering to cosmopolitan elites would be more efficacious. But what is clear throughout this book is that hunting defines how we relate to nature, and we are still learning how nature will respond.

John G. Robinson, PhD
Joan L. Tweedy Chair in Conservation Strategy
Wildlife Conservation Society
New York, USA

Preface

There is no doubt that the hunting of wild animals for their meat has been a crucial activity that has transformed the evolution of humans, and it continues to be an essential source of protein and a generator of income for millions of Indigenous and rural communities in tropical and subtropical regions worldwide. Conservationists fear that excessive hunting of many animal species, particularly large-bodied ones, will cause further demise, as already witnessed throughout the Anthropocene. Many species of large mammals and birds have already been decimated or completely annihilated by humans overhunting them. If such pressures continue, many other species, even smaller-bodied ones, will meet the same fate. Equally, if the use of wildlife resources by those who most need them (i.e., the poor) is to continue, sustainable practices must clearly be implemented. More importantly, these communities must be enabled to become, or to remain, the custodians and managers of the wildlife resources within their lands, for themselves as well as for bio-diversity in general. However, greater wildlife offtakes are now facilitated by the increased penetration of new lands by infrastructure, logging, mining and agriculture but also impacted by the emergence of new hunting technologies and by consumers in fast-growing urban centres demanding wild meat as a luxury item. More recently, the effects of zoonotic diseases linked to wild meat, including COVID-19, SARS and Ebola, have had devastating consequences on human health and econ-omies worldwide and are likely to be a persistent threat to wildlife and its users in the future.

All available evidence points to the importance of hunting and use of wild animals for their meat by humans worldwide, and to the ways that overhunting (alongside habitat fragmentation) will impact future habitat composition and the provision of ecosystem services such as carbon storage. Our aim in this book is to present an up-to-date review of the vast amount of literature that has been published since the early 1980s. We focus on themes ranging from why humans hunt wildlife and who are the hunters, to what humans hunt and how they hunt, to the extent of hunting in different environments and how uncontrolled hunting can affect wild animal populations and the food security of those people who depend on wild meat. We also focus on how hunters make decisions to hunt their prey and on the thorniest issue – how do we measure hunting sustainability. However, although this is not a book to guide policy actions or teach us how to improve wild meat governance and management, because there are a good number of documents that deal with these more applied issues, we only touch upon this topic in our concluding chapter.

This volume is divided into three distinct themes. The first part includes two introductory chapters that outline the topic at hand as well as the environmental background where hunting of wildlife takes place in the tropics and subtropics. The second part collates information on the hunting process itself. We start by reviewing how human hunters hunt and examine the variety of techniques used in the past and present to take animals (Chapter 3). We show this not just as a record of how animals are taken by people but also as a testament to the ingenuity and resourcefulness that human beings have developed to feed themselves. This is followed by two chapters, the first explaining what we know about how hunters go about making decisions on how and what to hunt (Chapter 4), and a second that explores how we define hunting sustainability (Chapter 5). The third part of the book contains three chapters about the threats and drivers affecting wild meat use. A first chapter summarizes our understanding of how wild meat is consumed and hunted but more importantly what we know of the spatial and temporal impact of overexploitation of wildlife (Chapter 6). Here we also define defaunation and the consequences on prey populations and ecosystems. The following chapter deals with the currently topical matter of the variety of diseases in humans that can be or are linked to wild animals, especially when these are butchered and consumed by human beings (Chapter 7). We end the book with our thoughts on how we can bridge the gap between science and action (Chapter 8) and suggest ways of achieving this.

We want our book to be seen as a 'go-to' reference work that arguably presents the most extensive compilation of current knowledge on wild meat biology in one single volume. Despite the fact that we have placed our emphasis on examples from the tropics and subtropics, all or most of the subjects we deal with are generic in that they apply to other environments. They relate as much to hunting in the Arctic as they do to any environment around the world where hunting for food is still practised.

We have written this book with the student in mind, but it is meant to reach a wide audience, requiring no university science to understand it. The book should guide any reader by providing the basics required to understand all topics involved, by providing the elementary learning blocks for the uninitiated and a bolster to those with some background. Our wish is that this book can also be a source of inspiration for those wanting to work towards mitigating the threat of unsustainable use of natural resources. As John Robinson and Elizabeth Bennett alluded to, in their seminal book, *Hunting for Sustainability in Tropical Forests,* now over two decades ago, our quest for sustainability is like the allegory to pursuing the absolute in Lewis Carroll's nonsense poem 'Hunting of the Snark', an elusive enterprise undertaken by a motley crew. We hope that through hard work and the good application of science, but always linked to an understanding of those communities that still rely on wildlife for food, this volume can inspire many to help come up with ways of ensuring a positive future for wildlife and people. Time is running out!!

Acknowledgements

This work is based on our many years of experience in the field working in a variety of human and natural environments and learning from these. Our work has been motivated also by our concern for the countless number of peoples we have met and worked with all over the world, Indigenous and rural, who are still trying to survive on a planet where resources are rapidly shrinking. We thank them all. We are also grateful to the many colleagues who have inspired us in our journey in understanding such a complicated and complex issue as wildlife exploitation. In particular, we need to mention our friends and colleagues John Robinson, Liz Bennett, David Wilkie, David Brown, Carlos Peres, E.J. Milner-Gulland, Guy Cowlishaw, Marcus Rowcliffe, Nathalie Van Vliet and Lauren Coad, for teaching us and challenging us. We would also like to thank our many colleagues from the Sustainable Wildlife Management Programme who are working on 'Closing the Gap' (Chapter 8) at project sites in Africa, Asia and the Pacific. Many collaborators across numerous organizations have motivated us and bettered our thinking over the years, we thank them all.

We are especially grateful to Michael Usher for his constant and wholehearted steer. Michael read and commented on all earlier drafts of the chapters. We also greatly appreciate the support and guidance of Dominic Lewis, Aleksandra Serocka, Jenny van der Meijden and Vicky Harley from CUP for smoothly enabling the process of turning manuscript into book. To Nikki Tagg, Sophie Von Dobschuetz, E.J. Milner-Gulland, Michael Alvard, Edmund Dounias, Daniel Ingram and Glyn Young we are thankful for taking the time to read all or separate chapters. Their insights, comments and positive criticism have improved the final manuscript incalculably. All views expressed in this book are entirely our own.

Finally, we would like to acknowledge the financial support from CGIAR Fund, USAID and European Commission. This book is part of the Bushmeat Research Initiative of the CGIAR research program on Forests, Trees and Agroforestry.

Abbreviations

ACTO	Amazon Cooperation Treaty Organization
AIDS	acquired immunodeficiency syndrome
AMH	anatomically modern humans
ASEAN	Association of Southeast Asian Nations
ASEANAPOL	ASEAN National Police Network
ASEAN-WEN	ASEAN-Wildlife Enforcement Network
AU	African Union
BCE	before the common or current era
BP	before present
CAR	Central African Republic
CBD	Convention on Biological Diversity
CCAD	Central American Commission for the Environment and Development
CECNA	Commission for Environmental Cooperation of North America
CIR	change-in-ratio
CITES	Convention on International Trade in Endangered Species of Wild Fauna and Flora
CJD	Creutzfeldt–Jakob disease
CMS	Convention on Migratory Species, also known as the Bonn Convention
COMIFAC	Commission on Forests of Central Africa
CoV	coronavirus
COVID-19	coronavirus disease of 2019
CPHD	catch per hunter per day
CPUE	catch per unit effort
CR	critically endangered (red list category)
DGI	Directorate-General for International Cooperation
DI	defaunation index
DRC	Democratic Republic of Congo

DRI	dietary reference intake
EBFM	ecosystem-based fisheries management
EBM	ecosystem-based management
ECOWAS	Economic Community of West African States
EN	endangered (red list category)
EU	European Union
EVD	Ebola virus disease
FAO	Food and Agriculture Organization of the United Nations
FCM	fuzzy-logic cognitive mapping
GDI	index of game depletion
GENuS	global expanded nutrient supply database
GIZ	German Development Cooperation
GSF	Guiana Shield Facility
HBV	hepatitis B virus
HCV	hepatitis C virus
HEV	hepatitis E virus
HF	human footprint
HIV	human immunodeficiency virus
HTLV	human T-lymphotropic virus
ICCWC	International Consortium on Combating Wildlife Crime
IEA	integrated ecosystem assessment
IF	intact forest
IUCN	International Union for Conservation of Nature
LDG	latitudinal diversity gradient
LFI	large fish indicator
LPI	living planet index
MARV	Marburg virus
MBMI	mean body mass indicator
MERS	Middle East respiratory syndrome
MEY	maximum economic yield
MHR	maximum sustainable harvest rate
MSY	maximum sustainable yield
MVT	marginal value theorem
NAFTA	North American Free Trade Agreement
NCT	niche construction theory
NOAA	United States' National Oceanic and Atmospheric Administration

NPE	Brazil's federal monitoring agency
NPP	net primary productivity
NTFP	non-timber forest product
OFT	optimal foraging theory
OIE	World Animal Health Organization
OPI	offtake pressure indicator
PBR	potential biological removal index
PRA	Amazon Regional Program
PVA	population viability analysis
SADC	Southern African Development Community
SARS	severe acute respiratory syndrome
SAWEN	South Asian Wildlife Enforcement Network
SBSTTA	Subsidiary Body on Scientific, Technical and Technological Advice to the Convention on Biological Diversity
SFV	simian foamy virus
SIV	simian immunodeficiency virus
TB	bovine tuberculosis
TCA	Treaty for Amazonian Cooperation
UNEP	United Nations Environment Programme
UNU	United Nations University
USAN	Union of South American Nations
VU	vulnerable (red list category)
WCS	Wildlife Conservation Society
WHO	World Health Organization of the United Nations

1 · *Eating Wild Animals*

1.1 Introduction

Wild animals, plants and their products are harvested for purposes ranging from food to medicine. Humans have exploited wild animals and plants throughout their evolution (Hill 1982) and contemporary aboriginal and rural peoples still rely on them for their daily needs (Wilkie *et al.* 2005). The meat of wild animals or wild meat (see Box 1.1) is still a crucial part of the staple diet of millions of families in the tropics and subtropics since it is often the most available and widely used source of animal protein (Abernethy *et al.* 2013; Fa *et al.* 2003), and is also important for its micronutrient content (Golden *et al.* 2011; Sarti *et al.* 2015; Sirén & Machoa 2008). Wild meat is central to the livelihood strategies of the poor since it can constitute a significant source of revenue, especially for rural families (Brown & Williams 2003; Milner-Gulland & Bennett 2003). It is also consumed regularly by urban peoples more as a commodity product than as a necessity.

In this book, we use the Coad *et al.* (2019) definition of wild meat as any non-domesticated terrestrial mammals, birds, reptiles and amphibians harvested for food. We concentrate on the consumption and trade of wild animals as food and the implications of these activities on the fauna in the region of the globe found within a band on either side of the equator from 23.5°N, and 23.5°S; the Tropic of Cancer and the Tropic of Capricorn, respectively. This portion of the world known more generally as the tropics is important in not just harbouring most of the Earth's biodiversity but also millions of peoples who still depend on wild animals for their food security and livelihoods. A more detailed description of the extent and characteristics of the tropics and subtropics are given in Chapter 2.

Although other animals comprise important dietary items in the tropics and subtropics, in this book we focus only on vertebrates because they constitute most of the terrestrial wild animal biomass consumed by

Box 1.1 *What is wild meat?*

For some time, the term bushmeat was used as a catchall phrase for the meat of wild animals. The term, which originated in Africa, referred to the meat from animals found in forests and savannas; these habitats are commonly referred to as 'bush', hence the name bushmeat. The expression is assumed to have originated in British colonial times but may pre-date this era. The native catechist, T. C. Brownell, in south-east Liberia, mentioned he was offered on 29 March 1857 something to eat by the head-man of the interior village of Nyambo 'which he called bush meat, but it had such a human aspect that I laid it aside, and awaited the repast which was preparing' (quoted in Scott 1858, p. 295). Liberia was the first African republic to proclaim its independence in 1822.

Nasi *et al.* (2008) defined bushmeat as any 'non-domesticated terrestrial mammals, birds, reptiles and amphibians harvested for food''. Insects, crustaceans, grubs, molluscs and fish are excluded from this classification. But, although the term has been employed to refer to the meat of wild animals from regions other than Africa, there has been a recent move towards using the more generic term 'wild meat', since it has no geographical associations. Thus, following its adoption by the IUCN-World Conservation Union General Assembly Resolution 2.64 (IUCN World Conservation Congress 2000), Coad *et al.* (2019) use the term wild meat as terrestrial animals used for food in all parts of the world. However, the Convention on Biological Diversity 's (CBD) (2012) description of wild meat hunting as 'the harvesting of wild animals in tropical and subtropical countries for food and for non-food purposes, including for medicinal use' is imprecise since wild meat is only one of the products derived from the hunting of wild animals anywhere in the world.

humans in these regions. Mammals make up the largest proportion of all animals eaten and traded, both in terms of weight (biomass) and numbers. The cultural preference for wild meat is not due to a lack of awareness or entrepreneurship but ultimately relates to the low productivity of domestic livestock in many tropical and even subtropical conditions. For poor farmers in tropical environments, as seen in the Brazilian Amazon (Carvalho *et al.* 2020), raising livestock for their meat has high risks and investment costs, making successful livestock husbandry rarely a feasible option. In situations where livestock can be kept, such as the ever-present domestic chicken, these animals are often more a form of reserve banking, or to satisfy cultural needs. In contrast, wild meat is a resource that is freely available for use, so the cost of its procurement is always lower than the cost of raising livestock. However, in recent decades the exploitation of wild animals for their meat has moved from just being a source of food and income for rural communities or Indigenous Peoples, to a commodity exploited for profit-making reasons by supplying the urban areas. Such increase in demand for wild meat has been brought about by accelerating population growth, use of more modern and efficient hunting techniques, and opening of remote areas to commercial hunters by extractive industries. As will be documented in detail in this book, there is an accumulation of evidence that this is seriously threatening wild animal populations and human food security in many areas.

For the millions of Indigenous and non-Indigenous communities in tropical and subtropical environments, often among the world's rural poor, wild meat is frequently the most consumed source of protein, vitamins and minerals (Van Vliet et al. 2017). Wild animal meat can also be traded by and between rural communities and transported beyond its point of extraction. Because of its value-to-weight ratio and great transportability if smoked, the wild meat trade has risen dramatically, fuelling in some cases unsustainable extraction rates (Chapter 6) as shown for West and Central African countries (Fa et al. 2003; Fa & Peres 2001). Commercial hunting for wild meat has grown in importance in recent decades (see Section 1.7), with increasing numbers of hunters currently either earning or supplementing their incomes with the sale of meat (Milner-Gulland & Bennett 2003). This intensifies hunting levels and reduces the sustainability of numerous wildlife species, largely because it enlarges the population density of consumers eating meat from a given habitat area (cf. Bennett & Robinson 2000). Hunting of wildlife is still the single most geographically widespread form of resource extraction in the tropics (Fa et al. 2002, 2005; Milner-Gulland & Bennett 2003).

Hunting refers to the act of pursuing and taking wild animals by several means and for different purposes. Wildlife can be hunted for food, trophies (most often skins, teeth, antlers and horns), medicines and other traditional uses (most hard and soft body parts) and as pets (especially primates, birds and reptiles). Hunting occurs in a variety of habitats worldwide (Nasi et al. 2008). Vulnerability of hunted species varies according to their biological characteristics and the state of the habitats they are found in. Coupled with threats from habitat loss (Laurance *et al.* 2006; Wright & Muller-Landau 2006), overhunting can result in the extinction of species, especially of larger-bodied species of mammals and birds that have a naturally low intrinsic rate of population increase (see Chapter 5 & 6). This process, referred to as defaunation (Chapter 2; Dirzo *et al.* 2014) is an anthropogenically driven cause of species and population extirpations and, critically, of declines in local species abundance of seed dispersers and 'habitat landscapers' such as in tropical forests. This changes the long-term dynamics and structure of these ecosystems and ecosystem services (Chapter 6).

As we show in Chapter 2, tropical and subtropical landscapes are heterogeneous, containing diverse animal and plant species that make up a variety of wildlife communities that differ in their dynamics, including contrasting human pressures. Important intercontinental differences exist between tropical and subtropical areas worldwide, but there are significant contrasts in how the faunas in each continent have been affected by unsustainable hunting. In Asian tropical forests, already more than 12 large vertebrate species are known to have become extinct in countries such as Vietnam (Bennett & Rao 2002). The problem is perceived to be presently more acute in the heartlands of West and Central Africa, but progressively worsening even in the remotest parts of Latin America (Peres 2001). Such dissimilar trajectories in actual and potential faunal loss between continents follow the major impacts of development and forest loss, essentially linked to human population growth that drive agricultural expansion, logging, development and other human activities. The situation in Asia is also unlike other continents, because of the reliance on large-scale wildlife trade involving long-distance, international supply chains (Duckworth *et al.* 2012). Demand for land, timber and non-timber forest resources has exploded throughout Asia as a result of rapid economic growth (Bennett & Rao 2002). The region is a key supplier to the international wildlife market, both legal and illegal. Despite there being intercontinental dissimilarities, at a global scale there is now sufficient evidence to highlight that the plight of many species, in particular mammals, is primarily due to overhunting (see Ripple *et al.* 2016 p. 20016). We discuss the impact of unsustainable hunting in Chapters 2 and more in detail in Chapter 6 in this book.

We begin this introductory chapter with a description of the importance of hunting and meat eating to humans and how this has influenced the evolution of the species. This is followed by a brief review of how prevailing ecological conditions influence dependence on plants or animals to survive at different latitudes. We then document which animal species and groups are currently hunted and used for food, discuss the issue of wild meat markets especially in Africa and present our current understanding of wild meat consumption by diverse groups of people in different parts of the world. The chapter ends with the reasons for writing this book and explains how we can use the accumulated knowledge on this subject to help reduce wild meat exploitation and ways of balancing human and wildlife needs in the future.

1.2 Meat Eating and Hunting in Human Evolution

Similar to modern chimpanzees, the earliest hominins consumed large quantities of fruit, leaves, flowers, bark, insects and some meat (Watts 2008). By at least 2.6 million years ago (YA), a remarkable expansion in this diet occurred; some hominins began incorporating meat and marrow from small to very large animals into their diet. Arguably, it was not until at least one million YA that hominids actively hunted animals for food (Potts 1996; Walker & Shipman 1996). Eating meat from hunted animals or from carcasses provides more calories per unit of search time than the collection of plant products (Hill 1982). Carrion is thought to have been an early source of high-quality protein for hominids (Binford 1981; Blumenschine *et al.* 1987), who may have lacked appropriate technology to capture vertebrate prey. However, populations of chimpanzees and baboons are known to hunt cooperatively (Stanford & Wrangham 1998). This suggests that hominids may also have been social hunters who shared the obtained prey, in addition to actively stealing carcasses, as do other carnivores.

Human hunters have followed a complex evolutionary process. Bipedalism provided greater autonomy for the search and transport of food. The development of intelligence favoured in the first instance the theft of carcasses from other predators, the formation of groups that operated in a coordinated manner to access larger prey, the sequential development of tools to work the carcasses and weapons to defend and hunt, and the establishment of rules for an equitable distribution of the obtained meat (Stanford 2001). Competition with other carnivores could have induced the observed increase in body size of primitive hunters (Arsuaga *et al.* 2014), strategic cooperation, diurnal habits, rapid manipulation of prey and selective capture of smaller ones, in parallel with the progressive expansion of the neocortex and the improvement of cognitive skills and intragroup communication (Pearce *et al.* 2013; Van Valkenburgh 2001).

The conversion of primitive opportunistic hunters into systematic predators could have taken place in a scenario where optimal prey was abundant and predictable, the availability of other food was scarce or unpredictable and would have led to catches providing meat in surplus to the needs of the hunters (Rose 2001). Such a change would have required the possession of certain intellectual capacities to make decisions, develop cooperative strategies, and to manufacture and manage tools for capturing and processing game (Pearce *et al.* 2013), separating them from other primates (Hill 1982).

Cooperative hunting represents a stable evolutionary strategy from the moment Palaeolithic hunters became specialized in the pursuit of large animals (Boesch 1994) – those whose systematic capture is difficult to imagine without adequate technology and social organization (Hill & Hawkes 1983; Stiner 1994). As a consequence, this success gave rise to the adequate capture and processing of carcasses, and the selective transport and distribution of the most desirable parts before being consumed. All this process implies the adoption of decisions related to the management of prey species as can be verified from the fossil record and, with appropriate reservations, inferred from the behaviour observed in current hunter–gatherers.

Beginning around 10,000 BP however, the shift from hunting and gathering to domesticated food sources, both animal and plant, resulted in a narrowing of the diet (Larsen 2003). The consequences of this diet shift, from evidence from archaeological human remains worldwide, was a decline in health, including poorer dental health, increased occlusal abnormalities, increased iron deficiency anaemia, increased infection and bone loss (Larsen 2003). New dietary pressures introduced since the Industrial Revolution some 200 years ago have been the result of people's diets changing far more quickly than genetic adaptation is able to keep up with this change (Eaton *et al.* 1997). This discordance hypothesis postulated by Eaton *et al.* (1997) has been suggested to explain many of the chronic 'diseases of civilization'. Modern trends in human nutrition, especially after the Second World War, indicate a greater reliance on high-fat meats that, when eaten in excess, promote cardiovascular disease, especially in combination with the more sedentary lifestyles typical of many modern societies.

1.3 Importance of Wild Animal Foods in Human Diets

The relative importance of wild meat and plant consumption patterns can be determined from information obtained from modern-day hunter-gatherer societies (Box 1.2). The emerging patterns reflect regional and ecological specializations that in some groups probably date back to the late Pleistocene Epoch. Data on what types of food are eaten, and the importance of wild meat in particular, result from research conducted within a wide variety of disciplines. While most dietary data collected are behavioural and quantitative, human biological samples (e.g. urine, stool, saliva, serum, blood, dental calculus and hair) allow further insights into the physiological parameters of various modes of human subsistence (e.g. Gurven *et al.* 2016; Leonard *et al.* 2015; Pontzer *et al.* 2012).

Few hunter-gatherer or forager societies exist today, but many are well documented in the ethnographic record. Forager studies have become more popular over the last several decades, being of particular interest to evolutionary, sociological, demographic and human health science studies, as populations increasingly transition into a wage economy (Headland & Blood 2002). Earlier research on these groups was undertaken by anthropologists who assumed that the modern forager existence was a good analogue of the lifestyle that endured everywhere before 10,000 BP. However, one of the greatest obstacles to using foragers as analogues of our ancient ancestors is that virtually all foragers in the ethnographic record have complex technology compared to premodern hominins (Marlowe 2005). Moreover, as Lee and DeVore (1968) suggest, the foragers described may be a biased sample that have persisted because they occupied marginal habitats less coveted by agricultural people, although this contention has later been refuted. Using global remote sensing data to estimate habitat productivity for a representative sample of societies worldwide Porter and Marlowe (2007) showed that foraging societies do not inhabit significantly more marginal habitats than agriculturalists. Nevertheless, forager societies have not remained static, and many have changed their habits and diets because of their association with more food productive agricultural societies. This is clearly the case for some Pygmy communities in the Congo Basin (Dounias & Froment 2011).

Overview papers detailing contemporary hunter-gatherer diets have emerged as comprehensive and definitive sources of information on forager diets (Binford 2002; Cordain *et al.* 2000; Marlowe 2005). An important source of calculations of dietary patterns of surviving hunter-gatherer societies have resulted from George P. Murdock's Ethnographic

Box 1.2 *Hunter-gatherers*

The earliest definition of a 'forager' or 'hunter-gatherer' by Woodburn (1980) is entirely based on their subsistence mode, describing them as members of societies that obtain their food and other requirements directly from the wild. We use both terms interchangeably in this book. Others elaborated the definition as those peoples who specifically collect wild plant foods and game animals with 'no deliberate alteration of the gene pool of exploited species' (Panter-Brick *et al.* 2001). This definition is difficult to apply to all of the food consumed by a given population.

In the 1960s, based on diet alone, foraging populations worldwide (as those who consumed 100% of their diet from wild foods) were considered to account for less than 0.001% of the world's population (Lee & DeVore 1968). By the mid-1990s, since few of the remaining hunting and gathering groups depended on an entirely wild diet, a population of foragers was redefined as one that ate approximately 10–15% of domesticated foods (Kelly 1995). Presently, if the criterion that foraging populations must consume a diet of more than 90% wild foods is used, no population would meet the designation (Apicella & Crittenden 2015). Therefore, in the twenty-first century, almost all forager populations consume a mixed diet that includes varying degrees of farmed foods, wild foods, and in some cases nutritional subsidies from governments and aid organizations (Headland & Blood 2002).

Importantly though, hunter-gatherers have also been classified as peoples exhibiting unique social lives, which includes a degree of mobility, group size and/or kinship systems that impact of the use and sharing of resources (Lee 1992). Thus, depending on the environments inhabited in line with their social systems, foragers have been classified as 'generalized' or 'immediate return' *versus* 'complex' or 'delayed return.' Immediate return foragers consume their yield shortly after procurement and delayed return foragers store their food for varying lengths of time (Price & Brown 1985; Woodburn 1998).

Ecological factors that shape human population processes determine the distribution and abundance of hunter-gatherers worldwide. Using global ethnographic hunter-gatherer data from Binford (2001), Tallavaara *et al.* (2018) explored the effects of key environmental variables (net primary productivity, biodiversity and pathogen stress) on hunter-gatherer population densities. Primary and secondary productivity were shown, at least regionally, to have positive effects on hunter-gatherer population density as well as on population home ranges. Hunter-gatherers access food directly from their surroundings (which can vary widely in energy availability) and thus depend on the productivity of wild plant and animal species, where they appropriate only a small fraction of the production. Additionally, biodiversity was shown to play an important role since it influences ecosystem stability – higher biodiversity is linked to temporal stability of aggregate ecosystem properties, such as biomass and productivity. For hunter-gatherers, increased stability of ecosystem-level biomass production decreases subsistence-related risk, and therefore positively affects hunter-gatherer population densities. In contrast, the effects of pathogens on hunter-gatherer abundance are, as expected, negative. Tallavaara *et al.* (2018) conclude that subtropical and temperate forest biomes in particular, rather than tropical forests, have the highest carrying capacity potential for hunter-gatherer populations as a result of the balance between disease risk and habitat productivity. These findings document that environmental factors play a key role in shaping global population density patterns of pre-agricultural humans.

Atlas; a database on 1,167 societies coded and published in 29 successive instalments in the journal *Ethnology*, 1962–1980. While valuable, some critics (e.g. Milton 2000) suggest that because the data used in these compilations are non-standardized tabulations from ethnically and geographically widespread human populations, this limits finer-scale comparisons. Despite several limitations, data contained in reviews such as Cordain *et al.* (2000) are a valuable entry point for discussion of variation among foragers from different latitudinal living environments. Listed populations are categorized by the percentage of their subsistence dependence on various categories of foods (i.e., wild plant foods and wild meat) even though no consistent unit of measurement has been used for each instance of data collection, as explicitly acknowledged by Cordain *et al.* (2000).

As expected, the composition of the human diet is extrinsically conditioned by biogeographical and ecological factors. The majority of hunter-gatherer societies, as used in Cordain *et al.* (2000), obtained 56–65% of their subsistence (energy) from animal foods (Fig. 1.1a), and predicted macronutrient energy intake ranges were carbohydrate

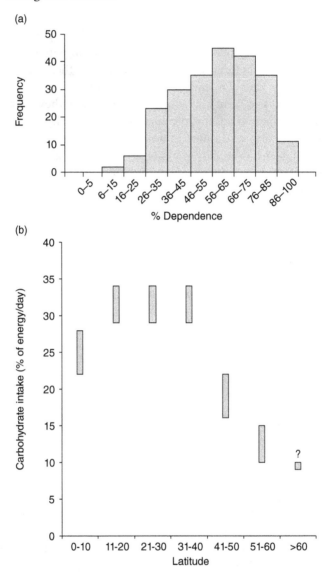

Figure 1.1 (a) Frequency distribution of subsistence dependence upon total (fished and hunted) animal foods in worldwide hunter-gatherer societies (*n* = 229). Frequency indicates the number of societies at that percentage dependence on animal foods. Median = 56–65%, mode = 56–65% (data from Cordain et al. 2000; figure adapted from Mann 2007 with permission from John Wiley & Sons). (b) Effects of latitude on carbohydrate intake (% of energy) for 229 hunter-gatherer diets shown as the minimum and maxiimum percentage recorded for each latitude intervals; maximum values were not available for >60 latitude (redrawn from data in Ströhle & Hahn 2011).

22–40%, protein 19–35% and fat 28–47% (Mann 2007). Because humans target different prey species depending on latitude and habitat type Marlowe (2005) suggests, from a trophic point of view, that they resemble different species more than conspecific populations. This adaptation of the diet to the regional and local availability is typical of predatory species that have a wide geographical distribution. As a corollary, plant-to-animal subsistence ratios vary significantly by latitude in response to differences in available primary productivity and biodiversity. Estimates of carbohydrate intake as a percentage of the total energy in 229 hunter-gatherer diets throughout the world vary from approx. 3% to 50% (Ströhle & Hahn 2011). Over a wide range of latitude intervals (11°–40° north or south of the equator) carbohydrate intake remains similar (30–35%) but decreases markedly from around 20% to 9% or less of the total energy with increasing latitude intervals from 41° to greater than 60° (Fig. 1.1b). Hunter-gatherers living in desert and tropical grasslands consumed the most carbohydrates (approx. 29–34% of the total energy). Diets of hunter-gatherers living in northern areas (tundra and northern coniferous forest) contained a very low carbohydrate content ($\leq$15% of the total energy) where hunting and fishing predominate over the collection of plant products (Mussi 2007; Ströhle & Hahn 2011). Hunter-gatherers in higher latitudes, where plant growth is greatly curtailed, have adapted to living largely or entirely on raw animal matter, both meat and fat. As shown for the Indigenous Peoples in Greenland, the Inuit, genetic and physiological adaptations to a diet rich in polyunsaturated fatty acids are clearly reflected in their genome (Fumagalli et al. 2015).

1.4 Species Hunted for Wild Meat

Animals as small as caterpillars and land snails to the largest land mammal, the elephant, are consumed throughout the tropics and subtropics (Fig. 1.2). According to Redmond et al. (2006), a total of 2,000 different animals are hunted for wild meat across the world. Of these, as many as 55% are terrestrial vertebrates (amphibians, reptiles, birds, mammals), of which 638 species are hunted in the world's tropical and subtropical regions (Table 1.1). Almost 50% of all vertebrates used for wild meat are mammals, followed by birds (34.8%), then reptiles (13.8%) and amphibians (5.6%). The distribution of the different taxonomic groups by region reflects the biogeographic idiosyncrasies of each area of the world (Table 1.1). For example, because Oceania is composed primarily of

Figure 1.2 Examples of animal species consumed by peoples in tropical forest areas in different parts of the world. (a) Frogs on skewers for sale at the Vientiane market, Republic of Lao (photo: J. M. Touzet); (b) Lowland tapir dressed for sale in Amazonia (photo: H. El Bizri); (c) Lizards for sale at the Vientiane market, Republic of Lao (photo: J. M. Touzet).

Table 1.1 *Number of terrestrial vertebrate species hunted and consumed for their wild meat in tropical and subtropical regions (data from Redmond et al. 2006)*

Vertebrate group	Oceania	South America	South/SE Asia	Sub-Saharan Africa	Total
Amphibians	3	3	14	16	36
Reptiles	0	6	76	6	88
Birds	34	53	75	60	222
Mammals	6	53	23	210	292

islands it is species-rich in birds but species-poor in reptiles and amphibians, with most mammals being bats. Also, as sub-Saharan Africa includes open, mammal-rich savannas, not common in Asia or South America (see Chapter 2), the numbers of mammal species hunted for wild meat in this region is significantly higher than in the others.

1.4.1 Mammals

Most hunted mammals are large-bodied primates, ungulates and rodents, with an average adult body mass equal to or greater than 1 kg (Robinson & Bennett 2004; Robinson & Redford 1991b). These species are considered to provide a greater return for the energy invested in hunting because of their size, but also because of their greater susceptibility to the more commonly used hunting techniques, such as snares and projectile weapons, particularly firearms (Chapter 3). As larger animals are often the most lucrative species to hunt, they are typically targeted first by hunters (Chapter 4). As populations of the larger animals decline, the time and effort required to hunt these species will eventually outweigh the potential gain. As a result, hunters change to targeting mid-size species until finally, if overexploitation is sustained, the hunt will primarily target small species (Jerozolimski & Peres 2003). However, throughout this process, the largest species will continue to be opportunistically captured whenever encountered, preventing their recovery, even though the primary target is now a smaller species (Robinson & Bennett 2004). In addition, snares, which are largely indiscriminate in what they catch, extensively deployed in Africa and Asia, are able to almost empty areas of a large number of animals in a short space of time (Fa *et al.* 2005; Harrison *et al.* 2016; Noss 1998b). The use of snares varies by continents in relation to the availability and

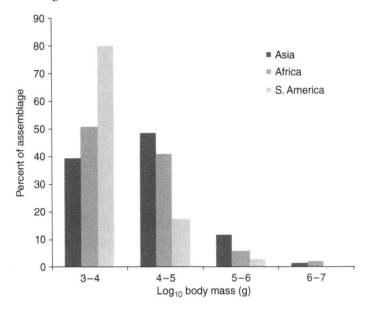

Figure 1.3 Distribution of body mass of hunted mammal species in Asian, African and South American forests (data from Corlett 2007 and Fa & Peres 2001).

distribution of ground and arboreal prey species. In South American moist forests, because there are relatively fewer abundant ground-dwelling species than in African and Asian forests, ground snares are consequently less profitable and not widely employed (see Chapter 2). The distribution of hunted mammals in South American, African and Asia moist forests clearly indicates the preponderance of smaller prey species in South America compared to Africa and Asia (Fig. 1.3, Corlett 2007; Fa & Peres 2001).

Thus, larger prey size and greater accessibility to hunters may explain the wider range of mammal species hunted in African forests compared to South American ones; 55% of a total of 284 African forest mammals are hunted in contrast to only 28% of the 192 species recorded in South American (Amazonian) forests (Fa & Peres 2001). The predominance of terrestrial large-bodied mammals in African forests can also explain their greater vulnerability to indirect hunting techniques, e.g. traps, nets, snares (Chapter 3). The use of snares has been a widespread practice in African forests, accounting for the extraction of more species (and biomass) than firearms (Kümpel 2006; Noss 2000, 1998b). Similarly, home-made snares are increasingly used across large areas of Southeast

Asia (O'Kelly 2013; Wilkinson 2016) with devastating effects on the fauna (Gray *et al.* 2018). In contrast, snare hunting is virtually absent in the Amazon Basin, probably because lower population densities recorded for Neotropical forest mammals render this trapping method relatively unprofitable (Fa & Purvis 1997; Peres 2000).

1.4.2 Birds

Primarily large but also smaller birds are hunted and eaten in tropical regions worldwide. In large areas of Latin America, some birds contribute significantly to the subsistence of rural families that depend on wildlife for their food. Groups such as cracids, large arboreal galliform birds (chachalacas, guans and curassows), are traditionally considered the most important birds for subsistence hunting for many Indigenous Amazonian communities. In a 5-year study of 35 Pano villages in Acre State, Brazilian Amazon, as many as 25 different bird taxa were hunted (Constantino 2016). Although the preferred prey were typically large species of ungulates, primates and reptiles, over the study period birds supplied 11% of all animals taken and 2% of all animal biomass hunted. Of all the bird taxa hunted, four species, the Spix's guan, large tinamou, pale-winged trumpeter and razor-billed curassow, contributed almost all the bird numbers and biomass. Macaws, parrots, toucans, rails, doves, wood quails, ducks, kites, aracari, jabiru stork and even harpy eagles were also recorded as hunted. In other areas of the Amazon, such as in the Pacaya-Samiria National Reserve (Peru) and its surroundings as many as 47 bird species are hunted for food (Gonzalez 2004). The most commonly hunted bird species included tinamou, anhinga, razor-billed curassow, Muscovy ducks and olivaceous cormorants but bird eggs are also an important source of food (Gonzalez 2004). In contrast to the moist forests regions, in the semi-arid habitats, the Caatinga in Brazil for example (de Albuquerque *et al.* 2012), although wild mammals still make up most of the animals and biomass hunted, doves, pigeons and tinamous are common birds used for food (Barboza *et al.* 2016).

Although birds are less commonly hunted in African forests, a large number of species are killed and traded for both meat and traditional medicine. Petrozzi (2018) documented a total of 302 different species of 24 orders on sale in wild meat markets in 10 sampled West African countries. Most recorded species were Least Concern, with 23% Threatened according to the IUCN Red List. However, in a study of semi-permanent hunting camps in the Ebo Forest, Cameroon, birds constituted 55%, more than mammals (43%) and other taxa (2%). The study recorded several species of birds rarely reported elsewhere (Whytock *et al.* 2016). Offtake of larger bird species was greater than for smaller taxa, but some bird species may be hunted more frequently than previous research suggests. This has important conservation implications for larger-bodied species such as raptors and hornbills (see Trail 2007).

1.4.3 Reptiles and Amphibians

Reptiles serve as an important source of animal protein for people around the world, but exploitation of this group for food is heaviest in the tropical and subtropical regions. By contrast, although amphibians are consumed on a smaller scale than reptiles, Mohneke *et al.* (2009) highlighted that at least 32 species (3 Urodela and 29 Anura) are used as food globally.

Of all reptiles, chelonians (turtles and tortoises) are the most heavily exploited (Klemens & Thorbjarnarson 1995). High levels of exploitation for food but also for pets and medicine are directly responsible for the precarious conservation status of as many as 11 (44%) of the 25 most threatened taxa (species and subspecies combined) of turtle and tortoise species in the world (Stanford *et al.* 2020). Crocodile and alligator meat are considered a delicacy in many parts of the tropics and subtropics (Huchzermeyer 2003), and are consumed extensively (Hoffman & Cawthorn 2012). The consumption of snakes is generally opportunistic, but in Asian countries (China, Taiwan, Thailand, Indonesia, Vietnam and Cambodia) and West Africa, these animals are important sources of wild meat (Brooks *et al.* 2010; Hoffman & Cawthorn 2012).

Within the Amazon region, a number of chelonian species, but also their eggs, are heavily exploited for food (Alves *et al.* 2012; Pezzuti *et al.* 2010). The giant Amazon River turtle, the largest South American river turtle, but especially the more abundant, yellow-spotted river turtle are widely harvested for their eggs and adults for food (Arraes *et al.* 2016). Similarly, in many tropical regions of sub-Saharan Africa, tortoises alongside other reptiles, but also amphibians, are collected for food. For example, in the Niger Delta in Nigeria, Akani *et al.* (1998) reported 4 frog species and 14 reptiles for sale in wild meat markets, that are consumed regularly; the latter group included two crocodiles, five snakes, one lizard and two tortoises. In this study, the Goliath frog, the largest living frog, was commonly consumed, as reported in other parts of Africa (Gonwouo & Rödel 2008).

Information on reptile and amphibian consumption in Asia, although less formally documented, points to numerous species of chelonians, snakes and lizards being used as locally important food sources. By contrast, the medicinal trade of reptiles, especially turtles and snakes in Southeast Asia, poses a greater threat to this group than consumption.

1.5 Regional Differences in Species Hunted for Wild Meat

A meta-analysis of the characteristics of vertebrates hunted and consumed in West and Central African moist forests showed that a total of 129 species were recorded in the literature over a 40-year period (1971–2010) in five countries (Petrozzi *et al.* 2016). By class, significant differences in the number of species appeared; 91 mammals dominating, followed by reptiles ($n = 19$), birds ($n = 14$) and amphibians ($n = 2$). Mammals were also the most numerous in terms of the number of individuals and overall biomass traded, ungulates and large rodents in particular. Herbivores and frugivores were the most common trophic animal guild. Forest-specialists were the most abundant, and in riverine habitats reptile biomass was almost as important as mammals. Most species and individuals were non-threatened according to the IUCN Red List.

Information on species hunted for wild meat in African savannas has received comparatively little attention in comparison to forests (Lindsey *et al.* 2013). Because of their high abundance in these more open habitats, ungulates are the most hunted species (Lindsey *et al.* 2011b, 2011a). The more commonly hunted species in these habitats include abundant species such as impala and blue wildebeest but also plains zebra, as recorded in the Savé Valley Conservancy in the southeast Lowveld of Zimbabwe (Lindsey *et al.* 2011a). In a nationwide study in Tanzania, Ceppi and Nielsen (2014) showed that a total of 25 taxa were consumed in 10 tribal areas. Antelope was the most frequently mentioned type of wild meat in all ecoregions, with dik-dik and duikers making up the majority of records. This was followed by hare and Guinea fowl. Dik-diks and duikers make up most records but larger species such as the bushbuck and the African buffalo are consumed only rarely. The larger animals require more sophisticated hunting techniques and adequate firearms which are often limited and more difficult to acquire.

There is a large number of studies on the hunting and gathering of vertebrates in Latin America (Alves & Van Vliet 2018). In a meta-analysis of 78 different hunting studies, from sites in Central America, Amazonia and the Guiana Shield, a total of 90 hunted mammal species were recorded (Stafford *et al.* 2017a). This number included 12 genera of primates, 6 of ungulates and 8 rodent genera. As in Africa, ungulates and rodents make up the majority of the wild meat offtake in Neotropical communities. Within the Amazon Basin, the largest rainforest block in the world, much of the wild meat offtake is comprised of medium-sized ungulates such as white-lipped peccary, collared peccary, white-tailed deer and various brocket deer species, but also large rodents like the paca and agoutis (Fa & Peres 2001; Mesquita & Barreto 2015; Stafford *et al.* 2017b). Tapirs (South American tapir in lowland South American forests, Baird's tapir in Central America and Andean tapir in Andean forests) are the largest mammals in South and Central American forests (ca. 200 kg), and a sought-after prey species (Jerozolimski & Peres 2003; Nasi *et al.* 2011; Suárez *et al.* 2009). Primates are also the main targets for hunters in Central and South America, but overall standing biomass is less than ungulates and rodents combined. Typically, primates such as large cebid monkeys of which there are six Alouttinae monkey species and seven Atelinae species, are actively hunted for meat throughout their ranges (Ráez-Luna 1995). Species hunted and consumed will vary according to habitat and region but also according to the type of hunter involved. In the Amazon, colonists and Indigenous Peoples pursue different animals (Redford & Robinson 1987), the latter group concentrating on primates (Cormier 2006; Ojasti 1996). The Wai Wai indigenous communities in Guyana mostly hunt black spider monkeys, paca and curassow (Shaffer *et al.* 2017).

Regional differences in animals hunted occur, as observed in the different regions of Colombia (Vargas-Tovar 2012). For all regions pooled, only three species, the collared peccary, the tapir and the paca contributed more than half of all the hunted biomass, but other species such as caiman appear important in the Orinoco region and iguanas and white-tailed deer in the Pacific region (Vargas-Tovar 2012). A study by Van Vliet *et al.* (2017) of animals on sale in markets in the five main ecoregions in Colombia indicated that even though as many as eighty five different species were sold for food, three or four out of six main species for the entire country (the paca, red and grey brocket deer, capybara, armadillo and black agouti) dominated markets in each region. In the more open Brazilian cerrado, tapir, white-lipped and collared peccary as well as various deer species (marsh deer, pampas deer, grey brocket deer, red brocket deer) and the giant anteater were commonly hunted (Welch 2014).

Information on wild meat extraction in Asian habitats remains scant (Lee *et al.* 2014) but some general patterns are available. According to Corlett (2007), over 160 species of mammal species of >1 kg are hunted in Asian forests where pigs contribute the largest proportion both in terms of individuals and biomass (Gray *et al.* 2018; Harrison *et al.* 2016; Morrison *et al.* 2007; Wilcove *et al.* 2013). As in other tropical and subtropical regions in Africa and the Neotropics, hunting of vertebrates, not just mammals in Asia and especially in Southeast Asia is common; hunting constitutes the greatest current threat to wild vertebrates in the region. This is primarily to supply ever-expanding local, regional and even global markets. Even in areas where good-quality forest remains intact, only a small proportion of the former vertebrate diversity and abundance is still found (Harrison *et al.* 2016). Only 1% of the land supports an intact fauna of mammals >20 kg (Morrison *et al.* 2007) and defaunation effects have been confirmed in a number of different localities (Aiyadurai *et al.* 2010; Johnson *et al.* 2003; Rao *et al.* 2010).

1.6 Indigenous and Rural Peoples Hunt Differently

Rural and Indigenous Peoples throughout the world still rely, to varying extents, on terrestrial animals (and fish) as food in the different habitats they inhabit. Levels of dependence on wildlife for food are affected by the ecological conditions in which people live. Where systematic comparisons have been undertaken for mammals in rainforest ecosystems, the most hunted group, in the Congo Basin in Central Africa and in the Amazon Basin in South America, inter-continental differences can be largely explained by the productivity of these ecosystems (see Chapter 2). However, because the standing biomass of mammals in Central African forests is considerably higher than in South America (Fa & Peres 2001), reliance on terrestrial wild meat is potentially greater for hunters in the former ecosystem. Yet, the high ratio of land area to rivers in the Amazon Basin, increases the possibility for penetration by inland fisheries and thus accounts for the higher proportion of fish. The possibility of exploiting more fish actually compensates for the lower contribution of mammalian meat in the diets of Amazonian peoples compared to those in Central African forests (Robinson & Bennett 1999b). Beyond the ecological reasons for the availability of wild meat for peoples living in tropical environments, understanding the cultural and socioeconomic drivers of different hunter groups may help determine levels of wildlife extraction and the motives for these. In the following section, we describe the differences in prey species and extraction levels of Indigenous and non-Indigenous Peoples living in Amazonian and Congo Basin forests.

Differences in the types of prey species hunted by Indigenous Peoples and rural communities have been studied in Neotropical and African settings. Using an index of the number of animals taken per consumer year, Redford and Robinson (1987) and later Redford (1993) described contrasts in the nature and intensity of hunting by Indigenous Peoples and colonists in tropical and subtropical forests in South America. For Indian communities in the Amazon, mammals constituted the most important type of game, with birds second and reptiles third; during a comparable time period, data for colonists, mammals were first, reptiles second and birds third. However, indigenous groups took on average a higher number of animals per consumer year than did colonists. Moreover, preferences between Indian and colonist groups in the types of mammals hunted were different, with primates being the most frequently taken order for Indians and rodents for colonists. In another meta-analysis in the Congo Basin, Fa *et al.* (2016) showed that there were significant differences in species hunted and extraction rates between indigenous Pygmy and non-Pygmy groups. Overall, Pygmies hunted a smaller range of taxa but took a higher proportion of prey of a greater mean body mass than non-Pygmies. Harvest rates, animals per inhabitant, were almost twice as high in non-Pygmy sites than in Pygmy sites, as were extraction rates, the number of animals hunted per unit area. There were no significant differences in biomass values, due to the higher body mass of species hunted by Pygmies. However, when converted to extraction per hunter per km^2, non-Pygmy sites harvested more per unit area than Pygmy groups.

The general picture that emerges from these two contrasting studies is that although variation in what Indigenous Peoples and other groups hunt may be to some extent explained by differences in the ecological context and hunting technologies used by each group, contrasting preferences for prey animals can also account for such variation. Although estimates of hunting impact by indigenous *versus* non-indigenous groups in different parts of the world are still lacking, Fa *et al.* (2016) have shown that given their lower numbers and estimated extraction rates, Pygmies in the Congo Basin have a substantially lower impact on prey populations than other groups. The most alarming difference between these two groups is in the proportion of hunted animals that are traded for profit with significantly higher volumes of game sold by non-Pygmies than by Pygmies (Fa *et al.* 2016).

1.7 Understanding Urban Wild Meat Markets

The sale of hunted animals, often to neighbours or passersby, is motivated by the need to earn some income for the family to buy goods (Nasi *et al.* 2008; Ávila Martin *et al.* 2020). In other circumstances, hunters can be driven or choose to sell their quarry to middlemen for sale beyond their immediate neighbourhoods. If hunters enter the broader and more elaborate commercialization of wild meat, they participate in a commodity chain driven primarily by demand by urban residents who are willing to pay a premium (Bowen-Jones *et al.* 2003). Although reliable information on the scale of the international wild meat trade is still patchy, in Europe some studies suggest that the amount of wild meat imported here is substantial (Chaber *et al.* 2010; Falk *et al.* 2013). For example, in a survey at Roissy-Charles de Gaulle airport (Paris, France), 7% of the inspected passengers from West and Central African countries were carrying wild meat (over 20 kg on average and up to 51 kg), and 25% had domestic meat (average 4 kg) in their luggage (Chaber *et al.* 2010). These and more recent studies (Gombeer *et al.* 2021) indicate that wild meat is not only imported for personal use but also to supply an organized illegal luxury market for African wild meat in many cities in Europe. Moreover, as suggested by Morrison-Lanjouw *et al.* (2021) in the Netherlands and Walz *et al.* (2017) in the USA, culture, taste preferences, the perception that wild meat is more healthy than other meats (and therefore of lower disease risk) as well as an increase in disposable income may all be driving the local demand for African wild meat in expatriate communities.

There is little evidence that exports of wild meat from Latin America or Asia are significant. Even though the international wild meat trade may be minimal in these continents, there is growing proof that there has been a clear rise in commercial hunting within tropical countries. Although urban wild meat was originally considered a more important issue in the African context, increased urbanization within other parts of the tropics is resulting in a greater demand for wild meat from cities and large towns. In South America, for example, the consumption of wild meat in urban centres had been considered minimal compared to in

Africa (Nasi *et al.* 2011; Rushton *et al.* 2005). However, recent studies suggest that there are non-negligible city markets in which a large number of wild animals are sold for human consumption (Bodmer & Lozano 2001; Chaves Baía Júnior *et al.* 2010; Parry *et al.* 2014; Van Vliet *et al.* 2015, 2017). In a recent study in cities in Amazonas, Brazil, El Bizri *et al.* (2019) demonstrated that wild meat is an important item in the diet of residents in urbanized Central Amazonia since a very large proportion of interviewees in the study ate wild meat and large numbers of animals are harvested every year to supply urban consumers. But, as shown in a study of the availability of wild meat and domestic meats in Kinshasa and Brazzaville − the two capital cities in Central Africa accounting for around 15 million inhabitants (Fa *et al.* 2019) − wild meat consumption can be considerable, despite the offer of domestic meat. The often-repeated suggestion that the solution could be the replacement of wild meat by domestic meat at more affordable prices, as suggested by Rushton *et al.* (2005) and others, may not be sufficient to solve the problem.

The greatest impact of commercial hunting on native vertebrate fauna is arguably occurring in Central Africa. In this region, populations of many hunted species are rapidly extirpated and sanctuaries for wildlife are dwindling since almost all Central Africa's forests are now accessible to hunters (Abernethy *et al.* 2013). Based on wild mammal meat removal rates estimated for the Amazon and Congo Basins (Nasi *et al.* 2011), Central African forests are subjected to four times higher extraction of wild animals than in the Amazon. This contrast is not just a reflection of the greater standing mammalian biomass in African moist forests but the higher density of people which drives the demand for wild meat. Historic data on changes in hunting pressure in Central Africa are not available but hunter numbers are likely to have increased relative to the rise in overall human population densities. In parallel, while only 1 in 10 people lived in urban areas in 1900, almost half of all sub-Saharan inhabitants now live in towns and cities (United Nations 2014). Urban inhabitants, especially those recently arrived from rural areas into cities, have a desire to carry on consuming wild meat (because it something they are accustomed to) even though domestic meats are more available and for most families affordable (Cowlishaw *et al.* 2004; Cronin *et al.* 2015; Wilkie *et al.* 2005). Consequently, urban wild meat markets thrive in Central Africa, even in countries where it may be illegal to sell some wild species as food. As a result, demand for wild meat in towns and cities has increased and is expected to grow even more with increasing urbanization. The urban population in Africa is projected to rise to 1.339 billion in 2050 from 395 million in 2010, 21% of the world's projected urban population (Güneralp *et al.* 2017). Much of the upsurge is taking place in small- and medium-sized provincial towns in mid-latitude Africa, as rural youth leave to seek a better life (Lwasa 2014). This demographic change implies a much greater demand on domesticated and wild food production systems, which can have far-reaching impacts.

Urban consumers of wild meat live either in (a) provincial towns close to sources of wildlife where livestock production is uncommon and market access makes imported animal source foods unavailable or unaffordable, or (b) large metropolitan areas far from sources of wildlife where wild meat is no longer a dietary necessity and more a cultural desire to connect to a rural past (Wilkie *et al.* 2005). Vigorous trading of wild meat to satisfy urban demand is widespread in all major West and Central African cities (Bennett Hennessey & Rogers 2008; Chausson *et al.* 2019; Edderai & Dame 2006; Luiselli *et al.* 2017; Malonga 1996; Mbayma 2009; Mbete *et al.* 2011) and the purchase of wild meat is common in even relatively small towns. The certainty of demand, ease of entering the market and low risk of penalties have encouraged villagers in subsistence economies across the region to use local wildlife as a cash crop.

In large metropolitan cities in Africa, consumers usually have the choice of several sources of domestic animal protein, but many opt for wild meat for reasons other than its nutritional importance. City dwellers may eat wild meat as a means of culturally reconnecting to their place of origin, where they or their parents consumed wild meat (Luiselli *et al.* 2017, 2018, 2019). Although consumers in some provincial towns (particularly isolated ones) may buy wild meat because it is the cheaper meat and more readily available (Fargeot *et al.* 2017; Van Vliet *et al.* 2010b), wild meat in metropolitan cities throughout the tropics for some groups of consumers is more of a luxury item and status symbol (Cao Ngoc & Wyatt 2013; Shairp *et al.* 2016; Wilkie *et al.* 2016). As a luxury commodity, city dwellers pay higher prices than rural consumers for the same animal. Urban consumer willingness to pay relatively high prices encourages rural hunters to increase the amount they take and the proportion they sell to gain income as well as food (Bennett *et al.* 2007; de Merode *et al.* 2004; Grande-Vega *et al.* 2016). It also encourages non-local hunters to enter the market. Perhaps more significantly, many rural peoples have shifted from being traditional subsistence hunters to supplying cities.

Although there are clear multigenerational issues affecting consumption of wild meat in cities, younger generations are less predisposed as shown in a study in West African cities by Luiselli *et al.* (2018, 2019), most people eat wild meat because they prefer its taste. The perception that wild meat is a luxury item is often cited but studies such as Kümpel *et al.* (2007) in the city of Bata in Equatorial Guinea, showed that consumption of fresh foods, including wild meat, increased with income while eating of frozen produce tended to decline. In some situations, however, such as in post-depletion scenarios (see Cowlishaw *et al.* 2005), wild meat is consumed as a bonus. In Ghana, wild meat was more expensive than domestic meat or fish since wild meat production was low in volume and occurred at considerable distances from urban centres, whereas domestic meat production was high in volume and near city markets (Cowlishaw *et al.* 2005). In Nigeria and Gabon, wild meat is also a luxury item, more expensive than imported beef, for which individuals are willing to pay a premium over other sources of animal protein (Ladele *et al.* 1996; Starkey 2004). Wealth is known to affect wild meat consumption in some rural settings where intake was higher in wealthier households (de Merode *et al.* 2004; Wilkie *et al.* 2005) because poorest households could not afford hunting tools or somebody able to hunt. In contrast, in cities like Kisangani in the Democratic Republic of Congo (DRC) where households no longer have access to free natural resources, the poorest seek the most inexpensive source of protein available in the market. Smoked wild meat is one of the cheapest sources of protein year-round but other sources of animal protein, except pork and caterpillars, are significantly more expensive. In the Kisangani market, wild meat was sold in small piles costing <USD 0.10 each, whereas domestic meat was sold in piles of 500 g to 1 kg (Van Vliet *et al.* 2012). Despite the existence of sharp socioeconomic structuring between rural and urban consumers, but also within them, there is the acceptance that the burgeoning urban populations, not just in Africa (see El Bizri *et al.* 2019 for the Amazon), fuels an ever-increasing, lucrative trade of wild animals from rural and protected areas (Chapter 5). This trade is now the most significant immediate threat to wildlife but also to the food security of people who have hunted them. Subsistence hunting and fishing do not usually pose a significant threat at low human densities to the abundant wildlife species living around rural forest communities.

Wild meat is sold as fresh carcasses or smoked meat in markets, at roadsides, in hunters' homes or as cooked dishes in restaurants. In all continents where wild meat is traded, it is available at several entry points in the commercial chain, where it passes from the hunter to the consumer. In some situations, hunters may sell their kill as whole animals to a trader or directly to a restaurant operator, who then retails it in smaller pieces. Hunters may also dress the carcass and sell pieces direct to consumers in their village. But, more commonly hunters or their emissaries may carry the meat to the point of sale, often the nearest town or city, though in the case of professional hunters operating from hunting camps, traders may travel to the camp to buy the smoked meat.

The main concentration sites for the sale of wild meat, on a regular basis, are without any doubt within markets. In Africa, such public gatherings, where the buying and selling of merchandise, including wild meat take place, occur in almost every sizeable village or town. Here, wild meat can be traded and displayed on makeshift counters, or in larger cities on more permanent stalls within purpose-built market buildings. Some, like the Atwemonon market in Ghana (Crookes et al. 2014; Ntiamoa-Baidu 1997), are highly organized and the wild meat trade and associated chain of small restaurants, known as chop bars, are handled as small-scale family businesses handed down from parents to children. In all studied areas in Africa (Cowlishaw et al. 2005; East et al. 2005; Fa 1999), there are five main actor groups identified in the wild meat trade: farmer hunters or mainly subsistence hunters, commercial hunters, wholesalers, market traders and small restaurant operators. Commonly, hunters and intermediaries are men, whilst sellers are women (Tagg et al. 2018). Hunters live and work in rural areas and capture their prey using snares and shotguns. Commercial hunters depend entirely on wild meat for their livelihood, whereas farmer hunters sell wild meat to supplement their income from agricultural produce. The women traders – wholesalers, market traders and restaurant and bar operators – live and work in the city. Wholesalers work from home. They buy meat in bulk from the hunters and sell to the retailers: the market traders and small restaurants or bars. Market traders operate from stalls in the market, whereas chop bars, a term used in West Africa for small establishments, are scattered across the city. Women form the main clientele for market traders, whereas men are more likely to frequent chop bars. The primary route of trade is from commercial hunters to restaurants and bars via wholesalers, although there is also substantial trade along other routes. Each trader has her own set of hunters who supply her with meat and whom she rewards by granting loans. The trade provides income for a large number of people – hunters and traders – but it is a fairly closed system. Most wild meat markets are largely unregulated by either state or local institutions.

In a number of countries, some wildlife species (e.g. endangered species) nominally protected from hunting by legislation are still consumed as wild meat. Wild meat sold openly to the public is a typical feature of many African countries, and markets are found in almost every village or town in the region. Wild meat markets are particularly well developed in West and Central Africa, which is also the area where the trade has been best documented since as long ago as the 1970s (see Asibey 1977; Jeffrey 1977).

The study of wild meat markets in urban and rural spaces can provide researchers with relatively easily obtainable data on carcass numbers and price by species, and sometimes information on the origin of the meat (see e.g. Dupain *et al.* 2012). Such data has been used to infer hunting sustainability although there are limitations to their use (Chapter 5). This is because there are varying reasons why animals are traded or retained by hunters e.g. the hunters need for cash (de Merode *et al.* 2004) or the relative prices of wild meat species and domestic meat (Wilkie *et al.* 2005; Wilkie & Godoy 2001) and transport costs to town (Crookes & Milner-Gulland 2006). As a result, the numbers and species appearing in markets is a subset of the total hunted in the production habitats. Despite potential drawbacks, the data emerging from wild meat market studies can be informative in assessing trends, such as the impact of Ebola on consumption of different species (Funk *et al.* 2021) and as argued by Fa (2007) if large market numbers can be monitored, these represent the best compromise between economy of collection effort, and precision and accuracy of estimates based on population indices. By standardizing data collection protocols and optimal sampling periods (as indicated in Fa *et al.* 2004) comparisons between areas and with other studies are possible. Data quality ultimately depends on the continued dedication and adequate training of observers, the cooperation of various agencies and the rapid and accurate compilation of results.

The sale of wild meat in different parts of the tropics and subtropics merits particular attention since this activity has important implications for the livelihood strategies of the poor, and it is relevant to wider issues of public governance (Brown & Williams 2003). Although these issues will be discussed further in Chapter 5, in this section we focus on the phenomenon of wild meat trade from the viewpoint of who sells wild meat and which wild meat is commercialized. At a landscape level, at least in tropical forest areas, evidence points to wild meat consumption and hunting being positively associated with increasing forest cover (both correlated with greater animal prey availability) which in turn is often negatively related with access to markets. As demonstrated by Carignano Torres *et al.* (2018) for households in post-frontier Amazonia, people living in remote, forested areas are likely to be the most dependent on wild meat. However, those living in more populous, peri-urban areas are likely to be the actors contributing most to total hunting effort, due to the greater market access. Market access also increases the opportunity for hunters to transition from a barter-based to a monetary economy, leading to greater wealth and livelihood diversification for them (Chaves *et al.* 2017). By increasing the supply of wild meat to markets, these hunters are effectively changing consumer behaviour, ultimately boosting the demand from consumers.

Data on actual wild meat volumes for sale, taken from the literature, generally indicate a very large variation in amounts traded per site. From more extensive, multiple-site studies (Fa *et al.* 2006; Starkey 2004; Wilkie *et al.* 2005) amounts traded ranged from about 100 to 9,000 carcasses per annum. When wild meat volume traded per site is adjusted by the number of inhabitants in each site (data from Fa *et al.* 2006), about 20 kg (median 7.7, range 0.1–392) is available per person per annum, but highly skewed, as 45% of all studied sites had between 0 and 4 kg of wild meat per inhabitant per annum. The more populated sites did not have more wild meat on sale (in fact, wild meat availability fell with larger settlements), but wild meat volume on sale per site was negatively correlated with mean body mass of the animals on sale (Fa 2007).

Market studies encompassing large numbers of monitored sites, as in the Cross-Sanaga region of Nigeria and Cameroon (35,000 km^2), estimated that over a million carcasses were traded in 89 urban and rural markets in a year (Fa *et al.* 2006). Typically (see Section 1.4), almost all animals traded were mammals, of which around 40% were ungulates (duikers and pigs), 30% rodents and close to 15% were primates. Information on wild meat volume traded within other markets in African forest areas has been published for Ghana (Cowlishaw *et al.* 2005; Crookes *et al.* 2014; Ntiamoa-Baidu 1997), Bioko (Cronin *et al.* 2015; Fa *et al.* 1995), Rio Muni (East *et al.* 2005; Fa *et al.* 1995), DRC (Colyn *et al.* 1987), the Cross-Sanaga region of Nigeria and Cameroon (Fa *et al.* 2006) and Gabon (Starkey 2004). From these sources, most markets sell largely ungulates and rodents, but primates can constitute more than 20% (Fig. 1.4). As indicated above, these three taxonomic groups are the most important for human consumption in all areas where the trade has been documented (see also studies in Bennett & Robinson

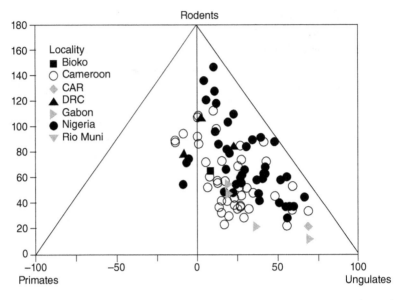

Figure 1.4 Ternary plot of proportions of the three most common mammal taxa for sale in wild meat markets in West and Central Africa. A ternary plot is a specialization of a barycentric plot for three variables, which graphically depicts the ratios of three proportions. (Data sources: Bioko, Fa et al. 1995; Cameroon, Fa et al. 2006; Central African Republic (CAR), Noss 1995; Democratic Republic of Congo (DRC), Colyn et al. 1987; Gabon, Steel 1994; Nigeria, Fa et al. 2006; Rio Muni, Fa et al. 1995; figure from Fa 2007, adapted with permission from John Wiley & Sons.)

2000), but significant variation in the proportions of ungulates, rodents and primates is typical. The relative contributions of these taxa are highly uneven, as often a limited number of taxa alone – small duikers such as blue duiker in Central Africa and Maxwell's duiker in West Africa, large rodents such as the cane rat and the brush-tailed porcupine – constitute over 50% of the total weight traded.

Observed differences in the volume of wild meat traded may of course reflect hunting pressure, the number of hunters operating, which in turn may be related to the population status of the prey species in the area (Fa *et al.* 2005). As Ling and Milner-Gulland (2006) argue, because open-access hunting is a dynamic system in which individual hunters respond to changes in hunting costs and prices obtained for their catch, resulting offtakes will reflect human processes as well as ecological ones, for example, prey abundance. Assessing underlying factors rather than prox-imate outcome variables is complicated, but the trade-off in choosing to assess one or the other is between the potential for reduced monitoring frequency due to longer-term predictions and greater uncertainty through the introduction of additional assumptions (Ling & Milner-Gulland 2006). Investing in characterizing supply and demand functions may not be essential if they are likely to change rapidly because of external economic or social processes or if effort and offtake can be manipulated directly. Assessing supply and demand, on the other hand, may be easier in a commercial market setting, because point demand is readily measured, and elasticity of demand can be inferred from knowledge of cultural and economic conditions. Ling and Milner-Gulland (2006) suggest that to determine sustainability reliably, some investment into modelling alternative monitoring and management strategies (with appropriate treatments of measurement error, system uncertainty and stochasticity), similar to those already being developed for fisheries, is necessary. Although this is an approach that definitely requires developing, its application may be more suited to small-scale analyses. In order to scale up to the level of large geographical areas, it may be necessary to sacrifice accuracy to gain a broader picture of the impact of hunting on wild meat species.

1.8 How Much Wild Meat Do People Eat?

Per capita wild meat consumption in different tropical regions has been measured in a number of studies in the Congo Basin and for Central and South America (Table 1.2). For Asia, there are no published studies on amounts of wild meat consumed by tropical forest peoples. Recent assessments of amounts of wild meat consumed by rural or indigenous communities in tropical and subtropical areas are scant. Most available estimates are dated (Table 1.2) and are somewhat problematic to compare since methods used differ in terms of level of accuracy of quantities eaten (ranging from less precise interview techniques such as 24-hour recalls to weighed amounts of foods consumed). Moreover, emerging values of wild meat consumed could reflect differences in the study population's dependence on game meat *versus* fish (or other non-vertebrate protein such as caterpillars), but also could reflect differences in the time of year in which the studies were undertaken. Often, there is not sufficient information reported to assess these potential sources of error. Despite these caveats, the data existing from the 40 published studies in Table 1.2 can be used to give an approximation of amounts of wild meat consumed per person per day by forest communities in South America and Africa. In general, we would assume that

Table 1.2 *Reported amounts of fresh edible wild meat and protein intake from hunting in selected rural South American and African communities. Values are in grams per person per day. We used a meat to protein conversion of 0.194 g of protein per gram of meat from Ojasti (1996)*

Group or locality	Country	Fresh meat	Protein	Source
South America				
Cuiba	Colombia	525.0	105.0	Arcand (1976)
Siona, Secoya	Ecuador	326.0	65.0	Vickers (1980)
Río Pachitea	Peru	299.0	49.5	Pierret and Dourojeanni (1966)
Jívaro	Peru/ Ecuador	278.0	56.0	Ross (1978)
Sharanahua	Peru	273.0	54.0	Siskind (1973)
Sirinó	Bolivia	219.0	44.0	Holmberg (1969)
Siona-Secoya	Ecuador	205.0	41.0	Vickers (1984)
Yékwana	Venezuela	159.0	32.0	Hames (1979)
Río Pachitea	Peru	153.0	20.6	Pierret and Dourojeanni (1966)
Yanomano	Venezuela	143.0	29.0	Hames (1979)
Trio	Suriname	130.0	26.0	Lenselink (1972)
Bari	Colombia	98.0	19.0	Beckerman (1980)
Kaingang	Brazil	95.0	19.0	Henry (1964)
Miskito	Nicaragua	86.0	17.0	Nietschmann (1972)
Jenaro Herrera	Peru	75.8	15.2	Ríos et al. (1975)
Río Ucayali	Peru	52.0	10.4	Pierret and Dourojeanni (1967)
Shipibo	Peru	47.0	9.0	Bergman (1974)
Río Ucayali	Peru	35.0	7.1	Pierret and Dourojeanni (1967)
Leonardo da Vinci	Brazil	31.0	6.2	Smith (1976)
Yukpa	Venezuela	28.0	6.5	Paolisso and Sackett (1985)
Nova Fronteira	Brazil	26.0	5.2	Smith (1976)
Rio Paragua	Venezuela	25.0	5.2	Ojasti et al. (1986)
Rio Aripuana, Dardanelos	Brazil	22.0	4.4	Ayres and Ayres (1979)
Coco Chato	Brazil	3.6	0.7	Smith (1976)
Africa				
Kola Pygmies	Cameroon	290.0	56.3	Koppert et al. (1993)
Liberia	Liberia	280.0	54.3	Anstey (1991)
Bomass	Republic of Congo	230.0	44.6	Auzel (1996)

Table 1.2 (*cont.*)

Group or locality	Country	Fresh meat	Protein	Source
Forest Mvae	Cameroon	200.0	38.8	Koppert and Hladik (1990)
Farmers, Campo Reserve	Cameroon	190.0	36.9	Koppert et al. (1993)
Ituri forest	DRC	160.0	31.0	Bailey and Peacock (1988)
Diba	CAR	160.0	31.0	Del Vingt (1997)
Ogooué-Ivindo	Gabon	140.0	27.2	Lahm (1993)
Ituri forest	DRC	120.0	23.3	Aunger (1992)
Oleme	CAR	120.0	23.3	Del Vingt (1997)
Dja	Cameroon	120.0	23.3	Del Vingt (1997)
Kenare	CAR	90.0	17.5	Del Vingt (1997
Coastal Mvae	Cameroon	90.0	17.5	Koppert et al. (1993)
Ekom	CAR	80.0	15.5	Del Vingt (1997)
Babenjele	CAR	50.0	9.7	Noss (1995)
Yassa	Cameroon	30.0	5.8	Koppert et al. (1993)

consumption of wild meat is likely to vary due to differences in: (a) the productivity and depletion levels of the landscape; (b) the price and availability of alternatives; (c) the wealth of the consumer and (d) consumer preference for wild meat.

For all South American tropical forest communities (Table 1.2), average amounts of wild meat were 138.9 ± 128.1 g/person/day (median = 96.5) or 27.0 ± 25.1 g/person/day (median = 19.0) of animal protein. In African communities, amounts of wild meat consumed (146.9 ± 75.9 g/person/day, median = 130.0) were higher than in the studied South American localities. Protein consumption in African sites was 28.5 ± 14.7 g/person/day (median = 25.2). Differences between the groups appear in both continental comparisons. In the South American sites, consumption varies from 3 to over 500 g/person/day, despite all localities occurring within similar tropical forest types. These disparities may be attributable to differences in the availability of wild meat. Availability of these resources will depend on the productivity of the habitat and perhaps more importantly on the existing or past hunting pressure. Hunting pressure is likely to be inversely correlated with the availability of animal protein other than terrestrial game species (Jerozolimski & Peres 2003). In these terms, a settlement close to a highly productive river and enjoying a reliable source of fish would be less reliant on forest wildlife than those deprived of this resource (Calouro 1995; Endo *et al.* 2016; Ross *et al.* 1978). Although a few tribal communities of native Amazonians may acquire as much as 45% of their protein from fish, for most upland communities fish may be highly seasonal, and contributes only 20% or less of their protein intake (Balée 1985).

Differences in wild meat consumption in the Congo Basin are much more attributable to contrasts in lifestyles, although the effect of different habitats or hunting pressure cannot be overruled. For example, the amount of wild meat consumed by Efe foragers in the Ituri forest of northeastern DRC) was estimated at 160 g/person/day (Bailey & Peacock 1988); not that different to farmers reported to consume around 120 g/person/day (Aunger 1994). In contrast, estimates for different localities given in Chardonnet *et al.* (1995) show that amounts of wild meat consumed by different groups vary considerably, from an average of 104 g/person/day in foragers to 430 g/person/day in farmers. Similar differences between foragers and farmers can be seen when comparing Lahm's (1993) value's for wild meat consumption in the Ogooué-Ivindo, Gabon (100–170 g/person/day) with the much lower amounts eaten by Babenjele net-hunters in Mossapoula, Central African Republic (CAR) of 50 g/person/day (Noss 1995). Wild meat consumption in villages surrounding the Dja Biosphere Reserve in Cameroon, Odzala National Park in the Republic of Congo and the Ngotto forest in the CAR range from 80 to 160 g/person/day (Del Vingt 1997) while farmers in the Campo Reserve in southwestern Cameroon consume on average around 19 g/person/day (Koppert *et al.* 1993). The Yassa, Mvae and Bakola from coastal southern Cameroon consume between 20 and 200 g/person/day of wild meat (Koppert *et al.* 1993). Higher wild meat consumption rates have been reported by Auzel (1996) for families living in northern Congo (160–290 g/person/ day); by Koppert *et al.* (1993) for forest hunter-gatherers (290 g/person/day) and by Anstay (1991) for rural Liberians (280 g/person/day). Chardonnet *et al.* (1995) report that urban populations in Gabon, DRC and the CAR consumed, on average, 13 g/person/day – which is less than 10% of the wild meat eaten by hunter-gatherers living in the forest. However, total meat consumption was higher in urban areas compared with rural areas (Chardonnet *et al.* 1995), given their higher population density.

Presently available estimates indicate that 5–8 million people in South America (ca. 1.4–2.2% of the total population) regularly rely on wild meat as a protein source, with many being amongst the poorest of the region (Rushton et al. 2005). Among the Caiçaras people in the Atlantic forest of Brazil, the dependency on wild meat is not constant throughout the year, but occasional hunting represents a complimentary source of animal protein (Nasi et al. 2008). In Venezuela, a study by Señaris and Ferrer (2012) found that hunting fulfilled mainly subsistence purposes in indigenous communities and contributed between 40% and 100% of the meat consumed, whereas in mestizo (mixed heritage) communities, wild meat contributed to 10–30% of meat intake. In semi-arid regions, such as the Brazilian Caatinga, wild mammal meat can be a vital source of animal protein for human communities since freshwater fish is limited in the region. Here, wild meat can be especially critical during the early drought periods, when crops are scarce and domestic animals may die from starvation and dehydration (Alves et al. 2009; Barboza et al. 2016; Fernandes-Ferreira et al. 2012; Miranda & Alencar 2007; Pereira & Schiavetti 2010). Similarly, in the Yucatan Peninsula of southern Mexico, a less arid area but still water-limited because of the predominant limestone soils which restrain the occurrence of surface water bodies and agriculture, wildlife is an important food resource for people living in small, isolated and poor villages surrounding extensive forest areas (Santos-Fita et al. 2012). Because hunting is also practiced to prevent or mitigate crop damage by wildlife, a high proportion of abundant and generalist species, such as doves, armadillos, coatis, collared peccaries and white-tailed deer, are taken in agricultural areas, surrounding fallows, gardens and forest patches (Santos-Fita et al. 2012). Several studies have shown that wild meat from the most commonly hunted Neotropical species contributes to healthy diets (see Van Vliet et al. 2017 for a review) and that the nutritional content of wild meat is difficult to replace by most affordable sources of meat from domestic and industrial origin (Gálvez et al. 1999). In addition, wild meat constitutes what could be called a festival food (León & Montiel 2008; Sirén 2012; Van Vliet et al. 2015), understood as a food choice that may be related to identifying with one's ethnic background (Chapman et al. 2011), or as a comfort food consumed in positive social contexts and resulting in an affirmative association between food and emotional well-being.

Estimates of wild meat consumption by a number of rural communities in the Amazon and the Congo Basin in Nasi et al. (2011) suggest that as much as 63 kg/year/person (170 g per day) and 51 kg/year/person (140 g/person/day) of wild meat is consumed respectively. The authors indicate that the total protein requirement is almost entirely satisfied by wild meat for these communities. A study by Fa *et al.* (2003) calculated that meat supply from wild meat hunting in Central Africa might be higher (at 48 g/person/day) than the non-wild meat protein supply locally generated or imported (34 g/person/day) in the region. These general approximations of the importance of wild meat to people's food security can be reinforced by making comparisons between the recommended daily amounts of protein required to maintain a healthy person and the reported amounts of wild meat protein consumed, albeit with known methodological limitations.

According to the FAO/WHO/UNU Expert Consultation on Protein and Amino Acid Requirements in Human Nutrition (FAO/WHO/UNU 2007) the dietary reference intake (DRI), is 0.8 g of protein per kilogram of body weight. This amounts to 56 g/day for the average sedentary man and 46 g/day for the average sedentary woman. From the available information in Table 1.2, we note that the minimum requirement is unmet in 20 out of the 24 studies for South America, and not covered in any sites for Africa, except one. As mentioned above, it is possible that the DRI for Amazonian sites in Table 1.1 is likely met given the importance of fish these Amazonian communities. Thus, the consumption of wild meat by rural communities in South America, and even throughout Latin America, is not high in terms of quantity, but remains an important component of household food security, and a key element in diet, income diversification, and socially and culturally.

1.9 The Aim of This Book

As suggested at the beginning of this chapter, the overexploitation of wild meat in many parts of the world is a concern for conservationists, development scientists, policy makers and NGOs dealing with wildlife exploitation and human livelihoods issues. In the tropics and subtropics, increasing human populations and the rising trade of wild meat from rural to urban areas, often compounded by the lack of any sizeable domestic meat sector, drive unsustainable hunting levels. Evidence from the Congo and Amazon Basin forests suggests that annual levels of wild meat extraction in these environments are unsustainable. Solving this worldwide problem is one that must embrace ecological, socioeconomic and cultural perspectives. These priorities need to be in balance in order to ensure that wild meat consumption does not lead to the extirpation of wildlife, and that its ongoing rational use continues to provide food security and livelihoods for the millions of rural and Indigenous Peoples that still depend on it. The study of wild meat use in all parts of the world is therefore as important as disciplines relating to the dynamics of disease, wildfire, carbon sequestration, invasive species and biogeochemical cycles (Terborgh & Estes 2010). 'Wild meat biology', if we were to give this discipline a name, is not just understanding the impact of global, local or functional extinction of animal populations or species on ecosystem functioning – defaunation processes primarily driven by overhunting (Chapter 2) – but also the consequences on food security of those still dependent on wild meat as a source of food.

Research on any aspect of wild meat use and hunting has been distributed over a large number of academic journals. As of 31 December 2021 a total of 1,243 papers have been published containing the key words 'bushmeat' or 'wild meat' as a topic in the Web of Science. These papers were published in 308 academic journals. A total of 284 journals published eight or fewer papers whilst only 24 journals published more than eight (Fig. 1.5).

Although all publications focused on wild meat, quite a broad spectrum of academic disciplines is involved. The first research paper was published in 1983. Since the turn of the millennium, the yearly number of papers has increased steadily and has now reached over 100 per annum (Fig. 1.6). Additionally, there are many papers that deal with the consequences of wild meat hunting, especially zoonotic transmission of diseases (e.g. anthrax, HIV/AIDS, Ebola, monkeypox, SARS, COVID-19 and many more). Moreover, numerous papers in the hunting literature deal with wild meat without explicitly mentioning 'bushmeat' or 'wild meat' in the title or abstract, and thus are not included in Fig. 1.5 or Fig. 1.6.

Early studies were mostly descriptive, but the assortment of subjects covered has increased considerably. Alongside this burgeoning scientific interest, there has been much interest in advancing policies and actions that remedy the growing concern for the loss of biodiversity due to overexploitation of species for food. Campaigns around the so-called 'bushmeat crisis', that emerged in the early 1990s (e.g. the Bushmeat Task Force, Eves et al. 2008) were primarily ensconced in protectionist measures toward wildlife consumption or an understandable concern for the fate of great apes. These initiatives have been replaced with

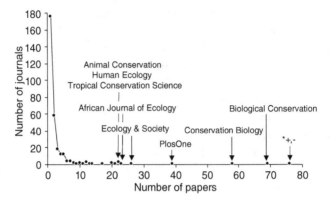

Figure 1.5 Number of scientific articles published on bushmeat and wild meat from 1983 until 2021 appearing in different journals (data from citations in the Web of Science). The most important journals in terms of papers published are shown on the graph.

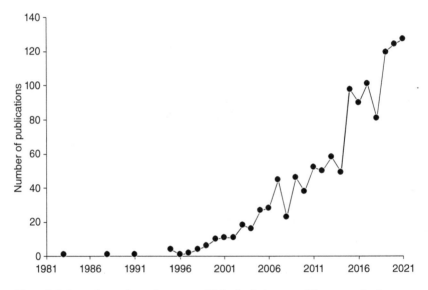

Figure 1.6 Annual number of papers published relating to wild meat or bushmeat since 1983 (data from citations in Web of Science).

those that seek to develop alternative livelihoods to replace the demand for wild meat (Alves & Van Vliet 2018; Wicander & Coad 2018) and to discover more comprehensive and context-specific biological and policy responses to prevent wildlife declines and to promote human well-being (CBD 2017; Nasi & Fa 2015). Technical documents have summarized our knowledge of the wild meat issue, such as Robinson and Bennett's (1999a) seminal book. Bakarr's *et al.* (2001) collection of papers on wild meat use in West and Central Africa has been followed by others aimed at providing guidance for better governance towards a more sustainable wild meat sector (Coad *et al.* 2019; Nasi *et al.* 2008). The latter document was presented to the Subsidiary Body on Scientific, Technical and Technological Advice (SBSTTA), to the CBD at their 21st meeting, 11–14 December 2017, with recommendations for consideration by the Parties to the Convention.

This book summarizes a large volume of information related to what is known about wild meat use in tropical and subtropical regions of the world (Chapters 1, 2 and 3). It also focuses on two key biological and sociological topics: what decisions hunters make when hunting (Chapter 4) and on the more intractable subject of how to measure sustainability (Chapter 5). The following chapters reviews what we know of the impact of overhunting on wildlife and the people that depend on it (Chapter 6) and the link between zoonotic diseases and wild meat (Chapter 7). We end the book (Chapter 8) by offering reflections on how best science and policy can intertwine to come up with possible solutions to the problem at hand. This textbook is not a policy recommendation document but a more updated primer that can find itself in the hands of students and of practitioners who are still developing their paradigms and perspectives.

2 · *The Backdrop*

2.1 Introduction

As we define in Chapter 3, humans hunt wildlife to procure meat for their own consumption or to sell, to enjoy recreation, to remove animals that are dangerous to humans or domestic animals, or to eliminate pests that destroy crops or kill livestock. Though we describe the different modalities of hunting in Chapter 3 in this book, we do not explicitly deal with sports, recreational or trophy hunting (Baker 1997; Lindsey *et al.* 2007; Naidoo *et al.* 2016). We focus on the hunting of animals for food. This is a practice that occurs throughout the globe, within different ecosystems, and by different groups of peoples. The meat of hunted wild animals provides nourishment for many millions of people (see Chapter 1).

Any treatise on wild meat hunting by humans could embrace a multitude of settings, from the Arctic, through temperate climates to tropical forests, and many cultures. Here, we concentrate on documenting and discussing the hunting of animals for food in the tropical and subtropical regions of the world. These regions occupy 40% of the Earth's surface area and contain 36% of the Earth's landmass. They are the most important areas in the globe in terms of biodiversity (Brown 2014) and are inhabited by the largest proportion of humans who still depend on wildlife as a source of food. This dependence on wild meat has been recently highlighted in the debate fostered by the COVID-19 pandemic in which some discussants suggest the permanent banning of wildlife consumption so as to prevent further public health threats (see Yang *et al.* 2020). As argued by Medeiros Jacob *et al.* (2020) and others (SWM Sustainable Wildlife Management Programme 2020), prohibiting hunting of wildlife for food in developing countries that rely on wild meat to subsist, will compromise the status of food and nutrition security of many people (Booth *et al.* 2021; FAO 2019).

To clearly define the environmental conditions in which our analyses of wild hunting are based we first define the climatic envelope which determines the tropics and subtropics. We then highlight the main biomes found in these areas, namely tropical and subtropical forests and open grasslands, and proceed to present an overview of the availability of huntable animals found in these habitats. Because mammals are the most important hunted group, most of our analyses refer to these. We also focus our descriptions of wildlife communities and hunting primarily on African and South American habitats since 94% of all publications (over 500 since the 1980s, see Chapter 1) focused on these two continents; only 6% were on Asia. We proceed by summarizing the anthropogenic pressures acting on biodiversity worldwide. We describe the available data on wild meat use in the tropics and subtropics compared to other parts of the world, and underline how pressures from growing populations in these areas can jeopardize the future of wildlife and impact the food security for many millions of humans. We end the chapter by introducing the consequences of overhunting on wild animals, which cause defaunation. The latter topic will be dealt in more detail in Chapter 6 and will examine the impact of the loss of wild animals on the functioning of ecosystems.

2.2 Defining Tropics and Subtropics

Understanding the extension of the global regions in which we concentrate our attention in this book allows us to appreciate better the variety of environments in which animal prey populations thrive and how this in turn determines the hunting methods and approaches developed by humans to access wild meat. As shown in Chapter 1, the reliance of humans on wild meat, in comparison to plant foods, varies latitudinally across the globe: it is in the tropical and subtropical regions that the greatest wild meat extraction is realized. Defining what we mean by the tropics is relatively straightforward. These are the regions of the planet close to the Equator whose main climatic characteristics are determined by the overhead sun. Numerous authors, primarily German scientists, have defined the tropics (e.g. Köppen, von Wissman, Troll & Paffen, Lauer & Frankenberg, Flohn, and Huang, all in Domroes 2003; Holdridge 1978; Trewartha 1968), using climatic features, chosen for their correlation with the distribution of important crops or major vegetation types. Bioclimatic definitions, such as multiple possible values of absolute minimum temperature, mean temperature of the coldest month, heat sum, mean annual temperature or a greater diurnal than annual temperature range, have been widely accepted. However, using the biologically arbitrary 'solar' definition removes the problem that emerges from temperature-based definitions (Domroes 2003).

Even though the subtropics are universally recognized as the zones immediately north and south of the tropic zone, precisely defining the subtropics is more difficult (Corlett 2013b). The term subtropics can be used to describe the regions outside, but bordering, the tropics though the main disagreement is with the poleward limits. Some authors, physical geographers in particular, have set broad limits, extending to 35° or 40°, or have defined the limits climatically (e.g. Marsh & Kaufman 2012; Petersen *et al.* 2010). According to the Köppen or Köppen-Geiger climate classification (Peel *et al.* 2007), subtropical climates extend to 45°N in some places, but this scheme has been recently modified by removing the colder half of this broad belt. The northern limit of the subtropics has also been set by Griffiths (1976) using a coldest month mean of 6°C, rather than Köppen-Geiger's 3°C. By contrast, Trewartha (1968) used eight months above 10°C.

Köppen' s definition of the subtropics does not include arid climates, whereas Griffiths used the same temperature scale as the other climates. Holdridge (1978) employed equal logarithmic divisions of the mean annual temperature (the mean with all temperatures $<0°C$ adjusted to $0°C$ and $>30°C$ adjusted to $30°C$) to classify into 'life zones', splitting the $12–24°C$ zone into two (subtropical and warm temperate) at the frost line. As a result, most of the area of 'subtropical' life zones lies within the solar tropics.

For our purposes here, we regard the subtropical areas as the regions from about 10°N and S of the tropic zone. Here the sun is never directly overhead, summer days are longer, so weather can be even hotter. Winter is relatively warm, though the nights are long relative to the tropic zone. The subtropics are geographic and climate zones located roughly between the tropics at latitude 23.5° (the Tropic of Cancer and Tropic of Capricorn) and temperate zones (normally referring to latitudes 35–66.5°) north and south of the Equator.

2.3 Main Biomes within the Tropics and Subtropics

The World Wide Fund for Nature Terrestrial Ecoregions map delimits 14 major biomes within which as many as 867 distinct terrestrial ecoregions are found (Olson *et al.* 2001). Biomes range from the wettest of forest types to the driest and hottest desert conditions. Six major biomes out of the 14 are found within the geographical limits of the subtropics and tropics, as we define above. These include: (1) tropical and subtropical moist broadleaf forests (also referred to as evergreen wet and moist forests, and both types denominated as rainforests, see also below), (2) tropical and subtropical dry broadleaf forests, (3) tropical and subtropical coniferous forests, (4) tropical and subtropical grasslands, savannas and shrublands, (5) Mediterranean forests, woodlands and scrub and (6) deserts and xeric shrublands. In this book we focus only on tropical and subtropical forests, savannas and shrublands since wild meat is crucial to many inhabitants of these biomes.

The largest expanses of land within the tropics and subtropics belt are occupied by the two main tropical broadleaf forest formations and by open habitats (Fig. 2.1). Tropical and subtropical moist broadleaf forests are found in large, discontinuous patches along the equatorial belt and between the Tropics of Cancer and Capricorn. These forests are characterized by low variability in annual temperature and high levels of rainfall (>200 cm annually). Forest composition is dominated by semi-evergreen

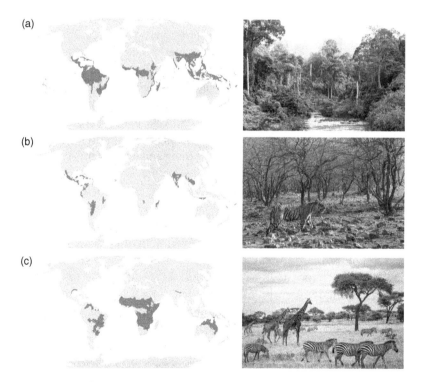

Figure 2.1 Distribution of the three main biomes found within the tropics and subtropics belt. (a) tropical and subtropical moist broadleaf forests, (b) tropical and subtropical dry broadleaf forests and (c) tropical and subtropical grasslands, savannas and shrublands (data from Olson et al. 2001).

and evergreen deciduous tree species. These trees number in their thousands and contribute to the highest levels of species diversity in any terrestrial major habitat type. Biodiversity is highest in the forest canopy. These forests are home to half of the world's species. They are found around the world, particularly in the Indo-Malayan Archipelagos, the Amazon Basin, and Central and West Africa.

Tropical and subtropical dry broadleaf forests occur in southern Mexico, southeastern Africa, the Lesser Sundas, central India, Indochina, Madagascar, New Caledonia, eastern Bolivia and central Brazil, the Caribbean, valleys of the northern Andes, and along the coasts of Ecuador and Peru. Though these forests occur in climates that are warm year-round and may receive several hundred centimetres of rain per year, they are subject to long dry seasons which last several months and vary with geographic location. These seasonal droughts impact all animals and plants in this biome. As an adaptation to seasonal droughts, deciduous trees predominate. The most diverse dry forests in the world occur in southern Mexico and in the Bolivian lowlands. Dry forests of the Pacific Coast of northwestern South America are unique due to their isolation and have a high endemism. Similarly, subtropical forests of Maputoland-Pondoland in southeastern Africa are diverse and include many endemics. The dry forests of central India and Indochina are notable for their diverse large vertebrate faunas. Dry forests of Madagascar and New Caledonia are also highly distinctive for a wide range of taxa and at higher taxonomic levels. Dry forests are highly sensitive to excessive burning and deforestation; overgrazing and exotic species can also quickly alter natural communities.

Tropical and subtropical grasslands, savannas and shrublands include large expanses of land in the tropics that do not receive enough rainfall to support extensive tree cover. They are characterized by rainfall levels between 90 and 150 cm per year. However, there may be great variability in soil moisture throughout the year. Grasses dominate the landscape, and large grazing mammals have evolved to take advantage of the ample primary productivity in these habitats. The typical large aggregations of grazers and their associated predators track seasonal rainfall or migrate to new areas during periodic droughts.

2.4 Wildlife Communities in Tropical and Subtropical Habitats

The geographical pattern of increasing biodiversity from the poles to the equator is one of the most pervasive features of life on Earth. That biodiversity is greatest in the tropics has been known for more than three centuries by Western science ever since European explorers and traders returned from Africa, Asia and the Americas with thousands of specimens of previously unknown kinds of animals and plants. Within the last few decades, this latitudinal diversity gradient (LDG), as referred to by biogeographers is better understood, though a number of hypotheses have proliferated to explain the reasons for this (see Brown 2014). The LDG occurs in nearly all kinds of organisms – plants, animals and microbes – and environments – terrestrial, freshwater and marine. It is now clear that the tropics also harbour the most diverse genomes, clades of higher taxa (e.g. Lomolino *et al.* 2010; Willig *et al.* 2003), and even languages and cultures of subsistence human societies (Collard & Foley, 2002a; Gavin & Stepp 2014; Pagel & Mace 2004). The pattern is ancient, apparent in the fossil record dating back hundreds of millions of years (e.g. Crame 2001; Crane & Lidgard 1989; Stehli *et al.* 1969).

Any explanation for the LDG essentially revolves around the balance between new species being added via speciation and the loss of species due to extinction or emigration (Gaston 1996, 2000). Reasons as to why the tropics are highly speciose have generated more than 25 different mechanisms to explain systematic latitudinal variation (Brown *et al.* 2000). They include explanations based on chance, historical perturbation, environmental stability, habitat heterogeneity, productivity and interspecific interactions. Many of these mechanisms merely offer different levels of explanation but a number are not mutually exclusive.

One factor known to be important in determining latitudinal gradients in species richness is the relationship between the number of species in an area and ambient available ('usable') environmental energy. This energy is usually estimated from models or indirectly from other variables, and often used interchangeably with 'net primary productivity'. Although much debated, at a relatively local scale (spatial resolution and extent) species richness increases from low to moderate levels of energy and then declines again towards high levels of energy (Evans *et al.* 2005). At least across temperate to polar areas, at geographical scales, there is substantial evidence for a broadly positive monotonic relationship between species richness and energy availability (Blackburn & Gaston 1996). For plants, the best correlates are measures of both heat and water (such as actual evapotranspiration and net primary productivity), whereas for terrestrial, and perhaps marine, animals the best correlates are measures of heat (such as mean annual temperature and potential evapotranspiration). The explanation for the broadly positive relationship between species richness and energy availability at geographical scales are believed to be reasonably straightforward (Hawkins *et al.* 2007). Greater energy availability is assumed to enable a greater biomass to be supported in an area. In turn, this enables more individual organisms to coexist, and thus more species at abundances that enable them to maintain viable populations. The result is an increase in species richness with energy availability. This assumes a basic equivalence between species in their energetic requirements at different levels of energy availability.

A good measure of the energy stored as biomass by plants or other primary producers and made available to the consumers in the ecosystem is the net primary productivity (NPP) (Tallavaara *et al.* 2018). This is the gross primary productivity minus the rate of energy loss to metabolism and maintenance (Fig. 2.2a). Reflecting the NPP across the globe is the distribution of biodiversity (Fig. 2.2b) showing the concentration of species along the tropics and subtropics.

2.5 Wildlife Biomass and Primary Productivity

Because species diversity is greatest in the tropics and subtropics, there is a greater variety of animals that are hunted by humans living in these regions compared to other parts of the world (see Redmond *et al.* 2006). Even though a wider range of taxa are consumed in the tropics and subtropics, indeed anything from caterpillars and land snails to the largest land mammal, the elephant, as already mentioned in Chapter 1, mammals of an average adult body mass equal to or greater than 1 kg are the mainstay of most hunts (Robinson & Bennett 2004). These groups of species, nonetheless, vary in their standing biomass, that is the total amount of living material in a specified population at a particular time (Table 2.1), related to the energy available in the ecosystems they inhabit. Mammalian standing biomass can be predicted from total rainfall, seasonality of rainfall, latitude, altitude and edaphic conditions.

Plant biomass, and therefore primary productivity, is negatively correlated with rainfall. In areas with rainfall above 4,000 mm, under conditions of low seasonality and at low altitudes, 'evergreen wet forests' appear. As rainfall declines to 2,000–4,000 mm, 'moist forests' are typical, and 'dry forests' are found at 1,000–2,000 mm. Savanna, scrub and even dry woodlands appear between 100 mm and 1,000 mm of rainfall, but little plant biomass can be found under arid conditions of less than 100 mm of rainfall a year. Rainfall, and in consequence primary productivity, affects the standing biomass of mammalian species, and thus

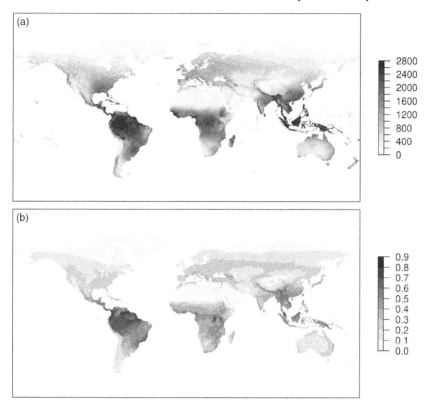

Figure 2.2 Global distribution of (a) net primary production (NPP) and (b) biodiversity (combined plant, mammal and bird richness) (figures taken from Tallavaara et al. 2018). NPP was calculated as the climatic NPP using the empirical Miami model (Leith 1973). Overall biodiversity values were generated from the combined mammal, bird, and vascular plant richness. See Tallavaara et al. (2018) for more details.

availability of the main hunted animals, as shown by Robinson and Bennett (2004). But the three most important taxa for human consumption, that is, large-bodied ungulates, primates and rodents, occur at contrasting comparative and absolute densities in different ecosystems in relation to rainfall. Higher primate biomass is typical of areas with higher rainfall (more forested zones) but ungulate biomass declines with rainfall, where higher biomass is typical of open habitats (in which rainfall is intermediate (Mandujano & Naranjo 2010; Robinson & Bennett 2004); Fig. 2.3). Overall mammalian biomass increases with rising rainfall but drops as forest canopy occupies habitat suitable for herbivorous ungulates. In evergreen wet and moist forests, much of the plant biomass

Table 2.1 *Biomass of large-bodied (>1 kg) rodents, primates and their totals at sites of different rainfall (from Robinson & Bennett 2004)*

Site	Rainfall (mm)	Rodents (kg/km^2)	Primates (kg/km^2)	Ungulates[a] (kg/km^2)	Total (kg/km^2)	Reference
Evergreen wet and moist forest						
Urucu, Brazil	3,256	70	391	341	891	Peres (1991)
Teiu, Brazil	2,850	?	?	?	1,087	Ayres (1986)
BCI, Panama	2,656	300	482	542	2,264	Eisenberg (1980)
Yavari Miri, Peru	2,337	63	441	319	823	Bodmer et al. (1994)
Ogooué-Maritime, Gabon	2,200	2	247	765	1,050	Prins and Reitsma (1989)
Manu, Peru	2,028	129	655	403	1,400	Janson and Emmons (1990)
Northwest Liberia	2,000		2076	933	3,009	Barnes and Lahm (1997)
Parc des Volcans, Rwanda	1,975	?	?	?	3,100	Plumptre and Harris (1995)
Northeast Gabon	1,798		692	1,521	2,213	Barnes and Lahm (1997)
Ituri, DRC	1,700		710	633	1,344	Barnes and Lahm (1997)
Lopé, Gabon	1,506	5	319	2,776	3,101	White (1994)
Deciduous dry forest						
Guatopo, Venezuela	1,500	280	139	270	946	Eisenberg (1980)
Deciduous dry forest and grassland savanna						
Piñero, Venezuela	1,470	36	20	7,952[b]	8,008	Polisar et al. (2003)
Masaguaral, Venezuela	1,462	445	175	7,875[b]	8,684	Eisenberg (1980)
Nagarahole, India	1,200	0	236	14,860[b]	15,094	Karanth and Sunquist (1992)
Acurizal, Brazil	1,120	50	20	3,750[b]	4,130	Schaller (1983)
Manyara, Tanzania	1,150			16,933	16,933	Runyoro et al. (1995)
Katavi, Tanzania	1,100	?	?	?	23,139	Caro (1999)

Grassland savanna

					Reference
El Frio, Venezuela	1,399	2564		18,804[b]	22,405	Eisenberg (1980)
Mara, Kenya	1,000			19,200[b]	19,200	Stelfox et al. (1986)
Serengeti Unit, Tanzania	811			4,222	4,222	Schaller (1972)
Serengeti, Tanzania	750	11		11,595	11,606	Campbell and Hofer (1995); Hofer et al. (1996); Dublin (1995)
Ngorongoro, Tanzania	630			10,982[b]	10,982	Runyoro et al. (1995)
Siminjaro, Tanzania	600			8,209[b]	8,209	Kahurananga (1981)
Cerro Cortado, Bolivia	500	520	10	343	873	A. Noss, pers. comm.
West Ngamiland, Botswana	405	?	?	?	203	Yellen and Lee (1976); Hitchcock (2000)

In all sites hunting is negligible, so mammals are assumed to be at or near carrying capacity (K). Blanks indicate that the biomass of this taxon at the site was negligible; question marks indicate that biomass was not specified.

[a] Includes elephants and buffalo at African sites, elephant and gaur at Asian sites.

[b] Includes domestic livestock.

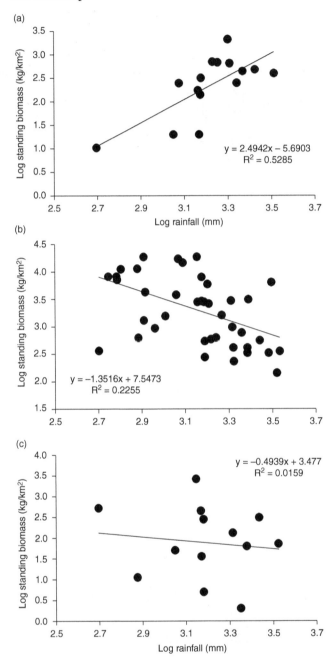

Figure 2.3 Relationship between rainfall (mm) and standing biomass (kg/km²) for: (a) primates; (b) ungulates and (c) rodents. All species are > 1 kg (data from Mandujano & Naranjo 2010 and Robinson & Bennett 2004).

is inedible to most mammals because lignins (tree trunks) are indigestible and toxic plant secondary compounds are found in leaves (McKey *et al.* 1981;Waterman & McKey 1989; Waterman *et al.* 1988). In tropical forests, most primary production is in the canopy and is only consumed by relatively small mammals, such as primates, sloths and rodents; food availability for large ungulates in tropical forests is low (e.g. Glanz 1982; Hart 2000). From data available from various sources, mammalian standing biomass varies from $16{,}404 \pm 13{,}494$ kg/km^2 in grasslands, $12{,}665 \pm 6989$ kg/km^2 in deciduous dry forests and grassland savannas through $1{,}844 \pm 918$ kg/km^2 in moist forests to 909 ± 52 kg/km^2 in dry forests (Mandujano & Naranjo 2010; Robinson & Bennett 2004; Fig. 2.4).

As previously suggested by Eisenberg (1980) and confirmed by Robinson and Bennett (2004) the association between mammalian biomass and rainfall is non-linear. In this relationship, mammalian standing biomass in areas receiving below 100 mm of rainfall is low, but grasslands and tropical dry forests with rainfall above 500 mm can support large mammalian biomasses ranging from 15,000 to 20,000 kg. However, Mandujano and Naranjo's (2010) analysis of variation in ungulate biomass across a rainfall gradient showed that rainfall was a good predictor of ungulate biomass in Neotropical ecosystems compared

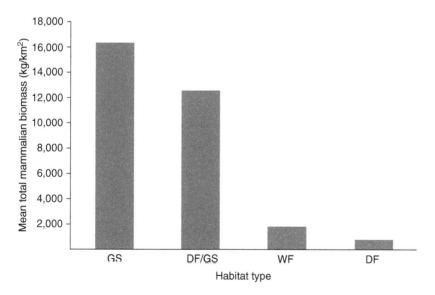

Figure 2.4 Mean total mammalian biomass (kg/km^2) according to habitat types. Habitat: WF, evergreen wet and moist forest; DF, deciduous dry forest; GS, grassland savanna (data from Mandujano and Naranjo 2010 and Robinson and Bennett 2004).

to palaeotropical ones under similar precipitation regimes but it did not correctly predict observed ungulate biomass at local level if data outside the Neotropics were included in the model. This overappraisal particularly affected predicted ungulate biomass in Neotropical dry forests since these ecosystems sustain different ungulate biomass values even when rainfall is similar. Mandujano and Naranjo's (2010) study suggests that even though overall relationships between rainfall (as a surrogate of productivity) and ungulate (or overall mammalian) biomass can be confirmed using data for different regions of the world, differences in the composition of the mammalian communities at a local level are important to understand. In the Neotropics, ungulate aggregations are of species with similar diet compositions resulting from the loss of large, native grazers during the Pleistocene thus maintaining ungulate richness and standing biomass relatively low. These historical transitions should be accounted for when comparing data sets from different regions (Mandujano & Naranjo 2010).

2.6 Available Huntable Mammalian Biomass Variation

2.6.1 General

Almost all mammals of the 28 orders (over 5,400 species) have forest representatives (Corlett & Hughes 2015). Different types of forests are occupied by an assortment of species of varying body sizes, and a large number of them play important ecological roles. Species richness of the large orders is greatest in the tropics (Rolland *et al.* 2014), and over 120 mammals have been recorded from the richest tropical rainforest sites (e.g. Corlett & Primack 2011; Happold 1996; Voss & Emmons 1996). Outside Africa, tropical forests in other continents have lost large mammals since the Middle Pleistocene (Corlett 2013a), and the number of threatened species has accelerated in recent decades (Di Marco *et al.* 2014; Hoffmann *et al.* 2011). Understanding the composition and organization of extant tropical mammalian communities in different regions of the world can provide valuable insights not only on the drivers of species diversity but also on which animals are available to hunters and what methods hunters would need to use (see Chapter 3). In this section, we describe the characteristics of mammal faunas in rainforests in the tropics and their differences across the globe.

Despite not being a highly productive environments in terms of hunted mammal biomass, tropical forests, as demonstrated by Jetz and Fine (2012), possess one of the highest numbers of vertebrate species because these biomes are highly productive (they are warm and have high rainfall), cover large areas and have a long evolutionary history. Studies of the differences and similarities in the mammalian faunas found in tropical forests worldwide are instructive to understand huntable biomass and hunter strategies. In a fine-scale study, using standardized camera trap data from the Tropical Ecology, Assessment and Monitoring (TEAM) Network (TEAM Network 2011), Rovero *et al.* (2020) compared mammal species community composition in 16 tropical rainforests in protected areas in Latin America, Africa and Southeast Asia. Their results indicated a surprising similarity in the composition of trophic guilds of the studied communities as well as body mass distributions. Further analyses showed that the average community mass (i.e., large animals were less common) was negatively related to proximity to human settlements (see Chapter 6 for more on this topic). Rovero *et al.* (2020) uncovered both a similarity in functional composition and sensitivity to changes among the mammal communities found in each site, despite taxonomic dissimilarities and variation in habitat and in anthropogenic pressures. These findings validate the broader-scale study by Penone *et al.* (2016) and an earlier meta-analysis by Fa and Purvis (1997) of the similarities between tropical forest mammal communities in different realms.

As Rovero *et al.* (2020) has pointed out, similar habitat characteristics and anthropogenic pressure induce comparable functional responses in mammal communities in tropical rainforests where they exploit resources in similar ways (Jetz & Fine 2012; Ricklefs 2010). It is therefore not unexpected to find that tropical forest vertebrates with similar ecological roles on different continents possess similar morphological features, an observation made as early as the 1970s by Bourlière (1973). However, a conspicuous difference between the tropical forest faunas of Asia, Africa and Central and South America is in the number of vertebrates that evolved specialized locomotory adaptations such as gliding membranes or prehensile tails (Emmons & Gentry 1983). Most gliding vertebrates are found in the Asian tropics, most with prehensile tails in the Neotropics, and few of either in Africa. Such differences in arboreal vertebrate locomotion modes are likely to have resulted from adaptations to contrasting forest structures in different parts of the world. Emmons and Gentry (1983) explicitly suggested that liana scarcity in tropical Asia aids gliding and high liana densities in tropical Africa correlates with no specialized locomotory adaptations, whereas the presence of many palms, an intermediate number of lianas and even the abundance of more fragile branches in the Neotropics favours prehensile tails.

Although differences and similarities exist among taxonomic groups in how they adapt to living in tropical forests, species numbers are not just determined by the availability of energy in the system but the past climatic changes as drivers of mammalian evolution (see Moreno Bofarull *et al.* 2008). Local environmental factors and anthropogenic pressures also differentiate communities uniquely.

2.6.2 Comparing Continents

More refined censusing techniques, such as the more cost-effective camera trapping (such as in Rovero *et al.* 2020), reveal more precisely, the distribution and abundance of medium to large mammals in tropical forests worldwide. Measuring the standing biomass of medium to large mammals in Neotropical and Palaeotropical forests (but also grasslands) has been of interest to scientists attempting to better understand similarities and differences of faunas living in these habitats. As early as the 1980s, Eisenberg (1980) was one of the first to gather and review information on numbers and biomass of mammals in habitats as distinct as the Venezuelan llanos grasslands or Sri Lankan forests (McKay & Eisenberg 1974). Analyses of ungulate biomass and species composition in different habitats, such as Eisenberg and Seidensticker's (1976) study in southern Asia, taken from census data national parks and wildlife sanctuaries in India, Nepal, Sri Lanka and Indonesia (Java), were significant in advancing our understanding of Asian faunas. Eisenberg and Seidensticker (1976) observed that information on numbers and biomass of mammals in Asian habitats fell behind African studies. These authors suggested that factors including funding difficulties, research politics and a relatively small number of scientists at the time engaged in long-term research projects were to blame. Although, of course, much more research has been conducted in Asia in recent times, as indeed in other tropical areas, data on mammalian standing biomass in Asian forests is still limited. Part of the reason for this is that research on this topic has been superseded by more elaborate studies employing camera trapping techniques to answers more pressing questions such as the impact of defaunation, for example studies in Malaysian Borneo (Brodie *et al.* 2015) and Northeast China (Feng *et al.* 2021), or human–wildlife conflict affecting high-profile species (e.g. Wang *et al.* 2017). These recent studies rely on advances in non-invasive survey methods and statistical modelling techniques to address the status of mammalian communities and guild conservation actions.

Although research on mammalian faunas in tropical forests is currently much more focused, comparisons of existing data on population densities of individual species or groups and estimates of total mammalian biomass data are still valuable. The caveat, of course, is that these tropical areas have without doubt been affected by human actions and the precise numbers will not be the same as when the studies were undertaken. Given that available estimates on mammalian species composition and standing biomass within tropical forests are mostly for African lowland forests, particularly for the Congo Basin, and for forests in the Amazon Basin, in this section we will review these data to comprehend the availability of mammal meat to hunters. Here we present information on non-volant medium and large-sized terrestrial mammals that are hunted for wild meat (see Chapter 1). Bats, which are the most widespread mammals in the world, are not included in our review, since although hunted and consumed, are relatively less important (except one or two species that flock in large numbers) and often not included in forest animal censuses.

There is an overall similarity in the numbers of mammal families, genera and species inhabiting tropical forests in South America, Africa and Southeast Asia (Corlett & Hughes 2015). Native rodents, a group widely distributed throughout the world like bats, are important as wild meat, particularly the larger species. Ungulates inhabit most forests, but primates only naturally occur in warmer regions: both groups are important providers of wild meat. Elephants, which are still hunted, and their relatives were once widely distributed throughout most climates and regions of the globe until the late Pleistocene when the megafaunal extinctions took place, except in tropical and subtropical forests of Asia and Africa where they are now confined. True insectivores are also widespread in forests in the tropics, except in New Guinea, Australia and Madagascar, and are restricted to the northern Andes in South America. Carnivores and all other orders are geographically more restricted, although many are regionally important.

More than 90% of the non-volant mammalian faunas in the tropical forests of South America (Amazon) and Africa (Congo Basin) are endemic at the species level; 29% and 54% of the families are exclusive to Africa and the Neotropics, respectively (Fa & Peres 2001). Marsupials, edentates, pangolins, aardvarks, elephants and hyraxes are represented in only one continent. Forest mammalian communities in Africa possess the highest species richness in the world, paralleled only by some communities in Asian forests. By comparison, South American communities, despite their similar latitudinal position have a much lower species richness. These differences have been related not just to current determinants but to biogeographic-historic factors. Overall the difference in mammal composition between the two regions is related to the high diversification of large mammals in Africa, which greatly contributes to the high local community richness in this region. The absence of extant large mammals in the South American region is the result of Pleistocene–Holocene extinctions, which affected large mammals all over the world. Since the late Miocene and through the Pliocene, a decrease in the abundance of large mammal species has been observed in almost all regions except Africa (Nieto *et al.* 2007).

Overall, larger-bodied taxa, even excluding the elephant (>1,000 kg), are characteristically more common in Africa than in the Neotropics (Fa & Purvis 1997). There is a wider size range of diurnal primates, lorisids, squirrels, carnivores and hornbills in African forests compared with their ecological analogues in the Neotropics, namely capuchin monkeys (primates), didelphid possums, raccoons and toucans (Cristoffer 1987). The largest Neotropical forest mammal is the lowland tapir (over 50 kg) whereas 13 frugivorous and browsing mammals can be assigned to this size class in African forests.

In the Neotropics, the more modest cervid radiation contrasts with that of African bovids where more than 20 species occupy equatorial forest environments (Kingdon *et al.* 2013). Indeed, the most species-rich Neotropical forests typically contain only five sympatric ungulates (i.e., two peccary species, two brocket deer species and the South American tapir), whereas as many as 10 ungulate species (*Cephalophus* spp., *Tragelaphus* spp., *Neotragus* spp., *Hyemoschus* sp., *Potamochoerus* sp., *Hylochoerus* sp., *Syncerus* sp.) can inhabit African forests. A similar phenomenon can be observed among the primates. In South America, prehensile-tailed (ateline) genera (members of subfamily of New World monkeys that includes the various spider and woolly monkeys) rarely exceed 10 kg, whereas several living or extinct Palaeotropical primate genera exceed 100 kg, including *Pongo* in Southeast Asia, *Gorilla* in mainland Africa, and *Archaeoindris* and other giant lemurs in Madagascar (Peres 1994). This difference cannot be explained as an artefact of a less complete primate fossil record in the Neotropics (Fleagle *et al.* 1997). The largest known New World primate species was a giant ateline from the Plio-Pleistocene boundary equivalent in size to only twice the weight of modern woolly spider monkeys

(Hartwig & Cartelle 1996). In any case, environmental changes since then could have altered selection pressure on body size differentially.

Average body mass of present-day non-volant forest mammals in African rainforests is 37.45 ± 17.19 kg, n = 284 (data from Kingdon 1997), significantly larger than those in Amazonian rainforests of 4.80 ± 1.44 kg, n = 192 (data from Da Fonseca et al. 1996). More large-bodied species are found in Africa compared to the Neotropics; in African forests 60% of species are >1 kg and 22% are > 10 kg, whereas in the Neotropics the equivalent figures are 38% and 7% (Fa & Peres 2001). Furthermore, whilst the body size of mammalian primary consumers of a forest in northeast Gabon (n = 66 species) are uniformly distributed across five orders of magnitude (Emmons et al. 1983), those of a typical terra firme forest of central Amazonia are markedly skewed towards small- and mid-sized species (Peres 1999b). These continental patterns are also reflected in the larger size of fruits consumed by vertebrate frugivores occurring in tropical Africa and Asia, i.e., the tropics of the Old World, compared with those in the Neotropics (Mack 1993). Various ecological hypotheses have been proposed to account for the narrower size range of Neotropical birds and mammals (Cristoffer 1987; Fleming et al. 1987; Terborgh & Van Schaik 1987). However, differences between African and South American species assemblages may be related to the impact of humans on forest habitats and their faunas during the Pleistocene–Holocene. The postulated overkill of most South American Pleistocene megafauna by the earliest human colonists did not occur in Africa, where human hunters and large vertebrates evolved side by side (see Section 6.1). Nevertheless, extinctions of large-bodied mammals have occurred in all continents during the Holocene (Turvey & Fritz 2011), with such losses impacting ecosystem structure and function (Malhi et al. 2016).

Although cause and effect may be confounded, forest structure could also have contributed to the contrast in size structure of the mammal fauna between continents. In Africa, forest elephants and other large mammals play a key role in the functioning and structure of rainforests (Malhi et al. 2016; Prins & Reitsma 1989; Western 1989). In the large gaps created by logging or natural disturbance these mammals are attracted to areas with dense stands of herbaceous growth (Chapman & Chapman 1997). Gaps in African forests may also be more long-lived, allowing herb and shrub layers to take hold in favour of large terrestrial browsers due to a lack of aggressive colonizing tree species that can take advantage of large gaps, unlike Neotropical ones (Struhsaker et al. 1996). Neotropical forests also appear to be generally more 'fragile' than those in

Africa (Emmons & Gentry 1983), since megaherbivores like forest elephants have a long history of structural influence on vegetation (Tutin et al. 1997). Although tapirs can excavate salt-licks and selectively kill understorey saplings (Montenegro 2004), large forest 'landscapers' that can uproot small and medium-sized trees are conspicuously absent in the Neotropics.

Average total crude primary consumer biomass of non-volant mammals in African forest sites (mean $\pm$ SD = 2,848 $\pm$ 1,129 kg/km^2, n = 9) far exceed that in Neotropical sites (1,109 $\pm$ 245 kg/km^2, n = 5) (Fa & Peres 2001). Biomass figures taken from these areas may not necessarily be representative of forests in the whole region, since there are considerable differences in soil type, elevation and climate. For example, total biomass among different sites within the Lopé Reserve (White 1994) and the Virungas (Plumptre 1991) in Africa, varied between 1,000 and 6,000 kg/km^2. This enormous range in productivity was attributed largely to differences in densities of ungulates and elephants (Barnes 1993). However, in some areas duikers can attain a biomass higher than that of elephants (Dubost 1978, 1979), where human disturbance is minimal (e.g. Yao et al. 2017). Primates have been observed to dominate the mammalian biomass in several other sites (Oates et al. 1990), probably typical of tropical rainforest communities, where folivorous primates are most abundant (colobines, Colobus and Procolobus spp., in mainland Africa and howler monkeys in South America). Primates are the most significant arboreal consumers in rainforests in Africa (Emmons et al. 1983; Oates et al. 1990) and South America (Peres 1999b). Although significant variations at intra- and the intercontinental levels do occur primate biomass is highest in sites with low levels of hunting and logging. In Central African forests primate biomass can vary from approx. 700 kg/km^2 (Thomas 1991) in the Ituri Forest, DRC, to ca. 3,000 kg/km^2 in the Kibale Forest, Uganda, just 250 km to the East of Ituri (Struhsaker 1975, 1997). Similar differences exist in Southeast Asia (Gupta & Chivers 1999) and South America (Peres 1997, 1999b).

Factors that determine the density of primate populations are difficult to identify because primate communities in rainforests include species with diversified niches (Fleagle & Reed 1996). Primate biomasses are the result of complex interactions among the composition, seasonal behaviour and structural heterogeneity of vegetation and soil conditions, intercommunity competition, disease and parasitic pressures, and historical events (Chapman et al. 1999; Oates et al. 1990). Although a broad link can be established between ecological variables (e.g. food supply) and primate abundance, the picture is complicated by the influence of human disturbance (logging and hunting), and historical and biogeographical factors (Oates 1995). The considerable variation in primate density and biomass across a wide range of non-hunted and lightly hunted forest sites in Africa ($n = 7$; Chapman et al. 1999), and South America ($n = 29$; Peres 1999b) is therefore not surprising. However, overall primate community biomass in Africa is on average significantly larger than that in the Neotropics: African forests sustain a mean primate density of 194.8 ($\pm$ 210.5) individuals/km^2 (range 53–657 individuals/km^2), and a mean biomass of 857.8 $\pm$ 839.2 kg/km^2 (range 318– 2,710 kg/km^2), whereas South American sites exhibit much lower densities (123.6 $\pm$ 78.1 individuals/km^2, range 24–355 individuals/km^2) and biomass of 277.0 $\pm$ 177.7 kg/km^2 (range 70–953 kg/km^2). In general, most African forest sites are dominated by folivorous colobines, thus inflating figures of the number of animals present and their biomass. In Africa and Asia, colobines account for an average of 60% (range 28–91%, $n = 10$) of the primate community biomass (Bourlière 1985; Oates et al. 1990). In Neotropical forests, the equivalent arboreal folivores often represent over half of the biomass of non-volant mammals (Eisenberg & Thorington 1973; Peres 1997).

Many case studies suggest that the quality, quantity and seasonal availability of food are the most important proximate factors that limit primate populations (Chapman & Chapman 1999; Gupta & Chivers 1999; Mendes Pontes 1999; Milton 1982; Peres 1994, 1997). Because of the alternation of dry and wet seasons in rainforests, the availability of plant reproductive and vegetative parts is irregular and induces periods of abundance and scarcity of food for consumers (Gautier-Hion et al. 1980; van Schaik et al. 1993). In addition, long-term studies underscore interannual variability in production of plant foods (Gautier-Hion et al. 1985; Struhsaker 1997; Tutin & Fernandez 1993). However, in Africa, Chapman et al. (1999) indicated that forest type correlates better with primate biomass than does forest productivity (as gauged from rainfall); biomass in the wettest locality (Douala-Edea, Cameroon) with 4,000 mm of rainfall is six times lower than that of Kibale (1,662 mm). Differences in primate biomass in these two localities are marked by contrast in the abundance of colobines. Folivorous primates are likely to be regulated by the lowest level of food availability rather than by the overall level of productivity (see e.g. Tutin et al. 1997). Moreover, colobine populations have been shown to be limited by leaf quality, especially during periods of food scarcity (Davies 1994; Ganzhorn 1992). In forests dominated by leguminous trees of the Caesalpiniaceae (which do not produce succulent fruitsbut often containing secondary vegetation of trees with fleshy fruits, as in Makandé, Gabon, primate community biomass has been shown to be one of the lowest in Central Africa (Table 2.2).

Peres (1999a) has shown that forest type, hydrology and geochemistry were key determinants of primate biomass in Amazonia. Thus, forests on nutrient-rich soils, and perhaps with a higher fruit production, sustain a greater primate biomass, even when differences in hunting pressure are considered (Peres 1999b). Total annual food abundance but particularly seasonal availability has been shown to determine the biomass and species richness of frugivorous primates on three continents (Hanya *et al.* 2011). Using data from fruit fall from South American, African and Asian sites, best-fit models for predicting primate biomass included total annual fruit fall (positive), seasonality (negative) and biogeography (Old World>New World and mainland>island), explaining 56–67% of the variation (Fig. 2.5). For the number of species, the best-fit models include seasonality (negative) and biogeography (Old World>New World and mainland>island) but not total annual fruit fall. Annual temperature has additional effects on primate biomass when the effects of fruits and biogeography are controlled, but there is no such effect on species richness.

Studies in Africa, however, have suggested that soil chemistry is less important than growth stage, heterogeneity, taxonomic composition and history of the vegetation in determining the abundance of colobines (Oates *et al.* 1990). In fact, Maisels *et al.* (1994) and Maisels and Gautier-Hion (1994) showed that the primate biomass can still be high in forests on nutrient-poor white-sand soils, where legume seeds and young leaves become prominent in their diets. The foraging plasticity of African monkeys may also explain why no clear relationship between frugivore primate biomass (guenons and mangabeys) and fruit availability has been found (Tutin *et al.* 1997); frugivorous primates will increase their seed and leaf intake in forests where fleshy fruits are less diverse or absent (Brugiere *et al.* 2002; Maisels & Gautier-Hion 1994).

The distribution of mammalian biomass in rainforests, according to whether the species belong to arboreal or terrestrial guilds, differs significantly between continents. African forests are dominated by terrestrial species, whereas this trend is reversed towards arboreal taxa in Neotropical forests (Fig. 2.6).

Table 2.2. *Monkey biomass estimates in 10 African rainforests with low or no hunting pressure (data from Brugiere et al. 2002)*

	No. of monkey species		Colobine biomass (standardized)		Total community biomass (kg/km^2)		Reference
	Guenons	Colobines	(kg/km^2)	% total	Standard	Given by authors	
Kibale, Uganda	4	2	2,100	78	2,705	2,877	Struhsaker (1997)
Tai, Ivory Coast	4	3	1,108	77	1,436	NA	R. Noë (pers. comm.)
Tiwaï, Sierra Leone	4	3	602	55	1,112	1,221	Oates et al. (1990)
Minkébé, Gabon	4	1	36	6	622	NA	Lahm (1993)
Lomako, DRC	3	1	39	6	615	964	McGraw (1994)
Ituri, DRC	8	3	176	45	394	682	Thomas (1991)
Douala, Cameroon	5	1	218	55	395	384	Oates et al. (1990)
Lopé North, Gabon	5	1	114	43	268	268	White (1994)
Lopé South, Gabon	6	1	89	43	208	208	Brugiere (1998)
Makandé, Gabon	6	1	57	28	204	204	Brugiere et al. (2002)

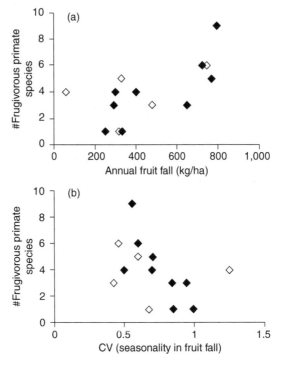

Figure 2.5 Effect of (a) annual fruit fall and (b) seasonality of fruit fall (assessed by the coefficient of variation of the 12 consecutive/average of 12 months' data) on the number of frugivorous primate species. Closed symbols indicate New World, and open symbols indicate Old World. (Figure from Hanya et al. 2011. Adapted with permission from John Wiley & Sons.)

Arboreal species account for more than 20% of the mammalian biomass in the few African forests surveyed to date, whereas this figure is typically 50–90% in the Neotropics. As a point of contrast, the terrestrial community of mammals in seasonally dry forests in the Amazon is more abundant than the arboreal one, with ungulates contributing to the bulk of the biomass, because of the strong seasonality. In Maracá in the Brazilian Amazon (Mendes Pontes 2004), biomass, due to the contribution of large mammals, was much higher (2,613 kg/km^2 in mixed forest, and 4,351 kg/km^2 in *terra firme* forest) than in the less seasonal Amazonian forests mentioned above. This study confirms that the animals surviving in larger numbers in these highly seasonal forests, where food productivity may be very low during the dry season, are those that have larger home ranges and travel longer distances in search of food.

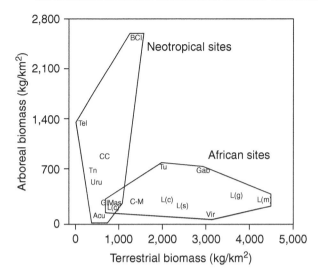

Figure 2.6 Relationship between the crude standing biomass of arboreal and terrestrial mammals in Neotropical and African forest sites. BCI, Barro Colorado Island, Panama; Tei, Teiú, Brazil; Tin, Tinigua, Brazil; Uru, Urucú, Brazil; CC, Cocha Cashu, Peru; Gua, Guatopo, Venezuela; Mas, Masaguaral, Venezuela; Acum Acurizal, Brazil; Itu, Ituri, Democratic Republic of Congo; Gab, Makokou, northeast Gabon; O-M., Ogooué-Maritime, Gabon; Vir, Virungas, Rwanda; L(g), Lopé Reserve, galleries and bosquets; L(m), Lopé Reserve Marantaceae forest, Gabon; L(c), Lopé Reserve, closed canopy forest, Gabon; L(s), Lopé Reserve, Sacoglottis forest, Gabon. (Figure redrawn from Fa and Peres 2001.)

The structure and distribution of plant production in these forests may explain, to some extent, the spread of mammalian consumers. In general terms, continuous close-canopy forests, which are more typical of the Neotropics, will have more of their plant production in the tree canopy (Fittkau & Klinge 1973; Lowman & Schowalter 2012), thus serving primarily the resource base of arboreal vertebrates. On the other hand, the terrestrial mammal biomass is expected to increase as large canopy gaps become increasingly common, allowing greater primary productivity for understorey shrubs and herbaceous layer. This trend is clearly uncovered when South American semi-open forest sites are compared with those under closed canopy (cf. Peres 1999b). Indeed, these appear to converge with African forests in terms of their terrestrial mammal biomass. Canopy structure at these sites is far more heterogeneous, allowing a greater proportion of total solar radiation to filter through to the understorey and ground layers, favouring the primary production that sustains the large-bodied terrestrial fauna. Although large frugivores and browsers occur at relatively low densities in both Neotropical (Peres 1999b; Robinson & Redford 1986) and African forests (Fa & Purvis 1997), these taxa can adjust to a relatively low quality diet, and hence harvest a greater fraction of the forest primary production. As we shall see, African forests should be able to sustain a relatively higher harvest rate per unit area, particularly at the higher end of the prey size spectrum, because they can support a far greater number of large-bodied herbivores.

2.7 Pressures Affecting Wild Species

Estimates of the percentage of Earth's surface that is directly influenced by activities of modern humans, in particular agriculture, grazing, forestry and logging, mining, infrastructure expansion and urban development, vary but are all alarmingly high (Box 2.1). By now, we have directly modified and transformed more than half of the Earth's land surface through agriculture and forestry, jointly modifying 47% of the land (Hooke & Martín-Duque 2012). Only less than quarter of terrestrial, ice-free lands shows no evidence of alteration and can thus still be considered 'wildlands' (Ellis & Ramankutty 2008). Daily (1995) estimates that approx. 43% of the surface experienced degradation by the mid 1990s and Bai et al. (2008) contend that approximately a quarter of the global land area has already been degraded.

Over the last century, terrestrial and coastal marine ecosystems have experienced significant reductions of quality and extent, and the losses are continuing. Excluding Antarctica and regions with predominantly rock and ice, only 23% of the world's terrestrial expanses remain as wilderness areas that remain fairly free from direct human impact (Watson et al. 2016). Most of the remaining wilderness areas occur in remote or inhospitable areas, such as northern North America, Siberia, Sahara and the Australian dry ecosystems. 'Fairly free' means that there are no areas in the world free of direct or indirect human impacts, especially since microplastics are now found in the most remote regions of Antarctic ocean and the deep sea, areas which are generally considered to be still pristine (Reed et al. 2018). A staggering 10% of terrestrial wilderness areas have been lost worldwide over the last two decades, especially in the Amazon Basin with 30% loss and Central Africa with 14% loss (Watson et al. 2016). At the same time, protection has been achieved for only half of the area that has been lost. Examples from wetland and forest areas highlight the extent of losses.

Box 2.1 *Assessing pressures on global biodiversity*

The framework of planetary boundaries includes the Biodiversity Intactness Index (BII) that estimates changes in community structure at a biome or ecosystem level from pre-industrial times until now (Steffen *et al.* 2015b). Pre-industrial levels result in a BII of 100%, values below 100% reflect reduced abundance of a taxonomically and ecologically broad set of species in an area and values above 100% reflect increases in the abundance of those species due to anthropogenic modifications to ecosystems. Because the relationship between BII and earth system responses remains poorly understood a preliminary boundary at 90% with a very large uncertainty range (90–30%) has been proposed (Steffen *et al.* 2015b). The global BII indicates that 75% of all loss occurred from the nineteenth century onwards and the value for 2015 is 78.5%, thus below the 'safe operating space' in the planetary boundaries (Hill *et al.* 2018). There is large regional variation but the BII is below 90% in all regions except Central Africa. The average for tropical forest biomes was 57.3% in 2001 and this fell to 54.9% by 2012 (Palma *et al.* 2021).

The most authoritative assessment of extinctions and extinction risks comes from the Red List prepared and regularly updated by the International Union for Conservation of Nature (IUCN) (IUCN 2020a). On average, about a quarter of assessed animal and plant species are threatened with extinction unless action is taken to stem their decline. Across the assessed groups of amphibians (40% threatened), birds (14%), conifers (34%), mammals (25%), reef corals (33%) and selected crustaceans (27%), more than 28,000 species are susceptible. No global estimates of past extinctions and current extinction risks exist for the most diverse, species rich and biologically important group – the insects. The most detailed data comes from selected insect orders from the Red List for Europe where 9.2% of bee species, 8.6% of butterflies and 17.9% of saproxylic beetles are threatened with extinction (Nieto & Alexander 2010; Nieto *et al.* 2014; Swaay *et al.* 2010). In terrestrial vertebrates, 322 species are listed by the IUCN as having become extinct with another 279 species either 'extinct in the wild' or listed as 'possibly extinct' since 1500 (Ceballos *et al.* 2015). During the same time period, approx. 1.4% of species of birds and mammals, the two best known groups, have become extinct, most of them since the beginning of the twentieth century. At least 3.1% of frogs have disappeared since the 1970s (Alroy 2015). These values are likely underestimates in particular because of time lags in confirming extinction events and taxonomic uncertainties, especially in less well-investigated groups, such as reptiles and amphibians. The number of eukaryotic species remains uncertain and it is conservatively estimated between 7.5 and 10 millions of which approx. 11,000–58,000 species are being lost annually (Dirzo *et al.* 2014; Mora *et al.* 2011). The global rate of extinctions exceeds by about 100–1,000 times the background rate of extinctions over past millennia indicating that we are at the start of the sixth mass extinction (Ceballos *et al.* 2015; Pimm *et al.* 2014). This estimate is likely an underestimate too because it does not include unknown extinctions, which are likely high for poorer known taxa and even for well-known ones. Moreover, the estimates do not include accrued extinction debt (Kuussaari *et al.* 2009) nor the negative trajectories of widespread population declines and extirpations even in species that are currently considered of low conservation concern (Ceballos *et al.* 2017; Dirzo *et al.* 2014).

A survey of 189 reports of change in wetland areas from around the world demonstrated that as much as 87% has been lost since the beginning of the eighteenth century (Davidson 2014). Losses accelerated during the twentieth and early twenty-first centuries with 64–71% of wetlands being lost since the beginning of the twentieth century. The extent of such dramatic loss of wetlands has also been confirmed by the Wetland Extent Trend Index (Dixon *et al.* 2016), which is another approach to estimate global change in wetland areas. This index is based on time-series reports of 1,100 wetlands from around the world. For the period 1970–2008 wetland declines vary between regions, from about 50% in Europe to about 17% in Oceania with an average decline of approx. 30% (Dixon *et al.* 2016).

Between 1990 and 2015, the total forest land area in the world dropped by 1–31% while the area of planted, secondary forest increased from 2% to 7% for the same period (Payn *et al.* 2015). Indicators relating to land-system change, expressed as the area of forested land as percentage of original forest cover, have reached and partially exceeded the precautionary safe boundary proposed by the framework of planetary boundaries (Steffen *et al.* 2015b). This framework defines a safe operating space for humanity regarding global biophysical processes. It uses deforestation as a key variable for land-use change because forest cover losses play a crucial role in understanding how anthropogenic land-system change affects biophysical climate regulation exceeding the importance of other biomes. The exact danger point for the reduction of forests that risks dangerous reduction in biotic regulation of global climate remains uncertain and has been estimated between 54% and 75% globally. The current value is 62%, thus indicating that deforestation is in a zone of uncertainty and increased risk of dangerous reduction in biotic regulation of global climate. So far, South America and the western parts of North America remain in the safe zone, northern North America, Northern Asia and Europe are in the zone of uncertainty and increased risk, but Africa and Southeast Asia are beyond the zone of uncertainty and are, therefore, at high risk.

Extinction debt refers to the future extinction of species due to events in the past. These species are impacted by past habitat loss, habitat alterations or invasions of non-autochthonous competitive species and are likely to become extinct in the future even without further deteriorating conditions. It is only the implementation of conservation measures that can remove them from the extinction vortex (Kuussaari *et al*. 2009). Estimates of current extinction debts range from 9% to 90% of current local species richness (Figueiredo *et al*. 2019). For example, deforestation in the Amazon has led to the local extinctions of 1% of species, but a further 80% or more extinctions are predicted from historical habitat loss (Wearn *et al*. 2012). Projections of the total period required to settle an extinction debt can extend to 1,000 years (Figueiredo *et al*. 2019).

An analysis of nearly half of the described vertebrate species shows that there has been around 32% average decline in abundance and range size during the twentieth century (Ceballos *et al*. 2017). All of the 177 intensively monitored mammal species have lost 30% or more of their geographic ranges and severe range declines of more than 80% were observed in more than 40% of species (Ceballos *et al*. 2017). Invertebrates are less well known but long-term monitoring data on a sample of 452 invertebrate species around the world indicate an overall 45% drop in abundance over the past 40 years albeit with large variance between insect orders (Dirzo *et al*. 2014). Indirect estimators of population declines using a variety of indices show similar declines. For example, the Living Planet Index (LPI), points to a 58% decline in vertebrate species between 1970 and 2012 (McRae *et al*. 2017).

Extrapolating to the future, the Geometric Mean Abundance Index, which is similar to the LPI, indicates that population abundance will decline by a further 18–35% while extinction risk increases for 8–23% of the species (Visconti *et al.* 2016). This model predicts future scenarios based on the extent of suitable habitat, projected land-cover and land-use and using different assumptions about species responses to climate change under the business-as-usual scenario.

2.8 Global Consumption of Wild Meat and Future Trends

Estimates of country-wide levels of wild meat consumption are scarce. Commonly used global datasets, such as the Food and Agriculture Organization of the United Nations (FAO) food balance sheets, have been applied to regional assessments (see Ziegler 2010 for Central Africa). These databases, although suffering from some limitations in terms of their accuracy, can still be used to compare annual consumption of wild meat in comparison to domestic meats for a number of countries. Using the Global Expanded Nutrient Supply (GENuS) database (Smith *et al.* 2016) amounts of wild meat (referred to as 'game meat' in the database) and domestic meats (Table 2.3) indicate that there is significant variation in amounts consumed by country, although the data contained in GENuS may underestimate wild meat consumption as it may not capture some types of wildlife consumed for food such as farmed reptiles, and there may have been reporting biases which vary by country, especially in places where wild meat is an informal sector or hunted illegally. The most significant difference can be seen when tropical and subtropical country data are compared with the other countries. In tropical/subtropical countries consumption of wild meat averaged 2.01 g/person/day compared to 4.88 g/person/day of domestic meats (only those countries are included where wild meat is also consumed). By contrast, in non-tropical/subtropical countries, an average of 22.48 g/person/day of domestic meats was typical, but only 0.79 g/person/day of wild meat/ was consumed. Wild meat consumed in tropical/subtropical countries accounted from 2.8% to 78.2% of all meats consumed, whereas in non-tropical/subtropical countries it was 0.0% to 8.0%. A quarter (25.8%) of consumed meat in tropical/subtropical countries was from wild meat, but only 1.2% in those non-tropical/subtropical countries where any wild meat was eaten. Cote d'Ivoire, Botswana, Republic of Congo, Cameroon, Ghana and Rwanda rely on wild meat for more than 35% of their protein intake. The dependence on wild meat in tropical/

Table 2.3 Amounts of domestic and wild meat consumed in a sample of tropical/subtropical and non-tropical/subtropical countries

Country	Domestic meat (g/person/day)	Game meat (g/person/day)	Game meat %	2020 census (persons/1,000)	Estimated game meat (kg)	Cattle equivalents
Tropical and subtropical countries						
Cote d'Ivoire	1.70318677	6.0995	78.2	26,172	58,267,182	261,204
Botswana	5.90501	9.7246	62.2	2,416	8,575,541	38,443
Republic of Congo	9.19758007	8.0824	46.8	5,687	16,777,082	75,209
Cameroon	3.8863377	2.618	40.3	25,958	24,804,686	111,196
Ghana	4.01481	2.4932	38.3	30,734	27,968,493	125,379
Rwanda	1.59589	0.98654	38.2	13,087	4,712,460	21,125
Central African Republic	9.1951	3.7551	29	4,921	6,744,779	30,236
Ethiopia	2.0599276	0.79195	27.8	112,759	32,594,314	146,116
Zimbabwe	5.63478	2.1336	27.5	17,680	13,768,548	61,723
Niger	4.367221	1.3872	24.1	24,075	12,189,847	54,646
Nigeria	2.72351	0.82683	23.3	206,153	62,215,522	278,904
Gambia	2.49804	0.61446	19.7	2,293	514,269	2,305
Namibia	10.13061843	2.4033	19.2	2,697	2,365,821	10,606
Mali	7.204667	1.3692	16	20,284	10,137,091	45,443
Guinea	2.4339	0.43278	15.1	13,751	2,172,173	9,738
Tanzania	2.85151	0.37731	11.7	62,775	8,645,257	38,756
Kenya	4.167496	0.51525	11	53,492	10,060,040	45,098
Benin	5.6920927	0.68129	10.7	12,123	3,014,637	13,514
Burkina Faso	4.841256	0.33325	6.4	20,903	2,542,563	11,398
Madagascar	4.3365243	0.27661	6	27,691	2,795,757	12,533
South Africa	18.843998	0.71549	3.7	58,721	15,335,215	68,746
Angola	9.92413	0.36732	3.6	32,827	4,401,175	19,730
Peru	6.709025	0.19438	2.8	33,312	2,363,443	10,595
Sudan (former)	6.48411	0.18741	2.8	57,151	3,909,394	17,525

(cont.)

Table 2.3 (*cont.*)

Country	Domestic meat (g/person/day)	Game meat (g/person/day)	Game meat %	2020 census (persons/1,000)	Estimated game meat (kg)	Cattle equivalents
Non-tropical and subtropical countries						
Morocco	10.229778	0.89328	8	37,071	12,086,896	54,184
Sweden	21.38267202	1.2017	5.3	10,122	4,439,717	19,903
New Zealand	36.63521	1.9008	4.9	4,834	3,353,791	15,035
Argentina	32.006247	0.82402	2.5	45,510	13,687,920	61,361
Germany	22.993859	0.59686	2.5	82,540	17,981,661	80,609
Mauritius	17.091997	0.4215	2.4	1,274	196,002	879
Norway	18.326832	0.41176	2.2	5,450	819,094	3,672
Denmark	20.9760395	0.45904	2.1	5,797	971,285	4,354
Switzerland	20.35068	0.42209	2	8,671	1,335,879	5,989
Austria	27.707007	0.52131	1.8	8,782	1,671,023	7,491
Cyprus	22.24949	0.28311	1.3	1,207	124,726	559
United States of America	33.5635315	0.444	1.3	331,432	53,711,870	240,783
Portugal	24.750034	0.29051	1.2	10,218	1,083,477	4,857

Protein from domestic meat (summed over different types of domestic animals; excluding offal) and game meat worldwide. Protein data from Smith 2016. Population census data from UN Department of Economic and Social Affairs, 2021. The cattle equivalent of is based on the average carcass weight of 326.8 kg from 436 young bulls of 15 Western European breeds, including specialized beef and dairy breeds and local breeds (Alberti *et al.* 2008) minus 30% for weight loss due to bones, trimming, shrinkage and other losses in the distribution system (Putnam & Allshouse 1999).

Countries with game consumption, but less than 1% of domestic meat: Belgium, Bulgaria, China, Czech Republic, Finland, France, Greece, Iran, Ireland, Italy, Kazakhstan, Lithuania, Luxembourg, Malta, Netherlands, Poland, Romania, Russian Federation, Senegal, Slovakia, Slovenia, Spain, Tunisia, United Arab Emirates, United Kingdom, Uruguay.
Countries without game consumption: Albania, Australia, Azerbaijan, Bahamas, Bangladesh, Bosnia and Herzegovina, Cabo Verde, Canada, Ecuador, Estonia, Georgia, Haiti, Hungary, Indonesia, Jordan, Kuwait, Kyrgyzstan, Latvia, Lebanon, Mauritania, Nepal, Republic of Korea, Republic of Moldova, Saudi Arabia, Serbia, Thailand, Yemen.

subtropical countries is orders of magnitude greater than in other parts of the world. These figures, although tentative, suggest that any increases in consumer populations would put even more pressure on the supplying wildlife.

If the amounts of wild meat eaten in each country are converted – for illustrative purposes – to cattle equivalents (see Table 2.3 for the conversion), then between 2,300 and 260,000 national cattle equivalents would be necessary to replace wild meat with domestic meat. As the cattle equivalent includes only slaughtered cattle, many more would need to be raised to achieve this number. Significant amounts of land would be needed to be converted to agriculture to raise that number of domestic animals. The required land conversion would not only destroy the habitat for the very same species that a conversion to domestic meat would aim to address, but it would increase zoonotic risk through habitat conversion and degradation (Chapter 7). Moreover, the required additional cattle raising would produce a significant carbon footprint and greenhouse gas emissions and would, thus, add to climate change (Nunes *et al.* 2021)

2.9 Overhunting: The Consequences of Increasing Demand

Evidence of increasing demand for wild meat, not just to supply the burgeoning numbers of potential consumers in rural areas but also to source urban markets is mounting throughout the tropics and subtropics. Such rise in hunting pressure, particularly on mammals, which are the most important source of wild meat as mentioned above, will increase the risk of extinction for many hunted species. Comparative studies have shown that extinction risk varies markedly across taxa and that species' biological characteristics can be an important determinant of this variation (Isaac & Cowlishaw 2004). An analysis of threat information gathered for more than 8,000 species in the IUCN Red List by Maxwell *et al.* (2016) revealed that by far the biggest drivers of biodiversity decline are overexploitation, agriculture and forestry. Of these 8,000 or so species, 19% (1,680) were directly affected by hunting and close to half (3,986) simultaneously by overexploitation and agricultural activity (Maxwell *et al.* 2016).

A global assessment of the impact of the hunting of species for wild meat consumption (and in some cases for medicinal products) has been more explicitly undertaken for terrestrial mammals (Ripple *et al.* 2016). The overall conclusion of this analysis was that a large number of terrestrial mammals are experiencing a massive collapse in their population sizes and geographical ranges around the world as a result of over-hunting. Ripple *et al.* (2016) identified 301 mammal species for which a primary threat is hunting by humans. This group of heavily hunted mammals represents 12 of the 26 extant terrestrial orders, approximately 7% of all assessed terrestrial mammals and approximately 26% of all threatened terrestrial species worldwide. Endangerment categories for these 301 species include 115 vulnerable (VU = 38%), 114 endangered (EN = 38%) and 72 critically endangered (CR = 24%). Orders with the most species threatened by hunting include primates (Primates, 126 species), even-toed ungulates (Cetartiodactyla, 65 species), bats (Chiroptera, 27 species), diprotodont marsupials (Diprotodontia, 26 species), rodents (Rodentia, 21 species) and carnivores (Carnivora, 12 species). Orders with the highest percentages of species threatened by hunting include pangolins (Pholidota, 100%), platypus and echidnas (Monotremata, 60%), odd-toed ungulates (Perissodactyla, 50%), primates (31%) and even-toed ungulates (30%). Mammal species threatened by hunting consist predominantly of ungulates for large-sized mammals (more than 10 kg), primates for medium-sized mammals (1–10 kg) and bats for small-sized mammals (less than 1 kg) (Fig. 2.7).

Almost all (95%) of the 301 threatened mammal species are affected by humans hunting these species for their meat, most of these species occurring in Africa, South America and particularly Southeast Asia (Ripple *et al.* 2016). Other reasons for hunting, such as the consumption of body parts for traditional medicine, for the pet trade or for ornamental use of body parts, were less common. Primates ($n = 25$) and ungulates ($n = 25$), but also various other taxa such as carnivores ($n = 8$) and pangolins ($n = 8$) were affected by use for medicinal purposes. Live trade mostly includes primates ($n = 31$), while ornamental uses (ivory, horns, antlers, skins etc.) largely involve ungulate ($n = 17$), carnivore ($n = 7$) and primate ($n = 6$) species.

Studies that have attempted to upscale local data with models based on quantitative relationships between impacts on wildlife populations and the main drivers of hunting pressure have resulted in useful impact maps. Regional impact maps for the entire Congo Basin (Ziegler *et al.* 2016) and for the Brazilian Amazon (Peres *et al.* 2016), described in Chapter 6, are excellent extrapolations of landscape use by hunters. Although similar analyses have not been undertaken for Southeast Asia, a simple model of hunter accessibility by Dieth and Brodie (2020) has proved valuable in understanding and predicting threats from hunting for Malaysian

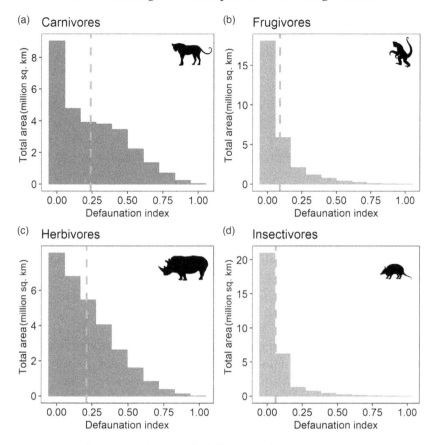

Figure 2.7 Defaunation Index (DI) for different trophic groups: (a) carnivores, (b) herbivores, (c) frugivores and (d) insectivores. The dashed grey line indicates the mean DI across the pantropical forest zone. The *y*-axes have different scales. (Figure taken from Benítez-López et al. 2019.)

Borneo. At a global scale, Benítez-López *et al.* (2019) have modelled hunting-induced mammal defaunation in the tropics to predict large-scale biodiversity loss, particularly in understudied areas. Using data for the main drivers of hunting, the authors developed a modelling framework based on a suite of important socioeconomic drivers of hunting pressure and taking into account the vulnerability of species to hunting. These drivers included hunters' accessibility to wildlife resources via road development and settlement establishment, hunters' preferences for certain species and proximity to urban markets (Benítez-López *et al.* 2010, 2017). Additional factors are human population growth and subsequent increases in wild meat demand, socioeconomic status, food security and governmental controls on hunting via law enforcement in protected areas. Subsequently, these models were used to map defaunation gradients across the tropics and to quantify the magnitude and spatial extent of the population declines of 3,923 mammal species. The declines were averaged across species into a Defaunation Index (DI) (Chapter 5). Areas with a DI > 0.1 (more than 10% average reduction in mammal abundance across all species) were considered to be partially defaunated, and areas with DI >0.7 to be severely defaunated. Defaunation hotspots were identified in areas where at least one third of the species had declines >70%. After overlaying the defaunation maps with intact forest (IF) (Potapov *et al.* 2017) and human footprint (HF) (Allan *et al.* 2017), the extent to which pristine landscapes could be defaunated are even clearer.

An average abundance decline of 13% across all tropical mammal species was estimated, with medium-sized species being reduced by >27% and large mammals by >40%. Mammal populations were predicted to be partially defaunated in approx. 50% of the pantropical forest area (14 million km^2), with severe declines in West Africa. Moreover, 52% of the IFs and 62% of the wilderness areas are partially devoid of large mammals, and hunting may affect mammal populations in 20% of protected areas in the tropics, particularly in West and Central Africa and Southeast Asia. Declines (shown in Fig. 2.8) were more severe for carnivores (DI: 0.24 ± 0.2, median: 0.19) and herbivores (DI: 0.22 ± 0.2, median: 0.17) than for frugivores (DI: 0.09 ± 0.1, median: 0.03) and insectivores (DI: 0.06 ± 0.1, median: 0.02).

In a meta-analysis of 82 studies on 254 mammal and 1,640 bird species from across the tropics, Osuri *et al.* (2020) assessed the effects of hunting, forest degradation and forest conversion, on measures of abundance for tropical mammal and bird species of different dietary guilds and IUCN conservation status groups. They found that mammal species across dietary guilds either declined or did not change, on average, in response to the three drivers, with hunting having the most consistent negative impacts on carnivores, frugivores, herbivores/granivores, large-bodied species and species of high conservation importance. By contrast, bird species declined most strongly in response to forest conversion, with responses varying widely across different dietary and conservation importance groups and not consistently related to body size. The results of this analysis reveal that hunting, forest degradation and conversion are associated with distinct types of defaunation of mammal and bird species and are therefore likely to have distinct implications for animal-mediated

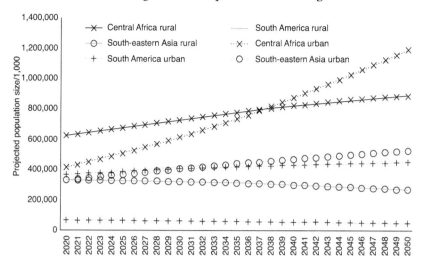

Figure 2.8 Human population sizes predicted by the FAO (2021) for 2020 to 2050.

interactions and processes, ecosystem functions and conservation of tropical forests. A follow-up study by Gallego-Zamorano *et al.* (2020), to understand how land use and hunting and their combined impacts affect tropical mammals found that, as expected, land use is the main driver reducing the distribution of the 1,884 studied mammal species. Yet, hunting pressure also causes considerable additional reductions in large-bodied species' distributions by 29% on average. Hence, large mammals suffered a disproportionate amount of area loss from both pressures combined. Areas of the world that were more affected by land use and hunting (hotspots) were the Gran Chaco, the Atlantic Forest and Thailand. In contrast, the Amazon and Congo Basins, the Guianas and Borneo were identified as coldspots. Any effort to protect tropical mammals must ensure that conservation policies address both pressures simultaneously, as their effects are highly complementary.

Importantly, we can safely assume that demand for wild meat, and thus the risk for over-exploitation will increase over the next decades. Figure 2.8 shows the changes in human populations for Central Africa, Southeastern Asia and South America, stratified according rural and urban populations predicted by the FAO (2021). Increases in rural populations are predicted to be high for Africa, slight for South America and slightly decreasing in Southeastern Asia. This indicates that the highest urgency to develop mechanisms to reduce wild meat in rural settings will be for Africa in order that the problem does not escalate.

Policies and management to control and decrease wild meat demand for urban areas must be very different than for that for rural areas because of the different driving factors for wild meat consumption (Chapter 6). Figure 2.8 shows high urgency to address urban wild meat consumption on all continents because of the foreseen increases in human numbers on all of these continents, but especially in Africa.

3 · *How Human Hunters Hunt*

3.1 Introduction

Hunting of wild animals, for meat and other body parts (e.g., pelts, horns, antlers) has been part of the human story for millennia. In this book, we focus only on the hunting of wild animals by humans for food. In this chapter we describe how humans hunt with a focus on technology and on the cultural and anthropological aspects of hunting; the topic of optimal hunting is addressed in Chapter 4. In broad terms, hunting can be subsistence, commercial, or recreational (Fig. 3.1, Ojasti 1996). We do not address recreational hunting, which refers to activities in which the main objective is the personal enjoyment of the hunter, rather than food or profit (e.g. trophy lion hunting, Whitman *et al.* 2004). Recreational hunting may have roots in traditional subsistence hunting or commercial hunting activities (McCorquodale 1997). We also do not address the removal of predators that can be dangerous to people or domestic animals, or the removal of pests that destroy crops or kill livestock, except when these animals are being used as wild meat.

Only in subsistence hunting is the sole purpose to provide food for the hunters and their families and hence it plays a vital role in their sustenance and even survival (Peres 2000). By contrast, commercial hunting takes place when natural products are exploited to be sold for profit. The consequences of unsustainable commercial harvesting of marine and terrestrial wild animals are now clearly felt throughout the globe (Di Minin *et al.* 2019). The impacts of uncontrolled commercial hunting on wildlife in the tropics and subtropics are also significant; these topics are discussed more in depth in Chapters 2 and 6 of this book.

In some countries, subsistence hunting is defined by law as just hunting for personal consumption, and it is often considered illegal to sell any surplus. Conversely, the sale of some of the animals hunted but not eaten by the hunters or their families, sometimes the most valuable species, can be an important source of income (Alexander *et al.* 2015; Coad *et al.* 2010; Schulte-Herbrüggen *et al.* 2013). However, Van Vliet

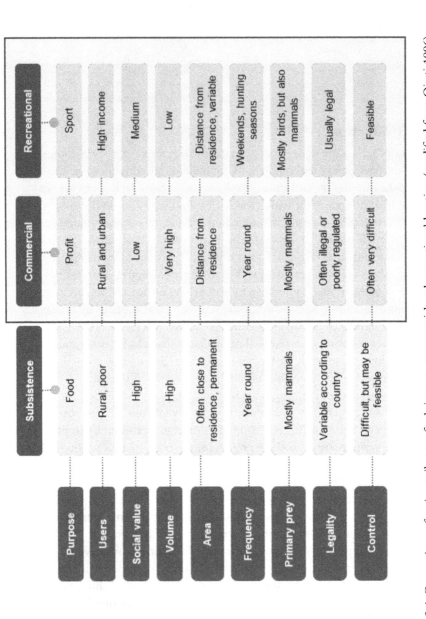

Purpose	Users	Social value	Volume	Area	Frequency	Primary prey	Legality	Control
Subsistence								
Food	Rural, poor	High	High	Often close to residence, permanent	Year round	Mostly mammals	Variable according to country	Difficult, but may be feasible
Commercial								
Profit	Rural and urban	Low	Very high	Distance from residence	Year round	Mostly mammals	Often illegal or poorly regulated	Often very difficult
Recreational								
Sport	High income	Medium	Low	Distance from residence, variable	Weekends, hunting seasons	Mostly birds, but also mammals	Usually legal	Feasible

Figure 3.1 Comparison of main attributes of subsistence, commercial and recreational hunting (modified from Ojasti 1996).

et al. (2019) argue strongly that formal regulations in many tropical countries are ill adapted to the reality in which rural and Indigenous Peoples live and that reforms which clarify the rights to sell surplus of meat and align land tenure rights with wildlife use rights are imminently needed. Many rural families sell surplus wild meat (see e.g. El Bizri *et al.* 2020b), and this can provide a very important source of income; if the right regulations are in place, surplus sale of wild meat should be permitted in rural settings (see also Chapter 8). Frequency of wild meat consumption and sale of wild meat are positively associated with proximity to markets, especially in urban centres (e.g. Sierra *et al.* 1999).

3.2 Hunting Technology

Since at least the past 200,000 years, when modern humans evolved, subsistence hunting for protein acquisition has dominated (Stanford & Bunn 2001). In fact, humans have spent more time as hunter-gatherers than as agriculturalists, industrialists or post-industrialists. This not only emphasizes the importance of hunting animals for our survival over many millennia but also highlights its role in the emergence and evolution of individual and social behaviour in our species. Because human beings are ill-adapted predators, lacking fangs, claws or high speed, hunting technology has filled this gap. Tools for hunting allow humans to expand the range of prey captured, reduce pursuit times and extend diet breadth by the use of methods for killing at a distance (spears, nets etc.), passive forms of animal capture (traps) and the use of methods to lure prey (decoys). In particular, projectile weaponry (such as the bow and arrow, and spearthrower and dart) has been a key strategic innovation that has aided ecological niche broadening and has allowed the dispersal of humans throughout the world (Shea 2006; Shea & Sisk 2010).

Numerous depictions of animals in prehistoric cave art clearly manifest the importance of hunting for human beings. Prehistoric cave art provides the most direct insight that we have into the earliest storytelling (Mithen 1989). One of the most primitive is the image portraying several figures that appear to represent therianthropes (human beings who metamorphose into other animals by means of shapeshifting) hunting wild pigs and dwarf bovids, the latter probably anoa, in the Leang Bulu' Sipong 4 cave in the limestone karsts of Maros-Pangkep, South Sulawesi, Indonesia (Fig. 3.2). The animals are being hunted by figures with animal characteristics who carry long thin objects that the authors interpret as spears and/or ropes. The interpretation of the scene is that it is a communal hunt, likely a game drive

Figure 3.2 Drawings found in Leang Bulu'Sipong 4 cave, south of Sulawesi, showing a buffalo being hunted by part-human, part-animal creatures holding spears and possibly ropes (from Aubert et al. 2019; reprinted with permission from Nature Springer and M. Aubert).

where animals of any species are driven from cover and directed towards waiting hunters. This image, created at least 43,900 years ago and described in 2019 (Aubert *et al.* 2019), has already been replaced as the oldest-known painting by the discovery of a figurative painting of a Sulawesi warty pig, dated to be 45,500 years old (Brumm *et al.* 2021).

In the following sections we describe the available evidence for the different forms of weapons and techniques used in hunting animals in the past and highlight both the importance hunting has had in the sustenance of humans over millennia but also how hunting technology itself has impacted their physical, social and cognitive evolution.

3.2.1 Projectile Hunting: Changes for the Better

Like most aspects of early biological and cultural evolution (e.g. Groucutt *et al.* 2015), the origin and development of projectile technology remain poorly understood. The earliest evidence for launched weapons used in both hunting and warfare for any hominid comes from several wooden spears found in Schöningen, Germany. These spears, dated ~400,000 BP, that is before the emergence of modern humans (Thieme 1997), were either hand-held, short-ranged thrusting weapons (Shea 2006; Thieme 1997) or throwing weapons for distances up to 20 metres (Milks *et al.* 2019). Relatively large, heavy spears sometimes tipped with stone armatures were typical of Neanderthal hunting, where Neanderthal upper limb and upper body morphology has been suggested to be an adaptation to the energetic and mechanical requirements of using thrusting spears (Churchill 2014). Thrusting and short-distance throwing spears preconditioned hunting strategies, and hunting with spears has often been equated with large hunter group size (Wadley 2010). The subsequent appearance of distance weapons is a critical development in human hunting technology. As a result, the arsenal of spears used by AMH was considerably larger, compared to Neanderthals who only used thrusting spears (Churchill 2014) or short-distance throwing lances (Milks *et al.* 2019). What were previously thought to be the oldest-known spears, those found in Clacton-on-Sea, UK (Oakley *et al.* 1977), and Lehringen, Germany (Movius 1950), dated to the Middle Pleistocene, have been debated because associated faunal remains do not necessarily demonstrate hunting (Klein 1987). For example, the Lehringen spear was found between the ribs of an elephant skeleton, but some authors have suggested that these sites are spring-, stream- or lakeside localities where it is difficult to separate bones that may represent natural deaths from human kills (Klein 1987). By contrast, the association of the Schöningen spears with stone tools and butchered remains of more than ten horses confirms them as hunting weapons, suggesting that systematic hunting that employed projectile technology was already present in pre-modern hominids.

The oldest backed stone blades have been found at Twin Rivers, Zambia, in deposits of approximately 300,000 BP (Barham 2002). Backed stone blades have one thick, blunt side suitable for hafting, with the attachment of the blades to wooden spears or arrows (Fig. 3.3). The design and preparation of backed tools, the preparation of hafts and the final hafting require problem-solving and planning that is usually associated with modern humans (Ambrose 2001). Indeed, new fossil finds, identified as *Homo sapiens,* from Jebel Irhoud, Morocco, place backed tool preparation at the same time as the emergence of AMH in Africa. These fossils, dated 315,000 ± 34,000 BP, show a mosaic of key modern human morphological features of early or recent AMH and more primitive cranial morphology (Hublin *et al.* 2017). The new technology together with new behaviour, including syntactic language, possibly allowed modern humans to expand their range into previously unoccupied Congo Basin tropical

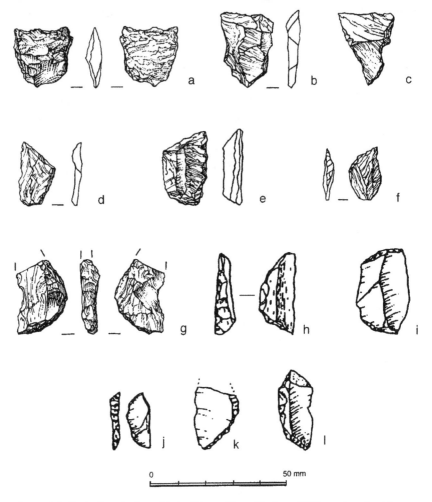

Figure 3.3 Backed tools from Twin Rivers (from Barham 2002 reprinted with permission from Elsevier).

forests (Barham 2001). Backed stone blades have been confirmed in East Africa at ~130,000 BP (Mehlman 1990) and in southern Africa between ~70,000 and ~60,000 BP (Wadley & Mohapi 2008). The latter paper describes Howiesons Poort Industry tools from Sibudu in South Africa, which are particularly interesting as they comprise diverse stone projectiles linked to different types of hunting tools. Tools made from dolerite were relatively large, too large for arrow heads, but suitable for darts and spearheads. Quartz tools were of a size of arrowheads, whilst hornfels tools varied in size and appear to have been reused during their lifetime for different purposes by reshaping. Trace analyses suggest that most tools were parts of hunting weapons, in particular bows and arrows (Lombard & Phillipson 2010; Wadley & Mohapi 2008).

Although lithic projectile weaponry has been confirmed across Africa before ~50,000 BP, it appears not to have been widespread or in regular use in this continent, in Europe or the Levant (Shea 2006). However, by 45,000–40,000 BP, lithic projectiles were in use in most parts of the world occupied by humans (Knecht 1997), after dispersing out of Africa and arriving at the periphery of the Old World, Australia, Siberia and northwest Europe by 50,000–40,000 BP (Groucutt *et al.* 2015). This widespread use of distance weapons for large animal hunting and warfare is regarded as an epiphenomenon of the 'Upper Palaeolithic' behavioural revolution as it involves planning, social organization and the application of suitable technology. Such use of projectile weapons allowed the more accurate killing of large, potentially dangerous prey at a safe distance compared to hand-delivered thrusting methods. The contention is that these technological changes diminished the need for muscular strength, thus affording the more gracile anatomically modern humans a competitive advantage over Neanderthals (Churchill & Rhodes 2006). Moreover, the development of mechanically delivered projectile weapons, spearthrower-darts or bows and arrows, further improved hunting efficiency in modern humans. The earliest evidence of mechanically delivered projectile weapons was found at Grotta del Cavallo in southern Italy, discovered alongside signs of hunting of young horses (Sano *et al.* 2019). These projectiles, dated to between 40,000 and 45,000 BP, correspond to the early migration period of modern humans into Eurasia (Groucutt *et al.* 2015; O'Connell *et al.* 2018). The Grotta del Cavallo projectiles pre-date the previously known spearthrowers and arrows from France and Germany by more than 20,000 years (Cattelain 1997; Sano *et al.* 2019).

3.2.2 Nets, Traps, Snares and Other Methods

In contrast to lithic artefacts and, in some cases, larger wooden fragments, materials such as fibres do not preserve well in the archaeological record. Evidence for hunting with nets, traps and snares is therefore rare; such information is, however, of importance for our understanding of human evolution. The operation of these techniques constitutes a significant milestone in the development of memory and cognition in planning across space and time (Wynn & Coolidge 2003). Nonetheless, indirect evidence from the Sibudu site in South Africa points to the use of snares during the Howiesons Poort Industry ~65,000–60,000 BP, possibly even ~70,000 BP (Wadley 2010). The high frequency and the relatively high taxonomic diversity of comparatively small mammals found at the site are consistent with modern snare hunting (Chapter 6) and not with hunting with projectile weaponry (bows and arrows or spears). This follows from our understanding of optimal foraging strategies (Chapter 4), which indicates that hunters prefer larger prey, especially when faunal assemblages are not depleted by overhunting, since during the Pleistocene human population density was likely to have been low. In Sibudu, the high frequency of small carnivores (including felids, viverrids, mongooses, mustelids and canids) does not suggest net hunting as these species are difficult to capture with this method but are easily caught with snares or traps. Trapping of carnivores often requires bait, often living. Using one prey animal to catch another presupposes a certain commitment to catch the carnivore. Generally, catching carnivores is more about protection against physical harm by such animals than for food since their meat is rarely preferred (see Section 3.4). The high number of carnivore remains in Sibudu suggest that they may have been caught for symbolic, medicinal or magic reasons, e.g. for their fur, teeth and claws. The high frequency of bushpig remains in Sibudu also suggests snare hunting because the species is nocturnal and dangerous to hunt. Although net hunting for bushpigs could have occurred, as demonstrated by Pygmy net hunters (Dounias 2016), these animals are strong enough to tear nets or break through the line of beaters rather than be cornered (Skinner & Chimimba 2005). The abundant remains of blue duiker, a common forest antelope, may point also to snaring since this relatively small animal is widely caught nowadays with snares throughout West and Central Africa (Fa *et al.* 2005) but is more difficult to hunt with bow and arrow or spears. However, duikers can be attracted in to the open by hunters imitating the call of a distressed animal (Brosset 1966; van Vliet et al. 2009). Finally, there is evidence that faunal assemblages in Sibudu became less diverse during the more recent Pleistocene, with fewer small mammals, bushpig or blue duiker remains being found. Wadley (2010) explains this change to be the result of larger hunter group sizes appearing as a result of population growth, thus allowing the hunting of large prey with spears. It is possible that, as observed in modern hunter-gatherers, as human group sizes increased large animals may have been primarily targeted by men, with the added benefit for the more skilled hunters to attain social prestige and kudos (see Section 3.4). Although in some contexts women are known to participate in active hunts with men (e.g. Aka Pygmy net hunting, Noss & Hewlett 2001), until recently when snaring has become commonplace due to the use of more affordable and accessible cable (Noss 1998b), trapping animals may have been largely pursued by women. This division of labour between the sexes has been postulated in Fa *et al.* (2013) to explain the difference in hunting techniques used by Neanderthals and AMH in Pleistocene Iberia. Snare hunting therefore introduces an alternative to large prey hunting which increases food security when men are unable to bring prey home. For the Hadza in East Africa, the chances of obtaining large prey was only 3% or 45 days of failure between successes, whereas snaring was successful with only one to three days of failure in-between and an overall success rate 40 times higher than that for large prey (Hawkes *et al.* 1991, 2001).

It is possible that pit trap hunting may have occurred as early as 40,000 BP. In a study in the Japanese Archipelago as many as 376 traps were excavated from 51 Pleistocene sites (Sato 2012). These were pits of about 1–2 metres in diameter, which may have been used for medium-sized prey such as wild boar and deer. Similarly, pit traps of over 20 metres in diameter have been discovered in Mexico containing a large assemblage of mammoth bones (Instituto Nacional de Antropología e Historia (Mexico) 2019). With an age of ~15,000 years they stem from the period of the peopling of the Americas and attest the versatility of humans hunting animals for food.

The oldest known confirmed evidence of the use of poison for hunting purposes dates to about 24,000 BP from the Border Cave in South Africa (d'Errico *et al.* 2012a). Although the identification and interpretation of archaeological micro-residuals of arrow poison is notoriously difficult (Bradfield *et al.* 2015), biochemical traces have been identified as arrow poison (d'Errico *et al.* 2012b). The technical and symbolic items also found at the site suggest that the Border Cave inhabitants used the same material culture 44,000 BP as today's San people, predating by 24,000 years the current consensus for the emergence of San hunter-gatherer cultural adaptations. The findings include bone points that are identical to San poisoned arrow points. Arrow points dated 37,000–35,000 BP, which could have been used with poison, have also been found at the White Paintings Rock Shelter in Botswana (Robbins *et al.* 2012). Today, San use beetle larvae and plant extracts to prepare poison for their arrow heads (Lee *et al.* 1976).

Another technological revolution appeared with the use of nets for hunting small and medium-sized prey. The first evidence for net hunting comes from the Pavlov and Dolní Věstonice sites in the Czech Republic (Pringle 1997; Soffer 2000, 2004) where clay fragments have been found bearing impressions of nets woven from wild plants and dated ~27,000 to ~25,00 BP. Evidence of the use of these nets is the large number of hare, fox and other small mammal bones found in the same site. The suggestion is that net-hunting is likely to have played an important role for food acquisition, introducing communal hunting practices that allowed children and women to participate (Soffer 2000). In the case of Aka Pygmy forest foragers of the Central African Republic women net-hunt more frequently than men (Noss & Hewlett 2001). In this particular context, women participated in net hunts when game was relatively abundant, they received relatively high caloric returns from hunting, they had access to the means/technology just as men, and importantly, Aka men did not prohibit them from participating. Thus, systems that are flexible between the sexes and ages and that adapt to prey abundance are likely to have been advantageous. When large prey was less abundant, the possibility of obtaining large numbers of small and medium-sized prey might have contributed to the development of larger, more settled populations as indicated from numerous archaeological finds for the Gravettian hunter-gatherers from Spain to southern Russia (Soffer 2000). This new technology may have also contributed to the diminishing selection pressure for muscularity, vital for large mammal hunting without mechanically delivered projectiles (see Soffer, cited in Pringle 1997).

3.3 Modern Hunting Techniques

Table 3.1 gives an overview of hunting methods from a total of 125 study populations where adequate information has been published. Available data reflects a strong bias towards Africa ($n = 90$) compared to South/Central America ($n = 21$) and Asia ($n = 13$). In Africa, much research interest has been directed towards hunter-gatherer societies, in particular the different Pygmy communities ($n = 33$). Information on the proportions of different hunting methods encountered is often not directly comparable with each other because they refer to different baseline units such as hunters (e.g. 10% of hunters used guns only) or the number of animals killed with each method. Moreover, some studies distinguish between technology used to kill animals, such as firearms and traps, from techniques such as hunting with dogs and horses, whilst some studies combine both, especially hunting with dogs (dogs may be used to chase and corner animals but also to kill their prey). For example,

Table 3.1 *Overview of hunting methods from a total of 125 study populations. When the mix of hunting methods differed or when different combinations of hunting methods were observed either over time or between study communities, studies are listed with separate entries for time or location*

Country, population, study period	Firearms	Modern snares	Explosives	Dogs	Traps	Bow & arrow	Spear	Club, stick	Knives / machetes / axes	Crossbow	Catapult/slingshot	Blowpipes	Fire	Trad. snares	Net	Hand	Others	Reference
Africa																		
Benin, 2017	x																	Ahmadi et al. (2018)
Botswana, review	x			x	x													Barnett (2000b)
Botswana, San, 1987/8				x		x	x	x										Ikeya (1994)
Botswana, San, 1990–2001		x		x	x	x	x	x										(Liebenberg (2006)
Botswana, 2014/5	x	x		x			x	x							x	x	x	Rogan et al. (2017)
Cameroon, mostly Badjoué, some Baka Pygmies, 2002/3/9/16	x	x			x												x	Ávila et al. (2019)
Cameroon, 2013	x	x		x			x									x		Bobo et al. (2015)
Cameroon, 1996	x	x																Delvingt (1997)
Cameroon, Fang (Bantu), 1984–91	x	x			x									x				Dounias (2016)

(cont.)

Table 3.1 (*cont.*)

Country, population, study period	Firearms	Modern snares	Explosives	Dogs	Traps	Bow & arrow	Spear	Club, stick	Knives / machetes / axes	Crossbow	Catapult/slingshot	Blowpipes	Fire	Trad.snares	Net	Hand	Others	Reference
Cameroon, Baka Pygmies, 2012/3	x	x			x		x		x				x				x	Duda *et al.* (2017)
Cameroon, Baka Pygmies, 2013		x																Fa *et al.* (2016)
Cameroon, Baka Pygmies, 2002		x					x		x							x		Fa *et al.* (2016)
Cameroon, Pygmies & non-Pygmies, 1994–6	x	x								x								Fimbel *et al.* (1999)
Cameroon, 1997	x	x																Fotso and Ngnegueu (1998)
Cameroon, Baka Pygmies, 2001/2	x	x		x			x		x							x		Hayashi (2008)
Cameroon, 1988	x	x																Infield (1988)
Cameroon, 1994/5	x	x																Muchaal and Ngandjui (1999)

Location								Reference
Cameroon, Fang (Bantu), 1904–9	x	x		x	x			Tessmann (1913a, 1913b)
Cameroon, Banyangi, 1999–2002	x	x	x		x			Willcox and Nambu (2007)
Cameroon, Mbo, 1999–2002	x	x	x					Willcox and Nambu (2007)
Cameroon, Banyangi, 2007	x	x						Wright and Priston (2010)
Cameroon, Baka Pygmies, 2002	x	x		x				Yasuoka (2006a)
Cameroon, non-Pygmy visitors, 2002	x							Yasuoka (2006a)
Cameroon, Baka Pygmies, 2002/3	x	x		x		x		Yasuoka (2006b)
Cameroon, Baka Pygmies, 2005	x			x		x		Yasuoka (2009)
Cameroon, Baka Pygmies, 2002–14	x			x				Yasuoka et al. (2015)
Cameroon, Konabembe, site 1, 2012/13	x			x			x	Yasuoka et al. (2015)
Cameroon, Konabembe, site 2, 2012/13	x						x	Yasuoka et al. (2015)
Central African Republic, Bofi & Aka Pygmies, 1999–2003	x			x		x		Lupo and Schmitt (2005, 2017)
Central African Republic, 1994	x							Noss (1998a, 1998b)

(cont.)

Table 3.1 (*cont.*)

Country, population, study period	Firearms	Modern snares	Explosives	Dogs	Traps	Bow & arrow	Spear	Club, stick	Knives / machetes / axes	Crossbow	Catapult/slingshot	Blowpipes	Fire	Trad.snares	Net	Hand	Others	Reference
Central African Republic, Baka Pygmies, 1994/5	x	x							x						x	x	x	Noss (2000)
Central African Republic, 2005	x	x																Remis and Kpanou (2011)
Côte d'Ivoire, 2012	x	x						x	x									Gonedelé Bi et al. (2017)
DRC, Mbuti Pygmies, 1984–8						x	x		x					x	x		x	Carpaneto and Germi (1989)
DRC, Mbuti Pygmies, 1985					x										x			Fa et al. (2016)
DRC, Mbuti Pygmies, 1985					x	x	x								x		x	Fa et al. 2016
DRC, Mbuti Pygmies, 1988					x	x	x										x	Fa et al. (2016)
DRC, Mbuti Pygmies, 1985					x		x								x			Fa et al. (2016)
DRC, Mbuti Pygmies, 1988					x	x	x								x	x		Fa et al. (2016)
DRC, Mbuti Pygmies, 1987					x	x	x								x		x	Fa et al. (2016)
DRC, Mbuti Pygmies, 1985					x	x	x								x		x	Fa et al. (2016)
DRC, Mbuti Pygmies, 1988					x	x	x								x		x	Fa et al. (2016)

Location, year							Reference
DRC, Mbuti Pygmies, 1985					x	x	Fa et al. (2016)
DRC, Mbuti Pygmies, 1985	x				x	x	Fa et al. (2016)
DRC, Mbuti Pygmies, 1985	x			x		x	Fa et al. (2016)
DRC, Mbuti Pygmies, 1985	x		x		x	x	Fa et al. (2016)
DRC, Mbuti Pygmies, 1974/5/80/1			x				Ichikawa (1983)
DRC, 2014	x	x		x	x	x	Spira et al. (2019)
DRC, Mbuti Pygmies, 1978/9				x			Terashima (1983)
DRC, Efe Pygmies &, 1982/1983	x			x	x	x	Wilkie (1987, 1989)
DRC, Efe Pygmies & Lese horticulturalists, 1982/3	x		x	x	x	x	Wilkie (1987, 1989)
DRC, Lese horticulturalists, 1982/3	x						Wilkie (1987, 1989)
Equatorial Guinea, 1986/90	x						Butynski and Koster (1994)
Equatorial Guinea, 1997–2010	x						Cronin et al. (2010)
Equatorial Guinea, 1998/99	x					x	Fa and García Yuste (2001)
Equatorial Guinea, 2003	x		x				Gill et al. (2012)
Equatorial Guinea, 2010	x		x				Gill et al. (2012)
Equatorial Guinea, 2002–4	x						Kümpel (2006); Kümpel et al. (2009)
Gabon, 1992	x		x			x	Carpaneto et al. (2007)
Gabon, 1988	x		x				Lahm (1994)

(cont.)

Table 3.1 (*cont.*)

Country, population, study period	Firearms	Modern snares	Explosives	Dogs	Traps	Bow & arrow	Spear	Club, stick	Knives / machetes / axes	Crossbow	Catapult/slingshot	Blowpipes	Fire	Trad.snares	Net	Hand	Others	Reference
Gabon, Pouvi, Bateke, 2004–10	x	x			x													Walters et al. (2015)
Liberia, review	x			x	x												x	Bene et al. (2013)
Madagascar, 2010	x	x		x	x						x							Gardner and Davies (2014)
Madagascar, 2004	x	x		x	x		x				x				x			Golden (2009)
Madagascar, review (bats)	x				x			x			x				x	x	x	Jenkins and Racey (2009)
Malawi, review	x	x		x												x		Barnett (2000a)
Nigeria, 2012	x			x	x				x									Friant et al. (2015)
Republic of Congo, Mbuti Pygmies, 1992/3						x	x								x			Carpaneto and Germi (1989)
Republic of Congo Aka Pygmies, 1991/2	x	x		x	x		x	x	x	x				x	x	x		Kitanishi (1995)
Republic of Congo,	x	x																Marrocoli et al. (2019)

Location										Source
Republic of Congo, Pygmies, 2009/10	x									Mbete et al. (2010)
Republic of Congo, Aka Pygmies, 2007/8	x				x			x		Riddell (2013)
Republic of Congo, Aka Pygmies, 1992/3	x				x			x		Riddell (2013)
Republic of Congo, Kaka, Bondongo, 2007/8	x									Riddell (2013)
Republic of Congo, Kaka, Bondongo, 1992/3	x									Riddell (2013)
South Africa,	x			x	x				x	Grey-Ross et al. (2010)
South Africa, 2003	x			x	x					Hayward (2009)
South Africa, review	x			x	x					Martins and Shackleton (2019)
Tanzania, review	x			x						Barnett (2000a)
Tanzania, review	x			x	x				x	Barnett (2000a)
Tanzania, 1998/9	x			x	x					Holmern et al. (2006)
Tanzania, 2007	x		x		x					Knapp (2012)
Tanzania, 2004/5	x			x	x		x		x	Magige et al. (2009)
Tanzania, 2009/10	x			x	x					Martin et al. (2013)
Tanzania, Hadza, 1985/6	x		x	x	x					O'Connell et al. (1988)
Zambia, review	x			x	x					Barnett (2000a)
Zimbabwe, review	x			x						Barnett (2000a)
Zimbabwe, 2009	x		x	x	x					Gandiwa (2011)
Zimbabwe, 2005–9	x			x	x				x	Lindsey et al. (2011b)
Zimbabwe, 2009	x			x	x				x	Gandiwa (2011)

(cont.)

Table 3.1 (*cont.*)

Country, population, study period	Firearms	Modern snares	Explosives	Dogs	Traps	Bow & arrow	Spear	Club, stick	Knives / machetes / axes	Crossbow	Catapult/slingshot	Blowpipes	Fire	Trad. snares	Net	Hand	Others	Reference
Asia																		
China, 2015/6	x	x																Chang et al. (2017)
India, Indigenous	x	x		x	x	x	x											Aiyadurai (2007); Aiyadurai et al. (2010)
India, 2006	x	x	x	x				x			x				x	x		Gubbi and Linkie (2012)
India, 2002	x																	Kaul et al. (2004)
India, 2002	x	x																Kaul et al. (2004)
India, Shertukpen, 2012	x			x														Velho and Laurance (2013)
Indonesia, 2011	x	x		x	x													Luskin et al. (2014)
Indonesia, 2005/6	x	x		x		x	x											Pangau-Adam et al. (2012)
Indonesia, 1995–9	x	x										x			x			Riley (2002)
Malaysia, Semaq Beri, 1978/9									x			x						Kuchikura (1988)
Malaysia, Temuan, 2004	x				x						x	x						Naito et al. (2005)
Myanmar, 2002/3	x	x			x					x								Rao et al. (2005)

Location, group, year								Reference
Vietnam, Katu, 2011	x		x		x			MacMillan and Nguyen (2014)
Latin America								
Bolivia, Brazil, Colombia, Ecuador, Peru, Suriname, Venezuela, Indigenous, review	x		x		x		x	Jerozolimski and Peres (2003)
Brazil, mixed,	x	x	x			x		Alves et al. (2009)
Brazil, Kaxinawa, 2006–9	x			x			x	de Araujo Lima Constantino (2015)
Brazil, Indigenous, 2001/2	x		x					de Mattos Vieira et al. (2015)
Brazil, 2004/5	x		x		x		x	Jean Desbiez et al. (2011)
Brazil, Guajá	x		x		x			Forline (1997)
Brazil, 1973/4	x	x						Smith (1976)
Ecuador, Huaorani, 2002	x	x	x	x		x	x	Franzen (2006)
Ecuador, Huaorani	x		x		x			Lu (1999)
Ecuador, Huaorani, 1989/90	x			x		x		Rival (2003)
Ecuador, Huaorani,	x		x		x			Yost and Kelley (1983)
Ecuador, Shuar, 2001–3	x		x	x		x		Zapata-Ríos et al. (2009)
Latin America, Indigenous, review	x		x			x	x	Redford and Robinson (1987)
Latin America, Mestizo, review	x		x					Redford and Robinson (1987)

(cont.)

Table 3.1 (*cont.*)

Country, population, study period	Firearms	Modern snares	Explosives	Dogs	Traps	Bow & arrow	Spear	Club, stick	Knives / machetes / axes	Crossbow	Catapult/slingshot	Blowpipes	Fire	Trad.snares	Net	Hand	Others	Reference
Mexico, Maya	x								x									Jorgenson(1993)
Nicaragua, Mayangna and Miskito, 2004/5	x			x														Koster(2008b)
Nicaragua, Mayangna, Miskito,	x			x			x		x									Koster(2007)
Panama, Mestizos, Buglé, Ngöbe, 1999/2000	x			x	x	x					x							Smith(2008)
Peru, Machiguenga, 1988–91						x												Alvard (1993a, 1995b,)
Peru, Piro, 1988–91	x					x												Alvard (1993a, 1995b)
Peru, Matses	x			x		x	x	x	x									Romanoff(1984)
Worldwide																		
Review (bats)	x				x	x	x	x			x				x	x	x	Mickleburgh *et al.* (2009)
Total	93	72	2	41	42	36	40	18	18	9	8	9	2	5	30	19	25	
Percentage	77	60	2	34	35	30	33	15	15	7	7	7	2	4	25	16	21	

Friant *et al.* (2015) report that techniques included traps (75%), guns (71%), machetes (71%) and dogs (18%). Elsewhere, they refer to 'hunting with a gun and dog', raising the question of how the prey was killed. Since hunters with dogs typically use other hunting technologies at the same time (Koster 2009) and the use of ammunition is expensive, the question is how to interpret the data listed in publications. In the case of Friant *et al.*'s study (2015), did dogs kill 18% of prey and guns kill 71% or were guns even more important by killing 89% of prey? Hunting with nets is a similar problem because it remains often unclear how the netted animals were killed. Dounias (2016) points out that spears are mainly used to deliver the coup de grace to animals cornered by dogs or nets and are rarely used as the sole hunting technique, but studies are often not clear whether spears are supporting net hunting or constitute separate strategies. Most studies imply but do not clearly indicate whether snares refer to modern snares that use wire cable made of metal or nylon. Snares made with plant fibres were recorded alongside snares made using metal wire in the Republic of Congo (Kitanishi 1995). Marrocoli *et al.* (2019) refer to snare hunting throughout their document without specifying whether modern or traditional snares are used, but their reference to the Congolese law forbidding hunting with metal snares implies that the snare hunting in question refers to modern ones. Only three studies explicitly referred to traditional snares or snares made from vegetable fibres. Use of snares is generally illegal. Although all studies were careful to work on the basis of anonymity, the response especially regarding snares might be biased and may underestimate the general use of trapping with this method. Casual and unreliable reporting is a general problem with questionnaires, especially when illegal methods are involved. For example, in the state of Arunachal Pradesh in India, hunters reported 11 mammalian species hunted during formal interviews but another 22 species were observed during casual visits, festivals and informal discussions (Aiyadurai *et al.* 2010). Notwithstanding these shortcomings, several key features are discernible from Table 3.1, as examined below.

3.3.1 Hunters Use Many Different Technologies

Almost all studies list more than one technology used, their mix depending on the type of animals hunted and local traditions (Fig. 3.4). This variation is best illustrated by the broad spectrum of how bats are caught and killed. Bats are common wild meat items in Africa and Asia, but are rarely targeted in South and Central America with the exception

Figure 3.4 (a) Asurini do Tocantins tribe member from the region between the Xingu and Tocantins rivers holding bow and arrow (WIN-Initiative/The Image Bank Unreleased/Getty Images); (b) Huaorani hunter from Ecuador using blowgun in forest (WIN-Initiative/The Image Bank Unreleased/Getty Images); (c) Bayaka or Aka tribesman holding spear in a forest in the Central African Republic (Timothy Allen/The Image Bank Unreleased/Getty Images); (d) Yangoru Boiken bat catcher retrieves a giant fruit bat from his net in the foothills of Mount Turu, East Sepik Province, Papua New Guinea (Timothy Allen/The Image Bank Unreleased/Getty Images).

of one Indigenous tribe, the Nambiquara of Western Brazil, who actively hunt three Phyllostomid bat species for food (Jenkins & Racey 2009; Mickleburgh et al. 2009; Setz & Sazima 1987). Bats are usually hunted either at roosting sites or at feeding sites by a wide variety of methods – bait and hook, bamboo poles with thorns or fish hooks on the end, barbed burrs of some plant species, birdlime, bow and arrow, by hand, catapults and slingshots, fire, firearms including guns, rifles and airguns, funnel traps to catch bats emerging from caves, hand nets, kites with hooks, nylon lines and ropes with hooks, snares, specialized large nets or fishing nets at roost or feeding trees, sticks, stoning and thorny bushes (Mickleburgh et al. 2009).

3.3.2 Techniques Differ between Neighbouring Villages and Regions

Hunting techniques seem to be determined by a mix of tradition, prey species and their densities, but also by the motivations of the hunters themselves. Mbuti Pygmy hunters of the Ituri forest in the Northeastern Congo Basin can be divided according whether they preferentially use bows and arrows or net hunting (Carpaneto & Germi 1989, 1992; Ichikawa 1983; Terashima 1983). The use of bows and arrows is the original subsistence hunting strategy of all the Mbuti Pygmies and involves either solitary hunts in which the archer walks in the forest or lies in ambush, and communal beat-hunt hunting, the so-called *mota*. This Mbuti Efe subgroup in the northeastern parts of the Ituri forest is in social contact with local Sudanic Lese agriculturalists and has adopted iron arrowheads and spear blades from the Lese but never engages in net hunting. The Mbuti Swa use nets alongside bows and arrows. Living in the central, southern and western parts of the Ituri forest, they are in social contact with local Bantu Bira and Ndaka agriculturalists, from whom the Swa have adopted net technology when they invaded the forest about 1,000–3,000 BP.

The impact of the motivation to hunt with different methods is demonstrated by the four different ethnic groups living around the Banyang-Mbo Wildlife Sanctuary in southwestern Cameroon (Willcox & Nambu 2007). The Mbo are almost exclusively hunters and gatherers while the Banyangi are hunters, gatherers and also cash-crop farmers. Both groups use shotguns and wire snares at almost the same rate (Banyangi 55% and 37%, respectively; Mbo 56% and 38%, respectively). The Bakossi and Basossi primarily farm cash crops (coffee and cocoa) and do not hunt, but their cash income allows them to buy domestic meat, wild meat and fish. In the oil palm plantation-dominated landscapes of Sumatra motivations and weapon choice are also aligned with the different ethnic groups (Luskin *et al.* 2014). Subsistence hunting is predominant in Javanese immigrants and Malay smallholder farmers, who used snare hunting and air rifles to hunt macaques and wild boar for both pest control and consumption. Professional Chinese and Batak hunters specialized in herding wild boar into wire net traps for subsequent sale. Social and cultural reasons are also the motivations for weekly large social day hunts with dogs by ethnic Minangkabau. Finally, wealthy members of a sport hunting group used hunts with firearms from pick-up trucks at night for sport.

The choice of weapon can depend on which prey hunters pursue. For example, Rogan *et al.* (2017) demonstrates that prey size and weapon choice are significantly correlated with firearms preferred for large game. Optimal foraging theory (Chapter 4) predicts a broad prey profile when a less efficient hunting technology is used compared to a narrower profile for firearms. Indeed, Aché bow hunters' prey profile is broad and includes less profitable species typically not targeted by shotgun hunters (Alvard, 1993; Hill & Hawkes 1983). Although firearm usage is not always correlated with the mean body mass of the target prey (Fa & García Yuste 2001; Gonedelé Bi *et al.* 2017), the general trend is the focus on large animals, one of the main threats against wildlife in Central Africa (Kümpel 2006). This is especially problematic for arboreal primates which are preferentially targeted with firearms (Bobo *et al.* 2015; Mittermeier 1987). Dounias (2016) reports that Fang hunters shoot 82% of harvested primate biomass, although firearms contributed 37% of the hunted biomass overall. Traditional weapons may be superior for animals moving in large groups since silent weapons such as blowguns allow the pursuit of several group-members unlike rifles which will invariably disperse the targeted group after hearing the shot (Peres 1990). However, shotguns can be used to kill several animals in large dense groups that remain in the same location, for example, the shooting of numerous individual mandrills who will remain on a refuge tree without dispersing, (see Fa and García Yuste (2001).

Prey density can also determine the hunting methods employed. In a study of hunting in two villages by Indigenous Central African foragers, Lupo and Schmitt (2017) observed that although hunters used the same range of technology there were differences in the frequency of hunting strategies depending on prey density. Hunters from the village in whose area the mean encounter rates with blue duikers, a preferred prey species, was low, would use more individualized technologies such as hand capture, spears and snares. Village hunters from the area with overall high wildlife encounter rates would use nets more often, predominantly targeting blue duikers. In two adjacent Community Hunting Zones in Cameroon, the more densely populated and thus the more heavily hunted zone would be primarily hunted using firearms, providing 79% of the hunted prey, whereas the less densely populated zone was targeted by snares, providing 82% prey (Bobo *et al.* 2015).

3.3.3 Firearms Are the Dominant Hunting Technology Today

Firearms were used in three quarters of the study sites in Table 3.1. Wild animals are hunted with shotguns, rifles, airguns, modern automatic weapons such as the AK47 (Barnett 2000a) and ancient muzzle-loader guns (Barnett 2000a; Martin *et al.* 2013; Sirén & Wilkie 2016). There is limited information to determine when firearms started being used for hunting in the tropics. In Gabon, guns were traded in the late 1800s, but they only became common in the 1960s (Bernault, 1996, cited in Walters *et al.* 2015). In the Congo Basin, guns were imported from the 1840s onwards, but they did not become widespread until the twentieth century (Savorgnan de Brazza, 1888, cited in Dounias 2016). Technical advances in the mid 1800s, such as the invention of the breech-loading rifle, spread slowly because of the cost and restrictions imposed by the colonial masters. The price of gunpowder also remained prohibitive and delayed the advance of firearms for hunting until the 1930s (Dounias 2016). The subsequent change from black gun powder to the much more powerful smokeless powder improved hunting efficiency substantially as it dramatically increased shooting distance and, thus, outcompeted bows and arrows (Faure, 2002, cited in Dounias 2016). The final technical innovation making firearms highly detrimental for wildlife has been the introduction of flashlights (Dounias 2016), and more recently the even more efficient LED lights (Bowler *et al.* 2019). Lighting allows hunting at night, preferred by many hunters (e.g. Ahmadi *et al.* 2018; Holmern *et al.* 2006; Yasuoka *et al.* 2015) because many prey species are more easily detected due to eye reflection of light. Moreover, species such as duikers freeze when targeted by flashlights, making them especially easy prey for night hunters (Yasuoka *et al.* 2015).

Despite the cost of firearms having come down dramatically and the availability of relatively cheap, locally produced weapons, initial purchase and cost of ammunition remains prohibitive for many people in the tropics (Sirén & Wilkie 2016). Gun hunting is the prime activity of soldiers and of wealthier individuals, often from regional cities, such as in Madagascar (Golden 2009) and Cameroon (Yasuoka 2006b). In many hunter-gatherer societies, gun hunting appears only secondary to snaring because of the higher cost and the greater skill involved (Kümpel 2006; Kümpel et al. 2008). This is borne out for most studies on Indigenous Peoples where there is quantitative data (Table 3.1). For example, Baka Pygmy hunters need to sell six duiker carcasses to buy a single rifle cartridge (Yasuoka 2006b). None of the Aka Pygmy hunters owned firearms, but most of their non-Pygmy neighbours owned shotguns and sometimes rifles (Kitanishi 1995). To overcome the problem of excessive costs of hunting with firearms, three strategies are often adopted. First, many hunters reload their cartridges with locally produced gunpowder (de Mattos Vieira et al. 2015) or use muzzle-loaders (Sirén & Wilkie 2016). Second, Baka Pygmy and Aka Pygmy hunters provide services for their richer, non-Pygmy neighbours who provide them with firearms and ammunition in exchange for meat (Duda et al. 2017; Kitanishi 1995; Yasuoka 2006b; Yasuoka et al. 2015). Here the main parts of a carcass are kept by the owner of the ammunition, thus making the social relationships between the parties involved also a strong social regulator (Hayashi 2008). In the case of the Aka Pygmies, the hunter is given the head, neck and internal organs plus two cigarettes (Kitanishi 1995). Third, increased market participation can increase cash income and make firearms and ammunition more affordable (Levi et al. 2011a). For those who decide to follow this avenue, the extra cost forces hunters to maximize the amount of meat per shot (Jerozolimski & Peres 2003), and to provide meat for sale rather than for their own consumption.

There are also social barriers against adopting hunting with firearms, especially amongst hunter-gatherers. Baka Pygmy hunters fear conflicts with the owners and lenders of guns, fear anti-poaching controls, fear the physical risks posed by old weapons and often do not have the required skills to use firearms (Duda 2017; Duda et al. 2017). On the other hand, firearm hunting bestows high social status. In Baka Pygmy society, shotgun hunters are often considered 'the best hunters' (Duda 2017). When Baka hunters have access to guns, their success can exceed the success of non-Pygmy hunters dramatically (Fa et al. 2016). Where poaching carries the risk of detection, such as in protected areas, firearms are generally avoided as gunshots alert ranger patrols to the presence of the hunter (Gandiwa 2011). A new development in areas where hunting with firearms is illegal is the replacement of firearms by running prey down with motorbikes or horses and then killing the animals with axes, clubs, spears or machetes to avoid the sound of shots, for example, in Tanzania (Kiffner *et al.* 2014) and Botswana (Rogan *et al.* 2017).

Firearm use in the surveyed studies can vary from none to all hunters using firearms and none to all animals killed with firearms, indicating that a multitude of factors impact gun use. There is a general, but not uniform, trend of increasing gun usage over time. Gill *et al.* (2012) visited the same site during a period of rapid national economic growth in Equatorial Guinea and reported that hunters using guns increased from 2% in 2003 to 22% by 2010. Percentage of animals taken by shotgun rose over a 14-year period on Bioko Island in Equatorial Guinea (Cronin *et al.* 2010). In Cameroon, gun use increased, replacing snares, in both a 15-year study in the Lebialem Division, in the southwest of the country (Wright & Priston 2010) and in three villages near the Dja Biosphere Reserve (southeast Cameroon) between 2003 and 2016 (Ávila *et al.* 2019).

Gun use differs amongst ethnicities, reflecting changes in socio-economic systems and lifestyle. Shotgun use in Aka Pygmy hunters increased as a percentage of livelihood activities from 5–29% in 1992/3 to 18–56% in 2007/8. By contrast, their farmer-fisher neighbours kept shotgun use at a similar level; 7–29% in 1992/2 and 7–27% in 2007/8 (Riddell 2013). Yasuoka *et al.* (2015) report on gun use of Konabembe in Cameroon in two adjacent areas and found that at one site 17% of hunters used guns (killing 16% of prey) whilst at a second site 58% of hunters used guns and killed 70% of prey. The two sites differed in their prey density, species composition, forest disturbance, hunting pressure and human density, but it remains unclear what caused the difference in gun use.

In Liberia, ancestral hunting methods have all disappeared and have been replaced by cable snares and shotguns since the civil conflict from 1989 to 2003 (Bene *et al.* 2013). Similarly, civil conflicts which have ravaged the Congo Basin for decades have collapsed many economies and the easy access to firearms may have enabled even more wild meat hunting. In the Amazon Basin, Western contact has led to a rapid change from traditional methods to guns and dogs across all Indigenous societies (Jerozolimski & Peres 2003). Amongst the Huaorani living in the Yasuní National Park, Ecuador, changes in hunting practices were reported in Papworth *et al.* (2013b). The only two South American studies that did not record the use of firearms were both from the 1980s and are for the Huaorani in Ecuador (Rival 2003; Yost & Kelley 1983). All studies from the 1990s and 2000s reported the use of firearms (Franzen 2006; Lu 1999).

There is clear evidence that hunting with guns is much more efficient than hunting with bow and arrow or blowpipes in terms of the number of animals killed at least in the short term. Alvard and Kaplan (1991) compared two Indigenous communities in southeastern Peru, one of which hunted with guns and the other with traditional bow and arrow. Shotgun hunters had relatively short pursuits, averaged 1.3 shots per kill, killed prey often with a single shot, and had uniformly high return rates ranging between 1.2 and 1.5 kg per hour of hunting. In contrast, bow hunters had relatively long pursuits, averaged 30 shots per kill, often missed their target or wounded but did not kill the prey and had low return rates of 0.10 kg per hour of hunting. Wherever there is a mix of modern and traditional hunting technology used, guns attain higher prey kills in study sites in South America (Alvard & Kaplan 1991), Africa (e.g. Baka Pygmy hunters, Duda *et al.* 2017) and Asia (e.g. in Arunachal Pradesh, northeast India Aiyadurai *et al.* 2010).

The problem with hunting with guns lies in its long-term impact on prey populations if commercial hunting is the main aim. Guns allow the killing of many more animals in a shorter time than traditional hunting methods. When prey is hunted for hunters' own consumption only, the increased efficiency afforded by guns reduces the required time for subsistence hunting and can allow hunters to reinvest spare time in other activities. When prey is being sold, however, the time saved can be invested in killing more animals. When animals and prey are not privately but communally owned, the Tragedy of the Commons dictates that as many animals as possible should be killed, leading to severe overhunting and unsustainability (Chapters 4 and 5).

3.3.4 Modern Snares Are the Second Most Utilized Hunting Technology Globally

Traditional snares are encountered rarely, with only five study sites reporting snares made of vines, mostly from the last century (Carpaneto & Germi 1989; Dounias 2016; Fa *et al.* 2016; Kitanishi 1995; Tessmann, 1913a). Modern cable snares were used in 57% of study sites. Snare hunting is rare in the Neotropics, where only 2 out of 20 study sites listed them as a hunting technique, compared to 75% in Asia and 68% in Africa. Although snares appear to be a major cause of prey declines across tropical Asia, information on snare hunting is still sketchy (Gray *et al.* 2018; Harrison *et al.* 2016). Their relative absence in the Neotropics might be related to the generally lower prey population densities of forest mammals,

Figure 3.5 Blue duiker caught using nylon rope snares in Bioko Island, Equatorial Guinea (photo: M. Grande-Vega).

making snares comparatively unprofitable (Fa & Purvis 1997; Peres 2000). However, although snares are illegal in most countries in Africa, they still account for most prey killed, as well as biomass, compared to firearms (Fa & Peres 2001). Their popularity is based on the fact that the material used, wire or nylon cord (Fig. 3.5), is easy to obtain, inexpensive, durable and strong enough for larger animals. Snares can be set under cover of darkness and their low detectability makes them a prime choice for poachers (Gandiwa 2011; Knapp 2012; Lindsey *et al.* 2011b). Snare hunting also requires relatively little skill compared to guns, but experienced hunters may be much more successful than inexperienced ones (Kümpel 2006). In some cases, wire can be stolen from wildlife and domestic fences, as in the Savé Valley Conservancy in Kenya, where rangers removed almost 85,000 snares, all of which were thought to have been made from the perimeter fence (Lindsey *et al.* 2015). In Zimbabwe, stolen telephone copper cables and steel wire from a veterinary fence along a National Park have been used (Gandiwa 2011).

As for firearms, snares have become more popular over time. Wire cable was introduced in Cameroon after the Second World War and has almost totally replaced vegetal fibre, which rots with moisture, or elephant hair that is only suitable for small prey, although snares made of rattan are still used for small prey (Dounias 2016). As a result, the Fang in Cameroon have changed from more traditional methods to focus on snares, now accounting for 54% of the hunted prey biomass (Dounias 2016). Traditionally, Baka Pygmies used mainly spears for hunting (Bahuchet 1992), but wire snares were introduced in the 1960s after contact with neighbouring cultivators to replace traditional, plant-based snares (Hayashi 2008; Yasuoka 2006b; Yasuoka *et al.* 2015). Nowadays, cable snares are the most common hunting technique amongst Pygmy hunters including Baka since this allows for a larger number of captures, therefore suitable for commercial wild meat production (Hayashi 2008; Noss 2000).

Snares are typically set, left unsupervised and then checked periodically (Fig. 3.5). The passive nature of snaring allows farmers to set and check snares in and at the margin of their fields. Their passive nature can result in indiscriminate capture of animals (Becker *et al.* 2013; MacMillan & Nguyen 2014) although relatively targeted setting of snares is possible (Coad 2007). The non-selectiveness is demonstrated by sex ratios of 1:1 in any captured species as predicted in a study in Equatorial Guinea (Fa & García Yuste 2001). Although daily checks are desirable from an animal welfare point of view, longer periods appear to be the norm rather than the exception. For example, Baka hunters checked snares on average every three days (Yasuoka *et al.* 2015). The consequence of leaving snares unchecked or checking these sporadically can lead to significant animal welfare issues and loss of carcasses. But even when checked regularly, animals may suffer from injury and stress. Up to a quarter of total captures can be lost to scavengers and decomposition (Noss 1998b), and around one third of animals can escape with injury (Lindsey *et al.* 2011b). In Zimbabwe, 59% of snared animals were found rotten or scavenged, 27% recovered by scouts and only 14% were extracted by poachers out of the 2,398 animals recorded as killed in snares from August 2005 to July 2009 (Lindsey *et al.* 2011b). In hunting zones around a study village in the Dja Biosphere Reserve in Cameroon, snare density was inversely related to distance from the village, but despite a 64% lower snare density in the farthest hunting zone compared to the closest zone, overall capture rate was four times higher and the number of rotting carcasses three times greater in the farthest zone (Muchaal & Ngandjui 1999). Dobson *et al.* (2019) modelled the amount of usable harvest when 20 snares are checked daily versus only once over a 30-day snaring period to find a three-fold increase for the daily-check scenario.

Two main categories of snares exist – foot snares and neck snares, – whereby the latter constitute the vast majority (Kümpel *et al.* 2009; Noss 2000; Yasuoka *et al.* 2015). When animals are entangled with their heads in neck snares, they are normally strangled to death. Larger animals can be caught by their feet in neck snares. After an animal steps into a typical foot snares, a bent rod springs loose, causing a wire fastened to the rod to wrap around the animal's foot and lift it into the air (Yasuoka *et al.* 2015). Animals larger than those targeted by any type of snare can still be caught but can escape – often with injuries. The two methods are characterized by different prey profiles. For example, in a study in Equatorial Guinea carnivores were only captured in neck snares and rodents solely in foot snares, but a large proportion of duikers were caught in both types though some were also shot (Kümpel *et al.* 2009). Ungulates, rodents and carnivores are relatively more vulnerable to snares than to firearms (Fa & García Yuste 2001). Medium-sized mammals are significantly more vulnerable to snaring (Duda *et al.* 2017; Fa *et al.* 2005; Fa & García Yuste 2001; Noss 1998b). Rodents, for example, represented 92% of snared animals in southeastern Cameroon (Bobo *et al.* 2015). A review of 36 tropical moist forests sites in seven countries in West and Central Africa revealed higher harvest rates for snared than for shot species, significantly smaller body size of snared *versus* shot species, higher extraction rates for terrestrial *versus* arboreal species, higher extraction rates for fast and medium speed species *versus* slower ones and higher extraction rates for frugivore–herbivores *versus* other dietary categories (Fa *et al.* 2005).

Snares are typically set along trails and often in clusters. Densities can vary widely with values of up to $56/km^2$ as reported from Equatorial Guinea (Fa & García Yuste 2001). In a private property near the Savé Valley Conservancy in Zimbabwe, 1.16 and 0.68 snares/km^2 were removed in 1998 and 1999, respectively, but the number increased dramatically to around 90 snares/km^2 per year from 2005 to 2009 after the settlement of adjacent land (Lindsey *et al.* 2011b). Whilst almost 85,000 snares were detected in a period of eight years in the Savé Valley Conservancy, 170,000 snares were removed from just two protected areas in Vietnam and Cambodia between 2011 and 2015 (Gray *et al.* 2018). The effects of snaring can be chilling. In Asia and in Africa, snaring is a major contributor to defaunation (Becker *et al.* 2013; Gray *et al.* 2018; Noss 1998b). This not only affects target species but also by-catch. Becker *et al.* (2013) analysed by-catch data from 1,038 antipoaching patrols in Zambia's Luangwa valley focusing on savanna elephants and large carnivores, to show that additional mortalities of 32% for elephants, 20% for adult (>4 years) male lions and 14–50% of adult and yearling pack members of African wild dogs were inflicted.

3.3.5 Traditional Hunting Technology Generally Augments Modern Technology Today

In only 15% of sites in Table 3.1 neither firearms nor cable snares were used. This proportion is biased towards traditional hunting methods such as bow and arrow and nets because 11 of the 19 sites in the table stem from a single study on Mbuti Pygmies in the DRC that documented a different mix of hunting technologies at different sites (see Fa *et al.* 2016). Here, we introduce the five most important traditional techniques: spears, dogs, bow and arrow, nets and blowpipes.

3.3.5.1 Spears

Spears are the oldest hunting weapons discovered and predate the emergence of modern man. As outlined above (see Section 3.2.1) the 400,000 year old Schöningen spears were likely used for thrusting or hand-thrown at close quarters (Shea 2006; Thieme 1997; Fig. 3.6). Virtually all historically known hunter-gatherers used spears but none employed spears alone without projectile weapons (Churchill 2014). In an extensive survey of small-scale hunter-gatherer societies across the world, Churchill (1993) observed that almost all had spears in their arsenal, but only half used them for terrestrial hunting. Other uses include hunting marine mammals, spearing fish, warfare and defence from predators. Most spears are thrusting spears and only some groups in Australia and Tasmania are known to use thin, light spears to hunt wallabies and kangaroos. Excluding these thin spears, the distance when thrown is 5.7 ± 0.9 m (Churchill 1993) or up to 20 m (Milks *et al.* 2019), depending on the thrower's skill. Typical use of thrusting spears is as a dispatching tool after prey has been driven by hunters, with or without accompanying dogs, into a disadvantaged position when using nets, snow drifts or geographical features such as valleys, rocks and swamps, or have been caught in traps. Spears were used as part of pitfall traps, but this technology has been replaced by snaring (Lewis & Phiri 1998). The

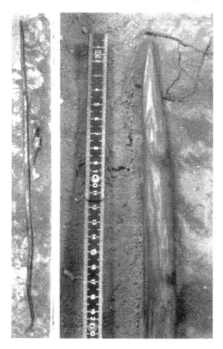

Figure 3.6 Spear II. The 2.30 m long spear is shown to the left of an incomplete pelvis of a horse, and the base has been broken off. Inset shows a detail of the tip of spear II. Scale in cm. (From Thieme 1997; reprinted with permission from Springer Nature.)

spearthrower, also called the atlatl, is a tool that uses leverage to throw a spear or dart at longer distances with a range of about 40 metres (Churchill 1993). The earliest known example is from the upper Palaeolithic in the Dordogne, France; it is made of reindeer antler and dated approx. 17,500 BP (Cattelain 1989). As a hunting weapon, it is used for marine mammals and waterfowl in Oceania, the Arctic and part of the Americas, but terrestrial hunting is known only from Australia (Cattelain 1997; Churchill 1993).

Spears have been reported for wild meat hunting in Africa, the Americas and Asia (Table 3.1). In the early twentieth century, spears were extensively used by the Fang during collective hunting expeditions (Tessmann 1913a). Like weapons of war, spears were richly carved and ornamented, thus expressing a special cultural importance. Elevation into the mythical level was also observed elsewhere, such as the Huaorani in South America. With the advent of firearms, spears were slowly replaced and the Fang do not have spears in their arsenal any longer (Dounias 2016). Today, spears are a Pygmy specialty in the rainforest where non-Pygmy people do not use them, but are also still encountered in Madagascar, Eastern Africa savannas and amongst the San in the Kalahari desert (Dounias 2016; Fa *et al.* 2016; Golden 2009; Holmern *et al.* 2006; Ikeya 1994). Pygmy groups use spears to kill larger and more aggressive mammals like elephants, African buffaloes, bushbucks, gorillas and wild pigs or as a dispatching tool, especially in net hunts and whenever any opportunity arises (Bahuchet 1992; Carpaneto & Germi 1989; Hayashi 2008; Kitanishi 1995; Yasuoka 2006a).

3.3.5.2 Dogs

Wild and domestic animals have been widely used as 'auxiliary animals' to assist in foraging generally and hunting in particular (Dounias 2018). Several birds of prey, ungulates, elephantids and felids have been tamed as hunting auxiliaries. For example, horseback falconry is still actively performed in Central Asia today and can be traced back to the second millennium BCE (Soma 2012). Indian hunters used tamed Indian antelope and Indian gazelle as decoys by sending them into a wild herd with nooses attached to their horns. Once an intruder was engaged by a wild animal its horns would easily become entangled with the tame animal's noose and could then be easily caught (Menon 2000). Similarly, tame female Asian elephants serve as decoys in Sri Lanka, India, Myanmar, Cambodia and Thailand, to attract wild individuals into places where they can more easily be trapped (Baker & Manwell 1983).

Domestic dogs are the undisputedly most important hunting auxiliary worldwide. Hunting has been discussed as one of the principle factors motivating the domestication of the dog from the wolf (Lupo 2011; Olsen 1985). Hunting dogs are used by numerous subsistence hunters in a broad range of locations and habitats across the world (Koster 2009). An exception appears to be in the tropical New World, where many Amazonian societies apparently lacked dogs until the historical period, though dogs may have been brought to South America by Paleoindians (Fiedel 2005). However, because bones do not preserve well in Neotropical settings it is difficult to make firm conclusions from the absence of archaeological evidence (Koster 2009). Hunting with dogs is both a traditional and a modern technology. Parallel to the introduction of firearms many of the previously isolated Neotropical societies acquired dogs (Koster 2009). Dogs are now common throughout Latin America, emphasizing their versatility and importance for hunting. Dogs were likely introduced to the Mbuti Pygmy hunters by agriculturalists (Carpaneto & Germi 1989) and have recently been used more frequently by numerous societies

(Barnett 2000b; Franzen 2006; Ikeya 1994). For example, hunting with dogs was once only of relatively low importance for the San in the Kalahari, but became more common as hunting with bow and arrows declined. This increase has been facilitated by a general increase in the dog population, by the ease of using these animals, by the convenience of having accompanying dogs when walking long distances and by the increase in market demand in a developing commercial economy (Ikeya 1994). In Table 3.1, the percentage of hunts with dogs varied dramatically from no dogs to 86% by Mayangna and Miskito hunters in Nicaragua (Koster 2008b) and 85% of hunts alongside hunters on horseback in the Brazilian Pantanal (Jean Desbiez et al. 2011). While Piro shotgun hunters brought dogs on only 3% of the hunts, the Machiguenga bow hunters living just 90 km away brought dogs on three quarters of their hunts (Alvard & Kaplan 1991); this difference may have been caused by different prey densities (Koster 2009). Among poachers, for example on farmland in KwaZulu-Natal, South Africa, some prefer using dogs over other methods such as hand-weapons, in this case 'knobkerries', traditional strong, short wooden clubs with a heavy rounded knob on one end used by Southern African tribes (Grey-Ross et al. 2010). Hunting with dogs in some areas includes more women and juveniles than in other forms of hunting, which are primarily dominated by adult males (Koster 2009).

Dogs are used to directly kill small prey but, more importantly and more frequently, are used to flush out or corner prey to be dispatched by the hunters or to drive prey into nets or traps. Sometimes, dogs are the only means to target species that are rare or are otherwise not susceptible to other hunting methods. For example, hunters in Lebialem Division, Cameroon, could only locate drills by hunting with dogs (Wright & Priston 2010). Poachers in Zimbabwe primarily target hyrax (100%), warthog (93%), bushpig (85%) and baboons (79%) with dogs, whilst buffalo (100%), zebra (98%), wildebeest (97%), impala (97%) and eland (90%) are primarily killed with snares (Lindsey et al. 2011b). Advantages of dogs vary. An increased encounter rate with prey and, thus, a higher efficiency has been described in several studies (Alves et al. 2009; Koster 2008b; Nobayashi 2016). Among the San in the Kalahari, dogs are not reported to increase encounter rates, but they decrease handling time between detection and kill of prey such as gemsbok (Ikeya 1994). In Nicaragua, the return rates of hunting tapirs, the largest prey species in the study, with dogs, with rifles, and with both guns and dogs were comparable (Koster 2008b). On the other hand, hunters with dogs encounter more than eight times as many agoutis as hunters without dogs in the same study, indicating that hunting dogs can rival firearms in their overall effectiveness.

3.3.5.3 Bow and Arrow

Bows and arrows are used across the world, mainly in traditional hunter-gatherer societies (Table 3.1). The technique is very versatile, allowing ambush, pursuit and disadvantage hunting. Bow hunting allows the hunter to focus on the behavioural characteristics of a given prey species without the constraints of prey size and terrain features encountered when hunting with spears or atlatl (Churchill 1993). However, to kill the prey, the arrow must be precisely lodged between ribs or behind the shoulder blade, thus resulting in short effective distance of 25.8 m on average (Churchill 1993) and in low success rates (Liebenberg 2006). Iron-tipped arrows are deadlier than simple wooden arrows but are heavy and, thus, limited by short distances. Mbuti archers use iron-tipped arrows for terrestrial animals and light wooden arrows, often with poisoned tips, for arboreal prey, because they are light and can be used at larger distances than iron-tipped arrows, but they often require that wounded animals are tracked (Carpaneto & Germi 1989). Mbuti archers hunt either individually or in groups in forest environments (Carpaneto & Germi 1989), but Hadza, the hunter-gatherers of savannahs in Tanzania, usually hunt alone to be able to approach prey in open habitats close enough without being detected to be able to shoot (Marlowe 2005). The prey portfolio of bow hunters differs from gun hunters. When Piro shotgun hunters used bows, they consistently pursued many species ignored when hunting with shotguns (Alvard 1993), which is consistent with foraging theory which predicts a broader prey selection when hunting with less efficient bow technology (Hill & Hawkes 1983). Although bows and arrows are still used by traditional hunters, they are largely been superseded by the more efficient firearms. The specialist knowledge and traditional skills required for bow and arrow hunting, such as how to prepare poison, has often vanished, for example in the Katu ethnic group in Vietnam (MacMillan & Nguyen 2014).

3.3.5.4 Blowpipes

Blowpipes, also called blowguns, are long narrow tubes for shooting light darts, seeds or clay pellets primarily used for hunting wildlife. They have been used by many Indigenous Peoples in Eastern regions of North America (Riley 1952), in tropical forests in Southeast Asia (Alvard 1999a; Bennett et al. 1999; Kuchikura 1988; Naito et al. 2005), South and Central America (Papworth et al., 2013a, b; Riley 1952; Rival 2003; Yost & Kelley 1983), and in Madagascar (Andrianaivoarivelo et al. 2012; Jenkins & Racey 2009). Blowpipes are exclusively employed by men who hunt typically alone or in small groups (Naito et al. 2005; Rival

2003; Yost & Kelley 1983). The Semaq Beri hunter-gatherers of Peninsular Malaysia sometimes hunt in pairs with one specialized blow-pipe hunter accompanied by a 'carrier' who only gathers and carries the killed animals (Kuchikura 1988). Several types of blowpipes exist. In North and Central America, it is a simple tube; in the Guyana region of Northeastern South America, it is a tube fitted into a protective sheath; in the Amazon Basin, it is a composite of two longitudinal half-tubes, but there are also intermediate types (Riley 1952). In Southeast Asia, double tubes are reported in which both the inner and outer tubes are composites of longitudinal half-tubes (Kuchikura 1988). Darts are either not poisoned, in North America, or poisoned with curare, a toxic extract from various plant species including the *Curarea* vine, in South and Central America. In Southeast Asia, poison from the sap of the ipoh tree is used (Kuchikura 1988). The poison is highly effective and relatively fast. In one reported case, it took the curare of 11 darts to bring a puma crashing down from a tree in just over half an hour (Yost & Kelley 1983).

Blowpipes are typically used for overhead hunting of arboreal species, such as bats, birds, primates and squirrels, but terrestrial vertebrates, such as pigs and peccaries, can also be targeted (Piper & Rabett 2009; Rival 2003). The technological differences between the blowpipes and darts and the effectiveness of the poison used impact prey choice of blowpipe hunters as demonstrated by the comparison of the different hunting strategies of the Huaorani of Ecuador (Yost & Kelley 1983) and the Semaq Beri of Malaysia (Kuchikura 1988). The Semaq Beri focus on hunting dusky and banded leaf monkeys but occasionally also kill large-sized Malayan and cream-coloured giant squirrels. Middle-sized and small-sized squirrels and birds are, however, ignored. In contrast, the Huaorani's prey included not only monkeys such as the Venezuelan red howler monkeys but also birds of all sizes (nearly 45% of the total catches) and ground-dwelling animals (15% of catches), whereby small-sized animals of less than 2 kg contribute nearly 60% of the total number of animals killed. The Huaorani's blowpipes are longer and produce higher velocities and higher penetration for their darts than those of the Semaq Beri. Success rate for the Huaorani is approximately 2.4 times higher and return rate 4 times higher. Crucially, the preparation time for darts is half for Huaorani than for Semaq Beri allowing the Huaorani to carry and use more darts than the Semaq Beri (100–300 *versus* 10–50, respectively). Thus, the Huaorani do not conserve darts and shoot even at small birds of less than 50 g including hummingbirds whereas the Semaq Beri save darts until they encounter larger primates, their prey of choice.

Blowpipe hunter groups produce a diversity of blowpipe darts depending on the prey. Some dart types are easy to make in great quantities and can be used without moderation; some others should not be lost and are saved carefully for appropriate prey.

3.3.5.5 Nets

Hunting with nets mainly occurs in three main contexts. First, nets have been reported to be used to hunt bats and birds. For example, bat hunting is practiced in Benin, Cameroon, Madagascar and the Seychelles in Africa, and in India, Indonesia, Malaysia, Myanmar, Philippines, Thailand and Vietnam in Asia (Golden 2009; Jenkins & Racey 2009; Mickleburgh *et al.* 2009; Riley 2002; Struebig *et al.* 2007). Specialized mist nets are used in China, India, Indonesia and Laos (Mickleburgh *et al.* 2009). Second, nets can be components of traps, either underground for small mammals or as net traps to capture terrestrial mammals. Third, net hunting of terrestrial animals has been practiced by a variety of Indigenous Peoples in the Congo Basin (Dupré 1976) and is today a specialty of some Pygmy populations. Up to the 1950s, the Fang used nets, but abandoned them for modern hunting technology (Dounias 2016; Koch 1968). According to Dounias (2016), it is not surprising that 'Pygmies have become the natural depositories of net hunting since this activity exacerbates egalitarian values like mutual aid, food sharing, social links between communities, spatial mobility and demographic fluidity.' Mbuti Pygmies use large collective beat-hunts with women as beaters (Carpaneto & Germi 1989). The nets are between 1 m and 1.5 m high and between 30 m and 100 m long and belong to the man who wove it (Ichikawa 1983). Animals are driven into a circular array of individual nets where men hide near their own nets ready to kill the game running towards them. Those Mbuti who sell their prey animals to Muslim Bantu kill the animals by cutting their throat with a knife in order to adhere to Muslim requirements for slaughter (Carpaneto & Germi 1989). The gender role in the Aka is opposite to the Mbuti as the adult and adolescent men set the nets and beat the bush, whereas women capture the animals caught in the net, waiting around the nets; sometimes they lead net hunting and also beat the bush when no adult men participate in the hunt (Bailey & Aunger 1989; Kitanishi 1995; Noss 2000). In Gabon, game was driven into nets by fire, but this practice has been abandoned and fire is mainly being used to promote growth of grass to which grazing game is attracted (Walters *et al.* 2015). Whilst the Mbuti specialize in net hunting and the Aka use nets alongside cable snares, the sympatric Efe do not practice net hunting (Carpaneto & Germi 1989; Fa *et al.* 2016; Kitanishi 1995). Bailey and Aunger (1989) argue that the Efe never adopted net hunting because their neighbouring farmers do not use them whereas the Mbuti adopted net hunting from their neighbours. Baka pygmies might have used nets in the past, but do not carry out net hunting today (Hayashi 2008; Yasuoka 2006b). In general, net hunting is declining and being replaced by snare hunting even amongst the Aka and Mbuti because of higher individual returns of snare hunting, greater involvement in formal employment and agriculture, and enforcement of regulations in protected areas (Noss 1997). However, it has not been abandoned completely because of the growing demand for wild meat (Noss 1997) and its suitability for illegal hunting, such as in communities adjacent to National Parks (Gandiwa 2011).

3.4 The Hunters

The typical profile of a hunter corresponds to any adult male with most hunters being around 25–50 years old (Bene et al. 2013; Fimbel et al. 1999; Kamins et al., 2011a; Martins & Shackleton 2019; Pailler et al. 2009; Pangau-Adam et al. 2012; Rogan et al. 2018; Wright & Priston 2010). Women hunters are generally very rare (Rogan et al. 2018) but can sometimes contribute to traditional hunting by checking traps, contributing to dog and net hunting (Sections 3.1.2 and 3.2.5.5) and helping to make weapons (Duda et al. 2017; Fimbel et al. 1999; Smith 2005). Amongst Baka Pygmies, all shotgun hunters and most snare trappers are men but half of the traditional hunters can be women (Duda et al. 2017). Except for the remaining hunter-gatherers, hunting wild meat is typically a secondary occupation alongside farming or employment and full-time hunters are rarely encountered, typically less than 10% (Ahmadi et al. 2018; Bene et al. 2013; Loibooki et al. 2002; Pailler et al. 2009; Pangau-Adam et al. 2012; Rao et al. 2005; Spira et al. 2019; Tumusiime et al. 2010). Socio-economic variables and a hunter's personal profiles, such as skills, income security, number of dependants and physical ability, are typically correlated with hunting behaviour (Kümpel et al. 2009). For example, Rogan et al. (2018) report from South Africa that in contrast to other studies, households with some form of formal employment were 1.6 times more likely to hunt than unemployed households and seasonal employment had the strongest correlation with the likelihood of hunting. In Uganda, the probability for an individual to set snares in the forest decreased with rising levels of formal education and subsistence farmers were 10 times more likely to set snares as compared to those who had some other main occupation (Tumusiime et al. 2010).

Marlowe (2005) used the most extensive dataset of known Indigenous forager and hunter-gatherer societies worldwide contained in Binford (2001). The majority of these societies were located in sub-Saharan Africa, India and Southeast Asia, Australia, South America and North America. Marlowe observed that the percentage contribution of hunting to their diet was positively correlated with local group area and how often camps moved. Figure 3.7a displays the relationship between area size and percentage hunting, whereby area size is log-transformed, and percentage hunting was logit transformed (logit is the appropriate transformation for percentages). The correlation coefficient is $r = 0.66$ with $n = 257$, explaining 43% of the observed variance. Using the dataset, we also analysed the relationship between population density and hunting and found a strong negative correlation with $r = -0.63$ with $n = 338$, explaining 40% of the variance (Fig. 3.7). Local group area and population density are also negatively correlated with $r = -0.90$ with $n = 258$, explaining 81% of the variance. Fitting a linear model with both population density and local group area size as independent variables, reveals no significance for the former ($p = 0.5$) but significance for the latter ($p < 0.0001$). In other words, it is local group area size which best explains the percentage of hunting in the diet. Less land corresponds with higher input from agriculture and fishing.

In the wild meat literature, hunting by children is rarely mentioned (Bonwitt *et al.* 2017). However, children learn hunting skills often from an early age and they also can actively engage in the hunting of wild meat. The vast cultural and environmental diversity of hunter gatherers results in a variety of learning and teaching subsistence skills during childhood. A meta-analysis of the anthropological literature has demonstrated several common trends across different societies (Lew-Levy *et al.* 2017). Across these, learning foraging begins in infancy when children are taken to foraging expeditions and when they are given toy versions of the tools used in hunting, such as baskets, spears and bows. Children then transition through multi-age playgroups where social peer-to-peer learning is important, but they also continue to observe their parents' subsistence activities and learn through participation. Small-animal hunting and trapping is primarily learned in playgroups. While children can become proficient at small-animal hunting relatively early in life, more complex hunting methods to take down larger animals are normally taught by adults, not necessarily the parents, from adolescence onwards. Learning to hunt big game may continue through life. There is a controversial debate whether teaching takes place in small-scale societies, including among foragers, but some research suggests that teaching rarely occurs (MacDonald 2007). However, in many hunter-gatherer societies, hunting

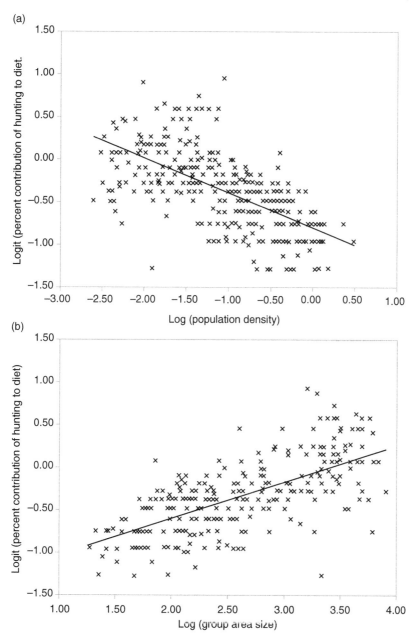

Figure 3.7 (a) Local group area size *versus* percent hunting contribution to diet; (b) population density *versus* percent hunting contribution to diet (data from Binford 2001).

skills are generally taught through direct instructions, likely because of the complexity of hunting, demonstrating that teaching does indeed exist amongst these societies (Lew-Levy *et al.* 2017). For example, San boys learn hunting skills through play, from five years old onwards, by imitating their playmates and not by overt instruction from adults (Imamura 2016). While they learn the use and construction of tools through observational learning and trial and error, teaching is very rare and, if it happens, it is limited to older children assisting younger children in tool making. Similarly, Chabu children in Ethiopia start learning to spear hunt at young age, 6–7 years of age, through role-playing and collaborative learning with their peers; they also actively listen to stories and verbal instructions from their fathers and learn skills by active participation under guidance of adults, mostly uncles (Dira & Hewlett 2016).

Regarding active hunting, an example are older children and juveniles in the Serengeti National Park and adjoining protected areas, who hunt small animals irrespective whether they are boys or girls (Magige *et al.* 2009). In a survey of rural children in the Eastern Cape of South Africa, 62% of the children surveyed were supplementing their diets with wild foods by gathering and by hunting, predominantly by setting snares (McGarry & Shackleton 2009). In a study on Fang People in Cameroon, snare hunting in forest edges, agroforests, swiddens, fallows or home gardens near or within or near villages (so-called garden trapping) is an activity exclusively conducted by children (Dounias 2016). Children maintain the trapping and snaring knowledge, which is technically highly diversified, with little intervention from adults. Such hunted wild meat is generally eaten by the children as snack food and constitutes a valuable part of their diet. Also children of the Baka Pygmies in Cameroon participate in snare hunting not only for garden trapping but also together with adults during hunting expeditions in forest camps (Hayashi 2008). Importantly, Baka children can conduct snare hunting by themselves whilst adult men devote days to spear-hunting expeditions (Yasuoka 2014). The non-overlap between children and adult hunting is also observed in village children in Sierra Leone, who regularly hunt from about 7 years of age, but focussing, in contrast to adults, on small animals using traps and nets (Bonwitt *et al.* 2017). Boys were more likely to hunt than girls and they hunt alone or, especially for net hunting, in small groups.

3.5 Cultural Hunting Aspects

Hunting is shaped by prey type, density and distribution (i.e., the OFT, Chapter 4) and by cultural behaviours. Here we highlight the importance of food taboos and how costly signalling and taste of meat can determine which species are hunted and which are ignored. Taboos are considered here for they reveal ongoing changes affecting traditional hunting practices and the shift into more commercial hunting that not only deplete wildlife, but also deteriorate cultural systems that give a high value to animals. Another cultural factor is the taste of meat, which can bias prey selection contrary to the predictions of the OFT. Costly signalling in the context of hunting is hunting of prey that is dangerous or otherwise costly to hunt in terms of time, material investment, risk of failure and the opportunity to engage in more efficient foraging, but awards the specialized hunters an enhanced social status and reproductive advantage (Bahuchet 1990; Putnam 1948).

Food taboos and taboos against killing certain animal species were widespread amongst small-scale traditional societies worldwide. McDonald (1977) reviewed food taboos amongst South American hunter-gatherers and found such taboos in all of the 11 societies under investigation. Food taboos are also reported from additional sites in South America (Jerozolimski & Peres 2003; Redford & Robinson 1987; Rival 1993), Africa (Hall *et al.* 1998; Inogwabini *et al.* 2013; Jimoh *et al.* 2012; Wright & Priston 2010), the Indian subcontinent (Aiyadurai *et al.* 2010; Velho & Laurance 2013), Inuit in Canada and Alaska (Burch 2007), Southeast Asia (Tuck-Po 2000) and virtually everywhere in the world. De-tabooing is widespread and reported in many studies, such as brocket deer in Central America (Hames & Vickers 1982), the tapir in South America (Rival 1993), the bonobo in Africa (Inogwabini *et al.* 2013) or the gaur, Himalayan serow and tiger on the Indian subcontinent (Velho & Laurance 2013). Taboos are often connected with religious belief (Meyer-Rochow 2009). For example, Machiguenga hunters believe that certain monkeys (especially large adult males) and other prey species have vengeful spirits that can 'take revenge' on the hunter's family (da Silva *et al.* 2005).This association between religious belief and taboos triggers changes and disappearance of taboos once people or societies convert. For example, a shift towards Christianity in Indigenous communities of Arunachal Pradesh probably led to an erosion of hunting taboos (Aiyadurai *et al.* 2010). When Christianity replaced the traditional system of beliefs about predator–prey relations in Inuit, the taboo vanished which previously significantly constrained the pursuit, processing and consumption of prey, vanished (Burch 2007). In Africa, many who belong to a Western religion now see some of these taboos as satanic (Jimoh *et al.* 2012), demonstrating that the taboos have no inner connection with conservation. When taboos are based on religion, it does not guarantee protection. For example, in Cameroon the belief that people can transform into animals is widespread. Although 83% of those that believed in transformation did not shoot apes for fear of killing a person, there are others that had killed apes despite knowing about this traditional belief (Wright & Priston 2010). Moreover, those that spoke of the belief were in the minority and the belief in animal totems has especially declined among the younger generation (Etiendem 2008 cited in Wright & Priston 2010). Erosion of taboos other than by religion is widespread. Jerozolimski and Peres (2003) have demonstrated that a shift from large to small-bodied prey species has taken place in the Neotropics and that taboos seem to play a minor role in determining the overall composition of target species. Increased consumption of meat previously avoided amongst the Yuqui community of Bolivia expresses how cultural attitudes change when preferred prey becomes scarce (Jerozolimski & Peres 2003). Bonobos were not hunted historically in the DRC because of traditional taboos but the introduction of money, commodity hunting and commerce has caused bonobos to now be killed (Inogwabini *et al.* 2013). This change might have been triggered by immigration of newly established ethnic groups that did not have such taboos. Finally, taboos might have spiritual or medicinal purposes, which have nothing to do with conservation. Alternatively, some taboos might have evolved as a means to prevent hunters from wasting time searching for game species that are difficult to find (Jerozolimski & Peres 2003).

Taboos and the avoidance of some wild meat species have in common that the species are not hunted despite OFT's prediction that some of these species should be exploited. For example, Machiguenga hunters in the Amazonian Peru prefer large primates while avoiding deer and ocelot (Shepard 2002); Piro in the Amazonian Peru never pursue otters, sloths, and pumas (Alvard 1993); and Kaxinawá and Katukina prefer peccaries while otters, kinkajous, rats, and marsupials are considered inedible (Kensinger 1995a). Mayangna and Miskito hunters in Nicaragua generally focus on prey types that are in the optimal diet set and kill giant anteaters and northern tamanduas to protect their dogs, but they do not eat the meat despite both species being in the optimal diet set (Koster 2008b, 2008a). Mayangna and Miskito hunters also pursue the sympatric, similar sized, black-handed spider monkey and mantled howler monkey differentially despite both being in the optimal diet set (Koster *et al.* 2010). Spider monkeys are predominantly frugivorous and howler monkeys are primarily folivorous, which may determine the different taste of their meat for humans (Shepard 2002). The taste of the meat of howler monkeys is unappealing to the hunters and the species is generally not pursued during hunts (Koster *et al.* 2010). Moreover, several carnivore species including ocelots, pumas, jaguars and tayras are not pursued and eaten as they appear unpalatable to the hunters because these species eat raw meat which hunters associate with potentially harmful pathogens (Koster et al. 2010). Similar to howler monkeys in Nicaragua, black colobus monkeys in Gabon are normally not pursued due to their meat's bad taste despite their being easy to hunt because of their inactivity and large size (Brugière 1978). Nevertheless, they are heavily hunted if other, preferred species have become overhunted.

The pursuit of inefficient or expensive prey is a costly signalling strategy (Boone 2017; Hawkes & Bliege Bird 2002) that has been documented in many societies. Costly signalling theory has been applied to explain some seemingly maladaptive cultural practices, such as relatively inefficient or apparently suboptimal foraging behaviours, and generosity by the foragers' motivation to broadcast honest information about their abilities (Hawkes & Bliege Bird 2002). Spearfishing Meriam Islanders violate predictions of OFT when they bypass opportunities to harvest shellfish and focus on inefficient, thus costly, spearfishing instead (Bliege Bird et al. 2001). These foraging decisions can be explained by the social status associated with being known as a successful spearfisher. The motivation underlying modern trophy hunting and big-game fishing, which are while rarely costly in terms of danger or difficulty but can be extraordinarily expensive, can be explained by costly signalling (Darimont et al. 2017). Turtle hunting by the Meriam Islanders (Bliege Bird & Smith 2005) and torch fishing for dogtooth tuna in the Micronesian Ifaluk atoll are other outstanding examples (Sosis 2000). Differences between the sexes in the use of costly signalling have been documented. Bliege Bird and Bird (2008) showed that in Australian Martu hunters, women will optimize their hunting for consumption, while men will hunt to optimize their social and political status. Hunters involved in costly signalling can improve their reproductive success, enjoy larger networks of allies and/or trading partners, as well as increase their social and political standing (Bliege Bird & Smith 2005; Smith 2004; Sosis 2000). In prehistory there is some evidence that in some situations signallers (hunters) would have gained social and even reproductive benefits. This is the most plausible explanation for prehistoric dolphin hunting, as inferred from faunal collections from several archaeological sites in the California Channel Islands, and Baja California (Porcasi & Fujita 2000). The faunal remains reveal a distinctive maritime adaptation that is more heavily reliant on the riskier capture of pelagic dolphins than on near-shore pinnipeds, a phenomenon that cannot be explained by the OFT. Similarly, OFT does not explain the benefits accrued by big game hunters living in the whaling community of Lamalera, Indonesia (Alvard & Gillespie 2004). Results indicate that big game hunting provides males a strong selective advantage. Harpooners, and, to a lesser degree, hunters in general reap substantial fitness benefits from their activities. Hunters, especially harpooners, have significantly more offspring than other men after controlling for age. Harpooners marry significantly earlier and start reproducing at an earlier age unlike other hunt group members or non-hunting participants – the technicians and the boat managers. These results are consistent with data from other hunting societies that show significant reproductive benefits for good hunters. Harpooners receive significantly more meat even after controlling for the effort they expend hunting, while at the same time suffer an increased risk of mortality. Some forms of collective hunting do not translate into larger quantities of meat for hunters than for the rest of the group, but this is compensated by obtaining other types of benefits such as, reputation and reproductive success. This public recognition may allow hunters to have more wives, who raise their children better (Blurton-Jones *et al.* 1997), as well as being considered a desirable neighbour and ally (Hawkes 2001). Among cooperative Hadza hunters (Blurton-Jones *et al.* 1997), meat is shared almost evenly between all the households in camp. Men with a higher reputation have higher reproductive success. First, they tend to have wives who produce live children faster because these wives are more efficient foragers than other women. Second, older Hadza men with a high reputation have young wives, usually married after deserting older wife by whom they had fathered children, thus increasing reproductive success. Finally, the costly signalling theory might apply in situations where hunters elect to forfeit hunting profitable prey types if it is linked to social costs. Koster *et al.* (2010) argue it might be preferable to return home empty-handed than to be known as a hunter who must pursue species that are widely disliked because of bad taste of the meat in order to secure an adequate amount of meat.

3.6 The 'Ecologically Noble Savage' Debate

From the 1970s to the 1990s the issue of the 'ecologically noble savage' was controversially debated but the discussion has abated since the predictions from the thesis were tested using foraging theory for the prey choice by Piro shotgun hunters of Amazonian Peru, demonstrating that there is little evidence supporting the hypothesis (Alvard 1993). Moreover, the hypothesis has become more and more redundant because most hunter-gatherer societies do not practice their original lifestyle any longer. Thus, the debate appears dated, but we present it here for completion and also to introduce the related concept of 'autonomous conservation'.

Indigenous, small-scale societies have often been portrayed as natural conservationists who 'live in harmony with their environment' (Alvard 1993). For example, McDonald (1977) argues that food taboos facilitate conservation of prey species among South American tropical forest groups. Jean Jacques Rousseau's romantic view of a 'noble savage', the Indigenous person who has not been corrupted by civilization, was extended and adapted to the concept of the 'ecological noble savage', the popular belief assuming that 'primitive' humans existed in a state of equilibrium with the surrounding natural resources (for overview, see Alvard 1993). Amongst biologists, the hypothesis gained support by Wynne-Edwards' (1962) assumption of group selection whereby social species evolved adaptations that prevented them from degrading their habitat. Specifically, he assumed that hunter-gatherer remained in balance with their natural resources (Wynne-Edwards 1965). Since, the hypothesis has been thoroughly debunked (Alvard 1993; Krech 1999; Harkin & Lewis 2007; Smith & Wishnie 2000). For example, McDonald's (1977) argument that food taboos facilitate conservation does not hold as shown by the numerous examples outlined above. Nevertheless, the hypothesis periodically appears in the academic literature, such as in Stoffle (2005): 'For tens of thousands of years, the people of the New World sustainably used and managed these very old human ecosystems. Those peoples who remained in place for long periods coadapted with their ecosystems causing a new ecological order to emerge – an order often accompanied by increases in biodiversity and biocomplexity.' The strongest evidence against the 'ecological noble savage' hypothesis comes from the test of foraging theory on the prey choice by Piro shotgun hunters (Alvard 1993) and from mammal extinctions over the past 126,000 years (Chapter 6.1; Andermann et al. 2020). Foraging theory assumes that foragers will maximize their short-term harvesting rate rather than be driven by a concern for the sustainability of the harvest (Chapter 4). The data show that Piro hunters pursued prey consistent with predictions of foraging theory. They did not show any restraint from harvesting species vulnerable to over-hunting and local extinction. For example, howler and spider monkeys, which are most vulnerable to extinction, were always pursued. One could argue that hunter-gatherers in South America had less time to adapt to the local environment and that, consequently, conservation behaviour should be strongest in Africa, the cradle of humanity. However, the widespread adoption of firearms and snares by Aka Pygmies, Baka Pygmies and San and the connected increased extraction rates and unsustainability of hunting speak against this notion. The exception is the Mbuti Pygmies, but all studies are from the last century and Mbuti readily adopted the more efficient net hunting after contact with agriculturalist neighbours (see Section 3.3.2).

Much of the debate appears to be centred on the definitions of conservation. It is important to distinguish proactive conservation from epiphenomenal conservation, which Hames (2007) defines as a consequence of a human population's inability to cause resource degradation or a simple observation about long-term equilibrium with resources. In contrast, proactive conservation does not only prohibit or mitigate resource depletion and damage, but it is designed to do so. An extensive review suggests that proactive conservation amongst hunter-gatherers is rare (Smith & Wishnie 2000). However, it is clear that many small-scale hunter-gatherers have extracted prey as sustainable levels, thus fulfilling the definition of epiphenomenal conservation. In general, this appears an epiphenomenon of population density where demand remains sustainable. Where effective population density increases, for example by hunting for the market economy through selling wild meat outside their own group, increased extraction rate occurs and unsustainability is the norm rather than the exception even within hunter-gatherer societies (Chapter 8). In other words, hunter-gatherer societies exhibit all the ingenuity and self-interest as societies elsewhere, except that they belong to the most disenfranchised people of the world (The Lancet 2016).

Related to, but clearly distinct from the 'ecologically noble savage' hypothesis is the recently emerging concept of rural communities taking responsibilities for managing their resources in their own lands (Franco et al. 2021) and that recognizing Indigenous Peoples' rights to land, benefit sharing and institutions is essential to meeting local and global conservation goals (Garnett et al. 2018), often even forming alliances with conservation bodies (Schwartzman & Zimmerman 2005). The new approach argues that 'local people are effective in protecting large areas in a relatively natural state ' (Sheil et al. 2015), ensuring that autonomous management can lead to effective conservation. We discuss this in more detail in Chapter 8.

4 · *Hunting Optimally*

4.1 Introduction

Like other animals, humans engage in foraging tasks that involve the acquisition of multiple 'targets', in this case foods, from their environment. Different foods, whether they are berries or animal prey, are often distributed in fairly discrete 'patches' in space and time. Thus, humans and other animals face decisions on which items to harvest, when to quit searching and when to move on to the next patch.

Theories of optimality involve mathematical models of cost and benefit analysis that can give quantitative predictions about an animal's behaviour. Such proximate decision models, such as those jointly classified under the umbrella of optimal foraging theory (OFT) have been used to understand and to predict foraging behaviour in animals as well as humans. Optimal foraging theory allows researchers to develop a large set of fundamental hypotheses that predict which food resources foragers will pursue when encountered during a search, or where foragers will travel to search for resources and how long they will stay in these places before moving to other areas. The optimal strategy for each individual is to leave a patch when the instantaneous rate of return of food from the current patch falls below the mean return rate from the environment when following the optimal strategy. When a forager first enters a rich patch, gains from exploiting it are high, because the resources are initially plentiful and easy to find. As time passes, however, the forager depletes non-renewing resources, and it takes longer and longer to find the next item.

Optimal foraging theory models were first developed by ecologists to understand non-human foraging behaviour. Since the publication of seminal papers in the mid-1960s on the topic, the annual number of publications considering foraging theory has grown exponentially (Perry & Pianka 1997; Pyke 2010). The key hypothesis is that foragers make choices on the trade-off between the highest possible rate of return and the foraging effort. These decisions lead to the maximization of the net rates of energy intake while foraging (energy gained from foraging minus the pre-encounter energy spent for the search minus the post-encounter energy spent for pursuit, killing and handling). The assumption is that choices made by a forager, to maximize net energy intake, is evolutionarily selected and will impact the individual's fitness. In essence then, OFT models consist of: (1) a goal, normally the maximization of foraging efficiency such as food gathered over some period of time; (2) a currency, most often the calories inherent in the food collected and the energy spent for the collection; (3) a set of constraints, such as the maximum amount of time available for foraging, information available, technology available, and the distribution, density and nutritional content of the available resources and (4) a set of options such as the potential food resources to pursue and to harvest. These basic elements are applicable to human hunters particularly since optimal foraging decisions will lead to a good diet (and then increase the individuals' survival and fertility) and by managing the time dedicated to foraging, other activities can be incorporated that benefit the hunter groups (Alvard 1998).

4.2 Optimal Foraging Theory Models

The success of the exploitation of prey species by humans is clearly influenced by the different techniques used for hunting, a topic even discussed in relation to the emergence of more efficient technologies amongst ancient hominins (Dusseldorp 2012; Hill 1982). Because prey species vary in terms of the energy they provide, and in the time a human predator uses in searching and handling them, some species are more profitable than others. Higher prey profitability is often linked to greater size, greater abundance, greater accessibility, less danger or cost of acquisition or even better nutritional qualities. In standard OFT models, however, profitability is measured as the return divided by the handling costs, usually calories divided by time, after encounter. Abundance and accessibility are not factored in OFT models. The issue of hunting technology is also not directly addressed by standard OFT, but only indirectly in the set of constraints.

Recent applications of OFT models to human foraging are based on the assumption, as for any animal, that short-term decisions are made to maximize yields from prey; this optimization is quantified in the form of energy or calories (Alvard 1993). Each prey species has a singular value as determined by its particular size and is distributed heterogeneously, often patchily in time and space, with a density that is not constant. Prey abundance is limited and there is a cost associated with locating it, pursuing it, hunting it down and processing it before being consumed. According to OFT predictions, species are chosen in order to maximize return rates and avoided regardless of their density and their size (Stephens & Krebs 1986). Three basic variables are central to OFT models. Prey species can then be classified according to their: (1) search time, (2) handling time (pursuit + capture + processing + transportation) and (3) average net energy they provides (calories / hour of manipulation) (Fig. 4.1a). Derived from the basic tenets in the original Stephens and Krebs (1986) OFT model, a number of more specific models have been developed. These models, which focus on prey and patch choices, residence time and central place foraging, are applicable to human foragers:

> **The diet-breadth model**, also called **prey-choice model**, pre-
> dicts whether a forager will utilize a resource upon encounter by
> defining the optimal diet combination by stepwise addition of diets
> which have been ranked by their pursuit and handling profitability.
> It predicts whether a diet should be narrow, i.e. focused on a small
> number of food resources, or broad (Charnov & Orians 1973;
> Emlen 1966; MacArthur & Pianka 1966).
>
> **The patch-choice model**, similar to the diet-breadth model, sug-
> gests that the forager has a choice of an array of patches that differ in
> the energy they contain; patches are ranked according to the net
> rate of energy intake per unit of total foraging time rather than
> energy per unit handling time as for the diet-breadth model
> (MacArthur & Pianka 1966). An example of this is given in Box 4.1.
>
> **Patch residence time: marginal value theorem, MVT.** When
> food is patchily distributed, the MVT predicts when to best leave
> the currently utilized patch and move to a new one. It is an
> optimality model describing the feeding strategy that maximizes
> gain per time when resource availability decreases with time spent
> in the patch. Specifically, 'the predator should leave the patch it is
> presently in when the marginal capture rate in the patch drops to
> the average capture rate for the habitat' (Fig. 4.1b; Charnov 1976).
>
> **Central place foraging.** Choices about prey and patches are contin-
> gent not only on the energy content of each prey relative to
> handling time but also relative to travelling time and transport cost
> to a home base (Fig. 4.1c; Cannon 2000; Orians & Pearson 1979).

Due to its simplicity and versatility, the diet-breadth model is the most widely applied in ethnology (e.g. Hames & Vickers 1982; Hawkes *et al.*

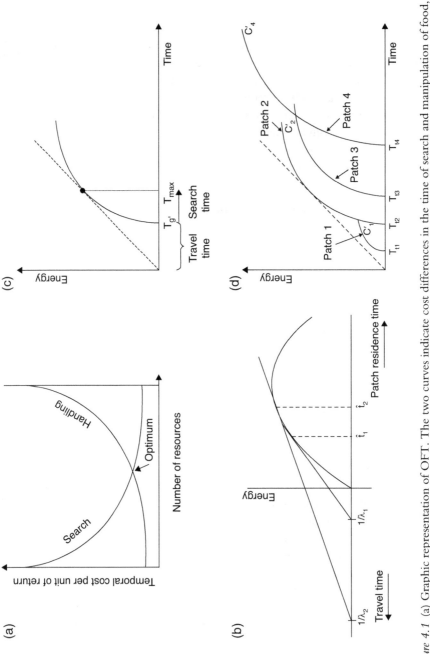

Figure 4.1 (a) Graphic representation of OFT. The two curves indicate cost differences in the time of search and manipulation of food, as well as the optimal diet corresponding to the cut-off point of both functions (from Stephens and Krebs 1986; adapted with permission from Princeton University Press); (b) The marginal-value theorem in the one-patch-type case. Two quantities are plotted on the abscissa: travel

1982; Hawkes & O'Connell 1985; Hill *et al.* 1987; Hill & Hawkes 1983; Smith *et al.* 1983; Winterhalder 1986a, 1986b) and archaeology (e.g. Bird & O'Connell 2006; Broughton 1999; Lupo 2007). This model has been used to successfully predict hunter-gatherer diets in different ecological settings, such as boreal forest (Winterhalder 1981), Amazonian forest (Hames & Vickers 1982), Southeast Asian forest (Kuchikura 1988), savanna (Hawkes *et al.* 1991), Australian desert (O'Connell & Hawkes 1984) and in the Arctic (Smith 1991). The two *crucial parameters* are (1) how long it takes to find each food resource *(search costs)* and (2) how long it takes to harvest and process each food source once it is found *(handling costs)*. These costs, and the resulting diet-breadth model, are demonstrated by one of the early classic OFT studies (Box 4.1). There are two important consequences of the diet-breadth model. First, lower ranked resources are not part of the optimal diet irrespective of their abundance. Second, all those in the optimal diet, i.e., the higher ranked resources, are always taken even when they are rare.

The MVT has been tested for humans only in one study, namely for Nahua mushroom foragers in Mexico (Pacheco-Cobos *et al.* 2019). The study analysed intrapatch and interpatch search behaviour, in particular the time for a transition to interpatch search after the last encounter with

---

Figure 4.1 (cont.) time increases and patch residence time. The optimal residence time is found by constructing a line tangent to the gain function that begins at the point $1/\lambda$ on the travel time axis. The slope of this line is the long-term average rate of energy intake, as $1/\lambda$ is the average time required to travel between patches. When travel time is long ($1/\lambda_2$), the rate-maximizing residence time ($\hat{t}_2$) is long. When travel time is short ($1/\lambda_4$), then rate-maximizing residence time ($\hat{t}_1$) is shorter (from Stephens and Krebs 1986; adapted with permission from Princeton University Press); (c) The patch choice model for central place foragers (after Orians and Pearson 1979). (d) For any patch i, T_{ti} is the round-trip travel time to the patch and $C'i$ is the gain function of the patch, which describes the expected energetic return from that patch per unit search time. Search time begins once the patch is entered. Gain functions are assumed to be negatively accelerated, which is to say that marginal energetic return diminishes as search time increases. Energetic return per total time (travel time plus search time) is maximized for any patch by foraging in that patch until time T_{maxi}, which is given by a line tangential to the gain function beginning at the origin of the graph. Patches with higher densities of high-return resources will, as a generalization, have 'taller' gain functions, or higher maximum profitabilities. The patch that provides the highest overall rate of energy delivery to the central place is the one that produces the steepest line between the origin and a point tangential to its gain function. Patch 2 is the delivery rate-maximizing patch for this hypothetical set of four patches. (From Cannon 2000; Adapted with permission from Elsevier.)

Box 4.1 *Optimal foraging by the Aché of eastern Paraguay*

The Indigenous Aché have lived as hunter-gatherers in the forests of eastern Paraguay since before the arrival of the Spanish. According to a study by Hawkes *et al.* (1982), Aché diet consisted of a large number of mammals (33+ species), reptiles and amphibians (at least 10 species), birds, fish (more than 15 species) and at least 5 adult insects and 10 types of larvae. Also, more than 14 kinds of honey and the edible products of 40 or more plant species were consumed. Researchers gathered data during seven foraging trips (lasting between 4 and 15 days), focussing on Aché groups consisting of 5–27 men, 4–15 women, 1–14 children and 2–8 infants. The most frequently hunted mammals were collared and white-lipped peccaries, red brocket deer and capuchin monkeys. Hunters used bows and arrows or shotguns for pursuing large mammals and birds. However, armadillos were dug from their burrows often by solitary hunters, and pacas were captured by groups of hunters in their dens. Most food processing was undertaken in overnight camp. Over the study period, average intake from foraging was about 3,600 calories per day per capita, 80% of which were from animals. OFT ranks resources according to the ratio of returns they provide (calories) *versus* the cost (handling time) of acquiring and processing the resources once they have been encountered, E_i/h_i (Fig. 4.2). Therefore, Aché should not take any resource with a post encounter return rate of less than 870 calories per hour, i.e., rank 13 or lower. It is important to note that the resource rankings say nothing about the quantitative importance of a resource to optimal foragers. In other words, however frequently a resource is below the critical return rate of 870 calories per hour, they should not harvest it. Indeed, the Aché were not observed to have harvested any resources ranked 13 or lower. However, palm fruit, which was just inside the optimal set on rank 12 were ignored on several occasions, whilst this never happened for oranges, ranked 4. By and large, however, the observed foraging patterns by the Aché is consistent with predictions derived from the optimal diet model. The authors also analysed the same data with the patch choice model and observed that the foraging pattern was also consistent with that model.

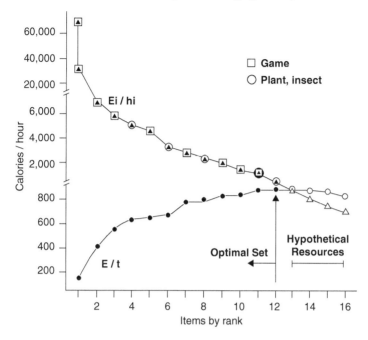

Figure 4.2 Example of the diet-breadth model. The figure shows the ratio of calories returned to handling time (Ei/hi) for each of the resources ordered by rank and the average returns for foraging in general (E/t) that result from the addition of each of these resources. From foraging data for Indigenous Aché in Paraguay the model predicts the optimal set that will be utilized. (From Hawkes *et al.* 1982; adapted with permission from the American Ethnological Society.)

a harvested mushroom within a patch. The empirically estimated 'giving-up times', i.e., the intrapatch search duration, was accurately predicted for the giving-up times as predicted by the MVT. For non-human organisms, Nonacs (2001) surveyed 26 studies that applied the MVT which is the dominant paradigm in predicting patch use. Whilst many studies have shown 'good qualitative support for MVT predictions', quantitative observations differed from the predicted MVT optima in 23 of 26 studies, whereby foragers consistently stayed too long in patches. Simulating state-dependent behaviour, Nonacs (2001) observed consistently longer patch residence times than predicted by the MVT, which were consistent with the observed deviations from the MVT. The suggested modifications for future predictive models of patch use are to consider: (1) the type of predator behaviour, e.g. sit-and-wait *versus* actively foraging; (2) activities that can occur simultaneously to foraging such as parental care; and (3) the nutritional states of the foraging animals. Cases of human hunting behaviour where observed deviations from the prediction of the OFT occur can be used to refine the models by incorporating the ecological settings. Case studies of historic resource depression (Box 4.2) and the question of hunting large-bodied species not for nutritional value but for social prestige are good examples (Section 3.4).

Overall, OFT has been tested in several settings. In a high percentage of studied cases, its predictions are consistent with what has been

---

Box 4.2 *Prehistoric prey resource depression*

Optimal foraging theory, particularly Charnov's (1976) MVT and Orians and Pearson's (1979) patch-choice model, predict that: (1) overhunting of 'high-return' species either leads to the decline in relative abundances, and changes in mean age of the overhunted species, if no alternative, high-productive patches occur, or (2) increases in both high-ranked prey abundances and mean age take place if alternative, high-productive patches exist. Both predictions are fulfilled in the archaeological late Holocene Emeryville Shellmound faunal sequences in California. Excavations of different horizons of the Shellmound demonstrate that the abundance of large-sized prey, such as the North American elk, white sturgeon and geese species declined through time relative to the smaller prey types that occurred in their respective patches (Fig. 4.3a). These large species were confined to the immediate vicinity of Emeryville, thus providing compelling evidence for the first prediction for resource depression. In contrast, the abundance of black-tailed deer, the second largest prey type from the terrestrial mammals' patch, first declined in the oldest strata but then increased across the younger strata (Fig. 4.3b). In contrast to the very localized red deer habitat, black-tailed deer habitat was not locally confined but extended uninterrupted far to the east, thus providing many productive patches. The result was an increased deer index after the first signature of local depletion. That the deer from the younger strata were hunted in more distant patches is supported from patterns in skeletal part representation indicating long-distance transport of high-value parts of carcasses to the central habitation at the Shellmound (Broughton 1999, 2002).

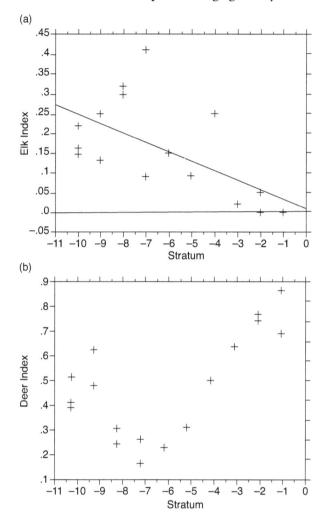

Figure 4.3 The distribution of (a) elk and (b) black-tailed deer abundance indices over archaeological strata at the Emeryville Shellmound, California, USA (from Broughton 2002; adapted with permission from Taylor & Francis).

observed in different hunter-gatherer societies (see the review by Alvard 1998, for example). This means that many Indigenous hunters maximize their short-term catch returns. A clear example of this is Alvard's (1995a) study of Piro hunters of Amazonian Peru. Alvard showed that these hunters do not select a particular age or sex class of prey, but act according to OFT. This is interesting since the alternative hypothesis, namely that hunters select certain age classes to minimize their impact on species or populations may not apply always (see Sections 4.3.1 and 4.8). Piro hunters therefore pursue larger animals, those weighing more than 4–5 kg, because species within this body mass are the commonest (see Chapter 2). However, hunters do not selectively target old, reproductively unimportant males, but would pursue any adult of reproductive age. For species whose immature animals are relatively small, hunters focus on adults but they are more likely to pursue immatures of large species. The result is that hunters choose an optimal set of species where according to the diet-breadth model, high value prey will always be hunted whenever encountered.

Prey body size is often assumed to be a proxy for profitability. However, different prey characteristics such as predator defence mechanisms and physical characteristics can impact handling costs. Lupo and Schmitt (2016), for example, showed that African forest elephants are ranked lower and are less efficient to hunt by Aka Pygmies, than many relatively smaller-sized animals. When measured by conventional currencies, elephants are relatively uneconomical to hunt, regardless of their encounter rates, and despite the fact that they are the largest terrestrial animal in the African forests. Congo Basin forest foragers normally do not hunt elephants when encountered but they are deliberately pursued by specialist hunters for whom hunting of very costly prey is worthwhile because they can gain social recognition (Section 3.4; Bahuchet 1990; Putnam 1948).

4.3 Cultural Settings and the Optimal Foraging Theory

Superimposed on optimal foraging behaviour, shaped by biological evolution, are cultural behaviours, shaped by social evolution. Hunters regularly sidestep profitable prey types despite their being part of the optimal diet set because of anthropological phenomena, such as taboos and religious belief, meat taste and costly signalling (see Section 3.4). In other cases, species in the optimal diet set are particularly valued and hunted because of add-on effects. For example, woolly monkeys are of large size with good returns of meat, but are particularly sought after by Amazonian Kichwa People in Ecuador as centrepieces for festivals and weddings (Sirén 2012). Good hunters earn high prestige that is unmatched by other occupations including fishing despite fish being a more important food source than wild meat (Sirén & Machoa 2008).

There is a large diversity of individual and communal hunting behaviour within the same habitats. Contrasting outcomes of the prey profile of colonist and Indigenous communities have been reported. In a comparison of 31 tribal and nontribal settlements in Neotropical forests, the prey species profiles obtained by hunters were influenced by the local availability of wildlife species rather than cultural aspects (Jerozolimski & Peres 2003). Similarly, the ethnic background of hunters (i.e., Indigenous vs mixed communities) had no detectable effect on how different primate populations were exploited in French Guiana (Thoisy *et al.* 2009). In contrast, 19 studies carried out between 1960 and 1980 in the Neotropics demonstrated differences in the number of prey species between Indigenous and colonist communities based on cultural factors such as hunting tools/methods, taboos/prohibitions, and or 'agreed upon' hunting rules within the community. Francesconi *et al.* (2018) observed hunting rate disparities in a study in Peru suggesting there are different types of hunters (specialized vs opportunistic) and that prey composition differs between Indigenous and colonist communities. Indigenous communities displayed higher take-off values and diversity of species than colonists. Specialized *versus* opportunistic hunting strategies have been observed in several studies including Van Vliet *et al.* (2015c) who observed that specialized hunters may spend more time in the forest and use more bullets compared to diversified hunters leading to a higher average game offtake. Individual foraging and hunting skills and their development with individual age also show cross-cultural variation across a vast spectrum of 23,000 hunting records generated by more than 1,800 individuals at 40 locations (Koster *et al.* 2019).

Stafford *et al.*'s (2017b) large cross-site analysis of neotropical hunting profiles confirmed the offtake for some species that appear to deviate from the predictions of OFT. In particular, woolly monkeys were more often targeted than would be predicted by their body size whereas capybaras were avoided despite their relatively large body size, possibly protected by the bad taste of their meat. Moreover, hunting profiles change substantially over short distances, but it remains unknown whether the observed dissimilarities are driven by differences in forest productivity over very small scales, rapidly diverging cultural preferences or both. Sympatric Panoan and Arawakan speaking Indigenous groups and non-indigenous communities in Southwestern Amazonia demonstrated that ethnolinguistic group identity significantly affected the taxa comprising the hunted assemblages, while the other predictors of country, ecoregion and watershed had no influence (de Araujo Lima Constantino *et al.* 2021). This reflects the pronounced cultural diversity and plasticity of hunting practices of overlapping communities living in the same environments, irrespective of OFT. Non-indigenous hunters targeted medium-sized rodents, and Indigenous hunters showed a preference for large species whereby the Pano typically hunted peccaries, and the Arawak preferentially consumed large primates and birds.

The observation that hunters regularly bypass profitable prey types or focus on prey more than their energetic value predicts, may be interpreted as contradicting the OFT. However, these deviations do not negate the heuristic value of the OFT as all the cited studies show that hunters pursue prey in the optimal diet set and that deviations are omissions from, not additions to the optimal diet set in some but not all hunter communities and in some but not all circumstances. Because of the plasticity of cultural factors impacting individual and communal hunting behaviour, conservation programmes need to tailor interventions closely to each community whereby even sympatric or close-by communities may require different wildlife management and conservation approaches.

4.4 Optimal Foraging Theory Applied to Human Foraging and Its Critics

Optimal foraging theory has advanced our understanding of subsistence patterns for individual human societies, helping us explain variability in the foraging behaviour between individuals and groups (Alvard 1995a; Begossi 1992; Belovsky 1987; Hawkes & O'Connell 1985; Hill 1988; Hill *et al.* 1987; Kelly 2013). The application of OFT models to human foraging has not been without its critics (e.g. Mithen 1989; Pierce & Ollason 1987; Pyke 1984). Criticism of optimization models in general and OFT in particular has ranged from the polemic – arguing that they are naïve, tautological and wrong (Ghiselin 1983; Gould & Lewontin 1979; Pierce & Ollason 1987) – to the more constructive deliberations that highlight problems and cases where deviations from the predictions of the OFT have been observed (Martin 1983; Nonacs 2001; Pyke 1984; Stephens & Krebs 1986). Critiques include:

- **Lack of 'true' testability**: If the predictions of an OFT model are not supported by observations, model parameters – which are notoriously difficult to estimate – are sometimes modified *a posteriori* until predictions and observations fit. This modification of models is standard scientific procedure to improve model outcomes, for example, it led to Chang and Drohan's (2018) optimal stopping diet choice model (see Section 4.5.4). However, some interpret such approaches as too bendable, 'tautological' or 'not scientific'. These critics question the usefulness of models because they can be modified whenever they do not fit the data (e.g. Ghiselin 1983; Gould & Lewontin 1979; Pyke 1984; Stephens & Krebs 1986). The argument is that OFT is then not truly testable (Gray 1987).

- **Optimality assumption is questionable**: Another line of criticism addresses the OFT's optimality assumption that the most economically advantageous resource is selected through evolutionary processes. Mithen (1989) argues that 'fitness is defined by doing better than other individuals, not by achieving some optimum'. Therefore, the concept of 'meliorizing' might be more adequate that the concept of 'optimizing' (Mithen 1989). Detractors indicate that deviations from the optimization assumptions are found in many culturally transmitted traits, where maladaptation is common. For example, Hallpike (1986) gives examples where there has been the 'survival of mediocre', such as stone axes and horse harnesses which have persisted despite being suboptimal or even maladaptive. In another study, Joseph (2000) discusses the Canadian Inuit as an example of the survival of the mediocre because different models predict that foraging is less profitable than alternative sources of livelihood, but foraging still endures (Smith 1991). But, as highlighted by Stephens and Krebs (1986), 'these criticisms amount to reasons why optimization models might be wrong but not why they are bound to be wrong'.

- **Contrasting conclusions**: Different researchers come to contrasting conclusions for the same ecological systems and evolutionary processes. For example, the transition from hunter-gathering to the first domestication of animals and plants has been explained with the OFT and the niche construction theory (NCT). The NCT's core principle is the deliberate engineered modification or enhancement of ecosystems, which provide organisms with a selective advantage. Smith (2015, 2016) argues that both theories constitute 'antithetical explanatory frameworks for initial domestication'. Discussing the archaeological and paleoenvironmental evidence for the Neotropics, he concludes that OFT does not predict the circumstances around which initial domestication occurred as well as NCT. Also for the Neotropics, Piperno et al. (2017) reject these conclusions and demonstrate that the available empirical evidence is fully in accord with hypotheses and predictions generated from OFT. Moreover, they reject the assumption that both theories are antithetical, but argue that they can be complementary, informing and explaining different aspects of human foraging behaviour.

- **Lack of formal testing**: Many studies do not explicitly or formally test the predictions derived from OFT but 'use the general ideas of foraging to organize data and ideas' (Stephens & Krebs 1986). Foraging by the Aché (Box 4.1) is by-and-large consistent with the predictions of the diet-breadth model (Hawkes *et al.* 1982) and is often cited as a prime example in favour of the OFT. Kelly (2013) also concludes that the diet-breath model 'predicts the Aché's choice of food items while on foraging treks'. However, the model did not explain why palm fruit, which is part of the optimal diet, albeit its lowest ranked item, is sometimes not utilized. The model explicitly does not include state-dependent behaviour, such as physiological or nutritional state, travel cost or opportunity costs, which might influence the Aché's decision to harvest palm fruit. Here, a refinement of the model that incorporates state-dependency, as suggested by Nonacs (2001), might explain why palm fruit is sometimes not taken.

For applied scientists and policy makers dealing with wild meat use, the critique of the OFT and, indeed the OFT framework itself, may appear rather academic and without direct applicability. Notwithstanding potential problems, OFT models have been successfully applied to human foraging behaviour of contemporary populations, archaeological settings and to other human behaviours such as how we visually search our environment (e.g. Cain *et al.* 2012; Dusseldorp 2012; Hawkes & O'Connell 1992; Martin 1983; Rode *et al.* 1999; Smith *et al.* 1983). An important conclusion from OFT is that hunters will pursue species whether they are abundant or rare. Thus, even when a species has been hunted to a low density, hunters will kill animals whenever encountered and not grant it temporary reprieve, which would allow it to recover. Moreover, as Alvard (1995a) has demonstrated for Piro people, hunters do not select species or specific age or sex class of prey to proactively conserve prey animals, but follow the predictions of the OFT (see Section 4.11).

4.5 Alternatives to the Optimal Foraging Theory Models

4.5.1 Theory of the Prudent Predator or Intelligent Predator

According to the prudent predator theory, the main objective of hunters is not the immediate maximization of hunting yields (as predicted by the OFT) but the sustainability of resources in the medium and long term

(Slobodkin 1974). This implies that a species will stop being hunted even if it is in the optimal diet when the population density falls below a certain risk threshold. Such behaviour would guarantee the sustainability of the prey species and implies the prioritization of catches towards other more abundant species. This can bring about a change away from the habitual hunting territory towards others with more abundant prey. This hypothesis is related to the concept of the 'ecologically noble savage' as defined by Redford (1991). This concept suggests that groups of hunter-gatherers live in harmony with nature and behave (as prudent predators) guided by their deep knowledge of the environment, which they culturally transmit from generation to generation (Alvard 1993; Hames 2007). Up until about the 1990s, the view of many anthropologists, academics and conservationists was that native people are knowledgeable stewards of natural resources (Alvard 1998; Hames 2007). It was Redford's (1991) book *The Ecologically Noble Savage* which firmly declared this view a myth. Since then, there have been many empirical studies rejecting the hypothesis (Sections 3.6 and 4.11).

4.5.2 Theory of Passive Selection of Prey

This little-known theory, due to Blondel (1967), was originally applied to explain prey selection by birds of prey (Falconiformes and Strigiformes), and proposes that prey species must meet three main requirements for the predator: (1) adequate size, (2) accessibility and (3) abundance. According to this hypothesis, there is no order of preference in how prey meet these three conditions, but rather prey items are selected opportunistically in relation to their space–time availability. Blondel (1967) argues that under these conditions, the energy spent by the raptor to capture its prey must be at least compensated for by the energy it derives from eating it. Unlike predictions of the OFT, the abundance or easy access to a prey can compensate for its suboptimal size and be captured, instead of refusing it in favour of searching other more energetically profitable prey. On the other hand, the passive selection of prey is not conditioned or directed by criteria of conservation of the prey species that are part of the diet, but by mere opportunism. However, the theory has found no empirical support and the OFT – notwithstanding its limitations – has in numerous studies shown, as outlined in the section above, that prey is taken non-randomly and not opportunistically as Blondel's (1967) theory assumes.

4.5.3 Robust-Satisficing Model

The concept of satisficing was suggested as an alternative to the OFT (Simon 1955; Ward 1992, 1993). According to Simon (1955), satisficing individuals, first, satisfy a minimum requirement and, second, will choose among a subset of behaviours when information-processing or time constraints limit their ability to make an optimal decision (Simon 1955). Ward (1992, 1993) introduced the idea that satisficing might constitute an alternative hypothesis to the OFT, but the concept lacked a testable mathematical model until Carmel and Ben-Haim (2005) formalized it by incorporating information gap decision theory. The latter is a non-probabilistic method for prioritizing alternatives and making choices and decisions under severe uncertainty; the 'information gap' is the disparity between what *is known* and what *needs to be known* for a responsible decision (Ben-Haim 2001, 2019). The predictions of the quantitative robust-satisficing model were compared with the predictions from the OFT's MVT, for 26 studies for a diverse range of taxa, including 24 in Nonacs' (2001) study (Carmel & Ben-Haim 2005). Nineteen studies reported significantly longer patch residence times than predicted by MVT but which were predicted by the robust-satisficing model. This contradiction of the prediction of OFT's MVT confirms Nonacs' (2001) review although he suggests that a refinement of the MVT was required rather than the rejection of the OFT.

4.5.4 Optimal Stopping Diet Choice Model

This model, due to (Chang & Drohan 2018), originates in economics and identifies a minimum threshold for a target trait such as body size, denoted by economists as a 'reservation value', that can define the cut-off for species to be included in the diet set. The stopping model requires less field data than the OFT, specifically the distribution of the trait under investigation and the opportunity cost for time spent hunting. In an application to hunter catch by sports hunters in Southwest China, the reservation values predicted by the optimal stopping model corresponded to catch data better than the diet threshold yielded by the OFT. Moreover, the optimal stopping model suggested that hunters should be less selective in their prey choice when they experience a larger opportunity cost for their time. Why the OFT performed worse remains unclear. The mismatch between the estimated and real handling times, important parameters for the tested OFT model, could be explained by the fact that handling times were simulated because they could not be collected in the field. Nevertheless, these results indicate that the optimal stopping diet choice model could be considered as an additional model to the OFT. Whilst Chang and Drohan (2018) regard the model as an alternative to the OFT, it can also be viewed as an extension to the OFT that incorporates opportunity cost.

4.6 Prey Selection

According to OFT, hunters will select, among all possible prey, those that minimize the cost of search and handling, while maximizing the amount of energy they provide. This implies the existence of one or several species in the optimal diet that will be searched for and captured, depending on their availability, size and handling ease (Dusseldorp 2012). However, when the density of the most desirable species decreases then the diet broadens leading to the consumption of other, lower ranked species (Madsen & Schmitt 1998). This may imply a change in the priority of the species within the optimal set but also include the incorporation of new prey species (Marín Arroyo 2009). This change is governed by the availability of preferred species, which will always be pursued by hunters even when the encounter rate is low and is reversible if population densities of these recover. This points to a dynamic and flexible foraging strategy. In general, specialization lengthens search time for prey but reduces handling time, in contrast to what happens when the diet is broadened. In the latter case, it is more efficient to improve the techniques of post-mortem manipulation (processing) than those of search, pursuit and capture (Hawkes & O'Connell 1992). Specialization can also be facilitated other than by OFT, such as through the accumulation of technical knowledge of search pursuit and kill, as well as improving the social structure that facilitates the cooperation required to kill a species that otherwise no one could kill alone (see Section 4.8; Alvard & Gillespie 2004).

As predicted by OFT, individual animals will be subject to intraspecific selection. Thus, although in most case males and females will be captured relative to their abundance, in sexually dimorphic species it becomes more profitable to target one or the other sex. Likewise, because adults have a greater intrinsic value than young animals, except when the size of the immature is comparable to that of adults as for large species, such as tapirs and capybaras (Alvard 1995a).

Prey selection is heavily impacted by the type of weapons used. Projectile weapons, in particular firearms, radically change the distance at which prey can be killed and its pursuit time, as well as the size of targeted animals. For example, a study of two Indian communities in southeastern Peru, one of which hunted with guns, the other with traditional weapons, showed that shotgun hunters averaged 1.3 shots per kill whereas bow hunters averaged 30 shots (Alvard & Kaplan 1991). Pursuits by shotgun hunters were also significantly shorter than bow hunter pursuits. Shotguns also bring into killing range animals that are difficult to target by arrows, such as arboreal primates. When a less efficient hunting technology is used, OFT predicts a broader prey profile compared to a more efficient hunting technology such as firearms. Indeed, the prey profile of Aché bow hunters is broad and includes smaller, less profitable species typically not targeted by hunters using guns (Alvard 1993b). Shotgun hunters primarily focus on large prey (Alvard 1993a; Kümpel 2006). Chapter 3 gives more details on hunters and technology.

4.7 Selection of the Foraging Space

Available food is not distributed uniformly throughout a landscape, and its abundance changes during the annual cycle. Therefore, according to OFT predictions, foragers must decide which area is more profitable in terms of distance, annual period and abundance of prey, and for how long to stay within it. As a result, as shown by Murdock (1967) for a sample of 168 societies, human hunter-gatherers can be divided into four distinct groups according to their mobility patterns of behaviour:

- Fully migratory or nomadic bands (75% in equatorial zones, 64% in semitropical zones, 42% in boreal zones, 10% in temperate zones and 8% in temperate-cold zones).
- Semi-nomadic communities, whose movements are interrupted by periods of permanence in stable camps.
- Semi-sedentary communities, where the tendency to remain tied to a camp takes precedence over mobile phases.
- Sedentary communities. Those that live fixed to a territory throughout the year.

Two dominant strategies can be distinguished: one that implies the displacement of consumers in search of resources (foragers) and one based on the total or partial transport of these resources to consumers (collectors) (Binford 1980). Generally, most forager groups are small, quite mobile, especially in temperate climates, and according to Marlowe (2005) undertake on average around seven trips every year. This also implies a cyclical and predictable use of different resources throughout the year. In favourable habitats, where food is more abundant and therefore can sustain a higher population density, local group size tends to remain fairly constant, around 30 individuals according to Marlowe (2005).

The collector model assumes a fixed camp from where hunters leave and to which they return. This strategy is followed, for example, by the !Kung (Binford 1980). In some cases, hunting parties use mobile camps for several days. In both situations, hunting effort tends to concentrate around the inhabited nucleus (Ohl-Schacherer et al. 2007; Smith 2008) causing an impoverishment of the peripheral area. The size of these depleted areas around settlements, termed an 'extinction envelope' (Levi et al. 2011b), is inversely proportional to the distance travelled by the hunters (Alvard 1994, 1998; Muchaal & Ngandjui 1999). Factors involved in this impoverishment are directly related to the size of the human population and its spatial distribution, types of weapons used and the average number of annual catches per hunter (Levi et al. 2011b). The existence of roads and rivers favours motorized transport, which allow travel of greater distances in less time than walking and thus causing resource depletion within a wider geographical area (De Souza-Mazurek et al. 2000).

The mobility and the size of areas used by human groups are positively related to how much hunting contributes to the total diet (Fig. 4.4). In temperate climates, mobility in hunter-gatherer populations differs from 14 km per day for men to 9.5 km per day for women (Marlowe 2005). Mobility is not necessarily related to food abundance or scarcity, although the number of trips varies according to the abundance of food in the environment. By contrast, sedentarism can result from local resource abundance in the context of regional scarcity, thus promoting territorial defence of resources and domestication (Alvard & Kuznar 2001). Hence, large home ranges and increased mobility are needed if hunting is the priority activity while fishing is associated with more sedentary lifestyles (Marlowe 2005). However, in some situations, by increasing resource productivity through environmental management, agriculture and livestock rearing, reducing mobility and even birth control, it is possible not to exceed the carrying capacity of a group's natural setting (Zeder 2012).

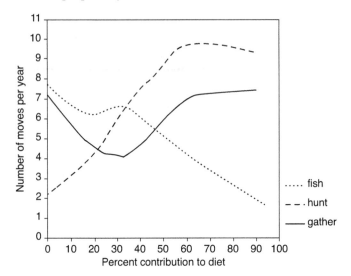

Figure 4.4 Number of residential moves per year by the percent contribution to the diet from hunting, gathering, and fishing (*n* = 340 forager samples); fitted lines are Lowess smoothed (from Marlowe 2005; adapted with permission from John Wiley & Sons).

Both foragers and collectors must make decisions on the choice of hunting range. According to OFT, this choice is conditioned by the availability of prey in the optimal diet set. The richest patches are used first, but are abandoned when benefits fall below the average of those obtained in other patches (Alvard 1995a). As a consequence, there is an inverse relationship between the number of trips made by foragers throughout the year and the average distance between the patches they visit. Therefore, distance between patches plays a very important role. Alvard (1994) found that the hunting pressure by the Piro (hunter horticulturists) was greater in the vicinity of their settlements. As a result, the average rate of return was 0.98 kg/h at a distance of no more than 4 km from settlements and 3.2 kg/h between 4–8 km. Greater distances are not covered, even when there are optimal hunting zones, since the energy cost of the displacements and transport of the prey does not compensate for the hunting yields obtained.

4.8 Group Hunting *versus* Individual Hunting

Group hunting allows the taking of more and larger prey and, in general, increases hunting success (Janssen & Hill 2014). In addition, it reduces the risk of confrontation with dangerous animals, makes it possible to ambush flocks and facilitates the isolation of gregarious individuals. Cooperative hunting is usually practiced by hunter-gatherers as different as !Kung, Mbuti Pygmies and Inujjuamiut, for example (Alvard 1999b). Packer and Ruttan (1988) argue that cooperative hunting occurs when it favours the probability of encountering or capturing optimal prey and compensates for having to distribute them, which is part of the predictions of OFT. In fact, an inverse relationship between the hunting success rate and the size of the prey has been observed. Among the Aché and Hadza, the success rate against prey weighing or exceeding 40 kg is 10 times lower than that obtained for prey less than 10 kg, and 5 times lower than the !Kung (Hawkes *et al.* 2001). Benefits provided by collective hunting have been quantified for the Lamalera whale hunters, who obtain 3 kg of meat / person / hour of collective hunting compared to 0.39 kg fishing alone of smaller species (Alvard 1999b).

Technological improvements brought about by the development of poison, bow and arrow, and firearms (Chapter 3) has favoured individual hunting or at least, the possibility of smaller hunting groups, as in the case of the Hadza. As a corollary, the probability of cooperation declines when the capture of the prey does not require the necessary participation of third parties (Scheel & Packer 1991). Vice versa, net hunting (see Chapter 3; Carpaneto & Germi 1989, 1992; Ichikawa 1983; Terashima 1983) or the technology required for whale hunting (Alvard & Gillespie 2004) requires larger groups.

4.9 Sexual Division of Hunting Roles

Hunting appears an eminently male activity although exceptions exist. Sexual division of labour is selected for where significant danger of injury, such as hunting mobile prey, exists and can expose infants to substantial risks when human mothers engage in this type of hunting. Differential costs of hunting for the two sexes has led to the sexual division of labour with subsequent sharing of resources and biparental investment within families (Hooper *et al.* 2015; Hurtado *et al.* 1985, 1992). Complementary strategies between both sexes seem to prevail, in which men and women pursue activities of a different nature (Hawkes *et al.* 1993; Hurtado & Hill 1992). In certain circumstances, men focus on hunting difficult-to-acquire prey, which often increases their social status and the dependence of other non-active members, while women concentrate on the collection of products that involve less effort but ensure a daily and sometimes constant supply of food (tubers in many cases: Speth 2010) for her, her offspring and other group members (Hawkes *et al.* 1997). Members of a group will perform different activities at different intensities according to their age, sex and reproductive status, and this in turn affects the size of the group. Ultimately, the way in which resources are distributed in the environment and their abundance has also a direct effect.

Foraging group size and composition is also impacted by the sexual division of labour, intergenerational division of labour and the economies of scale in production (Hooper *et al.* 2015). When groups are very small, generally fewer than 10 people, men and women are more equal in finding and obtaining resources increases (Binford 1980). This homogenization of tasks could have been favoured, in addition, by the use of tools that reduce the risk (net, traps) and the exclusive use of force to capture certain types of prey. This is the case, for example, of the Aka Pygmies (Hewlett 1993).

4.10 Handling and Distribution Strategies of Catches

The strategies which hunters employ for pursuing and handling prey depend on the technology used, as well as on the habits and customs of the group (Bright *et al.* 2002). Such strategies affect the amount of energy that can be made available to the hunters as well as to the rest of the group. For example, when multiple individuals cooperate to hunt the same prey, they can both increase the probability of successful prey capture and reduce the individual costs associated with hunting. Cooperative hunting provides mutualistic benefits only when the per capita intake rate increases with group size. Sharing of benefits resulting from cooperative hunting is common though not exclusive among hunter-gatherers who do not store food (Binford 1980); food storage occurs generally in environments where the effective temperature is below 15°C although meat can also be preserved at higher temperature by drying, marinating or curing (e.g. whale jerky by Lamalera whale hunters; Alvard & Gillespie 2004). Cooperative hunting is linked to the pursuit and capture of large prey species that are generally inaccessible to a lone hunter. Examples of cooperative hunting and sharing of meat are abundant (Hawkes 1990), and have been well studied in the !Kung, Mbuti Pygmies, Aché, Hadza and Nunamiut, for instance (e.g. Carpaneto & Germi 1992; Hawkes *et al.* 1991; Hawkes & O'Connell 1985; Hill & Hawkes 1983; Hurtado *et al.* 1992; Ichikawa 1983; Terashima 1983) or the technology required for whale hunting (Alvard & Gillespie 2004). Small catches are usually owned by the hunter and are not shared, although there are exceptions as in the Hadza (Hawkes *et al.* 2001).

The distribution of food within a social group reduces the risk of shortfall, since hunting is associated with a large variance in returns, and thus the risk of malnutrition and mortality amongst its members (Kaplan *et al.* 2000). There can either be an egalitarian sharing amongst hunters and other group members, but also situations in which certain group members gain a greater share (benefit) over others according to previously agreed rules (Barnes & Barnes 1996; Wiessner *et al.* 1996). Egalitarian sharing of meat, for example, is typical of hunter-gatherers groups in tropical forest environments, in which the hunters themselves do not control how a large prey animal is divided amongst their group, since this is considered a common good accessible to even those who have not participated in its capture (see Hawkes 2001).

4.11 Conservation and Sustainability

Many studied hunter-gatherer societies exploit their food sources in a sustainable manner but conservation is not their main *modus vivendi* (Section 3.5; Alvard 1995b). The active conservation of exploited resources by humans is a rational survival-linked decision that has a short-term cost for those who implement it, so as to maintain the long-term sustainability of resources (Alvard 1993). Therefore, this implies the deliberate manipulation of the environment to favour the production of resources (Balée & Erickson 2006), such as by restricting hunting activity of declining prey and impoverished territories. To achieve the expected results, actions must be intentional. The reality is that in a large number of societies, natural resources are considered inexhaustible since they are thought to depend on the generosity of supernatural forces. When resources become limited, mystical forces seem to have ceased their generosity, in which case it is necessary to implement magical expiatory rituals to appease the wrath of the spirits (Hames 2007; Krech 1999). Many of these societies do indeed adapt their behaviour to ensure that hunting continues in their territories, but often do not take direct actions that regulate prey extraction, even though they may be aware that overexploitation is harmful. Moreover, taboos cannot be interpreted as a primitive form of protection because, with some exceptions (Ross *et al.* 1978), their origin is usually not directly related to the conservation of overexploited species or places, but rather to cultural myths (Alvard 1998).

Living in harmony with nature does not necessarily reflect a 'conservationist' attitude (Alvard 1998), as many anthropologists argued between the 1960s and 1980s (FitzGibbon 1998). Many hunter-gatherer populations are in balance with their prey. But often this is not a fixed aim of these communities set in advance but a consequence of other factors (Alvard 1995b), an effect that has been named by Hunn (1982) as a 'conservationist epiphenomenon'. The balance with the environment can arise from low human population density, limited technology and high mobility. Indeed, human population size was significantly linked with mammalian extinctions over the past 126,000 years (Section 6.1; Andermann *et al.* 2020). In particular, low human population density results in the 'inability to overexploit' (Alvard 1995b). Therefore, it is not inconsistent to find a positive correlation between the presence of native peoples, often at low population densities, and areas of high diversity (Borgerhoff Mulder & Coppolillo 2005; Fa *et al.* 2020; Garnett *et al.* 2018).

Sustainability (Chapter 5) is possible in the absence of clear conservationist attitudes among users of a resource when the extraction rate does not exceed the intrinsic rate of growth of the target populations. The vulnerability of the species, the number of catches and the size of the population of consumers are factors to be taken into account (Alvard *et al.* 1997). Hence, in practice, sustainability depends on the behaviour of the hunter and the prey species, since they determine the number and type of animals collected (FitzGibbon 1998). Therefore, OFT and sustainability are compatible when overexploitation is spurious.

Currently, the idea prevails that many traditional societies have overexploited their prey and deteriorated the habitat (Alvard 1998; Diamond 1988). According to Krech (1999), there is little evidence of conservation among Native Americans prior to contact with Europeans and none during that period. Similarly, conservation among contemporary hunters is rare and occurs only when prey species are valuable and scarce: they constitute private goods (abundant and predictable resources) and are worth defending both in the short and long term (Alvard & Kuznar 2001). On the other hand, a study by Hames (1987) on various Amazonian peoples does not find support for the conservation hypothesis: the more decimated the target species are, the more time they invest in hunting them (Siona-Secoya and Yanomami hunters, among others). The Piro, for example, do not avoid hunting vulnerable species in fallow zones if they find them (Alvard 1995a). This does not obviate the existence of evidence in favour of proactive conservation by different hunter-gatherer societies (Ohl-Schacherer *et al.* 2007). For example, the transition of animal husbandry from hunting is a special case of resource conservation (see below). But these tests are scarce and those that point in the opposite direction are very abundant (Smith & Wishnie 2000). A recent review on the ecologically noble savage debate (Hames 2007) highlights the lack of empirical arguments in support of a generalized conservationism, concluding that the idea of 'proactive conservation' attributed to the hunter-gatherer communities is a myth. There is no doubt that Indigenous Peoples have extensive knowledge of the environment, but it is not clear whether they use it to maintain a balance with nature or to be more efficient hunters (Hames 1987). The causes of non-conservation are attributed to the fact that prey species are freely acquired (Hames 1991; Smith *et al.* 1983) or to the low impact caused by hunting on the biodiversity of the territory, which does not exclude the possibility that some species are overexploited (Alvard 1995b).

A very special case of conservation is the transition of animal husbandry from hunting. Alvard and Kuznar (2001) suggest that animal husbandry is prey conservation where the husbanded animals are prey that are not pursued upon encounter. At first, this appears to be in contrast to the diet-breadth model which predicts that foragers always pursue prey that are in the optimal diet set. The initiation of animal husbandry, however, does not involve immediate pursuit and killing of prey species and the benefits are deferred to the future by slaughtering the husbanded animals or their offspring. Alvard and Kuznar (2001) show that under certain, feasible conditions, OFT can explain the emergence of husbandry. The conditions are: (1) private ownership or territorial defence of animals, (2) sufficient value of animals to justify defence and (3) low opportunity cost of restraint of animals. Archaeological evidence for Neolithic transition in the Middle East indicates that these conditions were met. Alvard and Kuznar's (2001) OFT model predicts that animals below 40 kg should be husbanded under these conditions whilst larger animals should be hunted. The archaeological record indicates that the first domesticated animals, such as goat and sheep, fall within the range below 40 kg, whilst heavier animals such as cattle and pigs were only later domesticated (Alvard & Kuznar 2001).

One important conclusion from the emergence of animal husbandry is the crucial importance of property rights for conservation. Wild meat is typically extracted legally where ownership of animals does not exist or illegally where any ownership is ignored. Lack of ownership is the typical setting for the 'tragedy of the commons', where modern hunters and traditional hunter-gatherers have no incentive to limit their own harvesting when others can unilaterally maximize their own returns (e.g. Beckerman & Valentine 1996). Thus, property rights can contribute to successful conservation of prey species (see Chapter 8).

It is appropriate to remember that the conclusion that traditional hunter-gatherers generally follow the predictions of OFT and are not conserving prey species has a strictly academic value and does not justify inappropriate moral judgments. Because it is not about resurrecting the hunting–conservation dilemma, but to turn it into a conservation strategy where we are all part of the problem and together, we must contribute to its solution. According to Peres (1994), simply considering Indigenous peoples as ecologically noble is insufficient if other complementary measures are not adopted, without impositions and prior consensus.

Optimal foraging theory allows us to understand how those who depend on hunting for subsistence behave. Continuing to maintain the myth of the ecologically noble savage (Section 3.6) is as fallacious as it is dangerous and partly derives from confusing sustainability and conservation. Perhaps defending the view that they are the best guarantors of the rational use of resources is not condemning subsistence hunters involuntarily to remain in a cultural stasis that prevents population growth, technological modernization and the acquisition of consumer goods in exchange for raw materials alter the balance, whether circumstantially or voluntarily enter into this dynamic?

5 · *Estimating Sustainability*

5.1 Introduction

Sustainability is a concept widely used in science and politics, and it has myriad different definitions. The idea of sustainability first emerged at the start of the eighteenth century when von Carlowitz (1713), in the first book on forest sciences, wrote that timber should be used with caution, balancing timber growth and use. Much later, the broadest political vision of sustainability was expressed in the Brundtland Commission, as 'development that meets the needs of the present generation without compromising the ability of future generations to meet their own needs' (Brundtland 1987). The idea that sustainability should encompass the maximum use for humans is expressed in Tivy and O'Hare's (1981) description of sustainable yield as the 'management of a resource for maximum continuing production, consistent with the maintenance of a constantly renewable stock'. Different definitions emphasize the ecological, sociopolitical and economic pillars of sustainability. Highlighting ecology and socioeconomics, the Convention on Biological Diversity (CBD), the international legal instrument for the protection of global biodiversity, defines sustainable wildlife management as 'the sound management of wildlife species to sustain their populations and habitat over time, taking into account the socioeconomic needs of human populations' (CBD 2018). Whilst there are many nuances in how sustainability is conceptualized and underpinned by a theoretical framework (e.g. in bioeconomics, Clark 2010), the concept is often very difficult to apply and measure. A poignant reminder is fisheries management, which is much more advanced compared to wild meat management, despite there being many cases of fisheries collapse, even with careful management planning focused on sustainability (Bavington 2011; Roughgarden & Smith 1996). The most prominent example of fishery collapse is the disintegration of the Newfoundland Atlantic cod stocks (Bavington 2011). These stocks, like in fisheries in general, were managed based on the theory of maximum sustainable yield (MSY), which – under ideal conditions – can achieve the maximum possible harvest without depleting the species' stock over an indefinite period. This concept has limitations (see below); fisheries have now transitioned to ecosystems-based management, and in some parts of the world, at least, they seem to have achieved fisheries sustainability (e.g. Aswani *et al.* 2012; Pikitch *et al.* 2004; Section 5.7.1) It is the same concept that discussions of sustainability of wild meat hunting are currently emphasizing (Coad *et al.* 2019; Weinbaum *et al.* 2013), although more holistic concepts have recently emerged (Van Vliet *et al.* 2015b; Section 5.7.2). In this chapter, we introduce the different approaches and metrics that have been used or proposed to assess wild meat sustainability.

5.2 Growth Rate and Maximum Sustainable Yield

The MSY concept is based on a continuous time growth model according to which growth curves are density-dependent. The growth curve, that is, the recruitment that adds to a population, is parabolic, somewhat resembling an inverse U-shaped curve (Fig. 5.1). Growth rate is lowest at the two extremes of the possible densities of a population: at the carrying capacity, K, which is the maximum population size that the environment can support on a continuing basis and at very low population size. This means that the same levels of low sustainable yields exist when a population is unhunted, at K, as well as heavily hunted and close to extinction. Growth rate and, thus, sustainable yield increase when density either decreases from K or increases from very small values. The theoretical growth rate can be described with the following formula:

$$\text{growth rate} = \text{change in population size over time } \Delta N / \Delta t$$
$$= r \bullet N \bullet (1 - N / K)$$

with N = population size, ΔN = change of N, Δt change of time, r = intrinsic rate of population increase and K = carrying capacity. The two crucial parameters are r and K, which are both inherently difficult, if not virtually impossible, to measure in wild populations. At a given population size, the maximum amount that can be removed from a population equals the growth rate at that population size. In other words, harvest rates that are equal or below the growth rate can theoretically achieve ecological sustainability as the resulting growth will not be smaller than zero. There is a clear exception, namely at very low population density, because

environmental, demographic and genetic stochasticity and possibly biological processes such as the Allee effect (Courchamp *et al.* 2008) lead to a
high extinction probability – the 'extinction vortex' (Fagan & Holmes
2006). There is a point between the two extremes of K and population
extinction, at $K/2$, where growth is maximum, and this point is where
MSY occurs.

The effect of increases in the harvest rate depends on whether the
density is smaller or larger than $K/2$. If it is larger than $K/2$, the hunted
population will decline to a new equilibrium at a lower density (Fig. 5.1a
and c). Consequently, a population decline does not necessarily mean
unsustainability as it can mean that a declining population is on its way to
a new equilibrium. If the density is equal to or smaller than $K/2$,
however, then increase of hunting above the growth curve will eventually lead to population collapse because hunting takes away not only the
surplus but also the stock itself (Fig. 5.1b). If the density is only slightly
larger than $K/2$, an increase of hunting will decrease density towards
$K/2$, but density can also swing below $K/2$ because of stochasticity,
additional mortality or environmental variability (Fig. 5.1c). Any further
increase of hunting, even when small, would then cause a population to

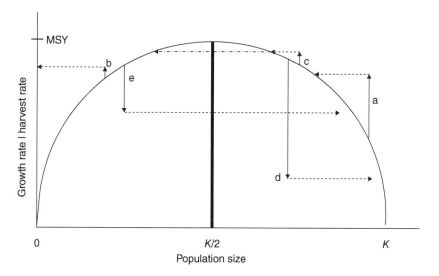

Figure 5.1 Parabolic relationship between population growth rate and population size
derived from the logistic equation for population growth. When harvest rate equals
growth rate, the population comes to an equilibrium at the associated population size.
Changes in harvest result in new equilibrium sizes, indicated by the heavy black line.
Further details in the text. Explanations of the letters are in the main text.

decline and collapse rather than achieve a new equilibrium. This applies when the harvest rate is constant. Once brought out of balance to the left side of $K/2$, the population is likely to crash except when hunting pressure is reduced; if hunting pressure is lowered, the population can grow until a new equilibrium above $K/2$ is reached (Fig. 5.1e and d; see also Clark 1976; Haddon 2011; Milner-Gulland & Mace 2009). When the harvest rate is proportional to the population size, then in principle any harvest rate is sustainable.

The CBD's (2018) definition of sustainable harvest implicitly points to MSY to balance ecological sustainability with socioeconomic sustainability to meet the needs of an increasing human population. Ecological sustainability could be at any point of the density-dependent continuum, but it must be stressed that at low population levels sustainability is unattainable (1) because of the potential for Allee effects (Courchamp et al. 2008) and the extinction vortex (Fagan & Holmes 2006) and (2) because the ecosystem may be disrupted as the species is no longer able to play its ecological role.

The most widely used method for assessing hunting sustainability – the Robinson & Redford (1991b) model – argues that sustainable harvesting should achieve the maximum possible level of extraction, which is a fraction of a species' maximum annual production, calculated from the carrying capacity and intrinsic population growth rate, whereby the fraction depends on the average lifespan of the species and an a priori precautionary factor (Section 5.4.2). Milner-Gulland and Akçakaya (2001) promote the full demographic harvesting model because it gives an accurate representation of the state of the population, unlike the Robinson and Redford (1991b) model, and is robust to uncertainty. It maximizes harvest whilst other simpler models incur substantial loss in offtake when estimating sustainable harvest levels. This means it is possible to hunt more without sending the population towards extinction but does not mean the maximum needs to be harvested.

Whilst the wild meat literature has introduced the MSY as an ideal to achieve (Coad et al. 2019), the suitability of MSY in fisheries management has long been rejected (Larkin 1977; Ludwig et al. 1993); the overwhelming criticisms against MSY were summarized by Larkin (1977). Even though the use of MSY approach has declined in fisheries, it has remained in use because it is a simple and easy-to-understand concept (Barber 1988). However, with the recent shift of the harvesting paradigm in fisheries towards ecosystem-based management (Section 5.7.1), MSY is now used as a reference point rather than as a target

(Mace 2001). In an analysis of managed fisheries collapses, Roughgarden and Smith (1996) stressed that the application of economic theory that aims to maximize sustainable harvest leads to an ecologically unstable equilibrium as 'difficult as to balance a marble on top of a dome'. To facilitate population stability, the emphasis should be on ecological stability rather than maximizing harvests. The authors argue that 'ecological stability is achieved if the target stock is above that producing maximum sustainable yield and harvested at less than the maximum sustainable yield'. In other words, the growth curve needs to stay on the right side of $K/2$. The apparent economic loss due to forfeiting MSY would act as a 'natural insurance' that is low in case of high productivity of the target species. However, this apparent economic loss under the MSY is not a loss under the concept of maximum economic yield (MEY), which is the long-term value of the largest positive difference between total revenues from fishing and total costs of fishing. Because it takes costs into account, MEY is almost always on the right-hand side of the parabola in Fig. 5.1, thus facilitating sustainability. Economists have argued that a fishery that maximizes its economic potential also usually will fulfil its conservation objectives. For example, Grafton *et al.* (2007) show that the biomass under MEY exceeds the biomass under MSY. However, to the best of our knowledge, the concept of MEY has not been applied as a management tool in wild meat hunting.

It is important to keep in mind that the logistic growth curve is an idealization. Real populations are more complex. This is because of demographic stochasticity, environmental variation, reproductive biases by age, sex and social structure, interdependence with other, often also hunted species (as in the case of predator–prey systems) and the influence of geographic structure, especially metapopulation dynamics and source–sink relationships. In the following sections, we introduce and critically discuss the commonly used methods to evaluate the sustainability of wildlife hunting. The selection of some of the benchmark example studies follows Weinbaum *et al.* (2013).

5.3 Indices Quantifying Population Trends over Time

Biological systems are multifaceted and are impacted by deterministic processes and stochastic events. There is usually also randomness and uncertainty in estimating population density and hunting pressure, not to mention complex biological parameters such as growth rate and reproductive parameters of prey species that are difficult to obtain from wild populations (see Section 5.3.1). Thus, ultimately, a population can only be known to be sustainably harvested after there has been adequate time to observe if the population estimators are sufficiently precise, the predictions hold true and the system is stable. Therefore, indices quantifying population trends over time are, thus, the most practicable for evaluating sustainability. Although direct monitoring of prey populations may be the 'golden standard', there are a number of methods that continue to be used. We describe these, their advantages and disadvantages, as well as an example of each to demonstrate its application.

5.3.1 Direct Surveys of Population Density

In a review of sustainability indicators for wild meat hunting, Weinbaum *et al.* (2013) proposed monitoring of harvested populations through time as one of the gold standards in sustainability monitoring. The surveys provide indications whether a target population is stable, increasing or decreasing. For an overview of techniques to estimate absolute and relative densities, see Millner-Gulland and Rowcliffe (2007).

> **Pros:** The advantage is that it is the only method that directly estimates sustainability. The method is very powerful if monitoring is continuous and the results are fed into adaptive harvesting strategies.
>
> **Cons:** The major caution is that changes in population abundance are difficult to interpret if estimates of associated species (e.g. predator–prey systems), harvesting and external factors (e.g. habitat change or climate change) are not simultaneously estimated, or if spatial scales are too small to detect source–sink patterns. Time frames need to be sufficiently long to allow distinguishing stochastic change from systematic change, albeit sudden declines in population density can act as early warning systems to trigger more intensive monitoring. The major disadvantage is that it is time intensive and expensive, especially when remote, tropical locations are concerned. Whilst intensive monitoring is more likely for those species in logistically easy-to-monitor habitats (e.g. savannahs), where animals can be directly observed or trapped, monitoring prey populations in dense vegetation environments (e.g. tropical forests) is more difficult.

Example: Weinbaum *et al.* (2013) describe the earliest textbook example of this method as Larivière *et al.*'s (2000) grey wolf monitoring study in southern Québec, Canada. Here, wolves are found in a mosaic of wildlife reserves, where hunting is controlled by quotas on hunting licenses, unlike public and private lands where harvests are less restricted. Over a 15-year time period, starting with the onset of wolf trapping in the reserves, the study monitored wolf densities in nine wildlife reserves by a combination of questionnaires distributed to moose hunters and the usage of radio-tracking wolves. Aerial surveys were used to monitor moose densities. Pelt sales and tanning records for each trapping district were employed to quantify wolf harvest. Over the study period, although wolf densities fluctuated widely in seven reserves, these showed no indication of long-term declines. By contrast, wolf populations in two reserves declined steadily. Without continuous monitoring, estimates of sustainability would have been highly biased. Population variability was negatively correlated with reserve size, indicating that wolf populations in smaller reserves were more unstable than those in larger reserves. In the two smallest reserves, however, harvesting frequently exceeded wolf densities but without population decline. This points to the presence of a source–sink system in which wolves from adjacent reserves repopulated the smaller reserves. Previously it was thought that these reserves acted as sources for the surrounding public and private lands, but the Larivière *et al.* (2000) study showed the contrary. These results demonstrate the importance of investing in continuous population density surveys to provide information to local wildlife managers to ensure conservation of the target species alongside their exploitation. As mentioned above, population monitoring of species such as the grey wolf is possible because the target species is generally visible to the observer (and therefore can be counted using direct methods) or their numbers can be inferred indirectly from records of hunted animals.

5.3.2 Catch Per Unit Effort over Time

The yield or number of animals removed by hunting, H, depends on catchability, q, hunting effort, E, and population size, N:

$$H = q \cdot E \cdot N$$

The parameter q is a species-specific constant quantifying how difficult or easy it is to hunt the species. If the effort is independent of the yield and population density, then changes in H/E translate in variations in N. This is the catch per unit effort (CPUE) – the ratio of yield to the effort expended to achieve the yield. Hunting effort can be measured as duration of hunts that result in H hunted animals, number of hunted animals per trip, number of snares set or amount of ammunition used. Using interviews and hunting returns, Vickers (1994) was the first to estimate population density trajectories, but without calling it CPUE, for Siona-Secoya hunters in the northwest Amazonian Peru. More recently,

Rist *et al.* (2010) investigated the methodology in more detail by comparing data collected by hunters with more direct information gathered by accompanying hunters on hunting trips. By applying simulations, Rist *et al.* (2010) assessed the accuracy, power and resolution of the method.

Pros: CPUE values can be obtained directly from hunters, which is easier and cheaper than monitoring populations in the field. Hunters require little training for data recording.

Cons: Estimates resulting from CPUE data are unable to determine population density and thus yield. CPUE needs to be monitored over time to reliably identify whether it increases, decreases or stays stable. It requires an adequate and representative sample of hunters per area/region to account for differences in their hunting efficiencies and strategies and geographic substructure such as contrasts between villages. The sample must be sufficiently large to distinguish between measurement errors and stochasticity from 'true' changes in CPUE. Studies need to demonstrate this, for example by subsampling and modelling (Rist *et al.* 2010). Selecting a sufficiently large number of monitored hunters can be a challenge, especially where hunting is illegal (e.g. protected areas), or where specific hunting methods are prohibited (e.g. snares). Moreover, if CPUE is used for management of hunting quotas, reductions in quota will likely erode the hunters' willingness to participate and compromise the trustworthiness of the data provided. Rist *et al.* (2010) modelled CPUEs assuming a statistical power of only 80% and $\alpha = 0.05$ reporting that information on 1,000 hunts had to be collected to allow the detection of a 20% density change. As many as 3,000 hunts were required for a detection of a 10% change. The method relies on trust between all participants where trust-building is time consuming. Reported values must be unbiased, but experience from fisheries has shown that there is over-reporting of both catch and effort in some fisheries (Lunn & Dearden 2006). A crucial component of the equation is that yield is directly proportional to both effort and population size. CPUE assumes that no density-dependent changes occur in hunter effort, such as change in technology or strategy. However, hunters might change to night hunting with flashlights when densities decline, which would bias CPUE and might even result in a stable CPUE despite population declines (Bowler *et al.* 2019). Similarly, hunting yield needs to be proportional to density. Even the assumption that catchability is a constant might not hold for many species, for example, when animals respond behaviourally to the presence of humans as a reaction to hunting pressure and, thus, bias the yield (Keane *et al.* 2011; Papworth *et al.* 2013a). Aggregation behaviour, the tendency for animals to group together in flocks or herds as seen in many bird and ungulate species can result in similar hunter effort independent of whether density is stable or declining. This is because it is easier to hunt gregarious species than solitary, territorial ones and because aggregations occur despite changes in density. Finally, the same caveats apply to the interpretation of inferred population decline as for the direct surveys of population density.

Example: Hill *et al.* (2003) recorded harvest-rate data for 5,526 Aché hunter days during seven years in the Mbaracayu Reserve, Paraguay. CPUE, expressed as animals killed per hunting day, was seen to decline in seven of the ten prey species, which jointly contributed 95% of all individuals and 96% of biomass harvested. Only the drop in capuchin monkeys was significant but high variability in monthly harvest rates may have masked the negative trends. To be able to interpret the complexities of the observed fluctuations in CPUE, 7,535 km of diurnal random line transect surveys were conducted by teams of five observers. Encounter rates from the line transects showed negative trends in nine of the ten species, with four species exhibiting significant declines (Fig. 5.2). However, these four species did not include the capuchin monkey. The 95% confidence interval (CI) of the estimated maximum harvest rate was lower than 1% of the standing stock for six species including the capuchin monkey and was lower than 3.7% for the remaining four species. Overall, the declining CPUE and encounter rates of most species caused concern, but there was little evidence that hunting pressure by Aché hunters was the main cause of these observed decreases. However, there was support for considerable poaching by non-Aché hunters, which could explain the observed patterns. Regarding the capuchin monkey, CPUE was possibly misleading as the observed significant declines may have been caused by changes in hunting effort E, but possibly not in N. During the study, Aché hunters appeared to refocus their attention to peccaries rather than capuchin monkey, thus changing E for the species involved. Finally, the results demonstrate that the applicability and interpretability of the CPUE index in the study was limited without the inclusion of direct surveys of population density.

5.4 Indices Based on Full Demographic Models

Modelling populations based on their life history traits and demographic parameters allows us to determine how much additional mortality is

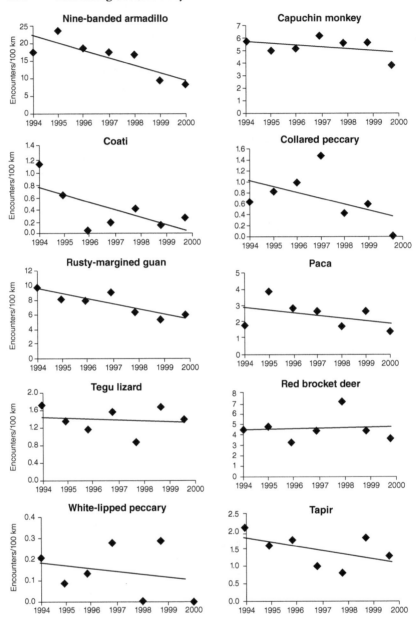

Figure 5.2 Crude encounter rates/100 km of ten important hunted species. Encounter rates were calculated as total encounters divided by total kilometres of transect walked in each 12-month period of the study. (From Hill *et al.* 2003; adapted with permission from John Wiley & Sons.)

compatible with population persistence. This can then be compared with the actual harvest. Milner-Gulland and Akçakaya (2001) introduced the full demographic harvesting model based on realistic demographic parameters and proportional harvest rates for each age class. Populations were simulated using RAMAS Metapop, a software package to analyse population viability (Akçakaya & Root 2002), under different demographic scenarios and then compared with simulations using different simple demographic algorithms (Section 5.4). The target was population persistence of 200 individuals during a 50-year period, with a likelihood of over 95%. Simulations indicated that the full demographic model outperformed all other models in population persistence and maximum harvest rates. It dramatically outperformed the Bodmer B method (Section 5.4.2), which was the next best performing model in terms of harvest, by a 7% greater harvest and a 95% lower risk of population collapse. It also outperformed the National Marine Fisheries Service algorithm (Section 5.4.3), which was the next-best performing model in terms of population persistence, by a 62% greater harvest.

Pros: Full models allow maximization of extraction rates whilst keeping extinction probabilities low. They allow the simulation of ranges of reasonable population parameters and, thus, make it possible to conduct sensitivity analyses. Population viability analysis (PVA) permits not only the modelling of deterministic parameters but also demographic, environmental and genetic stochastic events, which are of particular importance in small populations.

Cons: Full models are data-intensive, requiring life history information and knowledge of the many processes affecting populations. Attainment of such level of detail and precision is often not possible for most tropical, hunted species. Because such robust biological information is not available – even for well-studied species – such models do not adequately account for demographic complexities, in particular density-dependence. For example, in a study of sustainable harvest rates of the European hare, Marboutin *et al.* (2003) chose a simplified life cycle with three age classes and density-independence because of the lack of adequate data, despite the fact that sustained harvesting might indicate density-dependence. The absence of realistic reproductive and demographic data from wild populations has been pointed out as a major problem in applying sustainability models, even for widely hunted species. As a consequence, reproductive parameters are often taken from captive populations, which can be crude, biased towards *ex situ* conditions and in many cases outdated (Mayor *et al.* 2017; Van Vliet & Nasi 2018; see Chapter 8). For example, reproductive data used in sustainable hunting models (see Robinson & Redford 1986) for woolly monkeys, the Amazon's most hunted primates, have come primarily from captive populations for the 1960s, when they rarely reproduced, and before a major taxonomic revision split one supposed species into five different ones (Bowler *et al.* 2014). It is therefore essential not just to verify the suitability of demographic parameters from captivity for sustainability analysis, otherwise 'population modelling is based largely on guess-work' (Bowler *et al.* 2014). A relatively new approach is to utilize a citizen science approach with hunters themselves supplying the genitalia of prey animals to more precisely determine reproductive parameters of these species (see Section 8.2.1). Independent of data quality, computational issues can limit the reliability of the simulation outcomes. Diverse software packages and sometimes different versions of the same package may implement the modelling differently, sometimes producing results that are not concordant (Brook *et al.* 1999). Consequently, results from several modelling packages should be compared, albeit something rarely done in the literature. Modelling requires expertise in software applications and species biology and' 'must be a collaborative, trans-disciplinary and social process' (Lacy 2019).

5.4.1 Estimation of the Population Growth Rate

Another approach to using full demographic information is the modelling of net recruitment rates. Rather than modelling the likelihood of a population to persist as in the VORTEX software approach, the population growth rate lambda, λ, is estimated from the data including harvest whereby $\lambda \geq 1$ implies sustainability and $\lambda < 1$ unsustainability. Simulations allow us to evaluate the sensitivity of λ to the effects of parameter variations (Combreau *et al.* 2001; Marboutin *et al.* 2003).

Example: Lofroth and Ott (2007) assessed the sustainability of wolverine harvests across the Canadian province of British Columbia. Demographic parameters – survivorship estimates of juvenile, subadult and adult age classes and reproductive rates – were taken from the literature. The authors emphasized the caveats that reproductive output data are rare and that demographic parameters are not necessarily constant between habitats that differ in quality. But because

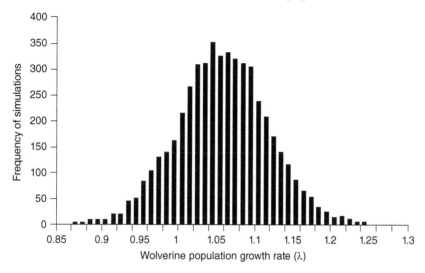

Figure 5.3 Frequency distribution of estimated wolverine population growth rate (λ) using simulation, British Columbia, Canada for 2007 (from Lofroth and Ott 2007; adapted with permission from John Wiley & Sons).

of lack of data, no density-dependence was modelled. Assuming an underlying normal distribution for all demographic parameters 5,000 estimates of population sizes were simulated by randomly drawing parameter values from their normal distributions. Subsequently, λ was mathematically calculated, resulting in a normal distribution with a mean $\pm$SE of 1.06 ± 0.06 (Fig. 5.3). Using spatially explicit density estimates and harvest rates from the province's 71 population units, annual net recruitment rates for the period 1985–2004 were then calculated. In 16% of simulations, net recruitment was negative, and 15 population units had negative net recruitment in more than half of the simulations, indicating unsustainable harvests. Overall, the simulations showed that the whole province was sustainably harvested between 1984 and 2004 despite the occurrence of 15 unsustainably harvested population units, emphasizing the importance of the spatial dimension of harvest for the assessment of sustainability. The study suggests the use of an adaptive management approach which advises wildlife managers to monitor mean harvest and recruitment rate for individual population units and then intervene when consecutive years of harvest are unsustainable. For a well-studied species such as the wolverine, monitoring recruitment might well be feasible, but it is information that is highly challenging to collect, particularly for many wild meat species. It is possible to estimate the reproductive status of harvested females, but this is still labour intensive and may not be a good guide to recruitment into the population if there is density-dependent juvenile mortality.

5.4.2 Population Viability Analysis and the Madingley General Ecosystem Model

Several software PVA packages are available, which can produce different results. These include GAPPS, INMAT, RAMAS Age, RAMAS Metapop, RAMAS Stage and VORTEX. The most often used software for PVA is VORTEX, an individual-based simulation of population demography (Lacy 1993, 2000). VORTEX is the PVA model of choice for use to simulate the fate of small populations threatened by extinction vortices and for complex models that include individual variation, spatial and metapopulation structure, and complex feedback between demography and genetics (Lacy 2019). Although hunting can be incorporated alongside other additional types of mortality, PVA's are essentially designed for single-species systems and are difficult to apply for multi-species ones, such as wild meat hunting. For multi-species systems, Barychka *et al.* (2020a) recently used a new approach, the Madingley General Ecosystem model, which allows simulation of ecosystem dynamics with multi-species harvesting. In computer simulations for duikers, the most heavily hunted species in sub-Saharan Africa (Chapter 1), the model adequately predicts yields, species extinction rates and ecosystem-level harvesting impacts compared to single-species models. Barychka *et al.* (2020a) suggest that this method should be used more widely for management, but so far it awaits implementation on the ground.

Example: Combreau *et al.* (2001) assessed the mortality rate of migrant Asian houbara bustards using VORTEX PVA modelling based on demographic data obtained from ringing, satellite tracking and a three-year study on the bird's breeding success (Combreau *et al.* 2002). The results of the PVA model demonstrated that the houbara population would become extinct within 50 years (with a probability of 94%) if current levels of hunting and poaching persisted.

5.5 Quantitative Indices Based on Surplus Production Models

Sustainability models that are able to use basic information of prey species' life-history traits are comparatively more accessible than those that depend on large amounts of population data being collected in the field. Since in situations where monitoring levels are minimal, and not long-term, less ambitious methods can still be useful in estimating sustainable production levels. These models employ the information available on life-history traits

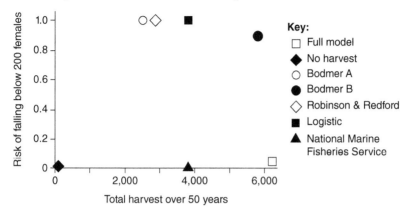

Figure 5.4 The trade-off between the risk of population decline and the number of individuals hunted, shown for a species with fast life history, high growth rate, depleted population, declining habitat and high variability (from Milner-Gulland and Akçakaya 2001; adapted with permission from Elsevier).

of the hunted species and take into account their average lifespan as a good index to which harvest takes the animals that would have died anyway. The proportion of animals that can be hunted will depend on whether the species is long or short-lived. Comparisons between the calculated sustainable production levels and the measured levels of hunting and additional mortality can then be used to point to whether a specific population is sustainably harvested or not. Perhaps the best exponent is the Robinson and Redford equation (Section 5.4.2) (see Weinbaum *et al.* 2013). Depending on the method, the underpinning calculation for the sustainable level of production, P, includes carrying capacity K, maximum rate of population increase (r_{max}), current population size, N, mortality or recovery factor, F, female survival to the average reproductive age, s, and female fecundity, φ. Milner-Gulland and Akçakaya (2001) simulated populations under a range of scenarios for two contrasting life histories and calculated the probability of falling below the threshold population size of 200 individuals when applying different models. For all scenarios, the simulations resulted in vastly differing model performances depending on the model used (example in Fig. 5.4).

Pros: These methods have been widely used as fallback when species are data-deficient as only a few parameters, not a full population model, are needed. The equations are easy to calculate and do not need modelling or specific software packages. Typically, the required life-history parameters are taken from the literature from *in situ* or *ex situ* populations, thus not requiring additional field work. By contrast to the Robinson and Redford method, the US National Marine Fisheries Service equation has been rarely used (Weinbaum *et al.* 2013) despite it being shown to generate robust, conservative estimates in simulation modelling (Milner-Gulland & Akçakaya 2001).

Cons: All algorithms use rudimentary sets of simplified parameters for life history traits because of the general paucity of the data available (Van Vliet & Nasi 2018; Weinbaum *et al.* 2013). General life history parameters taken from published lists (e.g. Robinson & Redford 1986) often do not adequately represent the populations under study (Bowler *et al.* 2014; Mayor *et al.* 2017; Van Vliet & Nasi 2018). Results from different sites are not comparable even when calculated with the same algorithm as a variety of methods can be used to calculate the parameters of the same model and each of the methods has different sources of error (Van Vliet & Nasi 2008b). The US National Marine Fisheries Service equation has been criticized as being too precautionary, and thus not facilitating maximum harvest, whereas other methods have been criticized because they are not precautionary enough (Milner-Gulland & Akçakaya 2001; Weinbaum *et al.* 2013).

5.5.1 Maximum Sustainable Yield Model

The standard logistic growth rate model introduced in Section 5.1 allows the calculation of maximum sustainable yield (MSY) as

$$MSY = (r \cdot K)/4$$

and a maximum sustainable harvest rate, (MHR), of

$$MHR = r/2$$

Whenever an observed harvest is larger than MSY, it is considered unsustainable. However, a harvest that is smaller or equal to MSY is not necessarily sustainable as we do not know whether the harvest yield is on the left side or the right side of the parabola; in case of the first, it would be unsustainable (see Fig. 5.1). This model is mainly used in fisheries (Weinbaum *et al.* 2013).

Example: Brook and Whitehead (2005) estimated r and the associated MHR using published information on fecundity and credible estimates of survival in magpie geese in northern Australia. They show that the range of reasonable r estimates is from $r = 0.035$, derived under the assumption of 'average environmental conditions', to $r = 0.498$, where all reproductive rates and survival rates are at maximum capacity. This range corresponds to MHR that spans from 2% to 25%. This assessment demonstrated that the previous estimate of $r = 0.78$ and MHR $= 39\%$ from a time-series analysis of aerial count data, before the best information was available, was not plausible and constituted a gross overestimate of the possible sustainable harvest. Instead, the authors argued that the overestimate of r constituted an example of 'extravagant claims of population resilience, and correspondingly excessive levels of exploitation'. They suggested an MHR of no more than 5–14% of total population size per annum for magpie geese.

5.5.2 Robinson and Redford Index

This algorithm has been the most widely used for wild meat species in tropical settings, despite some concerns being raised about its application (Weinbaum *et al.* 2013). The index is relatively easy to calculate according the equation:

$$P = 0.6 \cdot K \cdot (r_{max} - 1) \cdot F$$

with an ad hoc mortality factor F dependent on the species' life history ($F = 0.2$ for long-lived species whose age of last reproduction is over 10 years, $F = 0.4$ for short-lived species those whose age of last reproduction is between 5 and 10 years and $F = 0.6$ for short-lived species whose age of last reproduction is less than five years). The value of $0.6\,K$ is merely a precautionary factor that stems from the assumption that the maximum produced would be achieved when population density (N_i) was at 60% of carrying capacity K. This is a subjective percentage and could be adjusted according to density estimates and knowledge of the population. To assess the species' intrinsic rate of increase Robinson and Redford (1991b) use Cole's (1954) equation to calculate r_{max} from the age at first reproduction, the age at last reproduction and the annual birth rate of female offspring, b:

$$1 = -e^{-rmax} + b \cdot e^{-rmax(\text{age at first reproduction})} - b \cdot e^{-rmax(\text{age at last reproduction} + 1)}$$

This equation does not consider mortality, 'which is a very strong assumption" (Milner-Gulland & Akçakaya 2001). Estimates of these reproductive parameters are available for many commonly hunted forest species (e.g. Robinson & Redford 1986) but vary in their accuracy depending on their origin (see above). For example, in a comparison between published ex situ data and empirical in situ information for the ten most-hunted hunted Amazonian mammal species, the authors found concordance, underestimation and overestimation of species' r_{max} values, resulting in different biases for those studies that used the various estimates (Mayor *et al.* 2017). The discrepancies can be so wide that new assessments of these parameters which relate to various ecological conditions are urgently needed (Van Vliet & Nasi 2018). According to Milner-Gulland and Akçakaya's (2001) the index performed rather badly under realistic conditions simulation experiments (Section 6.3). Population persistence of 200 individuals during a 50-year period was never achieved and harvest was less than half of that of the best performing model, the National Marine Fisheries Service algorithm. Weinbaum at al. (2013) identified five publications which calculated the Robinson and Redford index alongside at least one other index. From 86 population comparisons, 23 (27%) resulted in divergent conclusions of sustainability.

Example: Zapata-Ríos *et al.* (2009) assessed the sustainability of mammal hunting by the Shuar within a 243 km^2 hunting catchment area in the Ecuadorian Amazon. The authors assessed sustainability of hunting of mammals by comparing the Robinson and Redford model, the Bodmer B model (Section 5.4.2) and the MSY index (Section 5.4.3). Harvest rates were obtained from hunter interviews and hunter self-monitoring data, animal density data from line-transects, and r_{max} and fecundity rates (litter size and gestations per year) were derived from the literature (Robinson & Redford 1986). Of the 21 mammal species hunted there were sufficient data to assess 15, 12 of which were hunted above maximum sustainable levels. All three methods produced the same conclusions.

5.5.3 Bodmer A and B Indices

The equation for the two Bodmer indices (Bodmer 1994a), also called the 'unified harvest model', is the same:

$$P = 0.5 \cdot N \cdot \varphi \cdot s$$

and requires information on the female part of the population, $0.5 \cdot N$, female fecundity, φ, and female survival to the average reproductive age, s. The latter is either estimated as $s = 0.2$ for long-lived species and $s = 0.6$ for short-lived species in case of the Bodmer A model or estimated from actual data in case of the Bodmer B model. Fecundity is typically estimated from ex situ populations that have the same associated problems, as already discussed for the Robinson and Redford index. Sustainability is achieved if the observed harvest is smaller or equal to the estimated P (Weinbaum *et al.* 2013). In Milner-Gulland and Akçakaya's (2001) simulation experiments, the Bodmer B model performed better in terms of yield, but led almost as often to a high risk (approx. 90%) of the population falling below 200 individuals during a 50-year period as the Bodmer A model (100%).

Example: Altrichter (2005) investigated the sustainability of collared, white-lipped and Chacoan peccary hunting in the Argentine Chaco by contrasting results from the Bodmer B model with comparisons of population densities in hunted versus unhunted sites (Section 5.5). Harvest data was obtained from hunter interviews, estimates of peccary density from transect counts and from published data from similar sites in the Chaco. Reproductive parameters for the three species were obtained by examining genitalia of hunted animals and from published data. Results showed the collared peccary was harvested sustainably according to both algorithms but findings were ambiguous for the Chacoan peccary. Estimates for the latter species showed that major differences appeared when density and reproductive parameters are based on field and published data resulting in an estimate of 74% versus 18% of production taken, which is either unsustainable or sustainable. Comparing unhunted with hunted sites showed that peccary populations were unsustainability harvested if density in hunted sites was only 35% of the unharvested density. For the white-lipped peccary, results were also ambiguous as the percent production taken in Bodmer B was below 50%, that is 'sustainable' according to Weinbaum's (2013), and according to Altrichter's (2005) cut-off point. However, the comparison of unhunted with hunted sites suggested unsustainability as the density of the harvested population was only 32% of the unharvested one. In conclusion, the study demonstrates, first, that there is no agreement how the Bodmer B method is interpreted and, second, that the discrepancies of the interpretations between the two methods stipulates the need for additional monitoring and refined reproductive parameter estimates for the site.

5.5.4 US National Marine Fisheries Service Index

The algorithm, also called the potential biological removal index (PBR), was developed for cetacean bycatch (Wade 1998):

$$PBR = N_{min} \cdot 0.5 \cdot r_{max} \cdot F_R$$

with N_{min} = minimum population estimate, F_R = recovery factor between 0.1 and 1, and r_{max} = maximum rate of population increase.

The index specifically calls for the minimum population estimate rather a mean estimate, thus accounting for uncertainty of density estimates. This is one of the main strengths of the index. The recovery factor allows for the implementation of different management strategies but needs to be assigned with care. Importantly, current knowledge of the species in general and the targeted population in particular, conservation goals, harvesting requests and the feasibility of further monitoring the population, need to be taken into consideration. The smallest value of $F_R = 0.1$ allows a population to be maintained close to its carrying capacity, to minimize extinction risk for depleted and small populations, or to delay the recovery of a depleted population only slightly. The largest value of $F_R = 1$ allows a healthy population to be maintained at its maximum net productivity at the MSY density. A recovery factor of $F_R = 0.5$ accounts for unknown bias or estimation problems such as overestimating r_{max} or underestimating mortality.

The risk of extinction is low in simulations and the algorithm performs best amongst the indices based on surplus production models. In Milner-Gulland and Akçakaya's (2001) simulation experiments, the algorithm performed best in its ability to have a no risk of the population falling below 200 individuals during a 50-year period. Total harvest was lower than the full demographic model (Section 6.3) because of its precautionary approach, which has been listed as a potential disadvantage since the algorithm is not designed to maximize yield (Weinbaum *et al.* 2013). Notwithstanding the favourable performance of this index and its popularity in fisheries and marine mammal, turtle and seabird bycatch studies, the approach remains very rarely used, despite its potential favourability over the Robinson and Redford and the Bodmer indices (Weinbaum *et al.* 2013).

Example: Dillingham and Fletcher (2008) compared the US National Marine Fisheries Service index with demographic models in two well-studied birds, the greater snow goose and the magpie goose. Both methods performed similarly giving comparable results for both species, further validating the algorithm. The authors also explored the sustainability of high mortality rates of the white-chinned petrel as bycatch in fisheries; a species with limited demographic information to apply demographic modelling. Because of data deficiency and history of high losses of this bird due to fisheries, the authors suggested the application of a F_R value between 0.1 and 0.3. The resulting PBR was lower than the known mortality from fisheries at $F_R = 0.1$ and possibly $F_R = 0.3$. Considering that mortality is strongly biased towards males, which constitute 80% of the bycatch, male-specific PBR was lower than male mortality at both F_R levels, suggesting unsustainable mortality. The high sex bias in bycatch of the white-chinned petrel highlights that the index might need to be adapted if applied to other life-histories other than the species it was designed for, namely cetaceans and pinnipeds, which are characterized by long life, delayed maturity and low fecundity.

5.5.5 Modelling Parameter Uncertainty

Barychka *et al.*'s (2020b) model allows the implementation of parameter uncertainty, which is pertinent in all field situations for the planning of sustainable hunting. The model centres on the Beverton–Holt population model which is widely used in fisheries (Beverton & Holt 1957):

$$N_{t+1} = r_t N_t / (1 + [(r_t - 1)/K]N_t)$$

with N_t and N_{t+1} = the population densities at time t and the following time step, respectively; K = the equilibrium population size without harvesting; r_t = the density-independent intrinsic rate of natural increase (i.e., the balance of births and deaths) for year t. Uncertainty for the parameters r_t and K are modelled based on prior belief. The prior belief is ideally based on field data for the studies populations and, failing that, on expert judgement. Barychka *et al.* (2020b) implemented two harvesting strategies at a constant rate, set either as a quota or proportional to the population size, N_t.

Example: Barychka *et al.* (2020b) simulated harvesting over a 25-year harvest period for three hypothetical duiker populations. Duikers are relatively well studied but population estimates vary considerably between localities (Van Vliet & Nasi 2008b), emphasizing the importance of modelling parameter uncertainty to assess sustainable harvesting. Figure 5.5 compares the modelled quota-based harvest yields and population survival probabilities for the blue duiker under scenarios without and with consideration of parameter uncertainties. At a harvesting level of four animals/km^2/year the survival probability was 100% over 25 years and the median yield was between 3 and 5 when no parameter uncertainty was considered, but survival probabilities (50% to 80%) and yield were markedly smaller (1–5) when parameter uncertainty was modelled. Thus, modelling uncertainty revealed a trade-off between yield and extinction probability whereas ignoring uncertainty implies higher yields and lower extinction probabilities that are unrealistic under field conditions where parameter uncertainty prevails (Van Vliet & Nasi 2008b). Moreover, with uncertainty there was no target quota that resulted in 100% survival probability in the investigated case. No such trade-off between yield and survival probability was evident for the blue duiker when a proportional harvesting strategy was implemented. However, such a proportional strategy is much more difficult to implement as

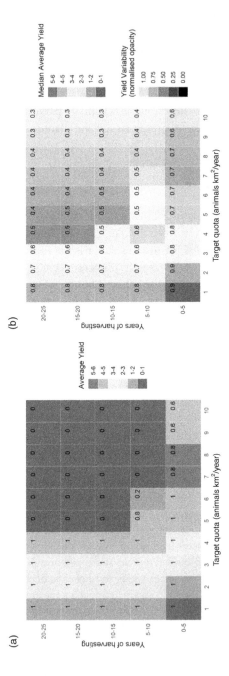

Figure 5.5 Estimated yields (animals/km²/year) from quota-based harvesting of blue duiker without (a) and with (b) parameter uncertainty. Yields are estimated over 25 years in 5-year increments. The survival probabilities are shown in top-right corner of each rectangle. (From Barychka *et al.* 2020b; reprinted with permission from PLOS ONE.)

it requires yearly field-based estimates of population size. The model demonstrates that considering model uncertainty is crucial to develop sustainable harvesting strategies.

5.6 Early Warning Systems

Several measurements indicate, but cannot demonstrate, whether wild meat hunting is sustainable or not. However, collecting these data is important in data-deficient situations as they act as early warning systems, identifying situations where more detailed monitoring is urgently advisable. Such indicators can use the comparison of population density and/ or population structure between sites subjected to different hunting pressure, changes in harvest characteristics and or changes in number of carcasses appearing in markets. The reasons underpinning the observed differences or changes can be problematic to interpret because hunter and animal populations are multivariate, dynamic and complex systems, which these indices do not measure or can take into account. The most realistic outcome is that the differences and changes obtained can be used as early warning systems which can trigger further monitoring and analysis.

5.6.1 Comparing Populations between Sites

The comparison of population density and/or population structure, especially age and sex, between hunted and non-hunted or lightly hunted sites has been used to assess harvesting sustainability. It is assumed that significant differences in density or age and sex composition can be interpreted as the result of unsustainable harvest in the exploited area.

Pro: Population density can be relatively easily estimated using line transects or camera traps for some species (Milner-Gulland & Rowcliffe 2007). Age and sex structure can be determined from direct observations of the hunted carcasses brought back by the hunters and requires little training. Differences can be statistically tested.

Cons: In dense tropical and subtropical habitats, the estimation of population density and age and sex structure can be challenging. Sites must be ecologically comparable, but that can often be verified only by intensive field work. Even when differences are significant and large, the data indicate only local depletion, but not sustainability. As indicated in Fig. 5.1, sustainable harvesting is possible in a large

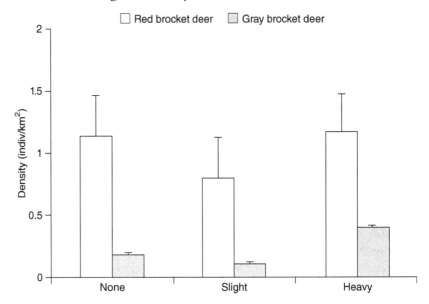

Figure 5.6 Densities of red and gray brocket deer according to different hunting pressures in the study site. Densities were estimated by line transect surveys. (From Hurtado-Gonzales and Bodmer 2004; adapted with permission from Elsevier.)

range of population densities. Thus, differences in population density per se do not prove unsustainability. Also, differences in sex and age structure per se do not prove unsustainability but the absence of differences does not demonstrate sustainability either. For example, Fitzgibbon *et al.* (1995) observed significant differences in density estimates in hunted versus unhunted areas in four-toed elephant shrews, squirrels and Syke's monkeys, but not for yellow baboons. Conversely, comparing current harvest levels reported by hunters with the estimated maximum potential sustainable harvest rates according to the Robinson and Redford (1991b) model (Section 5.4.2) indicated non-sustainability of yellow baboons and Syke's monkeys but not the other species.

Example: Hurtado-Gonzales and Bodmer (2004) assessed the sustainability of red and gray brocket deer hunting in unhunted, slightly hunted and heavily hunted sites in Peru. For the two species, gross productivity was higher in the heavily hunted site compared to the unhunted site as measured by the number of foetuses recorded per female. The heavily hunted area had a higher density of gray brocket deer compared to the non-hunted area (Fig. 5.6) but differences in age structure were not tested. No significant differences in density and age structure were found for red brocket deer. To solve this ambiguity, the Bodmer B algorithm (Section 5.4.2) was applied revealing that the harvest of both species was sustainable.

5.6.2 Differences in Harvest Characteristics

Changes in the characteristics of harvest data over time or differences between the characteristics of harvest data between ecologically similar sites might indicate depletion of populations or overharvesting. Such changes may encompass changes in hunting pressure, that is, number of animals killed per area, increasing distances required to reach profitable hunting grounds, and changes of species composition over time (Albrechtsen *et al.* 2007; Hurtado-Gonzales & Bodmer 2004; Smith 2008).

Pros: Data directly from hunters can be used, thus, relatively easy to obtain.

Cons: As discussed for CPUE (Section 5.2.2) the application of this method requires an adequate and representative sample of hunters involved in data generation. This may be a challenge in some situations, especially if hunting is illegal. Moreover, the sample obtained may be biased if offtake differs by age or sex of the hunter, or if hunting is for subsistence rather than for trade, factors often overlooked in harvest studies (Ingram *et al.* 2015). Moreover, hunters may under-report or fail to report the hunting of protected species. A suite of different factors can impact the system, other than hunting. These could include biological factors, such as climate or vegetation structure, and anthropogenic impacts, such as logging or road development, hunting motivations, hunting technology, market supply and demand, or law enforcement. There are neither standardizations nor any quantitative or even qualitative generalized guidelines or agreement on how to accept or reject the hypothesis of sustainability.

Example: Smith (2008) mapped the spatial patterns of hunting yields in Panama within a community of Indigenous Buglé and Ngöbe hunters. Kill sites were concentrated within just 2 km of the hunters' homes; nearly 90% of the total harvest originated here (Fig. 5.7). Hunting at larger distances occurred less often and depends on the availability of firearms, whereas other methods including slingshots and bow and arrow are more common near the settlements. While most species were killed near settlements, other species, in particular the

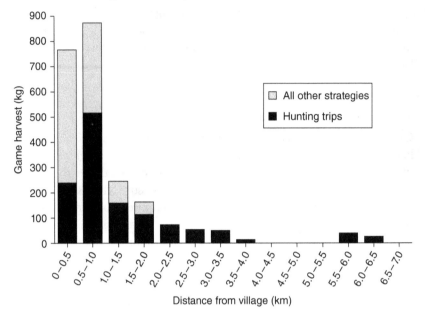

Figure 5.7 Hunting yields as a function of distance from hunters' primary residences in 500-m intervals. (From Smith 2008; adapted with permission from Elsevier.)

black-handed spider monkey, were hunted only further away. Smith (2008) argues that this pattern suggests that some degree of localized depletion may have occurred due to overhunting close to human settlements. Based on the local ecological knowledge of rural hunters, population depletion of hunted forest wildlife close to villages has been clearly demonstrated by Parry and Peres (2015) in the Brazilian Amazon. Similarly, mammal and bird population densities declined with their proximity to infrastructure such as roads (Benítez-López et al. 2010). For example, abundance of several species including duikers, sitatungas and forest elephants in Central Africa were depressed by the presence of roads. (Laurance et al. 2006)

The special case of duikers. Duikers (genera *Philantomba* and *Cephalophus*) are amongst the most hunted mammals for wild meat throughout the Congo Basin (Fa et al. 2016; Kingdon et al. 2013; Wilkie & Carpenter 1999; Yasuoka 2006b). Thus, there is a much interest in ascertaining the hunting sustainability for these species. Yasuoka et al. (2015) suggested that the catch ratio between the smaller blue duikers and the larger duikers, especially red duikers, could be used as an indicator of depletion in a site; higher numbers of red duikers denoting a less-affected system. The different duiker species respond distinctly to increased hunting pressure with the smaller blue duiker being less affected at a population level. This is because this species reaches reproductive age earlier than medium-sized duikers and have, thus, a higher reproductive output. The other reason is that they are more tolerant to and thrive in human-modified landscapes (Hart 1999). These predictions were fulfilled in Yasuoka et al.'s (2015) study on duiker densities in southeastern Cameroon. However, duiker densities in central African forests can vary from 3.5 to 59.8 individuals/km^2 for blue duikers and 2.6 to 64.5 individuals/km^2 for red duikers but explanations for these differences are likely to be related to a combination of habitat type, hunting history and hunting pressure factors (Breuer et al. 2021). Since the interactions of these factors has not been adequately determined in African forests, unlike studies for the Amazon for other species (see Peres 1999a), trends of the few studied duiker populations have been shown to decline with increases in hunting pressure (Grande-Vega et al. 2016; Hart 1999) but the impact of habitat or hunting history is unknown. Moreover, hunting methods can impact small- and medium-sized duikers differently with gun hunting, especially at night, making blue duiker easier prey than the medium-sized red duikers (Yasuoka et al. 2015). However, the large variance of the blue to red duiker ratios ranged from 0.39 to 22. 5 ($n = 5$, median = 1.33) in hunted areas and from 0.23 to 1.66 ($n = 4$, median = 1.4) for unhunted areas. Breuer et al. (2021) suggest to use them only with precaution as an indicator of hunting pressure or habitat type. Thus, the catch ratio as a means to estimate sustainability remains uncertain and for the time inapplicable.

5.6.3 Changes in Body Mass

A drop in the mean body mass of harvested species in a site can be used as an indicator of depletion. Trends in species composition and the average size of prey have been used in monitoring fish exploitation, a phenomenon known as 'fishing down marine food webs' (Pauly 1998) where fisheries increasingly rely on the smaller, short-lived fishes as the larger ones are depleted. This phenomenon has been measured by the large fish indicator (LFI), which captures changes over time in the contribution of biomass from large fish to the catch (Greenstreet et al. 2011; Shephard et al. 2011). The mean body mass of hunted terrestrial prey within each sample can also be used as a proxy of species composition, where a drop from larger to smaller species may indicate a process of defaunation of a habitat (Dirzo *et al.* 2014). In hunted terrestrial systems, the decrease in mean body mass of prey can reflect the increase in the proportion of small-bodied species over time, either because large-bodied species were extirpated, or more small-bodied species are being harvested. Based on these premises, Ingram *et al.* (2015) used the mean body mass indicator (MBMI) to integrate taxonomically, spatially and temporally disparate data collated from multiple sources over a period of 40 years. The MBMI can be used to offer insights into wildlife exploitation dynamics and is useful in understanding trends in hunted wildlife. In addition to the MBMI, Ingram *et al.* (2015) used an index of hunting pressure, the offtake pressure indicator (OPI) providing a measure of relative change in the number of harvested individuals indexed across multiple sites and species.

> **Pros:** As suggested by Ingram *et al.* (2015), these two indicators offer potentially useful approaches to assess wildlife offtake in the absence of comprehensive monitoring schemes, especially once further calibrated. For example, because each index is calculated differently, with the former employing an arithmetic mean and the latter a geometric mean, MBMI will change more rapidly compared to the OPI. With more time series at multiple sites available, it would be possible to calculate both indicators for the same sites and compare them. However, identifying causal links between changes in pressure on and the state of wild animal populations is often difficult. Wild animal offtake indicators have the potential to establish such linkages when combined with indicators of state to potentially estimate sustainable exploitation.
>
> **Cons:** Long-term data are required, which are rarely collected. As discussed for CPUE (Section 5.2.2) and for monitoring changes in harvest characteristics (Section 5.2.2), recruitment of hunters can be a challenge, especially when long-term monitoring is involved, as required here.

Example: Using data available for West and Central African mammals and birds, Ingram *et al.* (2015) demonstrated the indexed number of individuals harvested, OPI, of both mammals and birds increased dramatically between 1998 and 2010, indicating increasing hunting pressure (Fig. 5.8). During the same time span average body mass of harvested mammals declined significantly between 1966 and 2010, whereas that of birds increased between 1975 and

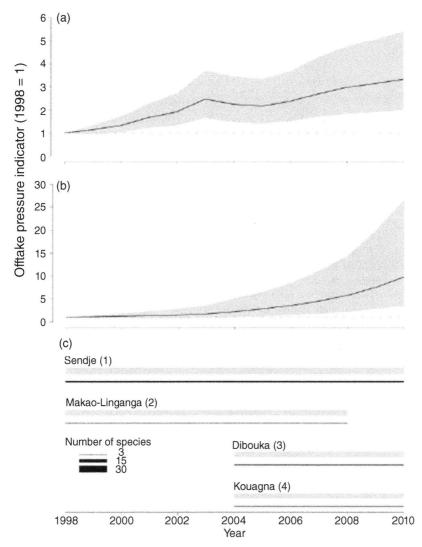

Figure 5.8 Offtake pressure indicator for (a) mammals and (b) birds in Central Africa and (c) the distribution of time-series data at four sites The indicator is set to 1 in the first year for which data were available (dotted horizontal line). Shading (a and b) represents ±95% confidence intervals generated with 1,000 bootstrap replicates. Width of bars (c) represents the number of mammal (grey) and bird (black) species sampled at four sites. (From Ingram *et al.* 2015; reprinted with permission from the Resilience Alliance.)

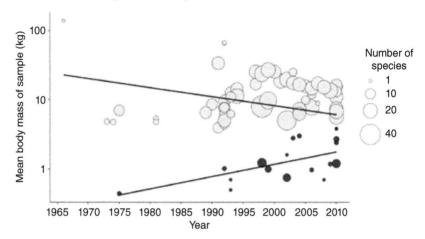

Figure 5.9 Mean body mass indicator for mammals (grey circles) and birds (black circles) in West and Central Africa. Circles represent offtake samples and are scaled by the number of species harvested within each sample; lines are fitted using linear mixed effects models. Samples are plotted on a logarithmic scale. (From Ingram *et al.* 2015; reprinted with permission from the Resilience Alliance.)

2010, indicating changed compositions of hunting bags (Fig. 5.9). This difference may indicate that whilst mammal prey were being depleted, in birds larger species were progressively being targeted, reflecting either the change in the demand for larger birds and their bills, such as the black-casqued hornbill, or in response to the decline in mammalian prey, although these effects are difficult to determine. The latter difficulty emphasizes that the trends in MBMI and OPI need careful interpretation because species might be hunted because of differing demands, for example, subsistence *versus* trophy hunting.

5.6.4 Market Indices

Among all different types of data required for sustainability assessments, market data are the easiest to collect. Surveys of wild meat markets over time allow monitoring of different aspects that might indicate unsustainability: price trends, quantity of species available, species composition and wildlife source distance. It is considered unsustainable whenever prices increase, quantity of available species decrease, species composition change and the distance where wildlife is sourced increase (Albrechtsen *et al.* 2007; Cowlishaw *et al.* 2005; Damania *et al.* 2005; Milner-Gulland & Clayton 2002; Rowcliffe *et al.* 2003). The hypothesis is that the composition of species for sale in wild meat markets, as influenced by hunting history in their catchment areas (Cowlishaw *et al.* 2005), will indicate the level of exploitation in the supply areas since vulnerable taxa (slow reproducers such as large ungulates and primates) are depleted first and are replaced by smaller-bodied robust taxa (fast reproducers), such as rodents and small antelopes. Consequently, there is increased prominence of species with high reproductive potential (as defined by their intrinsic rate of natural increase r_{max}) sold in markets characterizes heavily exploited catchments as shown in Dupain *et al.* (2012).

Pros: Requires monitoring of market stalls that sell wild meat, which is more easily conducted by local people than any other method of surveying sustainability. Changes can be statistically tested.

Cons: Data collection is not advised for foreigners in many settings because of safety concerns. Supply and demand of traded wild meat are impacted by a complex mixture of factors, such as taste preferences, tradition, economic settings, supply, demand and price of domestic meat and fish, environmental changes or law enforcements. There are neither standardizations nor any quantitative or even qualitative generalized guidelines or agreement on how to accept or reject the hypothesis of sustainability. The difficulties in interpreting the data make these changes more an early warning system than a decision-making system on sustainability.

Example: Albrechtsen *et al.* (2007) explored market data at the main wild meat market in Bioko Island, Equatorial Guinea, in 1996 and 1998. There was an increase in price, a significant decline in total and individual animal group carcass volumes, the species composition differed, and the diversity indices changed. Whilst the first three parameters indicate overhunting, the diversity index changed towards more diversity, which is surprising as the classic depletion model predicts the decrease of diversity. The authors argue that this is a transient phase and will be followed by a decrease of diversity once only the more resilient species are left as shown elsewhere in Bioko (Fa *et al.* 2000). Subsequent, independent market surveys showed that the numbers of these animals entering the market have not increased (BBPP 2006; Reid *et al.* 2005), thus indicating a sustained vulnerability of animal populations to extensive hunting.

The study by Fa *et al.* (2015a)shows a clear relationship between anthropogenic pressures in catchment areas and the profile of species appearing in wild meat markets from data for 79 markets (covering 30,000 km^2) in the Cross-Sanaga region in Nigeria and Cameroon (Fa *et al.* 2006; Macdonald *et al.* 2011, 2012). The hypothesis tested was that the percentage composition of various mammal groups (ungulates, rodents, primates and carnivores) in a market can be a crude measure of depleted faunas of the areas supplying that market. Results indeed confirmed that markets in heavily exploited areas (defined by indirect anthropogenic metrics such as high human population densities), the percentage contribution of larger-bodied prey (slow-reproducing species), especially ungulates and primates, to markets was characteristically lower than the percentage contribution of smaller fast-reproducing prey, such as rodents. Carnivores (mostly smaller taxa) become more numerous in markets as areas become more depleted of wild meat. Research from other sites in Central Africa are consistent with these results, especially the observation that species hitherto unimportant in the wild meat trade gain prominence when ungulates become scarce (Ingram *et al.* 2015; Wilkie 1989). In lightly hunted rural sites, duikers and other antelopes are the more common prey (Lahm 1993; Noss 1998a). Although factors, such as habitat quality and human pressures, will jointly impact the wildlife supplying markets (Fa & Brown 2009), the most parsimonious interpretation of the composition of traded species in wild meat markets in the Fa *et al.* (2015a) study was the contrasting ability of ungulate and rodent populations to recover from hunting. Thus, at sites where larger species have been severely depleted, hunters would extract fewer of the preferred larger red and blue duikers and more of the smaller species such as the Emin's and the African giant pouched rats or the cane rat. In most continental sites in Africa (unlike Bioko Island, see Fa *et al.* 2000), rodents only become important prey items in disturbed areas (Eves & Ruggiero 1999). Therefore, increases in rodents hunted suggest reductions in the availability of more preferred wild meat species. The relative proportions of ungulates and rodents in the offtake can be used as indicators of site over-exploitation. Fa *et al.* (2015a) showed that the relationship between ungulates and rodents was related to a number of prominent anthropogenic factors, rather than environmental variables *per se*. Higher road densities were linked to reduced abundance of a number of mammal species due to higher hunting pressure. Heavily populated and accessible areas have fewer duikers, forest buffalos and red river hogs (Laurance *et al.* 2006). Moreover, using an index of game depletion (GDI) for each market (the sum of the total number of carcasses traded per annum and species, weighted by the intrinsic rate of natural increase (r_{max}) of each species, divided by individuals traded in a market), Fa *et al.* (2015a) showed that this index increased as the proportion of fast-reproducing species (highest r_{max}) rose and as the representation of species with lowest

r_{max} (slow-reproducing) declined. The GDI is akin to indicators used for fishery catches and, as noted for the MBMI and OPI, can be used as a framework for discerning the status of hunted prey (particularly mammals) in a catchment area from observations of the composition of species for sale in markets (Section 5.5.3).

5.7 Ecosystem-Based Management

5.7.1 Ecosystem-Based Fisheries Management

The harvesting of any wildlife resource, whether wild meat and fisheries, should strive for the sustainable use of exploited species on land and in the sea. Because of the much longer history of industrial exploitation of marine life, and accompanying research on how to achieve sustainable exploitation of marine fish and stop fisheries collapses (Pauly *et al.* 2002), lessons learnt in fisheries can be applied to wild meat (Section 5.4.4; Milner-Gulland & Akçakaya 2001). Given this, we briefly describe some of the latest developments in fisheries management that are relevant to wild meat.

The failure of several fisheries, such as the notorious collapse of the Newfoundland Atlantic cod fishery (Bavington 2011), has led to the recognition that traditional management has failed to lead to sustainable exploitation of marine resources. These have caused a clear paradigm shift in fisheries research leading to a change in focus from a single species and MSY approach towards ecosystem-based management (EBM) (Lidström & Johnson 2020; Pikitch *et al.* 2004; Townsend *et al.* 2019). EBM has been defined by the FAO as aiming 'to balance diverse societal objectives, by taking into account the knowledge and uncertainties about biotic, abiotic and human components of ecosystems and their inter-actions and applying an integrated approach to fisheries within ecologic-ally meaningful boundaries' (FAO Fisheries Department 2003). Similarly, the United States' National Oceanic and Atmospheric Administration (NOAA), has adopted ecosystem-based fisheries management (EBFM), as the agency's strategic policy. NOAA defines EBFM as: 'a systematic approach to fisheries management in a geographically specified area that contributes to the resilience and sustainability of the ecosystem; recog-nizes the physical, biological, economic, and social interactions among the affected fishery-related components of the ecosystem, including humans; and seeks to optimize benefits among a diverse set of societal goals' (NOAA 2016).

EBM and EBFM differ from the conventional management of single species by describing management strategies for entire ecosystems, to explicitly achieve not only sustainability of target species but ensure the ecological sustainability of the species' ecosystems, including economic and social sustainability. These holistic approaches take into account natural marine resources' interactions with their environment as well as human interactions with these resources and the environment. The implementation of policies reflecting these new approaches must necessarily rely on the support of ecosystem science, continuing population monitoring, modelling and analysis and crucially the collaboration and consultation between scientists, policy makers, stakeholders and the public. Despite these encouraging innovations, there is still little practical advice on how to better select specific management measures to achieve EBFM goals. The main operational problems with implementing EBM/EBFM are: (1) defining proper long-term ecosystem related objectives, (2) identifying meaningful indicators and reference values for sustainable use and (3) developing appropriate data collection, analytical tools and models (Cury *et al.* 2005). As a response to these issues, Levin *et al.* (2009) suggested the adoption of integrated ecosystem assessments (IEAs), as a framework of 'formal synthesis and quantitative analysis of information on relevant natural and socioeconomic factors, in relation to specified ecosystem management objectives'. This framework is a looping workflow composed of scoping, indicator development, risk analysis, management strategy evaluation and ecosystem assessment repeated in an adaptive manner (Fig. 5.10). Importantly, the mechanistic indicators and estimators for population sustainability discussed in this chapter still remain important in indicator development, embedded in this adaptive management loop. Several example cases exist of successful implementation of the IEA framework under the EBFM policy, in particular outside the tropics (Townsend *et al.* 2019). In these cases, such as the Gulf of Alaska Pacific cod harvest, the use of ecosystem models in a management process has improved the health or status of particular fish stocks or habitats. These examples highlight the importance of collaboration between modellers, stakeholders and resource managers to ensure sustainable management. For fisheries in the tropics, however, an additional series of challenges and problems exist, resulting from undeveloped or inappropriate governance structures, poor science, lack of political will in many cases and often economic development overriding biodiversity protection (Aswani *et al.* 2012). Moreover, many developing countries have property rights which do not grant local coastal communities any legal rights to establish and enforce control over the coastal resources.

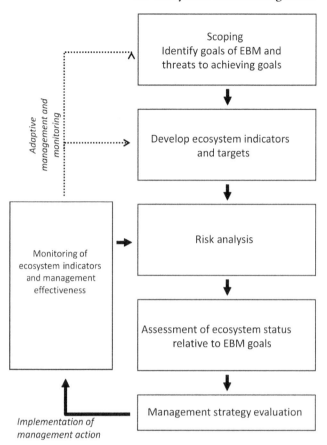

Figure 5.10 The Five-Step Process of Integrated Ecosystem Assessment. It begins with a scoping process to identify key management objectives and constraints of the ecosystem-based management, identifies appropriate indicators and management thresholds, determines the risk that indicators will fall below management targets and combines risk assessments of individual indicators into a determination of overall ecosystem status. The potential of different management strategies to alter ecosystem status is evaluated, and then management actions are implemented, and their effectiveness monitored. The cycle is repeated in an adaptive manner. (From Levin *et al.* 2009; adapted with permission from PLOS Biology.)

Problems associated with the implementation of EBM approaches to fisheries in tropical countries also apply to wild meat hunting. A holistic system such as EBM can be the gold standard for wild meat, but we are still far from pursuing this goal. Data-deficiency for most wild-meat-producing areas is not necessarily a limiting factor in implementing EBM because in such situations natural history and general knowledge can be used to develop precautionary safety margins as a starting point for more comprehensive EBM in the future (Pikitch *et al.* 2004). However, economic underdevelopment and local poverty can prevent the implementation of more sophisticated monitoring, modelling and management systems. For example, solid frameworks of population assessments and monitoring which are the foundation of EBM, are exceedingly rare in the tropics and subtropics. In fact, in many tropical countries, monitoring programmes are often short-lived, largely research projects limited by funds and unable to be extended over longer time periods. Even the basic acknowledgement of the need for monitoring is often missing at local, regional and national levels. Nevertheless, the idea of managing wildlife populations within a clear ecosystem and social context has been raised by some authors (Van Vliet *et al.* 2015b).

5.7.2 Shifting from Biological Indicators to Resilience Analysis for Wild Meat

In line with the EBM approach, Van Vliet *et al.* (2015b) have argued that wild meat hunting must be considered as a social-ecological system, and by so doing managers must move towards resilience analysis, adaptive resource management and participatory governance. Although this notion has been critiqued by Sirén (2015) who argues that MSY is seldom, if ever, the goal, most approaches to resolving wild meat hunting systems have been caught up in assessing rather achieving sustainability, as we show in Section 5.8. Because hunting systems involve human actions and include social structures, as well as biological processes (prey species, ecosystems), the distinction between the social and the natural is arbitrary (Berkes *et al.* 2002); hence a social-ecological system. Van Vliet *et al.* (2015b) argue that the emphasis should move away from just assessing stocks of prey populations, to considering the complex and dynamic relationships between the hunting ground, its resources, the stakeholders in play and the different exogenous drivers of change affecting the system. This new way of looking at hunting systems incorporates uncertainty and stochasticity inherent to complex systems. It also recognizes that systems evolve over time, adapt and transform.

The main implication of changing the theoretical understanding of hunting systems is that one–off biological indicators are not useful for the estimation of sustainability. Other methodologies that integrate complexity, for example, theoretical models, such as agent-based models, companion modelling approaches, fuzzy cognitive mapping, and resilience analysis tools, among others, are advantageous. Spatially explicit multi-agent-based models are particularly adapted to understanding wild meat hunting sustainability (Bousquet *et al.* 2001; Iwamura *et al.* 2013; Van Vliet *et al.* 2010a). Agent-based models are a class of computational models for simulating the actions and interactions of autonomous agents, both individual and collective entities such as organizations or groups, with a view to assessing their effects on the system as a whole. These models combine elements of game theory, complex systems, emergence, computational sociology, multi-agent systems and evolutionary programming (Grimm *et al.* 2005).

A number of methods are available for use in addressing the complexity of social-ecological systems. Firstly, collective decision-making processes in complex situations can be better understood with the application of participatory models (Barreteau *et al.* 2014). This approach facilitates collective decision-making processes by making more explicit the various points of view and subjective criteria to which the different stakeholders refer implicitly. As demonstrated in past research (Funtowicz *et al.* 1998; Mermet 1992; Ostrom *et al.* 1994), when a complex situation exists, the decision-making process is evolving, iterative and continuous. This process always produces imperfect 'decision acts', but by following each iteration they are less imperfect and more shared. Participatory scenario planning allows the description of how the future might unfold on the basis of coherent assumptions about the relations among drivers of change and key aspects of the system. The method also allows the participation of a great diversity of stakeholders.

Graphical stock-and-flow modelling, such as fuzzy-logic cognitive mapping (FCM), is a simple and easy method that allows groups to share and negotiate knowledge collaboratively and build semi-quantitative conceptual models. Fuzzy-logic cognitive mapping facilitates the explicit representation of group assumptions about a system being modelled through parameterized cognitive mapping (Gray *et al.* 2014). Specifically, FCM allows cognitive maps to be constructed by defining the most relevant variables that constitute a system, the dynamic relationships between these variables and the degree of influence, either positive or negative, that one variable can have on another. In group settings, FCM models are constructed based on combining group beliefs in a similar format as individuals share their experiences and understanding (Gray *et al.* 2014). The strength of using FCM in this context is the ability to extract, combine and represent group knowledge in a sensitive situation for comparison between or among groups. Nyaki *et al.* (2014) used FCM to understand the drivers of wild meat trade in four Tanzanian villages bordering Serengeti National Park.

Resilience analysis explicitly allows for sustainable use options (Box 5.1). Traditional one-off biological models applied to hunting

---

Box 5.1 *The Resilience Assessment Workbook*

The resilience assessment workbook (Resilience Alliance 2010) may also be useful to provide insight into developing strategies for buffering both known and unexpected change in hunting systems. The workbook was developed by Resilience Alliance to apply resilience thinking (Walker *et al.* 2002). It operationalizes resilience for practitioners and following its first release in 2007, it has been applied in multiple contexts around the world (Resilience Alliance 2021) primarily in natural resource management contexts (Bennett *et al.* 2005; Biggs *et al.* 2012; Peterson *et al.* 2003) and more recently in urban planning (Sellberg *et al.* 2015). The workbook guides researchers and practitioners in identifying the focal social-ecological system, describing threats and the impacts of those threats, and identifying the current and new strategies to strengthen the resilience of the system. It also guides the identification of potential thresholds that represent a breakpoint between two alternative system states and helps reveal what is contributing to or eroding system resilience.

As Van Vliet *et al.* (2015b) have further suggested, the resilience approach introduces the need to adopt an adaptive management process, which embraces uncertainties. In more classic forms of management, precautionary principles are put forward, interpreting precaution as the need to avoid impacts until wild meat stocks are estimated with precision and risks are measured. In fisheries, the practical challenge of giving advice when evidence is uncertain was solved by moving toward a better quantification of uncertainty (Getz & Bergh 1988). Recent experiences of adaptive management in temperate hunting systems can also provide inspiration for the sustainable use of wild meat in tropical areas (Brown *et al.* 2015; Carter *et al.* 2014; Fiorini *et al.* 2011; Hunt 2013). Weinbaum *et al.* (2013) suggest that learning how to manage under uncertainty is fundamental to achieving sustainable wild meat hunting and requires putting in place efficient monitoring processes. The creation of participatory monitoring systems often triggers a process of collective action (e.g. in Amazonian communities, see El Bizri *et al.* 2020a; Mayor *et al.* 2017) which can be included in any strategic action aimed at managing wild meat resources (Garcia & Lescuyer 2008). The hypothesis stating that the information generated by the system is inserted into the decision-making process so as to approach sustainability is only possible when resource management is completely decentralized and when a direct link is established between the monitoring results and the management decisions taken (Garcia & Lescuyer 2008).

Strategies for improving forecasts about the behaviour of hunted systems will require a combination of tools but under the assumption that sufficiently thorough understanding of ecosystems is needed to reduce deep uncertainties is probably not achievable. Therefore, as suggested by Schindler and Hilborn (2015), research should integrate more closely with policy development to identify the range of alternative plausible futures and develop strategies that are robust across these scenarios and can respond adequately to unpredictable ecosystem dynamics. Moving away from the assumption that developing richer mechanistic appreciation of ecological interactions will improve forecasts is now fundamental, and hunting sustainability models as described above, are heuristic tools for communication and for developing new ideas on how hunted systems respond. Managing ecosystems for multiple ecosystem services and balancing the well-being of diverse stakeholders will involve the development of multiple systems that also contain different kinds of trade-offs (Daw *et al.* 2015). Such trade-offs involve non-economic and difficult-to-evaluate values, such as cultural identity, employment, the well-being of poor people, or particular species or ecosystem structures. Management and policy decisions demand approaches that can explicitly acknowledge and evaluate diverse information flows, that take science into account but that involve more than this.

systems, which were based on a binary yes/no question, do not allow the system to be brought back to sustainability in case of a 'no' answer. In such cases, the response would be to ban hunting, reinforcing the protection of wildlife by prohibiting its use through legal prohibitions. In contrast, the resilience focus provides the opportunity for identifying strategies that strengthen resilience when the system is close to a given threshold. By recognizing the benefits that wild meat use generates for people, especially indigenous and local people who live with wildlife, and therefore bear associated costs (e.g. danger to life, damage to crops, restrictions on land use), the resilience approach can incorporate the diverse views and value systems of stakeholders, as well as different knowledge sources, including experimental or scientific knowledge and experiential or local ecological knowledge (Cooney & Abensperg-Traun 2013). As a result, resilience approaches recognize multiple objectives, design mechanisms for incorporating them, weigh trade-offs and establish conflict resolution mechanisms that are fair to all parties. Identifying areas of agreement and disagreement between actors helps in understanding and overcoming obstacles between them (Biggs *et al.* 2011).

5.8 Putting the Theory into Practice

The importance of developing reliable methods for evaluating the sustainability of wildlife offtake and assessing the status of hunted wildlife populations is unquestioned (Milner-Gulland & Akçakaya 2001; Robinson & Redford 1994; Sutherland 2001). Indices and models are available that provide a preliminary measurement of hunting sustainability in tropical forest systems. These allow the determination of whether the population production exceeds or is less than harvest demand at a given moment in time. These assessments do not imply that the harvest will continue to be sustainable over the long term, since the relationship between game population density and game harvest is a dynamic one. Hunting is sustainable in the long term only if the harvest is both biologically and socioeconomically sustainable (Robinson 1993). One of the main challenges is how to obtain realistic and timely information to adequately describe the basic components of demography of the hunted species as well as hunting effort. Even if this is possible, most assessments of sustainability for hunted species are still based on a posteriori comparison of actual *versus* estimated sustainable offtake. For example, Weinbaum *et al.* (2013) reviewed 750 separate evaluations of harvest sustainability of mostly mammal populations (but also birds and some reptiles) and found that all assessments measured the sustainability of harvests in theory. In other words, the conclusion that a large proportion of all reviewed studies were deemed sustainable by the authors may have depended on the model used but more importantly were not used in real time to guide the efforts of hunters to exploit wildlife more sustainably. So, even though in the literature the importance of theory informing data collection and management planning is frequently advo- cated, the reality is that because the methods for determining sustainable exploitation are highly sophisticated, most hunting schemes are based on limited science and data. This is the case even for resource management agencies in developed countries. For example, even though wildlife agencies in the USA and Canada commonly defend controversial policy by claiming adherence to science-based approaches, Artelle *et al.* (2018) provided limited support for the assumption that wildlife management in 62 US state and Canadian provincial and territorial agencies across 667 management systems were guided by science. Most management systems lacked indications of the basic elements of a scientific approach to management.

Even if a framework that provides guidance for adopting a science- based approach is adopted as suggested by Artelle *et al.* (2018), there is a case for arguing that for very many species simple methods that can be applied by non-specialists will be the most practical. Pretending that hunting communities in the tropics have the time and resources to compile prey population data so as to populate full demographic models, which incidentally are not even regularly applied by agencies in developed countries, is unrealistic. Assessing effort or demographic components such as density dependence or population growth rates are often too difficult to provide estimates that are sufficient to form the basis for sufficiently accurate exploitation. Milner-Gulland and Rowcliffe (2007) may have argued that long-term population monitoring programmes are the most informative approach to provide baseline information against which any hunting effects and/or conservation interventions can be monitored. But, although scientifically interesting and useful to understand exploitation processes, indicators of sustainability are the most realistic way forward to ensure practical management of wildlife populations will have to be based on sustainability indicators. This may mean that resource management by communities in the tropics will have to be based on perhaps less scientific- ally robust data, especially in countries where investment in research is limited. Community-led monitoring systems of hunting are becoming more common (see El Bizri *et al.* 2020a). These schemes may shorten decision-making time frames while promoting local autonomy in resource management and strengthen community resource rights (Brook & McLachlan 2008; Danielsen *et al.* 2014).

Participatory, adaptive management of wildlife use requires efficient monitoring systems designed to address impacts at appropriate temporal and spatial scales, while involving both scientific experts and local resource users (Luzar *et al.* 2011). Ideally, metrics that allow conservation managers or communities themselves to understand patterns, track changes, and revise and update regulations affecting hunting, are fundamental. However, collecting data on spatial and temporal changes in hunting offtake to assist a community to regulate their impact on prey numbers can be demanding if hunters are required to provide daily data on hunter effort and number of animals killed. The difficulty of convincing hunters to partake in self-monitoring activities is exemplified by a study of hunters in five communities in the Piagaçu-Purus Sustainable Development Reserve in Brazil in which only 37 out of 74 (50%) potential monitors, and 36% of initially interested families, participated (de Mattos Vieira *et al.* 2015). If monitoring of hunters is to be assisted by researchers (e.g. Coad *et al.* 2013) the costs of this would increase dramatically, especially if hunter follows are undertaken. Data on each hunting event, such as time dedicated to hunting and location of hunt, are more time-consuming to collect for every hunter especially if long-term trends are required. Thus, more cost-effective means of recording and using data on hunter offtake are required for hunting monitoring systems to be maintained over long periods. A practical way forward may comprise describing hunting offtake by gathering data that are simpler to collect, pertaining to animals hunted (number of animals taken by species, sex and relative age of animals) and hunter identity within a village or camp. In a study of three villages in Cameroon, Avila *et al.* (2019) argued that even though these types of data are imperfect, indicators such as catch per hunter per day (CPHD) and MBMI can be used alongside more basic hunter interviews at different intervals to ascertain whether hunters are increasing their hunting effort by using indirect methods such as those employed by Parry and Peres (2016). Testing how much the coarser CPHD index differs from the more costly to obtain CPUE measures may provide the information required to allow practitioners and communities to sustainably manage their wildlife resources. As Sutherland (2001) suggests, the simplest method is probably often the best method. Nowhere is this more urgent than in the places where people rely directly on wildlife meat for protein, calories, micronutrients and livelihoods. In such regions, the precautionary principle alone will not be sufficient to balance the needs of wildlife species and the people who depend on them; therefore, efforts to maximize harvests and the persistence of harvested populations must be improved.

5.9 Final Considerations

Quite a number of approaches exist to evaluate sustainability of wild meat hunting. All have their unique parameter requirements and assumptions and their own advantages and disadvantages. All methods require careful parameter selection and data interpretation. Ideally, studies employ two or more methods alongside each other. With the exception of the defaunation index, which quantifies the effects of any parameter on population and species survival, none of the methods explicitly considers the effects of animal predation and competition on population dynamics and hunting sustainability. The competition/predation release of smaller species when larger species are hunted down, for example, smaller duikers or monkeys, might actually increase in density when larger antelopes or carnivores are depleted (e.g. Prins 2016). Moreover, whilst the estimators for sustainability are a tool to assist wildlife management, they are not tools to assist the setting of management policies. Even the very term 'sustainability' has different meanings ranging from any level of exploitation that does not endanger population survival, as in the Brundtland (1987) definition, to aiming at maximum sustainable exploitation, as in the Tivy and O'Hare (1981) definition. Diametrically opposite is a conservation approach characterized by the total exclusion of humans from protected areas rejecting any notion of sustainable wildlife utilization, so-called 'forest conservation' (e.g. Adams & Hutton 2007; Brockington 2002; Pemunta 2019). For example, the expansion of protected area networks in Cameroon caused the eviction, displacement and widespread multiple human rights violations from armed guards/forest protection forces on the traditional way of life – hunting and gathering – of indigenous Baka people (Pemunta 2014, 2019). Only recently, the Rainforest Foundation UK (2020) voiced concerns that the Conference of Parties to the Convention on Biodiversity (CBD) is set to agree in 2021 on a new conservation target to place at least 30% of the earth's surface into conservation status by 2030, which could 'dispossess millions'. Although many in the conservation and sustainable development communities have diametrically opposite and mutually exclusive approaches to values of wildlife in general and sustainable hunting in particular, this apparent conflict is solvable as many examples of successful community conservation, for example in the Amazon Basin, have demonstrated (Kothari et al. 2013; Redpath et al. 2013). We outline these issues further in Chapter 8.

6 · Use and Overuse

6.1 Introduction

The exploitation of wild animals for their meat continues throughout the tropics and subtropics. This is an activity of crucial importance that continues to buttress the food security and livelihoods of many millions of people (Chapter 1). Even at varying stages of transition to agriculture, modern hunter-gatherers still exploit animal populations for food (Chapter 1), being able to continue doing this if extraction is in balance with production. Likewise, numerous rural peoples still depend on wild meat, as we show in Chapter 2. Ensuring that supply matches demand for wild meat from those human populations still living in or near natural ecosystems remains a central question; we discuss the issue of sustainability in more detail in Chapter 5.

In this chapter we offer an overview of the impact of hunting on prey populations in the world's tropical and subtropical regions. We first present what estimates are available of wild meat extraction levels for areas where information exists, followed by a discussion of spatial patterns of wild meat extraction at a regional scale. We then focus on the existing evidence for how overhunting can reduce prey populations and change species assemblages. What drives wild meat exploitation is then discussed and we end the chapter by summarizing the evidence on the effects of anthropogenic faunal loss, or defaunation, on wider ecosystem processes and functions.

6.2 Global Wild Meat Extraction Estimates

Data on the biomass of animals harvested in different localities throughout the tropics and subtropics are generally rare, particularly for Southeast Asia. Most published hunting studies tend to concentrate on listing the animal species that are removed from a particular study area but often do not specify the number of animals or the biomass (kg) extracted per unit hunting area. This is because information on the numbers of animals hunted is often taken from hunter reports and hunting territories are not generally measured. However, from a compilation of studies, albeit relatively small, Robinson and Bennett (2004) examined the supply of and demand for wildlife resources across the rainfall gradient in relatively undisturbed ecosystems, generating estimates of the biomass of wild mammals (rodents, primates and ungulates) in evergreen wet and moist forests (rainforests), deciduous dry forest and grassland savanna. From these results, extraction rates were highest ($744 \pm 1{,}030$ kg/km^2, $n = 4$ sites) in grasslands, followed by evergreen wet and moist forests (168 ± 193 kg/km^2, $n = 14$ sites) and lowest in deciduous dry forests (126 ± 150 kg/km^2, $n = 4$ sites). In evergreen wet and moist forest sites where human population sizes are available (from Robinson & Bennett 2004), the biomass harvested per person is positively correlated with rainfall (Fig. 6.1).

Information from 36 African rainforest sites compiled in Fa *et al.* (2005) show that from 40 to 12,168 carcasses are extracted annually per site (average 2,060 carcasses/yr per site or 240 kg/yr to 84,100 kg/yr), translating into a mean harvest rate per hunter of between 101 to 165

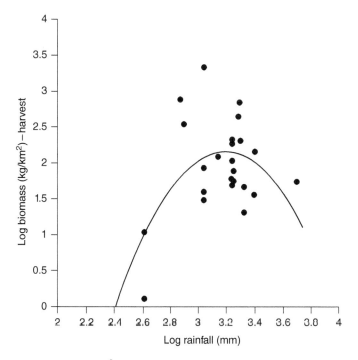

Figure 6.1 Biomass (kg/km^2) of ungulates, primates and rodents harvested in different tropical habitats in relation to rainfall (from Robinson and Bennett 2004; adapted with permission from John Wiley & Sons).

carcasses/yr and biomass of 946–1,610 kg/yr. Such variation in the number of carcasses hunted per year is a function of hunter numbers and provisioning conditions of each habitat. The impact of hunting intensity, forest structure and hunting history clearly influences prey standing biomass and the extraction potential in each habitat. But, even though habitat type and disturbance may affect animal numbers (see Chapter 2) there are major differences in populations of large-bodied vertebrates in hunted and unhunted Neotropical forests (Bodmer *et al.* 1997; Cullen Jr *et al.* 2000; Glanz 1991; Mena *et al.* 1999; Peres 1990, 1996, 2000; Wright *et al.* 2000), suggesting that the impact of hunters is paramount.

In all tropical regions where hunting of wildlife for meat occurs (Chapter 1), most prey animals are mammals, and among these the highest proportion is of ungulates (Coad *et al.* 2019). In a meta-analysis of hunting in Afrotropical forests in West and Central Africa, Fa *et al.* (2005) showed that as many as 71 mammal species were hunted in a total of 30 sites in 7 countries: 22 primates (5 families), 18 ungulates (4 families), 13 rodents (4 families), 12 carnivores (4 families), 3 pangolins, and 1 species each of elephant, hyrax and aardvark. For all sites pooled, ungulates (47%), followed by rodents (37%), were the most frequently taken taxonomic groups. Ungulates provided 73% in weight, while other groups significantly less. Small- (2.0–4.9 kg) and medium-sized (5–14.9 kg) species supplied more carcasses to the total kills (32.4% and 30.0%, respectively) than larger-bodied (15.0–99.9 kg) ones (21.6%). Large mammals alone made up 54.5% of total biomass extracted per year. Overall, the average estimated mammalian biomass extracted per year per site was almost 16,000 kg. Because most hunting is undertaken by non-discriminatory snares (where very few species, most of them primates, are shot), the relationship between the estimated average harvest rates per species correlated with body mass of the hunted groups. The smallest prey were arboreal species whilst the heaviest were almost exclusively terrestrial and a total of 32 out of the 36 terrestrial species were snared, whereas 13 of the 21 arboreal species were shot. The resulting pattern was a negative correlation between body mass and harvest rates for carnivores and ungulates, positive for rodents and curvilinear (inverted U-shape) for primates (Fig. 6.2). Smaller carnivores and ungulates but larger rodent species are therefore more susceptible to being caught in snares, whereas mid-sized primates are more likely to be shot. Smaller primates, mostly nocturnal (e.g. galagos) and larger ones (gorillas and chimpanzees) are rarely sought out by hunters, the former because of their lower cost-effectiveness and the latter because it requires

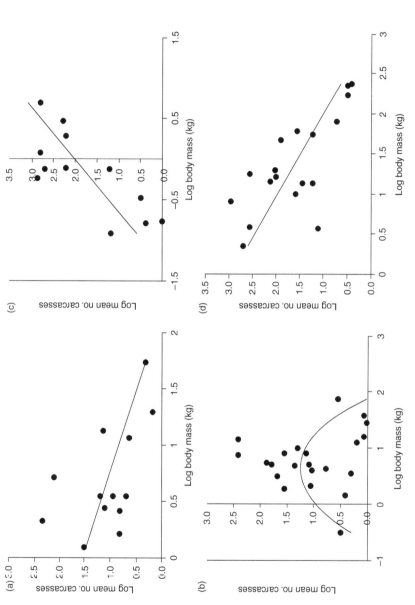

Figure 6.2 Regressions showing the relationship between species body mass and mean number of carcasses extracted per year of: (a) carnivores, (b) Primates; (c) rodents; (d) ungulates. (From Fa *et al.* 2005; adapted with permission from PLOS Biology.)

more specialized hunting abilities to take down. Overall, there is some evidence that wild meat extraction, according to the data in Fa *et al.* (2005), is less driven by hunters choosing which prey to hunt, but by the hunting method employed.

As a consequence of mostly using snares and the effects of these as shown above, harvest rates are not correlated with the abundance of the species in the habitat except for ungulates (Fa *et al.* 2005). This can be explained by the fact that in West and Central African forests most of the terrestrial mammalian faunas are bovids (see Chapter 2), which are highly abundant particularly the smaller duikers, their larger densities saturating traps before other terrestrial species. In terms of which dietary categories of mammals were hunted in West and Central Africa, Fa *et al.* (2005) and later confirmed by Petrozzi *et al.* (2016) showed that frugivore–herbivores and frugivore–granivores were mostly impacted, both in terms of number of carcasses and biomass, with most harvested species being rodents and ungulates. Not surprisingly, the average number of hunters operating per 100 days (hunter presence in Fa *et al.* 2005) in a site is significantly positively correlated with biomass harvested. Biomass hunted is also highly correlated with the susceptibility of a species to be hunted, or hunter ease, in Fa *et al.* (2005), as a measure of the vulnerability of a species to hunting as determined by the size of the prey animal (since larger animals are more conspicuous), whether arboreal or terrestrial, and the species' speed of movement. Similarly, carcass numbers were not correlated with hunter presence, but were highly correlated with hunter ease, pointing to the overriding importance of vulnerability of prey species.

In a more recent meta-analysis of 82 studies on 254 mammal and 1,640 bird species from across the tropics, hunting was shown to be less intense for larger-bodied than smaller-bodied species of mammals, particularly among carnivores and frugivores, than for herbivores, insectivores and generalists/omnivores (Osuri *et al.* 2020). In the same study, body size was either unrelated or weakly negatively related among birds across disturbance types (hunting, forest conversion and forest degradation) and across most dietary guilds, with the exception of herbivore/granivore and carnivore species. The most significant generalization is that large forest mammals make up the bulk of the hunted biomass in most sites and these large-bodied species are the most susceptible to over-exploitation. Such vulnerability may not be only due to the size of the animal but also due to its behaviour, for example, living in social groups or loud vocalizations may make the species more easily found by hunters (Fitzgibbon 1998; Infield 1988). Nonetheless, extraction levels will logically correlate with the density of hunters operating in an area, thus if hunter presence is not too intense, adjacent large tracts of undisturbed forest can replenish exploited areas, restocking prey populations and therefore contributing to the sustainability of hunting (Fa & Peres 2001). But, heavy hunter presence, deforestation and habitat fragmentation in an area disrupts such source–sink dynamics (Novaro *et al.* 2000), leading to over-exploitation of animal populations. Often, large mammals and birds, which tend to disappear first, are frugivores (including frugivore–granivores, frugivore–herbivores and frugivore–omnivores) and important in seed dispersal (Abernethy *et al.* 2013; Wright *et al.* 2000). Their absence can have severe impacts on the long-term future of tropical forests.

6.3 Evidence of Sustainability

Published studies of the sustainability of extraction in tropical forests (Table 6.1), which have compared estimated productivity and offtake rates, show that in most cases hunting appears to be unsustainable. In most cases, more than half of the species considered in each study was unsustainably hunted; in situations where the number of species was low, more than 50% and up to 100% of these were unsustainably hunted. These figures attest to unsustainable extraction of wildlife in all circumstances where hunting has been studied. How representative these studies are cannot be assessed. Sustainability in most of the studies included in Table 6.1 has been measured using the Robinson and Redford (1991b) index, which has inherent problems (see Mayor *et al.* 2016; van Vliet & Nasi 2008a; Chapter 5) that may affect the results. Sustainable extraction is thus likely to occur in very remote locations, areas sparsely populated by humans, or beyond the influence and attraction of external markets. By contrast, locations such as 'mature' markets in Ghana (Cowlishaw *et al.* 2004) can still contain a number of sustainably hunted species, large rodents in particular, given that larger species have been overhunted and smaller species can be exploited for longer. Evidence that animal populations are impacted by hunting can be derived from population density estimates of target species have been suggested as an indicator of sustainability (see e.g. Cawthorn & Hoffman 2015; Chapter 5). This assertion is perhaps equivocal since it is expected that hunted areas will be lower in density but the decline in stocks may not reflect unsustainable use. Estimates of standing stocks of mammals in a large number of Amazonian localities that have been hunted to varying degrees clearly show that they are affected by hunting pressure and forest type (Peres 1999a; Fig. 6.3). Thus, it is not

Table 6.1 *Estimated sustainability and decline in population densities of mammals due to hunting (taken from Cawthorn and Hoffman 2015)*

Country/region – site	Main reason for hunting	Column I	Column II	Reference
Africa				
Congo Basin	Subsistence/trade	60% (57)		Fa et al. (2002)
CAR, Mossapoula	Subsistence/trade	100% (4)	43.90%	Noss (2000)
Cameroon	Subsistence/trade	100% (2)		Fimbel et al. (1999)
Cameroon	Subsistence/trade	50–100% (6)		Delvingt et al. (2001)
DRC, Ituri I	Subsistence		42.10%	Hart (1999)
DRC, Ituri II	Subsistence		12.90%	Hart (1999)
Gabon, Makokou			43–100%	Lahm (2001)
Equatorial Guinea, Bioko	Subsistence/trade	30.7% (16)		Fa (1999)
Equatorial Guinea, Rio Muni	Trade	36% (14)		Fa and Garcia Yuste (2001)
Equatorial Guinea, Rio Muni	Trade	12% (17)		Fa et al. (1995)
Ghana	Trade	47% (15)		Cowlishaw et al. (2004)
Kenya	Subsistence/trade	42.9% (7)		Fitzgibbon et al. (1999)
Madagascar – Makira Forest	Subsistence	100% (5)		Golden (2009)
Latin America				
Brazil, 101 Amazon sites	Subsistence		90%	Peres (1999a); Peres and Palacios (2007)
Brazil, Mata de Planalto			27–69%	Cullen et al. (2000)
Bolivia	Subsistence	50% (10)		Townsend (2000)
Ecuador, Quehueiri-ono	Subsistence	30% (10)	35.30%	Mena et al. (1999)
Paraguay, Mbaracayu	Subsistence	0% (7)	53%	Hill and Padwe (1999)
Paraguay, Mbaracayu	Subsistence		0–40%	Hill et al. (2003)
Peru, Manu National Park	Subsistence	26% (19)		Ohl-Schacherer (2007)
South/Southeast Asia				
Indonesia, Sulawesi	Subsistence/trade	66.7% (6)		O'Brien and Kinnaird (1999)
Indonesia, Sulawesi	Subsistence/trade	74% (4)		Lee (1999)
India, Nagarahole			75%	Madhusudan and Karanth (2018)

Abbreviations: CAR = Central African Republic; DRC = Democratic Republic of Congo.
Column I: percentage of species hunted unsustainably (number of species studied). Sustainability indicators reported here are generally determined through the examination of the relationship between estimated productivity and off-take rates.
Column II: percentage by which densities of target species are lower in moderately to heavily hunted forests than in un-hunted forest.

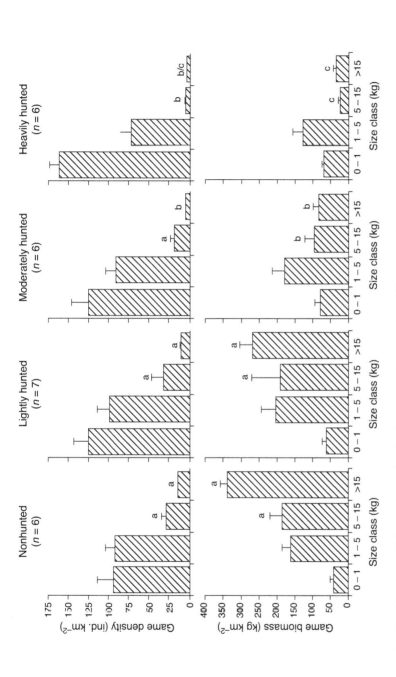

Figure 6.3 Total density and biomass (mean ±SD) of game populations in four different size classes subjected to varying levels of hunting pressure. For significant analyses of variance of log(e)-transformed density and biomass data, means are compared within each size class and across different levels of hunting; means that share the same letter do not differ significantly ($p < 0.005$) according to a Tukey multiple comparison test. (From Peres 2000a; adapted with permission from John Wiley & Sons.)

possible to determine whether these species assemblages have been hunted unsustainably or otherwise, since sustainability can only be determined as the difference between production and extraction.

6.4 Drivers of Extraction

Given the trends in human populations and infrastructure growth, impending large-scale degradation of ecosystem structure and content are underway in tropical forest regions. However, understanding what drives the ever-increasing extraction of wild meat, currently the most pervasive human activity in large forest blocks, is essential.

6.4.1 Wealth and Proximity to Wildlife Areas

Wild meat extraction patterns as described above are driven by a number of economic, social, geographic or other factors that reflect the scale of human reliance on wildlife. Brashares *et al.* (2011) point out that wild meat can be viewed as an 'inferior good' or a 'normal good'. As an 'inferior good', poorer, rural households would typically consume more wild meat than wealthier, urban households because wildlife provides a cheap and accessible source of food and income. In contrast, as a 'normal good', wild meat, like most household goods, would increase as household wealth grows. These two perspectives, although informative, over-simplify the reasons for wildlife consumption since there are a number of interacting and dynamic factors involved (Brashares *et al.* 2011). Overall, inhabitants of poorer rural areas have greater access to wildlife and the price of wild meat relative to alternative foods is lower. Using data across 2,000 households and 96 settlements in four countries in Africa Brashares *et al.* (2011) present evidence of the link between household wealth and wildlife consumption. Results from this study indicate that the least wealthy households in rural settings consistently consume greater amounts of wild meat (Fig. 6.4a), whereas wealthier households show higher rates of consumption in urban settings (Fig. 6.4b). The split between urban and rural settings, as suggested by Brashares *et al.* (2011), reflects considerable spatial variation in access to wildlife, as well as wild meat prices relative to those of alternative foods, and opportunity costs of time spent hunting, all of which are correlated with wealth measures. Conflicting results obtained in other studies may be due to the impact of the co-occurrence of spatial differences in wealth and wild meat consumption patterns.

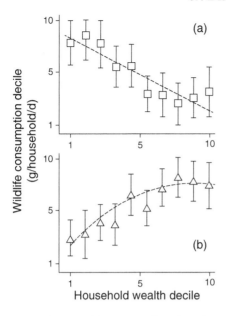

Figure 6.4 Household wealth is (a) significantly and negatively related to consumption for the 500 most rural households and (b) positively related to consumption for the 500 most urban households. (From Brashares *et al.* 2011; adapted with permission from the National Academy of Sciences, USA.)

Most available information on amounts of wild meat consumed relate to rural people (see Chapter 1) with only a few studies concentrating on urban settings (East *et al.* 2005; Fa *et al.* 2019; Wilkie *et al.* 2005). Comparisons between rural and urban wild meat consumption in Gabon showed that rural populations consumed significantly more wild meat (and less domestic meat) than did urban people (Wilkie *et al.* 2005). In a number of towns in Rio Muni, Equatorial Guinea, Fa *et al.* (2009) found that availability of wild meat differed substantially among localities, primarily depending on their location relative to forest areas. Despite these differences, overall meat intake was greater in wealthier households in all studied localities. However, because wealth distribution profiles differed significantly between sites, socio-economic conditions in the largest settlement, the city of Bata, influenced wild meat consumption in a distinct manner from the smaller, more rural sites. Reasons for this may be related to the fact that the substantially wealthier groups in Bata were consuming wild meat exclusively for prestige reasons. In contrast, wealth did not affect the likelihood of consuming domestic meats, and there was strong evidence that both site and wealth affected fish consumption: wealthier families were less likely to consume fish.

Until recently, urban consumption within the Amazon was not considered important and much of the emphasis had been placed on urban wild meat consumption in one city, Iquitos, in Peru (Bodmer & Lozano 2001). Based on this perception, for some time, urban wild meat consumption in Amazonia was regarded as negligible (Nasi 2001; Rushton *et al.* 2005). Recent studies suggest that this is not the case since there are significant city markets in the region where many wild animal species are sold for human consumption. For example, in the Brazilian Amazon well-established wild-meat markets have been documented in Abaetuba (Chaves Baía Júnior *et al.* 2009) and in two pre-frontier cities in the region (Parry *et al.* 2014). Estimates of about 473 tonnes of wild meat have been calculated as annually traded in a number of cities in the Amazonian tri-frontier (Brazil, Colombia and Peru) region according to Van Vliet *et al.* (2014). Although studies documenting sale of wild meat in urban centres in Latin America are mounting, factors affecting wild meat consumption and trade in this region are still largely undescribed in comparison to African cities (Fa *et al.* 2009). However, a few studies point to how the economic and cultural background of consumers in Amazonian cities, for example, affect how much wild meat is eaten (Chaves *et al.* 2017; Morsello *et al.* 2015). El Bizri *et al.* (2020b) found that in a study of six urban wild-meat markets in Amazonas state, a significant proportion (80%) of urban dwellers buy and consume wild meat. In Brazilian cities close to forest areas, Parry *et al.* (2014) showed that the poorest urban households hunt to obtain wild meat, whereas wealthier residents buy it. This is because hunting is the cheaper option for poorer people in cities, but also because the lack of formal employment, more common among this group allows them to spend more time in this activity. In some Amazonian cities, urban hunters profit from the sale of up to 97% of their game to closed markets (Van Vliet *et al.* 2015). According to a further study by El Bizri *et al.* (2020b) only a low number of urban residents declared hunting wild meat in the study, indicating that rural hunters are the most active supplying city markets. This is because hunters from rural areas in Amazonia are mainly subsistence hunters, but may sell part of their hunting yields, to generate money to buy urban goods, such as clothes and foods (Antunes *et al.* 2019). For instance, in the Peruvian Amazon, Bodmer and Lozano (2001) found that rural hunters sell around 7% of mammals hunted, whereas

Morcatty and Valsecchi (2015) found that around 21% of yellow-footed tortoises harvested by rural hunters in Amazonia were traded in urban wild meat markets. What is clear is that hunting wildlife for urban markets is a prerogative of rural inhabitants. The El Bizri *et al.* (2020b) study found that the proportion of rural inhabitants within a municipality was correlated with the proportion of inhabitants that declared consuming wild meat in cities, the reported frequency of consumption, and the prices per kilogram in the market. This pattern may be a result of the economic connectivity between urban and rural sectors in these municipalities. Thus, in municipalities where the rural population is larger, urban people are able to buy wild meat more frequently from rural people who hunt. Because these small cities are often isolated and only accessible by boat, domestic and processed products become more expensive due to higher transportation costs. As a consequence, wild meat prices are higher in small cities, where rural inhabitants outnumber urban ones, because trading in wild meat is one of the most prevalent and cost-effective activities in localities where agricultural commodities do not have a large local market and are uncompetitive due to high costs and long transportation times (Wilkie *et al.* 2016).

Wild meat extraction (and therefore consumption) is related to proximity to harvestable wildlife populations (Brashares *et al.* 2011). According to the data in Brashares *et al.* (2011) the effect of distance seems to disappear at 30 km or more, that is, consumption rates in settlements as close as 30 km to a wildlife harvest area were like those as far as 150 km away (Fig. 6.5a). Wild meat prices were cheaper around sites nearer to harvest areas, but higher in urban markets since having travelled some distance from its source after being sold to middlemen (Fig. 6.5b). From data for wild meat and domestic meat and fish in 52 markets Brashares *et al.* (2011) showed this effect (Fig. 6.5b). The price of wild meat relative to alternative meat also increased with increasing distances from hunting areas.

Because wild meat prices increase with proximity to urban areas, those hunters who harvest wild meat nearer cities should gain relatively more from selling their catch than those hunters in more remote areas. Consequently, hunters closer to cities are more likely to sell rather than consume their quarry. Brashares *et al.* (2011) showed that a high proportion (75–95%) of wildlife harvested in the settlements most isolated from commerce networks was consumed locally by the hunter's household or neighbour. In contrast, hunters who lived within 10 km of an urban market sold more than 80% of their catch to outsiders.

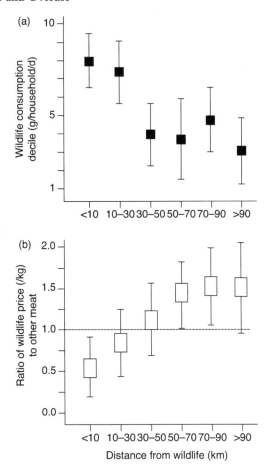

Figure 6.5 (a) Distance of human settlements from harvestable wildlife populations in Ghana, Tanzania, Madagascar and Cameroon was a strong predictor of the amount of wild meat that households in those communities consume annually as well as (b) the price that consumers paid for wild meat in Ghana and Tanzania (from Brashares et al. 2011; adapted with permission from the National Academy of Sciences, USA).

6.4.2 Non-wealth Factors

As outlined in the section above, wild meat is consumed primarily by the rural poor who live closer to wildlife areas. People eat wild meat in rural localities because it is cheaper than other meat sources or simply because no alternatives are available in the marketplace (Apaza *et al.* 2002; Wilkie & Godoy 2001). Some studies have indicated that consumers prefer the taste of wild meat (Chardonnet *et al.* 1995; Trefon & de Maret 1999) or wish to add variety to their diet and consume it for special social events and occasions (Njiforti 1996). Despite this variety of possible reasons that may motivate buyers to eat wild meat, most studies have focused on the socioeconomic background of consumers as the main reason underpinning their choice (Brashares *et al.* 2011; Wilkie & Godoy 2001). Findings relating to wealth show price and income have significant roles in determining the level of consumption of wild meat, fish, chicken and beef (Apaza *et al.* 2002; Wilkie & Godoy 2001; Wilkie *et al.* 2005). Nonetheless, as Brashares *et al.* (2011) has indicated, household wealth is only weakly associated with eating wildlife, and, thus, such a lack of a strong correlation could be explained by the undisclosed importance of other factors. Wild meat consumption can therefore be affected by other factors such as age, gender and geographical setting (Hema *et al.* 2019; Luiselli *et al.* 2017). Luiselli *et al.* (2019), using face-to-face interviews in Togo, Nigeria, Burkina Faso and Niger, examined the possible links between wild meat consumption frequency and types eaten relative to the age and gender of consumers as well as the influence of settlement type, ecological and country setting. Significant differences were evident in consumption between rural and urban areas in all four countries but the proportion of persons not consuming any wild meat was highest in urban areas. This observation was explained not by gender differences but by young people consistently avoiding wild meat, especially in urban areas. The complicated interplay between tradition and evolution of social systems (especially the trends towards Westernization) may explain the different perceptions that people have towards consuming wild meat in the four studied countries. Hence, a unifying theory of wildlife consumption will require taking into account the many drivers underlying different peoples' consumption practices, even specific to an intervention area, as suggested by Chausson *et al.* (2019). An in-depth understanding of behaviours and practices is also needed. For example, in a study of urban settlements in the Colombian Amazon, Morsello *et al.* (2015) argue that beliefs, attitudes and social norms explained consumption and preference of wild meat in the study locations. They argue that, as in Nardoto *et al.* (2011) for Amazonian towns, that even though wild meat was not the preferred source of animal protein, it was routinely consumed in the studied towns because it was the local custom.

6.5 Spatial Patterns of Extraction

Data on the spatial extraction of different species used for food can be obtained from either wild meat market studies (Fa 2007) or from records of prey taken by hunters in villages or camps (see Taylor *et al.* 2015). Most studies documenting offtake, consumption and trade of wild meat in tropical forests have focussed on West and Central Africa with much less information for South American and Asian forests (see Coad *et al.* 2019). Although the number of publications on wild meat use since the 1960s has increased significantly (see Chapter 1), most studies have targeted small catchment areas (often around single sites) over short time periods (but some regional assessments such as Fa *et al.* 2002 have been published) and limited data of wild meat extraction rates are available at a larger scale (and over longer time frames). Although such research may be affected by the lack of comparability between the studies used in the analysis, they still allow us to generate a broad understanding of wild meat extraction and availability patterns over large geographical areas. No doubt, these approximations will be further enhanced as more data becomes available. However, there is still a paucity of biological and socioeconomic data at a regional scale that can be used for determining patterns of wildlife exploitation to help decision-makers highlight areas that are at greater from unsustainable hunting (Ziegler 2010). Thus, developing regional maps delimiting hotspots of wild meat extraction can pinpoint areas requiring conservation interventions, and ultimately assist in protecting forest ecosystem and their biodiversity. Such maps are a useful data visualization tool for communicating the current situation of wildlife subjected to hunting, of use for decision-makers, protected area managers and researchers. Such maps are useful representations of the state and future of the wild meat resource and the pressures acting upon it.

A first attempt to project large-scale wild meat extraction in a large region is the spatial analyses performed in Ziegler *et al.* (2016) for Central Africa. These authors used data on the number of carcasses and species of mammals hunted in 27 sites between 1990 and 2007 in Cameroon, Central African Republic, Democratic Republic of Congo, Equatorial Guinea, Gabon and Republic of Congo. By examining the relationship between environmental and anthropogenic variables, they mapped (Fig. 6.6a) the intensity of wild meat extraction. Mean ($\pm$SD) annual total biomass offtake per recorded site was 25,657 $\pm$ 23,538 kg/yr (303–84,093 kg/yr). Catchment area sizes ranged between 45 km^2 and

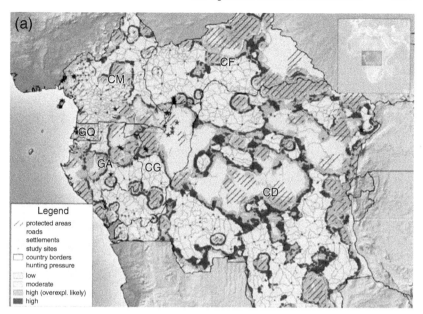

Figure 6.6 (a) Spatial prediction of hunting pressure using distance to protected areas, roads, and population density. From Ziegler *et al.* (2016) reprinted with permission from John Wiley & Sons. Risk zones: See legend for key to low, moderate, high (over exploitation likely) and high risk. CD, Democratic Republic of Congo; CG, Republic of Congo; CM, Cameroon; CF, Central African Republic; GA, Gabon; GQ, Equatorial Guinea. (b) Anthropogenic pressures (i) above median areas of rural human population density. (ii) below median areas of distance to urban areas. (iii) below median areas of distance to roads. (iv) above median areas of distance to protected areas. (v) Wild meat extraction patterns emerging from the overlay of urban areas, road networks, protected areas and densely populated rural areas (areas with a total score of 4 had the highest wild meat extraction potential, whereas areas with a total score of a 0 had the lowest). From Fa *et al.* (2015a) reprinted with permission from John Wiley & Sons.

1,010 km^2. The highest annual biomass extraction was 294 kg/km^2 but lowest recorded was 1 kg/km^2; mean annual offtake was 92 kg/km^2 ± 78.9 kg/km^2. Mean (±SD) number of hunted species per site was 20 ± 8.7 (7–39 species). A number of different anthropogenic variables used to construct the map included road density and distance from the hunting locality to the nearest protected area. These proved to be adequate proxies to predict annual offtake. Lower annual offtake in areas with higher road densities explained almost 23% of the variation in annual biomass offtake per km^2 and distance from the hunting locality alone, 17%.

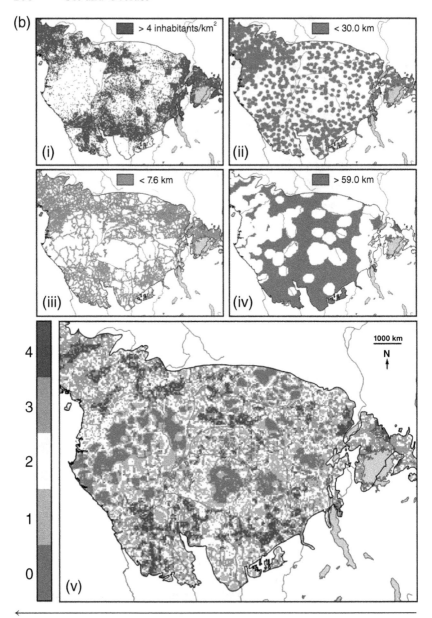

Figure 6.6 (cont.)

As expected, total annual wild meat offtake and distance to protected areas was significantly negatively correlated (Ziegler *et al.* 2016). Similarly, the number of species recorded in each site (= species richness) and road density and human population density were significantly correlated, explaining 64% of the variance. Using the median of the predicted values for annual offtake (156 kg/km²) and hunted species (n = 16), hunting pressure was divided into four classes: (1) lower pressure (annual offtake <156 kg/km²; number of hunted species <16), (2) moderate pressure (annual offtake >156 kg/ km²; number of hunted species <16), (3) high pressure (annual offtake <156 kg/km²; number of hunted species >16), and (4) very high pressure (annual offtake >156 kg/km²; number of hunted species >16). Predicted hunting pressure areas within the study area indicated a patchy distribution (Fig. 6.6a) where many protected areas are located in predicted higher hunting pressure zones accounting for approx. 1.5 million km² (39%) of the total area of the Congo Basin and concentrated along three main broad zones. Approximately 36% of the Congo Basin (371,740 km²) was characterized as zones of moderate hunting pressure, encompassing Cameroon and half of the land area of Republic of Congo and Central African Republic as well as the southern part of Democratic Republic of Congo.

Because wild meat hunters are typically central place foragers (Section 4.2), their hunting patterns should be distributed on the landscape according to how easily they can reach forested areas that support game (Levi *et al.* 2011a; Sirén *et al.* 2004). As shown in Ziegler *et al.* (2016), a well-developed infrastructure, including roads, rail- and waterways, in tropical forests, improves accessibility and transportation and therefore facilitates the extraction of wild meat in the Congo Basin. In fact, estimated hunting offtake in Ziegler *et al.* (2016) was not explained by any single environmental factor but by increased road density values and proximity to protected areas. Similar effects of road networks on hunting were found by Fuentes-Montemayor *et al.* (2009), and Benítez-López *et al.* (2019) developed a map of hunting pressure across the tropics where the distance to the nearest access point and market were used as a predictor of the spatial distribution of hunting pressure.

Simple Euclidean distance measures can successfully describe coarse patterns of game depletion even if hunting information is not considered. For example, Fa *et al.* (2015a) inferred wild meat extraction patterns using only the overlap of urban road networks, protected areas and densely populated rural areas resulting in similar patterns to the map in Zeigler *et al.* (2016) which also used hunting offtake data (Fig. 6.6b). However, according to Deith and Brodie (2020), fine-scale environmental features like topography and land cover influence hunter movement decisions while foraging and may offer more realistic and generalizable predictions of the distribution of hunting effort. These authors compared simple, commonly used measures of landscape accessibility against a novel, high-resolution accessibility model based on circuit theory and assess their ability to predict camera-trap detections of hunters across tropical forests in Malaysian Borneo. Deith and Brodie (2020) show that hunter movements are strongly correlated with the accessibility of different parts of the landscape, and these are most informative when they integrate fine-scale habitat features like topography and land cover.

Similar to extraction maps produced for the Congo Basin and Borneo, Peres *et al.* (2016) mapped the potential extent of large primate extirpation in the Brazilian Amazon. Because human hunters concentrate hunting effort near households, highly susceptible game species, such as large primates, are extirpated first near human settlements. Peres *et al.* (2016) assumed central place hunting by a single forest hunter for a total of 915,877 georeferenced rural households within different forest phytogeographic boundaries in the region. Population density, biomass density, or another abundance metric for 16 game and non-game primate species functional groups, from pygmy marmosets to the largest atelines (*Ateles* spp. and *Lagothrix* spp.) was calculated from line-transect surveys at 166 Amazonian forest sites (Fig. 6.7). This unprecedented dataset was used by the authors to determine the impact of defaunation of the most harvest-sensitive species that would lead to losses in aboveground biomass, given that primates are one of the main tree seed dispersers. The resulting map shows that areas that are heavily settled in the southern and eastern Amazon and along the main tributaries of the Amazon River are depleted (Fig. 6.8a and b), but that non-hunted refugia exist within inaccessible regions and large protected areas that are depopulated or sparsely populated. The actual spatial extent of overhunting varies regionally due to local food taboos that affect primate hunting, or the actual areas accessible to hunters; the latter may diverge due to topographic differences (see Deith & Brodie 2020). Overall, the study indicates that large primate frugivores would be completely extirpated in 103,022 km^2 and over-hunted in 236,308 km^2 across Brazilian Amazonia; 3.3% and 7.5% of the total remaining forest area, respectively. The total area affected by any

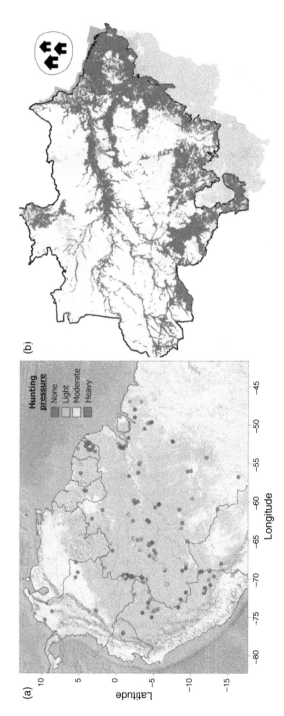

Figure 6.7 (a) Geographic location of 166 Amazonian and peri-Amazonian forest sites across eight of the nine Amazonian countries on which forest primate population density estimates were available; (b) spatial distribution of all georeferenced rural households across the phytogeographic boundaries of Brazilian Amazonia. (From Peres *et al.* 2016 reprinted with permission from the National Academy of Sciences, USA.)

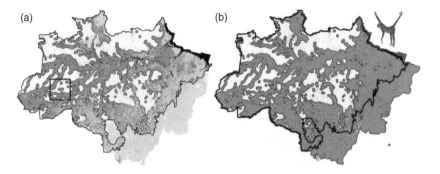

Figure 6.8 Maps (a) of the overall distribution of depletion envelopes excluding all deforested areas as of 2013 (shown in lighter grey); (b) of the population depletion envelopes for a game species that is highly sensitive to hunting (spider monkey, *Ateles* spp.) based on a biodemographic model that considers both the behaviour of central place hunters and the population dynamics of prey species. (From Peres *et al.* 2016 reprinted with permission from the National Academy of Sciences, USA.)

level of hunting represents 32.4% (1,017,569 km^2) of all remaining forest areas, approx. 1.34-times larger than the cumulative area deforested across this region over the 1970–2014 period (Peres *et al.* 2016).

The Peres *et al.* (2016) map for the Brazilian Amazon as well as Ziegler's *et al.* (2016) for the Congo Basin clearly show that there are hotspots of greater hunting pressure in those areas with more roads and with higher human population density. Similar regional assessments of hunting pressure for Southeast Asia are not available. For the Congo Basin, Ziegler *et al.* (2016) also show that the proportion of small- and medium-sized rodents in the recorded offtake studies increased significantly in areas of higher human presence. This finding is not unexpected as there is evidence that hunting pressure is likely to be higher where there are more hunters (areas of higher human population density) or where hunters have better access to hunting sites, often facilitated by more roads (Fa *et al.* 2015a). As a result, sites in less disturbed habitats will still have more intact species assemblages, with more large-bodied species present (Dupain *et al.* 2012). The higher proportion of rodents in hunter bags in African sites is an indication of a decline in slow-breeding large-bodied taxa and a replacement by faster-breeding species (see Section 5.5.3).

Differences in the composition of fauna, often related to habitat type and disturbance history, will impact the hunting potential of a region. Moreover, accessibility to hunters as well as the actual number of hunters in the region will influence the biomass of wildlife extracted. Studies of how habitat type and hunting history may explain the structure of the mammalian community in an area have been undertaken extensively for Amazonian forests (Peres 1999a, 2000). However, few studies are available for African moist forests (Effiom *et al.* 2013, 2014). As has been observed for the Amazon (Fa & Brown 2009), it is likely that type of habitat and history will affect mammalian assemblages in Africa in a similar way. In both the Amazon and the Congo Basin, environmental perturbations, such as selective logging, slash-and-burn agriculture, surface wildfires and forest fragmentation as well as hunting, can lead to marked changes in relative abundances of tropical forest vertebrates. Despite this, given the broad geographic spread in the analyses by both Peres *et al.* (2016) and Ziegler *et al.* (2016), the maps are likely to be a good reflection of the spread of hunting pressure in such large forest blocks. However, there are differences in their accuracy based on the type and quality of data used. Studies such Ziegler *et al.* (2016) employed hunting data exclusively drawn from the literature. As these data were neither random nor systematic, but determined by the contemporaneous studies that were available, the map is likely to comprise some bias. The dataset in Peres *et al.* (2016), in contrast, is drawn from field data systematically collected through line transects and, therefore, is not a reflection of game extraction but of the abundance of the game remaining. The ideal of generating data from a large sample of sites during a similar time period is not only time-consuming but also cost-prohibitive. Thus, even though literature-based or prey abundance data assessing spatial patterns of extraction may suffer some constraints (e.g. linked to the comparability of field methods and study periods, validation of study site geolocations, and determination of hunting catchment areas), results for Central Africa and the Amazon corroborate other published studies that show, as expected, higher anthropogenic activities and population densities to generate greater hunting pressure (Fa *et al.* 2015).

6.6 Estimates of Overextraction

Estimates of wild meat offtake in tropical forests range from global appraisals of what proportion wild animal protein contributes to people's diets (Prescott-Allen & Prescott-Allen 1982), to more precise extrapolations of numbers and biomass consumed within the Congo and Amazon Basins (Fa & Peres 2001; Fa *et al.* 2003). From these latter studies, extraction rates were calculated for 57 reported mammalian taxa, for a rural human population of 24 million within a forest area of 1.8 million km² in the Congo Basin (taken from Wilkie & Carpenter 1999). Resulting numbers suggest that as many as 579 million animals were consumed in the Congo Basin annually, producing around 4 million tonnes of dressed wild meat (Fa *et al.* 2003). This figure contrasts with Wilkie and Carpenter's (1999) study, which estimated only 1 million tonnes. The latter figure is based on extrapolations of actual meat consumed from figures assembled by Chardonnet *et al.* (1995) to estimate an average consumption of meat per person in the region. Using data on production and extraction for all mammal species exploited, Fa *et al.* (2003) calculated harvest rates from empirical data derived from hunting studies in 36 sites in seven West and Central African countries (Cameroon, Equatorial Guinea, Gabon, Republic of Congo, Democratic Republic of Congo, Central African Republic and Ghana). Although the magnitude of extraction in the two studies are different, these figures are likely to still be underestimates, since sample sizes are low. Despite this caveat, the amount of wild meat extracted and consumed per unit area in the Congo Basin is still orders of magnitude higher than in the Amazon. In terms of actual yields of dressed carcasses (given that muscle mass and edible viscera account on average for 55% of body mass), Fa and Peres (2001) estimate that 62,808 tonnes are consumed in the Amazon and around 2 million tonnes in the Congo Basin. More specifically, estimated hunting rates for Amazon and Congo Basin species, shown in a graph of production *versus* extraction (Fig. 6.9) indicate that most are exploited unsustainably in the Congo, whilst most hunted Amazonian taxa are still within the sustainable part of the graph. Congo Basin primates appear more heavily hunted than other species; 12 of the represented 17 species (>70%) fall above the 20% line.

These differences in species exploitation between the two continents are predominantly a result of larger human population sizes within a smaller forest area in the Congo Basin, and the fact that a large proportion of what hunters kill is sold in towns and villages for profit. Therefore, per capita harvest rates (kg/person/yr) in relation to number of consumers, show a lower variation for South American settlements than for Africa where they decline significantly from an average of approx. 500 kg/person/yr in smaller settlements to 1 kg/person/yr in the largest settlements (Robinson & Bennett 2004). This does not indicate greater consumption rates of wild meat per person but the fact the wild meat is commercialized.

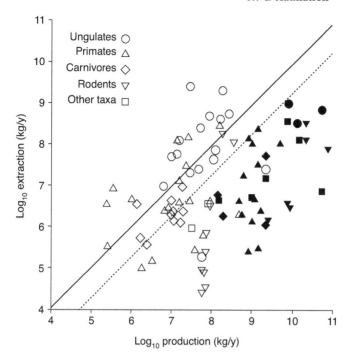

Figure 6.9 Hunting rates are unsustainably high across large tracts of tropical forests as seen in the relationship between extraction and total production of wild meat throughout the Amazon and Congo basin (solid and open symbols, respectively) by mammalian taxa. (From Fa *et al.* 2002; adapted with permission from John Wiley & Sons.)

6.7 Defaunation

The archaeological and paleontological evidence suggests that premodern peoples might have driven animal species to extinction. Mass extinction events of large-bodied vertebrates in Europe, parts of Asia, North and South America, Madagascar and several archipelagos are relatively well documented in the fossil and subfossil record (Young *et al.* 2016). Whether they are attributable to post-Pleistocene human overkill and/or climatic and environmental change remains controversial, although the latest analyses (Andermann *et al.* 2020) strongly imply that increasing human population size caused past extinctions (Box 6.1). In more recent times, extinction events induced by overexploitation have also been common as European settlers wielding superior technology expanded their territorial frontiers and introduced market and sport

Box 6.1 *Prehistoric megafaunal extinctions*

There has been a long and controversial debate on the extent of human contributions to prehistoric species extinctions, especially the late-Quaternary extinctions of megafauna. Based on different data sets, diverging assumptions and conflicting interpretations of several schools of thought have emerged:

- Humans have been driving species to extinction since the beginning of the late Pleistocene after their expansion from Africa into Europe, Asia, Australia and the Americas (Diniz-Filho 2004; Fiedel & Haynes 2004; Haynes 2007; Johnson 2002; Johnson *et al.* 2016; Klapman & Capaldi 2019; Martin & Klein 1984; Raczka *et al.* 2019; Sandom *et al.* 2014; Smith *et al.* 2018; Surovell *et al.* 2005, 2016). Key is a strong human hunting pressure leading to overkill, particularly of megafauna mammals (Whittington & Dyke 1984); blitzkrieg, that is rapid overkill (Mosimann & Martin 1975); and a sitzkrieg, that is hunting alongside habitat fragmentation, fire and introduction of exotic species and diseases (Diamond 1989).

- Others have argued that there is insufficient evidence for hunting as the cause of human-caused extinctions or that extinction models are highly sensitive to underpinning assumptions about the extinction dynamics (Grayson & Meltzer 2003, 2004; Lima-Ribeiro *et al.* 2013; Lima-Ribeiro & Diniz-Filho 2017). On the other hand, Emery-Wetherell (2017) highlights that maps of last megafaunal occurrence in North America are consistent with climate as a primary driver in some areas, but the analysis cannot reject human activities as contributing causation in all regions.

- Some argue that rapid or synchronous continental-wide extinction is not human-mediated but extinctions are associated with sustained climatic and environmental change especially due to glacial-interglacial cycles during the late Quaternary (Hocknull *et al.* 2020; Lorenzen *et al.* 2011; Wroe & Field 2006; Wroe *et al.* 2004).

- Some data indicate situation-specific extinction dynamics with differing underpinning causations whereby the importance of hunting and other factors such as climatic and environmental change varied considerably between sites and continents (Wroe *et al.* 2004). For example, Broughton and Weitzel (2018) concluded that the causes for extinctions in North America varied across taxa and by region whereby either extinctions are linked to hunting (mammoth, horse, sabre-toothed cat); to climate and ecological change (Shasta ground sloth, mastodon, mammoth in the Great Lakes region); or to both (mammoth in the Southwest region).

- A synthetic model ascribes extinctions to the combined effect of humans and climate change (Barnosky 2004; Bartlett *et al.* 2016; Gibbons 2004; Haynes 2018; Mondanaro *et al.* 2019; Prescott *et al.* 2012; Saltré *et al.* 2019).

- In a study applying Bayesian models to the fossil record to estimate how mammalian extinction rates have changed over the past 126,000 years, Andermann *et al.* (2020) showed that human population size is able to predict past extinctions with 96% accuracy. This study combined data of prehistoric extinctions of 271 mammal species since the beginning of the late Pleistocene and 80 mammal extinctions since the year 1500. Predictors based on past climate, in contrast, perform no better than expected by chance, suggesting that climate had a negligible impact on global mammal extinctions.

hunting. A prime example is the catastrophic loss of wildlife driven by uncontrolled market hunting, and unrelenting subsistence killing suffered in North America at the end of the nineteenth century (Mahoney & Geist 2019). Such unbridled hunting for meat, skins or merely recreation led to near extinction of once-vast bison herds in North America. There is also the notorious example of the extinction of what was once the most numerous bird in the world, the passenger pigeon (Bucher 1992).

Highly visible anthropogenic threats, such as deforestation, habitat degradation and climate change, have been the focus of much of our attention on biodiversity loss, often overshadowing the effects of direct exploitation. But overhunting is at least as serious a problem, often resulting in environments that might appear to be pristine but are devoid of wildlife, especially large-bodied wildlife (Peres *et al.* 2006). The meta-analysis of 176 hunting studies by Benítez-López *et al.* (2017) revealed that bird and mammal abundances were 58% (25% to 76%) and 83% (72% to 90%) smaller in hunted compared with unhunted areas. Abundances were reduced within 7 and 40 km from roads and settlements for birds and mammals, respectively. The commercial aspect of defaunation was evident by the fact that accessibility to major towns where wild meat could be traded impacted depletion.

Remote sensing data have indicated that only 23.5% of the current extent of forest ecosystems was considered intact in 2008, defined as containing an unbroken expanse of natural ecosystems within areas of current forest extent, without signs of significant human activity (Potapov *et al.* 2008). However, whilst remote sensing can identify habitat loss, conversion and degradation, it does not account for 'empty forests' (sensu Redford 1992) due to hunting. Benítez-López *et al.* (2019) mapped the spatial patterns of mammal defaunation in the tropics in what appear intact forests using a database of 3,281 mammal abundance declines from local hunting studies. They found an average abundance decline of 13% across all tropical mammal species, but there were large differences regarding mammals of different body size (Fig. 6.10). Medium-sized species were being reduced by >27% and large mammals by >40%. Defaunation, defined here as declines of 10% or more (see Section 6.7.1), was predicted on half of the pantropical forest area, 52% of the intact forests, 62% of the wilderness areas and 20% of protected areas in the tropics, particularly in West and Central Africa and Southeast Asia.

As an example, unprecedented rates of local extinctions of medium to large-bodied mammals have been demonstrated from the Atlantic Forest biome in eastern South America. This biome is one of the world's most important tropical biodiversity hotspots and one of the 'hottest' of the global biodiversity hotspots (Myers *et al.* 2000). Only 10.8% of the original forest cover in the surveyed four biogeographic subregions has been converted to other land-uses (Ribeiro *et al.* 2009). What remains of the original forest has only 767 from a possible 3,528 populations of ten terrestrial and seven arboreal mid- to large-bodied mammal species still persisting (Canale *et al.* 2012). Patchiness of remaining forest fragments makes populations especially vulnerable as fragments are highly accessible to hunters. Forest patches retained only 3.9 out of 18 potential species occupancies on average. Geographic ranges had contracted to 0–14.4% of their former distributions. In the Atlantic rainforest's Serra do Mar bioregion, mammalian biomass declined by up to 98% in intensively hunted sites (Galetti *et al.* 2017). This level of overkill was also confirmed by using the fate of selected surrogate Neotropical large mammal species to map the level of defaunation. Jorge *et al.* 2013) mapped the occurrence of the jaguar, tapir, white-lipped peccary and the muriqui – the largest apex predator, herbivore, seed predator and arboreal seed disperser, respectively – in 94 locations of Atlantic Forest remnants. They observed that 96% of these sites are depleted of at least one of the four surrogate species and 88% are completely depleted of all four surrogate species.

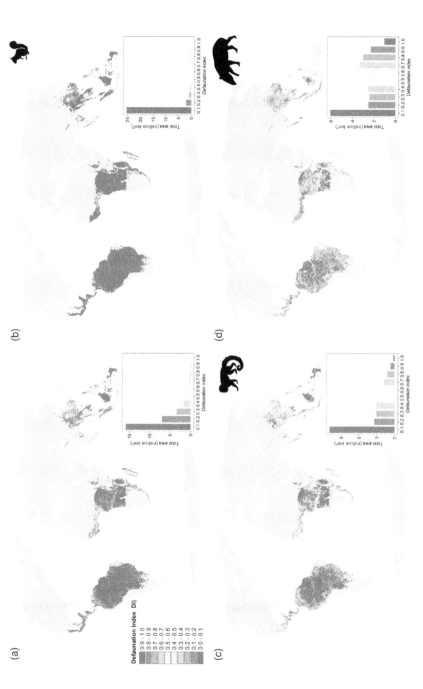

Figure 6.10 Geographic variation in hunting-induced defaunation for (a) all species, (b) small-sized species (<1 kg, e.g. *Sciurus* spp.), (c) medium-sized species (1–20 kg, e.g. *Alouatta* spp.), and (d) large-sized species (>20 kg, e.g. *Tapirus* spp.). The insets represent the total area (y-axis) under different levels of defaunation (x-axis, from D = 0 to D = 1). Note that the y-axes in the four insets have different scales. (From Benítez-López et al. 2019; adapted with permission from PLOS Biology.)

6.7.1 Defaunation Index

The defaunation index (DI) of Giacomini and Galetti (2013) quantifies the loss of species richness through matched site comparisons between an affected contemporary site and a reference site which represents a non-affected contemporary or historic site (e.g. in a forest fragment and a nearby protected area as a reference site). The index ranges from 0.0 for a completely intact faunal assemblage in the study area to 1.0 for a completely defaunated study site to −1.0 for a completely defaunated reference site. A defaunated reference site may seem counterintuitive as the reference site is supposed to be non-affected by species loss but negative DI values might arise due to species reintroductions or invasive species in the affected site. The index can be applied to different types of data − species occurrence, biomass, or site occupancy −depending on practical limitations and data availability.

It is the only index that allows quantification of the effects of hunting on the reduction of species richness in a given area. Even when a contemporary reference site is not available, probable occurrences can be estimated using known distribution maps for species assessed by the Red List (IUCN 2020b). Although these range maps are estimated themselves based on often limited available information, the use of the IUCN polygons is a widely established methodology (Bogoni *et al.* 2018). The index can be geared towards the importance of species for different biological aspects, such as ecosystem function or conservation importance by the weight parameter for species importance that is part of the equation to calculate DI.

The index quantifies species loss for any reason and cannot distinguish whether the loss occurred because of hunting, habitat alteration, habitat fragmentation or the non-synergistic or synergistic combination of these. Moreover, the index is unsuited for the practical assessment of sustainability of hunting for management purposes as it is an a posteriori assessment of species loss that has already occurred rather than a method that can flag-up non-sustainable hunting whilst the target species still occur and intervention is still possible. Depending on the choice of the weight parameter, different DI values might be calculated for the same data set; thus, DI values are not always directly comparable between studies and sites. For example, species importance might be equal for any species, resulting in DI values that follow an exact monotonically decreasing function of richness. If, however, species' body size is taken as weight to act as a proxy for vulnerability to extinction and conservation concern, the resulting DI values can vary substantially at the same richness. Other choices for the assumed weight are possible. Giacomini and Galetti (2013) point out that the criteria for its choice must be justified on a priori grounds and not on a posteriori inspection of resulting index values.

Example: Bogoni *et al.* (2018) calculated the DI for the entire mammal assemblage and for functional groups within the Atlantic Forest of South America which is one of the most endangered major ecoregions worldwide. Because only 11.7% of its original vegetation cover remains and the remaining habitat fragments are mostly highly disturbed (Ribeiro *et al.* 2009), historic species assemblages were reconstructed from the probable species occurrences calculated from the Red List geographic range polygons. A total of 105 studies provided data on 497 mammal assemblages from 164 independent clusters of study sites from which mammal inventories are available. The results showed high levels of defaunation of $DI > 0.5$ for most of the Atlantic forest. Comparing contemporary and historical mammal assemblages at any given site for all mammal taxa yielded a mean total defaunation index of 0.71 ± 0.25 ranging from 0.61 for small-bodied species to 0.76 for large-bodies species and to 0.79 for apex-predators (Fig. 6.11). Accounting for possible overestimation of the historical baseline through existing mammal distribution polygons, smaller but still very large DI values were estimated with a mean overall index of 0.57 ± 0.20. The geographic distribution of DI values across the entire Atlantic Forest biome was interpolated from the geographic distribution of the DI values in the separate clusters of study sites by kriging which accounts for spatial autocorrelation of the data. The eastern portions of the Atlantic Forest contain the regions with the highest levels of defaunation (see Bogoni *et al.* 2018, fig. 4).

6.7.2 Ecological Consequences of Defaunation

Defaunation not only has the above-described devastating effects on the species involved, but also on a plenitude of cascading effects that result in changed and depauperated environments, ecosystem services and human food security. Defaunation has long-term cascading effects on animal and plant community structure and ecosystem functioning, which manifests in a myriad way.

In predator–prey systems, prey species benefit from the removal of their predators, which can trigger further effects on various ecosystem

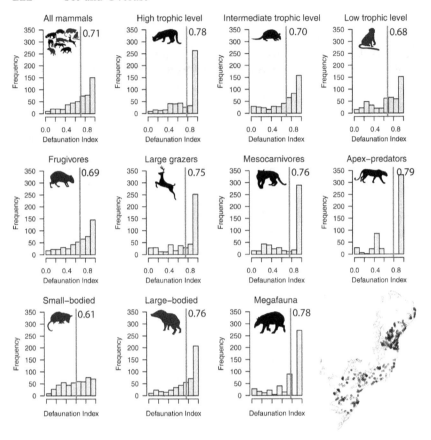

Figure 6.11 Frequency distribution of the overall defaunation index for medium- to large-bodied mammals across the Atlantic Forest biome of South America. The heavy vertical lines indicate mean values. Inset map (lower right) shows the geographic distribution of study sites in eastern Brazil. (From Bogoni *et al.* 2018; reprinted with permission from PLOS ONE.)

services. For example, sea otters on the northern Pacific coast of North America are sensitive to overhunting and became almost extinct in the nineteenth and twentieth centuries (Estes 1990). Sea otters prey on sea urchins, which in turn feed on kelp. Wilmers *et al.* (2012) calculated that kelp net primary productivity is 25–70 g C/m^2/year in the absence of otters, but over 10-fold higher when they are present (313–900 g C/m^2/year). The ecosystem service by increase in carbon storage is estimated to be worth US\$205 million to \$408 million on the European Carbon Exchange for the otter's ecosystem area of approximately 5.1 × 10^{10} m^2.

Another reduced ecosystem service by defaunation involves changes to prevalence and transmission of some zoonotic disease (Chapter 7). Young et al. (2014) experimentally excluded large wildlife from a savanna ecosystem in East Africa. Consequently, rodent population density doubled and with it the density their flea vectors infected with *Bartonella* spp., which causes bartonellosis in humans. Similar cascading effects by reductions in predator abundance increase the zoonotic risk of hantavirus and Lyme disease (Levi et al. 2012; Suzán et al. 2009). Human welfare is also impacted by ecosystem services such as the suppression of pest insects and, to a lesser extent, pollination services by birds and bats. Maas et al. (2013) observed in their exclusion experiments in Indonesian cacao agroforestry fields that insect herbivore abundance increased leading to the decrease of 31% of crop yield in this billion dollar per year industry.

A growing body of studies has demonstrated a significant impact of the defaunation of mid- and large-sized animals on plant regeneration and thus carbon storage through changes in seed dispersal, pre- and post-dispersal seed predation, leaf herbivory or browsing. Exclusion experiments have demonstrated increased seedling density, survival, recruitment and increased understory vegetation cover through reduced seed predation and herbivory (Aliaga-Rossel & Fragoso 2014; Beck et al. 2013). Whilst such experiments can demonstrate that plant community structure depends on vertebrate community structure, they are no analogues for real-world defaunation because they impact vertebrate communities differently. Exclusion experiments also exclude herbivores (e.g. ungulates) or seed predators (e.g. rodents), which are not hunted or hunted but not critically depressed in their abundance in real-world settings. Moreover, they fail to exclude arboreal and volant species such as primates, birds and bats, many of which are seed dispersers. Contrary results were observed by Rosin and Poulsen (2016) in experiments that excluded large animals but not rodents. Here, rodents caused the greatest seed mortality for all species, removing 60% of accessible seeds, leading to a reduction of seedling establishment by 42% compared to sites with intact fauna. Gardner et al. (2019) conducted a meta-analysis of real-world defaunation and manipulation experiments and confirmed these contrasting findings. Observed defaunation was associated with reduced forest regeneration whilst experiments were associated with increased forest regeneration. Overall, defaunation caused decreases in seedling density and richness. The defaunation of primates and birds caused the greatest declines in forest regeneration.

Defaunation changes the spatial structure and dynamics of tree populations and leads to a decline in local tree diversity over time (Harrison *et al.* 2013) because hunting directly impacts tree species whose seeds are dispersed by animals. For example, defaunation causes population genetic changes in the large-seeded queen palm in the Atlantic Forest of South America whereby trees in hunted forest fragments show lower allelic richness and stronger fine-scale spatial genetic structure compared to protected forest (Giombini *et al.* 2017). In a meta-analysis, Kurten (2013) confirmed that larger-seeded species consistently experience reduced primary seed dispersal when large seed-dispersing animals are absent. Resilient frugivores, such as small birds, bats and marsupials, which are not targeted by hunters, can disperse seeds up to 12.0 ± 1.1 mm in width, but larger animal-dispersed seeds are dispersed only by larger animals (Bello *et al.* 2015). Moreover, there is a functional relationship between seed diameter and traits related to carbon storage, with trees that produce seeds larger than 12 mm having a high carbon stock capacity. Thus, large seed dispersers are functionally linked to forest carbon storage (Bello *et al.* 2015). Consequently, overhunting of larger seed-dispersing animal species shifts plant species composition towards species, including lianas and low wood-density tree species, that are abiotically dispersed or dispersed by small animals(Kurten *et al.* 2015). Defaunation can negatively impact carbon storage in tropical forests by favouring the latter species as they store much less carbon than high wood density trees, which have typically large seed size (Bello *et al.* 2015; Jansen *et al.* 2010; Putz 1983). There is a relationship between wood volume and seed size with large-seeded animal-dispersed trees being larger than small-seeded animal-dispersed species, but smaller than abiotically dispersed species (Osuri *et al.* 2016). Because defaunation impacts preferentially large-bodied animal species, which disperse large seeds and, thus, large trees, defaunation shifts tree populations towards species with smaller trees. Consistent with this are simulations which demonstrate that African, American and South Asian forests, which have high proportions of animal-dispersed species, consistently show carbon losses (2–12%) when becoming defaunated, whereas Southeast Asian and Australian forests, where there are more abiotically dispersed species, show little to no carbon losses (Osuri *et al.* 2016). Field studies in Africa (Effiom *et al.* 2013, 2014; Poulsen *et al.* 2013; Vanthomme *et al.* 2010), Mesoamerica (Kurten *et al.* 2015; Wright *et al.* 2007), southern Asia (Brodie *et al.* 2009) and Southeast Asia (Chanthorn *et al.* 2019) corroborate that defaunation of large frugivore, seed–dispersing species affects the recruitment, relative abundance and population growth rate of animal-dispersed large-seeded trees. Loss of dispersal is also substantiated by the increase of genetic similarity in tree communities due to defaunation (Pérez-Méndez et al. 2016). In an Afrotropical forest, hunting reduced the mean dispersal distances of nine mammal-dispersed tree species by 22% (Poulsen et al. 2013). Hunted forest also had significantly lower above-ground biomass than logged and undisturbed forests. Using field data and models to project the impact of hunting on large primates in the Brazilian Amazon, Peres et al. (2016) found that loss of large primates alone leads to losses in aboveground biomass of 2.5–5.8% on average, with some losses as high as 26.5–37.8%. Such changes in plant structure, dynamics, regeneration, etc., affect the forest's ability to store carbon which impacts us globally.

7 · *Wild Meat and Zoonotic Diseases*

7.1 Introduction

The coronavirus disease of 2019 (COVID-19) that became pandemic in 2020 reminds us poignantly about the possible consequences of spillover events of diseases from wildlife. Over recent decades, we have experienced the emergence of new or newly identified infectious disease such as severe acute respiratory syndrome (SARS), Ebola, Nipah, human immunodeficiency virus infection and acquired immunodeficiency syndrome (HIV/AIDS), human 'mad cow disease' (variant Creutzfeldt–Jakob disease, CJD) and West Nile fever to name but a view. These diseases are directly or indirectly connected to wild and domestic meat and to wildlife in general. There is a huge variety of pathogens of animal origin including viruses, bacteria and parasites, all having different impacts ranging from mild to lethal. Because of the dramatic impact on the wider human population, we will focus in this chapter on those emerging zoonotic diseases which are directly linked to wild meat and which have the most serious impact on humans (mainly viral diseases). We will not focus on diseases which have had animal origins but are currently not directly linked with wild meat hunting. For example, malaria, caused by the parasite *Plasmodium falciparum*, had its likely origin in gorillas (Liu *et al.* 2010) and wild meat hunters will be particularly exposed to mosquitos that carry the malaria parasite, but there is no increased zoonotic risk by wild meat hunting to the resident human population. Similarly, we will not focus on parasites, such as helminths or bacteria, because their spillover risk is local, possibly affecting hunters and consumers (Kurpiers *et al.* 2016), but without a direct health risk for the broader society.

A total of 1,415 species of human infectious organism has been described, of which 61% are zoonotic (Taylor *et al.* 2001). Amongst all these pathogens, 175 are emerging, of which 75% are zoonotic. Whilst helminths are unlikely to cause emerging diseases, viruses and protozoa are overrepresented (Fig. 7.1). Almost all recent pandemics have a viral

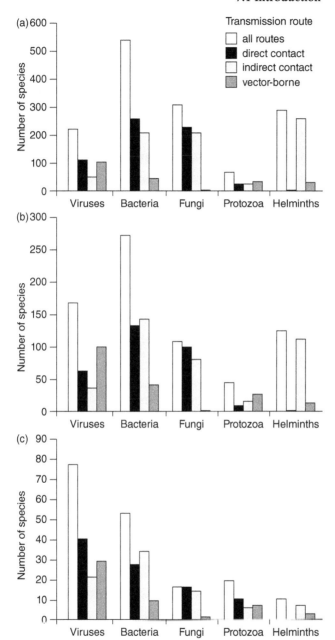

Figure 7.1 Numbers of species of infectious agent causing human disease, by taxonomic division and transmission route (noting that some species have more than one transmission route and for some the transmission route is unknown): (a) all

origin (Geoghegan *et al.* 2016; Jones *et al.* 2008). The next pandemics will likely be caused by viruses again. About 263 viruses are known to affect humans (King *et al.* 2012). In mammals and birds about 1.67 million yet-to-be-discovered viral species from key zoonotic viral families are likely to exist of which between 631,000 and 827,000 have zoonotic potential (Carroll *et al.* 2018). Currently, about one new disease is being detected per year (Cleaveland *et al.* 2007; Woolhouse 2002). Thus, the potential for the emergence of new zoonotic diseases is enormous. In fact, the total number and diversity of zoonotic outbreaks and richness of causal diseases has increased significantly since 1980 even after controlling for disease surveillance, communications, geography and host availability (Smith *et al.* 2014).

Major anthropologic transitions with changes in human socio-economic and spatial organization, especially increases in human population density and concentration, increase of human–animal contacts, increase in human mobility and increase in anthropogenic movements of live domestic and wild animals have caused three historic and the current phases of emergence of new zoonotic diseases (McMichael 2005). Some diseases which spilled over into humans during the historic transitions are re-emerging again, including measles, plague and yellow fever.

7.2 Re-emergent Zoonotic Diseases

A re-emerging pathogen is one 'whose incidence is increasing in an existing host population as a result of long-term changes in its underlying epidemiology' (Woolhouse & Dye 2001). These pathogens emerged during the first three major historical phases of emerging infectious zoonotic disease (McMichael 2005). Before the domestication of livestock about 10,000–15,000 BP, hunter-gatherer-fisher communities were too small to maintain pathogens that spilled over from wildlife, let alone sustain epidemic or pandemic spread (Dobson & Carper 1996). The first opportunity for zoonotic pathogens to spillover into humans and then to adapt to and remain in human populations arose during the transition to agriculture and livestock herding and the period of early human settlements with emerging diseases staying on a local scale some 5,000–10,000 BP. The second phase was generated by increased military

Figure 7.1 (cont.) infectious organisms ($n = 1415$); (b) zoonotic organisms ($n = 868$); (c) emerging organisms ($n = 175$). (From Taylor *et al.* 2001; adapted with permission from the Royal Society (Great Britain).)

and commercial contact around 3,000–1,500 BP, triggering continent-wide spread of diseases. The third phase is marked by European expansionism over the past five centuries resulting in intercontinental disease spread. For example, measles seem to have emerged in humans around 8,000 BP spilling over from sheep or goats when they were domesticated, but the infection chain stayed within humans ever since (Weiss 2001). Thus, the formerly zoonotic disease adapted to person-to-person transfer and became anthroponotic. Together with smallpox and other diseases, their effect on Amerindian people after colonization by Europeans was highly devastating (McNeill 1976). These diseases likely allowed Cortéz to defeat the Aztec empire. Smallpox, whose exact animal origin remains unknown (Weiss 2001), has afflicted humans at least for 3,500 years but it has now been eradicated thanks to efforts that began with Edward Jenner's pioneering vaccine prepared from cowpox in 1798 and were completed with the WHO-led programme to eliminate the disease (Fenner *et al.* 1988; Mühlemann *et al.* 2020). In contrast, measles is now re-emerging around the world (Misin *et al.* 2020).

7.2.1 Plague

The plague-causing bacillus *Yersinia pestis* is endemic among some species of rodents and is transmitted through human-to-human contact (pneumonic plague) or via fleas and lice between rodents, rodents-to-human and between humans as a common vector (bubonic or septicaemic plague). It emerged in humans at least 5,000 to 6,000 BP during the Neolithic decline in Asia and Europe followed by three major pandemics starting during the second historic disease period (Feldman *et al.* 2016; Rascovan *et al.* 2019; Rasmussen *et al.* 2015). The Justinian plague from 541 to around 750 BCE is the first detailed pandemic described in human history although mortality rates and socio-economic impact remain controversially discussed (Mordechai *et al.* 2019). Socio-economic devastation and a mortality of up to 50% during the Black Death has remained in public consciousness as the most widespread fatal pandemic in human history since it swept through Asia, the Middle East, North Africa and Europe in the 1340s (Benedictow 2004). This pandemic lasted until the eighteenth century with several recorded waves such as London's Great Plague (1665–1666 AD). The third epidemic started in the nineteenth century in China, spread around the world – over eight million people died in India between 1895 and 1914 – and is since a re-emerging infectious disease worldwide (Campbell & Hughes 1995;

WHO 2004a). Reservoir species are not only black rats, the principal species during the Black Death, but also diverse burrowing rodents such as chipmunks and woodchucks in the New World and marmots in Asia. Only in 2020, a teenage boy died of the disease in Mongolia after eating marmot hunted as wild meat (Associated Press 2020). Africa remains endemic for the pathogen with sporadic outbreaks (Davis *et al.* 2006; Forrester *et al.* 2017).

7.2.2 Yellow Fever

Mosquito-borne yellow fever, caused by the yellow fever virus, arose in Africa during the last 1,500 years and became to prominence after it invaded the Americas from Africa via the slave trade in the seventeenth century (Bryant *et al.* 2007). Its natural reservoir is monkeys in Africa, but yellow fever established itself successfully in New World monkeys (Weiss 2001). Although largely under-researched and categorized as a neglected tropical disease, recent outbreaks in Angola in 2015–2016 and in Brazil in 2016–2017 have highlighted the threat posed by this zoonotic disease (Butler 2016; Grobbelaar *et al.* 2016; Kleinert *et al.* 2019). The zoonotic threat to hunters is not via consuming wild meat but being exposed to mosquitos whilst hunting.

7.3 Pandemic Zoonotic Emerging Infectious Diseases

An emergent disease is an 'infectious disease whose incidence is increasing following its first introduction into a new host population' (Woolhouse & Dye 2001). During the last quarter century, we have witnessed not only the resurgence of infectious disease but the emergence of novel or newly identified diseases. Rapidly increasing human population densities, social-economic and behavioural changes, the globalized economy, increased mobility, the ever increasing encroaching in and modification of the natural environment and ecological changes have triggered a fourth great transition phase which fosters the emergence of infectious disease (McMichael 2005). Whilst the first three periods were local, continental and intercontinental, this time the impact is global as the rapid pandemic spread of COVID-19 or the 2009 H1N1 swine-flu clearly demonstrate. Importantly, we encroach more and more on the last remaining pristine wilderness areas thereby destabilizing ecosystems, changing the population dynamics of animal reservoirs for pathogens and increasing human-pathogen contacts. These changes are particularly well demonstrated by COVID-19, HIV/AIDS, Ebola and SARS, which all have direct connections to wild meat exploitation and animal trade (see Loh *et al.* 2015). After the original zoonotic transmission, all four diseases became anthroponotic and pandemic. A pandemic is 'an epidemic occurring over a very wide geographic area, crossing international boundaries, and usually affecting a large number of people. The agent must be able to infect humans, to cause disease in humans, and to spread easily from human to human' (Porta *et al.* 2014).

7.3.1 COVID-19

The coronaviruses SARS-CoV-2, SARS-CoV and MERS-CoV cause severe infections: COVID-19, the Severe Acute Respiratory Syndrome (SARS) and the Middle East respiratory syndrome (MERS), respectively. SARS-CoV-2, first termed 2019-nCoV, is the causative agent of COVID-19 and the seventh known coronavirus affecting humans. Except the above three, the other known coronaviruses affecting humans cause mild infections (Van der Hoek 2007). All have animal origins with SARS-CoV-2, SARS-CoV, MERS-CoV, HCoV-NL63 and HCoV-229E likely originating from bats and HCoV-OC43 and HCoV-HKU1 from rodents (Cui *et al.* 2019). MERS-CoV and HCoV-229E have camelids, HCoV-OC43 cattle and SARS-CoV civets as intermediate hosts whilst intermediate hosts for HCoV-NL63, HCoV-HKU1 and SARS-CoV-2 are unconfirmed (Fig. 7.2). Since the spillover into humans, SARS-CoV-2 has been transmitted human-to-human. Genetic and epidemiological analysis have shown that the virus is not a laboratory construct or a purposefully manipulated virus, thus debunking the conspiratory hypothesis expressed by many that the virus is of artificial origin (Andersen *et al.* 2020; Pekar *et al.* 2022; Worobey *et al.* 2022). SARS-CoV-2 and coronaviruses discovered in bats are genetically very similar, making it likely that SARS-CoV-2 or its progenitor evolved in horseshoe bats with other mammals as a plausible conduit for transmission to humans (Boni *et al.* 2020; Zhou *et al.* 2020). After the emergence of SARS-CoV and MERS-CoV in the early twenty-first century, Afelt *et al.* (2018a) predicted a new coronavirus to spillover from bats in Southeast Asia. The region is the world's most affected region of deforestation. The human demographic growth – the human population in the region increased by 130 million between 2001 and 2011 – causes strong pressures on the land, increases demand on domestic and wild meat and is an ideal environment to sustain an epidemic once a zoonotic pathogen spilled over into humans. Afelt *et al.* (2018a) also observed that

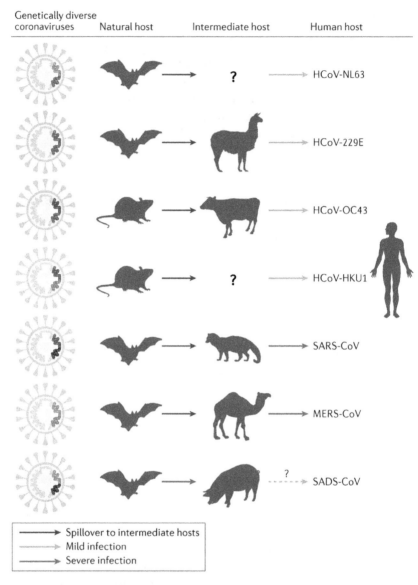

Figure 7.2 Animal origins of human coronaviruses prior the emergence of SARS-CoV-2 (From Cui *et al.* 2019; reprinted with permission from Springer Nature.)

the land-use changes triggered bat populations to move closer to human dwellings, in turn increasing the number and diversity of bat-borne viruses next to human dwellings and thus zoonotic risk (Afelt *et al.* 2018b;

Plowright *et al.* 2015). Whilst intermediate animal hosts for SARS-CoV-2 remain unknown, the virus can infect some other wildlife such as monkeys, rabbits and racoon dogs, and some domestic animals, such as cats, dogs, farmed American mink, ferrets and hamsters, but not pigs, chickens or ducks (El Masry *et al.* 2020; Shi *et al.* 2020). While experimentally infected cats, ferrets and hamsters infected other animals of the same species, dogs did not transmit the virus to other dogs in experimental settings (El Masry *et al.* 2020).

Since early December 2019, patients presenting with viral pneumonia due to an unidentified microbial agent were reported in Wuhan, China. Most patients worked at or lived around the local Huanan seafood wholesale market, where live animals were also on sale. The agent was subsequently identified as SARS-CoV-2 (Chen *et al.* 2020). Although COVID-19 was first detected officially at this market, epidemiological data indicate that early cases were not related to the market and thus that it may not necessarily be the site of emergence (Frutos *et al.* 2020). In November 2000, the WHO announced a Global Study of the origins of SARS-CoV-2 with field work to commence in China in early 2021. This study emphasizes that the origin of the virus and the spillover event remains unknown: 'some countries have retrospectively identified cases of COVID-19 weeks before the first case was officially notified through surveillance, and unpublished reports of positive sewage samples could suggest that the virus may have circulated undetected for some time'" (WHO 2020). The market might have acted as an amplification chamber for the human-to-human spread. The COVID-19 pandemic had caused 101,562,751 cases with 2,193,403 deaths worldwide as of 29 January 2021 and 456,956,790 cases with 6,042,210 deaths as of 13 March 2022 (https://coronavirus.jhu.edu).

7.3.2 HIV/AIDS

The first documented human HIV-1 infection dates from 1959 in Kinshasa (Worobey *et al.* 2008) and the AIDS was first recognized as a disease in 1981 (Barré-Sinoussi *et al.* 1983). All the genetic evidence indicates that the human immunodeficiency virus type 1 (HIV-1) and the related type 2 (HIV-2) evolved after zoonotic transmission from non-human primates, specifically chimpanzee for HIV-1 and sooty mangabey for HIV-2, in West-Central Africa (Gao *et al.* 1999; Van Heuverswyn & Peeters 2007). To account for the HIV's genetic diversity (Fig. 7.3), at least 12 zoonotic transmission events must have occurred, four to

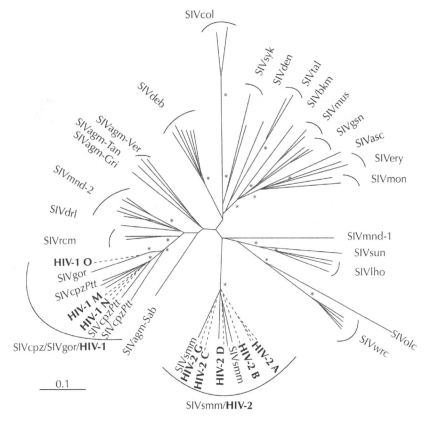

Figure 7.3 Evolutionary relationship among the different SIV and HIV lineages based on neighbour joining phylogenetic analysis of partial *pol* sequences. This phylogeny represents 26 of the 32 infected nonhuman primate species, for whom (partial) sequences are available. Asterisks indicate bootstrap replicates supporting the cluster to the right with values >85%. Within the branches with HIV sequences are sequences from gorilla (SIVgor), chimpanzee (SIVcpzPtt) and Sooty mangabey (SIVsmm). (From Van Heuverswyn and Peeters 2007; reprinted with permission from Springer Nature.)

account for the diversity of HIV-1 (Plantier *et al.* 2009) and eight to account for the diversity of HIV-2 (Van Heuverswyn & Peeters 2007). HIV's genetic diversity indicates that the zoonotic transmission of simian immunodeficiency viruses, (SIV), which then evolved into the respective HIV strains, is an ongoing, dynamic process and that new zoonotic transfers are real possibilities. A serological study of monkeys that were hunted in the rainforests of Cameroon for wild meat or kept as pets showed that a substantial proportion are SIV infected, thus exposing people to a plethora of genetically highly divergent SIV viruses (Peeters *et al.* 2002). Although the exact circumstances of the zoonotic transmissions of SIV remain unknown, hunting and butchering of primate wild meat is the most parsimonious explanation (Hahn 2000; Van Heuverswyn & Peeters 2007). Wild meat hunters in Central Africa continue to be exposed to and possibly infected with SIV (Kalish *et al.* 2005). Molecular clocks indicate that HIV-1 originated sometime near the beginning of the twentieth century (Worobey *et al.* 2008). This time frame corresponds with a period of the founding and rapid growth of colonial administrative and trading centres in West-Central Africa which might have facilitated the spread of the viruses in the human population, which eventually led to the global AIDS pandemic. The most dramatic effect is among the world's poorest and most underprivileged communities, in which life expectancy has dropped by 20 years on average (Weiss 2003). By the year 2020, it is estimated that between 55.9 and 100 million people have become infected with HIV and that between 24.8 and 42.2 million people have died from AIDS-related illnesses since the start of the pandemic (UNAIDS 2020).

7.3.3 Ebola

Six species of ebolavirus have been identified in West and Central Africa: Bombali virus, Bundibugyo ebolavirus, Reston ebolavirus, Sudan ebolavirus, Taï Forest ebolavirus and Zaire ebolavirus (Ebola virus) of which Bombali virus is the latest to be discovered (Goldstein *et al.* 2018). Note that the term 'Ebolavirus' can refer to the genus, when written in italics, and to the common name of the Zaire ebolavirus, if not written in italics. Only Bundibugyo ebolavirus, Sudan ebolavirus, and Ebola virus have caused disease outbreaks of severe haemorrhagic fever in humans with overall case fatality of 25%, 50% and 80%, respectively (Malvy *et al.* 2019). Outbreaks of Ebola virus disease (EVD) have been recorded since 1976 when two consecutive outbreaks of fatal haemorrhagic fever occurred, first in the former Zaire in what is now the Democratic Republic of Congo, caused by the Ebola virus, and second in what is now South Sudan, caused by the Sudan ebolavirus (Fig. 7.4, Centers for Disease Control and Prevention 2020). Since then, an additional 26 outbreaks have been registered mostly caused by the Ebola virus. However, at least half of EVD spillover events were likely not being reported (Glennon *et al.* 2019). Fatalities ranged from zero in Ivory Coast in 1994, caused by the Taï Forest ebolavirus, up to 11,325 for the most

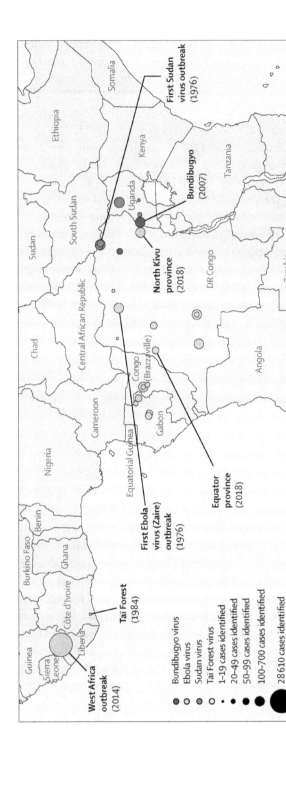

Figure 7.4 Outbreaks of Ebola disease in sub-Saharan Africa. (From Malvy *et al.* 2019; reprinted with permission from Elsevier.)

Figure 7.5 Ebola virus transmission. Fruit bats are considered natural reservoirs of Ebolaviruses EBOVs and these seem to infect non-human primates and duikers, which mostly constitute the spillover event. The virus disseminates from person to person, potentially affecting a large number of people. The virus spreads through direct contact with broken skin or mucous membranes in the eyes, nose, or mouth and semen. However, Ebolaviruses may spread through the handling and consumption of wild meat. (From Rojas *et al.* 2020; reprinted with permission from Elsevier.)

severe outbreak across multiple countries in West Africa from 2014 to 2016, caused by the Ebola virus. The number of deaths recorded in the 2016 outbreak was 11,310 in the three most affected countries, Guinea, Liberia and Sierra Leone (WHO 2016a). This EVD outbreak was the largest amongst all outbreaks with almost ten times more fatalities than all previous outbreaks combined. In addition to West Africa, imported cases were reported from the seven countries (Italy, Mali, Nigeria, Senegal, Spain, UK and USA (WHO 2016b)). Ebola virus disease is also a rapidly fatal disease for non-human primates, for example killing 90–95% of the gorilla population at the Lossi Sanctuary in northwest Republic of Congo during a 2002–2003 outbreak (Bermejo *et al.* 2006; Walsh *et al.* 2003).

Wild meat has been implicated as a source of zoonotic spillover (Fig. 7.5, Rojas *et al.* 2020). All five human EVD outbreaks during 2001–2003 in the forest zone between Gabon and Republic of Congo began after humans handled the carcasses of gorillas, chimpanzees, and duikers (Rouquet *et al.* 2005). In each case, mortality events in these species, which are also susceptible to Ebolavirus, began before each of the human outbreaks. These animal populations declined markedly during human EVD outbreaks. The first human victim of an EVD outbreak in the Democratic Republic of Congo in 2007 died after purchasing freshly killed fruit bats in a market (Leroy *et al.* 2009; Mann *et al.* 2015). Circumstantial evidence points to the source of the West African 2014–2016 outbreak to contact with secretions from wild fruit bats (Mann *et al.* 2015). Whilst all these species can harbour Ebola viruses the natural reservoirs of this virus remain unknown but is likely to be found amongst bats (Malvy *et al.* 2019; Spengler *et al.* 2016).

7.3.4 SARS

SARS was first recognized at the end of February 2003 in Hanoi, Vietnam involving a patient who had extensively travelled in Southeast Asia (WHO 2003). In the same year, SARS spread to more than 30 countries across five continents (Guan *et al.* 2003). The coronavirus SARS-CoV was identified as the causative agent (Drosten *et al.* 2003). This virus was much more pathogenic than the human coronaviruses (HCoV) known until then, which mainly cause mild respiratory disease (Section 7.3.1). The virus was traced back to a live-animal market in Guangdong, Southwest China, where it appears to have jumped from traded Himalayan palm civets that tested positive for a virus highly similar (99.8%) to SARS-CoV. Evidence of virus infection was also detected in other animals including a raccoon dog and Chinese ferret badger and in humans working at the same market (Guan *et al.* 2003). Furthermore, 40% of animal traders and 20% of animal slaughterers had detectable serum antibodies, compared to only 5% of vegetable traders. Subsequently, genetically diversified CoVs related to SARS-CoV were then found in diverse Chinese bat families albeit the reservoir population of bats for SARS has not been definitively identified (Drexler *et al.* 2014; Lau *et al.* 2005; Li 2005). The likely infection scenario is that bats infected civets as intermediate and amplifying hosts, which then triggered the zoonotic spillover (Guan *et al.* 2003; Song *et al.* 2005). The 2003–2004 pandemic infected 8,096 people worldwide and killed 774 (9.5%) of them (Drexler *et al.* 2014).

7.4 Other Zoonotic Infectious Diseases

A number of zoonotic diseases are emerging but have not become pandemic or are endemic (see Jones *et al.* 2008; Loh *et al.* 2015). These include viruses, bacteria, helminths, protozoans, fungi and prions (Kurpiers *et al.* 2016). The list of pathogens is so large that we restrict us here to some important and representative examples.

7.4.1 Anthrax

Anthrax is one of the oldest known zoonotic diseases, caused by the spore-forming bacterium *Bacillus anthracis*, which infects ruminants worldwide (De Vos & Bryden 1996; Dragon *et al.* 1996; Lindeque & Turnbull 1994).Through direct contact, inhaling spores or by consuming meat from infected animals other species can be infected, including humans and primates (Leendertz *et al.* 2004; Sirisanthana & Brown 2002). Use of contaminated carcasses and hides, which is a widespread practice amongst wild meat hunters, is the principle zoonotic risk (Beatty *et al.* 2003; Hang'ombe *et al.* 2012).

7.4.2 Hepatitis Viruses

Hepatitis E virus (HEV), transmission from wild boar meat to a human was reported in Japan confirming its zoonotic potential (Li *et al.* 2005). Hepatitis E virus prevalence in Japanese wild boar and deer was 9% and 2%, respectively (Sonoda *et al.* 2004). Non-human primates harbour a range of hepatitis viruses, some of them closely related to human hepatitis B and C, HBV and HCV, respectively, but the zoonotic origin of human hepatitis viruses remains unclear (Simmonds 2000). Hepatitis B-related viruses are also found in a range of other species, including rodents and birds (Marion *et al.* 1980; Mason *et al.* 1980). Whilst HBV can be transmitted to non-human primates, there is no evidence of zoonotic transmission of the diverse primate hepatitis viruses even for zookeepers who are in close contact with primates (Noppornpanth *et al.* 2003). However, given the zoonotic transmission of HEV and the intensive contact of wild meat hunters with animal body fluid there is a clear existent zoonotic risk.

7.4.3 Lassa Virus

Lassa fever is endemic to West Africa and causes in approx. 30% of cases illness ranging from mild, flu-like symptoms to haemorrhagic fever with a mortality rate of 1–2%, but occasionally of 50% (McCormick *et al.* 1987; ter Meulen *et al.* 1996). It has been known since the 1950s (Richmond & Baglole 2003). The only known natural host is the multimammate mouse, a hunted rodent that associates closely with humans and is commonly found in and around African villages (Lecompte *et al.* 2006). Three risk factors affect Lassa virus transmission: rodent infestation, uncovered storage of food and hunting the mouse for wild meat (ter Meulen *et al.* 1996).

7.4.4 Marburg Virus

The virus constitutes with *Ebolavirus* the family Filoviridae with insectivorous bat species as natural reservoirs (Allocati *et al.* 2016; Leendertz *et al.* 2016). It causes severe, often fatal, haemorrhagic fever in humans and primates. Marburg virus (MARV), is transmitted to humans through contact with body fluids and dead bodies of infected animals. Marburg virus was first identified in laboratory workers who had dissected an imported African green monkey (Martini *et al.* 1968). The reservoir host is the Egyptian fruit bat with antibodies and viral DNA also found in other insectivorous and fruit bats (Amman *et al.* 2012; Swanepoel *et al.* 2007). Egyptian fruit bats are hunted in West Africa for wild meat (Mickleburgh *et al.* 2009). Marburg virus is a prime example demonstrating that attempts to control the disease by persecuting the host species can fail (Amman *et al.* 2014): after MARV infected gold miners in southwest Uganda at the Kitaka mine, the miners exterminated the bat colony. However, the bat colony re-established itself albeit at lower total size. The re-established colony had a significantly higher level of active infection than before the eradication and other studies in Uganda and Gabon have yielded similar results. Such failures are not without precedent. For example, badger culling in the UK to control bovine tuberculosis (TB) not only failed to control but also seems to increase TB incidence in cattle (Donnelly *et al.* 2003).

7.4.5 Mayaro Virus

Mayaro fever is a non-fatal dengue-like acute viral disease of tropical rainforest in Central and South America and the Caribbean, first detected in the 1950s (Anderson *et al.* 1957). The mosquito-borne virus is suspected to have monkeys as the principal reservoir (Pinheiro & Travassos da Rosa 1994). However, this illness being largely neglected, there is inadequate surveillance in endemic areas and limited epidemiological data available (Mota *et al.* 2015). People who are frequently within forest environments, such as wild meat hunters, are at a higher risk of being bitten by numerous mosquito species that can carry the virus. A study in Ecuador showed that mainly Amazonians are infected by the virus, indicating that deep forest hunting may selectively expose local men to zoonotic spillover (Izurieta *et al.* 2011).

7.4.6 Monkeypox Virus

Monkeypox is an emerging zoonotic disease with clinical symptoms of fever and a severe rash similar to smallpox (Parker *et al.* 2007; Sklenovská

& Van Ranst 2018). Mortality rates can be as high as 17%, but a vaccine exists (Di Giulio & Eckburg 2004). It is endemic in the Democratic Republic of Congo, but human and animal cases have also been reported from elsewhere in Central and West Africa (Rimoin *et al.* 2010). The disease was imported once into the USA (Hutson *et al.* 2007). Frequency and geographical spread of human monkeypox have increased in recent years (Rimoin *et al.* 2010), but the epidemiology and ecology remain understudied (Sklenovská & Van Ranst 2018). Transmission likely occurs by direct contact with infected animals or their bodily fluids (Jezek *et al.* 1986). The virus was first isolated in primates (Arita & Henderson 1968), but the main host appears to be wild squirrels (Hutin *et al.* 2001; Parker *et al.* 2007). It has been isolated from diverse rodents, including imported and domestic rodents during a US monkeypox outbreak (Hutson *et al.* 2007). The virus's broad host range may permit additional species to become reservoirs or incidental hosts, increasing the zoonotic risk (Parker *et al.* 2007). Human-to-human transmission occurs but the disease requires continuous reintroduction from the wild reservoir to be maintained in a human population (Hutin *et al.* 2001; Jezek *et al.* 1986).

7.4.7 Nipah Virus

The paramyxovirus causes encephalitis and respiratory disease (Chua *et al.* 2000). It spilled over in 1998 from fruit bats first to pig livestock and then from pigs to farm workers in Malaysia causing 265 cases of encephalitis, including 105 deaths (Chua *et al.* 2000). Since, it has spread in Southeast Asia, especially to Bangladesh where spillover events now occur regularly (Gurley *et al.* 2017). Nipah is a prime example of how habitat change can cause spillover events. Deforestation and climate change are likely drivers for these events (Chua *et al.* 2002). Following decades of deforestation combined with a severe drought following an El Niño Southern Oscillation event, Pteropid fruit bats, which are the natural reservoir of the virus, compensated for the loss of flowering and fruiting forest trees by an unprecedented encroachment into cultivated fruit orchards. These orchards also house ever increasing piggeries, allowing the transmission from fruit bats to pig livestock (Chua *et al.* 2002; Field 2009). In Bangladesh, areas with reported Nipah outbreaks are characterized by higher human density and forest fragmentation than areas without outbreaks (Epstein *et al.* 2014). Although the outbreak did not involve wild meat hunters in this case, these are likewise at risk as fruit bats are regularly hunted across Africa and Asia (Mickleburgh *et al.* 2009).

Moreover, antibodies and henipavirus-related RNA, that is RNA from the same virus genus as Nipah, has been identified in straw-coloured fruit bat, the largest and most abundant African fruit bat species, in Ghana and in a wild meat market in the Republic of Congo (Drexler et al. 2009; Hayman et al. 2011; Weiss et al. 2012). In Africa, no human infection associated with bat henipavirus has been reported but continuing monitoring is advised to diminish the threat of a novel zoonotic disease especially as Nipavirus is associated with high mortality rates.

7.4.8 Simian Foamy Virus

Although there is no disease reported in humans (Switzer et al. 2004), Simian foamy virus,(SFV), infections are an increasing public health concern (Calattini et al. 2007). Simian foamy virus is endemic in most African primates (Peeters & Delaporte 2012; Switzer et al. 2005; Wolfe et al. 2004). It is transmitted by intensive contact between non-human primates and hunters (Calattini et al. 2007; Wolfe et al. 1998, 2004), zookeepers, veterinarians and scientists (Switzer et al. 2004) and people living near macaques in Asia (Jones-Engel et al. 2005, 2008). In southern Cameroon, less than 0.4% of the general population was seropositive to SFV, but 24% of those people who had contact with great apes (gorillas or chimpanzees) and 3.6% of those who had contact with monkeys, highlighting the zoonotic potential of SFV (Calattini et al. 2007). A serological survey of 1,099 rural Cameroonian villagers that had contact with primates identified that 1% had antibodies to SFV (Wolfe et al. 2004), suggesting a constant exposure to animal reservoirs (Pike et al. 2010). Simian foamy virus is one of the pathogens that were diagnosed in confiscated primates at US airports, highlighting the global zoonotic risk posed by the illegal wild animal trade (Smith et al. 2012).

7.4.9 T-lymphotropic Viruses

Two lineages of human T-lymphotropic viruses, HTLV-1 and HTLV-2, are anthroponotic transmitted via body fluids and can cause adult T-cell lymphoma or one of several inflammatory disorders (Proietti et al. 2005). Wild meat hunters and primate pet owners in Central Africa are infected not only with HTLVs including the newly discovered HTLV-3 and

HTLV-4 lineages, but also with a wide variety of simian T-lymphotropic viruses (STLVs) of non-human primates (Wolfe *et al.* 2005b). The lineage HTLV-3 falls into the phylogenetic clade of STLV-3, supporting the suspected multiple zoonotic origin of the different HTLV lineages (LeBreton *et al.* 2012; Wolfe *et al.* 2005b). Prevalence of HTLV-1 in Pygmy hunter-gatherers was higher than amongst non-hunting villagers in Cameroon (Ndumbe *et al.* 1992), confirming the observation that HTLVs are more prevalent in populations which are exposed to wild primates (Delaporte *et al.* 1989).

7.4.10 Tularaemia

Described in the 1910s, the tularaemia-causing bacterium *Francisella tularensis* has been reported in a range of vertebrates including mammals – in particular rodents and especially rabbits and hares – birds, amphibians and fish, and in invertebrates across the northern hemisphere (Ellis *et al.* 2002; Yeatter & Thompson 1952). A wide range of arthropod vectors have been implicated in the transmission between mammalian hosts. Infection can occur by handling animal skins or carcasses and less frequently from tick or deer fly bites; it is also possible to acquire the disease from drinking water contaminated with animal faeces and urine, or by eating undercooked contaminated meat (Higgins *et al.* 2000). Rural people, especially hunters but also farmers, walkers and forest workers, are most at risk of contracting tularaemia. Therefore, it is also variously known as rabbit fever, hare fever and deerfly fever. A study in a suspected endemic region of Germany showed a seroprevalence among hunters (1.7%) that was higher than in the general population (0.2%) (Jenzora *et al.* 2008). Outbreaks of disease in humans often parallel disease occurrences in wildlife as seen in Sweden where an association between peaks in vole and hare populations and outbreaks of tularaemia in humans have been reported (Tärnvik *et al.* 1996).

7.4.11 Others

Besides the above-listed diseases, many more pathogens with zoonotic risk are found in species used as wild meat. For example an unknown proportion of the about 25,000 yearly fatalities from rabies in Africa, caused by a lyssavirus, might be via wild meat species although the majority of cases stems from domestic dogs (Dodet *et al.* 2015; Kurpiers *et al.* 2016). Rabies also occurs in a variety of species other than canids, including primates that are hunted as wild meat (Gautret *et al.* 2014) and bats (Kuzmin *et al.* 2011). Many other lyssaviruses exist including Duvenhage virus, which causes fatal encephalitis and is transmitted by bats (Allocati *et al.* 2016; van Thiel *et al.* 2009).

In addition to the already mentioned, *B. anthracis* and *F. tularensis*, a large variety of bacteria can affect wild meat species and can be transmitted to humans. Bacteria constitute 54% of emerging infectious diseases (Jones *et al.* 2008). Bachand *et al.* (2012) confirmed the intestinal-infection causing *Campylobacter*, *Salmonella* and *Shigella* at low frequencies from wild meat carcasses in two markets in Gabon, emphasizing the potential transmission risk although the overall risk is low. Transmission of bacteria can occur through direct exposure to faeces or bodily fluids, to which hunters are exposed, or indirectly via fleas and ticks as in the case of *F. tularensis* or for ticks collected from duikers and a pangolin that harboured the bacterium *Rickettsia africae*, which causes African tick-bite fever, and, thus, pose a zoonotic risk (Mediannikov *et al.* 2012). Another example of bacterial infection is *Mycobacterium ulcerans* that is transmitted from plants to grasscutters (greater cane rats) and then to people who hunt and use them as wild meat, causing Buruli ulcer in the skin and subcutaneous tissues (Hammoudi *et al.* 2020). The disease is endemic especially in West Africa, but the impact is much more small-scale compared to the above introduced viral emerging zoonoses as it is noncontagious.

Spillover of many helminth species is likely (Kurpiers *et al.* 2016). For example, very high prevalence rates of helminth ova were found in greater cane rats and bush duikers from wild meat markets in Nigeria (Adejinmi & Emikpe 2011). Because humans and non–human primates share susceptibility to many parasitic helminth species (Pedersen *et al.* 2005), it is highly relevant that high loads of gastrointestinal parasites were present in the monkey species traded in a wild meat market in Cameroon (Pourrut *et al.* 2011). A similar risk as helminths is posed by protozoans, for example the diarrheal disease-causing Amoebozoa which have been confirmed in wild meat species (Pourrut *et al.* 2011). No transmissions of fungi and prions have been documented, but these constitute potential zoonotic risk nevertheless (Kurpiers *et al.* 2016). It has not only been difficult to find undisputable evidence to demonstrate the zoonotic transmission of specific pathogens from specific host species, but the exact risk and the frequency of transmission to wild meat hunters remains unknown for many pathogens.

7.5 Risk Factors for Zoonotic Disease Emergence

7.5.1 Hosts

In terms of numbers of pathogens, rodents, followed by bats are the most abundant and most species-rich mammal order (Fig. 7.6, Han *et al.* 2016). They also include a greater number of zoonotic hosts than any other order, carrying 85 known zoonotic diseases. However, zoonotic viruses are most abundant in domesticated species, primates and bats (Johnson *et al.* 2020). The relative risk of disease emergence is highest for bats, followed by primates and then ungulates and rodents (Cleaveland *et al.* 2007). More than 200 viruses are harboured in bats, many of them causing zoonotic disease (Allocati *et al.* 2016). For example, coronaviruses including SARS-CoV, SARS-CoV-2 and MERS-CoV likely originated in bats, but dromedary camels are intermediate hosts, a current natural reservoir and potential source for zoonotic transmission of MERS-CoV. Because bats host many coronaviruses, which represent 31% of their virome (Chen *et al.* 2014), and because they are remarkably resistant to viruses (Storm *et al.* 2018), the risk of emergence of a novel bat-CoV disease is high (Afelt *et al.* 2018a). Bats are widely hunted in Africa and Asia (Kamins *et al.* 2014; Mickleburgh *et al.* 2009; Mildenstein *et al.* 2016).

7.5.2 Wild Meat Hunting and Trade

In the early stages of the COVID-19 pandemic, China banned wildlife trade and consumption of wild meat through the 16th meeting of the Standing Committee of the 13th National People's Congress, on 'Comprehensively Prohibiting the Illegal Trade of Wild Animals, Eliminating the Bad Habits of Wild Animal Consumption, and Protecting the Health and Safety of the People' of 24 February 2020. The Wildlife Conservation Society hailed the decision 'for not only solving the COVID-19 outbreak but in preventing future risks through legislative reform and improved enforcement and management' (WCS 2020). On 25 February 2020, one of the first international actions to address the danger of zoonotic disease in the wake of the COVID-19 pandemic was the demand to close wildlife markets as outlined in an open letter to the World Health Organization, the UN Environment Programme and the Office International Epizoologie (Born Free Foundation 2020). The letter, undersigned by 236 international organizations and individuals, emphasizes the increasing risks to global human and animal health and the animal welfare problems. Whilst the open

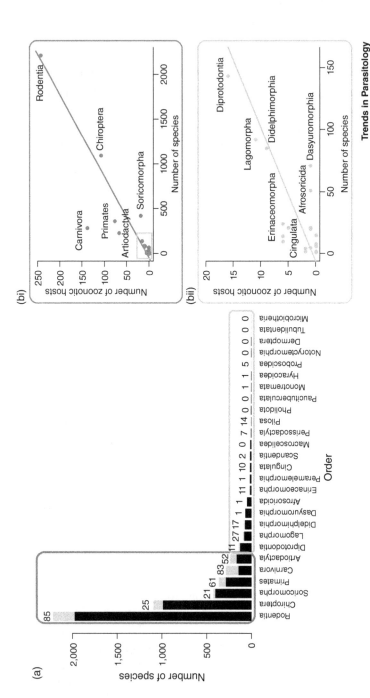

Figure 7.6 The number of zoonotic hosts increases with total species richness of the order. (a) This split bar plot shows the total number of host species (black plus grey) and the fraction of species that are confirmed zoonotic hosts for one or more zoonotic diseases (grey). The number above each bar represents a tally of the total unique zoonoses per order. Mammal orders are arranged in descending order of species richness. (b) The number of zoonotic host species in each order is represented by scatterplots. (i) The most-speciose orders being are shown in the upper chart (regression $R^2 = 0.81$); (ii) all other orders in lower chart (regression $R^2 = 0.63$). (From Han *et al.* (2016). Adapted with permission from Elsevier.

letter's primary demand is to close wildlife markets and to ban trade of live wild animals in order to protect human health, it implicitly extends to 'products derived from them', thus wild meat in general since wildlife markets primarily rely on animals taken from the wild but with slaughtering taking place at the market or the buyer's place rather than in the wild. Wild meat hunting and wildlife trade are two sides of the same coin. Indeed, subsequent bans on trade of wildlife included life wild animals and any products derived from them, for example, in Vietnam (Ratcliffe 2020).

Although the exact pathways of the zoonotic emergence remain unsolved, the 2003 SARS and, possibly, the 2019/20 COVID-19 coronavirus outbreaks demonstrate the wildlife trade's zoonotic disease risk. Especially when markets sell live animals, the so-called 'wet' markets, the combination of high wildlife volumes, taxonomic diversity, crammed and stressful conditions for the captive wildlife, taxa with high risk for zoonoses, poor biosafety and close contact between wildlife, domestic animals and humans contribute to a high potential for pathogen transmission. Often, live wild animals and domestic animals are housed alongside each other, with domestic animals also implicated in the transmission of zoonotic disease such as the avian influenza A H7N9 virus (Li et al. 2014; Yu et al. 2014). Turnover of live and dead animals is enormous. For example, after the outbreak of SARS in November 2002 more than 800,000 endangered animals were confiscated from the markets in China's southern province of Guangdong, where SARS originated, up to April 2003 (BBC 2003). During 25 weekends of the Bangkok Weekend Market approx. 70,000 birds of 276 species and approx. 3,500 native animals of at least 24 species were sold (Round 1990). Numbers of wild meat outlets, that is markets, restaurants, butchers and street vendors, in the Kinshasa–Brazzaville metropolitan area are estimated at 366 wild meat outlets per 100,000 inhabitants in Brazzaville and just over 700 per 100,000 inhabitants in Kinshasa (Fa et al. 2019). Only the trade in narcotics exceeds illegal wildlife trade in volume in the worldwide black market (Toledo et al. 2012).

These conditions in wet markets create perfect storms for pathogen cross-species and zoonotic transmission. Taxa sold as wild meat in restaurants, roadside stalls and markets in Malaysia potentially contain 51 zoonotic pathogens (16 viruses, 19 bacteria and 16 parasites), highlighting the extent of the problem (Fig. 7.7, Cantlay et al. 2017). All samples from illegally imported African wild meat confiscated at Paris Charles de Gaulle airport

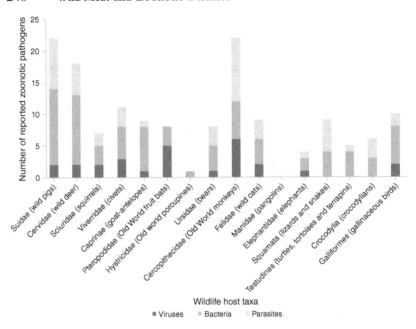

Figure 7.7 Total numbers of viral, bacterial and parasitic pathogens reported in traded wildlife taxa in Malaysia. (From Cantlay *et al.* 2017; adapted with permission from EcoHealth Alliance.)

had viable counts of bacteria above levels considered safe for human consumption including the pathogens *Staphylococcus aureus* and *Listeria monocytogenes* which are associated with food-borne illnesses (Chaber & Cunningham 2016). Trade of West African rodents to the USA triggered a local outbreak of monkeypox in prairie dogs and eventually zoonotic transmission to humans (Reed *et al.* 2004). The potential effect of trading activities along the market chain is demonstrated by a study on the prevalence of SARS-CoV in civets, the likely intermediate host responsible for the initial zoonotic SARS-CoV spillover. Whilst civets on farms were largely free from SARS-CoV infection, the prevalence in one animal market in China's Guangzhou was approx. 80% (Tu *et al.* 2004). Another study demonstrated that the transmission risk increases along wildlife supply chains for human consumption in Vietnam (Huong *et al.* 2020): for field rats, the odds of coronavirus RNA detection significantly increased along the supply chain from animals sold by traders by a factor of 2.2 for animals sold in large markets and by a factor of 10.0 for animals sold and served in restaurants.

The opportunities for zoonotic spillover have increased in parallel with the increase in the intensity and extent of wild meat trade over the last decades (Karesh & Noble 2009). Encroaching of remaining intact forests by road building, forestry and mining have made vast new areas accessible for wild meat hunting, thus increasing the zoonotic risk by not only bringing humans in contact with hitherto undisturbed host and pathogen populations, but also by increased wild meat hunting. For example, Poulsen et al. (2009) monitored the supply and household consumption of wild meat in a logging concession in the Congo Basin and observed a 69% increase in the population of logging towns and a 64% increase in wild meat supply. It is not only the increasing human population density in the logging areas, but also the increase of disposable incomes and few other dietary options which drives demand for wild meat in logging camps (Auzel & Wilkie 2000). Commercial logging has encouraged subsistence hunters to engage in or contribute to hunting as a commercial enterprise (Walsh et al. 2003). Armed conflicts also contributed to the scaling up of wild meat extraction. For example, the sales of protected species in urban markets in the Congo Basin increased five-fold in wartime (De Merode & Cowlishaw 2006).

Wild meat hunting certainly carries a high zoonotic risk, whether it is the hunting activity in the forest such as in the case of Mayaro virus and tularaemia, the butchering of infected animals, such as in the case of zoonotic emergence of HIV via spillover of SIV to humans, or whether by capture of wild animals who then enter the live animal markets, such as likely in the case of SARS and COVID-19. A pre-COVID-19 review of transmission pathways for emerging zoonoses from 1940 onwards identified only four cases where wild meat was likely the causative agent for the spillover: Monkeypox virus, SARS, Sudan Ebola virus and Zaire Ebola virus (Loh et al. 2015). This places wild meat only in ninth place, which is shared with the breakdown of public health services, of 11 primary drivers of zoonotic disease events (Loh et al. 2015). Figure 7.8 shows the geographic distribution of zoonotic diseases and the underpinning drivers (Keesing et al. 2010).

The report by UNEP and the International Livestock Research Institute (2020) on preventing the next pandemic lists seven human-mediated factors as the most likely driving the emergence of zoonotic diseases:

- increasing human demand for animal protein;
- unsustainable agricultural intensification;
- increased use and exploitation of wildlife;

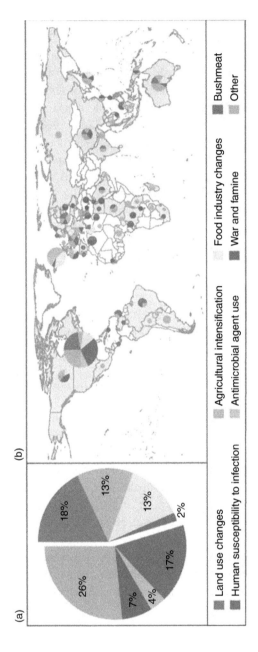

Figure 7.8 Drivers and locations of emergence events for zoonotic infectious diseases in humans from 1940 to 2005. (a) Worldwide percentage of emergence events caused by each driver. (b) Countries in which the emergence events took place, and the drivers of emergence. (From Keesing *et al.* 2010; reprinted with permission from Nature Springer.)

- unsustainable utilization of natural resources accelerated by urbanization, land use change and extractive industries;
- increased travel and transportation;
- changes in food supply; and
- climate change.

Wild meat features in the factor 'increasing human demand for animal protein' as intensified forestry and mining causes increased demand for wild meat. It also features in 'increased use and exploitation of wildlife alongside recreational hunting and consumption of wildlife as a status symbol, trade in live animals for recreational use (pets, zoos) and for research and medical testing, and use of animal parts for decorative, medicinal and other commercial products. Nevertheless, the majority of these factors are not related to wild meat, whether dead or alive.

7.5.3 Environmental Change

An analysis of correlates with zoonotic diseases demonstrated that zoonotic risk is elevated in forested tropical regions with high mammal species biodiversity which experience land-use changes (Allen *et al.* 2017). Risk of disease emergence is elevated in tropical regions in North and Central America, Asia, Central Africa, and regions of South America (Fig. 7.9). The mechanisms underlying this process are complex. Greater host biodiversity and their associated larger diversity of pathogens increase the potential for novel zoonotic disease emergence (Murray & Daszak 2013). On the other hand, increased biodiversity has been hypothesized to decrease zoonotic risk and vice versa because of a dilution effect. This has been demonstrated for Lyme disease (Allan *et al.* 2003), hantavirus (Suzán *et al.* 2009) and West Nile virus (Ezenwa *et al.* 2006). However, the general applicability of this has been widely refuted (Clay *et al.* 2009; Salkeld *et al.* 2013). Empirical and modelling data have demonstrated high complexity with declining habitat, and thus declining biodiversity, leading to either increasing or decreasing infectious disease risk, depending on the pathogen transmission mode and how host competence scales with body size (Faust *et al.* 2017). Lyme disease is the best-known example that has been assumed to follow the dilution effect (Allan *et al.* 2003). The pathogen is a spirochete bacterium *Borrelia burgdorferi,* which is transmitted by ixodid ticks vectors. These ticks feed on white-footed mice when young and on white-tailed deer as the primary host when adult. Detailed analyses have

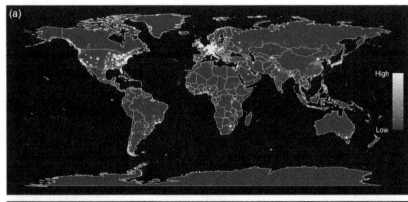

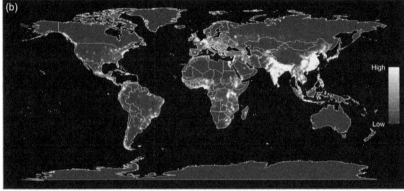

Figure 7.9 Heat maps of predicted relative risk distribution of zoonotic emerging infectious disease events: (a) the predicted distribution of new events being observed; (b) the estimated risk of event locations after factoring out reporting bias. (From Allen *et al.* 2017; reprinted with permission from Nature Springer.)

now shown a much more complex and scale-dependent disease dynamics for Lyme disease (Wood & Lafferty 2013). The recent hypothesis of the 'coevolution effect' suggests that anthropogenically created forest fragments serve as islands harbouring wildlife hosts of pathogens that undergo rapid genetic diversification, leading to greater probability that one of these pathogens will spillover into human populations (Keesing *et al.* 2010; Zohdy *et al.* 2019).

A meta-analysis of publications on the effect of anthropogenic land use change on infectious disease dynamics revealed that 57% of studies documented increased pathogen transmission, 10% decreased pathogen transmission, 30% demonstrated complex pathogen responses and 2% showed no detectable changes (Gottdenker *et al.* 2014). Examples for increased pathogen transmission include Ebola and Nipah as outlined above. Others are yellow fever and rabies with expansion into the forest by human settlements being a frequent cause of outbreaks (Wilcox & Ellis 2006), or the tapeworm *Echinococcus multilocularis* which is correlated with overgrazing of pastures resulting in increases of small mammal and disease densities (Craig 2006) to name but a few. The mosquito genera *Aedes*, *Anopheles* and *Culex*, which include the most important vectors for mosquito-borne diseases such as malaria, dengue and yellow fever, were more commonly encountered in disturbed habitats and had higher virus prevalence than forest mosquitoes did (Junglen *et al.* 2009). An analysis of 6,801 ecological assemblages and 376 host species worldwide showed that sites under substantial human use had wildlife hosts of human-shared pathogens and parasites with a greater proportion of local species richness (18–72% higher) and total abundance (21–144% higher) compared with nearby undisturbed habitats (Gibb *et al.* 2020). The effect was strongest for rodent, bat and passerine bird zoonotic host species. Mammal species harbouring more pathogens overall are more likely to occur in human-managed ecosystems.

Ecotones, the boundary between ecological systems, play key roles in the ten diseases for which information exists (Despommier *et al.* 2007). These ten diseases are caused by viruses (sin nombre, yellow fever, Nipah, influenza, rabies), bacteria (Lyme disease, cholera, leptospirosis) and protozoa (malaria, sleeping sickness), and are in most cases zoonotic. These diseases are ecologically similar to about half of the known zoonotic emerging infectious diseases, indicating a general importance of ecotones, particularly their anthropogenic origination or modification (Despommier *et al.* 2007). Olivero *et al.* (2017) analysed 27 EVD outbreak sites and 280 comparable control sites and showed that outbreaks along the edges of the rainforest biome were significantly associated with forest losses within the previous three years (Olivero *et al.* 2017).

Gottdenker *et al.*'s (2014) meta-analysis identified the most common types of land use change related to zoonotic disease transmission as deforestation, habitat fragmentation, agricultural development, irrigation and urbanization. Human encroachment has caused some bat species to become peridomestic, thus making them more vulnerable to hunting and increasing the zoonotic risk such as in the case of Nipah and Hendra (Kamins *et al.* 2011b; Plowright *et al.* 2011). Bats are also highly susceptible to deforestation, which isolates or divides populations, changes contact rates with other bat species, alters behaviour, compromises ecosystem functions and increases emergence of pathogens (Willig *et al.* 2019). For example, in Brazil bats near human settlements in deforested areas have a viral prevalence of coronaviruses of 9.3% compared to 3.7% in forested areas (EcoHealth Alliance & University of Sao Paulo 2015). Changes of animal guild compositions such as for bats due to deforestation (Willig *et al.* 2019) also happen due to selective hunting. For example, the removal of large carnivores from a savanna ecosystem in East Africa caused rodent and, consequently, flea abundance to double and, thus, elevating the risk for zoonotic transmission of *Bartonella* bacteria, which cause bartonellosis (Young *et al.* 2014).

Climate change will not only alter climatic conditions but also habitat structure and distribution. Alongside, it is likely that the geographic distribution of zoonotic diseases will change, especially for vector-borne diseases, such as Rift Valley fever, yellow fever, malaria and dengue, which are all highly sensitive to climatic conditions (Martin *et al.* 2008). For example, change in rainfall patterns triggered malaria re-emergence in Anhui Province, China (Gao *et al.* 2012). The geographic area of many infectious diseases will expand into previously disease-free areas. Between 1998 and 2005, changes in European climate have caused bluetongue virus, which causes an insect-borne disease of ruminants, to spread 800 km northward in Europe as a consequence of the northward expansion of the African midge *Culicoides imicola*, the main bluetongue virus vector, and the recruitment of indigenous European *Culicoides* species as vectors (Purse *et al.* 2005). Ecological niche modelling showed that the habitat range and distribution of the bat reservoir species for Nipah will likely change under climate change scenarios, increasing risk for zoonotic transmission (Daszak *et al.* 2013). Changes in avian migratory routes as a consequence of temperature changes of aerial streams can explain the outbreak of West Nile virus in Southeast Europe (Mills *et al.* 2010). Climate change will impose very complex changes on zoonotic disease distribution and evolution of novel susceptible immunocompromised populations including the very complex dynamics of evolution of virulence/resistance and genomic variability of zoonotic agents (Cascio *et al.* 2011).

7.5.4 Poverty

A number of zoonotic diseases disproportionately affect poor and marginalized populations but are largely ignored by public health and veterinary services. The WHO has designated them as 'neglected diseases' (Molyneux *et al.* 2011). Although treatments exist, action is often lacking (Wielinga & Schlundt 2013). For example, rabies remains a neglected disease in Africa and Asia and, despite that there being vaccinations for humans and wildlife, the mortality rate is about 55,000 per year (Knobel *et al.* 2005). Parasitic diseases including schistosomiasis, cysticercosis, trematodiasis, taeniasis and echinococcosis are predominant amongst the neglected tropical diseases. Wild meat hunters are amongst the poorest people and any zoonotic infection remains often treated only with traditional and not modern medicine. For example, the factors that best predict lemur hunting are poverty, poor health and child malnutrition, whereas knowledge of laws, level of education, involvement in ecotourism, traditional cultural values, taste preferences, opportunity and human–wildlife conflict had no impact (Borgerson *et al.* 2016). In Tanzania, questionnaires confirmed a strong linkage between poverty and poaching (Knapp *et al.* 2017). In Uganda, those arrested for unauthorized activities in a national park were significantly poorer than others (Twinamatsiko *et al.* 2014). Similarly, one of the most effective ways to reduce illegal wildlife hunting in Uganda is poverty alleviation (Harrison *et al.* 2015).

Poverty is linked with human health and access to health care systems. A study in Madagascar showed that consuming more wildlife was associated with significantly higher haemoglobin concentrations and that removing wild meat would triple anaemia cases among children in the poorest households (Fig. 7.10; Golden *et al.* 2011). Yet, wild meat hunters such as the Baka Pygmies face health challenges due to their limited access to and discrimination in public health centres and being more likely than their non-Pygmy neighbours to mention not using modern health care due to cost (Carson *et al.* 2019). Baka Pygmies in Cameroon are also particularly disadvantaged and in general exhibit poor health. They are the Indigenous group with the largest difference in life expectancy, 22 years, compared with their non-Indigenous neighbours amongst all studied populations (Anderson *et al.* 2016). For Indigenous Peoples, such as the Baka, consuming and also selling wild meat remains the backbone of their ways of life and food security (Fa *et al.* 2015b), despite the fact that numerous groups are no longer fully nomadic but

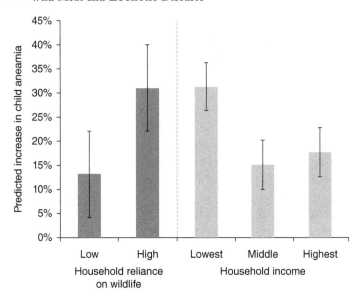

Figure 7.10 Wildlife loss induces major increases in childhood anaemia that is modified by household-level characteristics. Predictive models of the association between wildlife consumption and children's haemoglobin concentrations (*n* = 77) demonstrate that removing wildlife from the diet engenders a disproportionate risk of developing anaemia in households with a high reliance on wildlife and in low-income households. (From Golden *et al.* 2011; adapted with permission from the National Academy of Sciences, USA.)

have been dragged into our economic system. This reliance on wild meat combined with lack of access to modern health care means that Pygmy people are not only especially exposed to zoonotic diseases because of their hunting activities, but zoonotic spillovers will remain undetected until any resulting infectious disease has reached the non-Pygmy neighbours and people who can afford modern health care.

7.6 Solutions

The establishment of diseases throughout history has been described as 'a side effect of the growth of civilisation' (Dobson & Carper 1996). Yet, the enormous human and socio-economic costs cry for solutions. The pandemics of COVID-19, Ebola, HIV and SARS have sharpened humanities' perception of the worldwide misery caused by these diseases. It is not only the mortality rate, which can be very high (e.g. up to 88% for Ebola), but the disruption of society and commerce to control the disease as poignantly laid bare by COVID-19. Knock-on effects, such as loss of investment, reduced international tourism and unemployment, to name but a few make it notoriously difficult to estimate the total economic cost (Smith *et al.* 2019). For example, the 2014–2016 Ebola crisis in West Africa caused at least 28,616 suspected cases and 11,310 confirmed deaths in Guinea, Liberia and Sierra Leone, the mainly affected countries (WHO 2016a). The overall economic cost has been estimated at US$2.8 billion for these three countries including decreases of Gross Domestic Product (GDP) growth, declining government revenues and loss in private and foreign investors' confidence (World Bank 2016). The loss of investor confidence alone cost US$600 million. The international cost for fighting the epidemic by the end of 2015 was more than $3.6 billion (Centers for Disease Control and Prevention 2016). All these numbers, however, do not include indirect effects. For example in West Africa, the entire healthcare workforce declined and led to an estimated 10,600 additional deaths due to untreated conditions, childhood vaccination coverage decreased by 30%, 17,300 children lost one or both parents and more than 33 weeks of education were lost due to school closures (Centers for Disease Control and Prevention 2016). Moreover, local quarantine and travel restriction measures and enforcement led to illegal poaching, logging and mining and negatively impacted previous advances in environmental protection (Smith *et al.* 2019). All of these costs for Ebola are, however, overshadowed by COVID-19 whose economic damages have been estimated at US$8.1–15.8 trillion with at least US$5 trillion for 2020 (Dobson *et al.* 2020). The large uncertainty in the cost estimate is because the estimate was conducted only seven months into the pandemic and without knowledge whether and when a vaccine against COVID-19 would be available (Dobson *et al.* 2020).

Finding a solution to the zoonotic crisis is difficult because so many stakeholders and competing interests are involved. For example, China's ban on trade and consumption of terrestrial wild animals has met with support from various quarters, especially the international conservation and animal welfare lobby (Born Free Foundation 2020; Diamond & Wolfe 2020; WCS 2020). Others have called for much more cautionary approaches (FAO 2020a,b; SWM 2020). A successful regulation or ban of live and butchered wild meat will indeed avoid zoonotic risk especially for those involved in the wild meat chain and provide a cost-effective approach to decrease the risks for disease for humans, domestic animals, wildlife and ecosystems (Karesh *et al.* 2005). However, there are three major problems with the approach.

First, such bans have been implemented in many countries, but limited law enforcement have either rendered these laws as paper tigers or enforcement actually drove the trade into illegality. For example, following the 2014–2016 outbreak of Ebola virus disease in West Africa, governments imposed such bans on the hunting and consumption of meat from wild animals jointly with information campaigns on the infectious potential of wild meat (Bonwitt *et al.* 2018). The three mainly affected countries Guinea, Liberia and Sierra Leone banned the sale of wild meat (Samb & Toweh 2014). However, the criminalization of wild meat consumption entrenched distrust towards outbreak responders and governments whilst messaging contradicted people's own experience because they had always eaten wild meat without any incident (Bonwitt *et al.* 2018). Subsequently, informal and thus illegal networks of wild animal trade proliferated and undercut any meaningful 'development of acceptable, evidence-based surveillance and [made] mitigation strategies for zoonotic spillovers almost impossible' (Bonwitt *et al.* 2018). Indeed, informality and illegality are major obstacles to implementing policies on health and sustainable wildlife management.

Second, a generalized ban ignores both the dependency on wild meat of many people and the rights of Indigenous Peoples, who have hunted for millennia. Consumption of wild meat is the basis for food security in many rural communities (Friant *et al.* 2020). Overhunting and unsustainability are driven by modern market economies by people who buy wild meat as luxury items (Wolfe *et al.* 2005a) whilst Indigenous Peoples reacting to rather than causing the excessive demand. Under the pressures of poverty 'it is no wonder that hunters are lured into commercial' wild meat (Volpato *et al.* 2020). Therefore, we have to distinguish hunters and subsistence hunting on one hand and buyers and commercial hunters on the other hand. We need to find solutions for each group.

Buyers from urban, national and international markets are typically driving unsustainable exploitation where income generated from this livelihood activity will likely be short-lived, following a boom–bust cycle but where the depletion of wildlife is long-lasting (Fa *et al.* 2003). This ultimately risks increasing malnutrition and poverty for rural populations who rely on this resource for their subsistence and cultural identity. Here we need adequate legislation that limits trade to sustainable levels. Legislation must enable management and monitoring of harvesting, use and trade of wildlife. To avoid the pitfalls of illegality, which are difficult to counteract as amply demonstrated by the narcotics trade, 'well-regulated and well monitored wildlife use and trade will encourage the long-term conservation of biodiversity, ensure good animal and human health, as well as combat illegal, unhealthy or unsustainable practices' (FAO 2020a,b). Moreover, total bans will often drive the market into illegality as demonstrated by the unintended consequences of the wild meat ban in West Africa following the 2014–2016 Ebola epidemics (Bonwitt *et al.* 2018).

From the hunters' perspective we first of all need to acknowledge that Indigenous Peoples, who have hunted for millennia and critically depend on wild meat for their protein intake, have an inalienable right to harvest wild meat akin to Indigenous whaling rights (Fitzmaurice 2010). According to the UN Secretary-General: 'It is critical for countries to marshal the resources to respond to their needs, honour their contributions and respect their inalienable rights' (Guterres 2020). Consequently, it is essential that Indigenous Peoples are not only included in the COVID-19 response but that they are consulted and empowered to contribute and participate in policy planning and the drafting and execution of new laws that aim to avoid or better manage future spillovers. However, the use must be sustainable. Sustainable use of biodiversity is a key component of the UN Convention on Biological Diversity. The sustainable use should also include a trading component that is geographically restricted to the rural areas of origin. However, unsustainable use of wild meat may also decrease human welfare where people are dependent on wild meat (Duffy *et al.* 2016; Golden *et al.* 2011). The ultimate aim is to find a balance between people's rights and conservation whilst minimizing zoonotic risk. Concrete actions should include the following and see also (FAO 2020a,b), SWM (2020) and UNEP & International Livestock Research Institute (2020):

(i) Wildlife legislation needs to adequately protect and regulate the sustainable use of wildlife whilst taking into account the environmental and social needs and practices of local people and zoonotic risk. In Africa, such laws typically exist but wildlife is hunted as an unregulated open access resource (Bennett *et al.* 2007). Importantly, this legislation needs enforcement and monitoring but also needs to support the protection of livelihoods of those communities dependent on wild animals for food and income.

(ii) Animal health legislation for cases where trade in live animals remains permitted needs to be based on international standards and regulations as advocated by the World Animal Health Organization (OIE), founded in 1924. It is the intergovernmental organization responsible for improving animal health worldwide and has a total of 182 Member Countries as of 2018 (www.oie.int).

(iii) Legislation for food safety and surveillance along the wild meat chain are key factors in controlling zoonotic risks associated with wildlife meat consumption and trade. Again, it cannot be overstated that it is important to work with communities and stakeholders as one-sided imposition of laws and regulations can achieve the opposite of intended results (Grace *et al.* 2019).

(iv) Education and awareness building are cornerstones for behavioural change (Kuisma *et al.* 2019; Monroe & Willcox 2006). Often hunter behaviours – for example, eating animals found dead or sick (Smiley Evans *et al.* 2020) – are highly risky. Risk-reduction education programmes can help hunters and consumers minimize their risk, for example, by encouraging hunters not to butcher when there are injuries on their hands or limbs, to avoid all contact with animals found dead in the forest or to avoid riskier species, such as bats and primates (LeBreton *et al.* 2012; Pike *et al.* 2010). In general, awareness of zoonotic risk amongst hunters, butchers, vendors and consumers is, however, low (Kamins *et al.* 2015; Ozioko *et al.* 2018; Pruvot *et al.* 2019; Smiley Evans *et al.* 2020; Subramanian 2012). Where knowledge exists, people might be less likely to engage in wild meat hunting and butchering (LeBreton *et al.* 2006; Subramanian 2012), but knowledge is often not translated into behaviours which needs to be addressed by a culturally sensitive intervention programme, designed and implemented through collaboration between the education, public health, veterinary and wildlife authorities with wild meat stakeholders (Alhaji *et al.* 2018; LeBreton *et al.* 2006; Muehlenbein 2017; Wilkie 2006). For example, although the knowledge about anthrax was very high among butchers, owners, herdsmen and consumers in Ghana, 64% of respondents thought that meat from cattle suspected of having died from anthrax was suitable for consumption (Opare *et al.* 2000). The pitfalls are also highlighted by Ebola awareness campaigns which contradicted people's perceptions of low life-time risk of wild meat (Samb & Toweh 2014), thus squandering trust in governments and driving the wild meat market into illegality (Bonwitt *et al.* 2018). Behavioural change can be short-term. For example in Nigeria, wild meat consumption crashed after the 2014–2016 West African Ebola outbreak but immediately returned to pre-Ebola levels in some areas after the country was declared Ebola-free (Ogoanah & Oboh 2017; Onyekuru *et al.* 2018). On the other hand, trade of wild meat in other Nigerian markets did recover only slightly up to 2020 but never reaching pre-Ebola levels (Funk *et al.* 2021). Especially young and urban people stopped consuming wild meat, indicating that mild wild meat consumers can be highly sensitized and that further education campaigns might achieve long-term behavioural change (Funk *et al.* 2021). Education also needs to address the mistaken idea that persecution of animals suspected to transmit disease will solve the problem. We not only need to acknowledge that wildlife and humans are inter-dependent – for example, gorillas and chimpanzees suffered also from the same Ebola outbreak as humans or were infected by humans with respiratory pathogens (Spelman *et al.* 2013) – and that eradication measures might actually make the problem worse (as in the case of the Marburg virus, outlined above) but also that humans critically depend on the same species that carry pathogens, such as the pollination ecosystem service by bats. Often, education projects are implemented on the ground but fail to measure whether these efforts resulted in actually changed behaviour (e.g. Kuisma *et al.* 2019). Therefore, monitoring the effectiveness of education programmes and changing approaches, if applicable, are vital.

(v) Pathogen surveillance and research are needed to establish a sufficient knowledge basis on the diversity of pathogens in different guilds of wild and domestic animals in their concrete site-specific settings. Only this knowledge will allow the development of sufficiently accurate risk assessment models that predict pathogen transmission from wild animals to domestic animals and humans.

(vi) Because zoonotic diseases emerge not only from wildlife hunting but also from our modern livestock production systems, such as pig farming for Nipah virus or the 2009 H1N1 influenza pandemic, which originated in North American pig farms (Mena *et al.* 2016), a general reconsideration and restructuring of our food systems is required (FAO 2020a,b; IPES-Food 2020). The International Panel of Experts on Sustainable Food Systems highlights that intensive livestock production amplifies the risks of diseases emergence and spread and that commercial agriculture exacerbates zoonotic risk by commercial agriculture driving habitat loss and creating the conditions for viruses to emerge and spread (IPES-Food 2020). Increased substitution of wild meat with domestic animals, whether from global commercial systems or local subsistence husbandry, appears logical, but might accelerate the zoonotic problems because of the emergence of new pathogens and hosts. Commercial systems are intrinsically connected with the conversion of land for agricultural use, which constitutes the highest risk factor for the emergence of zoonotic disease. Even when domestic animals are raised locally in the tropics and subtropics in a sustainable manner, zoonotic risk may be increased, because these animals are raised in areas also frequented by wildlife.

Third, regarding the avoidance of future disease emergence and pandemics, the regulation or ban of live and butchered wild meat might demonstrate political actions and reassurance to the general public that something is being done by governments and politicians during an actual epidemic such as COVID-19. However, if the aim is to prevent pandemic zoonotic diseases, it will certainly not be sufficient – and might constitute nothing but a political smokescreen – considering that the vast majority of cases are based on anthropogenic environmental change and agricultural intensification. 'Although enforcement of hunting laws and promotion of alternative sources of protein may help curb the pressure on wildlife, the best strategy for biodiversity conservation may be to keep sawmills and the towns that develop around them out of forests' (Poulsen *et al.* 2009). The UN report prepared in the wake of COVID-19 highlights that we currently treat the symptoms of the COVID-19 pandemic but not the underlying issues (UNEP & International Livestock Research Institute 2020). Indeed the significantly increased number of incidences of emerging infectious diseases since the 1940s (Fig. 7.11; Jones *et al.* 2008; Smith *et al.* 2014) coincides with the increased acceleration of socioeconomic human activities (Steffen *et al.* 2015a). Habitat change and destruction is not only increasing the species richness and abundance of species sharing pathogens and parasites with humans (Gibb *et al.* 2020), but it also is driving species out of their natural habitats and into manmade environments, where they can interact and breed new strains of diseases such as in the case of Nipah. Therefore, the key to prevent or minimize future spillovers of zoonotic disease is that countries actively participate in the development and implementation of the CBD targets.

The accurate prediction of when, where and how a spillover will emerge is impossible because of the ecological complexity. However, it is clear that business-as-usual will inevitably lead to new zoonotic disease emergence. In 2018, the emergence of a new coronavirus was predicted to happen from bats in Southeast Asian areas most affected by deforestations (Afelt *et al.* 2018a) and this is, indeed, what happened. However,

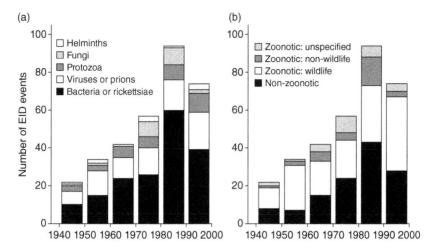

Figure 7.11 Number of emerging infectious disease events per decade according to (a) pathogen type and (b) transmission type. (From Jones *et al.* 2008; adapted with permission from Nature Springer.)

we have the knowledge – albeit the toolbox needs constant refinement by research and monitoring – to make better risk assessments and to reduce and mitigate the risk. According to UNEP Executive Director Inger Andersen: 'The science is clear that if we keep exploiting wildlife and destroying our ecosystems, then we can expect to see a steady stream of these diseases jumping from animals to humans in the years ahead' (Carrington 2020).

Many activities involving zoonotic disease control are at risk because of a failed investigative infrastructure or financial base (Murphy 1998). Yet in the face of the enormous cost, prevention is significantly more cost-effective than response (UNEP & International Livestock Research Institute 2020). Dobson *et al.* (2020) estimate that the gross annual costs of programmes to reduce deforestation and the wildlife trade and build pandemic surveillance in disease hotspots would be $17.7–26.9bn. The programmes would include monitoring wildlife trade, reducing spillovers from wildlife, early detection and control, reducing spillover via live-stock, reducing deforestation by half, and ending wild meat trade (see also Box 7.1) in China. This is more than three orders of magnitude smaller than the current estimated cost of Covid-19 economic damages, of $8.1–15.8 trillion (Dobson *et al.* 2020).

After Ebola and SARS, scientists hoped that these diseases would be eye-openers and warned that the next pandemic of zoonotic origin stood

Box 7.1 *Ending or managing wild meat trade?*

Whether it is possible or advisable to fully end the wild meat trade is debatable. From a public health point of view, trade in 'high-risk' species, particularly bats, which harbour a wide array of coronaviruses (Afelt *et al.* 2018a), and primates (see Section 7.5.1; Cleaveland *et al.* 2007), should no longer be permitted anywhere in the world. Moreover, wet markets are prone to promulgation of animal viruses and zoonotic disease spillovers (see Section 7.5.2) and need to be either severely restricted and controlled, or closed down altogether. Wildlife trade including trade in wild meat is a major cause of population decline. In a recent meta-analysis (Morton *et al.* 2021), species abundance declined by 62% on average with the reductions greatest when national or international trade was involved (76% and 66%, respectively). From a conservation point of view, improved management and control is trade is urgently required to stem the negative impacts of trade-related population declines.

Indeed, the worldwide ban of wild meat hunting and trade was suggested early in the COVID-19 pandemic because of the link between COVID-19 and wet markets (Born Free Foundation 2020). However, it is important to consider that a strict global ban on wild meat hunting and any type of market trade including local trade will affect the food security and livelihoods of millions of the poorest people (Fa *et al.* 2021; SWM 2020). For Indigenous Peoples and myriad rural communities, consumed and also sold wild meat remains the backbone of their ways of life (Fa *et al.* 2015b) despite the fact that numerous groups are no longer fully nomadic but have been dragged into our economic system. Hence, stopping short food supply chains can be a blunt tool which will imperil vulnerable peoples even more. This is not to say that urban wild meat consumption and any illegal and unregulated wildlife trade that endangers human health, animal welfare and biodiversity should not be banned, but extra care is required so that we can protect the already precarious food security of vulnerable Indigenous Peoples such as the Pygmies who rely on hunting and consumption of wild meat. For example, in the case of the Twa Pygmies in Uganda, exclusion from their traditional land in the 1990s caused severe poverty and hardship and high mortality rates amongst under-five year olds. It was only after Twa families were given land and hunting rights that mortality rates dropped from 59% to 18%, demonstrating the crucial importance of land for survival (Jackson 2006).

Allowing communities subsistence hunting and local trade requires effective laws to regulate subsistence and commercial hunting practices, which is lacking or remains unenforced in many countries. Wildlife legislation is often unclear in defining subsistence hunting for one's own food and local small-scale trade *versus* commercial hunting and trade. Moreover, legal guidance of disease risk assessment or public health protection is mostly lacking for informal or illegal hunting and trade. Thus, the development, promotion and enforcement of strong animal health guidelines and legislation are urgently required in many tropic and subtropic countries. The development of such animal health legislation can utilize the standards and recommendations of the OIE, including its Terrestrial and Aquatic Animal Health Codes, as a general framework. Training and education and investment in appropriate facilities are essential to translate such legislation into meaningful actions on the ground to prevent spillovers of zoonotic disease along the bush-to-table chain (hunting, slaughter, processing and handling, storage and distribution in food markets).

around the corner (Afelt *et al.* 2018a; Singh *et al.* 2017). Hopefully, COVID-19 will be the final trigger for implementing holistic solutions, whether under the umbrella of the 'One Health', 'EcoHealth' or 'Planetary Health' concepts (Lerner & Berg 2017). Future costs in dealing with zoonotic emerging infectious diseases, especially because of the pandemic risk, can be substantially reduced if global actions to lessen zoonotic risk are taken globally now to safeguard human health and conserve biodiversity.

8 · *Closing the Gap*

8.1 Introduction

As already highlighted in a number of global documents on the topic of sustainable use of wild meat in tropical and subtropical environments (e.g. Coad *et al.* 2019; Nasi *et al.* 2008), achieving this goal is challenging. Much data and many examples have emerged from research over more than four decades. From this information the overall recommendation is that with the right enabling environment and political will, and well-designed and multi-sectoral participation, it is possible to sustainably manage wild meat supply. There is no doubt that this is complex, but it is certain that under these conditions demand can be reduced to justifiable levels, at least for several species in some environments. Our intention in this book has been to primarily undertake a state-of-the-art review of the existing knowledge on the use of wild meat in a variety of tropical and subtropical environments. We present evidence on what species are consumed and how they are hunted; we explore the characteristics of the environments in which wildlife is exploited, and then discuss how sustainable hunting can be measured. In Chapters 6 and 7, we examined what is known about zoonotic diseases that are linked to wild meat use, an important topic considering the COVID-19 crisis and we then tackle how much we know about current hunting levels and the impact of overexploitation to set the scene for this final chapter. Here, we deliberate on ways we can 'close the gap' between knowledge and action, by a better understanding of sustainable wildlife use issues. We first concentrate on providing a comprehensive overview of what factors need to be considered to guarantee sustainable wild meat use, using the topics covered in previous chapters. We then end by providing guidelines on how we can improve wild meat governance and management worldwide. Our eventual purpose is to secure wildlife and food security for the benefit of biodiversity and humans.

8.2 Achieving Sustainable Wild Meat Use

In the following sections, we concentrate on a number of pivotal elements which we illustrate in Fig. 8.1. By understanding these major issues in an integrated manner, we can move closer to ensuring the long-term use of wild meat as a resource. We first expand on the need to determine the ecological determinants of wild animal numbers in the different habitats, learn about the reproductive biology and ecology of prey species, and then move towards understanding the demand side of the equation. The latter relates to how we can recognize who needs wild meat, and therefore puts pressure on wildlife and which factors enable this process. We present these different elements in a simple list within which we present the available information.

8.2.1 Improving the Sustainability of Local Wild Meat Supply

8.2.1.1 Knowing the Production Potential of Different Habitats
Overall productivity of hunted species (particularly mammals) in different habitats across the world is correlated primarily with rainfall (Chapters 2 and 6). Production of huntable species even within the same habitat type such as tropical forests can differ due to ecological parameters such as vegetation composition. Monodominant upland Amazonian *terra firme* forests or *Gilbertodendron* forests in the Congo Basin are less productive. Differences between sites in prey species richness and biomass, can also occur because of biophysical variation between areas, even within the arguably more uniform and productive landscapes, such as forest-savanna mosaics or fruit-rich forests. Some authors like Robinson and Bennett (1999b) have argued that only about 150 kg of vertebrate biomass per year are available for extraction per kilometre square but this amount will differ according to habitat type, as indicated above. Reported annual hunting rates are known to be substantially higher than these figures thus provoking declines in wildlife populations in both the medium and long term (Chapter 6). Further understanding what ecological factors explain the vertebrate species biomass in different habitats is essential to determine the natural capacity an environment has to supply wild meat. Although in the past some studies have attempted to measure animal numbers and their biomass in a variety of habitats (see Chapter 2), emphasis on these sorts of investigations has become less popular since John Eisenberg's seminal work in the 1970s (Wemmer & Sunquist 2005). As highlighted in Eisenberg and Thorington (1973),

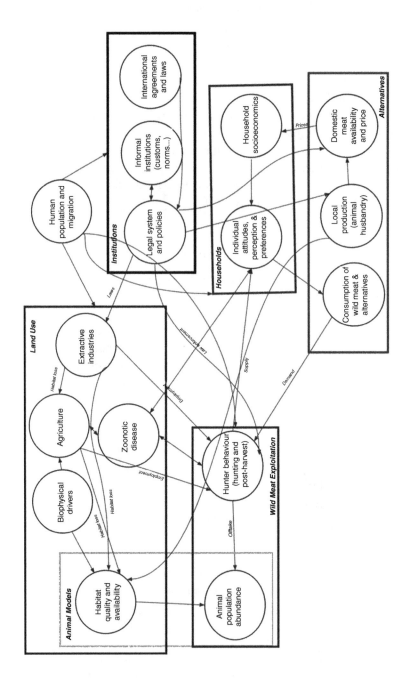

Figure 8.1 A simple conceptual diagram of some of the processes driving the direct use value of wild meat. The hunting decision is made at the small scale by individual hunters, but this decision is influenced by village and market-level factors; for example, consumer preferences and availability of substitutes influence consumer demand. Hunter offtake is a function of animal abundance, which is affected at a range of scales by habitat quality and availability. Modelling approaches to this system vary by scale and process type; for example, small-scale harvest models, market models, habitat models and village livelihoods models. These different components of the wild meat system have been modelled separately but not in an integrated manner.

assessing the numbers and biomass of different mammalian species (applicable to any other group of organisms) can shed light on the role these have in the functioning of an ecosystem. By determining the biomass present per taxon it is possible to establish the ecological dominance (and success) of different species and orders of mammals within a particular ecological context, compared to the more conventional use of number of species or genera per higher taxon in each geographic area. More importantly, comparisons of the biomass and numbers of the species found in different habitats and geographic areas, can be useful to highlight the ecological and anthropogenic factors involved in these environments.

8.2.1.2 Comprehending the Basic Ecology of Hunted Species

Although the existing variation at a macroecological level is important to understand the limits of exploitation possible in specific environments, information directly linked to a species' likelihood of being overharvested can allow researchers and conservation managers to better calculate sustainable exploitation levels. Generally, the intrinsic rate of population increase of a species, denoted as r_m (Caughley & Birch 1971) or r_{max} (see Skalski *et al.* 2005) or λ_{max}, which is the exponential of r_{max} (e.g. Robinson & Bodmer 1999) is very simply the number of births minus the number of deaths per generation time – the reproduction rate less the death rate. This index has been used as a useful measure of a species' vulnerability to overharvesting. A related general rule, Fenchel's law (Fenchel 1974), proposes that species with larger body sizes tend to have lower rates of population growth and these are more vulnerable to overharvesting. Sustainability of harvests therefore hinges on methods for estimating life-history parameters (Robinson & Redford 1986) alongside measurement of prey abundance (Chapter 5). Fundamental for assessing hunting sustainability using models such as the Robinson and Redford (1986) production model (Section 5.4.2), which has become a standard model in sustainability analyses, is the estimation of r_{max}. This parameter has often been calculated using Cole's (1954) equation. For populations not limited by food, space, resource competition, or predation and parasites, r_{max} is the maximum possible increase in number (Caughley 1977; Robinson & Redford 1986). Therefore, r_{max} can be used to predict how particular prey species will respond to different levels of harvesting (Greene *et al.* 1998), and it is used in models to determine the sustainability of hunting (see Chapter 5), such as the production model with survival probabilities (Slade *et al.* 1998), source-sink models (Joshi & Gadgil 1991) and spatial models (Levi *et al.* 2011b).

The key value used to estimate r_{max} is the annual birth rate of female offspring, which is also used in a range of hunting models such as Bodmer's (1994b), Robinson and Bodmer's (1999) and Robinson and Redford's (1991a) (Chapter 5). Annual birth rate is also used in population viability analyses (Section 5.3.2; Akçakaya & Sjögren-Gulve 2000) and calculations of minimum viable population size for several species, the results of which are used to determine International Union for Conservation of Nature threat status (IUCN 2020a). Nevertheless, inaccurate reproductive estimates can strongly influence sustainability calculations: basic biological data often does not exist for many species, so researchers cannot make accurate calculations (Milner-Gulland & Akçakaya 2001). The reality is that few reproductive life histories have been estimated in the field (Duncan *et al.* 2007) with Conde *et al.* (2019) showing that only 1.3% of 32,144 extant described mammals, birds, reptiles and amphibians have comprehensive information on birth and death rates. These authors suggest that data from zoos and aquariums in the Species360 network (Species 360 2020) can significantly improve knowledge for an almost eightfold gain.

Reproductive parameters used in the Robinson and Redford (1991a) production model or other algorithms to estimate r_{max} are in most cases based on data from captive populations. These are normally kept in low-density, high-resource settings (Fa *et al.* 2011) that may produce reproductive variations due to multiple factors, such as the stress of captivity, availability of resources, mates, territories and the composition of social groups. Furthermore, seasonal variations in food availability in the original habitats are often circumvented in captive populations and likely have strong impacts on reproduction (Goodman *et al.* 1999; Mayor *et al.* 2011). Because captive conditions may differ substantially from the wild, reproductive estimates obtained from captive systems may be appropriate for estimating maximum reproductive parameters (e.g. longevity), but even wild populations not limited by food, space and resource competition may not achieve these estimates. Furthermore, data on captive reproduction are unavailable for many, often endangered species, mainly because they do not reproduce well in captivity (Bowler *et al.* 2014). As a result of using reproductive values generated from captive populations, there is evidence that production estimates are consistently inflated and values of sustainable exploitation exaggerated (Milner-Gulland & Akçakaya 2001; Van Vliet & Nasi 2008b). In a sensitivity analysis with 33 comparisons, the production model failed to detect unsustainability, whereas unsustainability was detected by other methods, which do not use r_{max} estimates in 58% (n = 19) of the cases (Weinbaum et al. 2013). Thus, if models based on r_{max} are to be used to determine the sustainability of game harvests, reproduction parameters of game species should be derived from field studies or, at least, uncertainty should be modelled. Barychka et al. (2020b) used an approach that allows the integration of parameter uncertainty (Section 5.4.5).

When reproductive performance is studied in the wild, it is usually by directly examining animals after capture and restraint, or from direct field observations of births (e.g. Zhang et al. 2007). This is a difficult task to cover all hunted species since studies of their life histories (and especially long-lived ones) are beset by logistical, methodological and financial constraints. Because the application of researcher-led methods is challenging, especially for tropical forest animals (Fragoso et al. 2016), citizen science is becoming more widely applied to gather large amounts of biological and ecological data in the field (Dickinson et al. 2010). There are now numerous examples of non-professionals participating in obtaining vital information on a variety of subjects (Bonney et al. 2014; Steger et al. 2017). In the tropics, Indigenous and rural people have been involved in citizen-science projects, providing information on animal populations and trends, just as accurately as trained scientists (e.g. Danielsen et al. 2014). Since local communities in tropical forests have extensive knowledge of the environment and are the main direct users of natural resources, their participation in scientific monitoring is central (Pocock et al. 2015). Mayor et al. (2017) have demonstrated the effectiveness of citizen science through a community-based collection of organs of Amazonian forest mammals to determine reproductive parameters. In this study, local hunters collected and voluntarily donated complete viscera of hunted specimens over an uninterrupted 15-year period. Using this material, Mayor et al. (2017) were able to estimate annual birth rates of female offspring. These estimates differed significantly from those obtained in sustainability assessments that often use data from captive populations. Mayor et al. (2017) have shown that it is possible to collect accurate reproductive parameters of some hunted species over the long-term through the examination of biological materials brought back to researchers. This is possible for small-bodied animals but not for large species since their viscera are often not brought back from the forest due to their greater weight (see Mayor *et al.* 2017). El Bizri *et al.* (2020a) overcame this setback by training hunters to determine the reproductive status of the larger-bodied species in the field. By engaging local people in sample collection survey costs are lessened and involve locals in data processing and analysis, arguably allowing the collected data to be used directly in decision-making. Beyond providing more precise estimates of reproductive rates, larger sample sizes are also possible to better understand hunting impacts, for example by determining how variation in reproductive rates over time relates to density-dependent responses of populations to hunting. Local communities who depend on subsistence hunting for food could become active samplers of valuable biological material that is usually discarded. Alongside this, the involvement of hunters with scientists will also facilitate a better understanding between these often-disparate groups and create the much-needed trust and understanding that can lead to hunting sustainability. Importantly, results should be fed back to the people who provide the data.

8.2.1.3 Counting Animals

The management of wild populations for sport and subsistence harvest requires knowledge of both animal abundance and harvest success. Knowing the population size of harvested animals is crucial not just to monitor baseline populations but to follow the impact of hunting over time. Wildlife population size has been estimated using many models that require information on various population parameters such as carrying capacity (for logistic growth models), age structure, age-specific survival and reproduction rates (for age structure models), demographic and environmental stochasticities (for logistic growth models and age structure models), catch per unit effort (CPUE) and catch effort (for Poisson catchability models) (Skalski *et al.* 2005). Obtaining or estimating these population parameters, especially for species in tropical forests, is complicated, sometimes even impossible, due to the lack of direct observability of the study animals and the difficulties of undertaking mark–recapture studies.

Visual surveys are possible for animals in open habitats and such surveying is the most widely used non-tagging method to estimate and monitor wildlife abundance. Visual count surveys provide a relatively inexpensive and unintrusive approach to population surveys. Line-transect methods have seen a rapid development in statistical theory (Buckland *et al.* 2015). Detection functions estimated from right-angle distance data can be used to both test the assumptions of homogeneous detection probabilities and convert counts to absolute abundance and/or density. Extensive examples of the use of line transects in determining the impact of hunting of animals are available from the work of Peres and colleagues in the Amazon (e.g. Parry *et al.* 2009).

Methods that involve the collaboration of hunters to record the species hunted by them are more practical. Harvest data are relatively easy to collect, and at the same time, they avoid the high costs associated with more direct hands-on survey methods. Accompanying age-structure estimates can also provide crucial information on survival, productivity and age composition at relatively low cost. Data on the animals hunted over time can be used in CPUE estimates to monitor both hunter satisfaction and population trends. When carefully structured, CPUE data (Section 5.2.2) can also be used to estimate absolute abundance. Harvest counts can be employed in conjunction with change-in-ratio (CIR) methods and index-removal methods to estimate total abundance (Skalski *et al.* 2005). All of these methods rely on the impact of harvest removals on population responses which in turn can be linked to changes in animal abundance. The CIR and index-removal methods use auxiliary observations to relate harvest numbers to animal abundance. The CPUE methods use changes in success rate with known removals to estimate abundance. Alongside information of where hunting takes place harvest data can be used to assess sustainable harvests and denote hunting territories.

Long-term management of mammal populations, as for example emphasized by Newing (2001) for Central African populations, are likely to be more effective if the effects of different hunting management scenarios are monitored, and where solutions rely on trial-and-error models rather than scientific methods, the basis of which is still a matter of debate. Hunting management models that incorporate spatio-temporal rotation of hunting areas, as proposed by Vermeulen *et al.* (2009) in logging concessions, where non-hunted areas act as 'wildlife reserves', able to re-stock the hunted zones (see McCullough 1996), are a more realistic way forward. Alongside awareness programmes, the control of poaching, supply of alternative protein sources where needed and recognition of the rights of the local populations must be acknowledged if realistic hunting models are going to succeed. Monitoring by the actors of hunting offtake and the areas used is fundamental if an effective way forward is to succeed after its implementation.

8.2.2 Understanding the Drivers at a Landscape Level

8.2.2.1 Keeping an Eye on Human Population Increases

Extraction and use of wild meat resources is directly related to human population densities, both, where hunting takes place and where meat is being consumed. A higher human population will exert a proportionately greater pressure on wild animals hunted for wild meat and other natural resources. Understanding of the potential that habitats have to support human beings has been the concern of some researchers seeking to determine the carrying capacity, especially in tropical forests (Robinson & Bennett 1999b). Forest dwelling peoples have persisted in tropical forests for as many as 40,000 years in Asia (Hutterer 1988), 90,000 years in Africa (Bahuchet 1993; Verdu *et al.* 2009) and more recently in the Americas. These peoples would have depended significantly on animals for their protein needs (Chapters 1 and 3), and most hunted species may have persisted because hunter numbers were low, thus enabling sustainable human hunting. However, human harvest of wild species will depend on the harvestable biomass related to the overall standing biomass of the species, which in turn is linked to the available primary productivity of the different habitats (Chapter 2). Given these relationships, the maximum number of people solely depending on wild meat (i.e., with little or no dependence on agriculture and domestic animals) who can live in tropical forests has been calculated by Robinson and Bennett (1999b). According to these authors, if the maximum sustainable production of wild meat in tropical forests is around 150 kg/km^2 in most forests, the carrying capacity of humans in tropical forests should not exceed 1 person/km^2. This result is based on the per capita protein needs of 0.8 g of protein/day/kg (US recommended daily amount) or a daily protein need of a 70 kg man of 56 g of protein or approximately 180 g of meat/day, assuming that this protein comes from meat sources alone (Fa *et al.* 2003). Comparison of actual human population densities in tropical forests indicate that rural population densities in Central Africa are orders of magnitude higher than 1 person/km^2 (see Fa *et al.* 2003), almost equivalent to this figure for the Amazon (Fa & Peres 2001) but much higher in Asian forests (Corlett 2007). Trends of protein supply in all tropical forests are therefore highly pessimistic especially considering that human population densities are increasing (Chapter 2). Fa *et al.* (2003) in fact suggest that wild meat extraction in the Congo Basin is unsustainable and not only catastrophic for wildlife but also for the people who rely on it.

8.2.2.2 Containing Logging and Other Resource Extraction Activities

A major source of disruption of wildlife habitat is linked to the industrial exploitation of renewable resources as is the case of timber or non-renewable resources, such as minerals and oil. Extractive companies may directly destroy critical habitat, disturb movement patterns and alter behaviour of wildlife, but also indirectly facilitate hunting by opening forests to hunters and creating markets for wild meat. Once roads provide access to markets, wild meat becomes a market commodity, transforming hunting from a solely subsistence activity to a joint subsistence and commercial activity (Robinson *et al.* 1999; Wilkie *et al.* 2000). The extensive networks of roads created by logging companies open up remote forest areas – estimates suggest that 50,000–59,000 km^2 are opened every year (Grieser Johns 1997). The greater access to untouched forest areas accelerated by the large-scale operations of extractive industries can 'ring the death knell' for many hunted species.

The demand for natural resources is, in part, fuelled by emerging nations, such as China, India and Brazil, but also by many others which are propelling their economies by expanding their exploitation of natural resources (e.g. mining in Brazil in 2020; Vallejos & Veit 2020; Villén-Pérez *et al.* 2020). In particular, the accompanying rise in prices has led to the expansion of operations of extractive industries causing an increase in pressure on wildlife but also on Indigenous Peoples throughout the tropics (Butler & Laurance 2008). Logging concessions in Central Africa, the most extensive extractive industry in the region, occupy 30–45% of all tropical forests and over 70% of forests in some countries (Global Forest Watch 2002; Laporte *et al.* 2007). As a result, road construction for logging has intensified dramatically in the last decade, opening an additional 29% of Central African forests to increased hunting pressure (Laporte *et al.* 2007). Logging companies also attract large numbers of workers (and their family members) into formerly sparsely populated forest areas (Wilkie & Carpenter 1999). Since most logging companies do not provide their workers with animal protein, many have to survive on wild meat hunted by themselves and bought from others (Poulsen *et al.* 2009). Moreover, the better salaries offered in logging companies allow hunters to acquire more sophisticated hunting technologies (such as cartridges, guns, snare wires, outboard motors and headlamps), which in turn allows for

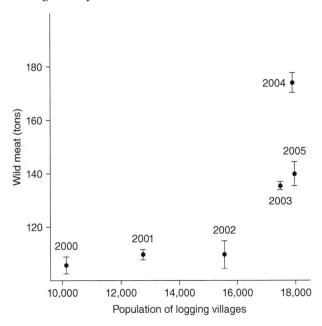

Figure 8.2 Annual biomass of wild meat entering logging towns in relation to the combined populations of the towns. Bars are bootstrapped 95% confidence intervals. (From Poulsen *et al.* 2009; adapted with permission from John Wiley & Sons.)

more efficient harvests. As a consequence, the per capita harvest rates in local communities within logging or oil-drilling infrastructures can be three to six times higher than other villages (Auzel *et al.* 2001: Cameroon; Auzel & Wilkie 2000: Congo; Robinson *et al.* 1999: Bolivia; Thibault & Blaney 2003: Gabon). In five logging towns in the northern Republic of Congo, Poulsen *et al.* (2009) found that industrial logging operations led to a 69% increase in population and a 64% increase in wild meat supply. Wild meat biomass entering logging towns was highly correlated with population increases of these settlements, around 10 kg per person per year (Fig. 8.2). Importantly, immigrants hunted 72% of all wild meat, suggesting that the short-term benefits of hunting accrue disproportionately to 'outsiders' and not to rural communities and Indigenous Peoples who have prior, legitimate claims to wildlife resources in the area.

Attempts to control the wild meat trade within lands occupied by logging concessions (but not for other extractive industries) have primarily focussed on coercing companies to ban their employees from hunting and prevent them from purchasing wild meat from forest villagers and transporting it to urban markets. To a lesser extent, logging companies have been encouraged to regulate the activities of forest villagers themselves such as by blocking off their channels for trade. Although the take up is still patchy, there are some promising examples of collaborations between conservation organizations and logging companies to curb illegal hunting and reduce the amount of wild meat trade (see Aviram *et al.* 2002; Butler & Laurance 2008; Elkan *et al.* 2006; Poulsen *et al.* 2007).

By promoting biodiversity conservation and human livelihoods, extractive companies can foster sustainable practices that explicitly consider the direct and indirect effects of their activities on wildlife (Milner-Gulland & Bennett 2003; Robinson *et al.* 1999). One way of achieving this, as Poulsen and Clark (2010) argue, is for forest certification granted to companies if they are able to raise management standards and improve practices in support of biodiversity conservation. A good example is the unprecedented partnership between the Wildlife Conservation Society, Congolese Industrielle des Bois (CIB), and the Congolese Ministry of Ministry of Sustainable Development, Forest Economy and the Environment (MDDEFE) in northern Republic of Congo. The result was the accreditation by the Forest Stewardship Council (FSC) of two timber concessions (750,000 ha) resulting in the largest tract of contiguous certified tropical forest in the world (Poulsen & Clark 2010). Aside from reducing the impact of logging practices, these concessions are managed for wildlife and biodiversity. Wildlife has increased in these concessions, comparable to adjacent Nouabalé-Ndoki National Park (Clark *et al.* 2009), and there has been a consistency in wild meat supply over time partially resulting from the conservation measures taken by the logging companies (Poulsen *et al.* 2009). These measures include: (1) companies guaranteeing the importation or development of protein sources for their workers and their families, keeping prices competitive with wild meat and fish; (2) companies should contribute to wildlife law enforcement (e.g. salaries of ecoguards who control transport of hunters and wild meat along logging roads); (3) companies should ensure that their workers hunt legally (with proper licences and permits) and impose penalties or fire workers who break the law; (4) traditional systems of resource management (e.g. hunting territories) should be formalized in land-use planning (e.g. management plans for logging concessions) and access to resources for indigenous people should be prioritized; (5) access to forest roads should be restricted to company vehicles, and roads should be closed when not actively used for logging. Poulsen *et al.* (2009) also suggest that urbanization should be avoided in logging concessions. If possible, sawmills and wood-finishing factories should be built and operated in or close to existing cities to avoid the growth of urban centres in the forest. Such a multi-pronged approach can address biodiversity and development interests, but acceptance by all extractive companies is still the major challenge. Of course, these measures only function for legal forestry and mining, but do not address the multitude of illegal wood extraction and mining that is widespread throughout the tropics and subtropics (e.g. Andrews 2015; Lawson 2014; Plummer 2014; Vallejos & Veit 2020; Villén-Pérez et al. 2020).

8.3 Governance and Legal Control of Wild Meat Use

8.3.1 International Conventions

A main channel for national governments to get involved in wildlife issues, including wild meat, is via international conventions and declarations. Such mechanisms, notably the CBD, Convention on Trade in Endangered Species (CITES) and Convention on Migratory Species (CMS), and the UN Declaration on the Rights of Indigenous Peoples (Table 8.1), but also other formally recognized international organizations that support or help implement the Decisions adopted by the Parties (i.e., Interpol, TRAFFIC, IUCN), attempt to control or regulate the international wildlife trade, including wild meat. Such agreements, which are between national parties have most authority over transboundary issues, but also promote food security and conservation through the sustainable use of wild fauna within national boundaries. Conventions are important platforms for intergovernmental policy outcomes, particularly relating to curbing the illegal wildlife trade. For those governments that ratify these global conventions, they are legally binding. However, Parties are not legally bound by the decisions of the Conference of Parties, known as COP, the decision-making body responsible for monitoring and reviewing the implementation of United Nations conventions, but should work toward implementing them.

In most cases, conventions have concentrated on species for which rapid or critical declines have been recorded, usually as recognized by the IUCN Red List framework. The illegal wildlife trade for products other than meat, ivory or rhino horn, as examples, is of major concern for many governments and international/regional institutions, as it generates large sums of untraceable money, often used to fund other international crime (UNODC 2016) and can also drive wildlife to extirpation very rapidly. The expansion of pangolin scales in the international trade

Table 8.1 *Description of the main international conventions relating to wildlife and use of wild meat (taken from Coad et al. 2019)*

International convention	Description
UN Convention on Biological Diversity (CBD)	The CBD does not regulate trade in wildlife but is interested in the sustainable use of biodiversity and its components, including wild meat. In 2010, the COP to the CBD adopted the Strategic Plan of the Convention on Biological Diversity at their 10th meeting. The Strategic Plan is a 10-year framework for action by all countries and stakeholders to save biodiversity and enhance its benefits for people. It comprises a shared vision, a mission, strategic goals and 20 ambitious yet achievable targets, collectively known as the Aichi Biodiversity Targets. Specifically, Target 4 states that: 'By 2020, Governments, business and stakeholders at all levels have taken steps to achieve or have implemented plans for sustainable production and consumption and have kept the impacts of use of natural resources well within safe ecological limits'.
	After publishing a CBD Technical Series report (Nasi *et al.* 2008) on conservation and use of wildlife resources, the CBD established a Liaison Group on Bushmeat. The Liaison Group provided recommendations for the sustainable use of wild meat which were adopted by the CBD COP 11 in 2012 (Decision XI/25), with further recommendations adopted by the CBD COP 12 in 2014 (Decision XII/18). The work of the Liaison Group culminated in support for the creation of the Collaborative Partnership on Sustainable Wildlife Management (CPW) in 2013, a voluntary partnership of international organizations with substantive mandates and programmes for the sustainable use and conservation of wildlife resources. In addition, the CBD Action Plan on Customary Sustainable Use (UNEP/CBD/COP/DEC/XII/12, B, Annex) was adopted in 2014. It aimed to promote, within the framework of the Convention, a just implementation of Article 10(c)4 at local, national, regional and international levels and to ensure the full and effective participation of indigenous and local communities at all stages and levels of implementation. Article 10(c) of the CBD states that Parties shall: 'protect and encourage customary use of biological resources in accordance *(cont.)*

Table 8.1 (*cont.*)

International convention	Description
	with traditional cultural practices that are compatible with conservation or sustainable use requirements.'
Convention on Trade in Endangered Species (CITES or Washington Convention)	CITES monitors and authorizes the international trade among its parties of all species listed in its appendices. The wild meat trade impacts several of these species, such as sharks, rays and pangolins, which are killed for both trade in wildlife parts (teeth, gill rakes and scales) and their meat. The current CITES position on wild meat is explained in Resolution Conf. 13. 11 (Rev. CoP 17) and encourages Parties to implement CBD Decisions XI/25 and XII/18 where appropriate and take advantage of the guidance and other materials provided by the CPW in relation to the sustainable management and use of wildlife. CITES is also part of the CPW, which is dedicated to developing improved policies and practices for sustainable wildlife management (see below and Section 1.3). Transport channels, such as seaports or airports, provide focused control points for CITES enforcement of international trade between distant countries; this is less the case for trade between neighbouring countries with porous borders (UNODC 2016). More consideration should be given to how trade across such borders could be effectively regulated. In 2016, the COP adopted Resolution Conf. 16.6 (Rev. CoP17) on 'CITES and livelihoods', recognizing that the implementation of CITES is better achieved when the national governments of the parties seek the engagement of rural communities, especially those traditionally dependent on CITES-listed species for their livelihoods. In 2000, CITES supported the creation of a Central Africa Wild Meat Working Group (CBWG). The group held two meetings including a joint meeting with the CBD Liaison Group on Bushmeat in 2011. However, the CBWG is no longer active after the 2012 decision (CoP15 Doc.61) that no further action was required on the subject.
Convention on Migratory Species (CMS)	The CMS lists threatened migratory species in two appendices, very much like the three CITES appendices, and seeks protection of these listed species against their 'taking' (with some exceptions). Appendix 1 lists endangered species and Appendix

Table 8.1 (*cont.*)

International convention	Description
	2 lists other species of unfavourable conservation status and the need for international agreements to protect them during migrations. Wild meat hunting of species listed on either appendix is not prohibited if it accommodates the needs of traditional subsistence users. The COP 12 document on unsustainable use of terrestrial vertebrates and birds gives the most relevant CMS position on wild meat use, and in 2016 their Scientific Council championed the concept of aquatic wild meat, which requested some action by the CMS on the issue of overexploitation of fisheries. The CMS is a member of the CPW.
UN Declaration on the Rights of Indigenous Peoples (UNDRIP)	The UNDRIP, passed in 2007, elaborates on existing human rights standards and fundamental freedoms as they apply to the specific situation of Indigenous Peoples. It sets minimum standards that should be adhered to by nation-states and broader society to ensure the survival, dignity and well-being of the Indigenous Peoples of the world. Articles particularly relevant to wild meat management are Article 8 on preventing dispossession from territories, Article 18 on the right to participate in decision making, Article 19 relating to free, prior and informed consent (FPIC), and Article 26 on the right to own, use, develop and control traditional territories. Further policy principles and commitments relevant to the rights of IPLCs in managing wildlife are provided in Table 1 of Wildlife, Wild Livelihoods, published by the UN Environment Programme (UNEP; Cooney *et al.* 2018).

exemplifies how hunting of these species for their meat has also resulted in the illegal flow of a more lucrative secondary product resulting in even greater pressures on these species (Heinrich *et al.* 2016; Ingram *et al.* 2019; Mambeya *et al.* 2018).

Another international channel concerned with regulating the use of wildlife resources involves the regional cooperation bodies such as the European Union (EU), African Union (AU), Association of Southeast Asian Nations (ASEAN), Union of South American Nations (USAN), and the Commission for Environmental Cooperation of North America (CECNA) and associated specialized wildlife bodies, such as the Interministerial Commission on Forests of Central Africa (COMIFAC) or the South Asian Wildlife Enforcement Network (SAWEN). Within these intergovernmental conventions, there is a tacit acceptance that wildlife should be sustainably used. Some regional intergovernmental bodies have also translated this mandate into policies promoting sustainable use within their own regions. This move indicates a clear shift toward wildlife as a resource that can be managed by and for humans, with the right enabling environment and resources and a step away from 'fortress conservation' policies. Yet, despite the clear positioning expressed by all these bodies that sustainable use must govern access to wildlife and other natural resources, policies resulting from these are often not adequately implemented on the ground. Moreover, in the case of conventions, their secretariats have not yet adopted technical standards for measuring sustainability in wildlife harvests, nor methods for moving toward improved sustainability should this be needed. As sustainability of a wildlife population can only be assessed over relatively long timeframes, there is also a need for standards in monitoring and measuring change over time. Such lack of international standards leaves national governments reliant on their own technical expertise, or that proffered by their NGO community. De facto, this leaves poorer nations with fewer technical resources to develop new approaches and revise governance structures.

8.3.2 Regional Governance Related to the Wild Meat Sector

8.3.2.1 Africa

Unsustainable hunting has been generally understood to be a threat to wildlife and livelihoods in most African countries. More explicit policies have been developed in Central and Southern African countries to manage subsistence hunting and to control illegal poaching of wildlife for meat. The AU adopted the Convention on the Conservation of Nature in 2003, and an 'African Strategy on Combating Illegal Exploitation and Illegal Trade in Wild Fauna and Flora in Africa' was drafted in May 2015. Revised and adopted in 2017, it became the Convention on the Conservation of Nature and Natural Resources, expanding on elements related to sustainable development. Through sustainable management tools their position calls for wildlife conservation and protection of traditional access to wildlife.

In Central Africa, COMIFAC has united six central African countries under a Convergence Plan for environmental management. The plan's objectives include conservation and sustainable use of biodiversity and socioeconomic development through multi-actor strategies. COMIFAC has supported several national and regional initiatives to improve the sustainability of wild meat and non-timber forest product harvests, as well as regulation of their trade. Together the COMIFAC and the Central African Forests Observatory have produced a State of the Forests report every 2–3 years, including an overview of hunting impacts and policy guidelines. Similarly, the Southern African Development Community, (SADC) developed and signed a Protocol on Wildlife Conservation and Management in 1999. This agreement promotes community-based management of wildlife and sustainable use for local consumption focussing on regulating use of wildlife for tourism, including trophy hunting, to improve local livelihoods. In conjunction with the Government of the Republic of Botswana the SADC Secretariat hosted a Ministerial Workshop on Illegal Trade in Wildlife, in Gaborone, Botswana, on 8 July 2016. In West Africa, the Economic Community of West African States (ECOWAS) and the West African Economic and Monetary Union have agriculture and environment sectors, but projects and expertise are heavily weighted toward agricultural crop production. Neither organization has formulated a clear position on wild meat management or use. The East African Community identifies three sectors potentially influencing the governance of wildlife and fisheries: agriculture and food security, tourism and wildlife management, and environment and natural resources. Under the environment and natural resources sector, member states agree to adhere to sustainable use policies, including for forests and wildlife, and to promote regional cooperation for cross-border management.

8.3.2.2 Latin America

South American regional policies unanimously recognize the need for sustainable use of all wild resources though the reality is that implementation of these rules is often ineffective. In Brazil alone, June 2019 saw an 88% rise in Amazon deforestation over the same month in 2018. In the first half of July 2019, deforestation was 68% above that for the entire month of July 2018, according to INPE, Brazil's federal monitoring agency. In the case of hunting, or rather overhunting, and its potential threat to biodiversity, regulations are rarely available. In particular, there is a need to fully integrate and manage subsistence hunting as part of regional environmental governance. The Amazon Cooperation Treaty Organization (ACTO) coordinates the policies and practices undertaken in respect of the Treaty for Amazonian Cooperation (TCA), and streamlines the execution of its decisions through its Permanent Secretariat. The Program for Sustainable Use and Conservation of Forests and Biodiversity in the Amazon Region, called the Amazon Regional Program (PRA), was born out of a joint cooperation between ACTO, the Directorate-General for International Cooperation (DGI), of the Netherlands, the German Federal Ministry of Economic Cooperation and Development (BMZ) and the German Development Cooperation (GIZ). It promotes the sustainable use of forest resources but refers to hunting only within projects to protect the rights of Indigenous Peoples. The Guiana Shield Facility (GSF) is a multi-donor funding facility for the long-term financing of national and regional activities to conserve ecosystems, protect biodiversity and sustain human livelihoods within the Guiana Shield ecoregion. The GSF priority setting workshop did not identify hunting as a major threat to biodiversity conservation in the region.

In 1993, Mexico, Canada and the USA signed the North American Agreement on Environmental Cooperation to address environmental issues of common concern, prevent environmental conflicts arising from the commercial relationships and promote the effective application of environmental legislation in the three countries. The agreement complements the North American Free Trade Agreement (NAFTA) and promotes sustainable development based on cooperation and mutually supportive environmental and economic policies. This applies to wild meat hunting; however, most hunting in this region is for sport rather than subsistence.

The Central American Commission for the Environment and Development (CCAD) is the organ responsible for the environmental agenda in Central America. Its main objectives are to contribute to the sustainable development of the region and strengthen cooperation and integration for the management of environmental resources. Although CCAD encourages the participation of indigenous communities and local farmers in activities compatible with conservation and sustainability, it does not express a specific policy on hunting, citing only water, ecosystem services, timber and non-timber plant resources as the objectives of sustainable management.

The Southern Common Market (Mercado Común del Sur, or Mercosur) is a regional integration process, established by Argentina, Brazil, Paraguay and Uruguay, and then more recently joined by Venezuela by the Treaty of Asunción in 1991 and Protocol of Ouro

Preto in 1994. Associate countries are Bolivia, Chile, Colombia, Ecuador, Guyana, Peru and Suriname. The stated objective of Mercosur is to promote a common space that generates business and investment opportunities through the competitive integration of national economies into the international market. The parties signed a specific agreement on environmental issues within Mercosur, reaffirming their commitment to the principles enunciated in the Rio de Janeiro Declaration on Environment and Development. The agreement aims to promote sustainable development and the protection of the environment through the articulation of economic, social and environmental dimensions, and to improve the quality of the environment and provide better lives for the population. This would clearly require sustainability to be part of any regulated hunting for trade, but Mercosur has not published specific wild meat policies.

8.3.2.3 Southeast Asia

Southeast Asian countries recognize an urgent need for improved hunting governance, and this is expressed as a priority at national and regional levels. However, hunting to supply the commercial trade in wildlife trophies and traditional medicines is at the forefront of policies. ASEAN is a regional intergovernmental organization comprising ten Southeast Asian countries. It promotes intergovernmental cooperation and facilitates economic, political, security, military, educational and sociocultural integration among its members. Members include Brunei, Cambodia, Indonesia, Lao PDR, Malaysia, Myanmar, the Philippines, Singapore, Thailand and Vietnam. ASEAN's overarching objectives and policies are detailed in three blueprint documents for community policies in economics, sociocultural affairs and politics–security. The socio-cultural blueprint for policies until 2025 includes environmental cooperation. It identifies several priority areas of regional importance, including sustainable use of terrestrial, marine and coastal ecosystems, and a halt to biodiversity loss and land degradation.

ASEAN member states have recognized the importance of action on wildlife crime, with ASEAN ministers adding wildlife and timber trafficking to the list of priority transnational crimes, mandating follow-up through the ASEAN Senior Officials Meeting on Trans-National Crime. Following this decision, the ASEAN National Police Network, (ASEANAPOL), is also seeking to work more closely with the International Consortium on Combating Wildlife Crime's (ICCWC) ASEAN-Wildlife Enforcement Network (ASEAN-WEN).

8.3.3 The Challenge of Legislating for Subsistence Hunting and Limited Sale

In numerous countries, there are still inconsistencies in national laws with regards to rural and Indigenous communities' rights to hunt wildlife for self-consumption, and to sell some of the meat (Van Vliet *et al.* 2019). Although hunting is often to satisfy the need for food for most families, hunters may sell some of the animals killed as a source of income. The proportion and volumes of meat sold varies depending on the cultural and socioeconomic contexts of the hunters thus making it difficult to establish simple categories. A practical definition of subsistence hunting could include selling (mostly locally) part of the game hunted for consumption to purchase other subsistence goods (e.g. soap, gasoline, oil). However, in legal terms, the concept of subsistence hunting is defined differently and refers to often contrasting realities. As shown by the diversity of terms used in legal frameworks in examples from Latin America (Mexico, Brazil, Colombia, Guyana) and Africa (Republic of Congo, Gabon, Democratic Republic of Congo) Van Vliet *et al.* (2019) attest to the difficulty of developing a unified concept of subsistence hunting (Table 8.2). These authors argue that formal regulations are ill adapted to the contexts in which they should be applied and are characterized by gaps and contradiction that maintain hunting for meat and the sale of its surplus in an equivocal legal space, a limbo according to Van Vliet *et al.* (2019).

Though most legal instruments allow Indigenous or rural peoples to hunt wildlife for food, the sale of surplus meat is not permitted. Differences exist across countries, but a common denominator is the lack of clarity concerning the right to sell wild meat hunted by local communities. Currently, the sale of surplus meat is either under-regulated, or over-regulated to a point where enforcement becomes nearly impossible. For example, in Brazil, it is forbidden to transport, sell or acquire eggs, larvae or specimens of fauna and by-products from hunting and harvesting or from unauthorized breeding sites (Antunes *et al.* 2019; Pezzuti *et al.* 2019) but within indigenous territories Amerindians have rights over aboveground natural resources and there are no commercial legal restrictions. An interesting contrast is the case of Gabon, which is the only country that, following a forest law reform in 2008, has introduced the concept of 'economic user rights' (Sartoretto *et al.* 2017). These are rights, recognized by the State, to market locally and without intermediaries, part of the collection of products derived from their customary use rights. Customary hunters selling game products outside their community must apply for a hunting permit and a commercial capture license.

Table 8.2 *Comparison of national regulations regarding the use and trade of wild meat in Colombia, Brazil, Guyana, Mexico, Republic of Corgo, Gabon, and Democratic Republic of Congo (taken from Van Vliet et al. 2019).*

Country	Hunting rights	Wild meat trade rights	Relevant legal code
Colombia	Subsistence hunting allowed for any resident except for protected species in protected areas (unless specified by a management plan in the case of overlap with indigenous reserves).	Trade allowed in theory for species listed by the Ministry of Environment (no list has been issued to date) provided permit being issued by the regional environmental agency after submission of an Environmental Assessment Study (EIS).	Decree-Law 2811 of 1974–National Code on Natural Renewable Resources Environment Protection. Decree 1076 pf 2015–Regulatory Decree of the Environment Sustainable Development Sector. Law 17 of 1981–Approves the CITES Convention, Resolution 705 of 2015–Establishes safety requirements for commercial hunting. Decree 1272 of 2016–Establishes regulation on wildlife hunting compensatory fees.
Brazil	Only explicitly allow for Indigenous people (Amerindians) within titled land. Generally tolerated for other ethnic groups and rural populations if intended 'to quench the hunger' in remote regions.	Trade is forbidden in the entire Brazilian territory, except inside titled Indigenous lands where Amerindians have management rights over aboveground natural resources and there are no legal restrictions on internal commercialisation of meat surplus. Commercial extensive management can be permitted	Law 5197/03 January 1967–Wildlife Protection Act. Law 6001/19 December 1973–Indian Statute. Law 9605/12 February 1998–Law of Environmental Crimes. Law 9985/18 July 2000–National System of Conservation Units (SNUC). Law 10826/22 December 2003–Disarmamen Statute. Decree 5051/19 April 2004–Promulgation of ILO Convention 169. Law 11346/15 September 2006–National

(cont.)

Table 8.2 (*cont.*)

Country	Hunting rights	Wild meat trade rights	Relevant legal code
		in exceptional circumstances upon the existence of management plans and governmental licenses.	System of Food and Nutritional Security (SISAN). Decree 6040/08 February 2007-National Policy for the Sustainable Development of Traditional Peoples and Communities.
Guyana	Only allowed in Amerindian titled land. Outside Amerindian titled lands, hunters are required to request a permit delivered by the Guyana Wildlife Conservation and Management Commission.	Allowed for any citizen, pending the obtention of a commercial license.	Kaieteur National Park Act of 1930. Fisheries (Aquatic Wildlife Control) Regulations of 1966. Amerindian Act of 2006. Animal Health Act of 2011. Protected Areas Act of 2011. Wildlife Management and Conservation Regulations of 2013. Wildlife Conservation and Management Act of 2016.
Mexico	There is lack of clarity whether hunting can be practiced as part of the legally recognized 'subsistence uses' or if it is subjected to previous authorization by the Ministry in charge.	Trade is legal only if the meat comes from intensive or extensive breeding authorised centres (called Wildlife Management Units – UMA) and is sold in established and official markets.	General Law for Wildlife (Ley General de Vida Silvestre, LGVS) (SEMARNAT, 2016/2000). LGVS Regulations (SEMARNAT, 2014/2006). National Strategy foer Wildlife 1995–2000 (INE, 2000). Program of Wildlife Conservation and Productive Diversification in the Rural Sector 1997–2000 (SEMARNAP, 1997).

Republic of Congo	Hunting for the satisfaction of personal and community needs is allowed under customary rights.	No commercial trade is allowed under any circumstances.	Loi 37–2008 du 28 novembre 2008 sur la faune et les aires protégées. Loi 16–2000 portant code forestier. Loi 5–2011 du 25 février 2011 portant promotion et protection des droits de populations autochtones. Arrêté 3772 de 12 aout 1972 fixant les périodes d'ouverture et de fermeture de la chasse sportive en République du Congo. Arrêté 5053/MEF/CAB du 19 juin 2007 définissant les directives nationales d'aménagement durable des concessions forestières.
Gabon	Hunting for the satisfaction of personal and community needs is allowed under customary rights.	Trade within the community is allowed without restrictions following the economic user rights. For trade beyond the community boundaries, the trader should obtain a certificate of origin, a zoo-sanitary certificate and a certificate of harvest.	Loi 16–2001 portant code forestier. Décret 161/2001, fixant les conditions de délivrance des permis et licences de chasse et de capture. Décret 163/2011, fixant les conditions de détention, de transport, de commercialisation des espèces animaux sauvages, des trophées et produits de chasse.
Democratic Republic of Congo	Hunting, including by local communities, is subordinated to the acquisition of a collective hunting license, which authorises hunting 'within the strict limits of their food needs'.	Trade is allowed under a specific license or a 'commercial catch' permit, pending the obtention of a 'hunting ability test' and a hunting license.	Loi 82–002 portant règlementation de la chasse. Arrêté 014/CAB/MIN/ENV/2004.

In addition, the Gabonese legislation provides that the possession and transport of the remains of species requires a certificate of origin, a zoo-sanitary certificate and a certificate of harvest (Sartoretto *et al.* 2017): requirements that are far beyond the capacities of contemporary Gabonese hunters. Van Vliet *et al.* (2019) suggest that there is the need for much greater clarity on how the rights to sell surplus of meat and sustainable use of wildlife is defined in law that accounts for the realities and needs of communities from different cultural backgrounds. Without the revision of current inconsistencies, overlaps and gaps, there is little hope that investments in law enforcement will achieve tangible outputs for wildlife conservation and the livelihoods of marginalized groups.

8.4 Reducing the Demand for Wild Meat

8.4.1 Stemming Increased Commercialization of the Wildlife Harvest

Wild animals hunted may be consumed, sold locally or transported to urban markets where they fetch higher prices. Factors which determine which species are sold or consumed include the size of the animal, cultural inhibitions as well as personal or public appeal and demand. Hunters might sell a proportion of the wild meat extracted. However, the proportion of wild meat sold varies depending on the hunters' needs, access to market and even the individual's desire to monetize the resource if this is not cultural. For example, differences between the proportion of hunted game sold by Indigenous groups (Pygmies) and Bantu farmers in the Congo Basin indicate that whilst on average only 35% (range 0–90%) of the hunted game in Pygmy settlements was sold, significantly more prey (65.4%, range 11–95.3%) was commercialized in non-Pygmy settlements (Fa *et al.* 2016). Often, small-sized prey is more likely to be consumed locally while the more appealing and profitable species are sold in town and city markets.

As discussed in the previous chapters in this book, wild meat hunting is a major component of the livelihoods and food security of myriad rural and Indigenous Peoples. In some areas, unsustainable hunting is a major cause of wildlife declines even affecting many protected areas (see Tranquilli *et al.* 2014). These declines can have significant knock-on effects on ecological systems, impacting ecosystem services such as nutrient cycling and carbon capture (Chapters 2 and 6) and also affect human survival. Hunting in more remote rural areas is likely to be sustainable, primarily because human population densities (and thus hunter numbers) are low (see Ávila Martin *et al.* 2020) and source areas are likely to be larger. In high human density areas or where the focus of hunters is to supply urban markets, vulnerable species may be extirpated leading to larger numbers of smaller species making the bulk of the wild meat sold in these markets (Cowlishaw *et al.* 2005).

Generally, the demand for wild meat in fast-growing urban centres is considered by many researchers to be the main drive for unsustainable harvesting rates (Coad *et al.* 2019). Because many urban dwellers consume wild meat as a luxury item rather than as a nutritional staple in many cases, they pay higher prices than rural consumers do for the same animal. This encourages hunters in rural villages to hunt more animals for sale, to gain higher incomes resulting in a classic, unregulated Tragedy of the Commons problem. Likewise, this same urban demand drives the proliferation of purely commercial hunters, some forming parts of highly organized groups engaged in the illegal trade of wildlife products at the domestic or even international level. More income from wild meat will also allow these hunters to buy better and more powerful firearms, thus increasing the pressure on wild meat populations even more. The consensus is that this uncontrolled wild meat trade, together with the loss of intact habitat, threatens wildlife in all tropical and subtropical regions in all continents. In the Amazon, an area presumed by some in the past to have been exempt from the huge demand for wild meat by cities or town (Rushton *et al.* 2005), El Bizri *et al.* (2019) have shown that there has been a considerable switch from hunting wild meat for home consumption to supplying more lucrative city markets. Emerging evidence for large cities in Central Africa, for example, Kinshasa and Brazzaville (together representing more than 15 million people), suggests that if each inhabitant ate a minimum of 1–2 kg of wild meat per year (data for urban consumers from Wilkie & Carpenter 1999) between 15–30 million kilograms are likely to be consumed annually (Fa *et al.* 2019). Given that urbanization is growing in all tropical regions with large, even megacities emerging, the demand for wild meat is increasing rapidly (see Fig. 2.10, Chapter 2). Although most data on the flow of wild meat from rural to urban areas are from Africa (Chausson *et al.* 2019; Fa *et al.* 2019; Fargeot *et al.* 2017; Mbete *et al.* 2011) and increasingly from Latin America (El Bizri *et al.* 2019; Van Vliet *et al.* 2014, 2015a), increasing urban wild meat consumption in Asian cities also poses a major threat to faunal biodiversity (see Sandalj *et al.* 2016 for Vietnam). The reduction or even elimination of wild meat in cities and towns, if possible, is unlikely to affect access to other forms of animal protein. As shown in Fa *et al.* (2019) for Kinshasa and Brazzaville, and by Wilkie *et al.* (2005) for the Congo Basin, domestically produced and imported animal source foods (primarily chicken and fish) provide city dwellers with almost all their dietary protein, and that wild meat is sold irregularly by only a small percentage of vendors, and is not likely to be a dietary necessity. Research in poor neighbourhoods in sub-Saharan African cities shows high levels of household food insecurity and emphasizes the important role of informal food traders in meeting the needs of poor urban household (Crush & Riley 2019; Ingram 2020).

Tackling the problem of wild meat consumption in urban settlements is an urgent priority requiring a greater focus on social science research to compliment long-term ecological monitoring (Redman *et al.* 2004). Understanding better why different people in metropolitan areas consume wild meat is essential if we are to eliminate obstacles to creating policies that remove the need for these resources and promote the potential for other more abundant (and more affordable) animal protein sources to be available. Because food systems are complex entities, consisting of many different actors, their activities and interactions – the driving forces shaping these activities and the outcomes produced at the individual and system level – food systems research must move towards an integrated approach for analysis and new ways to communicate this complexity outside the research domain. Moving towards sustainable management requires interconnected interventions to target the management of rural supply but primarily the reduction of urban demand. This calls for work along the entire value chain, including local hunting communities, urban consumers and wider society.

8.4.2 Substituting with Other Meat Alternatives

Farming of wildlife species for their meat was proposed as a solution to reduce demand as early as the 1950s (e.g. Asibey 1974; de Vos 1977; Ntiamoa-Baidu 1997). Though there are known zoonotic risks linked to rearing of animals in restricted spaces, whether domestic animals or wild species (Chapter 7), the main assumption is that by providing people with farmed wild animal meat, pressure would be lessened on wildlife populations. Concerns about the viability of such farming, its cost effectiveness and its impact on wildlife populations has been much debated (Mockrin *et al.* 2005). Wildlife farming proponents envision fully controlled production systems, independent of wild populations for source animals, operating in urban, peri-urban and rural settings to supplement human protein intake without large investment costs. A wide array of vertebrate species has been investigated for farming to obtain meat (see Appendix 1 in Mockrin *et al.* 2005), either because they are preferred food species (Smythe & Brown de Guanti 1995), others because they command a high price in markets (Jori *et al.* 1995). However, raising wild species for food does not necessarily comprise domestication of the species – a long and intensive process whereby humans selectively control the animals' reproduction, with resulting genetic changes. Yet, notwithstanding the somewhat consistent emphasis on wildlife farming of a variety of tropical forest species (e.g. mini-livestock, see Hardouin 1995) in the past three decades, examples of successful wildlife farming are uncommon. Few wild vertebrate species native to the humid tropics are commonly farmed with perhaps the exception of large rodents such as grasscutters in West and Central Africa (Adu *et al.* 2013; Jori *et al.* 1995; Mensah 2000).

The possibility and eventual success in raising wild species in captivity depends on the species' biology (reproduction, productivity and vulnerability to disease) and the cost-effectiveness of farming it. The demands on source populations for new blood, genetic mixing with wild populations and potential introductions of invasive alien species are concerns that have to be taken into account. Aside from these issues, the reception of this production method by actors unfamiliar with farming wild animals will also influence the likely success of such efforts. Cultural norms and individual motivations will influence which community members participate in an activity, and throughout much of Central Africa mini-livestock rearing (e.g. chickens, cane rats) is often a women's activity (Hardouin *et al.* 2003; Thornton *et al.* 2002). Furthermore, even the lack of preference of the produced farmed over wild meats can impede progress. For example, a study of consumer preferences in Ghana showed that wild grasscutter meat was favoured over farmed animals because it was perceived to have better flavour, be more tender and had less fat content (Teye *et al.* 2020).

Wildlife farming is therefore a complex enterprise, involving aspects of rural development, agricultural production and conservation. However, the production of wild meat farming, even if economically viable, is unlikely to produce sufficient meat to satisfy the needs of consumers and ensure their food security. Wildlife farming also poses major conservation threats to existing wildlife populations. This is because of the need to acquire breeding stock from wild populations, increased risks of disease and genetic contamination of wild populations of the same or other species, as well as the risks of the spread of invasive alien species including diseases. Wildlife farms are also known to be a front for illegal trade of wild-caught animals (e.g. Livingstone & Shepherd 2016). Moreover, until wildlife numbers in the wild become so low that it is no longer worthwhile hunting them, wildlife farming is unlikely to reduce hunting, due to the high costs of farming compared to hunting, lack of appropriate technical skills and funds, and cultural constraints. However, as suggested by Tensen (2016), wildlife farming can benefit species conservation only if the following criteria are met: (1) the legal products will form a substitute, and consumers show no preference for wild-caught animals; (2) a substantial part of the demand is met, and the demand does not increase due to the legalized market; (3) the legal products will be more cost-efficient, in order to combat the black market prices; (4) wildlife farming does not rely on wild populations for re-stocking; (5) laundering of illegal products into the commercial trade is absent. Until these conditions are met, more efforts should be placed to create hardier breeds that are less susceptible to disease and choose appropriate locations and socio-economic strategies to expand domestic livestock farming as part of planning for a sustainable landscape (Robinson 1993). Any improvement of known domestic breeds must ensure that production is not extensive and thus does not encourage deforestation and soil erosion, for example. However, in certain economic and cultural conditions, wildlife farming should be conducted but strict guidelines are needed to ensure that the operations succeed as viable farming enterprises and do not harm wildlife populations.

Although the regulation of hunting practices in rural areas is likely to ensure a sustainable supply of wild meat to the local consumers, in some cases wildlife farms may be appropriate if domestic animal farming is not a viable option. Wildlife farming in peri-urban areas to satisfy the demand for wild meat could reduce the pressure on wildlife. The higher prices paid by some urban consumers will, in some cases, make this economically viable. Under these circumstances, the farms are not a food security solution since urban dwellers who can afford the higher-priced farmed wild meat inevitably have alternative, cheaper, sources of protein, usually fish or domestic meat. Such farms are also not a solution to a conservation problem, since they would not reduce hunting by rural peoples, or supply cheap meat to poorer urban dwellers. The farms might, however, be viable commercial concerns, and be supported politically.

8.5 Balancing Conservation and Needs of Rural and Indigenous Peoples

Reducing the rates of global deforestation and forest degradation would yield substantial gains for climate change mitigation and biodiversity conservation. However, forest loss caused by the rising and urbanizing non-forest human population will dramatically increase competition for natural resources with forest-living peoples. The exploitation of sub-surface commodities, namely mining, oil and gas resources, poses one of the greatest of the many threats facing Indigenous Peoples and the lands, territories and the resources that they depend on. As the global economy expands, pressure on indigenous lands to yield up these resources is intensifying. In the eyes of more socially minded conservationists, however, local people (and the improvement of their social, physical and economic well-being) are understood to be the focal point of holistic conservation efforts. Recent reviews suggest that this is a promising path to explore: evidence shows that local traditional and Indigenous Peoples are better custodians of forests and biodiversity than governments (Fa *et al.* 2020; O'Bryan *et al.* 2020; Stevens 2014), and a global survey of tropical forests found that government-protected forests were cut down four times faster than community-managed ones (Porter-Bolland *et al.* 2012).

There are at least 370 million people who define themselves as Indigenous (The World Bank 2020), are descended from populations who inhabited a country before the time of conquest or colonization, and who retain at least some of their own social, economic, cultural and political institutions (International Labour Organisation 1989). Irrespective of their global diversity, Indigenous Peoples often express deep spiritual and cultural ties to their land and contend that local ecosystems reflect millennia of their stewardship, with Indigenous Peoples' lands representing one of the oldest forms of conservation units (Garnett *et al.* 2018). Moreover, they assert that Indigenous rights do not require state-sanctioned approval to exist. While Indigenous Peoples' land rights are acknowledged and implemented to varying degrees across time and geography, even when refused or ignored, Indigenous Peoples frequently retain de facto influence over their ancestral lands. Using publicly available geospatial resources, Garnett *et al.* (2018) have shown that Indigenous Peoples manage or have tenure rights over at least approx. 38 million km^2 in 87 countries or politically distinct areas on all inhabited continents. This represents over a quarter of the world's land surface and intersects about 40% of all terrestrial protected areas and ecologically intact landscapes (Fa *et al.* 2020). These results add to growing evidence that recognizing Indigenous Peoples' rights to land, benefit sharing and institutions is essential to meeting local and global conservation goals. Alongside training, capacity and awareness building etc., we have the same problem as it is not being Indigenous *per se* which achieves conservation goals but population density (as opposite to the 'noble savage hypothesis'; Section 3.6).

International solutions to achieving the conservation of tropical forest biodiversity have historically followed three general approaches: (1) establishing parks and other protected areas (PAs) to safeguard wild species and natural systems, and (2) enforcing/promoting restraint in the harvest and (3) prohibiting consumption of wild species and their products. All three approaches affect rural and Indigenous People's access to natural resources, either by denying them the opportunity to use certain areas (as in PAs), or by reducing their harvest levels. In so doing, conservation actions can conflict with other ethical obligations, by curtailing, for instance, the ability of some people to make a living, an obligation and a core right recognized in the Universal Declaration of Human Rights (United Nations 1948): 'Everyone has the right to a standard of living adequate for [their] health and wellbeing'. If conservation activities have a negative impact on the autonomy and rights of Indigenous Peoples, then it might conflict with other ethical obligations such as the right of all peoples to self-determination enshrined in UN International Covenant on Economic, Social and Cultural Rights (1976) that 'recognizes the right of peoples to dispose freely of their wealth and natural resources to satisfy their needs' or, as identified in the UN Declaration on the Rights of Indigenous People (United Nations 2007), which states that Indigenous People have rights 'to the lands, territories and resources which they have traditionally owned, occupied, or otherwise used or acquired'. Other relevant international conventions include the Convention on Biological Diversity (article 8j); International Covenant on Civil and Political Rights (Article 1); the Charter of the United Nations (Article 1, 55 and 56); Rio Declaration on Environment and Development (Principles 1, 10, 22 and 23), and other international ethical standards such as the Principles of the Forest Stewardship Council or the International Labour Organisation Convention 169 (Articles 6, 7 and 15.2).

Indigenous Peoples lands are demarcated territories officially recognized as belonging to and managed by the first-comers. These

Indigenous Peoples are traditional groups who closely identify with their land and with a distinctive culture but who are marginalized by dominant society. Despite the potential spectrum of solutions available for balancing the needs of people with those of nature, it is the 'parks *versus* people' debate that has created the greatest tensions between and within the conservation and development communities (see e.g. Adams & Hutton 2007; Brockington 2002; Roe & Elliott 2004; Sanderson & Redford 2004; Schwartzman *et al.* 2000; Terborgh 1999, 2000). Such debate has, more often than not, concentrated on the value and efficacy of PAs or the alternative, Integrated Conservation and Development Projects (ICDPs), in protecting biodiversity – and promoting (or negatively impacting) human livelihoods (e.g. Terborgh *et al.* 2002; Wells & McShane 2004). For those within the 'strict preservation' camp, PAs are the most important means to achieve the primary task of conservation, that is, the protection of global biodiversity. Among conservation interventions in tropical forests, the establishment of PAs has been the most prominent and best funded (Chomitz *et al.* 2007). The Global Environment Facility reports that its investments in PAs included $1.6 billion of its own resources and $4.2 billion in co-financing; much of this has been implemented through the World Bank. Protected areas, mostly in the marine realm, have expanded rapidly in recent years (Coad *et al.* 2008) and now cover around 27.1% of the tropical forest estate, contributing to the reduction of tropical deforestation. As already mentioned, there is emerging evidence that forest reserves that allow for sustainable use by local people were even more effective, on average, than strictly protected areas focused exclusively on conservation. The most effectively protected areas of all were those within indigenous lands, which were estimated to reduce deforestation by about 16% more than all other conservation approaches between 2000 and 2008 (Nelson & Chomitz 2011). These findings are relevant in the context of ongoing global efforts to reward countries for reducing greenhouse gas emissions from deforestation pointing to the fact that the most effective forest conservation incorporates local livelihoods and recognizes indigenous land and resource rights. Collaborative partnerships involving conservation practitioners, rural and Indigenous Peoples and governments would yield significant benefits for conservation of ecologically valuable landscapes, ecosystems and genes for future generations. It is through these new alliances, where long-resident human populations who have a right to their lands and resources manage and protect biodiversity areas, including PAs, that protection and supply of human needs will be possible in the future.

8.6 Concluding Remarks

A clear understanding of the numerous factors which can lead to the unsustainable harvest of wild meat is needed to resolve the issue. From an applied perspective, we need to differentiate between commercial *versus* non-commercial hunting, the species we are dealing with, the zoonotic risk and the results of monitoring to devise management strategies (Fig. 8.3). Fundamental is the interpretation of the issues affecting the supply side, that is, the environment and the ecology of the hunted species, but also how the present and future demand by rural and urban populations puts pressure on the animal populations themselves. We use a simple conceptual diagram (see Fig. 8.1) of the key processes driving the direct use value of wild meat ranging from the decisions made at the small scale by individual hunters, the influence of village and market-level factors, for example, consumer preferences and availability of meat substitutes and how these in turn affect consumer demand. At the ecological level, hunter offtake is a function of animal abundance, which is affected at a range of scales by habitat quality and food resource availability. The productivity of these habitats is influenced by land use patterns at a local scale but also by global changes at a macro level. Although researchers may concentrate on approaches that vary by scale and process type, for example, small-scale harvest models, market models, habitat models and village livelihoods models, these different components of the wild meat system progress can only be made if we consider all these variables jointly.

This book concentrates on the science on wild meat use so we focus less on the regulatory aspects of how communities manage the resource although we mention issues of national governance of wild meat in Section 8.3. This is a key to the successful management of natural resources at the country level. A first step forward in regulating the use of wild meat in any country is to ensure the consultation with all stakeholders so national hunting laws and land tenure governance systems are adequate (see Van Vliet *et al.* 2019 and above). However, hunting regulations in many tropical and subtropical countries are based on legislation originally written for seasonal hunting in temperate regions and are not focused on subsistence needs (e.g. for laws with colonial legacy, see Morgera & Cirelli 2010). They are often ambiguous, as they do not fit well within the local context, making it difficult for local communities to act within the law, or use the law to support hunter adherence to sustainable practices (Van Vliet *et al.* 2019). Failure to

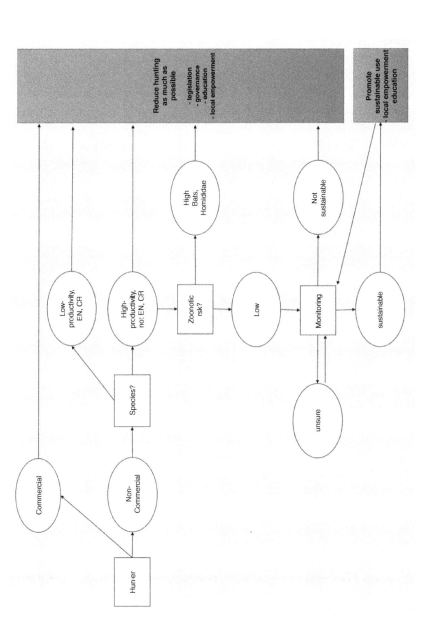

Figure 8.3 Simplified decision diagram to decide how wild meat hunting is managed. Non-commercial subsistence hunters might sell part of their hunted game; we consider this as 'non-commercial' as long as trade is local and does not involve intermediate buyer/sellers.

devolve land tenure and support Indigenous management, for example, how to enable them to restrict outside commercial hunters has also prevented many of these populations from acting as stewards of their landscapes, especially in Africa.

Political support for sustainable wild meat management is more likely if the circumstances for legitimate consumptive use of wildlife are recognized and formalized (Coad *et al.* 2019). Ensuring sustainability is genuinely achieved over the long term will require regional- and national-level monitoring and surveillance frameworks that respond to indicators of unsustainable use. Understanding what works and what does not in a specific context will allow the refinement of policies and measures over time, providing a pathway to ensure true sustainability for the future. Bringing together a series of actions that can ensure better governance towards a sustainable wild meat sector has been proposed by Nasi and Fa (2015), as shown in Box 8.1.

In this last chapter we have highlighted the ecological and socio-economic variables that are involved in the study and understanding of wild meat use and over-exploitation. Designing effective policies on sustainable wild meat use will require robust data on the indicators of overexploitation of wildlife – and the impacts of exploitation on ecosystems, human health and livelihoods – so that a legitimate case for sustainable use can be made. Such data should be commonly available to managers and decision makers. Thus, whilst we acknowledge that the sustainable management of the tropical wild meat sector is complex, we argue that with the right enabling environment and political will, well-designed and participatory multi-sectoral approaches that are based on solid science, we can effectively enable wild meat supply and reduce demand to sustainable levels. We are nonetheless realistic in acknowledging that this may be possible only for some species in some places.

Emphasized throughout the book is the fact that sustainable wildlife exploitation has to happen against a complex and changing backdrop because of human population growth. Talk of human population numbers in the tropics and subtropics, and its concomitant decline in space for wildlife from habitat loss, is the ever-present 'elephant in the room'. Thus, ultimately, and quite categorically, governments and development agencies must recognize that wild meat use must be reserved for those people and communities closest to the resource (and more dependent on it). Every effort should be made by them to reduce or even eliminate the demand for wild meat in urban areas as well as be given the support or power to stop others taking away their resources. Protected

Box 8.1 *A comprehensive roadmap for better governance towards a sustainable wild meat sector requires (Nasi & Fa 2015).*

- **Working with the upstream actors to improve the sustainability of supply**
  - Hunters: negotiate hunting rules and quotas allowing harvesting resilient species and banning vulnerable ones; design and agree on simple participatory monitoring tools
  - Extractive industries: enforce codes of conducts and include wildlife concerns in companies' standard operating procedures; forbid transportation on company's vehicles; establish adequately staffed checkpoints; provide alternative sources of protein at cost; organize, support community hunting schemes; adopt certification.
- **Reducing the demand**
  - Rural consumers: develop alternative sources of protein at a cost similar to wild meat; improve economic opportunities in productive sectors; use local media (e.g. radio) to deliver environmental education and raise awareness
  - Retailers, urban consumers: strictly enforce ban on protected/endangered species sales and consumption, confiscating and publicly incinerating carcasses; taxing sales of authorized species of international consumers: institute very heavy fines for transport (eventually targeting airline companies), possession or trade of wild meat (whatever the status or provenance of the species); raise awareness of the issue in airports or seaports; train custom personnel
- **Create an enabling environment for a controlled, sustainable wild meat sector**
  - Local institutions: negotiate full support of communities that have a vested interest in protecting the resource; increase capacity to setup and manage sustainable wild meat markets.
  - National level: enhance ownership, linked to tenurial and rights reform; legitimize the wild meat debate; make an economic assessment of the sector and include in national statistics; acknowledge contribution of wild meat to food security in national strategies; develop a framework to 'formalize' parts of the trade; review national legislation for coherence, practicality and to reflect actual practices (without surrendering key conservation concerns); include wild meat/wildlife modules in curricula.
  - International level: strictly enforce CITES with more consideration on regional trade; ensure wildlife issues are covered within

internationally supported policy processes; link international trade with increased emerging disease risks; impose tough fines and shame irresponsible behaviour.

- **Develop more targeted research**
  - Create a shift away from descriptive studies of wildlife exploitation to more incisive investigations on the roles which wild meat might play in poverty eradication in balance with the sustainable use of the resource.
  - Develop cost-effective systems for examining the importance of wild meat to human populations in different ecological and socio-economic settings. In particular, examine the further application of existing global mechanisms for data gathering on nutrition, such as FAO's Food Balance Sheets.
  - Determine causal links between alternative protein sources (e.g. marine and freshwater fish supply) and wildlife populations, and the ecological footprints of increasing accessibility to domestic meats (e.g. livestock, poultry).
  - Elaborate effective systems for monitoring the status of hunted wildlife that can be operated by local communities and managers.
  - In combination with the conservation sector, instigate original research on the role of source–sink dynamics of hunted wildlife, including the role of protected areas.
  - Understand the relationships and trade-offs between wild meat and other meat/protein sources for human populations inhabiting distinct faunal areas, such as those identified by Fa *et al.* (2015b) for Central Africa.

areas are no doubt refuges for wildlife and sources of wild meat for adjacent communities but envisaging these areas as fortress conservation spaces may work against the future of wildlife and of long-time resident peoples. Also, it is possible to facilitate sustainable hunting of species that reproduce quickly (such as small ungulates and large rodent species), and where necessary supplementing this with domestic meats at the same time as protecting threatened animals.

Sustainable management of wildlife resources will not happen if interconnected interventions are not deployed to target the management of rural supply of wild meat and most definitely achieve the reduction of urban demand. This needs to be achieved by involving local hunting communities, urban consumers and the wider society. Of vital importance is the involvement and stewardship of Indigenous Peoples and local communities who inhabit more than half of the world's land area. Despite these populations being the custodians of existing natural resources, including wildlife, they rarely have formal legal ownership. This lack of land tenure rights makes it hard for communities to protect their lands legally, especially against external commercial hunters and extractive industries (see Pemunta 2019 for Baka in Cameroon). A key prerequisite for ensuring sustainable management of wildlife resources has to be the devolution of land management and tenure rights to local communities. Additionally, government authorities must have the structures, capacities and budgets to support local communities in their management of wildlife, as well as enforce local and national hunting rules. A number of different community-based approaches for managing wildlife that are appropriate in different contexts are already in force including community- or co-managed protected areas, wildlife ranching and community conservancies, Payment for Ecosystem Services (PES) schemes and certification mechanisms (see Coad *et al.* 2019 for examples). Alongside these initiatives, extractive industries as well as extensive agriculture, which now affect a significant proportion of tropical and subtropical habitats should provide food alternatives (such as domestic meat) for staff working in concessions, help to enforce equitable hunting regulations in collaboration with local communities to ensure sustainable local use. Ultimately, they should also prevent the use of concession roads and vehicles by external commercial hunters aiming to supply urban demand.

As stressed by Van Vliet (2018) in all aspects of biodiversity use and protection, it is fundamental to carefully consider the value orientations toward wildlife, bringing often segmented perspectives away from hegemony, and closer to an overall vision for conservation that is broadly inclusive of a full range of wildlife values (Manfredo *et al.* 2016). Taking into account both hegemonic and marginalized ideas about wildlife will reduce the likelihood for conservation abuses in postcolonial contexts (McGregor 2005) and provide a unique opportunity to shift the paradigms in tropical wildlife management. The human stakeholders with the most to lose often have no voice in decision-making. Disturbingly, some conservation practitioners suggest that promoting cultural change regarding wildlife use amongst traditional users is legitimate based on evidence-based scientific knowledge about the 'bushmeat crisis'

(Dickman *et al.* 2015; Jepson & Canney 2003). Acknowledging the disparities in power relationships, providing the necessary grounds for a fair debate and supporting free decision-making by the legitimate constituency are all necessary steps to avoid 'cultural imperialism' in conservation practice. Failing to do so might increase the potential for social conflict over wild meat management issues. Embracing the richness and complexity of cross-cultural plurality will allow us to take disparate value orientations seriously without privileging anyone (Hovorka 2017). In a period of unparalleled social-ecological change, bringing together the differences in wildlife value orientations between local/international, rural/urban, traditional/western visions is a necessary step in radically reconstructing a new paradigm for a sustainable and culturally respectful wild meat sector.

Appendix 1

Species and Genera

In this appendix we only give the scientific names associated with common names if they refer to single species or genera. We do not list common names associated with several genera, such as in the case of hyrax or duiker.

African buffalo: *Syncerus caffer*
African giant pouched rat: *Cricetomys gambianus* and *C. emini*
African green monkey: *Chlorocebus aethiops*
African wild dog: *Lycaon pictus*
Agouti: *Dasyprocta* spp.
American mink: *Neovison vison*
Andean tapir: *Tapirus pinchaque*
Anhinga: *Anhinga anhinga*
Anoa: *Bubalus* spp.
Aracari: *Pteroglossus* spp.
Asian elephant: *Elephas maximus*
Atlantic cod: *Gadus morhua*
Baboon: *Papio* spp.
Baird's tapir: *Tapirus bairdii*
Banana: *Musa* spp.
Black colobus monkey: *Colobus satanas*
Black rat: *Rattus rattus*
Black spider monkey: *Ateles paniscus*
Black-casqued hornbill: *Ceratogymna atrata*
Black-handed spider monkey: *Ateles geoffroyi*
Black-tailed deer: *Odocoileus hemionus*
Blue duiker *Philantomba monticola*
Blue wildebeest: *Connochaetes taurinus*
Bonobo: *Pan paniscus*
Brocket deer: *Mazama* spp.
Brush-tailed porcupine: *Atherurus africanus*

Bush duiker: *Sylvicapra grimmia*
Bushbuck: *Tragelaphus sylvaticus*
Bushpig: *Potamochoerus larvatus*
Cane rat: *Thryonomys swinderianus*
Capuchin monkey: *Cebus apella*
Capybara: *Hydrochoerus hydrochaeris*
Cassava: *Manihot esculenta*
Chachalaca: *Phasianus motmot*
Chacoan peccary: *Catagonus wagneri*
Chimpanzee: *Pan troglodytes*
Chinese ferret badger: *Melogale moschata*
Chipmunk: *Neotamias* spp.
Cocoa: *Theobroma cacao*
Coffee: *Coffea* spp.
Collared peccary: *Pecari tajacu*
Dik-dik: *Madoqua* spp.
Dogtooth tuna: *Gymnosarda unicolor*
Domestic cat: *Felis catus*
Domestic chicken: *Gallus gallus domesticus*
Domestic dog: *Canis familiaris*
Domestic duck: *Anas platyrhynchos domesticus*
Domestic ferret: *Mustela putorius furo*
Domestic pig: *Sus scrofa domesticus*
Drill: *Mandrillus leucophaeus*
Egyptian fruit bat or Egyptian rousette: *Rousettus aegyptiacus*
Eland: *Taurotragus* spp.
Emin's pouched rat: *Cricetomys emini*
European hare: *Lepus europaeus*
Forest elephant: *Loxodonta cyclotis*
Four-toed elephant shrew: *Petrodomus tetradactylus*
Gemsbok: *Oryx gazella*
Geoffroy's spider monkey: *Ateles geoffroyi*
Giant Amazon river turtle: *Podocnemis expansa*
Giant anteater: *Myrmecophaga tridactyla*
Goliath frog: *Conraua goliath*
Grasscutter: *Thryonomys* spp.
Greater cane rat: *Thryonomys swinderianus*
Grey brocket deer: *Mazama gouazoubira*
Grey wolf: *Canis lupus*

Guenon: *Cercopithecus* spp.
Guinea fowl: *Numida meleagris*
Hare: *Lepus* spp.
Harpy eagle: *Harpia harpyja*
Himalayan palm civet: *Paguma larvata*
Horseshoe bat: *Rhinolophus* spp.
Houbara bustard: *Chlamydotis undulata*
Howler monkey: *Alouatta* spp.
Impala: *Aepyceros melampus*
Indian antelope: *Antilope cervicapra*
Indian gazelle: *Gazella bennettii*
Jabiru stork: *Jabiru mycteria*
Jaguar: *Panthera onca*
Kinkajou: *Potos flavus*
Lion: *Panthera leo*
Magpie goose: *Anseranas semipalmata*
Mandrill: *Mandrillus sphinx*
Mantled howler monkey: *Alouatta palliata*
Marmot: *Marmota* spp.
Marsh deer: *Blastocerus dichotomus*
Maxwell's duiker: *Philantomba maxwellii*
Moose: *Alces alces*
Multimammate mouse: *Mastomys natalensis*
Muscovy duck: *Cairina moschata*
Northern tamandua: *Tamandua mexicana*
Ocelot: *Leopardus pardalis*
Olivaceous cormorant: *Phalacrocorax olivaceus*
Paca: *Cuniculus paca*
Pale-winged trumpeter: *Psophia leucoptera*
Pampas deer: *Ozotoceros bezoarticus*
Passenger pigeon: *Ecopistes migratorius*
Peccary: *Tayassu* spp.
Plains zebra: *Equus quagga*
Plantain: *Musa* × *paradisiaca*
Puma: *Puma concolor*
Pygmy marmoset: *Cebuella pygmaea*
Queen palm: *Syagrus romanzoffiana*
Raccoon dog: *Nyctereutes procyonoides*
Razor-billed curassow: *Mitu tuberosa*

Red brocket deer: *Mazama americana*
Red deer: *Cervus elaphus*
Red duiker: *Cephalophus natalensis*
Red river hog: *Potamochoerus porcus*
Savanna elephant: *Loxodonta africana*
Sea otter: *Enhydra lutris*
Sea urchin: *Strongylocentrotus* spp.
Sitatunga: *Tragelaphus spekei*
Sooty mangabey: *Cercocebus atys*
South American tapir: *Tapirus terrestris*
Sperm whale: *Physeter macrocephalus*
Spider monkey: *Ateles* spp.
Straw-coloured fruit bat: *Eidolon helvum*
Sulawesi warty pig: *Sus celebensis*
Spix's guan: *Penelope jacquacu*
Syke's monkey: *Cercopithecus mitis*
Tapir: *Tapirus* spp.
Tayra: *Eira Barbara*
Undulated tinamous: *Crypturellus undulates*
Venezuelan red howler monkey: *Alouatta seniculus*
Warthog: *Phacochoerus* spp.
White-footed mouse: *Peromyscus leucopus*
White sturgeon: *Acipenser transmontanus*
White-lipped peccary: *Tayassu pecari*
White-tailed deer: *Odocoileus virginianus*
Wildebeest: *Connochaetes* spp.
Wolverine: *Gulo gulo*
Woodchuck: *Marmota monax*
Woolly monkey: *Lagothrix* spp.
Yellow baboon: *Papio cynocephalus*
Yellow-footed tortoise: *Chelonoidis denticulatus*
Zebra: *Equus* spp.

Appendix 2

Glossary

!Kung (Ju/'hoansi) are one of the San peoples. They are former foragers who live mostly on the western edge of the Kalahari Desert of north-eastern Namibia, southern Angola, and northwestern Botswana. They gather-hunted traditional up until the 1970s but are mainly sedentarised today (Konner & Shostak 1987).

Aché (Guayaki) of Paraguay are one of the few remaining hunter-gatherers groups with a total population size of about 1,200 persons (Callegari-Jacques *et al.* 2008). Archaeological data suggest that they might have inhabited what is now eastern Paraguay for at least 10,000 years (Hill & Padwe 1999).

Aka see Pygmy

Anatomically modern human, AMH. There has been a controversial discussion on what constitutes 'anatomically modern' morphology (Pearson 2008). The skeleton of Omo-Kibish 1 (Omo I) from southern Ethiopia was the oldest anatomically modern human skeleton (196,000 ± 5,000 BP) known up to recently (Hammond *et al.* 2017). New fossil finds, identified as *Homo sapiens*, from Jebel Irhoud, Morocco, dated 315,000 ± 34,000 BP show a mosaic of key modern human morphological features of early or recent AMH and more primitive cranial morphology (Hublin *et al.* 2017). The term typically contrasts to term 'archaic humans' which typically includes Neanderthals, Denisovans, *Homo rhodesiensis*, *Homo heidelbergensis* and others.

Arawakan is the most widespread family of languages that was spoken by Indigenous People in large parts of South and Central America and the Caribbean but has become extinct in some parts such as the Caribbean (Dixon & Aikhenvald 1999).

Banyangi (Bayang) are a Bantu people who are cash-crop farmers, hunters and gatherers. Together with the Mbo there are less than 10,000 people living in communities around the Banyang-Mbo Wildlife Sanctuary in southwest Cameroon (Willcox & Nambu 2007).

Baka see Pygmy

Batak is a collective term for related indigenous groups in Northern Sumatra, Indonesia, where they are the largest ethnic minority group, constituting about 6% of the population (Luskin *et al.* 2014).

Bakola see Pygmy

Bakossi live in Southwestern Cameroon including in the Banyang-Mbo Wildlife Sanctuary. They are subsistence farmers also producing farm cash crops, especially coffee and cocoa (Willcox & Nambu 2007).

Basossi ethnic group living around the Banyang-Mbo Wildlife Sanctuary in Southwestern Cameroon. Like the Bakossi they are subsistence farmers also producing farm cash crops especially coffee and cocoa (Willcox & Nambu 2007).

Biomass is the total quantity or weight of animals and plants in a given area or volume.

Bira, Ndaka and Lese are adjacent groups of originally immigrant farmers of Bantu (Bira, Ndaka) or Sudanic (Lese) speaking origin, living at the edge of the Ituri forest in the Democratic Republic of the Congo (Turnbull 2018). They came in contact with the Pygmies of the Ituri forest (Mbuti Efe and Swa) probably 2,000 years ago (Carpaneto & Germi 1989).

Body mass or body size of an animal is measured in terms of its weight. Body mass is an important character when studying interspecific variation in life-history patterns of living organisms and can be used to define assemblages of animal communities.

Buglé are a small indigenous group of about 20,000 people in Panama. They live in the same territories as the Ngöbe. Both indigenous people speak different, mutually unintelligible languages (Smith 2008).

Bushmeat see Box 1.1

Caiçaras are descendants of Amerindians and European colonizers with influences of other cultures such as from African slaves and Japanese immigrants. They live on the Southeastern coast area in Brazil. They practice artisanal fishery, small-scale agriculture and occasional hunting (Hanazaki *et al.* 2009).

Decision-makers involved in the exploitation of natural assets are individuals within an organization or management system who are responsible for making important pronouncements with regards to the fate of the resources used.

Defaunation is the global, local or functional extinction of animal populations or species from ecological communities.

Efe see Pygmy

Emerging zoonotic disease or emerging zoonosis is defined by the WHO, FAO and OIE as '*a zoonosis that is newly recognized or newly evolved, or that has occurred previously but shows an increase in incidence or expansion in geographical, host or vector range'* (WHO 2004b).

Endangered species is a species that is very likely to become extinct in the near future, either worldwide or in a particular political jurisdiction. The IUCN Red List registers the global conservation status of many species using various categories (see CR, EN, VU in the list of abbreviations).

Extraction when used in the context of hunted animals, e.g., game extraction, refers to the removal of animals in a defined area through hunting.

Fang are a group of southern Cameroon forest dwellers belonging to the Bantu ethnicity (Dounias 2016). They constitute a continuum of five ethnic groups, all speaking a Fang language characterized by mutual comprehension among speakers of the different languages. Fang populations of about 250,000 people are scattered widely and mixed with other linguistic groups in southern Cameroon and northern Equatorial Guinea and Gabon. They continue to live from slash-and-burn swidden agriculture, hunting and fishing.

Game is any animal hunted for food or sports.

Gravettian hunter-gatherers were widespread across most of Europe about 30,000 to 20,000 YA. They were specialized in the hunting of mammoths (Wojtal & Wilczyński 2015). The most distinctive features of the archaeological record of the Gravettian culture are stone tools and female figurines, often called 'Palaeolithic Venuses'.

Hadza are considered one of the last practicing hunter-gatherer tribes in Africa with approximately 1,300 people in 2012, living in the Rift Valley and in the neighbouring Serengeti Plateau of northern Tanzania (Skaanes 2015). They have lost between 75% and 90% of their land over the past 50 years. The minority still live almost exclusively from hunting and gathering, whilst the majority shift between foraging and various other activities including tourism and farm labour (Marlowe 2002).

Huaorani (Waorani) were a semi-nomadic Indigenous People living in South-Central Ecuador living from hunting, fishing, collecting and rotating agroforestry. First contacted by missionaries in 1958, they were granted the Huaorani Ethnic Territory Reserve adjacent to the Yasuní National Park. Today, the community of about 2,000 people (Moloney 2019) is largely sedentarised but they continue to hunt. However, hunting technology has rapidly changed with a switch from blowpipes to firearms and the introduction of dogs (Mena *et al.* 1999).

Hunter-gatherer see Box 1.2

Inujjuamiut are the Inuit residing in and around the village of Inujjuak in Northern Quebec. Whilst 600 Inuit are settled in Inujjuak, many families continue to camps in the warmer summer months along the coast, hunting, fishing and carving soapstone (Smith 1979). Today, Inuit mainly practice a mixed economy of traditional food procurement, fishing and hunting, and a modern market economy (e.g. Wenzel 2019).

Katu are an ethnic group living in forested areas of eastern Laos and central Vietnam. They have traditionally relied on wildlife utilization for their livelihood and continue hunting (MacMillan & Nguyen 2014).

Katukina is a generic term for what was at the beginning of the twentieth century five and today only three linguistically distinct and geographically proximate groups of Indigenous People in Northwestern Brazil (Coffaci de Lima 2021).

Kaxinawá (Huni Kuin) are an Indigenous People of about 1,300 persons inhabiting the tropical forest of eastern Peru and Northwestern Brazil. Hunting is widespread but the traditional bow and arrow was supplemented by firearms in the 1960s (Kensinger 1995b; Lagrou 2021).

Kichwa are a group of different Indigenous People in the Ecuadorian Amazon who all speak different Quechuan dialects. Amongst them are the Canelos Kichwa, who emerged as a fusion between various Amazonian Indigenous Peoples including the Shuar as a result of the activities of Catholic missionaries in the area by sedentarisation of Indigenous Peoples. They live from shifting cultivation, hunting and fishing. They also hunt for ceremonial purposes as part of a festival, celebrated annually until recently, which is a mixture of indigenous culture and Catholic religion (Sirén 2012).

Konabembe are a Bantu tribe living in Southeastern Cameroon. Around the Nki and Boumba-Bek National Park, they are the major farming communities living alongside communities of Baka Pygmies (Bobo et al. 2015). They practice small-scale subsistence and cash-crop farming but also hunt using mainly snares and firearms (Hirai 2014; Yasuoka et al. 2015).

Lamalera is a village on the island of Lembata, Indonesia. The people of Lamalera are complex marine foragers with revolves around cooperative hunting for large marine mammals, in particular sperm whale (Alvard & Gillespie 2004).

Lese see Bira

Machiguenga (Matsigenka) are an Indigenous People living in and outside the Manu National Park in the Amazon Basin of Southeastern Peru (Ohl-Schacherer *et al.* 2007). There are a settled Machiguenga population, poorly known and isolated Machiguenga and related communities, and unknown numbers of uncontacted hunter–gatherers (Shepard *et al.* 2010). Some remote communities have emerged from isolation since 1990, suffering from numerous respiratory epidemics as a consequence. The Machiguenga engage in hunting, fishing, foraging and swidden agriculture.

Markets of wild meat (sometimes known as bushmeat markets) refer to the regular gathering of people for the purchase and sale of live, dead processed (smoked, dried) wild animals brought to such localities by hunters themselves or by intermediaries who sell these to the market sellers. See also Wet markets.

Martu are indigenous, contemporary hunter-gatherers in Australia's Western Desert with a population size of about 1,000 people (Bird *et al.* 2009)

Mayangna and Miskito are two Indigenous People in the northeast regions of Nicaragua and Honduras. Along with the Rama, they are two of the last surviving Indigenous groups in the region, having lived there for more than 4,500 years (Perez & Longboat 2019). They live in relative isolation, e.g., in the Bosawas Biosphere Reserve, which has allowed them to preserve their culture and language. There is considerable intermarriage between the Mayangna and the Miskito. Currently, they are threatened by the rapidly increasing number of, often armed, colonists, extractive industries, commercial agriculture, forestry and cattle ranching (Perez & Longboat 2019). They are sedentary swidden horticulturalists but hunting and fishing provides the primary protein supply (Koster *et al.* 2010). They have adapted modern hunting technology, in particular dogs and firearms (Koster 2008b).

Mbo are a Bantu people who are almost exclusively hunters and gatherers. Together with the Banyangi there are less than 10,000 people living in communities around the Banyang-Mbo Wildlife Sanctuary in southwest Cameroon (Willcox & Nambu 2007).

Mbuti see Pygmy

Meriam Islanders are one of five distinct Indigenous Peoples of Melanesian origin living on a number of inner eastern Torres Strait Islands, Australia, including Mer. They are hunter–fisher–gatherers (Bliege Bird *et al.* 2001)

Middle Pleistocene: Since 2020 known under the name Chibanian as defined by the International Union of Geological Sciences. It is estimated to span the time between 770,000 and 126,000 years ago.

Minangkabau are an indigenous group in Western Sumatra, Indonesia, where they are, after the Batak, the second largest ethnic minority constituting about 5% of the population (Luskin *et al.* 2014).

Miskito see Mayangna

Mvae are a Bantu-speaking population in Cameroon. In coastal areas, they live sympatric with Bakola Pygmies and Yassa. They live from agriculture and hunting (mainly trapping) (Koppert *et al.* 1993).

Nambiquara are an Indigenous People inhabiting the tropical forest of eastern Peru and Northwestern Brazil (Miller 2021). Population size was about 5,000 to 10,000 at the beginning of the twentieth century but crashed to 1,300 people in 2002. They live in villages and practice swidden agriculture and hunting.

Ndaka see Bira

Ngöbe (Ngäbe) are the largest indigenous group in Panama. Smaller communities live also in Costa Rica. In the same territories lives a smaller indigenous group, the Buglé, who speak a different language. Total population size is about 200,000–250,000.

Overexploitation: the harvesting of species from the wild at rates that cannot be compensated for by reproduction or regrowth.

Panoan is a family of languages spoken by Indigenous People in Peru, western Brazil and Bolivia (de Araujo Lima Constantino *et al.* 2021).

Piro are Piro-speaking, an Arawakan language, Indigenous People in the lowland rainforests of southeastern Peru in an area which contains the Manu National Park. They are hunter–fisher–farmers and cultivate manioc and plantains. Most of the protein stems from hunting and fishing (Alvard 1993a). The Piro live in larger villages outside the Manu National Park, where they have access to non-traditional hunting technology, but also in traditional lifestyle in small riverside in and outside the National Park. Different Piro groups inhabit different river sheds including the Mashco-Piro tribe which has only recently emerged from isolation (Drake 2015; Gow 2012).

Pygmy People are an ethno-linguistically diverse group of hunter–gatherers or former hunter–gatherers which now have variable access to wild forest resources. These forager cultures are profoundly varied but some similarities exist. Most have a strong identity and association with the forest. Not all Pygmies are hunter–gatherers or foragers all year. Despite this, 80% or more of the Pygmy groups recognized by some authors (e.g. Bahuchet 2014) live in rainforests, and most groups are forest foragers and hunter–gatherers, even though some have taken up some form of agriculture. For example, from about the 1960s onwards, Baka in Cameroon became sedentarised following missionary activities and the 'development assistance' programmes by the State after independence (Bahuchet, McKey & de Garine 1991; Bailey, Bahuchet & Hewlett 1992; Leclerc 2012) although the adoption of agriculture and semi-sedentary lifestyle has been rather voluntary (Froment 2014). After relocation from the forest, Baka have opened their own plots growing crops such as plantain, banana, and cassava (Kitanishi 2003; Knight 2003; Leclerc 2012; Yasuoka 2012). Pygmy groups have witnessed the gradual reduction of access to forest resources (Pemunta 2019). However, the preeminent traditional way of life is associated with forest hunting and gathering.

They are broadly subdivided into Western groups, including Baka in Cameroon and Gabon, the Bakola of the coastal regions of Cameroon, and the Aka in the Republic of Congo and the Central African Republic, and Eastern groups including Mbuti in the Northeast of the Democratic Republic of Congo. Mbuti Efe and Mbuti Swa are two sub-groups in the Ituri forest who are distinguished from each other according whether they preferentially use bows and arrows or net hunting, respectively (Carpaneto & Germi 1989, 1992; Ichikawa 1983; Terashima 1983). The demographic and evolutionary split between Pygmy and non-Pygmy populations is amongst the oldest for modern humans with the divergence estimated from genetic data to roughly between 60,000 and over 100,000 years ago and the split between Western and Eastern Pygmy groups about 20,000 years ago (Hsieh *et al.* 2016; Lopez *et al.* 2018; Patin & Quintana-Murci 2018).

Although numerous alternative terms to Pygmy have been used to refer the rainforest hunter–gatherers of the Congo Basin, none have been agreed upon by academics or the people themselves to replace it. Although some academics and Central African government officers feel the term Pygmy is derogatory or does not adequately represent the people, the term Pygmy *sensu lato* to refer to all hunter–gatherer groups in Central Africa, is widely used by a broad group of people in Europe, Japan, the United States and Africa (e.g. Bahuchet 2014; Berrang-Ford *et al.* 2012; Betti 2013; Bozzola *et al.* 2009; Dounias & Leclerc 2006; Hewlett 2014; Hsieh *et al.* 2016; Jackson 2006; Meazza *et al.* 2011; Migliano *et al.* 2013; Patin *et al.* 2009; Ramírez Rozzi & Sardi 2010; Verdu *et al.* 2009). Moreover, international and local NGOs use the term in their titles or literature, e.g., Pygmy Survival Alliance, Forest Peoples' Programme.

Survival International, Rainforest Foundation, Reseau Recherches Actions Concerteees Pygmees, Centre d'Accompagnement des Autochtones Pygmees et Minoritaires Vulnerables and the Association for the Development of Pygmy Peoples of Gabon. Congo Basin conservation groups, such as World Wildlife Fund and Wildlife Conservation Society and international human rights groups working in the region, such as UNICEF and Integrated Regional Information Networks (IRIN), also regularly use the term Pygmy in their literature.

Resilience analysis focuses on the ability of a system to withstand stressors, adapt, and rapidly recover from disruptions.

San self-identify as hunter–gatherers but today the vast majority are small-scale agro-pastoralists, or hold other small jobs residing in both rural and urban areas. They live mainly in Botswana and to a smaller extend in Namibia, Angola, Zambia, Zimbabwe, Lesotho and South Africa. They are very diverse and speak different languages from different language families. The San are the first inhabitants of Southern Africa living there for at least the last 44,000 years (d'Errico *et al.* 2012a). San are also known as 'Bushmen', a name given by European colonialists, but this name is considered derogatory.

Semaq Beri are a small group of Indigenous People, numbering about 1700 persons, in Peninsular Malaysia, ethnically belonging to the Senoi, one of the three major categories of the Malayan aboriginal people, the Orang Asli (Kuchikura 1988). Some are nomadic hunter–gatherers, some are semi-nomadic practicing farming with shifting cultivation and some are settled farmers.

Shuar are Indigenous People of the neo-tropical lowland Amazonas region of Southeastern Ecuador, numbering about 40,000 to 110,000 people. They have traditionally lived in small, scattered households living from horticulture, foraging, hunting and fishing. Since the 1940s, centralized villages were gradually formed after Christian missionization, but some communities continue to practice a largely traditional way of life (Urlacher *et al.* 2016).

Siona-Secoya are an Indigenous People of the northwest Amazon in Ecuador, Colombia and Peru, numbering about 1,000 people at the beginning of the 1990s. They speak closely related and mutually intelligible dialects and both groups are descended from the Encabellado, a once large ethnic population in the Northwestern Amazon. They live in scattered households or small villages and practice a traditional subsistence economy of slash-and-burn gardening, hunting, fishing and collecting (Vickers 1994).

Sustainability is a widely applied concept that is often not specifically defined. The definitions can vary widely (e.g. Moore *et al.* 2017), especially when applied to different contexts such as ecological, socio-political and economic sustainability. Perhaps the broadest and most used political vision of sustainability was expressed in the Brundtland Commission, as *'development that meets the needs of the present generation without compromising the ability of future generations to meet their own needs'* (Brundtland 1987). A useful definition for sustainable wildlife use was coined by the US Wild Bird Conservation Act of 1992, federal regulation 50CFR Part 15: *'Sustainable use means the use of a species in a manner and at a level such that populations of the species are maintained at biologically viable levels for the long term and involves a determination of the productive capacity of the species and its ecosystem, in order to ensure that utilization does not exceed those capacities or the ability of the population to reproduce, maintain itself and perform its role or function in its ecosystem.'* Recommendations and strategies for wild meat management might differ when approached from the angle of ecological, socio-political or economic sustainability.

Swa Mbuti see Pygmy

Therianthropes are representations of people with animal features.

Wai Wai are an Indigenous People in Brazil and Guyana. In Guyana, they are the smallest Indigenous tribe with a single community (Edwards & Gibson 1979; Shaffer *et al.* 2017). They live off swidden horticulture of mainly cassava supplemented by hunting and fishing (Shaffer *et al.* 2017).

Wet markets are typically marketplaces selling fresh meat, fish, produce and other perishable goods in contrast to dry markets that sell durable goods. Not all wet markets sell live animals but because wet markets stock together animals of different kinds often in unsanitary conditions, these are potential breeding grounds for zoonotic diseases, such as COVID-19, SARS, and MERS. Wet markets are common in many parts of the world, but mostly associated with the Asia-Pacific.

Wild meat see Box 1.1

Yanomami are the largest relatively isolated Indigenous tribe in South America, living in the Amazon Basin of northern Brazil and southern Venezuela. They maintain a traditional lifestyle of hunting, fishing, gathering and swidden horticulture (Albert & Le Tourneau 2007).

Yassa are a Bantu-speaking population in coastal Cameroon. They live sympatrically with Bakola Pygmies and Mvae. They are principally a fishing population but also practice subsistence agriculture (Koppert *et al.* 1993).

Yuqui are an Indigenous People of the Amazon Basin in Eastern Bolivia. Having adopted a settled life-style and practicing some agriculture since the 1960s, they continue to rely on hunting as their sole source of protein (Stearman & Redford 1995).

Zoonotic diseases are defined by the WHO and FAO as '*those diseases and infections which are naturally transmitted between vertebrate animals and man*' (Joint FAO/WHO Expert Committee on Zoonoses *et al.* 1959).

References

Abernethy, K. A., Coad, L., Taylor, G., Lee, M. E., & Maisels, F. (2013). Extent and ecological consequences of hunting in Central African rainforests in the twenty-first century. *Philosophical Transactions of the Royal Society B: Biological Sciences*, **368**(1625), 20120303.

Adams, W. M., & Hutton, J. (2007). People, parks and poverty: Political ecology and biodiversity conservation. *Conservation and Society*, **5**(2), 147–183.

Adejinmi, J. O., & Emikpe, G. E. (2011). Helminth parasites of some wildlife in Asejire Game Reserve, Nigeria. *South African Journal of Wildlife Research*, **41**(2), 214–217.

Adu, E. K., Asafu-Adjaye, A., & Hagan, B. A. (2013). The grasscutter: An untapped resource of Africa's grasslands. In *International Grassland Congress Proceedings*, Orange, Australia: New South Wales Department of Primary Industry, 3.

Afelt, A., Frutos, R., & Devaux, C. (2018a). Bats, coronaviruses, and deforestation: Toward the emergence of novel infectious diseases? *Frontiers in Microbiology*, **9**, 702.

Afelt, A., Lacroix, A., Zawadzka-Pawlewska, U., Pokojski, W., Buchy, P., & Frutos, R. (2018b). Distribution of bat-borne viruses and environment patterns. *Infection, Genetics and Evolution*, **58**, 181–191.

Ahmadi, S., Maman, S., Zoumenou, R., *et al.* (2018). Hunting, sale, and consumption of bushmeat killed by lead-based ammunition in Benin. *International Journal of Environmental Research and Public Health*, **15**(6), 1140.

Aiyadurai, A. (2007). *Hunting in a Biodiversity Hotspot: A survey on hunting practices by indigenous communities in Arunachal Pradesh, North-east India (Report to Rufford Maurice Laing Foundation, UK)*, Mysore, India: Nature Conservation Foundation.

Aiyadurai, A., Singh, N. J., & Milner-Gulland, E. J. (2010). Wildlife hunting by indigenous tribes: A case study from Arunachal Pradesh, north-east India. *Oryx*, **44**(4), 564–572.

Akani, G. C., Luiselli, L., Angelici, F. M., & Politano, E. (1998). Bushmen and herpetofauna: Notes on amphibians and reptiles traded in bush-meat markets of local people in the Niger Delta (Port Harcourt, Rivers State, Nigeria). *Anthropozoologica*, **27**, 21–26.

Akçakaya, H. R., & Root, W. (2002). *RAMAS Metapop: Viability Analysis for Stage-Structured Metapopulations (Version 4.0)*, Setauket, NY: Applied Biomathematics.

Akçakaya, H. R., & Sjögren-Gulve, P. (2000). Population viability analyses in conservation planning: An overview. *Ecological Bulletins*, **48**, 9–21.

Albert, B., & Le Tourneau, F. (2007). Ethnogeography and resource use among the Yanomami: Toward a model of reticular space. *Current Anthropology*, **48**(4), 584–592.

Albertí, P., Panea, B., Sañudo, C., *et al.* (2008). Live weight, body size and carcass characteristics of young bulls of fifteen European breeds. *Livestock Science*, **114**(1), 19–30.

Albrechtsen, L., Macdonald, D. W., Johnson, P. J., Castelo, R., & Fa, J. E. (2007). Faunal loss from bushmeat hunting: Empirical evidence and policy implications in Bioko Island. *Environmental Science & Policy*, **10**(7–8), 654–667.

Alexander, J. S., McNamara, J., Rowcliffe, J. M., Oppong, J., & Milner-Gulland, E. J. (2015). The role of bushmeat in a West African agricultural landscape. *Oryx*, **49**(4), 643–651.

Alhaji, N. B., Yatswako, S., & Oddoh, E. Y. (2018). Knowledge, risk perception and mitigation measures towards Ebola virus disease by potentially exposed bushmeat handlers in north-central Nigeria: Any critical gap? *Zoonoses and Public Health*, **65**(1), 158–167.

Aliaga-Rossel, E., & Fragoso, J. M. (2014). Defaunation affects *Astrocaryum gratum* (Arecales: Arecaceae) seed survivorship in a sub-montane tropical forest. *Revista de Biología Tropical*, **63**(1), 57.

Allan, B. F., Keesing, F., & Ostfeld, R. S. (2003). Effect of forest fragmentation on Lyme disease risk. *Conservation Biology*, **17**(1), 267–272.

Allan, J. R., Venter, O., & Watson, J. E. M. (2017). Temporally inter-comparable maps of terrestrial wilderness and the Last of the Wild. *Scientific Data*, **4**(1), 170187.

Allen, T., Murray, K. A., Zambrana-Torrelio, C., *et al.* (2017). Global hotspots and correlates of emerging zoonotic diseases. *Nature Communications*, **8**(1), 1124.

Allocati, N., Petrucci, A. G., Di Giovanni, P., Masulli, M., Di Ilio, C., & De Laurenzi, V. (2016). Bat-man disease transmission: Zoonotic pathogens from wildlife reservoirs to human populations. *Cell Death Discovery*, **2**(1), 16048.

Alroy, J. (2015). Current extinction rates of reptiles and amphibians. *Proceedings of the National Academy of Sciences of the United States of America*, **112**(42), 13003–13008.

Althabe, G. (1965). Changements sociaux chez les Pygmées Baka de l'Est-Cameroun. *Cahiers d'études Africaines*, 561–592.

Altrichter, M. (2005). The sustainability of subsistence hunting of peccaries in the Argentine Chaco. *Biological Conservation*, **126**(3), 351–362.

Alvard, M. (1995a). Intraspecific prey choice by Amazonian hunters. *Current Anthropology*, **36**(5), 789–818.

(1995b). Shotguns and sustainable hunting in the Neotropics. *Oryx*, **29**(1), 58–66.

(1999a). The impact of traditional subsistence hunting and trapping on prey populations: Data from Wana horticulturalists of Upland Central Sulawesi, Indonesia. In J. G. Robinson, & E. L. Bennett, eds., *Hunting for Sustainability in Tropical Forests*, New York: Columbia University Press, 214–230.

Alvard, M., & Kaplan, H. (1991). Procurement technology and prey mortality among indigenous neotropical hunters. In M. Stiner, ed., *Human Predators and Prey Mortality*, Boulder, CO: Westview Press, 79–104.

Alvard, M. S. (1993). Testing the 'ecologically noble savage' hypothesis: Interspecific prey choice by Piro hunters of Amazonian Peru. *Human Ecology*, **21**(4), 355–387.

(1994). Conservation by native peoples. *Human Nature*, **5**(2), 127–154.

(1998). Indigenous hunting in the Neotropics: Conservation or optimal foraging. In T. Caro, ed., *Behavioral Ecology and Conservation Biology*, New York: Oxford University Press, 474–500.

(1999b). *Mutualistic hunting in the early human diet: The role of meat. Conference.* University of Wisconsin, 261–278.

Alvard, M. S., & Gillespie, A. (2004). Good Lamalera whale hunters accrue reproductive benefits. In M. Alvard, ed., *Research in Economic Anthropology*, Vol. **23**, Bingley: Emerald, 225–247.

Alvard, M. S., & Kuznar, L. (2001). Deferred harvests: The transition from hunting to animal husbandry. *American Anthropologist*, **103**(2), 295–311.

Alvard, M. S., Robinson, J. G., & Kaplan, H. (1997). The sustainability of subsistence hunting in the Neotropics. *Conservation Biology*, **11**(4), 6.

Alves, R. R., Mendonça, L. E., Confessor, M. V., Vieira, W. L., & Lopez, L. C. (2009). Hunting strategies used in the semi-arid region of northeastern Brazil. *Journal of Ethnobiology and Ethnomedicine*, **5**(1), 12.

Alves, R. R. N., Gonçalves, M. B. R., & Vieira, W. L. S. (2012). Caça, uso e conservação de vertebrados no semiárido Brasileiro. *Tropical Conservation Science*, **5**(3), 394–416.

Alves, R. R. N., & van Vliet, N. (2018). Wild fauna on the menu. In R. R. N. Alves, & U. P. Albuquerque, eds., *Ethnozoology*, Oxford: Elsevier, 167–194.

Ambrose, S. H. (2001). Paleolithic technology and human evolution. *Science*, **291**(5509), 1748–1753.

Amman, B. R., Carroll, S. A., Reed, Z. D., *et al.* (2012). Seasonal pulses of Marburg virus circulation in juvenile *Rousettus aegyptiacus* bats coincide with periods of increased risk of human infection. *PLoS Pathogens*, **8**(10), e1002877.

Amman, B. R., Nyakarahuka, L., McElroy, A. K., *et al.* (2014). Marburg virus resurgence in Kitaka mine bat population after extermination attempts., Uganda. *Emerging Infectious Diseases*, **20**(10), 1761–1764.

Andermann, T., Faurby, S., Turvey, S. T., Antonelli, A., & Silvestro, D. (2020). The past and future human impact on mammalian diversity. *Science Advances*, **6**(36), eabb2313.

Andersen, K. G., Rambaut, A., Lipkin, W. I., Holmes, E. C., & Garry, R. F. (2020). The proximal origin of SARS-CoV-2. *Nature Medicine*, **26**(4), 450–452.

Anderson, C. R., Downs, W. G., Wattley, G. H., Ahin, N. W., & Reese, A. A. (1957). Mayaro virus: A new human disease agent. II. Isolation from blood of patients in Trinidad, B.W.I. *The American Journal of Tropical Medicine and Hygiene*, **6**, 1012–1016.

Anderson, I., Robson, B., Connolly, M., *et al.* (2016). Indigenous and tribal peoples' health (The Lancet–Lowitja Institute Global Collaboration): A population study. *The Lancet*, **388**(10040), 131–157.

Andrews, N. (2015). Digging for survival and/or justice? The drivers of illegal mining activities in Western Ghana. *Africa Today*, **62**(2), 3.

Andrianaivoarivelo, R., Andriafidison, D., Rahaingonirina, C., *et al.* (2012). A conservation assessment of *Rousettus madagascariensis* (G. Grandidier, 1928, Pteropodidae) roosts in eastern Madagascar. *Madagascar Conservation & Development*, **6**(2), 78–82.

Anstey, S. (1991). Wildlife Utilization in Liberia: The Findings of a National Survey 1989–1990 (Report to WWF/FDA).

Antunes, A. P., Rebêlo, G. H., Pezzuti, J. C. B., et al. (2019). A conspiracy of silence: Subsistence hunting rights in the Brazilian Amazon. Land Use Policy, 84, 1–11.

Apaza, L., Wilkie, D., Byron, E., et al. (2002). Meat prices influence the consumption of wildlife by the Tsimane' Amerindians of Bolivia. Oryx, 36(4), 382–388.

Apicella, C. L., & Crittenden, A. N. (2015). Hunter-gatherer families and parenting. In D. M. Buss, ed., The Handbook of Evolutionary Psychology, Hoboken, NJ: John Wiley & Sons, 578–597.

Arcand, B. (1976). Cuiva food production. Canadian Review of Sociology, 13, 387–396.

Arraes, D. R. S., Cunha, H. F. A., & Tavares-Dias, M. (2016). Anthropogenic impacts on yellow-spotted river turtle Podocnemis unifilis (Reptilia: Podocnemididae) from the Brazilian Amazon. Acta Biológica Colombiana, 21, 413–421.

Arita, I., & Henderson, D. A. (1968). Smallpox and monkeypox in non-human primates. Bulletin of the World Health Organization, 39(2), 277–283.

Arsuaga, J. L., Martinez, I., Arnold, L. J., et al. (2014). Neandertal roots: Cranial and chronological evidence from Sima de los Huesos. Science, 344(6190), 1358–1363.

Artelle, K. A., Reynolds, J. D., Treves, A., Walsh, J. C., Paquet, P. C., & Darimont, C. T. (2018). Hallmarks of science missing from North American wildlife management. Science Advances, 4(3), eaao0167.

Asibey, E. O. (1974). Wildlife as a source of protein in Africa south of the Sahara. Biological Conservation, 6(1), 32–39.

(1977). Expected effects of land-use patterns on future supplies of bushmeat in Africa south of the Sahara. Environmental Conservation, 4(1), 43–49.

Associated Press. (2020). Teenage boy dies of bubonic plague in Mongolia after eating marmot Bubonic plague. The Guardian. 16 July, 2020.

Aswani, S., Christie, P., Muthiga, N. A., et al. (2012). The way forward with ecosystem-based management in tropical contexts: Reconciling with existing management systems. Marine Policy, 36(1), 1–10.

Aubert, M., Lebe, R., Oktaviana, A. A., et al. (2019). Earliest hunting scene in prehistoric art. Nature, 576(7787), 442–445.

Aunger, R. (1992). The nutritional consequences of rejecting food in the Ituri Forest of Zaire. Human Ecology, 20(3), 263–291.

(1994). Are food avoidances maladaptive in the Ituri forest of Zaire? Journal of Anthropological Research, 50(3), 277–310.

Auzel, P. (1996). Agriculture/Extractivisme et Exploitation Forestière. Etude de la Dynamique des Modes D'Exploitation du Milieu dans la Nord de IUFA De Pokola, Nord Congo. Wildlife Conservation Society/GEF Congo, Bomassa, Repulic of Congo.

Auzel, P., Fétéké, F., Fomété, T., Nguiffo, S., & Djeukam, R. (2001). Incidence de L'exploitation Forestière Illégale sur la Fiscalité, l'Aménagement et le Développement Local: Cas de l'UFA 10 030 dans l'Arrondissement de Messok, Province de L'Est, Cameroun, Université de Dschang, CED, Youndé.

Auzel, P., & Wilkie, D. S. (2000). Wildlife use in Northern Congo: Hunting in a commercial logging concession. In J. Robinson, & E. Bennett, eds., *Hunting for Sustainability in Tropical Forest*, Columbia University Press, 413–426.

Ávila, E., Tagg, N., Willie, J., *et al.* (2019). Interpreting long-term trends in bushmeat harvest in southeast Cameroon. *Acta Oecologica*, **94** (special issue), 57–65.

Ávila Martin, E., Ros Brull, G., Funk, S. M., Luiselli, L., Okale, R., & Fa, J. E. (2020). Wild meat hunting and use by sedentarised Baka Pygmies in southeastern Cameroon. *PeerJ*, **8**, e9906.

Aviram, R., Bass, M., & Parker, K. (2002). Extracting Hope for Bushmeat: Case studies of oil, gas, mining and logging industry efforts for improved wildlife management. Uncertain Future: The Bushmeat Crisis in Africa. Reports prepared for the Bushmeat Crisis Task Force by the Problem Solving Team of the Fall.

Ayres, J. M. C. (1986). Uakaris and Amazonian flooded forest. (PhD thesis), University of Cambridge.

Ayres, J. M., & Ayres, C. (1979). Aspectos da caça no alto rio Aripuana. *Acta Amazonica*, **9**, 287–298.

Bachand, N., Ravel, A., Onanga, R., Arsenault, J., & Gonzalez, J.-P. (2012). Public health significance of zoonotic bacterial pathogens from bushmeat sold in urban markets of Gabon, Central Africa. *Journal of Wildlife Diseases*, **48**(3), 785–789.

Bahuchet, S. (1990). Food sharing among the pygmies of Central Africa. *African Study Monographs*, **11**, 27–53.

(1992). *Dans la Forêt D'Afrique Centrale: Les Pygmées Aka et Baka*, Paris: Peeters-Selaf.

(1993). *La rencontre des Agriculteurs. Les Pygmées parmi les Peuples d'Afrique Centrale*, Paris: Peeters-SELAF.

(2014). Cultural diversity of African Pygmies. In B. S. Hewlett, ed., *Hunter-gatherers of the Congo Basin: Cultures, Histories and Biology of African Pygmies*, New Brunswick, NJ: Transaction Publishers, 1–29.

Bahuchet, S., McKey, D., & de Garine, I. (1991). Wild yams revisited: Is independence from agriculture possible for rain forest hunter-gatherers? *Human Ecology*, **19**(2), 213–243.

Bai, Z. G., Dent, D. L., Olsson, L., & Schaepman, M. E. (2008). Proxy global assessment of land degradation. *Soil Use and Management*, **24**(3), 223–234.

Bailey, R. C., & Aunger, R. (1989). Net hunters vs. archers: Variation in women's subsistence strategies in the Ituri Forest. *Human Ecology*, **17**(3), 273–297.

Bailey, R. C., & Peacock, N. R. (1988). Efe pygmies of northeast Zaire: Subsistence strategies in the Ituri forest. In I. de Garine, & G. A. Harrison, eds., *Coping with Uncertainty in Food Supply*, Oxford: Oxford University Press, 88–117.

Bailey, R. C., Bahuchet, S., & Hewlett, B. S. (1992). Development in the Central African rainforest: Concern for forest peoples. In K. M. Cleaver, ed., *Conservation of West and Central African Rainforest*, Gland: International Union for Conservation of Nature and Natural Resource, 202–211.

Bakarr, M., Oduro, W., & Adomako, E. (2001). West Africa: Regional overview of the bushmeat crisis. In N. D. Bailey, H. E. Eves, A. Stefan, & J. T. Stein, eds.,

Bushmeat Crisis Task Force Collaborative Action Planning Meeting Proceedings, Silver Spring, Maryland, USA, 110–114.

Baker, C. A., & Manwell, C. (1983). Man and elephant the 'dare theory' of domestication and the origin of breeds *Zeitschrift Für Tierzüchtung Und Züchtungsbiologie*, **100**(1-5), 55–75.

Baker, J. E. (1997). Trophy hunting as a sustainable use of wildlife resources in southern and eastern Africa. *Journal of Sustainable Tourism*, **5**(4), 306–321.

Balée, W. (1985). Ka'apor ritual hunting. *Human Ecology*, **13**, 485–510.

Balée, W. L., & Erickson, C. L. (2006). *Time and Complexity in Historical Ecology: Studies in the Neotropical Lowlands*, New York: Columbia University Press.

Barber, W. E. (1988). Maximum sustainable yield lives on. *North American Journal of Fisheries Management*, **8**(2), 153–157.

Barboza, R. R. D., Lopes, S. F., Souto, W. M. S., Fernandes-Ferreira, H., & Alves, R. R. N. (2016). The role of game mammals as bushmeat in the Caatinga, northeast Brazil. *Ecology and Society*, **21**(2), art2.

Barham, L. (2001). Central Africa and the emergence of regional identity in the Middle Pleistocene. In L. S. Barham, & K. Robson-Brown, eds., *Human Roots: Africa and Asia in the Middle Pleistocene*, Bristol: Western Academic and Specialist Press, 65–80.

(2002). Backed tools in Middle Pleistocene central Africa and their evolutionary significance. *Journal of Human Evolution*, **43**(5), 585–603.

Barnes, R. F. W. (1993). Indirect methods of counting elephants in forest. *Pachyderm*, **16**, 24–33.

Barnes, R. F. W., & Lahm, S. A. (1997). An ecological perspective on human densities in the Central African forest. *Journal of Applied Ecology*, **34**(1), 245.

Barnes, R. H., & Barnes, R. H. (1996). *Sea Hunters of Indonesia: Fishers and Weavers of Lamalera*, Oxford: Oxford University Press.

Barnett, R. (2000a). *Food for Thought: The Utilization of Wild Meat in Eastern and Southern Africa*, Nairobi: TRAFFIC East/Southern Africa.

(2000b). Regional overview on wild meat utilization. In *Food for Thought: The Utilization of Wild Meat in Eastern and Southern Africa*, Nairobi: TRAFFIC East/Southern Africa, 5–37.

Barnosky, A. D. (2004). Assessing the causes of late Pleistocene extinctions on the Continents. *Science*, **306**(5693), 70–75.

Barré-Sinoussi, F., Chermann, J.-C., Rey, F., *et al.* (1983). Isolation of a T-lymphotropic retrovirus from a patient at risk for acquired immune deficiency syndrome (AIDS). *Science*, **220**(4599), 868–871.

Barreteau, O., Bousquet, F., Étienne, M., Souchère, V., & d'Aquino, P. (2014). Companion modelling: A method of adaptive and participatory research. In M. Étienne, ed., *Companion Modeling: A Participatory Approach to Support Sustainable Development*, Dordrecht: Springer, 13–40.

Bartlett, L. J., Williams, D. R., Prescott, G. W., *et al.* (2016). Robustness despite uncertainty: Regional climate data reveal the dominant role of humans in explaining global extinctions of Late Quaternary megafauna. *Ecography*, **39**(2), 152–161.

Barychka, T., Mace, G. M., & Purves, D. W. (2020a). The Madingley General Ecosystem Model predicts bushmeat yields, species extinction rates and ecosystem-level impacts of bushmeat harvesting. *Oikos,* **130**(11), 1930–1942.

Barychka, T., Purves, D. W., Milner-Gulland, E. J., & Mace, G. M. (2020b). Modelling parameter uncertainty reveals bushmeat yields versus survival trade-offs in heavily-hunted duiker *Cephalophus* spp. *PLoS ONE*, **15**(9), e0234595.

Bavington, D. (2011). *Managed Annihilation: An Unnatural History of the Newfoundland Cod Collapse*, Vancouver: University of British Columbia Press.

BBC. (2003). Animals suffer in the war on Sars. *BBC News*, p. 3, 20 April 2003.

BBPP. (2006). Monkeys in Trouble: The Rapidly Deteriorating Conservation Status of the Monkeys on Bioko Island, Equatorial Guinea, Philadelphia, PA: Bioko Biodiversity Protection Program. http://bioko.org/assets/hearn-et-al_2006_monkeys-in-trouble-the-rapidly-deteriorating-conservation-status-of-the-monkeys-on-bioko-island%2C-equatorial-guinea.pdf

Beatty, M. E., Ashford, D. A., Griffin, P. M., Tauxe, R. V., & Sobel, J. (2003). Gastrointestinal anthrax: Review of the literature. *Archives of Internal Medicine*, **163**(20), 2527.

Beck, H., Snodgrass, J. W., & Thebpanya, P. (2013). Long-term exclosure of large terrestrial vertebrates: Implications of defaunation for seedling demographics in the Amazon rainforest. *Biological Conservation*, **163** (special issue), 115–121.

Becker, M., McRobb, R., Watson, F., *et al.* (2013). Evaluating wire-snare poaching trends and the impacts of by-catch on elephants and large carnivores. *Biological Conservation*, **158**(2013), 26–36.

Beckerman, S. (1980). Fishing and hunting by the Bari of Colombia. W. T. Vickers, & K. M. Kesinger, eds., *Working Papers on South American Indians*. Bermington College, Vermont, 67–109.

Beckerman, S., & Valentine, P. (1996). On Native American conservation and the Tragedy of the Commons. *Current Anthropology*, **37**(4), 659–661.

Begossi, A. (1992). The use of optimal foraging theory in the understanding of fishing strategies: A case from Sepetiba Bay (Rio de Janeiro State, Brazil). *Human Ecology*, **20**(4), 463–475.

Bello, C., Galetti, M., Pizo, M. A., *et al.* (2015). Defaunation affects carbon storage in tropical forests. *Science Advances*, **1**(11), e1501105.

Belovsky, G. (1987). Hunter-gatherer foraging: A linear programming approach. *Journal of Anthropological Archaeology*, **6**, 29–76.

Bene, J.-C. K., Gamys, J., & Dufour, S. (2013). The hunting practice in Northern Nimba County, Liberia. *Global Advanced Research Journal of Environmental Science and Toxicology*, **2**, 22–36.

Benedictow, O. J. (2004). *The Black Death, 1346–1353: The Complete History*, Woodbridge: Boydell & Brewer.

Ben-Haim, Y. (2001). *Information-Gap Decision Theory: Decisions under Severe Uncertainty*, London: Academic Press.

(2019). Info-gap decision theory (IG). In V. A. W. J. Marchau, W. E. Walker, P. J. T. M. Bloemen, & S. W. Popper, eds., *Decision Making under Deep Uncertainty: From Theory to Practice*, Cham: Springer International Publishing, 93–115.

Benítez-López, A., Alkemade, R., Schipper, A. M., *et al.* (2017). The impact of hunting on tropical mammal and bird populations. *Science*, **356**(6334), 180–183.

Benítez-López, A., Alkemade, R., & Verweij, P. A. (2010). The impacts of roads and other infrastructure on mammal and bird populations: A meta-analysis. *Biological Conservation*, **143**(6), 1307–1316.

Benítez-López, A., Santini, L., Schipper, A. M., Busana, M., & Huijbregts, M. A. J. (2019). Intact but empty forests? Patterns of hunting-induced mammal defaunation in the tropics. *PLoS Biology*, **17**(5), e3000247.

Bennett, E. L., Blencowe, E., Brandon, K., *et al.* (2007). Hunting for consensus: Reconciling bushmeat harvest, conservation, and development policy in West and Central Africa. *Conservation Biology*, **21**(3), 884–887.

Bennett, E. L., Nyaoi, A. J., & Sompud, J. (1999). Saving Borneo's bacon: The sustainability of hunting in Sarawak and Sabah. In J. G. Robinson, & E. L. Bennett, eds., *Hunting for Sustainability in Tropical Forests*, New York: Columbia University Press, 305–324.

Bennett, E. L., & Rao, M. (2002). Wild meat consumption in Asian tropical forest countries: Is this a glimpse of the future for Africa. In S. Mainka, & M. Trivedi, eds., *Links between Biodiversity, Conservation, Livelihoods and Food Security: The Sustainable Use of Wild Species for Meat*, Gland: IUCN, 39–44.

Bennett, E. L., & Robinson, J. G. (2000). *Hunting of Wildlife in Tropical Forests: Implications for Biodiversity and Forest Peoples* (Impact Studies, Paper no. 76), Washington DC: The World Bank Environment Department.

Bennett, E. M., Peterson, G. D., & Levitt, E. A. (2005). Looking to the future of ecosystem services. *Ecosystems*, **8**(2), 125–132.

Bennett Hennessey, A., & Rogers, J. (2008). A study of the bushmeat trade in Ouesso, Republic of Congo. *Conservation and Society*, **6**(2), 179.

Bergman, R. (1974). Shipibo subsistence in the upper Amazon. (PhD thesis), University of Wisconsin, Madison.

Berkes, F., Colding, J., & Folke, C. (eds.). (2002). *Navigating Social-Ecological Systems: Building Resilience for Complexity and Change*, Cambridge: Cambridge University Press.

Bermejo, M., Rodriguez-Teijeiro, J. D., Illera, G., Barroso, A., Vila, C., & Walsh, P. D. (2006). Ebola outbreak killed 5000 gorillas. *Science*, **314**(5805), 1564–1564.

Berrang-Ford, L., Dingle, K., Ford, J. D., *et al.* (2012). Vulnerability of indigenous health to climate change: A case study of Uganda's Batwa Pygmies. *Social Science & Medicine*, **75**(6), 1067–1077.

Betti, J. (2013). An ethnobotanical and floristical study of medicinal plants among the Baka Pygmies in the periphery of the Ipassa Biosphere Reserve, Gabon. *European Journal of Medicinal Plants*, **3**(2), 174–205.

Beverton, R. J., & Holt, S. J. (1957). *On the Dynamics of Exploited Fish Populations,*. Vol. **XIX**, London: Chapman and Hall.

Biggs, D., Abel, N., Knight, A. T., Leitch, A., Langston, A., & Ban, N. C. (2011). The implementation crisis in conservation planning: Could 'mental models' help? Mental models in conservation planning. *Conservation Letters*, **4**(3), 169–183.

Biggs, R., Schlüter, M., Biggs, D., *et al.* (2012). Toward principles for enhancing the resilience of ecosystem services. *Annual Review of Environment and Resources*, **37**, 421–448.

Binford, L. R. (1980). Willow smoke and dogs' tails: Hunter-gatherer settlement systems and archaeological site formation. *American Antiquity*, **45**(1), 4–20.

(1981). *Bones: Ancient Men and Modern Myths*, New York: Academic Press.

(2001). *Constructing Frames of Reference: An Analytical Method for Archaeological Theory Building Using Ethnographic and Environmental Data Sets*, Berkeley, CA: University of California Press.

(2002). *In Pursuit of the Past: Decoding the Archaeological Record*, Berkeley, CA: University of California Press.

Bird, D. W., Bliege Bird, R., & Codding, B. F. (2009). In pursuit of mobile prey: Martu hunting strategies and archaeofaunal interpretation. *American Antiquity*, **74**(1), 3–29.

Bird, D. W., & O'Connell, J. F. (2006). Behavioral ecology and archaeology. *Journal of Archaeological Research*, **14**(2), 143–188.

Blackburn, T. M., & Gaston, K. J. (1996). A sideways look at patterns in species richness, or why there are so few species outside the tropics. *Biodiversity Letters*, **3**(2), 279–313.

Bliege Bird, R., & Bird, D. W. (2008). Why women hunt: Risk and contemporary foraging in a Western Desert Aboriginal community. *Current Anthropology*, **49**(4), 655–693.

Bliege Bird, R., & Smith, E. A. (2005). Signaling theory, strategic interaction, and symbolic capital. *Current Anthropology*, **46**(2), 221–248.

Bliege Bird, R., Smith, E., & Bird, D. (2001). The hunting handicap: Costly signaling in human foraging strategies. *Behavioral Ecology and Sociobiology*, **50**(1), 9–19.

Blondel, J. (1967). Réflexions sur les rapports entre prédateurs et proies chez les Rapaces.—I. Les effets de la prédation sur les populations de proies. *La Terre et La Vie*, **1967**, 5–32.

Blumenschine, R. J., Bunn, H. T., Geist, V., *et al.* (1987). Characteristics of an early hominid scavenging niche [and comments and reply]. *Current Anthropology*, **28**(4), 383–407.

Blurton-Jones, N. G., Hawkes, K., & O'Connell, J. F. (1997). Why do Hadza children forage? In N. L. Segal, G. E. Weisfeld, & C. C. Weisfeld, eds., *Uniting Psychology and Biology: Integrative Perspectives on Human Development*, Washington DC: American Psychological Association, 279–313.

Bobo, K. S., Kamgaing, T. O. W., Kamdoum, E. C., & Dzefack, Z. C. B. (2015). Bushmeat hunting in southeastern Cameroon: Magnitude and impact on duikers (*Cephalophus* spp.). *African Study Monographs, Suppl.* **51**, 119–141.

Bodmer, R. E. (1994a). Managing wildlife with local communities in the Peruvian Amazon. In D. Western, & M. Wright, eds., *Natural Connections. Perspectives in Community-based Conservation*. Washington DC: Island Press, 113–134.

(1994b). Managing wildlife with local communities: The case of the Reserva Comunal Tamshiyacu-Tahuayo. In D. Western, M. Wright, & S. Strum, eds., *Natural Connections: Perspectives on Community Based Management*, Washington, DC: Island Press, 113–134.

Bodmer, R. E., Aquino, R., Puertas, P., Reyes, R., Fang, T., & Gottbenker, N. (1997). *Manejo y Uso Sustentable de Pecaríes en la Amazonía Peruana*, Quito, Ecuador: IUCN Regional Office for South America.

Bodmer, R. E., Fang, T. G., Moya, L., & Gill, R. (1994). Managing wildlife to conserve Amazonian forests: Population biology and economic considerations of game hunting. *Biological Conservation*, **67**(1), 29–35.

Bodmer, R. E., & Lozano, E. P. (2001). Rural development and sustainable wildlife use in Peru. *Conservation Biology*, **15**(4), 1163–1170.

Boesch, C. (1994). Cooperative hunting in wild chimpanzees. *Animal Behaviour*, **48**(3), 653–667.

Bogoni, J. A., Pires, J. S. R., Graipel, M. E., Peroni, N., & Peres, C. A. (2018). Wish you were here: How defaunated is the Atlantic Forest biome of its medium- to large-bodied mammal fauna? *PLoS ONE*, **13**(9), e0204515.

Boni, M. F., Lemey, P., Jiang, X., *et al.* (2020). Evolutionary origins of the SARS-CoV-2 sarbecovirus lineage responsible for the COVID-19 pandemic. *Nature Microbiology*, **5**, 1408–1417.

Bonney, R., Shirk, J. L., Phillips, T. B., *et al.* (2014). Next steps for citizen science. *Science*, **343**, 1436–1437.

Bonwitt, J., Dawson, M., Kandeh, M., *et al.* (2018). Unintended consequences of the 'bushmeat ban' in West Africa during the 2013–2016 Ebola virus disease epidemic. *Social Science & Medicine*, **200**, 166–173.

Bonwitt, J., Kandeh, M., Dawson, M., *et al.* (2017). Participation of women and children in hunting activities in Sierra Leone and implications for control of zoonotic infections. *PLoS Neglected Tropical Diseases*, **11**(7), e0005699.

Boone, J. L. (2017). The evolution of magnanimity. In D. J. Penn, & I. Mysterud, eds., *Evolutionary Perspectives on Environmental Problems*, Routledge, 183–200.

Booth, H., Clark, M., Milner-Gulland, E. J., *et al.* (2021). Investigating the risks of removing wild meat from global food systems. *Current Biology*, **31**(8), 1788–1797.

Borgerhoff Mulder, M., & Coppolillo, P. (2005). *Conservation: Linking Ecology, Economics, and Culture*, Princeton: Princeton University Press.

Borgerson, C., McKean, M. A., Sutherland, M. R., & Godfrey, L. R. (2016). Who hunts lemurs and why they hunt them. *Biological Conservation*, **197**(2016), 124–130.

Born Free Foundation. (2020, February 25). Live Wild Animal Markets, Human and Animal Health, and Biodiversity Protection. Open letter to the World Health Organisation, United Nations Environment Programme and Office International Epizoologie. www.bornfree.org.uk/storage/media/content/files/WildlifeMarketClosureLetter_Feb20_FINALV3_1.pdf

Bourlière, F. (1973). The comparative ecology of rain forest mammals in Africa and tropical America: Some introductory remarks. In B. J. Meggers, E. S. Ayensu, & W. D. Duckworth, eds., *Tropical Forest Ecosystems in Africa and South America: A Comparative Review*, Washington, DC: Smithsonian Institution Press, 279–292.

(1985). Primate communities: Their structure and role in tropical ecosystems. *International Journal of Primatology*, **6**, 1.

Bousquet, F., LePage, C., Bakam, I., & Takforyan, A. (2001). A spatially-explicit individual-based model of blue duikers population dynamics: Multi-agent simulations of bushmeat hunting in an eastern Cameroonian village. *Ecological Modelling*, **138**(1–3), 331–346.

Bowen-Jones, E., Brown, D., & Robinson E. J. Z. (2003). Economic commodity or environmental crisis? An interdisciplinary approach to analysing the bushmeat trade in Central and West Africa. *Area*, **35**(4), 390–402.

Bowler, M., Anderson, M., Montes, D., Pérez, P., & Mayor, P. (2014). Refining reproductive parameters for modelling sustainability and extinction in hunted primate populations in the Amazon. *PLoS ONE*, **9**(4), e93625.

Bowler, M., Beirne, C., Tobler, M. W., *et al.* (2019). LED flashlight technology facilitates wild meat extraction across the tropics. *Frontiers in Ecology and the Environment*, **18**(9), 489–495.

Bozzola, M., Travaglino, P., Marziliano, N., *et al.* (2009). The shortness of Pygmies is associated with severe under-expression of the growth hormone receptor. *Molecular Genetics and Metabolism*, **98**(3), 310–313.

Bradfield, J., Wadley, L., & Lombard, M. (2015). Southern African arrow poison recipes, their ingredients and implications for Stone Age archaeology. *Southern African Humanities*, **36**.

Brashares, J. S., Golden, C. D., Weinbaum, K. Z., Barrett, C. B., & Okello, G. V. (2011). Economic and geographic drivers of wildlife consumption in rural Africa. *Proceedings of the National Academy of Sciences of the United States of America*, **108**(34), 13931–13936.

Breuer, T., Breuer-Ndoundou Hockemba, M., Opepa, C. K., Yoga, S., & Mavinga, F. B. (2021). High abundance and large proportion of medium and large duikers in an intact and unhunted afrotropical protected area: Insights into monitoring methods. *African Journal of Ecology*, **59**(2), 399–411.

Bright, J., Ugan, A., & Hunsaker, L. (2002). The effect of handling time on subsistence technology. *World Archaeology*, **34**(1), 164–181.

Brockington, D. (2002). *Fortress Conservation: The Preservation of the Mkomazi Game Reserve, Tanzania*, Bloomington: Indiana University Press.

Brodie, J. F., Giordano, A. J., Zipkin, E. F., Bernard, H., Mohd-Azlan, J., & Ambu, L. (2015). Correlation and persistence of hunting and logging impacts on tropical rainforest mammals. *Conservation Biology*, **29**, 110–121.

Brodie, J. F., Helmy, O. E., Brockelman, W. Y., & Maron, J. L. (2009). Bushmeat poaching reduces the seed dispersal and population growth rate of a mammal-dispersed tree. *Ecological Applications*, **19**(4), 854–863.

Brook, B. W., Cannon, J. R., Lacy, R. C., Mirande, C., & Frankham, R. (1999). Comparison of the population viability analysis packages GAPPS, INMAT, RAMAS and VORTEX for the whooping crane (*Grus americana*). *Animal Conservation*, **2**(1), 23–31.

Brook, B. W., & Whitehead, P. J. (2005). Plausible bounds for maximum rate of increase in magpie geese (*Anseranas semipalmata*): Implications for harvest. *Wildlife Research*, **32**(5), 465.

Brook, R. K., & McLachlan, S. M. (2008). Trends and prospects for local knowledge in ecological and conservation research and monitoring. *Biodiversity and Conservation*, **17**(14), 3501–3512.

Brooks, S. E., Allison, E. H., Gill, J. A., & Reynolds, J. D. (2010). Snake prices and crocodile appetites: Aquatic wildlife supply and demand on Tonle Sap Lake, Cambodia. *Biological Conservation*, **143**(9), 2127–2135.

Brosset, A. (1966). Un comportement énigmatique: Pourquoi l'antilope vient-elle à l'appel du chasseur gabonais. *Biologica Gabonica*, **2**(3), 287–290.

Broughton, J. M. (1999). *Resource Depression and Intensification During the Late Holocene, San Francisco Bay: Evidence from the Emeryville Shellmound Vertebrate Fauna*, Berkeley: University of California Press.

(2002). Prey spatial structure and behavior affect archaeological tests of optimal foraging models: Examples from the Emeryville Shellmound vertebrate fauna. *World Archaeology*, **34**(1), 60–83.

Broughton, J. M., & Weitzel, E. M. (2018). Population reconstructions for humans and megafauna suggest mixed causes for North American Pleistocene extinctions. *Nature Communications*, **9**(1), 5441.

Brown, C. L., Kellie, K. A., Brinkman, T. J., Euskirchen, E. S., & Kielland, K. (2015). Applications of resilience theory in management of a moose-hunter system in Alaska. *Ecology and Society*, **20**(1), 16. http://dx.doi.org/10.5751/ES-07202-200116

Brown, D., & Williams, A. (2003). The case for bushmeat as a component of development policy: Issues and challenges. *International Forestry Review*, **5**(2), 148–155.

Brown, J. H. (2014). Why are there so many species in the tropics? *Journal of Biogeography*, **41**(1), 8–22.

Brown, J. H., Lomolino, M. V., & E-mail, U. S. A. (2000). Concluding remarks: Historical perspective and the future of island biogeography theory. *Global Ecology*, **6**.

Brugière, D. (1998). Population size of the black colobus monkey *Colobus satanas* and the impact of logging in the Lopé Reserve, Central Gabon. *Biological Conservation*, **86**(1), 15–20.

Brugiere, D. (1998). Facteurs de variation des densités et des biomasses de primates en milieu tropical forestier: l'exemple des communautés de Cercopithecidae d'Afrique Centrale (These de Diplome Doctoral), Universite de Rennes I, Rennes, France.

Brugiere, D., Gautier, J.-P., Moungazi, A., & Gautier-Hion, A. (2002). Primate diet and biomass in relation to vegetation composition and fruiting phenology in a rain forest in Gabon. *International Journal of Primatology*, **23**(5), 999–1024.

Brumm, A., Oktaviana, A. A., Burhan, B., *et al.* (2021). Oldest cave art found in Sulawesi. *Science Advances*, **7**(3), eabd4648.

Brundtland, G. H. (1987). *Report of the World Commission on Environment and Development: 'Our Common Future'*, New York: United Nations.

Bryant, J. E., Holmes, E. C., & Barrett, A. D. T. (2007). Out of Africa: A molecular perspective on the introduction of yellow fever virus into the Americas. *PLoS Pathogens*, **3**(5), e75.

Bucher, E. H. (1992). The causes of extinction of the passenger pigeon. In D. M. Power, ed., *Current Ornithology*, Vol. 9, New York: Plenum Press, 1–36.

Buckland, S. T., Rexstad, E. A., Marques, T. A., & Oedekoven, C. S. (2015). *Distance Sampling: Methods and Applications*, Cham: Springer International Publishing.

Burch Jr., E. S. (2007). Rationality and resource use among hunters: Some Eskimo examples. In M. E. Harkin, & D. R. Lewis, eds., *Native Americans and the*

Environment: Perspectives on the Ecological Indian, Lincoln: University of Nebraska Press, 123–152.

Butler, D. (2016). Fears rise over yellow fever's next move: Scientists warn vaccine stocks would be overwhelmed in the event of large urban outbreaks. *Nature*, **532**(7598), 155–157.

Butler, R., & Laurance, W. (2008). New strategies for conserving tropical forests. *Trends in Ecology & Evolution*, **23**(9), 469–472.

Butynski, T. M., & Koster, S. H. (1994). Distribution and conservation status of primates in Bioko Island, Equatorial Guinea. *Biodiversity and Conservation*, **3**(9), 893–909.

Cain, M. S., Vul, E., Clark, K., & Mitroff, S. R. (2012). A Bayesian optimal foraging model of human visual search. *Psychological Science*, **23**(9), 1047–1054.

Calattini, S., Betsem, E. B. A., Froment, A., *et al.* (2007). Simian foamy virus transmission from apes to humans, rural Cameroon. *Emerging Infectious Diseases*, **13**(9), 1314–1320.

Callegari-Jacques, S. M., Hill, K., Hurtado, A. M., Rodrigues, L. T., Bau, C. H. D., & Salzano, F. M. (2008). Genetic clues about the origin of Aché hunter-gatherers of Paraguay. *American Journal of Human Biology*, **20**(6), 735–737.

Calouro, A. M. (1995). Caça de subsistência: sustentabilidade e padrões de uso entre seringueiros ribeirinhos e não ribeirinhos do Estado do Acre (MSc Ecology thesis), Universidade de Brasília, Brasília, Brazil.

Campbell, G. L., & Hughes, J. M. (1995). Plague in India: A new warning from an old nemesis. *Annals of Internal Medicine*, **122**(2), 151–153.

Campbell, K. L. I., & Hofer, H. (1995). People and wildlife: Spatial dynamics and zones of interaction. In A. R. E. Sinclair, & P. Arcese, eds., *Serengeti II: Dynamics, Management, and Conservation of an Ecosystem*, Chicago: University of Chicago Press, 534–570.

Canale, G. R., Peres, C. A., Guidorizzi, C. E., Gatto, C. A. F., & Kierulff, M. C. M. (2012). Pervasive defaunation of forest remnants in a tropical biodiversity hotspot. *PLoS ONE*, **7**(8), e41671.

Cannon, M. D. (2000). Large mammal relative abundance in Pithouse and Pueblo Period archaeofaunas from Southwestern New Mexico: Resource depression among the Mimbres-Mogollon? *Journal of Anthropological Archaeology*, **19**(3), 317–347.

Cantlay, J. C., Ingram, D. J., & Meredith, A. L. (2017). A review of zoonotic infection risks associated with the wild meat trade in Malaysia. *EcoHealth*, **14**(2), 361–388.

Cao Ngoc, A., & Wyatt, T. (2013). A green criminological exploration of illegal wildlife trade in Vietnam. *Asian Journal of Criminology*, **8**, 129–142.

Carignano Torres, P., Morsello, C., Parry, L., *et al.* (2018). Landscape correlates of bushmeat consumption and hunting in a post-frontier Amazonian region. *Environmental Conservation*, **45**(4), 315–323.

Carmel, Y., & Ben-Haim, Y. (2005). Info-gap robust-satisficing model of foraging behavior: Do foragers optimize or satisfice? *The American Naturalist*, **166**(7), 633–641.

Caro, T. M. (1999). Abundance and distribution of mammals in Katavi National Park, Tanzania. *African Journal of Ecology*, **37**(3), 305–313.

Carpaneto, G., & Germi, F. (1989). The mammals in the zoological culture of the Mbuti Pygmies in north-eastern Zaire/I mammiferi nella cultura zoologica dei Pigmei Mbuti nello Zaire nord-orientale. *Hystrix, the Italian Journal of Mammalogy*, **1**(1), 1–83.

Carpaneto, G. M., Fusari, A., & Okongo, H. (2007). Subsistence hunting and exploitation of mammals in the Haut-Ogooué province, south-eastern Gabon. *Journal of Anthropological Sciences*, **85**, 183–193.

Carpaneto, G. M., & Germi, F. P. (1992). Diversity of mammals and traditional hunting in central African rain forests. *Agroecosystem Biodiversity*, **40**, 335–354.

Carrington, D. (2020, July 6). Coronavirus: World treating symptoms, not cause of pandemics, says UN. *The Guardian*, 7.

Carroll, D., Daszak, P., Wolfe, N. D., *et al.* (2018). The Global Virome Project. *Science*, **359**(6378), 872–874.

Carson, S. L., Kentatchime, F., Sinai, C., *et al.* (2019). Health challenges and assets of forest-dependent populations in Cameroon. *EcoHealth*, **16**(2), 287–297.

Carter, N. H., Viña, A., Hull, V., *et al.* (2014). Coupled human and natural systems approach to wildlife research and conservation. *Ecology and Society*, **19**(3), 43. http://dx.doi.org/10.5751/ES-06881-190343

Carvalho, R., de Aguiar, A. P. D., & Amaral, S. (2020). Diversity of cattle raising systems and its effects over forest regrowth in a core region of cattle production in the Brazilian Amazon. *Regional Environmental Change*, **20**(2), 44.

Cascio, A., Bosilkovski, M., Rodriguez-Morales, A. J., & Pappas, G. (2011). The socio-ecology of zoonotic infections. *Clinical Microbiology and Infection*, **17**(3), 336–342.

Cattelain, P. (1989). Un crochet de propulseur solutréen de la grotte de Combe-Saunière 1 (Dordogne). *Bulletin de la Société Préhistorique Française*, **86**(7), 213–216.

(1997). Hunting during the Upper Paleolithic: Bow, spearthrower, or both? In H. Knecht, ed., *Projectile Technology*, Boston, MA: Springer US, 213–240.

Caughley, G. (1977). Analysis of Vertebrate Populations. London: John Wiley & Sons.

Caughley, G., & Birch, L. C. (1971). Rate of increase. *Journal of Wildlife Management*, **35**(4), 658–663.

Cawthorn, D.-M., & Hoffman, L. C. (2015). The bushmeat and food security nexus: A global account of the contributions, conundrums and ethical collisions. *Food Research International*, **76**, 906–925.

CBD (Convention on Biological Diversity). (2012). Decision adopted by the conference of the Parties to the Convention on Biological Diversity at its Eleventh Meeting (XI/25). Hyderabad, India, 8–19 October 2012.

(Convention on Biological Diversity). (2017). Use of biodiversity scenarios at local, national and regional scales (No. CBD/SBSTTA/21/INF/3).

(Convention on Biological Diversity). (2018). Decision adopted by the conference of the parties to the convention on biological diversity 14/7. Sustainable wildlife management. Fourteenth meeting Sharm el-Sheikh, Egypt, 17–29 November 2018, Pub. L. No. CBD/COP/DEC/14/7 (2018).

Ceballos, G., Ehrlich, P. R., Barnosky, A. D., Garcia, A., Pringle, R. M., & Palmer, T. M. (2015). Accelerated modern human-induced species losses: Entering the sixth mass extinction. *Science Advances*, **1**(5), E1400253–E1400253.

Ceballos, G., Ehrlich, P. R., & Dirzo, R. (2017). Biological annihilation via the ongoing sixth mass extinction signaled by vertebrate population losses and declines. *Proceedings of the National Academy of Sciences of the United States of America*, **114**, E6089–E6096.

Centers for Disease Control and Prevention. (2016). Cost of the Ebola Epidemic. www.cdc.gov/vhf/ebola/pdf/cost-ebola-multipage-infographic.pdf

(2020). Ebola Virus Disease Distribution Map: Cases of Ebola Virus Disease in Africa Since 1976. www.cdc.gov/vhf/ebola/history/distribution-map.html

Ceppi, S. L., & Nielsen, M. R. (2014). A comparative study on bushmeat consumption patterns in ten tribes in Tanzania. *Tropical Conservation Science*, **7**(2), 272–287.

Chaber, A.-L., Allebone-Webb, S., Lignereux, Y., Cunningham, A., & Rowcliffe, J. M. (2010). The scale of illegal meat importation from Africa to Europe via Paris. *Conservation Letters*, **3**(5), 317–321.

Chaber, A.-L., & Cunningham, A. (2016). Public health risks from illegally imported African bushmeat and smoked fish: Public health risks from African bushmeat and smoked fish. *EcoHealth*, **13**(1), 135–138.

Chang, C. H., Barnes, M. L., Frye, M., *et al.* (2017). The pleasure of pursuit: Recreational hunters in rural Southwest China exhibit low exit rates in response to declining catch. *Ecology and Society*, **22**(1), 43. http://dx.doi.org/10.5751/ES-06881-190343

Chang, C. H., & Drohan, S. E. (2018). Should I shoot or should I go? Simple rules for prey selection in multi-species hunting systems. *Ecological Applications*, **28**(8), 1940–1947.

Chanthorn, W., Hartig, F., Brockelman, W. Y., Srisang, W., Nathalang, A., & Santon, J. (2019). Defaunation of large-bodied frugivores reduces carbon storage in a tropical forest of Southeast Asia. *Scientific Reports*, **9**(1), 10015.

Chapman, C. A., & Chapman, L. J. (1997). Forest regeneration in logged and unlogged forests of Kibale National Park, *Uganda. Biotropica*, **29**(4), 396–412.

(1999). Implications of small scale variation in ecological conditions for the diet and density of red colobus monkeys. *Primates*, **40**(1), 215–231.

Chapman, C. A., Gautier-Hion, A., Oates, J. F., & Onderdonk, D. A. (1999). African primate communities: Determinants of structure and threats to survival. In J. G. Fleagle, C. Janson, & C. K. Read, eds., *Primate Communities*, Cambridge: Cambridge University Press, 1–37.

Chapman, G. E., Ristovski-Slijepcevic, S., & Beagan, B. L. (2011). Meanings of food, eating and health in Punjabi families living in Vancouver, *Canada. Health Education Journal*, **70**(1), 102–112.

Chardonnet, P., Fritz, H., Zorzi, N., & Feron, E. (1995). Current importance of traditional hunting and major contrasts in wild meat consumption in sub-Saharan Africa. In J. A. Bissonette, & P. R. Krausman, eds., *Integrating People and Wildlife for a Sustainable Future. Proceedings of the First International Wildlife Management Conference*, Bethesda, MD: The Wildlife Society, 304–307.

Charnov, E. L. (1976). Optimal foraging, the marginal value theorem. *Theoretical Population Biology*, **9**, 129–136.

Charnov, E. L., & Orians, G. H. (1973). *Optimal Foraging: Some Theoretical Explorations*, Salt Lake City, UT: Department. of Biology, University of Utah.

Chausson, A. M., Rowcliffe, J. M., Escouflaire, L., Wieland, M., & Wright, J. H. (2019). Understanding the sociocultural drivers of urban bushmeat consumption for behavior change interventions in Pointe Noire, Republic of Congo. *Human Ecology*, **47**(2), 179–91.

Chaves Baía Júnior, P., Anelie Guimarães, D., & Le Pendu, Y. (2010). Non-legalized commerce in game meat in the Brazilian Amazon: A case study. *Revista de Biología Tropical*, **58**(3), 1079–1088.

Chaves, W. A., Wilkie, D. S., Monroe, M. C., & Sieving, K. E. (2017). Market access and wild meat consumption in the central Amazon, Brazil. *Biological Conservation*, **212**(2017), 240–248.

Chen, L., Liu, B., Yang, J., & Jin, Q. (2014). DBatVir: The database of bat-associated viruses. *Database*, **2014**(bau021). doi:10.1093/database/bau021

Chen, N., Zhou, M., Dong, X., et al. (2020). Epidemiological and clinical characteristics of 99 cases of 2019 novel coronavirus pneumonia in Wuhan, China: A descriptive study. *The Lancet*, **395**(10223), 507–513.

Chomitz, K. M., Buys, P., De Luca, G., Thomas, T. S., & Wertz-Kanounnikoff, S. (2007). *At Loggerheads? Agricultural Expansion, Poverty Reduction, and Environment In The Tropical Forests*, Washington, DC: The World Bank.

Chua, K. B., Bellini, W. J., Rota, P. A., et al. (2020). Nipah virus: A recently emergent deadly paramyxovirus. *Science*, *288*, 1432–1435.

Chua, K. B., Chua, B. H., & Wang, C. W. (2002). Anthropogenic deforestation, El Niiio and the emergence of Nipah virus in Malaysia. *Malaysia Journal of Pathology*, **24**(1), 15–21.

Churchill, S. E. (1993). Weapon technology, prey size selection, and hunting methods in modern hunter-gatherers: Implications for hunting in the Palaeolithic and Mesolithic. *Archeological Papers of the American Anthropological Association*, **4**(1), 11–24.

(2014). Red in tooth and claw: Neandertals as predators. In S. E. Churchill, ed., *Thin on the Ground: Neandertal Biology, Archeology, and Ecology*, Oxford: Wiley Blackwell, 219–250.

Churchill, S. E., & Rhodes, J. A. (2006). How strong were the Neandertals? Leverage and muscularity at the shoulder and elbow in Mousterian foragers. *Periodicum Biologorum*, **108**(4), 457–470.

Clark, C. J., Poulsen, J. R., Malonga, R., & Elkan, Jr., P. W. (2009). Logging concessions can extend the conservation estate for Central African tropical forests. *Conservation Biology*, **23**(5), 1281–1293.

Clark, C. W. (1976). *Mathematical Bioeconomics: The Optimal Management Renewable Resources*, New York: John Wiley & Sons.

(2010). *Mathematical Bioeconomics: The Mathematics of Conservation*, Hoboken, NJ: John Wiley & Sons.

Clay, C. A., Lehmer, E. M., Jeor, S. St., & Dearing, M. D. (2009). Sin Nombre virus and rodent species diversity: A test of the dilution and amplification hypotheses. *PLoS ONE*, **4**(7), e6467.

Cleaveland, S., Haydon, D. T., & Taylor, L. (2007). Overviews of pathogen emergence: Which pathogens emerge, when and why? In J. E. Childs, J. S.

Mackenzie, & J. A. Richt, eds., *Wildlife and Emerging Zoonotic Diseases: The Biology, Circumstances and Consequences of Cross-Species Transmission*, Vol. **315**, Berlin: Springer, 85–111.

Coad, L. (2007). Bushmeat hunting in Gabon: Socio-economics and hunter behaviour (PhD thesis), Emmanuel College, University of Cambridge; Imperial College London.

Coad, L., Abernethy, K., Balmford, A., Manica, A., Airey, L., & Milner-Gulland, E. J. (2010). Distribution and use of income from bushmeat in a rural village, Central Gabon: Bushmeat income in Gabon. *Conservation Biology*, **24**(6), 1510–1518.

Coad, L., Campbell, A., Miles, L., & Humphries, K. (2008). *The Costs and Benefits of Protected Areas for Local Livelihoods: A Review of the Current Literature*, Cambridge: UNEP World Conservation Monitoring Centre.

Coad, L., Fa, J. E., Abernethy, K., *et al.* (2019). *Towards a Sustainable, Participatory and Inclusive Wild Meat Sector*, Bogor, Indonesia: CIFOR.

Coad, L., Schleicher, J., Milner-Gulland, E. J., *et al.* (2013). Social and ecological change over a decade in a village hunting system, central Gabon. *Conservation Biology*, **27**(2), 270–280.

Coffaci de Lima, E. (2021). Katukina Pano. https://pib.socioambiental.org/en/Povo:Katukina_Pano

Cole, L. C. (1954). The population consequences of life history phenomena. *The Quarterly Review of Biology*, **29**(2), 103–137.

Collard, I. F., & Foley, R. A. (2002). Latitudinal patterns and environmental determinants of recent human cultural diversity: Do humans follow biogeographical rules? *Evolutionary Ecology Research*, **4**, 371–383.

Colyn, M., Dudu, A., & Mbaelele, M. (1987). Data on small and medium scale game utilization in the rain forest of Zaire. In *International Symposium & Conference on Wildlife Management in Sub-Saharan Africa. Harare, Zimbabwe.* UNESCO, Harare: World Wide Fund for Nature, 109–145.

Combreau, O., Launay, F., & Lawrence, M. (2001). An assessment of annual mortality rates in adult-sized migrant houbara bustards (*Chlamydotis [undulata] macqueenii*). *Animal Conservation*, **4**(2), 133–141.

Combreau, O., Qiao, J., Lawrence, M., *et al.* (2002). Breeding success in a Houbara Bustard *Chlamydotis [undulata] macqueenii* population on the eastern fringe of the Jungar Basin, People's Republic of China. *Ibis*, **144**, E45–E56.

Conde, D. A., Staerk, J., Colchero, F., *et al.* (2019). Data gaps and opportunities for comparative and conservation biology. *Proceedings of the National Academy of Sciences of the United States of America*, **116**(19), 9658.

Constantino, P. A. L. (2016). Deforestation and hunting effects on wildlife across Amazonian indigenous lands. *Ecology and Society*, **21**(2), 3. http://dx.doi.org/10.5751/ES-08323-210203

Cooney, R., & Abensperg-Traun, M. (2013). Raising local community voices: CITES, livelihoods and sustainable use: Raising local community voices. *Review of European, Comparative & International Environmental Law*, **22**(3), 301–310.

Cooney, R., Roe, D., Dublin, H., & Booker, F. (2018). *Wild life, Wild Livelihoods: Involving Communities in Sustainable Wildlife Management and Combatting the Illegal Wildlife Trade*, Nairobi: United Nations Environment Programme.

Cordain, L., Miller, J. B., Eaton, S. B., Mann, N., Holt, S. H., & Speth, J. D. (2000). Plant-animal subsistence ratios and macronutrient energy estimations in world-wide hunter-gatherer diets. *The American Journal of Clinical Nutrition*, **71**(3), 682–692.

Corlett, R., & Primack, R. B. (2011). *Tropical Rain Forests: An Ecological and Biogeographical Comparison*, 2nd ed, Chichester: Wiley-Blackwell.

Corlett, R. T. (2007). The impact of hunting on the mammalian fauna of tropical Asian forests. *Biotropica*, **39**(3), 292–303.

(2013a). The shifted baseline: Prehistoric defaunation in the tropics and its consequences for biodiversity conservation. *Biological Conservation*, **163**, 13–21.

(2013b). Where are the subtropics? *Biotropica*, **45**(3), 273–275.

Corlett, R. T., & Hughes, A. C. (2015). Mammals in forest ecosystems. In R. T. Corlett, & Y. Bergeron, eds., *The Routledge Handbook of Forest Ecology*. Oxford: Routledge, 264–278.

Cormier, L. (2006). A preliminary review of neotropical primates in the subsistence and symbolism of Indigenous Lowland South American Peoples. *Ecological and Environmental Anthropology*, **2**(1), 20.

Courchamp, F., Berec, L., & Gascoigne, J. (2008). *Allee Effects in Ecology and Conservation*, Oxford: Oxford University Press.

Cowlishaw, G., Mendelson, S., & Rowcliffe, J. M. (2004). The bushmeat commodity chain: Patterns of trade and sustainability in a mature urban market in West Africa. *ODI Wildlife Policy Briefing*, **7**, 1–4.

(2005). Evidence for post-depletion sustainability in a mature bushmeat market: Sustainability of bushmeat markets. *Journal of Applied Ecology*, **42**(3), 460–468.

Craig, P. S. (2006). Epidemiology of human alveolar echinococcosis in China. *Parasitology International*, **55**, S221–S225.

Crame, J. A. (2001). Taxonomic diversity gradients through geological time. *Diversity and Distributions*, **7**, 175–189.

Crane, P. R., & Lidgard, S. (1989). Angiosperm diversification and paleolatitudinal gradients in Cretaceous floristic diversity. *Science*, **246**(4930), 675–678.

Cristoffer, C. (1987). Body size differences between New World and Old World, arboreal, tropical vertebrates: Cause and Consequences. *Journal of Biogeography*, **14**(2), 165.

Cronin, D. T., Meñe, D. B., Butynski, T. B., *et al.* (2010). *Opportunities Lost: The Rapidly Deteriorating Conservation Status of the Monkeys on Bioko Island, Equatorial Guinea (2010) (A report to the Government of Equatorial Guinea)*, Philadelphia, PA: Bioko Biodiversity Protection Program, Drexel University.

Cronin, D. T., Woloszynek, S., Morra, W. A., *et al.* (2015). Long-term urban market dynamics reveal increased bushmeat carcass volume despite economic growth and proactive environmental legislation on Bioko Island, Equatorial Guinea. *PLoS ONE*, **10**(7), e0134464.

Crookes, D., Humphreys, D., Masroh, F., Tarchie, B., & Milner-Gulland, E. (2014). The role of hunting in village livelihoods in the Ashanti region, Ghana. *South African Journal of Economic and Management Sciences*, **10**(4), 457–469.

Crookes, D. J., & Milner-Gulland, E. J. (2006). Wildlife and economic policies affecting the bushmeat trade: A framework for analysis. *South African Journal of Wildlife Research*, **36**(2), 159–165.

Crush, J., & Riley, L. (2019). Rural bias and urban food security. In J. Battersby, & V. Watson, eds., *Urban Food Systems Governance and Poverty in African Cities*, Abingdon: Routledge, 42–55.

Cui, J., Li, F., & Shi, Z.-L. (2019). Origin and evolution of pathogenic coronaviruses. *Nature Reviews Microbiology*, **17**(3), 181–192.

Cullen Jr, L., Bodmer, R. E., & Pádua, C. V. (2000). Effects of hunting in habitat fragments of the Atlantic forests, Brazil. *Biological Conservation*, **95**, 49–56.

Cury, P. M., Mullon, C., Garcia, S. M., & Shannon, L. J. (2005). Viability theory for an ecosystem approach to fisheries. *ICES Journal of Marine Science*, **62**(3), 577–584.

d'Errico, F., Backwell, L., Villa, P., *et al.* (2012a). Early evidence of San material culture represented by organic artifacts from Border Cave, South Africa. *Proceedings of the National Academy of Sciences of the United States of America*, **109** (33), 13214–13219.

(2012b). Reply to Evans: Use of poison remains the most parsimonious explanation for Border Cave castor bean extract. *Proceedings of the National Academy of Sciences of the United States of America*, **109**(48), E3291–E3292.

Da Fonseca, G. A., Herrmann, G., Leite, Y. L., Mittermeier, R. A., Rylands, A. B., & Patton, J. L. (1996). *Lista Anotada dos Mamíferos do Brasil*, Washington, DC: Conservation International.

Da Silva, M. N. F., Shepard, G. H., & Yu, D. W. (2005). Conservation implications of primate hunting practices among the Matsigenka of Manu National Park. *Neotropical Primates*, **13**(2), 31–36.

Daily, G. C. (1995). Restoring value to the world's degraded lands. *Science*, **269**, 350–354.

Damania, R., Milner-Gulland, E. J., & Crookes, D. J. (2005). A bioeconomic analysis of bushmeat hunting. *Proceedings of the Royal Society B: Biological Sciences*, **272**(1560), 259–266.

Danielsen, F., Jensen, P. M., Burgess, N. D., *et al.* (2014). A multicountry assessment of tropical resource monitoring by local communities. *BioScience*. **64**(3), 236–251.

Darimont, C. T., Codding, B. F., & Hawkes, K. (2017). Why men trophy hunt. *Biology Letters*, **13**(3), 20160909.

Daszak, P., Zambrana-Torrelio, C., Bogich, T. L., *et al.* (2013). Interdisciplinary approaches to understanding disease emergence: The past, present, and future drivers of Nipah virus emergence. *Proceedings of the National Academy of Sciences of the United States of America*, **110**(Supplement_1), 3681–3688.

Davidson, N. C. (2014). How much wetland has the world lost? Long-term and recent trends in global wetland area. *Marine and Freshwater Research*, **65**(10), 934.

Davies, G. E. (1994). Colobine populations. In G. E. Conner, & J. F. Oates, eds., *Colobine Monkeys: Their Ecology, Behaviour and Evolution*, Cambridge University Press, 285–310.

Davis, S., Makundi, R. H., Machang'u, R. S., & Leirs, H. (2006). Demographic and spatio-temporal variation in human plague at a persistent focus in Tanzania. *Acta Tropica*, **100**(1–2), 133–141.

Daw, T. M., Coulthard, S., Cheung, W. W. L., *et al.* (2015). Evaluating taboo trade-offs in ecosystems services and human well-being. *Proceedings of the National Academy of Sciences of the United States of America*, **112**(22), 6949–6954.

De Albuquerque, U. P., de Lima Araújo, E., El-Deir, A. C. A., *et al.* (2012). Caatinga revisited: Ecology and conservation of an important seasonal dry forest. *The Scientific World Journal*, **2012**, 1–18.

De Araujo Lima Constantino, P. (2015). Dynamics of hunting territories and prey distribution in Amazonian Indigenous Lands. *Applied Geography*, **56**, 222–231.

De Araujo Lima Constantino, P., Valente-Neto, F., Nunes, A. V., & Campos-Silva, J. V. (2021). Culture still matters: Conservation implications of hunting by ethnolinguistic groups in Southwestern Amazonia after centuries of contact. *Biodiversity and Conservation*, **30**(2), 445–460.

De Mattos Vieira, M. A. R., von Muhlen, E. M., & Shepard, G. (2015). Participatory monitoring and management of subsistence hunting in the Piagaçu-Purus Reserve, Brazil. *Conservation and Society*, **13**(3), 254–264.

De Merode, E., & Cowlishaw, G. (2006). Species protection, the changing informal economy, and the politics of access to the bushmeat trade in the Democratic Republic of Congo: Politics of access to the bushmeat trade. *Conservation Biology*, **20**(4), 1262–1271.

De Merode, E., Homewood, K., & Cowlishaw, G. (2004). The value of bushmeat and other wild foods to rural households living in extreme poverty in Democratic Republic of Congo. *Biological Conservation*, **118**(5), 573–581.

De Souza-Mazurek, R. R., Pedrinho, T., Feliciano, X., Hilário, W., Gerôncio, S., & Marcelo, E. (2000). Subsistence hunting among the Waimiri Atroari indians in central Amazonia, Brazil. *Biodiversity & Conservation*, **9**(5), 579–596.

De Vos, A. (1977). Game as food. *Unasylva*, **29**, 2–12.

De Vos, V., & Bryden, H. B. (1996). Anthrax in the Kruger National Park: Temporal and spatial patterns of disease occurrence. *Salisbury Medical Bulletin*, **87** (Special Suppl.), 26–30.

Deith, M. C. M., & Brodie, J. F. (2020). Predicting defaunation: Accurately mapping bushmeat hunting pressure over large areas. *Proceedings of the Royal Society B: Biological Sciences*, **287**(1922), 20192677.

Del Vingt, W. (1997). *La Chasse Villageoise Synthèse régionale des études réalisées durant la première phase du Programme ECOFAC au Cameroun, au Congo et en République Centrafricaine.*

Delaporte, E., Peeters, M., Simoni, M., & Piot, P. (1989). HTLV-I infection in western equatorial Africa. *Lancet*, **2**(8673), 1226.

Delvingt, W. (1997). *La Chasse Villageoise Synthèse régionale des études réalisées durant la première phase du Programme ECOFAC au Cameroun, au Congo et en République Centrafricaine. Faculté Universitaire Des Sciences Agronimiques Des Gembloux: ECOFAC AGRECO-CTFT*, 73.

Delvingt, W., Dethier, M., Auzel, P., & Jeanmart, P. (2001). La chasse villageoise Badjoué, gestion coutumière durable ou pillage de la ressource gibier. In *La forêt des hommes: Terroirs villageois en forêt tropicale africaine*, In W. Delvingt, ed. Gembloux, Belgium: Presses Agronomiques de Gembloux, 65–92.

Despommier, D., Ellis, B. R., & Wilcox, B. A. (2007). The role of ecotones in emerging infectious diseases. *EcoHealth*, **3**(4), 281–289.

Di Giulio, D. B., & Eckburg, P. B. (2004). Human monkeypox: An emerging zoonosis. *The Lancet Infectious Diseases*, **4**(1), 15–25.

Di Marco, M., Boitani, L., Mallon, D., *et al.* (2014). A retrospective evaluation of the global decline of carnivores and ungulates: Global decline of carnivores and ungulates. *Conservation Biology*, **28**(4), 1109–1118.

Di Minin, E., Brooks, T. M., Toivonen, T., *et al.* (2019). Identifying global centers of unsustainable commercial harvesting of species. *Science Advances*, **5**(4), eaau2879.

Diamond, J. (1988). The golden age that never was. *Discover*, **9**(12), 70–79.

(1989). Quaternary megafaunal extinctions: Variations on a theme by Paganini. *Journal of Archaeological Science*, **16**(2), 167–175.

Diamond, J., & Wolfe, N. (2020, March 16). How we can stop the next new virus. The Washington Post, 10.

Dickinson, J. L., Zuckerberg, B., & Bonter, D. N. (2010). Citizen science as an ecological research tool: Challenges and benefits. *Annual Review of Ecology, Evolution, and Systematics*, **41**(1), 149–172.

Dickman, A., Johnson, P. J., van Kesteren, F., & Macdonald, D. W. (2015). The moral basis for conservation: How is it affected by culture? *Frontiers in Ecology and the Environment*, **13**(6), 325–331.

Dillingham, P. W., & Fletcher, D. (2008). Estimating the ability of birds to sustain additional human-caused mortalities using a simple decision rule and allometric relationships. *Biological Conservation*, **141**(7), 1783–1792.

Diniz-Filho, J. A. F. (2004). Macroecological analyses support an overkill scenario for late Pleistocene extinctions. *Brazilian Journal of Biology*, **64**(3a), 407–414.

Dira, S. J., & Hewlett, B. S. (2016). Learning to spear hunt among Ethiopian Chabu adolescent hunter-gatherers. In H. Terashima and B. S. Hewlett *Social Learning and Innovation in Contemporary Hunter-Gatherers*, Tokyo: Springer Japan, 71–81.

Dirzo, R., Young, H. S., Galetti, M., Ceballos, G., Isaac, N. J., & Collen, B. (2014). Defaunation in the Anthropocene. *Science*, **345**(6195), 401–406.

Dixon, M. J. R., Loh, J., Davidson, N. C., Beltrame, C., Freeman, R., & Walpole, M. (2016). Tracking global change in ecosystem area: The Wetland Extent Trends index. *Biological Conservation*, **193**, 27–35.

Dixon, R. M., & Aikhenvald, A. Y. (eds.). (1999). *The Amazonian Languages*, Vol. **20**, Cambridge: Cambridge University Press.

Dobson, A. D. M., Milner-Gulland, E. J., Ingram, D. J., & Keane, A. (2019). A framework for assessing impacts of wild meat hunting practices in the Tropics. *Human Ecology*, **47**(3), 449–464.

Dobson, A. P., & Carper, E. R. (1996). Infectious diseases and human population history. *BioScience*, **46**(2), 115–126.

Dobson, A. P., Pimm, S. L., Kaufman, L., *et al.* (2020). Ecology and economics for pandemic prevention. *Science*, **369**, 3.

Dodet, B., Tejiokem, M. C., Aguemon, A.-R., & Bourhy, H. (2015). Human rabies deaths in Africa: Breaking the cycle of indifference. *International Health*, **7**(1), 4–6.

Domroes, M. (2003). Climatological characteristics of the tropics in China: Climate classification schemes between German scientists and Huang Bingwei. *Journal of Geographical Sciences*, **13**(3), 271–285.

Donnelly, C. A., Woodroffe, R., Cox, D. R., et al. (2003). Impact of localized badger culling on tuberculosis incidence in British cattle. *Nature*, **426**(6968), 834–837.

Dounias, E. (2016). From subsistence to commercial hunting: Technical shift in cynegetic practices among Southern Cameroon forest dwellers during the 20th century. *Ecology and Society*, **21**(1), 23. http://dx.doi.org/10.5751/ES-07946-210123/

(2018). Cooperating with the wild. Past and present auxiliary animals assisting humans in their foraging activities. In C. Stépanoff, & J.-D. Vigne, eds., *Hybrid Communities: Biosocial Approaches to Domestication and Other Trans-species Relationship*, Abingdon,: Routledge, 197–220.

Dounias, E., & Froment, A. (2011). From foraging to farming among present-day forest hunter-gatherers: Consequences on diet and health. *International Forestry Review*, **13**(3), 294–304.

Dounias, E., & Leclerc, C. (2006). Spatial shifts and migration time scales among the Baka Pygmies of Cameroon and the Punan of Borneo. In W. de Jong, T. P. Lye, & A. Ken-Chi, eds., *The Social Ecology of Tropical Forest: Migration, Populations and Frontiers*, Kyoto: Trans Pacific Press, 147–173.

Dragon, D. C., Renniie, R. P., & Gates, C. C. (1996). Bison and anthrax in northern Canada. *Salisbury Medical Bulletin*, **87** (Special Suppl.), 22–23.

Drake, N. (2015, October 13). An isolated tribe is emerging from Peru's Amazonian wilderness. *National Geographic*, **2**.

Drexler, J. F., Corman, V. M., & Drosten, C. (2014). Ecology, evolution and classification of bat coronaviruses in the aftermath of SARS. *Antiviral Research*, **101**, 45–56.

Drexler, J. F., Corman, V. M., Gloza-Rausch, F., et al. (2009). Henipavirus RNA in African bats. *PLoS ONE*, **4**(7), e6367.

Drosten, C., Günther, S., Preiser, W., et al. (2003). Identification of a novel coronavirus in patients with severe acute respiratory syndrome. *New England Journal of Medicine*, **348**(20), 1967–1976.

Dublin, H. T. (1995). Vegetation dynamics in the Serengeti-Mara ecosystem: The role of elephants, fire, and other factors. In A. R. E. Sinclair, & P. Arcese, eds., *Serengeti II: Dynamics, Management, and Conservation of an Ecosystem*, Vol. **2**, Chicago, IL: University of Chicago Press, 71.

Dubost, G. (1978). Un aperçu sur l'écologie du chevrotain africain Hyemoschus aquaticus Ogilby, *Artiodactyle Tragulidé. Mammalia*, **42**(1), 1–62.

(1979). The size of African forest artiodactyls as determined by the vegetation structure. *African Journal of Ecology*, **17**(1), 1–17.

Duckworth, J. W., Batters, G., Belant, J. L., et al. (2012). Why South-east Asia should be the world's priority for averting imminent species extinctions, and a call to join a developing cross-institutional programme to tackle this urgent issue. *S.A.P.I.EN.S* (Online), 5.2 URL : http://journals.openedition.org/sapiens/1327

Duda, R. (2017). Ethnoecology of hunting in an empty forest: Practices, local perceptions and social change among the Baka (Cameroon) (PhD thesis), Universitat Autonoma de Barcelona, Barcelona, Spain.

Duda, R., Gallois, S., & Reyes-Garcia, V. (2017). Hunting techniques, wildlife offtake and market integration. A perspective from individual variations among the Baka (Cameroon). *African Study Monographs*, **38**, 97–118.

Duffy, R., St John, F. A. V., Büscher, B., & Brockington, D. (2016). Toward a new understanding of the links between poverty and illegal wildlife hunting. *Conservation Biology*, **30**(1), 14–22.

Duncan, R. P., Forsyth, D. M., & Hone, J. (2007). Testing the metabolic theory of ecology: Allometric scaling exponents in mammals. *Ecology*, **88**(2), 324–333.

Dupain, J., Nackoney, J., Mario Vargas, J., *et al.* (2012). Bushmeat characteristics vary with catchment conditions in a Congo market. *Biological Conservation*, **146**(1), 32–40.

Dupré, G. (1976). La chasse au filet chez les Nzabi (République Populaire du Congo). *ORSTOM Série Sciences Humaines*, **13**(4), 343–355.

Dusseldorp, G. L. (2012). Studying prehistoric hunting proficiency: Applying optimal foraging theory to the Middle Palaeolithic and Middle Stone Age. *Quaternary International*, **252**, 3–15.

East, T., Kümpel, N. F., Milner-Gulland, E. J., & Rowcliffe, J. M. (2005). Determinants of urban bushmeat consumption in Río Muni, Equatorial Guinea. *Biological Conservation*, **126**(2), 206–215.

Eaton, S., Eaton, S., & Konner, M. (1997). Review Paleolithic nutrition revisited: A twelve-year retrospective on its nature and implications. *European Journal of Clinical Nutrition*, **51**(4), 207–216.

EcoHealth Alliance & University of Sao Paulo. (2015). *An ecoHealth approach: Prediction and prevention of emerging infectious diseases from wildlife: final technical report.* https://idl-bnc-idrc.dspacedirect.org/bitstream/handle/10625/58827/IDL%20-%2058827.pdf

Edderai, D., & Dame, M. (2006). A census of the commercial bushmeat market in Yaoundé, Cameroon. *Oryx*, **40**(4), 472–475.

Edwards, W., & Gibson, K. (1979). An ethnohistory of Amerindians in Guyana. *Ethnohistory*, **26**(2), 161.

Effiom, E. O., Birkhofer, K., Smith, H. G., & Olsson, O. (2014). Changes of community composition at multiple trophic levels due to hunting in Nigerian tropical forests. *Ecography*, **37**(4), 367–377.

Effiom, E. O., Nunez-Iturri, G., Smith, H. G., Ottosson, U., & Olsson, O. (2013). Bushmeat hunting changes regeneration of African rainforests. *Proceedings of the Royal Society B: Biological Sciences*, **280**(1759), 20130246.

Eisenberg, J. F. (1980). The density and biomass of tropical mammals. In M. Soulee, & B. Wilcox, eds., *Conservation biology: An Evolutionary-Ecological Perspective*, Sunderland, MA: Sinauer Associates, 35–55.

Eisenberg, J. F., & Thorington, R. W. (1973). A preliminary analysis of a Neotropical mammal fauna. *Biotropica*, **5**(3), 150–161.

Eisenberg, J. F., & Seidensticker, J. (1976). Ungulates in southern Asia: A consideration of biomass estimates for selected habitats. *Biological Conservation*, **10**, 293–308.

El Bizri, H. R., Fa, J. E., Lemos, L. P., *et al.* (2020a). Involving local communities for effective citizen science: Determining game species' reproductive status to assess hunting effects in tropical forests. *Journal of Applied Ecology*, **58**(2), 224–235.

El Bizri, H. R., Morcatty, T. Q., & Ferreira, J. C. (2020b). Social and biological correlates of wild meat consumption and trade by rural communities in the Jutaí River Basin, Central Amazonia. *Journal of Ethnobiology*, **40**(2), 183–201

El Bizri, H. R., Morcatty, T. Q., Valsecchi, J., et al. (2019). Urban wild meat consumption and trade in central Amazonia. *Conservation Biology*, **34**(2), 438–448.

El Masry, I., Dobschuetz, S., Plee, L., et al. (2020). *Exposure of humans or animals to SARS-CoV-2 from wild, livestock, companion and aquatic animals*, Rome: FAO. doi:10.4060/ca9959en

Elkan, P. W., Elkan, S. W., Moukassa, A., Malonga, R., Ngangoue, M., & Smith, J. L. D. (2006). Managing threats from bushmeat hunting in a timber concession in the Republic of Congo. In C. Peres, & W. Laurance, eds., *Emerging Threats to Tropical Forests*, Chicago, IL: University of Chicago Press, 395–415.

Ellis, E. C., & Ramankutty, N. (2008). Putting people in the map: Anthropogenic biomes of the world. *Frontiers in Ecology and the Environment*, **6**(8), 439–447.

Ellis, J., Oyston, P. C. F., Green, M., & Titball, R. W. (2002). Tularemia. *Clinical Microbiology Reviews*, **15**(4), 631–646.

Emery-Wetherell, M. M., McHorse, B. K., & Byrd Davis, E. (2017). Spatially explicit analysis sheds new light on the Pleistocene megafaunal extinction in North America. *Paleobiology*, **43**(4), 642–655.

Emlen, J. M. (1966). The role of time and energy in food preference. *The American Naturalist*, **100**(916), 611–617.

Emmons, L. H., Gautier-Hion, A., & Dubost, G. (1983). Community structure of the frugivours-folivorous forest mammals of Gabon. *Journal of Zoology*, **199**(2), 209–222.

Emmons, L. H., & Gentry, A. H. (1983). Tropical forest structure and the distribution of gliding and prehensile-tailed Vertebrates. *The American Naturalist*, **121**(4), 513–524.

Endo, W., Peres, C. A., & Haugaasen, T. (2016). Flood pulse dynamics affects exploitation of both aquatic and terrestrial prey by Amazonian floodplain settlements. *Biological Conservation*, **201**, 129–136.

Epstein, J. H., Gurley, E. S., Patz, J. A., et al. (2014). The role of landscape composition and configuration on *Pteropus giganteus* roosting ecology and nipah virus spillover risk in Bangladesh. *The American Journal of Tropical Medicine and Hygiene*, **90**(2), 247–255.

Estes, J. A. (1990). Growth and equilibrium in sea otter populations. *Journal of Animal Ecology*, **59**(2), 385–401.

Etiendem, D. N. (2008). Traditional knowledge on Cross River gorilla conservation: A case study in the Bechati-Fossimondi-Besali area, southwest Cameroon (MSc dissertation), Vrije Universiteit Brussel, Brussels.

Evans, K. L., Greenwood, J. J., & Gaston, K. J. (2005). Dissecting the species–energy relationship. *Proceedings of the Royal Society B: Biological Sciences*, **272**(1577), 2155–2163.

Eves, H. E., Hutchins, M., & Bailey, N. D. (2008). The bushmeat crisis task force (BCTF). In T. S. Stoinski, H. D. Steklis, & P. T. Mehlman, eds., *Conservation in the 21st century: Gorillas as a Case Study*, Springer, 327–344.

Eves, H. E., & Ruggiero, R. G. (1999). Socioeconomics and the sustainability of hunting in the forests of northern Congo (Brazzaville). In J. G. Robinson, & E. L. Bennett, eds., *Hunting for Sustainability in Tropical Forests*, New York: Columbia University Press, 427–454.

Ezenwa, V. O., Godsey, M. S., King, R. J., & Guptill, S. C. (2006). Avian diversity and West Nile virus: Testing associations between biodiversity and infectious disease risk. *Proceedings of the Royal Society B: Biological Sciences*, **273**(1582), 109–117.

Fa, J. E. (1999). Hunted animals in Bioko Island, West Africa: Sustainability and future. In J. G. Robinson, & E. L. Bennett, eds., *Hunting for Sustainability in Tropical Forests*, New York: Columbia University Press, 168–198.

(2007). Bushmeat Markets - White Elephants or Red Herrings? In G. Davies, & D. Brown, eds., *Bushmeat and Livelihoods: Wildlife Management and Poverty Reduction*, Oxford: Blackwell, 47–60.

Fa, J. E., Albrechtsen, L., Johnson, P. J., & Macdonald, D. W. (2009). Linkages between household wealth, bushmeat and other animal protein consumption are not invariant: Evidence from Rio Muni, Equatorial Guinea: Bushmeat consumption and household wealth. *Animal Conservation*, **12**(6), 599–610.

Fa, J. E., & Brown, D. (2009). Impacts of hunting on mammals in African tropical moist forests: A review and synthesis. *Mammal Review*, **39**(4), 231–264.

Fa, J. E., Currie, D., & Meeuwig, J. (2003). Bushmeat and food security in the Congo Basin: Linkages between wildlife and people's future. *Environmental Conservation*, **30**(1), 71–78.

Fa, J. E., Funk, S. M., & O'Connell, D. (2011). *Zoo Conservation Biology*, Cambridge: Cambridge University Press.

Fa, J. E., & García Yuste, J. E. (2001). Commercial bushmeat hunting in the Monte Mitra forests, Equatorial Guinea: Extent and impact. *Animal Biodiversity and Conservation*, **24**(1), 31–52.

Fa, J. E., Johnson, P. J., Dupain, J., Lapuente, J., Köster, P., & Macdonald, D. W. (2004). Sampling effort and dynamics of bushmeat markets. *Animal Conservation*, **7**, 409–416.

Fa, J. E., Juste, J., Del Val, J. P., & Castroviejo, J. (1995). Impact of market hunting on mammal species in Equatorial Guinea. *Conservation Biology*, **9**(5), 1107–1115.

Fa, J. E., Nasi, R., & Funk, S. M. (2021). The COVID-19 pandemic endangers Africa´s indigenous Pygmy populations. *EcoHealth*, **18**(4), 403–440.

Fa, J. E., Olivero, J., Farfán, M. Á., et al.(2015a). Correlates of bushmeat in markets and depletion of wildlife. *Conservation Biology*, **29**(3), 805–815.

Fa, J. E., Olivero, J., Farfán, M. A., et al. (2016). Differences between Pygmy and non-Pygmy hunting in Congo Basin Forests. *PLoS ONE*, **11**(9), e0161703.

Fa, J. E., Olivero, J., Real, R., et al. (2015b). Disentangling the relative effects of bushmeat availability on human nutrition in central Africa. *Scientific Reports*, **5**(1), 8168.

Fa, J. E., & Peres, C. A. (2001). Game vertebrate extraction in African and Neotropical forests: An intercontinental comparison. In J. D. Reynolds, G. M. Mace, K. H. Redford, & J. G. Robinson, eds., *Conservation of Exploited Species*, Cambridge University Press, 203–241.

Fa, J. E., Peres, C. A., & Meeuwig, J. (2002). Bushmeat exploitation in tropical forests: An intercontinental comparison. *Conservation Biology*, **16**(1), 232–237.

Fa, J. E., & Purvis, A. (1997). Body size, diet and population density in Afrotropical forest mammals: A comparison with neotropical species. *Journal of Animal Ecology*, **66**(1), 98–112.

Fa, J. E., Ryan, S. F., & Bell, D. J. (2005). Hunting vulnerability, ecological characteristics and harvest rates of bushmeat species in afrotropical forests. *Biological Conservation*, **121**(2), 167–176.

Fa, J. E., Seymour, S., Dupain, J., Amin, R., Albrechtsen, L., & Macdonald, D. (2006). Getting to grips with the magnitude of exploitation: Bushmeat in the Cross–Sanaga rivers region, Nigeria and Cameroon. *Biological Conservation*, **129**(4), 497–510.

Fa, J. E., Stewart, J. R., Lloveras, L., & Vargas, J. M. (2013). Rabbits and hominin survival in Iberia. *Journal of Human Evolution*, **64**, 233–241.

Fa, J. E., Watson, J. E., Leiper, I., *et al.* (2020). Importance of Indigenous Peoples' lands for the conservation of Intact Forest Landscapes. *Frontiers in Ecology and the Environment*, **18**(3), 135–140.

Fa, J. E., Wright, J. H., Funk, S. M., *et al.* (2019). Mapping the availability of bushmeat for consumption in Central African cities. *Environmental Research Letters*, **14**(9), 094002.

Fa, J. E., Yuste, J. E. G., & Castelo, R. (2000). Bushmeat markets on Bioko Island as a measure of hunting pressure. *Conservation Biology*, **14**(6), 1602–1613.

Fagan, W. F., & Holmes, E. E. (2006). Quantifying the extinction vortex. *Ecology Letters*, **9**(1), 51–60.

Falk, H., Dürr, S., Hauser, R., *et al.* (2013). Illegal import of bushmeat and other meat products into Switzerland on commercial passenger flights. *Revue Scientifique et Technique (International Office of Epizootics)*, **32**, 727–739.

FAO. (2019). *Safeguarding against Economic Slowdowns and Downturns*, Rome: FAO.

(2020a). *Global Emergence of Infectious Diseases: Links with Wild Meat Consumption, Ecosystem Disruption, Habitat Degradation and Biodiversity Loss*, Rome: FAO. www.fao.org/documents/card/en/c/ca9456en

(2020b). *The COVID-19 Challenge: Zoonotic Diseases and Wildlife. Collaborative Partnership on Sustainable Wildlife Management's Four Guiding Principles to Reduce Risk From Zoonotic Diseases and Build More Collaborative Approaches in Human Health and Wildlife Management.* Rome: FAO. www.fao.org/3/cb1163en/CB1163EN.pdf

(2021). FAOSTAT- Annual Population. www.fao.org/faostat/en/#data/OA

FAO Fisheries Department. (2003). *The Ecosystem Approach to Fisheries* (No. 4, Suppl. 2.), Rome: FAO.

FAO/WHO/UNU. (2007). *Protein and Amino Acid Requirements in Human Nutrition: Report of a Joint FAO/WHO/UNU expert consultation*, Geneva: World Health Organization.

Fargeot, C., Drouet-Hoguet, N., & Le Bel, S. (2017). The role of bushmeat in urban household consumption: Insights from Bangui, the capital city of the Central African Republic. *Bois et Forêts Des Tropiques*, **(332)**, 31–42.

Faust, C. L., Dobson, A. P., Gottdenker, N., *et al.* (2017). Null expectations for disease dynamics in shrinking habitat: Dilution or amplification? *Philosophical Transactions of the Royal Society B: Biological Sciences*, **372**(1722), 20160173.

Feldman, M., Harbeck, M., Keller, M., *et al.* (2016). A high-coverage *Yersinia pestis* genome from a sixth-century Justinianic plague victim. *Molecular Biology and Evolution*, **33**(11), 2911–2923.

Fenchel, T. (1974). Intrinsic rate of natural increase: The relationship with body size. *Oecologia*, **14**(4), 317–326.

Feng, J., Sun, Y., Li, H., *et al.* (2021). Assessing mammal species richness and occupancy in a Northeast Asian temperate forest shared by cattle. *Diversity and Distributions*, **27**(50), 857–872.

Fenner, F., Henderson, D. A., Arita, I., Jezek, Z., & Ladnyi, I. D. (1988). *Smallpox and its Eradication*, Vol. **6**. Geneva: World Health Organization.

Fernandes-Ferreira, H., Mendonça, S. V., Albano, C., Ferreira, F. S., & Alves, R. R. N. (2012). Hunting, use and conservation of birds in Northeast Brazil. *Biodiversity and Conservation*, **21**(1), 221–244.

Fiedel, S., & Haynes, G. (2004). A premature burial: Comments on Grayson and Meltzer's 'Requiem for overkill.' *Journal of Archaeological Science*, **31**(1), 121–131.

Fiedel, S. J. (2005). Man's best friend – mammoth's worst enemy? A speculative essay on the role of dogs in Paleoindian colonization and megafaunal extinction. *World Archaeology*, **37**(1), 11–25.

Field, H. E. (2009). Bats and emerging zoonoses: Henipaviruses and SARS. *Zoonoses and Public Health*, **56**(6–7), 278–284.

Figueiredo, L., Krauss, J., Steffan-Dewenter, I., & Sarmento Cabral, J. (2019). Understanding extinction debts: Spatio–temporal scales, mechanisms and a roadmap for future research. *Ecography*, **42**(12) 1973–1990.

Fimbel, C., Curran, B., & Usongo, L. (1999). Enhancing the sustainability of duiker hunting through community participation and controlled access in the Lobéké region of southeastern Cameroon. In J. G. Robinson, & E. L. Bennet, eds., *Hunting for Sustainability in Tropical Forests*, New York: Columbia University Press, 356–374.

Fiorini, S., Yearley, S., & Dandy, N. (2011). Wild deer, multivalence, and institutional adaptation: The 'Deer Management Group' in Britain. *Human Organization*, **70**(2), 179–188.

Fittkau, E. J., & Klinge, H. (1973). On biomass and trophic structure of the Central Amazonian rain forest ecosystem. *Biotropica*, **5**(1), 2–14.

Fitzgibbon, C. (1998). The management of subsistence harvesting: Behavioral ecology of hunters and their mammalian prey. In T. Caro, ed., Behavioral Ecology and Conservation Biology, 449–473.

Fitzgibbon, C. D., Mogaka, H., & Fanshawe, J. H. (1995). Subsistence hunting in Arabuko-Sokoke Forest, Kenya, and its effects on mammal populations. *Conservation Biology*, **9**(5), 1116–1126.

Fitzgibbon, C. D., Mogaka, H., & Fanshawe, J. H. (1999). Threatened mammals, subsistence harvesting and high human population densities: A recipe for disaster? In J. G. Robinson, & L. E. Bennett, eds., *Hunting for Sustainability in Tropical Forests*, New York: Columbia University Press.

Fitzmaurice, M. (2010). Indigenous whaling, protection of the environment, intergenerational rights and environmental ethics. *The Yearbook of Polar Law Online*, **2**(1), 253–277.

Fleagle, J. G., Kay, R. F., & Anthony, M. R. L. (1997). Fossil New World monkeys. In R. D. Madden, R. L. Cifelli, & J. J. Flynn, eds., *Vertebrate Paleontology in the Neotropics: The Miocene fauna of La Venta, Colombia*, Washington, DC: Smithsonian Institution Press, 473–495.

Fleagle, J. G., & Reed, K. E. (1996). Comparing primate communities: A multivariate approach. *Journal of Human Evolution*, **30**(6), 489–510.

Fleming, T. H., Breitwisch, R., & Whitesides, G. H. (1987). Patterns of tropical vertebrate frugivore diversity. *Annual Review of Ecology and Systematics*, **18**(1), 91–109.

Forline, L. C. (1997). The persistence and cultural transformation of the Guajá Indians, foragers of Maranhão State, Brazil (PhD thesis), Gainesville: University of Florida.

Forrester, J. D., Apangu, T., Griffith, K., *et al.* (2017). Patterns of human plague in Uganda, 2008–2016. *Emerging Infectious Diseases*, **23**(9), 1517–1521.

Fotso, R. C., & Ngnegueu, P. R. (1998). *Commercial Hunting and its Consequences on the Dynamics of Duiker Populations*, Cameroon: ECOFAC.

Fragoso, J. M., Levi, T., Oliveira, L. F., *et al.* (2016). Line transect surveys underdetect terrestrial mammals: Implications for the sustainability of subsistence hunting. *PloS One*, **11**(4), e0152659.

Francesconi, W., Bax, V., Blundo-Canto, G., *et al.* (2018). Hunters and hunting across indigenous and colonist communities at the forest-agriculture interface: An ethnozoological study from the Peruvian Amazon. *Journal of Ethnobiology and Ethnomedicine*, **14**, 54.

Franco, C. L. B., El Bizri, H. R., de Souza, P. R., *et al.* (2021). Community-based environmental protection in the Brazilian Amazon: Recent history, legal landmarks and expansion across protected areas. *Journal of Environmental Management*, **287**, 112314.

Franzen, M. (2006). Evaluating the sustainability of hunting: A comparison of harvest profiles across three Huaorani communities. *Environmental Conservation*, **33**(1), 36–45.

Friant, S., Ayambem, W. A., Alobi, A. O., *et al.* (2020). Eating bushmeat improves food security in a biodiversity and infectious disease 'hotspot.' *EcoHealth*, **17**(1), 125–138.

Friant, S., Paige, S. B., & Goldberg, T. L. (2015). Drivers of bushmeat hunting and perceptions of zoonoses in Nigerian hunting communities. *PLoS Neglected Tropical Diseases*, **9**(5), e0003792.

Froment, A. (2014). Human biology and the health of African rainforest inhabitants. In B. S. Hewlett, ed., *Hunter-gatherers of the Congo Basin*, New Brunswick, NJ: Transaction Publishers, 117–164.

Frutos, R., Lopez Roig, M., Serra-Cobo, J., & Devaux, C. A. (2020). COVID-19: The conjunction of events leading to the Coronavirus pandemic and lessons to learn for future threats. *Frontiers in Medicine*, **7**, 223.

Fuentes-Montemayor, E., Cuarón, A. D., Vázquez-Domínguez, E., Benítez-Malvido, J., Valenzuela-Galván, D., & Andresen, E. (2009). Living on the edge: Roads and edge effects on small mammal populations. *Journal of Animal Ecology*, **78**(4), 857–865.

Fumagalli, M., Moltke, I., Grarup, N., *et al.* (2015). Greenlandic Inuit show genetic signatures of diet and climate adaptation. *Science*, **349**(6254), 1343–1347.

Funk, S. M., Fa, J. E., Ajong, S. N., *et al.* (2021). Pre- and post-Ebola outbreak trends in wild meat trade in West Africa. *Biological Conservation*, **255**, 109024.

Funtowicz, S., Ravetz, J., & O'Connor, M. (1998). Challenges in the use of science for sustainable development. *International Journal of Sustainable Development*, **1**(1), 99–107.

Galetti, M., Brocardo, C. R., Begotti, R. A., *et al.* (2017). Defaunation and biomass collapse of mammals in the largest Atlantic forest remnant. *Animal Conservation*, **20**(3), 270–281.

Gallego-Zamorano, J., Benítez-López, A., Santini, L., Hilbers, J. P., Huijbregts, M. A. J., & Schipper, A. M. (2020). Combined effects of land use and hunting on distributions of tropical mammals. *Conservation Biology*, **34**(5), 1271–1280.

Gálvez, H., Arbaiza, T., Carcelén, F., & Lucas, O. (1999). Valor nutritivo de las carnes de sajino (*Tayassu tajacu*), venado colorado (*Mazama americana*), majaz (*Agouti paca*) y motelo (Geochelone denticulata). *Revista de Investigaciones Veterinarias Del Peru*, **10**, 82–86.

Gandiwa, E. (2011). Preliminary assessment of illegal hunting by communities adjacent to the Northern Gonarezhou National Park, Zimbabwe. *Tropical Conservation Science*, **4**(4), 445–467.

Ganzhorn, J. U. (1992). Leaf chemistry and the biomass of folivorous primates in tropical forests. *Oecologia*, **91**(4), 540–547.

Gao, F., Bailes, E., Robertson, D. L., *et al.* (1999). Origin of HIV-1 in the chimpanzee. *Nature*, **397**(6718), 436–441.

Gao, H.-W., Wang, L.-P., Liang, S., *et al.* (2012). Change in rainfall drives malaria re-emergence in Anhui Province, China. *PLoS ONE*, **7**(8), e43686.

Garcia, C. A., & Lescuyer, G. (2008). Monitoring, indicators and community based forest management in the tropics: Pretexts or red herrings? *Biodiversity and Conservation*, **17**(6), 1303–1317.

Gardner, C. J., Bicknell, J. E., Baldwin-Cantello, W., Struebig, M. J., & Davies, Z. G. (2019). Quantifying the impacts of defaunation on natural forest regeneration in a global meta-analysis. *Nature Communications*, **10**(1), 4590.

Gardner, C. J., & Davies, Z. G. (2014). Rural bushmeat consumption within multiple-use protected areas: Qualitative evidence from Southwest Madagascar. *Human Ecology*, **42**(1), 21–34.

Garnett, S. T., Burgess, N. D., Fa, J. E., *et al.* (2018). A spatial overview of the global importance of Indigenous lands for conservation. *Nature Sustainability*, **1**(7), 369–374.

Gaston, K. J. (1996). Biodiversity-latitudinal gradients. *Progress in Physical Geography*, **20**(4), 466–476.

(2000). Global patterns in biodiversity. *Nature*, **405**(6783), 220–227.

Gautier-Hion, A., Duplantier, J.-M., Quris, R., *et al.* (1985). Fruit characters as a basis of fruit choice and seed dispersal in a tropical forest vertebrate community. *Oecologia*, **65**(3), 324–337.

Gautier-Hion, A., Emmons, L. H., & Dubost, G. (1980). A comparison of the diets of three major groups of primary consumers of Gabon (primates, squirrels and ruminants). *Oecologia*, **45**(2), 182–189.

Gautret, P., Blanton, J., Dacheux, L., *et al.* (2014). Rabies in nonhuman primates and potential for transmission to humans: A literature review and examination of selected French national data. *PLoS Neglected Tropical Diseases*, **8**(5), e2863.

Gavin, M. C., & Stepp, J. R. (2014). Rapoport's Rule revisited: Geographical distributions of human languages. *PLoS ONE*, **9**(9), e107623.

Geoghegan, J. L., Senior, A. M., Di Giallonardo, F., & Holmes, E. C. (2016). Virological factors that increase the transmissibility of emerging human viruses. *Proceedings of the National Academy of Sciences of the United States of America*, **113**(15), 4170–4175.

Getz, W. M., & Bergh, M. O. (1988). Quota setting in stochastic fisheries. In W. S. Wooster, ed., *Biological Objectives and Fishery Management*, Heidelberg: Springer, 259–277.

Ghiselin, M. T. (1983). Lloyd Morgan's canon in evolutionary context. *Behavioral and Brain Sciences*, **6**(3), 362–363.

Giacomini, H. C., & Galetti, M. (2013). An index for defaunation. *Biological Conservation*, **163**, 33–41.

Gibb, R., Redding, D., Qing Chin, K., *et al.* (2020). Zoonotic host diversity increases in human-dominated ecosystems. *Nature*, **584**(7821), 398–402.

Gibbons, R. (2004). Examining the extinction of the Pleistocene megafauna. *Scholarly Undergraduate Research Journal*, **3**, 22–27.

Gill, D. J. C., Fa, J. E., Rowcliffe, J. M., & Kümpel, N. F. (2012). Drivers of change in hunter offtake and hunting strategies in Sendje, Equatorial Guinea. *Conservation Biology*, **26**(6), 1052–1060.

Giombini, M. I., Bravo, S. P., Sica, Y. V., & Tosto, D. S. (2017). Early genetic consequences of defaunation in a large-seeded vertebrate-dispersed palm (*Syagrus romanzoffiana*). *Heredity*, **118**(6), 568–577.

Glanz, W. E. (1982). The terrestrial mammal fauna of Barro Colorado Island: Censuses and long-term changes. In E. G. Leigh Jr., A. S. Rand, & D. M. Windsor, eds., *The Ecology of a Tropical Forest*, Washington, DC: Smithsonian Institution Press, 455–468.

(1991). Mammalian densities at protected versus hunted sites in Central Panama. In J. G. Robinson, & K. H. Redford, eds., *Neotropical Wildlife Use and Conservation*, Chicago, IL: University of Chicago Press, 163–173.

Glennon, E. E., Jephcott, F. L., Restif, O., & Wood, J. L. N. (2019). Estimating undetected Ebola spillovers. *PLoS Neglected Tropical Diseases*, **13**(6), e0007428.

Global Forest Watch. (2002). *An analysis of access into Central Africa's rainforests*, Washington, DC: World Resources Institute.

Golden, C. D. (2009). Bushmeat hunting and use in the Makira Forest, north-eastern Madagascar: A conservation and livelihoods issue. *Oryx*, **43**(3), 386–392.

Golden, C. D., Fernald, L. C. H., Brashares, J. S., Rasolofoniaina, B. J. R., & Kremen, C. (2011). Benefits of wildlife consumption to child nutrition in a biodiversity hotspot. *Proceedings of the National Academy of Sciences of the United States of America*, **108**(49), 19653–19656.

Goldstein, T., Anthony, S. J., Gbakima, A., *et al.* (2018). The discovery of Bombali virus adds further support for bats as hosts of ebolaviruses. *Nature Microbiology*, **3**(10), 1084–1089.

Gombeer, S., Nebesse, C., Musaba, P., *et al.* (2021). Exploring the bushmeat market in Brussels, Belgium: A clandestine luxury business. *Biodiversity and Conservation*, **30**, 55–66.

Gonedelé Bi, S., Koné, I., Béné, J. C. K., *et al.* (2017). Bushmeat hunting around a remnant coastal rainforest in Côte d'Ivoire. *Oryx*, **51**(3), 418–427.

Gonwouo, L. N., & Rödel, M.-O. (2008). The importance of frogs to the livelihood of the Bakossi people around Mount Manengouba, Cameroon, with special consideration of the Hairy Frog. *Salamandra*, **44**, 23–34.

Gonzalez, J. A. (2004). Human use and conservation of economically important birds in seasonally flooded forests of the Northeastern Peruvian Amazon. In K. Silvius, R. Bodmer, & J. Fragoso, eds., *People in Nature: Wildlife Conservation in South and Central America*, New York: Columbia University Press, 344–361.

Goodman, S. J., Barton, N. H., Swanson, G., Abernethy, K., & Pemberton, J. M. (1999). Introgression through rare hybridization: A genetic study of a hybrid zone between red and sika deer (genus *Cervus*) in Argyll, Scotland. *Genetics*, **152**(1), 355–371.

Gottdenker, N. L., Streicker, D. G., Faust, C. L., & Carroll, C. R. (2014). Anthropogenic land use change and infectious diseases: A review of the evidence. *EcoHealth*, **11**(4), 619–632.

Gould, S. J., & Lewontin, R. C. (1979). The spandrels of San Marco and the Panglossian paradigm: A critique of the adaptationist programme. *Proceedings of the Royal Society of London. Series B. Biological Sciences*, **205**(1161), 581–598.

Gow, P. (2012). The Piro canoe. A preliminary ethnographic account. *Journal de La Société Des Américanistes*, **98**(98–1), 39–61.

Grace, D., Dipeolu, M., & Alonso, S. (2019). Improving food safety in the informal sector: Nine years later. *Infection Ecology & Epidemiology*, **9**(1), 1579613.

Grafton, R. Q., Kompas, T., & Hilborn, R. W. (2007). Economics of overexploitation revisited. *Science*, **318**(5856), 1601.

Grande-Vega, M., Farfán, M. Á., Ondo, A., & Fa, J. E. (2016). Decline in hunter offtake of blue duikers in Bioko Island, Equatorial Guinea. *African Journal of Ecology*, **54**(1), 49–58.

Gray, R. D. (1987). Faith and foraging: A critique of the 'Paradigm Argument from Design.' In A. C. Kamil, J. R. Krebs, & H. R. Pulliam, eds., *Foraging Behavior*, New York: Plenum Press, 69–140.

Gray, S. A., Zanre, E., & Gray, S. R. (2014). Fuzzy cognitive maps as representations of mental models and group beliefs. In E. I. Papageorgiou, ed., *Fuzzy Cognitive Maps for Applied Sciences and Engineering*, Heidelberg: Springer, 29–48.

Gray, T. N. E., Hughes, A. C., Laurance, W. F., *et al.* (2018). The wildlife snaring crisis: An insidious and pervasive threat to biodiversity in Southeast Asia. *Biodiversity and Conservation*, **27**(4), 1031–1037.

Grayson, D. K., & Meltzer, D. J. (2003). Clovis hunting and large mammal extinction: A critical review of the evidence. *Journal of World Prehistory*, **47**.

Grayson, D. K., & Meltzer, D. J. (2004). North American overkill continued? *Journal of Archaeological Science*, **31**(1), 133–136.

Greene, C., Umbanhowar, J., Mangel, M., & Caro, T. (1998). Animal breeding systems, hunter selectivity, and consumptive use in wildlife conservation. In T. Caro, ed., *Behavioral Ecology and Conservation Biology*, Oxford: Oxford University Press, 271–305.

Greenstreet, S. P. R., Rogers, S. I., Rice, J. C., et al. (2011). Development of the EcoQO for the North Sea fish community. *ICES Journal of Marine Science*, **68**(1), 1–11.

Grey-Ross, R., Downs, C. T., & Kirkman, K. (2010). An assessment of illegal hunting on farmland in KwaZulu-Natal, South Africa: Implications for Oribi (*Ourebia ourebi*) conservation. *South African Journal of Wildlife Research*, **40**(1), 43–52.

Grieser Johns, A. (1997). *Timber Production and Biodiversity Conservation in Tropical Rain Forests*, Cambridge University Press.

Griffiths, J. F. (1976). *Applied Climatology: An Introduction*, Oxford: Oxford University Press.

Grimm, V., Revilla, E., Berger, U., et al. (2005). Pattern-oriented modeling of agent-based complex systems: Lessons from ecology. *Science*, **310**(5750), 987–991.

Grobbelaar, A. A., Weyer, J., Moolla, N., Jansen van Vuren, P., Moises, F., & Paweska, J. T. (2016). Resurgence of yellow fever in Angola, 2015–2016. *Emerging Infectious Diseases*, **22**(10), 1854–1855.

Groucutt, H. S., Petraglia, M. D., Bailey, G., et al. (2015). Rethinking the dispersal of *Homo sapiens* out of Africa. *Evolutionary Anthropology*, **24**(4), 149–164.

Guan, Y., Zheng, B. J., He, Y. Q., et al. (2003). Isolation and characterization of viruses related to the SARS coronavirus from animals in southern China. *Science*, **302**(5643), 276–278.

Gubbi, S., & Linkie, M. (2012). Wildlife hunting patterns, techniques, and profile of hunters in and around Periyar tiger reserve. *Journal of the Bombay Natural History Society*, **109**(3), 165–172.

Güneralp, B., Lwasa, S., Masundire, H., Parnell, S., & Seto, K. C. (2017). Urbanization in Africa: Challenges and opportunities for conservation. *Environmental Research Letters*, **13**(1), 015002.

Gupta, A. K., & Chivers, D. J. (1999). Biomass and use of resources in south and south-east Asian primate communities. In J. G. Fleagle, C. Janson, & C. K. Read, eds., *Primate Communities*, Cambridge: Cambridge University Press, 38–54.

Gurley, E. S., Hegde, S. T., Hossain, K., et al. (2017). Convergence of humans, bats, trees, and culture in Nipah virus transmission, Bangladesh. *Emerging Infectious Diseases*, **23**(9), 1446–1453.

Gurven, M. D., Trumble, B. C., Stieglitz, J., et al. (2016). High resting metabolic rate among Amazonian forager-horticulturalists experiencing high pathogen burden. *American Journal of Physical Anthropology*, **161**(3), 414–425.

Guterres, A. (2020). Hard Hit by COVID-19 Pandemic, Indigenous Peoples' Input Must Be Part of Response, Recovery Strategies, Secretary-General Says in Observance Message (Press release). www.un.org/press/en/2020/sgsm20194 .doc.htm

Haddon, M. (2011). *Modelling and Quantitative Methods in Fisheries*, Boca Raton, FL: CRC Press.

Hahn, B. H. (2000). AIDS as a zoonosis: Scientific and public health implications. *Science*, **287**(5453), 607–614.

Hall, J. S., Saltonstall, K., Inogwabini, B.-I., & Omari, I. (1998). Distribution, abundance and conservation status of Grauer's gorilla. *Oryx*, **32**(2), 122–130

Hallpike, C. R. (1986). *The Principles of Social Evolution*, Oxford: Oxford University Press.

Hames, R. B. (1979). Comparison of the efficiencies of the shotgun and the bow in Neotropical forest hunting. *Human Ecology*, **7**, 219–251.

Hames, R. (1987). Game conservation or efficient hunting? In B. J. McCay, & J. M. Acheson, eds., *The Question of the Commons: The Culture and Ecology of Communal Resources*, Tucson: University of Arizona Press, 92–107.

(1991). Wildlife conservation in tribal societies. In A. Oldfield, ed., *Biodiversity: Culture, Conservation, and Ecodevelopment*, Boulder, CO: Westview Press, 172–199.

(2007). The ecologically noble savage debate. *Annual Review of Anthropology*, **3**, 177–190.

Hames, R. B., & Vickers, W. T. (1982). Optimal diet breadth theory as a model to explain variability in Amazonian hunting. *American Ethnologist*, **9**(2), 358–378.

Hammond, A. S., Royer, D. F., & Fleagle, J. G. (2017). The Omo-Kibish I pelvis. *Journal of Human Evolution*, **108**, 199–219.

Hammoudi, N., Dizoe, S., Saad, J., *et al.* (2020). Tracing *Mycobacterium ulcerans* along an alimentary chain in Côte d'Ivoire: A one health perspective. *PLoS Neglected Tropical Diseases*, **14**(5), e0008228.

Han, B. A., Kramer, A. M., & Drake, J. M. (2016). Global patterns of zoonotic disease in mammals. *Trends in Parasitology*, **32**(7), 565–577.

Hanazaki, N., Alves, R. R., & Begossi, A. (2009a). Hunting and use of terrestrial fauna used by Caiçaras from the Atlantic Forest coast (Brazil). *Journal of Ethnobiology and Ethnomedicine*, **5**(1), 36.

Hang'ombe, M. B., Mwansa, J. C. L., Muwowo, S., *et al.* (2012). Human–animal anthrax outbreak in the Luangwa valley of Zambia in 2011. *Tropical Doctor*, **42**(3), 136–139.

Hanya, G., Stevenson, P., van Noordwijk, M., *et al.* (2011). Seasonality in fruit availability affects frugivorous primate biomass and species richness. *Ecography*, **34**(6), 1009–1017.

Happold, D. C. D. (1996). Mammals of the Guinea–Congo rain forest. *Proceedings of the Royal Society of Edinburgh, Section B: Biological Sciences*, **104**, 243–284.

Hardouin, J. (1995). Minilivestock: From gathering to controlled production. *Biodiversity & Conservation*, **4**(3), 220–232.

Hardouin, J., Thys, É., Joiris, V., & Fielding, D. (2003). Mini-livestock breeding with indigenous species in the tropics. *Livestock Research for Rural Development*, **15**(4), 30.

Harkin, M. E., & Lewis, D. R. (eds.) (2007). *Americans and the Environment: Perspectives on the Ecological Indian*, Lincoln: University of Nebraska Press.

Harrison, M., Roe, D., Baker, J., *et al.* (2015). *Wildlife crime: a review of the evidence on drivers and impacts in Uganda* (IIED Research Report), London: International Institute for Environment and Development.

Harrison, R. D., Sreekar, R., Brodie, J. F., *et al.* (2016). Impacts of hunting on tropical forests in Southeast Asia: Hunting in Tropical Forests. *Conservation Biology*, **30**(5), 972–981.

Harrison, R. D., Tan, S., Plotkin, J. B., *et al.* (2013). Consequences of defaunation for a tropical tree community. *Ecology Letters*, **16**(5), 687–694.

Hart, J. A. (1999). Impact and sustainability of indigenous hunting in the Ituri Forest, Congo-Zaire: A comparison of unhunted and hunted duiker populations. In J. G. Robinson, & E. L. Bennett, eds., *Hunting for Sustainability in Tropical Forests*, New York: Columbia University Press, 106–153.

(2000). Impact and sustainability of indigenous hunting in the Ituri forest, Congo-Zaïre: A comparison of unhunted and hunted duiker populations. In J. G. Robinson, & E. L. Bennett, eds., *Hunting for Sustainability in Tropical Forests* New York: Columbia University Press, 106–153.

Hartwig, W. C., & Cartelle, C. (1996). A complete skeleton of the giant South American primate *Protopithecus*. *Nature*, **381**(6580), 307–311.

Hawkes, K. (1990). Why do men hunt? Benefits for risky choices. In E. Cashdan, ed., *Risk and Uncertainty in Tribal and Peasant Economies*, Boulder, CO: Westview Press, 145–166.

(2001). Is meat the hunter's property? Big game, ownership, and explanations. In C. B. Stanford, & H. T. Bunn, eds., *Meat-Eating and Human Evolution*, Oxford: Oxford University Press, 219–236.

Hawkes, K., Altman, J., Beckerman, S., *et al.* (1993). Why hunter-gatherers work: An ancient version of the problem of public goods [and comments and reply]. *Current Anthropology*, **34**(4), 341–361.

Hawkes, K., & Bliege Bird, R. (2002). Showing off, handicap signaling, and the evolution of men's work. *Evolutionary Anthropology*, **11**(2), 58–67.

Hawkes, K., Hill, K., & O'Connell, J. F. (1982). Why hunters gather: Optimal foraging and the Aché of eastern Paraguay. *American Ethnologist*, **9**(2), 379–398.

(1985). Optimal foraging models and the case of the !Kung. *American Anthropologist*, **87**(2), 401–405.

Hawkes, K., O'Connell, J. F., & Blurton Jones, N. G. (1991). Hunting income patterns among the Hadza: Big game, common goods, foraging goals and the evolution of the human diet. *Philosophical Transactions of the Royal Society of London. Series B: Biological Sciences*, **334**(1270), 243–251.

Hawkes, K., & O'Connell, J. (1992). On optimal foraging models and subsistence transitions. *Current Anthropology*, **(33)**, 63–66.

Hawkes, K., O'Connell, J. F., Blurton Jones, N. G., *et al.* (2001). Hunting and nuclear families: Some lessons from the Hadza about men's work. *Current Anthropology*, **42**(5), 681–709.

Hawkes, K., O'Connell, J. F., & Rogers, L. (1997). The behavioral ecology of modern hunter-gatherers, and human evolution. *Trends in Ecology & Evolution*, **12**(1), 29–32.

Hawkins, B. A., Albuquerque, F. S., Araújo, M. B., *et al.* (2007). A global evaluation of metabolic theory as an explanation for terrestrial species richness gradients. *Ecology*, **88**(8), 1877–1888.

Hayashi, K. (2008). Hunting activities in forest camps among the Baka hunter-gatherers of Southeastern Cameroon. *African Study Monographs*, **29**, 73–92.

Hayman, D. T. S., Wang, L.-F., Barr, J., *et al.* (2011). Antibodies to Henipavirus or Henipa-like viruses in domestic pigs in Ghana, West Africa. *PLoS ONE*, **6**(9), e25256.

Haynes, G. (2007). A review of some attacks on the overkill hypothesis, with special attention to misrepresentations and doubletalk. *Quaternary International*, **169–170**, 84–94. Hewlett, B. S.

(2018). The evidence for human agency in the Late Pleistocene megafaunal extinctions. In D. A. DellaSala, & M. I. Goldstein, eds. *Encyclopedia of the Anthropocene*, Oxford: Elsevier, 219–226.

Hayward, M. W. (2009). Bushmeat hunting in Dwesa and Cwebe Nature Reserves, Eastern Cape, South Africa. *South African Journal of Wildlife Research*, **39**(1), 70–84.

Headland, T. N., & Blood, D. (2002). *What Place for Hunter-Gatherers in Millennium Three?*, Dallas, TX: SIL International and the International Museum of Cultures.

Heinrich, S., Wittmann, T. A., Prowse, T. A. A., *et al.* (2016). Where did all the pangolins go? International CITES trade in pangolin species. *Global Ecology and Conservation*, **8**, 241–253.

Hema, E. M., Ouattara, V., Parfait, G., *et al.* (2019). Bushmeat consumption in the West African Sahel of Burkina Faso, and the decline of some consumed species. *Oryx*, **53**(1), 145–150.

Henry, J. (1964). *Jungle People. A Kaisang tribe of the Highlands of Brazil*. New York: Vintage Books.

Hewlett, B. S. (1993). *Intimate Fathers: The Nature and Context of Aka Pygmy Paternal Infant Care*, Ann Arbor: University of Michigan Press.

(ed.). (2014). *Hunter-Gatherers of the Congo Basin: Cultures, Histories and Biology of African Pygmies*, New Brunswick, NJ: Transaction Publishers.

Higgins, J. A., Hubalek, Z., Halouzka, J., *et al.* (2000). Detection of *Francisella tularensis* in infected mammals and vectors using a probe-based polymerase chain reaction. *The American Journal of Tropical Medicine and Hygiene*, **62**(2), 310–318.

Hill, K. (1982). Hunting and human evolution. *Journal of Human Evolution*, **11**(6), 521–544.

(1988). Macronutrient modifications of optimal foraging theory: An approach using indifference curves applied to some modern foragers. *Human Ecology*, **16** (2), 157–197.

Hill, K., & Hawkes, K. (1983). Neotropical hunting among the Aché of Eastern Paraguay. In R. Hames, & W. Vickers, eds., *Adaptive Responses of Native Amazonians*, New York: Academic Press, 139–188.

Hill, K., Kaplan, H., Hawkes, K., & Hurtado, M. (1987). Foraging decisions among Ach hunter-gatherers: New data and implications for optimal foraging models. *Ethology and Sociobiology*, (**8**), 1–36.

Hill, K., McMillan, G., & Farina, R. (2003). Hunting-related changes in game encounter rates from 1994 to 2001 in the Mbaracayu Reserve, Paraguay. *Conservation Biology*, **17**(5), 1312–1323.

Hill, K., & Padwe, J. (1999). Sustainability of Aché hunting in the Mbaracayu reserve, Paraguay. In J. Robinson, & E. L. Bennett, eds., *Hunting for Sustainability in Tropical Forests*, New York: Columbia University Press, 79–105.

Hill, S. L. L., Gonzalez, R., Sanchez-Ortiz, K., *et al.* (2018). Worldwide impacts of past and projected future land-use change on local species richness and the Biodiversity Intactness Index. *BioRxiv.* doi:10.1101/311787

Hirai, M. (2014). Agricultural land use, collection and sales of non-timber forest products in the Agroforest Zone in Southeastern Cameroon. *African Study Monographs*, Suppl. **49**, 169–202.

Hitchcock, R. K. (2000). Traditional African wildlife utilization: Subsistence hunting, poaching, and sustainable use. In H. H. T. Prins, J. G. Grootenhusi, & T. T. Dolan, eds., *Wildlife Conservation by Sustainable Use*, Dordrecht: Kluwer Academic Publishers, 389–416.

Hocknull, S. A., Lewis, R., Arnold, L. J., *et al.* (2020). Extinction of eastern Sahul megafauna coincides with sustained environmental deterioration. *Nature Communications*, **11**(1), 2250.

Hofer, H., Campbell, K. L., East, M. L., & Huish, S. A. (1996). The impact of game meat hunting on target and non-target species in the Serengeti. In V. J. Taylor, & N. Dunstone, eds., *The Exploitation of Mammal Populations*, London: Chapman and Hall, 117–146.

Hoffman, L. C., & Cawthorn, D.-M. (2012). What is the role and contribution of meat from wildlife in providing high quality protein for consumption? *Animal Frontiers*, **2**(4), 40–53.

Hoffmann, M., Belant, J. L., Chanson, J. S., *et al.* (2011). The changing fates of the world's mammals. *Philosophical Transactions of the Royal Society B: Biological Sciences*, **366**(1578), 2598–2610.

Holdridge, L. R. (1978). *Life Zone Ecology*, San Jose de Costa Rica: IICA, Tropical Science Center.

Holmberg, A. (1969). *Nomads of the Long Bow: The Sironó of Eastern Bolivia*. Garden City, NY: Natural History Press.

Holmern, T., Mkama, S., Muya, J., & Røskaft, E. (2006). Intraspecific prey choice of bushmeat hunters outside the Serengeti National Park, Tanzania: A preliminary analysis. *African Zoology*, **41**(1), 81–87.

Hooke, R. LeB., & Martín-Duque, J. F. (2012). Land transformation by humans: A review. *GSA Today*, **12**(12), 4–10.

Hooper, P. L., Demps, K., Gurven, M., Gerkey, D., & Kaplan, H. S. (2015). Skills, division of labour and economies of scale among Amazonian hunters and South Indian honey collectors. *Philosophical Transactions of the Royal Society B: Biological Sciences*, **370**, 20150008.

Hovorka, A. J. (2017). Animal geographies I: Globalizing and decolonizing. *Progress in Human Geography*, **41**(3), 382–394.

Hsieh, P., Veeramah, K. R., Lachance, J., *et al.* (2016). Whole-genome sequence analyses of Western Central African Pygmy hunter-gatherers reveal a complex demographic history and identify candidate genes under positive natural selection. *Genome Research*, **26**(3), 279–290.

Hublin, J.-J., Ben-Ncer, A., Bailey, S. E., *et al.* (2017). New fossils from Jebel Irhoud, Morocco and the pan-African origin of *Homo sapiens*. *Nature*, **546**(7657), 289–292.

Huchzermeyer, F. (2003). *Crocodiles – Biology, Husbandry and Diseases*, Wallingford: CABI Publishing,.

Hunn, E. S. (1982). Mobility as a factor limiting resource use in the Columbia Plateau of North America. In H. Williams, & E. S. Hunn, eds., *Resource Managers: North American and Australian Hunter-Gatherers*, New York: Westview Press, 17–43.

Hunt, L. M. (2013). Using human-dimensions research to reduce implementation uncertainty for wildlife management: A case of moose (*Alces alces*) hunting in northern Ontario, Canada. *Wildlife Research*, **40**(1), 61–69.

Huong, N. Q., Nga, N. T. T., Long, N. V., *et al.* (2020). Coronavirus testing indicates transmission risk increases along wildlife supply chains for human consumption in Viet Nam, 2013–2014. *PLoS ONE*, **15**(8), e0237129.

Hurtado, A. M., Hawkes, K., Hill, K., & Kaplan, H. (1985). Female subsistence strategies among Aché hunter-gatherers of eastern Paraguay. *Human Ecology*, **13**(1), 1–28.

Hurtado, A. M., Hill, K., Hurtado, I., & Kaplan, H. (1992). Trade-offs between female food acquisition and child care among Hiwi and Aché foragers. *Human Nature*, **3**(3), 185–216.

Hurtado, A. M., & Hill, K. R. (1992). Paternal effect on offspring survivorship among Aché and Hiwi hunter-gatherers: Implications for modeling pair-bond stability. In B. Hewlet, ed., *Father–Child Relations: Cultural and Biosocial Contexts*, Berlín: Aldine de Gruyter, 31–55.

Hurtado-Gonzales, J. L., & Bodmer, R. E. (2004). Assessing the sustainability of brocket deer hunting in the Tamshiyacu-Tahuayo Communal Reserve, north-eastern Peru. *Biological Conservation*, **116**(1), 1–7.

Hutin, Y. J. F., Williams, R. J., Malfait, P., *et al.* (2001). Outbreak of human monkeypox, Democratic Republic of Congo, 1996–1997. *Emerging Infectious Diseases*, **7**(3), 5.

Hutson, C. L., Lee, K. N., Abel, J., *et al.* (2007). Monkeypox zoonotic associations: Insights from laboratory evaluation of animals associated with the multi-state US outbreak. *The American Journal of Tropical Medicine and Hygiene*, **76**(4), 757–768.

Hutterer, K. L. (1988). The prehistory of the Asian rain forests. In J. S. Denslow, & C. Padoch, eds. *Peoples of the Tropical Rain Forest*, Los Angeles,: University of California Press, 63–72.

Ichikawa, M. (1983). An examination of the hunting-dependent life of the Mbuti Pygmies, Eastern Zaire. *African Study Monographs*, **4**, 55–76.

Ikeya, K. (1994). Hunting with dogs among the San in the central Kalahari. *African Study Monographs*, **15**(3), 119–134.

Imamura, K. (2016). Hunting play among the San Children: Imitation, learning, and play. In H. Terashima, & B. S. Hewlett, eds., *Social Learning and Innovation in Contemporary Hunter-Gatherers*, Tokyo: Springer Japan, 179–186.

Infield, M. (1988). *Hunting, Trapping and Fishing in Villages within and on the Periphery of the Korup National Park*, World Wide Fund for Nature.

Ingram, D. J. (2020). Wild meat in changing times. *Journal of Ethnobiology*, **40**(2), 117–130.

Ingram, D. J., Coad, L., Collen, B., *et al.* (2015). Indicators for wild animal offtake: Methods and case study for African mammals and birds. *Ecology and Society*, **20**(3), 40. http://dx.doi.org/10.5751/ES-07823-200340

Ingram, D. J., Cronin, D. T., Challender, D. W. S., Venditti, D. M., & Gonder, M. K. (2019). Characterising trafficking and trade of pangolins in the Gulf of Guinea. *Global Ecology and Conservation*, **17**, e00576.

Inogwabini, B.-I., Nzala, A. B., & Bokika, J. C. (2013). People and bonobos in the Southern Lake Tumba Landscape, Democratic Republic of Congo. *American Journal of Human Ecology*, **2**(2), 44–53.

Instituto Nacional de Antropología e Historia (Mexico). (2019). Descubren en Tultepec, Estado de México, contexto inédito de cacería y destazamiento de mamuts. https://unamglobal.unam.mx/descubren-en-tultepec-estado-de-mexico-contexto-inedito-de-caceria-y-destazamiento-de-mamuts

International Labour Organisation. (1989). *C169 - Indigenous and Tribal Peoples Convention, 1989 (No. 169)*, Geneva: International Labour Organisation. www.ilo.org/dyn/normlex/en/f?p=NORMLEXPUB:12100:0::NO:: P12100_ILO_CODE:C169

IPES-Food. (2020). COVID-19 and the crisis in food systems: Symptoms, causes, and potential solutions. Communiqué by IPES-Food, April 2020. www.ipes-food.org/_img/upload/files/COVID-19_CommuniqueEN.pdf

Isaac, N. J. B., & Cowlishaw, G. (2004). How species respond to multiple extinction threats. *Proceedings of the Royal Society of London. Series B: Biological Sciences*, **271**(1544), 1135–1141.

IUCN. (2020a). The IUCN Red List of Threatened Species v. 2015.2. www .iucnredlist.org

   (2020b, July 9). The IUCN Red List of Threatened Species. Version 2020-2. Spatial Data Download. www.iucnredlist.org

IUCN World Conservation Congress. (2000). Resolution 2.64, 2–4.

Iwamura, T., Guisan, A., Wilson, K. A., & Possingham, H. P. (2013). How robust are global conservation priorities to climate change? *Global Environmental Change*, **23**(5), 1277–1284.

Izurieta, R., Macaluso, M., Watts, D., *et al.* (2011). Hunting in the rainforest and mayaro virus infection: An emerging alphavirus in Ecuador. *Journal of Global Infectious Diseases*, **3**(4), 317.

Jackson, D. (2006, May 1). The health situation of women and children in Central African Pygmy Peoples. www.forestpeoples.org/es/node/942

Jansen, P. A., Muller-Landau, H. C., & Wright, S. J. (2010). Bushmeat hunting and climate: An indirect link. *Science*, **327**(5961), 30–30.

Janson, C. H., & Emmons, L. H. (1990). Ecological structure of the nonflying mammal community at Cocha Cashu Biological Station, Manu National Park, Peru. In A. Gentry, ed., *Four Neotropical Rainforests*, New Haven, CT: Yale University Press, 339–357.

Janssen, M. A., & Hill, K. (2014). Benefits of grouping and cooperative hunting among Ache hunter-gatherers: Insights from an agent-based foraging model. *Human Ecology*, **42**, 823–835.

Jean Desbiez, A. L., Keuroghlian, A., Piovezan, U., & Bodmer, R. E. (2011). Invasive species and bushmeat hunting contributing to wildlife conservation: The case of feral pigs in a Neotropical wetland. *Oryx*, **45**(1), 78–83.

Jeffrey, S. (1977). How Liberia uses wildlife. *Oryx*, **14**(2), 168–173.

Jenkins, R. K. B., & Racey, P. A. (2009). Bats as bushmeat in Madagascar. *Madagascar Conservation & Development*, **3**(1). doi:10.4314/mcd.v3i1.44132

Jenzora, A., Jansen, A., Ranisch, H., Lierz, M., Wichmann, O., & Grunow, R. (2008). Seroprevalence study of *Francisella tularensis* among hunters in Germany. *FEMS Immunology & Medical Microbiology*, **53**(2), 183–189.

Jepson, P., & Canney, S. (2003). Values-led conservation. *Global Ecology and Biogeography*, **12**(4), 271–274.

Jerozolimski, A., & Peres, C. A. (2003). Bringing home the biggest bacon: A cross-site analysis of the structure of hunter-kill profiles in Neotropical forests. *Biological Conservation*, **111**(3), 415–425.

Jetz, W., & Fine, P. V. A. (2012). Global gradients in vertebrate diversity predicted by historical area-productivity dynamics and contemporary environment. *PLoS Biology*, **10**(3), e1001292.

Jezek, Z., Arita, I., Mutombo, M., Dunn, C., Nakano, J. H., & Szczeniowski, M. (1986). Four generations of probable person-to-person transmission of human monkeypox. *American Journal of Epidemiology*, **123**(6), 1004–1012.

Jimoh, S. O., Ikyaagba, E. T., Alarape, A. A., Obioha, E. E., & Adeyemi, A. A. (2012). The role of traditional laws and taboos in wildlife conservation in the Oban Hill Sector of Cross River National Park (CRNP), Nigeria. *Journal of Human Ecology*, **39**(3), 209–219.

Johnson, A., Singh, S., Dongdala, M., & Vongsa, O. (2003). Wildlife hunting and use in the Nam Ha National Protected Area: Implications for rural livelihoods and biodiversity conservation. December 2003. In B. Bouahom, A. Glendinning, S. Nilsson, & M. Victor, eds. *Poverty Reduction and Shifting Cultivation Stabilisation in the Uplands of Lao PDR: Technologies, Approaches and Methods for Improving Upland Livelihoods - Proceedings of a Workshop held in Luang Prabang, Lao PDR, January 27–30, 2004.* Vientiane: National Agriculture and Forestry Research Institute, Lao PDR, 195–208.

Johnson, C. K., Hitchens, P. L., Pandit, P. S., et al. (2020). Global shifts in mammalian population trends reveal key predictors of virus spillover risk. *Proceedings of the Royal Society B: Biological Sciences*, **287**(1924), 20192736.

Johnson, C. N. (2002). Determinants of loss of mammal species during the Late Quaternary 'megafauna' extinctions: Life history and ecology, but not body size. *Proceedings of the Royal Society of London. Series B: Biological Sciences*, **269**(1506), 2221–2227.

Johnson, C. N., Alroy, J., Beeton, N. J., et al. (2016). What caused extinction of the Pleistocene megafauna of Sahul? *Proceedings of the Royal Society B: Biological Sciences*, **283**(1824), 20152399.

Joint FAO/WHO Expert Committee on Zoonoses, World Health Organization, & Food and Agriculture Organization of the United Nations. (1959). Joint WHO/FAO Expert Committee on Zoonoses [meeting held in Stockholm from 11 to 16 August 1958]: second report. https://apps.who.int/iris/handle/10665/40435

Jones, K. E., Patel, N. G., Levy, M. A., et al. (2008). Global trends in emerging infectious diseases. *Nature*, **451**(7181), 990–993.

Jones-Engel, L., Engel, G. A., Schillaci, M. A., et al. (2005). Primate-to-human retroviral transmission in Asia. *Emerging Infectious Diseases*, **11**(7), 1028–1035.

Jones-Engel, L., May, C. C., Engel, G. A., *et al.* (2008). Diverse contexts of zoonotic transmission of simian foamy viruses in Asia. *Emerging Infectious Diseases*, **14**(8), 1200–1208.

Jorge, M. L. S. P., Galetti, M., Ribeiro, M. C., & Ferraz, K. M. P. M. B. (2013). Mammal defaunation as surrogate of trophic cascades in a biodiversity hotspot. *Biological Conservation*, **163**, 49–57.

Jorgenson, J. P. (1993). Gardens, wildlife densities, and subsistence hunting by Maya Indians in Quintana Roo, *Mexico* (PhD dissertation), University of Florida.

Jori, F., Mensah, G. A., & Adjanohoun, E. (1995). Grasscutter production: An example of rational exploitation of wildlife. *Biodiversity and Conservation*, **4**(3), 257–265.

Joseph, S. (2000). Anthropological evolutionary ecology: A critique. *Journal of Ecological Anthropology*, **4**(1), 6–30.

Joshi, N. V., & Gadgil, M. (1991). On the role of refugia in promoting prudent use of biological resources. *Theoretical Population Biology*, **40**(2), 211–229.

Junglen, S., Kurth, A., Kuehl, H., *et al.* (2009). Examining landscape factors influencing relative distribution of mosquito genera and frequency of virus infection. *EcoHealth*, **6**(2), 239–249.

Kahurananga, J. (1981). Population estimates, densities and biomass of large herbivores in Simanjiro Plains, Northern Tanzania. *African Journal of Ecology*, **19**(3), 225–238.

Kalish, M. L., Wolfe, N. D., Ndongmo, C. B., *et al.* (2005). Central African hunters exposed to simian immunodeficiency virus. *Emerging Infectious Diseases*, **11**(12), 1928–1930.

Kamins, A., Baker, K., Restif, O., Cunningham, A., & Wood, J. L. (2014). Emerging risks from bat bushmeat in West Africa. In P. Paulsen, A. Bauer, M. Vodnansky, R. Winkelmayer, & F. J. M. Smulders, eds., *Trends in Game Meat Hygiene: From Forest to Fork*, Wageningen Academic Publishers, 239–240.

Kamins, A., Restif, O., Rowcliffe, M., Cunningham, A., & Wood, J. (2011b). Use of bats as bushmeat: Implications for human health in Ghana, West Africa. *Ecohealth*, **7**, S102–S102.

Kamins, A. O., Restif, O., Ntiamoa-Baidu, Y., *et al.* (2011a). Uncovering the fruit bat bushmeat commodity chain and the true extent of fruit bat hunting in Ghana, West Africa. *Biological Conservation*, **144**(12), 3000–3008.

Kamins, A. O., Rowcliffe, J. M., Ntiamoa-Baidu, Y., Cunningham, A. A., Wood, J. L. N., & Restif, O. (2015). Characteristics and risk perceptions of Ghanaians potentially exposed to bat-borne zoonoses through bushmeat. *EcoHealth*, **12**(1), 104–120.

Kaplan, H., Hill, K., Lancaster, J., & Hurtado, A. M. (2000). A theory of human life history evolution: Diet, intelligence, and longevity. *Evolutionary Anthropology*, 156–185.

Karanth, K. U., & Sunquist, M. E. (1992). Population structure, density and biomass of large herbivores in the tropical forests of Nagarahole, India. *Journal of Tropical Ecology*, **8**, 21–35.

Karesh, W. B., Cook, R. A., Bennett, E. L., & Newcomb, J. (2005). Wildlife trade and global disease emergence. *Emerging Infectious Diseases*, **11**(7), 3.

Karesh, W. B., & Noble, E. (2009). The bushmeat trade: Increased opportunities for transmission of zoonotic disease. *Mount Sinai Journal of Medicine*, **76**(5), 429–434.

Kaul, R., Hilaluddin, Jandrotia, J. S., & McGowan, P. J. K. (2004). Hunting of large mammals and pheasants in the Indian western Himalaya. *Oryx*, **38**(4), 426–431.

Keane, A., Jones, J. P. G., & Milner-Gulland, E. J. (2011). Encounter data in resource management and ecology: Pitfalls and possibilities: Encounter data in ecology. *Journal of Applied Ecology*, **48**(5), 1164–1173.

Keesing, F., Belden, L. K., Daszak, P., *et al.* (2010). Impacts of biodiversity on the emergence and transmission of infectious diseases. *Nature*, **468**(7324), 647–652.

Kelly, R. L. (1995). *The Foraging Spectrum: Diversity in Hunter-Gatherer Lifeways*, Washington: Smithsonian Institution Press.

(2013). *The Lifeways of Hunter-Gatherers*, 2nd ed., Cambridge: Cambridge University Press.

Kensinger, K. M. (1995). *How Real People Ought to Live: The Cashinahua of Eastern Peru*, Prospects Height, IL: Waveland PressInc.

Kiffner, C., Kioko, J., Kissui, B., *et al.* (2014). Interspecific variation in large mammal responses to human observers along a conservation gradient with variable hunting pressure: Animal behavioural response to human hunting pressure. *Animal Conservation*, **17**(6), 603–612.

King, A. M., Adams, M. J., Carstens, E. B., & Lefkowitz, E. J. (2012). Virus taxonomy. *Ninth Report of the International Committee on Taxonomy of Viruses*, 486–487.

Kingdon, J. (1997). *The Kingdon Field Guide to African Mammals*, San Diego, CA: Academic Press.

Kingdon, J., & Hoffmann, M. (2013). *Mammals of Africa. Volume VI, Pigs, Hippopotamuses, Chevrotain, Giraffes, Deer and Bovids*. London: Bloomsbury Publishing,.

Kingdon, J., Happold, D., Butynski, T., Hoffmann, M., Happold, M., & Kalina, J. (2013). *Mammals of Africa*, Vols. I–VI, London: Bloomsbury Publishing.

Kitanishi, K. (1995). Seasonal changes in the subsistence activities and food intake of the Aka hunter-gatherers in northeastern Congo. *African Study Monographs*, **16**(2), 73–118.

(2003). Cultivation by the Baka hunter-gatherers in the tropical rain forest of central Africa. *African Study Monographs, Suppl.* **28**, 143–157.

Klapman, M., & Capaldi, A. (2019). A simulation of anthropogenic Columbian mammoth (*Mammuthus columbi*) extinction. *Historical Biology*, **31**(5), 610–617.

Klein, R. G. (1987). Reconstructing how early people exploited animals: Problems and prospects. In M. Nitecki, & D. Nitecki, eds., *The Evolution of Human Hunting*, New York: Springer, 11–45.

Kleinert, R. D. V., Montoya-Diaz, E., Khera, T., *et al.* (2019). Yellow fever: Integrating current knowledge with technological innovations to identify strategies for controlling a re-emerging virus. *Viruses*, **11**(10), 960.

Klemens, M. W., & Thorbjarnarson J. B. (1995). Reptiles as a food resource. *Biodiversity & Conservation*, **4**, 281–298.

Knapp, E. J. (2012). Why poaching pays: A summary of risks and benefits illegal hunters face in Western Serengeti, Tanzania. *Tropical Conservation Science*, **5**(4), 434–445.

Knapp, E. J., Peace, N., & Bechtel, L. (2017). Poachers and poverty: Assessing objective and subjective measures of poverty among illegal hunters outside Ruaha National Park, Tanzania. *Conservation and Society*, **15**(1), 24.

Knecht, H. (1997). *Projectile Technology*, Boston, MA: Springer US..

Knight, J. (2003). Relocated to the roadside: Preliminary observations on the forest Peoples of Gabon. *African Study Monographs*, **28**, 81–121.

Knobel, D. L., Cleaveland, S., Coleman, P. G., *et al.* (2005). Re-evaluating the burden of rabies in Africa and Asia. *Bulletin of the World Health Organization*, **11**.

Koch, H. (1968). *Magie et chasse dans la forêt camerounaise*, Paris: Berget-Lerrault.

Konner, M., & Shostak, M. (1987). Timing and management of birth among the !Kung: Biocultural interaction in reproductive adaptation. *Cultural Anthropology*, **2**(1), 11–28.

Koppert, G. J. A., & Hladik, A. (1990). Measuring food consumption. In: C. M. Hladik, S. Bahuchet, & I. de Garine, eds. *Food and Nutrition in the African Rain Forest*, Paris: UNESCO, 58–61.

Koppert, G. J., Dounias, E., Froment, A., & Pasquet, P. (1993). Food consumption in three forest populations of the southern coastal area of Cameroon: Yassa-Mvae-Bakola. In C. Hladik, H. Pagezy, O. Linares, A. Hladik, A. Semple, & M. Hadley, eds., *Tropical Forests, People and Food. Bio-cultural Interactions and Applications to Development*, Vol. **13**, Paris: UNESCO/Parthenon, 295–295.

Koster, J. M. (2007). Hunting and subsistence among the Mayangna and Miskito of Nicaragua's Bosawas Biosphere Reserve (PhD dissertation), Penn State University.

(2008a). Giant anteaters (*Myrmecophaga tridactyla*) killed by hunters with dogs in the Bosawas Biosphere Reserve, Nicaragua. *The Southwestern Naturalist*, **53**(3), 414–416.

(2008b). Hunting with dogs in Nicaragua: An optimal foraging approach. *Current Anthropology*, **49**(5), 935–944.

(2009). Hunting dogs in the lowland Neotropics. *Journal of Anthropological Research*, **65**(4), 575–610.

Koster, J. M., Hodgen, J. J., Venegas, M. D., & Copeland, T. J. (2010). Is meat flavor a factor in hunters' prey choice decisions? *Human Nature*, **21**(3), 219–242.

Koster, J., McElreath, R., Hill, K., *et al.* (2019). The life history of human foraging: Cross-cultural and individual variation. *Science Advances*, **6**, eaax9070.

Kothari, A., Camill, P., & Brown, J. (2013). Conservation as if people also mattered: Policy and practice of community-based conservation. *Conservation and Society*, **11**(1), 1–15.

Krech, S. (1999). *The Ecological Indian: Myth and History*, New York: W. W. Norton & Company.

Kuchikura, Y. (1988). Efficiency and focus of blowpipe hunting among Semaq Beri hunter-gatherers of Peninsular Malaysia. *Human Ecology*, **16**(3), 271–305.

Kuisma, E., Olson, S. H., Cameron, K. N., *et al.* (2019). Long-term wildlife mortality surveillance in northern Congo: A model for the detection of Ebola virus disease epizootics. *Philosophical Transactions of the Royal Society B: Biological Sciences*, **374**(1782), 20180339.

Kümpel, N. F. (2006). Incentives for sustainable hunting of bushmeat in Río Muni, Equatorial Guinea (PhD thesis), Imperial College London.

Kümpel, N. F., East, T., Keylock, N., Rowcliffe, J. M., Cowlishaw, G., & Milner-Gulland, E. J. (2007). Determinants of bushmeat consumption and trade in Continental Equatorial Guinea: An urban–rural comparison. In G. Davies, & D. Brown, eds., *Bushmeat and Livelihoods: Wildlife Management and Poverty Reduction*, Oxford: Blackwell, 73–91.

Kümpel, N. F., Milner-Gulland, E. J., Rowcliffe, J. M., & Cowlishaw, G. (2008). Impact of gun-hunting on diurnal primates in continental Equatorial Guinea. *International Journal of Primatology*, **29**(4), 1065–1082.

Kümpel, N. F., Rowcliffe, J. M., Cowlishaw, G., & Milner-Gulland, E. J. (2009). Trapper profiles and strategies: Insights into sustainability from hunter behaviour. *Animal Conservation*, **12**(6), 531–539.

Kurpiers, L. A., Schulte-Herbrüggen, B., Ejotre, I., & Reeder, D. M. (2016). Bushmeat and emerging infectious diseases: Lessons from Africa. In F. M. Angelici, ed., *Problematic Wildlife*, Cham: Springer International Publishing, 507–551.

Kurten, E. L. (2013). Cascading effects of contemporaneous defaunation on tropical forest communities. *Biological Conservation*, **163**, 22–32.

Kurten, E. L., Wright, S. J., & Carson, W. P. (2015). Hunting alters seedling functional trait composition in a Neotropical forest. *Ecology*, **96**(7), 1923–1932.

Kuussaari, M., Bommarco, R., Heikkinen, R. K., *et al.* (2009). Extinction debt: A challenge for biodiversity conservation. *Trends in Ecology & Evolution*, **24**(10), 564–571.

Kuzmin, I. V., Bozick, B., Guagliardo, S. A., *et al.* (2011). Bats, emerging infectious diseases, and the rabies paradigm revisited. *Emerging Health Threats Journal*, **4**(1), 7159.

Lacy, R. (1993). Vortex - a computer-simulation model for population viability analysis. *Wildlife Research*, **20**(1), 45–65.

(2019). Lessons from 30 years of population viability analysis of wildlife populations. *Zoo Biology*, **38**(1), 67–77.

(2000). Structure of the VORTEX simulation model for population viability analysis. *Ecological Bulletins*, **48**, 191–203.

Ladele, A. A., Joseph, K., Omotesho, O. A., & Ijaiya, T. O. (1996). Sensory quality ratings, consumption pattern and preference for some selected meat types in Nigeria. *International Journal of Food Sciences and Nutrition*, **47**, 141–145.

Lagrou, E. M. (2021). Huni Kuin (Kaxinawá). https://pib.socioambiental.org/pt/Povo:Huni_Kuin_(Kaxinawá)

Lahm, S. A. (1993). Utilization of forest resources and local variation of wildlife populations in Northeastern Gabon. In C. Hladik, A. Hladik, H. Pagezy, O. Linares, G. Koppert, & A. Froment, eds., *Tropical Forests, People and Food*, Vol. **13**, Paris: UNESCO, 213–226.

(1994). Ecology and economics of human/wildlife interaction in northeastern Gabon (Dissertation), New York University.

(2001). Hunting and wildlife in Northeastern Gabon. Why conservation should extend beyond protected areas. In W. Weber, L. J. T. White, A. Vedder, & L. Naughton-Treves, eds., *African Rain Forest Ecology and Conservation. An Interdisciplinary Perspective*, New Haven, CT: Yale University Press, 344–354.

Laporte, N. T., Stabach, J. A., Grosch, R., Lin, T. S., & Goetz, S. J. (2007). Expansion of industrial logging in Central Africa. *Science*, **316**(5830), 1451–1451.

Larivière, S., Jolicoeur, H., & Crête, M. (2000). Status and conservation of the gray wolf (*Canis lupus*) in wildlife reserves of Québec. *Biological Conservation*, **94**(2), 143–151.

Larkin, P. A. (1977). An epitaph for the concept of maximum sustained yield. *Transactions of the American Fisheries Society*, **106**(1), 1–11.

Larsen, C. S. (2003). Animal source foods and human health during evolution. *The Journal of Nutrition*, **133**(11), 3893S–3897S.

Lau, S. K. P., Woo, P. C. Y., Li, K. S. M., *et al.* (2005). Severe acute respiratory syndrome coronavirus-like virus in Chinese horseshoe bats. *Proceedings of the National Academy of Sciences of the United States of America*, **102**(39), 14040–14045.

Laurance, W. F., Croes, B. M., Tchignoumba, L., *et al.* (2006). Impacts of roads and hunting on Central African rainforest mammals: Road and hunting impacts in Gabon. *Conservation Biology*, **20**(4), 1251–1261.

Lawson, S. (2014). Illegal logging in the Democratic Republic of the Congo. *Energy, Environment and Resources EER*, London: Chatham House.

LeBreton, M., Pike, B. L., Saylors, K. E., *et al.* (2012). Bushmeat and infectious disease emergence. In A. Alonso Aguirre, R. S. Ostfeld, & P. Daszak, eds., *New Directions in Conservation Medicine: Applied Cases of Ecological Health*, Oxford: Oxford University Press, 164–178.

LeBreton, M., Prosser, A. T., Tamoufe, U., *et al.* (2006). Patterns of bushmeat hunting and perceptions of disease risk among central African communities. *Animal Conservation*, **9**(4), 357–363.

Leclerc, C. (2012). *L'adoption de l'agriculture chez les Pygmées Baka du Cameroun.* Versailles: Editions Quae.

Lecompte, E., Fichet-Calvet, E., Daffis, S., *et al.* (2006). *Mastomys natalensis* and Lassa fever, West Africa. *Emerging Infectious Diseases*, **12**(12), 1971–1974.

Lee, R. B. (1992). Art, science, or politics? The crisis in hunter-gatherer studies. *American Anthropologist*, **94**, 31–54.

Lee, R. B., & DeVore, I. (1968). *Man the Hunter*, Chicago: Aldine.

Lee, R. B., Lee, R. B., & DeVore, I. (1976). *Kalahari Hunter-Gatherers: Studies of the !Kung San and their Neighbors*, Cambridge, MA: Harvard University Press.

Lee, R. J. (1999). Impact of subsistence hunting in North Sulawesi, Indonesia, and conservation options. In J. G. Robinson, & L. E. Bennett, eds., *Hunting for Sustainability in Tropical Forests*, New York: Columbia University Press, 455–472.

Lee, T. M., Sigouin, A., Pinedo-Vasquez, M., & Nasi, R. (2014). *The harvest of wildlife for bushmeat and traditional medicine in East, South and Southeast Asia:*

Current knowledge base, challenges, opportunities and areas for future research, Bogor: CIFOR.

Leendertz, F. H., Ellerbrok, H., Boesch, C., *et al.* (2004). Anthrax kills wild chimpanzees in a tropical rainforest. *Nature*, **430**(6998), 451–452.

Leendertz, S. A. J., Gogarten, J. F., Düx, A., Calvignac-Spencer, S., & Leendertz, F. H. (2016). Assessing the evidence supporting fruit bats as the primary reservoirs for Ebola viruses. *EcoHealth*, **13**(1), 18–25.

Lenselink, J. (1972). De Jachtopbrengst in een Surinaams Trio-dorp. *Suriname Landschap*, **20**, 3741.

León, P., & Montiel, S. (2008). Wild meat use and traditional hunting practices in a rural Mayan community of the Yucatan Peninsula, Mexico. *Human Ecology*, **36**(2), 249–257.

Leonard, C., Vashro, L., O'Connell, J. F., & Henry, A. G. (2015). Plant micro-remains in dental calculus as a record of plant consumption: A test with Twe forager-horticulturalists. *Journal of Archaeological Science: Reports*, **2**, 449–457.

Lerner, H., & Berg, C. (2017). A comparison of three holistic approaches to health: One health, ecohealth, and planetary health. *Frontiers in Veterinary Science*, **4**, 163.

Leroy, E. M., Epelboin, A., Mondonge, V., *et al.* (2009). Human Ebola outbreak resulting from direct exposure to fruit bats in Luebo, Democratic Republic of Congo, 2007. *Vector-Borne and Zoonotic Diseases*, **9**(6), 723–728.

Levi, T., Kilpatrick, A. M., Mangel, M., & Wilmers, C. C. (2012). Deer, predators, and the emergence of Lyme disease. *Proceedings of the National Academy of Sciences of the United States of America*, **109**(27), 10942–10947.

Levi, T., Lu, F., Yu, D. W., & Mangel, M. (2011a). The behaviour and diet breadth of central-place foragers: An application to human hunters and Neotropical game management. *Evolutionary Ecology Research*, **13**, 171–185.

Levi, T., Shepard, G. H., Ohl-Schacherer, J., Wilmers, C. C., Peres, C. A., & Yu, D. W. (2011b). Spatial tools for modeling the sustainability of subsistence hunting in tropical forests. *Ecological Applications*, **21**(5), 1802–1818.

Levin, P. S., Fogarty, M. J., Murawski, S. A., & Fluharty, D. (2009). Integrated ecosystem assessments: Developing the scientific basis for ecosystem-based management of the ocean. *PLoS Biology*, **7**(1), e1000014.

Lewis, D. M., & Phiri, A. (1998). Wildlife snaring – an indicator of community response to a community-based conservation project. *Oryx*, **32**, 111–121.

Lew-Levy, S., Reckin, R., Lavi, N., Cristóbal-Azkarate, J., & Ellis-Davies, K. (2017). How do hunter-gatherer children learn subsistence skills? A meta-ethnographic review. *Human Nature*, **28**(4), 367–394.

Li, Q., Zhou, L., Zhou, M., *et al.* (2014). Epidemiology of human infections with avian influenza A(H7N9) virus in China. *New England Journal of Medicine*, **370**(6), 520–532.

Li, T. C., Chijiwa, K., Sera, N., *et al.* (2005). Hepatitis E virus transmission from wild boar meat. *Emerging Infectious Diseases*, **11**(12), 1958–1960.

Li, W. (2005). Bats are natural reservoirs of SARS-like Coronaviruses. *Science*, **310**(5748), 676–679.

Lidström, S., & Johnson, A. F. (2020). Ecosystem-based fisheries management: A perspective on the critique and development of the concept. *Fish and Fisheries*, **21**(1), 216–222.

Liebenberg, L. (2006). Persistence hunting by modern hunter-gatherers. *Current Anthropology*, **47**(6), 1017–1026.

Lieth, H. (1973). Primary production: Terrestrial ecosystems. *Human Ecology*, **1**, 303–332.

Lima-Ribeiro, M. S., & Diniz-Filho, J. A. F. (2017). Climate change, human overkill, and the extinction of megafauna: A macroecological approach based on pattern-oriented modelling. *Evolutionary Ecology Research*, **18**, 97–121.

Lima-Ribeiro, M. S., Nogués-Bravo, D., Terribile, L. C., Batra, P., & Diniz-Filho, J. A. F. (2013). Climate and humans set the place and time of Proboscidean extinction in late Quaternary of South America. *Palaeogeography, Palaeoclimatology, Palaeoecology*, **392**, 546–556.

Lindeque, P. M., & Turnbull, P. C. B. (1994). Ecology and epidemiology of anthrax in the Etosha National Park, Namibia. *Onderstepoort Journal of Veterinary Research*, **61**(1), 71–83.

Lindsey, P., Balme, G., Becker, M., et al. (2015). *Illegal Hunting and the Bush-meat Trade in Savanna Africa: Drivers, Impacts and Solutions to Address the Problem*. New York: FAO, Panthera/Zoological Society of London/Wildlife Conservation Society.

Lindsey, P. A., Balme, G., Becker, M., et al. (2013). The bushmeat trade in African savannas: Impacts, drivers, and possible solutions. *Biological Conservation*, **160**, 80–96.

Lindsey, P. A., Romañach, S. S., Matema, S., Matema, C., Mupamhadzi, I., & Muvengwi, J. (2011a). Dynamics and underlying causes of illegal bushmeat trade in Zimbabwe. *Oryx*, **45**(1), 84–95.

Lindsey, P. A., Romañach, S. S., Tambling, C. J., Chartier, K., & Groom, R. (2011b). Ecological and financial impacts of illegal bushmeat trade in Zimbabwe. *Oryx*, **45**(1), 96–111.

Lindsey, P. A., Roulet, P. A., & Romanach, S. S. (2007). Economic and conservation significance of the trophy hunting industry in sub-Saharan Africa. *Biological Conservation*, **134**(4), 455–469.

Ling, S., & Milner-Gulland, E. J. (2006). Assessment of the sustainability of bush-meat hunting based on dynamic bioeconomic models: Dynamic modeling of bushmeat hunting. *Conservation Biology*, **20**(4), 1294–1299.

Liu, W., Li, Y., Learn, G. H., et al. (2010). Origin of the human malaria parasite *Plasmodium falciparum* in gorillas. *Nature*, **467**(7314), 420–425.

Livingstone, E., & Shepherd, C. R. (2016). Bear farms in Lao PDR expand illegally and fail to conserve wild bears. *Oryx*, **50**(1), 176–184.

Lofroth, E. C., & Ott, P. K. (2007). Assessment of the sustainability of wolverine harvest in British Columbia, Canada. *Journal of Wildlife Management*, **71**(7), 2193.

Loh, E. H., Zambrana-Torrelio, C., Olival, K. J., et al. (2015). Targeting transmission pathways for emerging zoonotic disease surveillance and control. *Vector-Borne and Zoonotic Diseases*, **15**(7), 432–437.

Loibooki, M., Hofer, H., Campbell, K. L. I., & East, M. L. (2002). Bushmeat hunting by communities adjacent to the Serengeti National Park, Tanzania: The importance of livestock ownership and alternative sources of protein and income. *Environmental Conservation*, **29**(3), 391–398.

Lombard, M., & Phillipson, L. (2010). Indications of bow and stone-tipped arrow use 64 000 years ago in KwaZulu-Natal, South Africa., *Antiquity*, **84**(325), 635–648.

Lomolino, M. V., Riddle, B. R., & Brown, J. A. (2010). *Biogeography*, 4th ed., Sunderland, MA: Sinauer Associates.

Lopez, M., Kousathanas, A., Quach, H., *et al.* (2018). The demographic history and mutational load of African hunter-gatherers and farmers. *Nature Ecology & Evolution*, **2**(4), 721–730.

Lorenzen, E. D., Nogu?s-Bravo, D., Orlando, L., *et al.* (2011). Species-specific responses of Late Quaternary megafauna to climate and humans. *Nature*, **479**(7373), 359–364.

Lowman, M. D., & Schowalter, T. D. (2012). Plant science in forest canopies - the first 30 years of advances and challenges (1980–2010): Tansley review. *New Phytologist*, **194**(1), 12–27.

Lu, F. E. (1999). Changes in subsistence patterns and resource use of the Huaorani Indians in the Ecuadorian Amazon (PhD dissertation), University of North Carolina at Chapel Hill.

Ludwig, D., Hilborn, R., & Walters, C. (1993). Uncertainty, resource exploitation, and conservation: Lessons from history. *Science*, **260**(5104), 17–36.

Luiselli, L., Hema, E. M., Segniagbeto, G. H., *et al.* (2018). Bushmeat consumption in large urban centres in West Africa. *Oryx*, **54**(4), 731–734.

et al. (2019). Understanding the influence of non-wealth factors in determining bushmeat consumption: Results from four West African countries. *Acta Oecologica*, **94**, 47–56.

Luiselli, L., Petrozzi, F., Akani, G. C., *et al.* (2017). Rehashing bushmeat–interview campaigns reveal some controversial issues about the bushmeat trade dynamics in Nigeria. *Revue d'Ecologie, Terre et Vie, Société nationale de Protection de la Nature*, **72**(1), 3–18.

Lunn, K. E., & Dearden, P. (2006). Monitoring small-scale marine fisheries: An example from Thailand's Ko Chang archipelago. *Fisheries Research*, **77**(1), 60–71.

Lupo, K. D. (2007). Evolutionary foraging models in zooarchaeological analysis: Recent applications and future challenges. *Journal of Archaeological Research*, **15**(2), 143–189.

(2011). A dog is for hunting. In U. Albarella, & A. Trentacoste, eds., *Ethnozooarchaeology: The Present and Past of Human-Animal Relationships*, Oxford: Oxbow Books, 4–12.

Lupo, K. D., & Schmitt, D. N. (2005). Small prey hunting technology and zooarchaeological measures of taxonomic diversity and abundance: Ethnoarchaeological evidence from Central African forest foragers. *Journal of Anthropological Archaeology*, **24**(4), 335–353.

(2016). When bigger is not better: The economics of hunting megafauna and its implications for Plio-Pleistocene hunter-gatherers. *Journal of Anthropological Archaeology*, **44**, 185–197.

(2017). How do meat scarcity and bushmeat commodification influence sharing and giving among forest foragers? A view from the Central African Republic. *Human Ecology*, **45**(5), 627–641.

Luskin, M. S., Christina, E. D., Kelley, L. C., & Potts, M. D. (2014). Modern hunting practices and wild meat trade in the oil palm plantation-dominated landscapes of Sumatra, Indonesia. *Human Ecology*, **42**(1), 35–45.

Luzar, J. B., Silvius, K. M., Overman, H., Giery, S. T., Read, J. M., & Fragoso, J. M. V. (2011). Large-scale environmental monitoring by Indigenous Peoples. *BioScience*, **61**(10), 771–781.

Lwasa, S. (2014). Managing African urbanization in the context of environmental change. *INTERdisciplina*, **2**(2). doi:10.22201/ceiich.24485705e.2014.2.46528

Maas, B., Clough, Y., & Tscharntke, T. (2013). Bats and birds increase crop yield in tropical agroforestry landscapes. *Ecology Letters*, **16**(12), 1480–1487.

MacArthur, R. H., & Pianka, E. R. (1966). On optimal use of a patchy environment. *American Naturalist*, **100**, 603–609.

Macdonald, D. W., Johnson, P. J., Albrechtsen, L., *et al.* (2011). Association of body mass with price of bushmeat in Nigeria and Cameroon: Association of body mass with price of bushmeat. *Conservation Biology*, **25**(6), 1220–1228.

et al. (2012). Bushmeat trade in the Cross–Sanaga rivers region: Evidence for the importance of protected areas. *Biological Conservation*, **147**(1), 107–114.

MacDonald, K. (2007). Cross-cultural comparison of learning in human hunting: Implications for life history evolution. *Human Nature*, **18**(4), 386–402.

Mace, P. (2001). A new role for MSY in single-species and ecosystem approaches to fisheries stock assessment and management. *Fish and Fisheries*, **2**(1), 2–32.

Mack, A. L. (1993). The sizes of vertebrate-dispersed fruits: A Neotropical-Paleotropical comparison. *The American Naturalist*, **142**(5), 840–856.

MacMillan, D. C., & Nguyen, Q. A. (2014). Factors influencing the illegal harvest of wildlife by trapping and snaring among the Katu ethnic group in Vietnam. *Oryx*, **48**(2), 304–312.

Madhusudan, M. D., & Karanth, K. U. (2018). Hunting for an answer: Is local hunting compatible with large mammal conservation in India? In J. G. Robinson, & L. E. Bennett, eds., *Hunting for Sustainability in Tropical Forests*, New York: Columbia University Press, 455–472.

Madsen, D. B., & Schmitt, D. N. (1998). Mass collecting and the diet breadth model: A Great Basin example. *Journal of Archaeological Science*, **25**(5), 445–455.

Magige, F. J., Holmern, T., Stokke, S., Mlingwa, C., & Røskaft, E. (2009). Does illegal hunting affect density and behaviour of African grassland birds? A case study on ostrich (*Struthio camelus*). *Biodiversity and Conservation*, **18**(5), 1361–1373.

Mahoney, S. P., & Geist, V. (2019). *The North American Model of Wildlife Conservation*, Baltimore, MD: Johns Hopkins University Press.

Maisels, F., & Gautier-Hion, A. (1994). Why are Caesalpinioideae so important for monkeys in hydromorphic rainforests of the Zaire basin? In J. I. Sprent, & D. C. McKey, eds., *Advances in Legume Systematics 5: The Nitrogen Factor*, Kew: Royal Botanic Gardens, 189–204.

Maisels, F., Gautier-Hion, A., & Gautier, J.-P. (1994). Diets of two sympatric colobines in Zaire: More evidence on seed-eating in forests on poor soils. *International Journal of Primatology*, **15**(5), 681–701.

Malhi, Y., Doughty, C. E., Galetti, M., Smith, F. A., Svenning, J.-C., & Terborgh, J. W. (2016). Megafauna and ecosystem function from the Pleistocene to the

Anthropocene. *Proceedings of the National Academy of Sciences of the United States of America*, **113**(4), 838–846.

Malonga, R. (1996). *Dynamique socio-economique du circuit commercial de viande de chasse a Brazzaville*, New York: Wildlife Conservation Society.

Malvy, D., McElroy, A. K., de Clerck, H., Günther, S., & van Griensven, J. (2019). Ebola virus disease. *The Lancet*, **393**(10174), 936–948.

Mambeya, M. M., Baker, F., Momboua, B. R., *et al.* (2018). The emergence of a commercial trade in pangolins from Gabon. *African Journal of Ecology*, **56**(3), 601–609.

Mandujano, S., & Naranjo, E. J. (2010). Ungulate biomass across a rainfall gradient: A comparison of data from neotropical and palaeotropical forests and local analyses in Mexico. *Journal of Tropical Ecology*, **26**(1), 13–23.

Manfredo, M. J., Teel, T. L., & Dietsch, A. M. (2016). Implications of human value shift and persistence for biodiversity conservation: Value Shift and Conservation. *Conservation Biology*, **30**(2), 287–296.

Mann, E., Streng, S., Bergeron, J., & Kircher, A. (2015). A review of the role of food and the food system in the transmission and spread of Ebolavirus. *PLoS Neglected Tropical Diseases*, **9**(12), e0004160.

Mann, N. (2007). Meat in the human diet: An anthropological perspective. *Nutrition & Dietetics*, **64**(s4), S102–S107.

Marboutin, E., Bray, Y., Péroux, R., Mauvy, B., & Lartiges, A. (2003). Population dynamics in European hare: Breeding parameters and sustainable harvest rates. *Journal of Applied Ecology*, **40**, 580–591.

Marín Arroyo, A. B. (2009). The use of optimal foraging theory to estimate Late Glacial site catchment areas from a central place: The case of eastern Cantabria, Spain. *Journal of Anthropological Archaeology*, **28**(1), 27–36.

Marion, P. L., Oshiro, L. S., Regnery, D. C., Scullard, G. H., & Robinson, W. S. (1980). A virus in Beechey ground squirrels that is related to hepatitis B virus of humans. *Proceedings of the National Academy of Sciences of the United States of America*, **77**(5), 2941–2945.

Marlowe, F. (2002). Why the Hadza are still hunter-gatherers. In S. Kent, ed., *Ethnicity, Hunter-Gatherers, and the 'Other': Association or Assimilation in Africa*, Washington D.C.: Smithsonian Institution Press, 247–275.

(2005). Hunter-gatherers and human evolution. *Evolutionary Anthropology*, **14**(2), 54–67.

Marrocoli, S., Nielsen, M. R., Morgan, D., van Loon, T., Kulik, L., & Kühl, H. (2019). Using wildlife indicators to facilitate wildlife monitoring in hunter-self monitoring schemes. *Ecological Indicators*, **105**, 254–263.

Marsh, W. M., & Kaufman, M. M. (2012). *Physical Geography: Great Systems and Global Environments*, Cambridge: Cambridge University Press.

Martin, A., Caro, T., & Kiffner, C. (2013). Prey preferences of bushmeat hunters in an East African savannah ecosystem. *European Journal of Wildlife Research*, **59**(2), 137–145.

Martin, J. F. (1983). Optimal foraging theory: A review of some models and their applications. *American Anthropologist*, **85**(3), 612–629.

Martin, P. S., & Klein, R. G. (eds.). (1984). *Quaternary Extinctions: A Prehistoric Revolution*, Tucson: University of Arizona Press.

Martin, V., Chevalier, V., Ceccato, P., *et al.* (2008). The impact of climate change on the epidemiology and control of Rift Valley fever. *Revue scientifique et technique / Office international des épizootie.*, **27**, 413–426.

Martini, G. A., Knauff, H. G., Schmidt, H. A., Mayer, G., & Baltzer, G. (1968). A hitherto unknown infectious disease contracted from monkeys. 'Marburg-virus' disease. *German Medical Monthly*, **13**(10), 457–470.

Martins, V., & Shackleton, C. M. (2019). Bushmeat use is widespread but under-researched in rural communities of South Africa. *Global Ecology and Conservation*, **17**, e00583.

Mason, W. S., Seal, G., & Summers, J. (1980). Virus of Pekin ducks with structural and biological relatedness to human hepatitis B virus. *Journal of Virology*, **36**(3), 829–836.

Maxwell, S. L., Fuller, R. A., Brooks, T. M., & Watson, J. E. M. (2016). The ravages of guns, nets and bulldozers. *Nature News*, **536**(7615), 143.

Mayor, P., Bodmer, R. E., & Bowler, M. (2016). Reproductive biology for the assessment of hunting sustainability of rainforest mammal populations through the participation of local communities. *Conservation Biology*, **31**(4), 912–923.

Mayor, P., Bodmer, R. E., López-Béjar, M., & López-Plana, C. (2011). Reproductive biology of the wild red brocket deer (*Mazama americana*) female in the Peruvian Amazon. *Animal Reproduction Science*, **128**(1–4), 123–128.

Mayor, P., El Bizri, H., Bodmer, R. E., & Bowler, M. (2017). Assessment of mammal reproduction for hunting sustainability through community-based sampling of species in the wild: Participatory reproductive monitoring. *Conservation Biology*, **31**(4), 912–923.

Mbayma, G. (2009). *Bushmeat Consumption in Kinshasa, DRC. Analysis at the Household Level*, New York: Wildlife Conservation Society.

Mbete, P., Ngokaka, C., Bonazebi, F. A. N., & Vouidibio, J. (2010). Evaluation of the depletion of game by hunting around the Park National of Odzala Kokoua and the impact on biodiversity degradation. *Journal of Animal and Plant Sciences*, **8**(3), 1061–1069.

Mbete, R. A., Banga-Mboko, H., Racey, P., *et al.* (2011). Household bushmeat consumption in Brazzaville, the Republic of the Congo. *Tropical Conservation Science*, **4**(2), 187–202.

McCormick, J. B., Webb, P. A., Krebs, J. W., Johnson, K. M., & Smith, E. S. (1987). A prospective study of the epidemiology and ecology of Lassa fever. *The Journal of Infectious Diseases*, **155**(3), 437–444.

McCorquodale, S. M. (1997). Cultural contexts of recreational hunting and native subsistence and ceremonial hunting: Their significance for wildlife management. *Wildlife Society Bulletin*, **25**, 568–573.

McCullough, D. R. (1996). Spatially structured populations and harvest theory. *Journal of Wildlife Management*, **60**, 1–9.

McDonald, D. R. (1977). Food taboos: A primitive environmental protection agency (South America). *Anthropos*, **72**, 734–748.

McGarry, D. K., & Shackleton, C. M. (2009). Children navigating rural poverty: Rural children's use of wild resources to counteract food insecurity in the Eastern Cape, South Africa. *Journal of Children and Poverty*, **15**(1), 19–37.

McGraw, S. (1994). Census, habitat preference, and polyspecific associations of six monkeys in the Lomako Forest, Zaire. *American Journal of Primatology*, **34**(4), 295–307.

McGregor, J. (2005). Crocodile crimes: People versus wildlife and the politics of postcolonial conservation on Lake Kariba, Zimbabwe. *Geoforum*, **36**(3), 353–369.

McKay, G. M., & Eisenberg, J. F. (1974). Movement patterns and habitat utilization of ungulates in Ceylon. In V. Geist, & R. Walther, eds., *The Behavior of Ungulates and its Relation to Management*. Volumn2e. IUCN Publication Number 24, 708–721.

McKey, D. B., Gartlan, J. S., Waterman, P. G., & Choo, G. M. (1981). Food selection by black colobus monkeys (*Colobus satanas*) in relation to plant chemistry. *Biological Journal of the Linnean Society*, **16**(2), 115–146.

McMichael, A. J. (2005). Environmental and social influences on emerging infectious diseases: Past, present, and future. In A. McLean, R. M. May, J. Pattison, & R. A. Weiss, eds., *SARS: A Case Study in Emerging Infections*, Oxford: Oxford University Press, 4–15.

McNeill, W. H. (1976). *Plagues and Peoples*, London: Penguin.

McRae, L., Deinet, S., & Freeman, R. (2017). The Diversity-weighted Living Planet Index: Controlling for taxonomic bias in a global biodiversity indicator. *PLoS One*, **e0169156**, 20.

Meazza, C., Pagani, S., & Bozzola, M. (2011). The Pygmy short stature enigma. *Pediatric Endocrinology Reviews*, **8**(4), 7.

Medeiros Jacob, M. C., Feitosa, I. S., & Albuquerque, U. P. (2020). Animal-based food systems are unsafe: Severe acute respiratory syndrome coronavirus 2 (SARS-CoV-2) fosters the debate on meat consumption. *Public Health Nutrition*, **23**(17), 3250–3255.

Mediannikov, O., Diatta, G., Zolia, Y., et al. (2012). Tick-borne rickettsiae in Guinea and Liberia. *Ticks and Tick-Borne Diseases*, **3**(1), 43–48.

Mehlman, M. J. (1990). Later Quaternary archaeological sequences in northern Tanzania. (PhD thesis), University of Illinois at Urbana-Champaign.

Mena, I., Nelson, M. I., Quezada-Monroy, F., et al., B. (2016). Origins of the 2009 H1N1 influenza pandemic in swine in Mexico. *Elife*, **5**, e16777.

Mena, V. P., Stallings, J. R., Regalado, J. B., & Cueva, R. L. (1999). The sustainability of current hunting practices by the Huaorani. In J. G. Robinson, & L. E. Bennett, eds., *Hunting for Sustainability in Tropical Forests*, New York: Columbia University Press, 57–78.

Mendes Pontes, A. R. (1999). Environmental determinants of primate abundance in Maraca Island, Roraima, Brazilian Amazonia. *Journal of Zoology*, **247**(2), 189–199.

   (2004). Ecology of a community of mammals in a seasonally dry forest in Roraima, Brazilian Amazon. *Mammalian Biology*, **69**(5), 319–336.

Menon, R. K. (2000). Nature watch-the quintessential Antelope – life of the Blackbuck. *Resonance*, **19**, 69–79.

Mensah, G. A. (2000). Présentation générale de l'élevage d'aulacodes, historique et état de la diffusion en Afrique. *Actes Séminaire International Sur l'élevage Intensif de Gibier à but Alimentaire à Libreville (Gabon), Projet DGEG/VSF/ADIE/CARPE/UE*, 45–59.

Mermet, L. (1992). *Stratégies pour la gestion de l'environnement: la nature comme jeu de société?* Paris: Éditions L'Harmattan.

Mesquita, G. P., & Barreto, G. P. (2015). Evaluation of mammals hunting in indigenous and rural localities in Eastern Brazilian Amazon. *Ethnobiology and Conservation*, **4**, 1–14.

Meyer-Rochow, V. B. (2009). Food taboos: Their origins and purposes. *Journal of Ethnobiology and Ethnomedicine*, **5**, e18.

Mickleburgh, S., Waylen, K., & Racey, P. (2009). Bats as bushmeat: A global review. *Oryx*, **43**(2), 217.

Migliano, A. B., Romero, I. G., Metspalu, M., Leavesley, M., & Pagani, L. (2013). Evolution of the Pygmy phenotype: Evidence of positive selection from genome-wide scans in African, Asian, and Melanesian Pygmies. *Human Biology*, **85**, 85(1–3), 251–284.

Mildenstein, T., Tanshi, I., & Racey, P. A. (2016). Exploitation of bats for bushmeat and medicine. In C. C. Voight, & T. Kingston, *Bats in the Anthropocene: Conservation of Bats in a Changing World*, Cham: Springer, 325–375.

Milks, A., Parker, D., & Pope, M. (2019). External ballistics of Pleistocene hand-thrown spears: Experimental performance data and implications for human evolution. *Scientific Reports*, **9**(1), 820.

Miller, J. (2021). Nambikwara. https://pib.socioambiental.org/en/Povo:Nambikwara

Mills, J. N., Gage, K. L., & Khan, A. S. (2010). Potential influence of climate change on vector-borne and zoonotic diseases: A review and proposed research plan. *Environmental Health Perspectives*, **118**(11), 1507–1514.

Milner-Gulland, E. J., & Akçakaya, H. R. (2001). Sustainability indices for exploited populations. *Trends in Ecology & Evolution*, **16**(12), 686–692.

Milner-Gulland, E. J., & Bennett, E. L. (2003). Wild meat: The bigger picture. *Trends in Ecology & Evolution*, **18**(7), 351–357.

Milner-Gulland, E. J., & Clayton, L. (2002). The trade in babirusas and wild pigs in North Sulawesi, Indonesia. *Ecological Economics*, **42**(1–2), 165–183.

Milner-Gulland, E. J., & Mace, R. (2009). *Conservation of Biological Resources*, Oxford: Wiley.

Milner-Gulland, E. J., & Rowcliffe, J. M. (2007). *Conservation and Sustainable Use: A Handbook of Techniques*, Oxford: Oxford University Press.

Milton, K. (1982). Dietary quality and demographic regulation in a howler monkey population. In E. G. Leigh, A. S. Rand, & D. M. Windsor, eds., *The Ecology of a Tropical Forest*, Washington, DC: Smithsonian Institution Press, 273–290.

  (2000). Hunter-gatherer diets—a different perspective. *The American Journal of Clinical Nutrition*, **71**(3), 665–667.

Miranda, C. L., & Alencar, G. da S. (2007). Aspects of hunting activity in Serra da Capivara National Park, in the state of Piauí, Brazil. *Natureza & Conservação*, **5**(1), 114–121.

Misin, A., Antonello, R. M., Di Bella, S., *et al.* (2020). Measles: An overview of a re-emerging disease in children and immunocompromised patients. *Microorganisms*, **8**(2), 276.

Mithen, S. J. (1989). Modeling hunter-gatherer decision making: Complementing optimal foraging theory. *Human Ecology*, **17**(1), 59–83.

Mittermeier, R. A. (1987). Effects of hunting on rain forest primates. In C. W. Marsh, & R. A. Mittermeier, eds., *Primate Conservation in Tropical Rain Forest*, New York: Alan R. Liss, 109–146.

Mockrin, M. H., Bennett, E. L., & LaBruna, D. T. (2005). *Wildlife farming: A viable alternative to hunting in tropical forests?* (WCS Working Paper NO. 2 3), New York: Wildlife Conservation Society.

Mohneke, M., Onadeko, A. B., & Rödel, M. O. (2009). Exploitation of frogs–a review with a focus on West Africa. *Salamandra*, **45**(4), 193–202.

Moloney, A. (2019, April 11). Ecuador's hunter-gatherers in court over oil drilling in Amazon. *Reuters*, 4.

Molyneux, D., Hallaj, Z., Keusch, G. T., *et al.* (2011). Zoonoses and marginalised infectious diseases of poverty: Where do we stand? *Parasites & Vectors*, **4**(1), 106.

Mondanaro, A., Di Febbraro, M., Melchionna, M., *et al.* (2019). Additive effects of climate change and human hunting explain population decline and extinction in cave bears. *Boreas*, **48**(3), 605–615.

Monroe, M. C., & Willcox, A. S. (2006). Could risk of disease change bushmeat-butchering behavior? *Animal Conservation*, **9**(4), 368–369.

Montenegro, O. L. (2004). Natural licks as keystone resources for wildlife and people in Amazonia. (PhD thesis), University of Florida.

Moore, J. E., Mascarenhas, A., Bain, J., & Straus, S. E. (2017). Developing a comprehensive definition of sustainability. *Implementation Science*, **12**(1), 110.

Mora, C., Tittensor, D. P., Adl, S., Simpson, A. G. B., & Worm, B. (2011). How many species are there on Earth and in the ocean? *PLoS Biology*, **9**(8), e1001127.

Morcatty, T. Q., & Valsecchi, J. (2015). Social, biological, and environmental drivers of the hunting and trade of the endangered yellow-footed tortoise in the Amazon. *Ecology and Society*, **20**(3), 3. http://dx.doi.org/10.5751/ES-07701-200303

Mordechai, L., Eisenberg, M., Newfield, T. P., Izdebski, A., Kay, J. E., & Poinar, H. (2019). The Justinianic Plague: An inconsequential pandemic? *Proceedings of the National Academy of Sciences of the United States of America*, **116**(51), 25546–25554.

Moreno Bofarull, A., Royo, A. A., Fernández, M. H., Ortiz-Jaureguizar, E., & Morales, J. (2008). Influence of continental history on the ecological specialization and macroevolutionary processes in the mammalian assemblage of South America: Differences between small and large mammals. *BMC Evolutionary Biology*, **8**(1), 97.

Morgera, E., & Cirelli, M. T. (2010). Wildlife law in the Southern African development community (No. 84), FAO.

Morrison, J. C., Sechrest, W., Dinerstein, E., Wilcove, D. S., & Lamoreux, J. F. (2007). Persistence of large mammal faunas as indicators of global human impacts. *Journal of Mammalogy*, **88**, 1363–1380.

Morrison-Lanjouw, S. M., Coutinho, R. A., Boahene, K., & Pool, R. (2021). Exploring the characteristics of a local demand for African wild meat: A focus group study of long-term Ghanaian residents in the Netherlands. *PLoS ONE*, **16**(2), e0246868.

Morsello, C., Yagüe, B., Beltreschi, L., *et al.* (2015). Cultural attitudes are stronger predictors of bushmeat consumption and preference than economic factors among urban Amazonians from Brazil and Colombia. *Ecology and Society*, **20**(4), 21. http://dx.doi.org/10.5751/ES-07771-200421/

Morton, O., Scheffers, B. R., Haugaasen, T., & Edwards, D. P. (2021). Impacts of wildlife trade on terrestrial biodiversity. *Nature Ecology & Evolution*, **5**, 540–548.

Mosimann, J. E., & Martin, P. S. (1975). Simulating overkill by Paleoindians: Did man hunt the giant mammals of the New World to extinction? Mathematical models show that the hypothesis is feasible. *American Scientist*, **63**(3), 304–313.

Mota, M. T. de O., Ribeiro, M. R., Vedovello, D., & Nogueira, M. L. (2015). Mayaro virus: A neglected arbovirus of the Americas. *Future Virology*, **10**(9), 1109–1122.

Movius, Hallam L. (1950). A wooden spear of Third Interglacial Age from Lower Saxony. *Southwestern Journal of Anthropology*, **6**(2), 139–142.

Muchaal, P. K., & Ngandjui, G. (1999). Impact of village hunting on wildlife populations in the Western Dja Reserve, Cameroon. *Conservation Biology*, **13**(2), 385–396.

Muehlenbein, M. P. (2017). Primates on display: Potential disease consequences beyond bushmeat. *American Journal of Physical Anthropology*, **162**(S63), 32–43.

Mühlemann, B., Vinner, L., Margaryan, A., *et al.* (2020). Diverse variola virus (smallpox) strains were widespread in northern Europe in the Viking Age. *Science*, **369**(6502), eaaw8977.

Murdock, G. P. (1967). Ethnographic atlas: A summary. *Ethnology*, **6**(2), 109–236.

Murphy, F. A. (1998). Emerging zoonoses. *Emerging Infectious Diseases*, **4**(3), 429.

Murray, K. A., & Daszak, P. (2013). Human ecology in pathogenic landscapes: Two hypotheses on how land use change drives viral emergence. *Current Opinion in Virology*, **3**(1), 79–83.

Mussi, M. (2007). Women of the middle latitudes. The earliest peopling of Europe from a female perspective. In W. Roebroeks, ed., *Guts and Brains an Integrative Approach to the Hominin Record*, Leiden: Leiden University Press, 165–183.

Myers, N., Mittermeier, R. A., Mittermeier, C. G., da Fonseca, G. A. B., & Kent, J. (2000). Biodiversity hotspots for conservation priorities. *Nature*, **403**(6772), 853–858.

Naidoo, R., Weaver, L. C., Diggle, R. W., Matongo, G., Stuart-Hill, G., & Thouless, C. (2016). Complementary benefits of tourism and hunting to communal conservancies in Namibia. *Conservation Biology*, **30**(3), 628–638.

Naito, D., Abe, K., Okuda, T., & Salleh, H. H. M. (2005). The changes of subsistence activities among Temuan communities in Negeri Sembilan, Peninsular Malaysia: Focus on hunting and gathering. In S. Masayoshi, & G. Yintiso, eds., *Environment, Livelihood and Local Praxis in Asia and Africa*, Kyoto: Center for African Area Studies, Kyoto University, 106–112.

Nardoto, G. B., Murrieta, R. S. S., Prates, L. E. G., *et al.* (2011). Frozen chicken for wild fish: Nutritional transition in the Brazilian Amazon region determined by carbon and nitrogen stable isotope ratios in fingernails. *American Journal of Human Biology*, **23**(5), 642–650.

Nasi, R. (2001). Biodiversity Planning Support Programme Integration of Biodiversity into National Forest Planning Programmes: The Case of Gabon,

Presented at the International workshop on 'Integration of Biodiversity in National Forestry Planning Programme,' Bogor, Indonesia.

Nasi, R., Brown, D., Wilkie, D., et al. (2008). *Conservation and Use of Wildlife-Based Resources: The Bushmeat Crisis*, Montreal: Secretariat of the Convention on Biological Diversity; Center for International Forestry Research (CIFOR).

Nasi, R., & Fa, J. E. (2015, September). The role of bushmeat in food security and nutrition, Presented at the XIV World Forestry Congress, Durban, South Africa.

Nasi, R., Taber, A., & Van Vliet, N. (2011). Empty forests, empty stomachs? Bushmeat and livelihoods in the Congo and Amazon Basins. *International Forestry Review*, **13**(3), 355–368.

Ndumbe, P. M., Okie, F., Nyambi, P., & Delaporte, E. (1992). Retrovirus infections in the south of Cameroon. *Annales de la Société Belge de Médecine Tropicale*, **72**, 141–144.

Nelson, A., & Chomitz, K. M. (2011). Effectiveness of strict vs. multiple use protected areas in reducing tropical forest fires: A global analysis using matching methods. *PLoS ONE*, **6**(8), e22722.

Newing, H. (2001). Bushmeat hunting and management: Implications of duiker ecology and interspecific competition. *Biodiversity and Conservation*, **10**(1), 99–108.

Nieto, A., & Alexander, K. (2010). *European Red List of Saproxylic Beetles*, Luxembourg: Publications Office of the European Union.

Nieto, A., Roberts, S. P. M., Kemp, J., et al. (2014). *European Red List of Bees*, Luxembourg: Publication Office of the European Union.

Nieto, M., Hortal J., Martínez-Maza, C., et al. (2007). Historical determinants of mammal diversity in Africa: Evolution of mammalian body mass distribution in Africa and South America during Neogene and Quaternary Times. In B. A. Huber, B. J. Sinclair, & K-H. Lampe, eds., *African Biodiversity: Molecules, Organisms, Ecosystems*, 287–295.

Nietschmann, B. (1972). Hunting and fishing focus among the Miskito Indians, eastern Nicaragua. *Human Ecology,* **1**, 41–67.

Njiforti, H. L. (1996). Preferences and present demand for bushmeat in north Cameroon: Some implications for wildlife conservation. *Environmental Conservation*, **23**(2), 149–155.

Nobayashi, A. (2016). An ethnoarchaeological study of chase hunting with gundogs by the aboriginal peoples of Taiwan. In L. Snyder, ed., *Dogs and People in Social, Working, Economic or Symbolic Interaction*, Oxford: Oxbow Books, 77–84.

Nonacs, P. (2001). State dependent behavior and the Marginal Value Theorem. *Behavioral Ecology*, **12**(1), 71–83.

Noppornpanth, S., Haagmans, B. L., Bhattarakosol, P., et al. (2003). Molecular epidemiology of gibbon hepatitis B virus transmission. *Journal of General Virology*, **84**(1), 147–155.

Noss, A. (2000). Cable snares and nets in the Central African Republic. In J. Robinson, & E. L Bennett, eds., *Hunting for Sustainability in Tropical Forest*, New York: Columbia University Press, 282–305.

Noss, A. J. (1995). Duikers, cables, and nets: A cultural ecology of hunting in a central African forest (PhD dissertation), University of Florida.

(1997). The economic importance of communal net hunting among the BaAka of the Central African Republic. *Human Ecology*, **25**(1), 71–89.

(1998a). Cable snares and bushmeat markets in a central African forest. *Environmental Conservation*, **25**(3), 228–233.

(1998b). The impacts of cable snare hunting on wildlife populations in the forests of the Central African Republic. *Conservation Biology*, **12**(2), 9.

Noss, A. J., & Hewlett, B. S. (2001). The contexts of female hunting in Central Africa. *American Anthropologist, New Series*, **103**(4), 1024–1040.

Novaro, A. J., Redford, K. H., & Bodmer, R. E. (2000). Effect of hunting in source-sink systems in the Neotropics. *Conservation Biology*, **14**(3), 713–721.

Ntiamoa-Baidu, Y. (1997). *Wildlife and food security in Africa*, Rome: FAO.

Nunes, A. V., Peres, C. A., Constantino, P. de A. L., Fischer, E., & Nielsen, M. R. (2021). Wild meat consumption in tropical forests spares a significant carbon footprint from the livestock production sector. *Science Reports*, **11**, 19001. https://doi.org/10.1038/s41598-021-98282-4

Nyaki, A., Gray, S. A., Lepczyk, C. A., Skibins, J. C., & Rentsch, D. (2014). Local-scale dynamics and local drivers of bushmeat trade: Participatory modeling in conservation. *Conservation Biology*, **28**(5), 1403–1414.

Oakley, K. P., Andrews, P., Keeley, L. H., & Clark, J. D. (1977). A reappraisal of the Clacton spearpoint. *Proceedings of the Prehistoric Society*, **43**, 13–30.

Oates, J. F. (1995). The dangers of conservation by rural development – a case-study from the forests of Nigeria. *Oryx*, **29**(2), 115–122.

Oates, J. F., Whitesides, G. H., Davies, A. G., *et al.* (1990). Determinants of variation in tropical forest primate biomass: New evidence from West Africa. *Ecology*, **71**(1), 328–343.

O'Brien, T. G., & Kinnaird, M. F. (1999). Differential vulnerability of large birds and mammals to hunting in North Sulawesi, Indonesia, and the outlook for the future. In J. G. Robinson, & L. E. Bennett, eds., *Hunting for Sustainability in Tropical Forests*, New York: Columbia University Press, 199–213.

O'Bryan, C. J., Garnett, S. T., Fa, J. E., *et al.* (2020). The importance of indigenous peoples' lands for the conservation of terrestrial mammals. *Conservation Biology*, **35**(3), 1002–1008.

O'Connell, J. F., Allen, J., Williams, M. A. J., *et al.* (2018). When did *Homo sapiens* first reach Southeast Asia and Sahul? *Proceedings of the National Academy of Sciences of the United States of America*, **115**(34), 8482–8490.

O'Connell, J. F., & Hawkes, K. (1984). Food choice and foraging sites among the Alyawara. *Journal of Anthropological Research*, **40**(4), 504–535.

O'Connell, J. F., Hawkes, K., & Jones, N. B. (1988). Hadza hunting, butchering, and bone transport and their archaeological implications. *Journal of Anthropological Research*, **44**(2), 113–161.

Ogoanah, S. O., & Oboh, I. P. (2017). Effect of Ebola virus on bush meat sales in Benin City, Edo State, Nigeria. *African Scientist*, **18**(2), 129–134.

Ohl-Schacherer, J., Shepard, G. H., Kaplan, H., Peres, C. A., Levi, T., & Yu, D. W. (2007). The sustainability of subsistence hunting by Matsigenka native communities in Manu National Park, Peru. *Conservation Biology*, **21**(5), 1174–1185.

Ojasti, F., Febres Fajardo, G., & Cova, O. M. (1986). Consumo de fauna por una comunidad indígena en el Estado Bolívar, Venezuela. In P. G. Aguilar, ed., *Conservación y manejo de la fauna silvestre en Latinoamérica*, Arequipa: Apeco.

Ojasti, J. (1996). *Wildlife Utilization in Latin America: Current Situation and Prospects for Sustainable Management*, Rome: FAO.

O'Kelly, H. J. (2013). Monitoring conservation threats, interventions and impacts on wildlife in a Cambodian tropical forest. (PhD thesis), Imperial College London.

Olivero, J., Fa, J. E., Real, R., & et al. (2017). Recent loss of closed forests is associated with Ebola virus disease outbreaks. *Scientific Reports* **7**, 14291.

Olsen, S. J. (1985). *Origins of the Domestic Dog: The Fossil Record*, Tucson: University of Arizona Press.

Olson, D. M., Dinerstein, E., Wikramanayake, E. D., et al. (2001). Terrestrial ecoregions of the worlds: A new map of life on Earth. *Bioscience*, **51**(11), 933–938.

Onyekuru, A. N., Ezea, C. P., & Ihemezie, E. J. (2018). Assessment of the structural effects of Ebola disease outbreak on bush meat enterprise in Nigeria: Implications on biodiversity conservation. *Journal of Agriculture and Ecology Research International*, **15**(4), 1–13.

Opare, C., Nsiire, A., Awumbilla, B., & Akanmori, B. D. (2000). Human behavioural factors implicated in outbreaks of human anthrax in the Tamale municipality of northern Ghana. *Acta Tropica*, **76**(1), 49–52.

Orians, G. H., & Pearson, N. E. (1979). On the theory of central place foraging. In D. J. Horn, R. D. Mitchell, & G. R. Stairs, eds., *Analysis of Ecological Systems*, Columbus: Ohio State University, 157–177.

Ostrom, E., Gardner, R., Walker, J., Walker, J. M., & Walker, J. (1994). *Rules, Games, and Common-Pool Resources*, Ann Arbor: University of Michigan Press.

Osuri, A. M., Mendiratta, U., Naniwadekar, R., Varma, V., & Naeem, S. (2020). Hunting and forest modification have distinct defaunation impacts on tropical mammals and birds. *Frontiers in Forests and Global Change*, **2**, 87.

Osuri, A. M., Ratnam, J., Varma, V., et al. (2016). Contrasting effects of defaunation on aboveground carbon storage across the global tropics. *Nature Communications*, **7**, 11351.

Ozioko, K. U., Okoye, C. I., Obiezue, R. N., & Agbu, R. A. (2018). Knowledge, attitudes, and behavioural risk factors regarding zoonotic infections among bushmeat hunters and traders in Nsukka, southeast Nigeria. *Epidemiology and Health*, **40**, e2018025.

Pacheco-Cobos, L., Winterhalder, B., Cuatianquiz-Lima, C., Rosetti, M. F., Hudson, R., & Ross, C. T. (2019). Nahua mushroom gatherers use area-restricted search strategies that conform to marginal value theorem predictions. *Proceedings of the National Academy of Sciences of the United States of America*, **116**(21), 10339–10347.

Packer, C., & Ruttan, L. (1988). The evolution of cooperative hunting. *American Naturalist*, **132**(2), 159–198.

Pagel, M., & Mace, R. (2004). The cultural wealth of nations. *Nature*, **428**(6980), 275–278.

Pailler, S., Wagner, J. E., McPeak, J. G., & Floyd, D. W. (2009). Identifying conservation opportunities among Malinké bushmeat hunters of Guinea, West Africa. *Human Ecology*, **37**(6), 761–774.

Palma, A. D., Hoskins, A., Gonzalez, R. E., *et al.* (2021). Annual changes in the Biodiversity Intactness Index in tropical and subtropical forest biomes, 2001–2012. *Scientific Reports,* **11**, 20249.

Pangau-Adam, M., Noske, R., & Muehlenberg, M. (2012). Wildmeat or bushmeat? Subsistence hunting and commercial harvesting in Papua (West New Guinea), Indonesia. *Human Ecology*, **40**(4), 611–621.

Panter-Brick, C., Layton, R. H., & Rowley-Conwy, P. (2001). *Hunter-Gatherers: An Interdisciplinary Perspective*, Vol. 13, Cambridge: Cambridge University Press.

Paolisso, M., & Sackett, R. (1985). Traditional meat procurement strategies among the Irapa-Yukpa of the Venezuela-Colombia border area. *Research in Economic Anthropology,* **7**, 177–199.

Papworth, S., Milner-Gulland, E. J., & Slocombe, K. (2013a). Hunted woolly monkeys (*Lagothrix poeppigii*) show threat-sensitive responses to human presence. *PLoS ONE*, **8**(4), e62000.

  (2013b). The natural place to begin: The ethnoprimatology of the Waorani. *American Journal of Primatology*, **75**(11), 1117–1128.

Parker, S., Nuara, A., Buller, R. M. L., & Schultz, D. A. (2007). Human monkeypox: An emerging zoonotic disease. *Future Microbiology*, **2**(1), 17–34.

Parry, L., Barlow, J., & Pereira, H. (2014). Wildlife harvest and consumption in Amazonia's urbanized wilderness: Wildlife consumption in urbanized Amazonia. *Conservation Letters*, **7**(6), 565–574.

Parry, L., Barlow, J., & Peres, C. A. (2009). Hunting for sustainability in tropical secondary forests. *Conservation Biology*, **23**(5), 1270–1280.

Parry, L., & Peres, C. A. (2015). Evaluating the use of local ecological knowledge to monitor hunted tropical-forest wildlife over large spatial scales. *Ecology and Society*, **20**(3), 15. http://dx.doi.org/10.5751/ES-07601-200315/

Patin, E., Laval, G., Barreiro, L. B., *et al.* (2009). Inferring the demographic history of African farmers and Pygmy hunter–gatherers using a multilocus resequencing data set. *PLoS Genetics*, **5**(4), e1000448.

Patin, E., & Quintana-Murci, L. (2018). The demographic and adaptive history of central African hunter-gatherers and farmers. *Current Opinion in Genetics & Development*, **53**, 90–97.

Patterson, B. D., & Norris, R. W. (2016). Towards a uniform nomenclature for ground squirrels: The status of the Holarctic chipmunks. *Mammalia*, **80**(3), 241–251.

Pauly, D. (1998). Fishing down marine food webs. *Science*, **279**(5352), 860–863.

Pauly, D., Christensen, V., Guénette, S., *et al.* (2002). Towards sustainability in world fisheries. *Nature*, **418**(6898), 689–695.

Payn, T., Carnus, J.-M., Freer-Smith, P., *et al.* (2015). Changes in planted forests and future global implications. *Forest Ecology and Management*, **352**, 57–67.

Pearce, E., Stringer, C., & Dunbar, R. I. M. (2013). New insights into differences in brain organization between Neanderthals and anatomically modern humans. *Proceedings of the Royal Society B: Biological Sciences*, **280**(1758), 20130168.

Pearson, O. M. (2008). Statistical and biological definitions of 'anatomically modern' humans: Suggestions for a unified approach to modern morphology. *Evolutionary Anthropology*, **17**(1), 38–48.

Pedersen, A. B., Altizer, S., Poss, M., Cunningham, A. A., & Nunn, C. L. (2005). Patterns of host specificity and transmission among parasites of wild primates. *International Journal for Parasitology*, **35**(6), 647–657.

Peel, M. C., Finlayson, B. L., & McMahon, T. A. (2007). Updated world map of the Köppen-Geiger climate classification. *Hydrology and Earth System Sciences*, **11**, 1633–1644.

Peeters, M., Courgnaud, V., Abela, B., *et al.* (2002). Risk to human health from a plethora of simian immunodeficiency viruses in primate bushmeat. *Emerging Infectious Diseases*, **8**(5), 451–457.

Peeters, M., & Delaporte, E. (2012). Simian retroviruses in African apes. *Clinical Microbiology and Infection*, **18**(6), 514–520.

Pekar, J. E. Magee, A., Parker, E., *et al.* (2022). SARS-CoV-2 emergence very likely resulted from at least two zoonotic events. *Zenodo*, https://doi.org/10.5281/zenodo.6291627

Pemunta, N. V. (2014). The impact of climate change on food security and health in northern Cameroon. In C. B. Keyes & O. C. Lucero *New Developments in Global Warming Research*, New York: Nova Science Publishers, 1–46.

(2019). Fortress conservation, wildlife legislation and the Baka Pygmies of southeast Cameroon. *GeoJournal*, **84**(4), 1035–1055.

Penone, C., Weinstein, B. G., Graham, C. H., *et al.* (2016). Global mammal beta diversity shows parallel assemblage structure in similar but isolated environments. *Proceedings of the Royal Society B: Biological Sciences*, **283**(1837), 20161028.

Pereira, J. P. R., & Schiavetti, A. (2010). Conhecimentos e usos da fauna cinegética pelos caçadores indígenas 'Tupinambá de Olivença'(Bahia). *Biota Neotropica*, **10**(1), 175–183.

Peres, C. A. (1990). Effects of hunting on western Amazonian primate communities. *Biological Conservation*, **54**(1), 47–59.

(1991). Humboldt's woolly monkeys decimated by hunting in Amazonia. *Oryx*, **25**(2), 89–95.

(1994). Primate responses to phenological changes in an Amazonian terra firme forest. *Biotropica*, 98–112.

(1996). Population status of white-lipped *Tayassu pecari* and collared peccaries *T. tajacu* in hunted and unhunted Amazonian forests. *Biological Conservation*, **77**(2–3), 115–123.

(1997). Primate community structure at twenty western Amazonian flooded and unflooded forests. *Journal of Tropical Ecology*, **13**(3), 381–405.

(1999a). Evaluating the impact and sustainability of subsistence hunting at multiple Amazonian forest sites. In J. G. Robinson, & E. L. Bennett, eds., *Hunting for Sustainability in Tropical Forests*, New York: Columbia University Press, 31–56.

(1999b). Primate communities. In J. G. Fleagle, C. H. Janson, & K. E. Reed, eds., *Primate Communities*, Cambridge: Cambridge University Press, 268–283.

(1999c). The structure of nonvolant mammal communities in different Amazonian forest types. In J. F. Eisenberg, & K. H. Redford, eds., *Mammals of the Neotropics*, **Vol. 3**, Chicago: University of Chicago Press, 564–581.

(2000). Effects of subsistence hunting on vertebrate community structure in Amazonian forests. *Conservation Biology*, **14**(1), 240–253.

(2001). Synergistic effects of subsistence hunting and habitat fragmentation on Amazonian forest vertebrates. *Conservation Biology*, **15**(6), 1490–1505.

Peres, C. A., Barlow, J., & Laurance, W. F. (2006). Detecting anthropogenic disturbance in tropical forests. *Trends in Ecology & Evolution*, **21**(5), 227–229.

Peres, C. A., Emilio, T., Schietti, J., Desmoulière, S. J. M., & Levi, T. (2016). Dispersal limitation induces long-term biomass collapse in overhunted Amazonian forests. *Proceedings of the National Academy of Sciences of the United States of America*, **113**(4), 892–897.

Peres, C. A., & Palacios, E. (2007). Basin-wide effects of game harvest on vertebrate population densities in Amazonian forests: Implications for animal-mediated seed dispersal. *Biotropica*, **39**(3), 304–315.

Perez, M. A., & Longboat, S. (2019). Our shared relationship with land and water: Perspectives from the Mayangna and the Anishinaabe. *Ecopsychology*, **11**(3), 1–8.

Pérez-Méndez, N., Jordano, P., García, C., & Valido, A. (2016). The signatures of Anthropocene defaunation: Cascading effects of the seed dispersal collapse. *Scientific Reports*, **6**(1), 24820.

Perry, G., & Pianka, E. R. (1997). Animal foraging: Past, present and future. *Trends in Ecology & Evolution*, **12**(9), 360–364.

Petersen, J., Trapaso, L. M., & Gabler, R. E. (2010). *Fundamentals of Physical Geography*, Belmont, CA: Brooks/Cole.

Peterson, G. D., Cumming, G. S., & Carpenter, S. R. (2003). Scenario planning: A tool for conservation in an uncertain world. *Conservation Biology*, **17**(2), 358–366.

Petrozzi, F. (2018). Bushmeat and fetish trade of birds in West Africa: A review. *Vie et Milieu*, **68**(1), 51–64.

Petrozzi, F., Amori, G., Franco, D., *et al.* (2016). Ecology of the bushmeat trade in West and Central Africa. *Tropical Ecology*, **57**(3), 545–557.

Pezzuti, J. C. B., Antunes, A. P., Fonseca, R., *et al.* (2018). A caça e o caçador: Uma análise crítica da Legislação Brasileira sobre o uso da fauna por populações indígenas e tradicionais na Amazônia. *BioBrasil,Biodiversidade Brasileira*, **2**, 42–74.

Pezzuti, J. C. B., Lima, J. P., da Silva, D. F., & Begossi, A. (2010). Uses and taboos of turtles and tortoises Along Rio Negro, Amazon Basin. *Journal of Ethnobiology*, **30**(1), 153–168.

Pierce, G. J., & Ollason, J. G. (1987). Eight reasons why optimal foraging theory is a complete waste of time. *Oikos*, **49**(1), 111–118.

Pierret, P. V., & Dourojeanni, M. J. (1966). La caza y la alimentación humana en las riberas del río Pachitea, Perú. *Turrialba*, **16**, 271–277.

(1967). Importancia de la caza y la alimentación humana en el curso del río Ucayali, Perú. *Revista Forestal del Perú*, **1**, 10–21.

Pike, B. L., Saylors, K. E., Fair, J. N., *et al.* (2010). The origin and prevention of pandemics. *Clinical Infectious Diseases*, **50**(12), 1636–1640.

Pikitch, E. K., Santora, C., Babcock, E. A., *et al.* (2004). Ecosystem-based fishery management. *Science*, **305**(5682), 346–347.

Pimm, S. L., Jenkins, C. N., Abell, R., *et al.* (2014). The biodiversity of species and their rates of extinction, distribution, and protection. *Science*, **344**(6187), 1246752.

Pinheiro, F. P., & Travassos da Rosa, A. P. (1994). Arboviral zoonoses of Central and South America. In G. Beran, ed., *Handbook of Zoonoses: Viral*, 2nd ed., Vol. 210, Boca Raton, FL: CRC Press, 201–225.

Piper, P. J., & Rabett, R. J. (2009). Hunting in a tropical rainforest: Evidence from the Terminal Pleistocene at Lobang Hangus, Niah Caves, Sarawak. *International Journal of Osteoarchaeology*, **19**(4), 551–565.

Piperno, D. R., Ranere, A. J., Dickau, R., & Aceituno, F. (2017). Niche construction and optimal foraging theory in Neotropical agricultural origins: A re-evaluation in consideration of the empirical evidence. *Journal of Archaeological Science*, **78**, 214–220.

Plantier, J.-C., Leoz, M., Dickerson, J. E., *et al.* (2009). A new human immunodeficiency virus derived from gorillas. *Nature Medicine*, **15**(8), 871–872.

Plowright, R. K., Eby, P., Hudson, P. J., *et al.* (2015). Ecological dynamics of emerging bat virus spillover. *Proceedings of the Royal Society B: Biological Sciences*, **282**(1798), 20142124.

Plowright, R. K., Foley, P., Field, H. E., *et al.* (2011). Urban habituation, ecological connectivity and epidemic dampening: The emergence of Hendra virus from flying foxes (*Pteropus* spp.). *Proceedings of the Royal Society B: Biological Sciences*, **278**(1725), 3703–3712.

Plummer, J. (2014). The Yanomami: Illegal mining, law, and indigenous rights in the Brazilian Amazon. *The Georgetown International Environmental Law Review*, **27**, 279–496.

Plumptre, A. J. (1991). Plant-herbivore dynamics in the Birungas (PhD thesis), University of Bristol.

Plumptre, A. J., & Harris, S. (1995). Estimating the biomass of large mammalian herbivores in a tropical montane forest: A method of faecal counting that avoids assuming a'steady state'system. *Journal of Applied Ecology*, **32**, 111–120.

Pocock, M. J. O., Newson, S. E., Henderson, I. G., *et al.* (2015). Developing and enhancing biodiversity monitoring programmes: A collaborative assessment of priorities. *Journal of Applied Ecology*, **52**(3), 686–695.

Polisar, J., Maxit, I., Scognamillo, D., Farrell, L., Sunquist, M. E., & Eisenberg, J. F. (2003). Jaguars, pumas, their prey base, and cattle ranching: Ecological interpretations of a management problem. *Biological Conservation*, **109**(2), 297–310.

Pontzer, H., Raichlen, D. A., Wood, B. M., Mabulla, A. Z. P., Racette, S. B., & Marlowe, F. W. (2012). Hunter-gatherer energetics and human obesity. *PLoS ONE*, **7**(7), e40503.

Porcasi, J. F., & Fujita, H. (2000). The dolphin hunters: A specialized prehistoric maritime adaptation in the southern California Channel Islands and Baja California. *American Antiquity*, **65**(3), 543–566.

Porta, M. S., Greenland, S., Hernán, M., *et al.* (eds.) (2014). *A Dictionary of Epidemiology*, 6th ed., Oxford: Oxford University Press.

Porter, C. C., & Marlowe, F. W. (2007). How marginal are forager habitats? *Journal of Archaeological Science*, **34**, 59–68.

Porter-Bolland, L., Ellis, E. A., Guariguata, M. R., *et al.* (2012). Community managed forests and forest protected areas: An assessment of their conservation effectiveness across the tropics. *Forest Ecology and Management*, **268**, 6–17.

Potapov, P., Hansen, M. C., Laestadius, L., *et al.* (2017). The last frontiers of wilderness: Tracking loss of intact forest landscapes from 2000 to 2013. *Science Advances*, **3**(1), e1600821.

Potapov, P., Yaroshenko, A., Turubanova, S., *et al.* (2008). Mapping the World's intact forest landscapes by remote sensing. *Ecology and Society*, **13**(2), 51. www.ecologyandsociety.org/vol13/iss2/art51

Potts, R. (1996). *Humanity's Descent: The Consequences of Ecological Instability*, New York: William Morrow & Co.

Poulsen, J. R., & Clark, C. J. (2010). Congo Basin timber certification and biodiversity conservation. In D. Sheil, F. E. Putz, & R. J. Zagt, eds., *Biodiversity Conservation in Certified Forests*, Wageningen: Tropenbos International, 55–60.

Poulsen, J. R., Clark, C. J., & Mavah, G. A. (2007). Wildlife management in a logging concession in Northern Congo: Can livelihoods be maintained through sustainable hunting? In G. Davies, & D. Brown, eds., *Bushmeat and Livelihoods: Wildlife Management and Poverty Reduction*,Malden: Blackwell, 140–157.

Poulsen, J. R., Clark, C. J., Mavah, G., & Elkan, P. W. (2009). Bushmeat supply and consumption in a tropical logging concession in Northern Congo. *Conservation Biology*, **23**(6), 1597–1608.

Poulsen, J. R., Clark, C. J., & Palmer, T. M. (2013). Ecological erosion of an Afrotropical forest and potential consequences for tree recruitment and forest biomass. *Biological Conservation*, **163**, 122–130.

Pourrut, X., Diffo, J. L. D., Somo, R. M., *et al.* (2011). Prevalence of gastrointestinal parasites in primate bushmeat and pets in Cameroon. *Veterinary Parasitology*, **175**(1–2), 187–191.

Prescott, G. W., Williams, D. R., Balmford, A., Green, R. E., & Manica, A. (2012). Quantitative global analysis of the role of climate and people in explaining late Quaternary megafaunal extinctions. *Proceedings of the National Academy of Sciences of the United States of America*, **109**(12), 4527–4531.

Prescott-Allen, R., & Prescott-Allen, C. (1982). *What's Wildlife Worth? Economic Contributions of Wild Plants and Animals to Developing Countries*, London: Earthscan.

Price, T. D., & Brown, J. A. (1985). Aspects of hunter–gatherer complexity. In T. D. Price, & J. A. Brown, eds., *Prehistoric Hunters-Gatherers*, Orlando, FL: Academic Press, 3–20.

Pringle, H. (1997). Ice Age communities may be earliest known net hunters. *Science*, **277**(5330), 1203.

Prins, H. H. T. (2016). Interspecific resource competition in antelopes. In J. Bro-Jørgensen, & D. P. Mallon, eds., *Antelope Conservation: From Diagnosis to Action*, Chichester: John Wiley & Sons, 51–77.

Prins, H. H. T., & Reitsma, J. M. (1989). Mammalian biomass in an African equatorial rain forest. *Journal of Animal Ecology*, **58**(3), 851–861.

Proietti, F. A., Carneiro-Proietti, A. B. F., Catalan-Soares, B. C., & Murphy, E. L. (2005). Global epidemiology of HTLV-I infection and associated diseases. *Oncogene*, **24**(39), 6058–6068.

Pruvot, M., Khammavong, K., Milavong, P., *et al.* (2019). Toward a quantification of risks at the nexus of conservation and health: The case of bushmeat markets in Lao PDR. *Science of the Total Environment*, **676**, 732–745.

Purse, B. V., Mellor, P. S., Rogers, D. J., Samuel, A. R., Mertens, P. P. C., & Baylis, M. (2005). Climate change and the recent emergence of bluetongue in Europe. *Nature Reviews Microbiology*, **3**(2), 171–181.

Putnam, J. J., & Allshouse, J. E. (1999). *Food consumption, prices, and expenditures, 1970–97*, Washington, DC: US Department of Agriculture.

Putnam, P. (1948). *Pygmies of the Ituri Forest*, New York: Henry Holt and Company.

Putz, F. E. (1983). Liana biomass and leaf area of a 'Tierra Firme' forest in the Rio Negro Basin, Venezuela. *Biotropica*, **15**(3), 185–189.

Pyke, G. H. (1984). Optimal foraging theory: A critical review. *Annual Review of Ecology and Systematics*, **15**(1), 523–575.

(2010). Optimal foraging theory: Introduction. In M. D. Breed, & J. Moore, eds., *Encyclopedia of Animal Behavior*, London: Elsevier, 601–603.

Raczka, M. F., Mosblech, N. A., Giosan, L., *et al.* (2019). A human role in Andean megafaunal extinction? *Quaternary Science Reviews*, **205**, 154–165.

Ráez-Luna, E. F. (1995). Hunting large primates and conservation of the Neotropical rain forests. *Oryx*, **29**(1), 43–48.

Rainforest Foundation UK. (2020, July). The 'post-2020 global biodiversity framework' – how the CBD drive to protect 30 percent of the planet could dispossess millions. www.mappingforrights.org/MFR-resources/mapstory/cbddrive/300_million_at_risk_from_cbd_drive

Ramírez Rozzi, F. V., & Sardi, M. L. (2010). Diversity among African Pygmies. *PLoS ONE*, **5**(10), e13620.

Rao, M., Htun, S., Zaw, T., & Myint, T. (2010). Hunting, livelihoods and declining wildlife in the Hponkanrazi Wildlife Sanctuary, North Myanmar. *Environmental Management*, **46**(2), 143–153.

Rao, M., Myint, T., Zaw, T., & Htun, S. (2005). Hunting patterns in tropical forests adjoining the Hkakaborazi National Park, north Myanmar. *Oryx*, **39**(3), 292–300.

Rascovan, N., Sjögren, K.-G., Kristiansen, K., *et al.* (2019). Emergence and spread of basal lineages of *Yersinia pestis* during the Neolithic decline. *Cell*, **176**(1–2), 295–305.

Rasmussen, S., Allentoft, M. E., Nielsen, K., *et al.* (2015). Early divergent strains of *Yersinia pestis* in Eurasia 5,000 years ago. *Cell*, **163**(3), 571–582.

Ratcliffe, R. (2020, July 24). Vietnam bans imports of wild animals to reduce risk of future pandemics. *The Guardian*, 4.

Redford, K. (1993). Hunting in Neotropical forests: A subsidy from nature. In C. M. Hladik, A. Hladik, O. F. Linares, H. Pagezy, A. Semple, & M. Hadley, eds., *Tropical Forests, People and Food: Biocultural Interactions and Applications to Development*, Paris: UNESCO-Parthenon, 227–248.

Redford, K. H. (1991). The ecologically noble savage. *Cultural Survival Quarterly*, **15**(1), 46–48.

(1992). The empty forest. *BioScience*, **42**(6), 412–422.

Redford, K. H., & Robinson, J. G. (1987). The game of choice: Patterns of Indian and colonist hunting in the Neotropics. *American Anthropologist*, **89**(3), 650–667.

Redman, C. L., Grove, J. M., & Kuby, L. H. (2004). Integrating social science into the Long-Term Ecological Research (LTER) network: Social dimensions of ecological change and ecological dimensions of social change. *Ecosystems*, **7**(2), 161–171.

Redmond, I., Aldred, T., Jedamzik, K., & Westwood, M. (2006). *Recipes for Survival: Controlling the Bushmeat Trade (Report)*, London: Ape Alliance; WPSA.

Redpath, S. M., Young, J., Evely, A., et al. (2013). Understanding and managing conservation conflicts. *Trends in Ecology & Evolution*, **28**(2), 100–109.

Reed, K. D., Melski, J. W., Graham, M. B., et al. (2004). The detection of monkeypox in humans in the Western Hemisphere. *New England Journal of Medicine*, **350**(4), 342–350.

Reed, S., Clark, M., Thompson, R., & Hughes, K. A. (2018). Microplastics in marine sediments near Rothera Research Station, Antarctica. *Marine Pollution Bulletin*, **133**, 460–463.

Reid, J., Morra, W., Bohome, C. P., & Sobrado, D. F. (2005). *The Economics of the Primate Trade in Bioko, Equatorial Guinea*. Santa Cruz and Washington, DC: Conservation Strategy Fund and Conservation International.

Remis, M. J., & Kpanou, J. B. (2011). Primate and ungulate abundance in response to multi-use zoning and human extractive activities in a Central African Reserve: Human impacts on wildlife. *African Journal of Ecology*, **49**(1), 70–80.

Resilience Alliance. (2010). *Assessing Resilience in Social-Ecological Systems: Workbook for Practitioners 2.0*, Resilience Alliance. www.resalliance.org/3871.php

Resilience Alliance. (2021). Assessment Projects. www.resalliance.org/assessment-projects

Ribeiro, M. C., Metzger, J. P., Martensen, A. C., Ponzoni, F. J., & Hirota, M. M. (2009). The Brazilian Atlantic Forest: How much is left, and how is the remaining forest distributed? Implications for conservation. *Biological Conservation*, **142**(6), 1141–1153.

Richmond, J. K., & Baglole, D. J. (2003). Lassa fever: Epidemiology, clinical features, and social consequences. *BMJ*, **327**, 1271–1275.

Ricklefs, R. E. (2010). Evolutionary diversification, coevolution between populations and their antagonists, and the filling of niche space. *Proceedings of the National Academy of Sciences of the United States of America*, **107**(4), 1265–1272.

Riddell, M. (2013). Assessing the impacts of conservation and commercial forestry on livelihoods in northern Republic of Congo. *Conservation and Society*, **11**(3), 199–217.

Riley, C. L. (1952). The blowgun in the New World. *Southwestern Journal of Anthropology*, **8**(3), 297–319.

Riley, J. (2002). Mammals on the Sangihe and Talaud Islands, Indonesia, and the impact of hunting and habitat loss. *Oryx*, **36**(3), 288–296.

Rimoin, A. W., Mulembakani, P. M., Johnston, S. C., *et al.* (2010). Major increase in human monkeypox incidence 30 years after smallpox vaccination campaigns cease in the Democratic Republic of Congo. *Proceedings of the National Academy of Sciences of the United States of America*, **107**(37), 16262–16267.

Ripple, W. J., Abernethy, K., Betts, M. G., *et al.* (2016). Bushmeat hunting and extinction risk to the world's mammals. *Royal Society Open Science*, **3**(10), 160498.

Ríos, M., Douroujeanni, M. J., & Tovar, A. (1975). La fauna y su aprovechamiento en Jenaro Herrera (Requena, Peru). *Revista Forestal del Perú*, **5**, 73–92.

Rist, J., Milner-Gulland, E. J., Cowlishaw, G., & Rowcliffe, M. (2010). Hunter reporting of catch per unit effort as a monitoring tool in a bushmeat-harvesting system. *Conservation Biology*, **24**(2), 489–499.

Rival, L. (1993). The growth of family trees: Understanding Huaorani perceptions of the forest. *Man*, **28**(4), 635–652.

(2003). Blowpipes and spears: The social significance of Huaorani technological choices. In D. Pescola, & G. Palsson, eds., *Nature and Society: Anthropoligical Perspectives*, London: Routledge, 155–174.

Robbins, L. H., Campbell, A. C., Brook, G. A., Murphy, M. L., & Hitchcock, R. K. (2012). The antiquity of the bow and arrow in the Kalahari Desert: Bone points from White Paintings Rock Shelter, Botswana. *Journal of African Archaeology*, **10**(1), 7–20.

Robinson, J. G. (1993). The limits to caring: Sustainable living and the loss of biodiversity. *Conservation Biology*, **7**(1), 20–28.

Robinson, J. G., & Bennett, E. L. (1999a). Carrying capacity limits to sustainable hunting in tropical forests. In J. G. Robinson, & E. L. Bennett, eds., *Hunting for Sustainability in Tropical Forests*, New York: Columbia University Press, 13–30.

Robinson, J. G., & Bennett, E. L. (eds.). (1999b). *Hunting for Sustainability in Tropical Forests*, New York: Columbia University Press.

(2004). Having your wildlife and eating it too: An analysis of hunting sustainability across tropical ecosystems. *Animal Conservation*, **7**(4), 397–408.

Robinson, J. G., & Bodmer, R. E. (1999). Towards wildlife management in tropical forests. *Journal of Wildlife Management*, **63**(1), 1–13.

Robinson, J. G., & Redford, K. H. (1986). Intrinsic rate of natural increase in Neotropical forest mammals: Relationship to phylogeny and diet. *Oecologia*, **68**(4), 516–520.

(eds.). (1991a). *Neotropical Wildlife Use and Conservation*, Chicago, IL: University of Chicago Press.

(1991b). Sustainable harvest of neotropical forest mammals. In J. G. Robinson, & K. H. Redford, eds., *Neotropical Wildlife Use and Conservation*, Chicago, IL: University of Chicago Press, 415–429.

(1994) Measuring the sustainability of hunting in tropical forests. *Oryx*, **28**(4), 249–256.

Robinson, J. G., Redford, K. H., & Bennett, E. L. (1999). Wildlife harvest in logged tropical forests. *Science*, **284**(5414), 595–596.

Rode, C., Cosmides, L., Hell, W., & Tooby, J. (1999). When and why do people avoid unknown probabilities in decisions under uncertainty? Testing some predictions from optimal foraging theory. *Cognition*, **72**(3), 269–304.

Roe, D., & Elliott, J. (2004). Poverty reduction and biodiversity conservation: Rebuilding the bridges. *Oryx*, **38**(2), 137–139.

Rogan, M. S., Lindsey, P. A., Tambling, C. J., *et al.* (2017). Illegal bushmeat hunters compete with predators and threaten wild herbivore populations in a global tourism hotspot. *Biological Conservation*, **210**, 233–242.

Rogan, M. S., Miller, J. R. B., Lindsey, P. A., & McNutt, J. W. (2018). Socioeconomic drivers of illegal bushmeat hunting in a Southern African Savanna. *Biological Conservation*, **226**, 24–31.

Rojas, M., Monsalve, D. M., Pacheco, Y., *et al.* (2020). Ebola virus disease: An emerging and re-emerging viral threat. *Journal of Autoimmunity*, **106**, 102375.

Rolland, J., Condamine, F. L., Jiguet, F., & Morlon, H. (2014). Faster speciation and reduced extinction in the Tropics contribute to the mammalian latitudinal diversity gradient. *PLoS Biology*, **12**(1), e1001775.

Romanoff, S. A. (1984). Matses adaptations in the Peruvian Amazon (PhD dissertation), Columbia University.

Rose, A. L. (2001). Social change and social values in mitigating bushmeat commerce. In M. Bakarr, G. Fonseca, R. Mittermeier, & A. B. Rylands, eds., *Hunting and Bushmeat Utilization in the African Rain Forest. Perspectives Toward a Blueprint for Conservation Action*, Washington DC: Conservation International, 59–74.

Rosin, C., & Poulsen, J. R. (2016). Hunting-induced defaunation drives increased seed predation and decreased seedling establishment of commercially important tree species in an Afrotropical forest. *Forest Ecology and Management*, **382**, 206–213.

Ross, E. B., Arnott, M. L., Basso, E. B., *et al.* (1978). Food taboos, diet, and hunting strategy: The adaptation to animals in amazon cultural ecology [and Comments and Reply]. *Current Anthropology*, **19**(1), 1–36.

Roughgarden, J., & Smith, F. (1996). Why fisheries collapse and what to do about it. *Proceedings of the National Academy of Sciences of the United States of America*, **93**(10), 5078–5083.

Round, P. D. (1990). Bangkok Bird Club survey of the bird and mammal trade in the Bangkok weekend market. *Natural History Bulletin of the Siam Society*, **38**, 1–43.

Rouquet, P., Froment, J.-M., Bermejo, M., *et al.* (2005). Wild animal mortality monitoring and human ebola outbreaks, Gabon and Republic of Congo, 2001–2003. *Emerging Infectious Diseases*, **11**(2), 283–290.

Rovero, F., Ahumada, J., Jansen, P. A., *et al.* (2020). A standardized assessment of forest mammal communities reveals consistent functional composition and vulnerability across the tropics. *Ecography*, **43**(1), 75–84.

Rowcliffe, J. M., Cowlishaw, G., & Long, J. (2003). A model of human hunting impacts in multi-prey communities: Modelling hunting in multi-prey communities. *Journal of Applied Ecology*, **40**(5), 872–889.

Runyoro, V. A., Hofer, H., Chausi, E. B., & Moehlman, P. D. (1995). Populations of the Ngorongoro Crater. In A. R. E. Sinclair, & P. Arcese, eds., *Serengeti II: Dynamics, Management, and Conservation of an Ecosystem*, Vol. 2, Chicago, IL: University of Chicago Press, 46–168.

Rushton, J., Viscarra, R., Viscarra, C., Basset, F., Baptista, R., & Brown, D. (2005). *How Important is Bushmeat Consumption in South America: Now and in the Future?* (Overseas Develoment Institute Wildlife Policy Briefing No. 11).

Salkeld, D. J., Padgett, K. A., & Jones, J. H. (2013). A meta-analysis suggesting that the relationship between biodiversity and risk of zoonotic pathogen transmission is idiosyncratic. *Ecology Letters*, **16**(5), 679–686.

Saltré, F., Chadoeuf, J., Peters, K. J., *et al.* (2019). Climate-human interaction associated with southeast Australian megafauna extinction patterns. *Nature Communications*, **10**(1), 5311.

Samb, S., & Toweh, A. (2014, March 27). Beware of bats: Guinea issues bushmeat warning after Ebola outbreak. www.reuters.com/article/us-ebola-bushmeat/beware-of-bats-guinea-issues-bushmeat-warning-after-ebola-outbreak-idUSBREA2Q19N20140327

Sandalj, M., Treydte, A. C., & Ziegler, S. (2016). Is wild meat luxury? Quantifying wild meat demand and availability in Hue, Vietnam. *Biological Conservation*, **194**(4), 105–112.

Sanderson, S., & Redford, K. (2004). The defence of conservation is not an attack on the poor. *Oryx*, **38**(2), 146–147.

Sandom, C., Faurby, S., Sandel, B., & Svenning, J.-C. (2014). Global late Quaternary megafauna extinctions linked to humans, not climate change. *Proceedings of the Royal Society B: Biological Sciences*, **281**(1787), 20133254.

Sano, K., Arrighi, S., Stani, C., *et al.* (2019). The earliest evidence for mechanically delivered projectile weapons in Europe. *Nature Ecology & Evolution*, **3**(10), 1409–1414.

Santos-Fita, D., Naranjo, E. J., & Rangel-Salazar, J. (2012). Wildlife uses and hunting patterns in rural communities of the Yucatan Peninsula, Mexico. *Journal of Ethnobiology and Ethnomedicine*, **8**(1), 38.

Sarti, F. M., Adams, C., Morsello, C., *et al.* (2015). Beyond protein intake: Bushmeat as source of micronutrients in the Amazon. *Ecology and Society*, **20**(4), 22. http://dx.doi.org/10.5751/ES-07934-200422

Sartoretto, E., Tomassi, A., & Karpe, P. (2017). Analyse comparative des cadres juridiques régissant la gestion de la faune par les collectivités lo-cales en Afrique Centrale. Diversités et limites. In N. Van Vliet, J. C. Nguinguiri, D. Cornelis, & S. Le Bel, eds., *Communautés locales et utilisation durable de la faune en Afrique Central*, Rome: FAO.

Sato, H. (2012). Late Pleistocene trap-pit hunting in the Japanese Archipelago. *Quaternary International*, **248**(1), 43–55.

Schaller, G. B. (1972). *The Serengeti lion: A Study of Predator-Prey Relations*, Chicago, IL: University of Chicago Press.

(1983). Mammals and their biomass on a Brazilian ranch. *Arquivos de Zoologia*, **31**(1), 1–36.

Scheel, D., & Packer, C. (1991). Group hunting behaviour of lions: A search for cooperation. *Animal Behaviour*, **41**(4), 697–709.

Schindler, D. E., & Hilborn, R. (2015). Prediction, precaution, and policy under global change. *Science*, **347**(6225), 953–954.

Schulte-Herbrüggen, B., Cowlishaw, G., Homewood, K., & Rowcliffe, J. M. (2013). The importance of bushmeat in the livelihoods of West African cash-crop farmers living in a faunally-depleted landscape. *PLoS ONE*, **8**(8), e72807.

Schwartzman, S., Nepstad, D., & Moreira, A. (2000). Arguing tropical forest conservation: People versus parks. *Conservation Biology*, **14**(5), 1370–1374.

Schwartzman, S., & Zimmerman, B. (2005). Conservation alliances with Indigenous Peoples of the Amazon. *Conservation Biology*, **19**(3), 721–727.

Scott, A. M. K. (1858). *Day Dawn in Africa: Or Progress of the Protestant/Episcopal Mission at Cape Palmas, West Africa*, New York: Protestant Episcopal Society.

Sellberg, M. M., Wilkinson, C., & Peterson, G. D. (2015). Resilience assessment: A useful approach to navigate urban sustainability challenges. *Ecology and Society*, **20**(1), 43. http://dx.doi.org/10.5751/ES-07258-200143

Señaris, J. C., & Ferrer, A. (2012). Síntesis preliminar del uso de la fauna en la Guayana venezolana. In *Carne de monte y consumo de fauna silvestre en la Orinoquia y Amazonis (Colombia y Venezuela) Memorias del Taller Regional Inirida, Guainia (Colombia)*, Instituto de Investigaciones de Recursos Biológicos Alexander von Humboldt, Universidad Nacional de Colombia, Sede Orinoquia, Instituto de Estudios de la Orinoquia y Corporación para el Desarrollo Sostenible del Norte y el Oriente Amazónico.

Setz, E. Z. F., & Sazima, I. (1987). Bats eaten by Nambiquara Indians in Western Brazil. *Biotropica*, **19**(2), 190.

Shaffer, C. A., Milstein, M. S., Yukuma, C., Marawanaru, E., & Suse, P. (2017). Sustainability and comanagement of subsistence hunting in an indigenous reserve in Guyana: Sustainability and comanagement. *Conservation Biology*, **31**(5), 1119–1131.

Shairp, R., Veríssimo, D., Fraser, I., Challender, D., & MacMillan, D. (2016). Understanding urban demand for wild meat in Vietnam: Implications for conservation actions. *PLoS ONE*, **11**(1), e0134787.

Shea, J. J. (2006). The origins of lithic projectile point technology: Evidence from Africa, the Levant, and Europe. *Journal of Archaeological Science*, **33**(6), 823–846.

Shea, J. J., & Sisk, M. L. (2010). Complex projectile technology and *Homo sapiens* dispersal into western Eurasia. *PaleoAnthropology*, **2010**, 100–122.

Sheil, D., Boissière, M., & Beaudoin, G. (2015). Unseen sentinels: Local monitoring and control in conservation's blind spots. *Ecology and Society*, **20**(2), 39. http://dx.doi.org/10.5751/ES-07625-200239

Shepard, G. H. (2002). Primates in Matsigenka subsistence and world view. In A. Fuentes, & L. D. Wolfe, eds., *Primates Face to Face: Conservation Implications of Human-Nonhuman Primate Interconnections*, Cambridge: Cambridge University Press, 101–136.

Shepard, G. H., Jr., Rummenhoeller, K., Ohl-Schacherer, J., & Yu, D. W. (2010). Trouble in paradise: Indigenous populations, anthropological policies, and biodiversity conservation in Manu National Park, Peru. *Journal of Sustainable Forestry*, **29**(2/4), 252–301.

Shephard, S., Reid, D. G., & Greenstreet, S. P. R. (2011). Interpreting the large fish indicator for the Celtic Sea. *ICES Journal of Marine Science*, **68**(9), 1963–1972.

Shi, J., Wen, Z., Zhong, G., *et al.* (2020). Susceptibility of ferrets, cats, dogs, and other domesticated animals to SARS–coronavirus 2. *Science*, **368**(6494), 1016–1020.

Sierra, R., Rodriguez, F., & Losos, E. (1999). Forest resource use change during early market integration in tropical rain forests: The Huaorani of upper Amazonia. *Ecological Economics*, **30**(1), 107–119.

Simmonds, P. (2000). 2000 Fleming Lecture. The origin and evolution of hepatitis viruses in humans. *Journal of General Virology*, **82**(4), 693–712.

Simon, H. A. (1955). A behavioral model of rational choice. *Quarterly Journal of Economics*, **69**(1), 99–118.

Singh, R. K., Dhama, K., Malik, Y. S., *et al.* (2017). Ebola virus – epidemiology, diagnosis, and control: Threat to humans, lessons learnt, and preparedness plans – an update on its 40 year's journey. *Veterinary Quarterly*, **37**(1), 98–135.

Sirén, A. (2012). Festival hunting by the Kichwa People in the Ecuadorian Amazon. *Journal of Ethnobiology*, **32**(1), 30–50.

Sirén, A. H. (2015). Assessing sustainability is just one component of many in the quest to achieve sustainability. *Ecology and Society*, **20**(4), http://dx.doi.org/10 .5751/ES-07932-200435

Sirén, A. H., & Wilkie, D. S. (2016). The effects of ammunition price on subsistence hunting in an Amazonian village. *Oryx*, **50**(1), 47–55.

Sirén, A., Hambäck, P., & Machoa, J. (2004). Including spatial heterogeneity and animal dispersal when evaluating hunting: A model analysis and an empirical assessment in an Amazonian community. *Conservation Biology*, **18**(5), 1315–1329.

Sirén, A., & Machoa, J. (2008). Fish, wildlife, and human nutrition in tropical forests: A fat gap? *Interciencia*, **33**, 186–193.

Sirisanthana, T., & Brown, A. E. (2002). Anthrax of the gastrointestinal tract. *Emerging Infectious Diseases*, **8**(7), 649–651.

Siskind, J. (1973). *To Hunt in the Morning*. Oxford: Oxford University Press.

Skaanes, T. (2015). Notes on Hadza cosmology. *Hunter Gatherer Research*, **1**(2), 247–267.

Skalski, J. R., Ryding, K. E., & Millspaugh, J. (2005). *Wildlife Demography: Analysis of Sex, Age, and Count Data*, Boston, MA: Elsevier.

Skinner, J. D., & Chimimba, C. T. (2005). *The Mammals of the Southern African Subregion*, Cambridge: Cambridge University Press.

Sklenovská, N., & Van Ranst, M. (2018). Emergence of monkeypox as the most important orthopoxvirus infection in humans. *Frontiers in Public Health*, **6**, 241.

Slade, N. A., Gomulkiewicz, R., & Alexander, H. M. (1998). Alternatives to Robinson and Redford's method of assessing overharvest from incomplete demographic data. *Conservation Biology*, **12**, 148–155.

Slobodkin, L. B. (1974). Prudent predation does not require group selection. *The American Naturalist*, **108**(963), 665–678.

Smiley Evans, T., Myat, T. W., Aung, P., *et al.* (2020). Bushmeat hunting and trade in Myanmar's central teak forests: Threats to biodiversity and human livelihoods. *Global Ecology and Conservation*, **22**, e00889.

Smith, B. D. (2015). A comparison of niche construction theory and diet breadth models as explanatory frameworks for the initial domestication of plants and animals. *Journal of Archaeological Research*, **23**(3), 215–262.

(2016). Neo-Darwinism, niche construction theory, and the initial domestication of plants and animals. *Evolutionary Ecology*, **30**(2), 307–324.

Smith, D. A. (2005). Garden game: Shifting cultivation, indigenous hunting and wildlife ecology in Western Panama. *Human Ecology*, **33**(4), 505–537.

(2008). The spatial patterns of indigenous wildlife use in western Panama: Implications for conservation management. *Biological Conservation*, **141**(4), 925–937.

Smith, E. A. (1979). Inujjuamiut hunting strategies: A preliminary report. *Études/Inuit/Studies*, **3**(2), 128–131.

(1991). *Inujjuamiunt Foraging Strategies: Evolutionary Ecology of an Arctic Hunting Economy*, New Brunswick, NJ: Transaction Publishers.

(2004). Why do good hunters have higher reproductive success? *Human Nature*, **15**(4), 343–364.

Smith, E. A., Bettinger, R. L., Bishop, C. A., *et al.* (1983). Anthropological applications of optimal foraging theory: A critical review [and comments and reply]. *Current Anthropology*, **24**(5), 625–651.

Smith, E. A., & Wishnie, M. (2000). Conservation and subsistence in small-scale societies. *Annual Review of Anthropology*, **29**, 493–524.

Smith, F. A., Elliott Smith, R. E., Lyons, S. K., & Payne, J. L. (2018). Body size downgrading of mammals over the late Quaternary. *Science*, **360**(6386), 310–313.

Smith, K. F., Goldberg, M., Rosenthal, S., *et al.* (2014). Global rise in human infectious disease outbreaks. *Journal of The Royal Society Interface*, **11**(101), 20140950.

Smith, K. M., Anthony, S. J., Switzer, W. M., *et al.* (2012). Zoonotic viruses associated with illegally imported wildlife products. *PLoS ONE*, **7**(1), e29505.

Smith, K. M., Machalaba, C. C., Seifman, R., Feferholtz, Y., & Karesh, W. B. (2019). Infectious disease and economics: The case for considering multi-sectoral impacts. *One Health*, **7**, 100080.

Smith, M. R., Micha, R., Golden, C. D., Mozaffarian, D., & Myers, S. S. (2016). Global Expanded Nutrient Supply (GENuS) Model: A new method for estimating the global dietary supply of nutrients. *PLoS ONE*, **11**(1), e0146976.

Smith, N. J. (1976). Utilization of game along Brazil's transamazon highway. *Acta Amazonica*, **6**(4), 455–466.

Smythe, N., & Brown de Guanti, O. (1995). *The domestication and husbandry of the paca (Agouti paca)* (FAO Conservation Guide No. 26), Rome: FAO.

Soffer, O. (2000). Gravettian technologies in social contexts. In W. Roebroeks, M. Mussi, & J. Svoboda, eds., *Hunters of the Golden Age: The Mid Upper Palaeolithic of Eurasia*, Leiden: University of Leiden Press, 59–75.

(2004). Recovering perishable technologies through use wear on tools: Preliminary Evidence for Upper Paleolithic weaving and net making. *Current Anthropology*, **45**(3), 407–413.

Soma, T. (2012). Ethnoarhchaeology of horse-riding falconry. In *The Asian Conference on the Social Sciences 2012: Official conference proceedings*, 167–182.

Song, H.-D., Tu, C.-C., Zhang, G.-W., *et al.* (2005). Cross-host evolution of severe acute respiratory syndrome coronavirus in palm civet and human. *Proceedings of the National Academy of Sciences of the United States of America*, **102**(7), 2430–2435.

Sonoda, H., Abe, M., Sugimoto, T., *et al.* (2004). Prevalence of hepatitis E virus (HEV) infection in wild boars and deer and genetic identification of a genotype 3 HEV from a boar in Japan. *Journal of Clinical Microbiology*, **42**(11), 5371–5374.

Sosis, R. (2000). Costly signaling and torch fishing on Ifaluk atoll. *Evolution and Human Behavior*, **21**(4), 223–244.

Species 360. (2020). Global information serving conservation. www.species360.org

Spelman, L. H., Gilardi, K. V. K., Lukasik-Braum, M., *et al.* (2013). Respiratory disease in mountain gorillas (*Gorilla beringei beringei*) in Rwanda, 1990–2010: Outbreaks, clinical course, and medical management. *Journal of Zoo and Wildlife Medicine*, **44**(4), 1027–1035.

Spengler, J. R., Ervin, E. D., Towner, J. S., Rollin, P. E., & Nichol, S. T. (2016). Perspectives on West Africa Ebola virus disease outbreak, 2013–2016. *Emerging Infectious Diseases*, **22**(6), 956–963.

Speth, J. D. (2010). *The Paleoanthropology and Archaeology of Big-Game Hunting*, New York: Springer.

Spira, C., Kirkby, A., Kujirakwinja, D., & Plumptre, A. J. (2019). The socio-economics of artisanal mining and bushmeat hunting around protected areas: Kahuzi–Biega National Park and Itombwe Nature Reserve, eastern Democratic Republic of Congo. *Oryx*, **53**(1), 136–144.

Stafford, C. A., Preziosi, R. F., & Sellers, W. I. (2017a). A cross-site analysis of Neotropical bird hunting profiles. *Tropical Conservation Science*, **10**, 194008291773689.

(2017b). A pan-neotropical analysis of hunting preferences. *Biodiversity and Conservation*, **26**(8), 1877–1897.

Stanford, C. B. (2001). A comparison of social meat-foraging by Chimpanzees and Human foragers. In C. B. Stanford, & H. T. Bunn, eds., *Meat-Eating and Human Evolution*, Oxford: Oxford University Press, 101–121.

Stanford, C. B., & Bunn, H. T. (2001). *Meat-Eating and Human Evolution*, Oxford University Press.

Stanford, C. B., & Wrangham, R. W. (1998). *Chimpanzee and Red Colobus: The Ecology of Predator and Prey*, Cambridge, MA: Harvard University Press.

Stanford, C. B. Iverson, J. B., Rhodin, A. G. J., *et al.* (2020). Turtles and tortoises are in trouble. *Current Biology*, **30**, R721–735.

Starkey, M. P. (2004). Commerce and subsistence: The hunting, sale and consumption of bushmeat in Gabon (PhD thesis), University of Cambridge.

Stearman, A. M., & Redford, K. H. (1995). Game management and cultural survival: The Yuquí Ethnodevelopment Project in lowland Bolivia. *Oryx*, **29**(1), 29–34.

Steel, E. A. (1994). Study of the value and volume of bushmeat commerce in Gabon WWF and Gabon Ministry of Forests and Environment, Libreville.

Steffen, W., Broadgate, W., Deutsch, L., Gaffney, O., & Ludwig, C. (2015a). The trajectory of the Anthropocene: The great acceleration. *The Anthropocene Review*, **2**(1), 81–98.

Steffen, W., Richardson, K., Rockstrom, J., *et al.* (2015b). Planetary boundaries: Guiding human development on a changing planet. *Science*, **347**(6223), 736.

Steger, C., Butt, B., & Hooten, M. B. (2017). Safari science: Assessing the reliability of citizen science data for wildlife surveys. *Journal of Applied Ecology*, **54**(6), 2053–2062.

Stehli, F. G., Douglas, R. G., & Newell, N. D. (1969). Generation and maintenance of gradients in taxonomic diversity. *Science*, **164**(3882), 947–949.

Stelfox, J. G., Peden, D. G., Epp, H., *et al.* (1986). Herbivore dynamics in southern Narok, Kenya. *The Journal of Wildlife Management*, 339–347.

Stephens, D. W., & Krebs, J. R. (1986). *Foraging Theory*, Princeton, NJ: Princeton University Press.

Stevens, S. (2014). *Indigenous Peoples, National Parks, and Protected Areas: A New Paradigm Linking Conservation, Culture, and Rights*, Tucson: University of Arizona Press.

Stiner, M. C. (1994). *Honor Among Thieves a Zooarchaeological Study of Neandertal Ecology*, Princeton, NJ: Princeton University Press.

Stoffle, R. W. (2005). Reviewed works: *Places That Count: Traditional Cultural Properties in Cultural Resource Management* by Thomas F. King; *Tribal Cultural Resource Management: The Full Circle to Stewardship* by Darby C. Stapp, Michael S. Burney. *American Anthropologist*, **107**(1), 138–140.

Storm, N., Jansen Van Vuren, P., Markotter, W., & Paweska, J. (2018). Antibody responses to Marburg virus in Egyptian rousette bats and their role in protection against infection. *Viruses*, **10**(2), 73.

Ströhle, A., & Hahn, A. (2011). Diets of modern hunter-gatherers vary substantially in their carbohydrate content depending on ecoenvironments: Results from an ethnographic analysis. *Nutrition Research*, **31**(6), 429–435.

Struebig, M. J., Harrison, M. E., Cheyne, S. M., & Limin, S. H. (2007). Intensive hunting of large flying foxes *Pteropus vampyrus natunae* in Central Kalimantan, Indonesian Borneo. *Oryx*, **41**(3), 390–393.

Struhsaker, T. T. (1975). *The Red Colobus Monkey*, Chicago, IL: University of Chicago Press.

(1997). *Ecology of an African Rain Forest: Logging in Kibale and the Conflict between Conservation and Exploitation.*, Gainesville: University Press of Florida.

Struhsaker, T. T., Lwanga, J. S., & Kasenene, J. M. (1996). Elephants, selective logging and forest regeneration in the Kibale Forest, Uganda. *Journal of Tropical Ecology*, **12**(1), 45–64.

Suárez, E., Morales, M., Cueva, R., *et al.* (2009). Oil industry, wild meat trade and roads: Indirect effects of oil extraction activities in a protected area in north-eastern Ecuador. *Animal Conservation*, **12**(4), 364–373.

Subramanian, M. (2012). Zoonotic disease risk and the bushmeat trade: Assessing awareness among hunters and traders in Sierra Leone. *EcoHealth*, **9**(4), 471–482.

Surovell, T. A., Pelton, S. R., Anderson-Sprecher, R., & Myers, A. D. (2016). Test of Martin's overkill hypothesis using radiocarbon dates on extinct megafauna. *Proceedings of the National Academy of Sciences of the United States of America*, **113**(4), 886–891.

Surovell, T., Waguespack, N., & Brantingham, P. J. (2005). Global archaeological evidence for proboscidean overkill. *Proceedings of the National Academy of Sciences of the United States of America*, **102**(17), 6231–6236.

Sutherland, W. J. (2001). Sustainable exploitation: A review of principles and methods. *Wildlife Biology*, **7**(1), 131–140.

Suzán, G., Marcé, E., Giermakowski, J. T., *et al.* (2009). Experimental evidence for reduced rodent diversity causing increased Hantavirus prevalence. *PLoS ONE*, **4**(5), e5461.

Swanepoel, R., Smit, S. B., Rollin, P. E., *et al.* (2007). Studies of reservoir hosts for Marburg virus. *Emerging Infectious Diseases*, **13**(12), 1847–1851.

Switzer, W. M., Bhullar, V., Shanmugam, V., *et al.* (2004). Frequent simian foamy virus infection in persons occupationally exposed to nonhuman primates. *Journal of Virology*, **78**(6), 2780–2789.

Switzer, W. M., Salemi, M., Shanmugam, V., *et al.* (2005). Ancient co-speciation of simian foamy viruses and primates. *Nature*, **434**(7031), 376–380.

SWM Sustainable Wildlife Management Programme. (2020). White paper: Building back better in a Post-COVID world – reducing future wildlife-borne spill-over of disease to humans, Sustainable Wildlife Management Programme (SWM), FAO.

(2020). Policy Brief - Build Back Better in a post COVID-19 world: Reducing future wildlife-borne spillover of disease to humans, FAO, CIRAD, CIFOR and WCS. www.fao.org/documents/card/en/c/cb1490cn

Tagg, N., Maddison, N., Dupain, J., *et al.* (2018). A zoo-led study of the great ape bushmeat commodity chain in Cameroon. *International Zoo Yearbook*, **52**(1), 182–193.

Tallavaara, M., Eronen, J. T., & Luoto, M. (2018). Productivity, biodiversity, and pathogens influence the global hunter-gatherer population density. *Proceedings of the National Academy of Sciences of the United States of America*, **115**(6), 1232–1237.

Tärnvik, A., Sandström, G., & Sjöstedt, A. (1996). Epidemiological analysis of tularemia in Sweden 1931–1993. *FEMS Immunology & Medical Microbiology*, **13**(3), 201–204.

Taylor, G., Scharlemann, J. P. W., Rowcliffe, M., *et al.* (2015). Synthesising bushmeat research effort in West and Central Africa: A new regional database. *Biological Conservation*, **181**, 199–205.

Taylor, L. H., Latham, S. M., & Woolhouse, M. E. J. (2001). Risk factors for human disease emergence. *Philosophical Transactions of the Royal Society B: Biological Sciences*, **356**, 983–989.

TEAM Network. (2011). *Terrestrial vertebrate protocol implementation manual, v. 3.1.*, Tropical Ecology, Assessment and Monitoring Network, Conservation International. https://figshare.com/articles/TEAM TV protocol/9730562

Tensen, L. (2016). Under what circumstances can wildlife farming benefit species conservation? *Global Ecology and Conservation*, **6**, 286–298.

ter Meulen, J., Lukashevich, I., Sidibe, K., *et al.* (1996). Hunting of peridomestic rodents and consumption of their meat as possible risk factors for rodent-to-human transmission of Lassa virus in the Republic of Guinea. *The American Journal of Tropical Medicine and Hygiene*, **55**(6), 661–666.

Terashima, H. (1983). Mota and other hunting activities of the Mbuti archers: A socio-ecological study of subsistence technology. *African Study Monographs*, **3**, 71–85.

Terborgh, J. (1999). *Requiem for Nature*, Washington DC: Island Press.

——— (2000). The fate of tropical forests: A matter of stewardship. *Conservation Biology*, **14**(5), 1358–1361.

Terborgh, J., & Estes, J. A. (eds) (2010). *Trophic Cascades: Predators, Prey and the Changing Dynamics of Nature*. Washington, DC: Island Press.

Terborgh, J., Pitman, N., Silman, M., Schichter, H., & Núñez, V. P. (2002). Maintenance of tree diversity in tropical forests. In D. J. Levey, W. R. Silva, & M. Galetti, eds., *Seed Dispersal and Frugivory: Ecology, Evolution and Conservation*, Wallingford: CABI Publishing, 1–17.

Terborgh, J., & Van Schaik, C. P. (1987). Convergence vs. nonconvergence in primate communities. In J. H. R. Gee, & P. S. Giller, eds., *Organization of Communities: Past and Present*, Oxford: Blackwell Scientific, 205–226.

Tessmann, G. (1913a). *Erster Band. Die Pangwe: Völkerkundliche Monographie eines westafrikanischen Negerstammes; Ergebnisse der Lübecker Pangwe-Expedition 1907 – 1909 und früherer Forschungen 1904 – 1907*, Vol. 1, Berlin: Ernst Wasmuth A.-G.

——— (1913b). *Zweiter Band. Die Pangwe: Völkerkundliche Monographie eines westafrikanischen Negerstammes; Ergebnisse der Lübecker Pangwe-Expedition 1907 – 1909 und früherer Forschungen 1904 – 1907*, Vol. 2, Berlin: Ernst Wasmuth A.-G.

Teye, M., Fuseini, A., & Odoi, F. N. A. (2020). Consumer acceptance, carcass and sensory characteristics of meats of farmed and wild cane rats (*Thryonomys swinderianus*). *Scientific African*, **8**, e00461.

The Lancet. (2016). Indigenous health: A worldwide focus. *The Lancet*, **388**(10040), 104.

The World Bank. (2020, October 1). Indigenous peoples. www.worldbank.org/en/topic/indigenouspeoples

Thibault, M., & Blaney, S. (2003). The oil industry as an underlying factor in the bushmeat crisis in Central Africa. *Conservation Biology*, **17**(6), 1807–1813.

Thieme, H. (1997). Lower Palaeolithic hunting spears from Germany. *Nature*, **385**(6619), 807–810.

Thoisy, B. de, Richard-Hansen, C., & Peres, C. A. (2009). Impacts of subsistence game hunting on Amazonian primates. In P. A. Garber, A. Estrada, J. C. Bicca-Marques, E. W. Heymann, & K. B. Strier, eds., *South American Primates*, New York: Springer New York, 389–412.

Thomas, S. C. (1991). Population densities and patterns of habitat use among anthropoid primates of the Ituri Forest, Zaire. *Biotropica*, **23**(1), 68–83.

Thornton, P. K., Kruska, R. L., Henninger, N., *et al.* (2002). *Mapping Poverty and Livestock in the Developing World*, Nairobi: International Livestock Research Institute.

Tivy, J., & O'Hare, G. (1981). *Human Impact on the Ecosystem*, Edinburgh: Oliver & Boyd.

Toledo, L. F., Asmüssen, M. V., & Rodríguez, J. P. (2012). Track illegal trade in wildlife. *Nature*, **483**(7387), 36–36.

Townsend, H., Harvey, C. J., deReynier, Y., *et al.* (2019). Progress on implementing ecosystem-based fisheries management in the United States through the use of ecosystem models and analysis. *Frontiers in Marine Science*, **6**, 641.

Townsend, W. R. (2000). The sustainability of subsistence hunting by the Sirionó Indians of Bolivia. In J. G. Robinson, & E. L. Bennett, eds., *Hunting for Sustainability in Tropical Forest*, New York: Columbia University Press, 267–281.

Trail, P. W. (2007). African hornbills: Keystone species threatened by habitat loss, hunting and international trade. *Ostrich*, **78**(3), 609–613.

Tranquilli, S., Abedi-Lartey, M., Abernethy, K., *et al.* (2014). Protected areas in Tropical Africa: Assessing threats and conservation activities. *PLoS ONE*, **9**(12), e114154.

Trefon, T., & de Maret, P. (1999). Snack nature dans les villes d'Afrique Centrale. In S. Bahuchet, D. Bley, H. Pagezy, & N. Vernazza-Licht, eds., *L'homme et la forêt tropicale*, Châteauneuf: Editions de Bergier.

Trewartha, G. T. (1968). *An Introduction to Climate*, New York: McGraw-Hill.

Tu, C., Crameri, G., Kong, X., *et al.* (2004). Antibodies to SARS Coronavirus in civets. *Emerging Infectious Diseases*, **10**(12), 2244–2248.

Tuck-Po, L. (2000). Forest, Bateks, and degradation: Environmental representations in a changing world. *Southeast Asian Studies*, **38**(2), 165–184.

Tumusiime, D. M., Eilu, G., Tweheyo, M., & Babweteera, F. (2010). Wildlife snaring in Budongo Forest Reserve, Uganda. *Human Dimensions of Wildlife*, **15**(2), 129–144.

Turnbull, C. M. (2018). Society and sociality: An expanding universe. In B. M. Du Toit, ed., *Ethnicity in Modern Africa*, New York: Routledge, 91–104.

Turvey, S. T., & Fritz, S. A. (2011). The ghosts of mammals past: Biological and geographical patterns of global mammalian extinction across the Holocene. *Philosophical Transactions of the Royal Society B: Biological Sciences*, **366**(1577), 2564–2576.

Tutin, C. E., & Fernandez, M. (1993). Relationships between minimum temperature and fruit production in some tropical forest trees in Gabon. *Journal of Tropical Ecology*, **9**(2), 241–248.

Tutin, C. E. G., White, L. J. T., & Mackanga-Missandzou, A. (1997). The use by rain forest mammals of natural forest fragments in an equatorial African savanna: Utilización de Fragmentos de Bosque Natural por Mamíferos de Selva Lluviosa en una Sabana Ecuatorial Africana. *Conservation Biology*, **11**(5), 1190–1203.

Twinamatsiko, M., Baker, J., Harrison, M., *et al.* (2014). *Understanding profiles and motivations of resource users and local perceptions of governance at Bwindi Impenetrable National Park, Uganda* (IIED Research Report), London: International Institute for Environment and Development.

UNAIDS. (2020). Global HIV & AIDS statistics — 2020 fact sheet. www.unaids .org/en/resources/fact-sheet

UNEP & International Livestock Research Institute. (2020). *Preventing the Next Pandemic- Zoonotic diseases and How to Break the Chain of Transmission*, Nairobi: UNEP.

United Nations. (1948). Universal Declaration of Human Rights. www.ohchr.org/ en/udhr/documents/udhr_translations/eng.pdf

(2007). United Nations Declaration on the Rights of Indigenous Peoples. www .un.org/development/desa/indigenouspeoples/wp-content/uploads/sites/19/ 2018/11/UNDRIP_E_web.pdf

(2014). A world of cities. Population Facts No. 2014/2, United Nations Department of Economics and Social Affairs, Population Division. www.un. org/en/development/desa/population/publications/pdf/popfacts/PopFacts_ 2014-2.pdf

UNODC. (2016). *World Wildlife Crime Report 2016: Trafficking in Protected Species*, United Nations Office on Drugs and Crime (UNODC).

Urlacher, S. S., Blackwell, A. D., Liebert, M. A., *et al.* (2016). Physical growth of the Shuar: Height, weight, and BMI references for an indigenous Amazonian population.. *American Journal of Human Biology*, **28**(1), 16–30.

Vallejos, P. Q., & Veit, P. (2020, October 7). Mining Threatens 20% of Indigenous Lands in the Amazon. www.wri.org/blog/2020/10/amazon-indigenous-land-mining

Van der Hoek, L. (2007). Human coronaviruses: What do they cause? *Antiviral Therapy*, **12**(4 B), 651–658.

Van Heuverswyn, F., & Peeters, M. (2007). The origins of HIV and implications for the global epidemic. *Current Infectious Disease Reports*, **9**(4), 338–346.

Van Schaik, C. P., Terborgh, J. W., & Wright, S. J. (1993). The phenology of tropical forests: Adaptive significance and consequences for primary consumers. *Annual Review of Ecology and Systematics*, **24**(1), 353–377.

Van Swaay, C., Cuttelod, A., Collins, S., *et al.* (eds.). (2010). *European Red List of Butterflies*, Luxembourg: Publications Office of the European Union.

Van Thiel, P.-P. A. M., de Bie, R. M. A., Eftimov, F., *et al.* (2009). Fatal human rabies due to Duvenhage virus from a bat in Kenya: Failure of treatment with coma-induction, ketamine, and antiviral drugs. *PLoS Neglected Tropical Diseases*, **3**(7), e428.

Van Valkenburgh, B. (2001). The dog-eat-dog world of carnivores. A review of past and present carnivore community dynamics. In C. B. Stanford, & H. T. Bunn, eds., *Meat-Eating and Human Evolution*, Oxford: Oxford University Press, 101–121.

Van Vliet, N. (2018). 'Bushmeat Crisis' and 'Cultural Imperialism' in wildlife management? Taking value orientations into account for a more sustainable and culturally acceptable wildmeat sector. *Frontiers in Ecology and Evolution*, **6**, 112.

Van Vliet, J. E. F. Schulte-Herbrüggen, N. B., Muhindo, J., Nebesse, C. Gambalemoke, S. and Nasi, R. (2017). Trends in bushmeat trade in a post-conflict forest town: Implications for food security. *Ecology and Society*, **22**(4), 35, https://doi.org/10.5751/ES-09780-220435

Van Vliet, N., Antunes, A. P., Constantino, P. de A. L., Gómez, J., Santos-Fita, D., & Sartoretto, E. (2019). Frameworks regulating hunting for meat in tropical countries leave the sector in the limbo. *Frontiers in Ecology and Evolution*, **7**, 280.

Van Vliet, N., Cruz, D., Quiceno-Mesa, M. P., *et al.* (2015a). Ride, shoot, and call: Wildlife use among contemporary urban hunters in Três Fronteiras, Brazilian Amazon. *Ecology and Society*, **20**(3), 8. http://dx.doi.org/10.5751/ES-07506-200308

Van Vliet, N., Fa, J., & Nasi, R. (2015b). Managing hunting under uncertainty: From one-off ecological indicators to resilience approaches in assessing the sustainability of bushmeat hunting. *Ecology and Society*, **20**(3), 7. http://dx.doi.org/10.5751/ES-07669-200307

Van Vliet, N., Gomez, J., Quiceno-Mesa, M. P., *et al.* (2015). Sustainable wildlife management and legal commercial use of bushmeat in Colombia: The resource remains at the cross-road. *International Forestry Review*, **17**(4), 438–447.

Van Vliet, N., Kaniowska, E., Bourgarel, M., Fargeot, C., & Nasi, R. (2009). Answering the call! Adapting a traditional hunting practice to monitor duiker populations. *African Journal of Ecology*, **47**(3), 393–399.

Van Vliet, N., Mesa, M. P. Q., Cruz-Antia, D., de Aquino, L. J. N., Moreno, J., & Nasi, R. (2014). The uncovered volumes of bushmeat commercialized in the Amazonian trifrontier between Colombia, Peru & Brazil. *Ethnobiology and Conservation*, **3**, 7.

Van Vliet, N., Milner-Gulland, E. J., Bousquet, F., Saqalli, M., & Nasi, R. (2010a). Effect of small-scale heterogeneity of prey and hunter distributions on the sustainability of bushmeat hunting: Heterogeneity of prey and hunter distributions. *Conservation Biology*, **24**(5), 1327–1337.

Van Vliet, N., Moreno, J., Gómez, J., *et al.* (2017). Bushmeat and human health: Assessing the Evidence in tropical and sub-tropical forests. *Ethnobiology and Conservation*, **6**(3), 1–45.

Van Vliet, N., Muhindo, J., Kambale Nyumu, J., Mushagalusa, O., & Nasi, R. (2018). Mammal depletion processes as evidenced from spatially explicit and temporal local ecological knowledge. *Tropical Conservation Science*, **11**, 194008291879949.

Van Vliet, N., & Nasi, R. (2008a). Hunting for livelihood in Northeast Gabon: Patterns, evolution, and sustainability. *Ecology and Society*, **13**(2), 33. www.ecologyandsociety.org/vol13/iss2/art33/

(2008b). Why do models fail to assess properly the sustainability of duiker (*Cephalophus* spp.) hunting in Central Africa? *Oryx*, **42**(3), 392–399

(2018). What do we know about the life-history traits of widely hunted tropical mammals? *Oryx*, **53**(4), 670–676.

Van Vliet, N., Nebesse, C., Gambalemoke, S., Akaibe, D., & Nasi, R. (2012). The bushmeat market in Kisangani, Democratic Republic of Congo: Implications for conservation and food security. *Oryx*, **46**(2), 196–203.

Van Vliet, N., Nebesse, C., & Nasi, R. (2010b). The dynamics of bushmeat trade in the market of Kisangani. Presented at the XXIII IUFRO Congress, Seoul, South Korea, 23–28.

Van Vliet, N., Quiceno, M., Moreno, J., Cruz, D., Fa, J. E., & Nasi, R. (2017). Is urban bushmeat trade in Colombia really insignificant? *Oryx*, **51**(2), 305–314.

Van Vliet, N., Quiceno, M. P., Cruz, D., *et al.* (2015c). Bushmeat networks link the forest to urban areas in the trifrontier region between Brazil, Colombia, and Peru. *Ecology and Society*, **20**(3), 21. http://dx.doi.org/10.5751/ES-07782-200321

Vanthomme, H., Bellé, B., & Forget, P.-M. (2010). Bushmeat hunting alters recruitment of large-seeded plant species in Central Africa: Hunting and Central African forest regeneration. *Biotropica*, **42**(6), 672–679.

Vargas-Tovar, N. (2012). Carne de monte y seguridad alimentaria: Consumo, valor nutricional, relaciones sociales y bienestar humano en Colombia. In S. Restrepo, ed., *Carne de Monte y Seguridad Alimentaria: Bases Técnicas para una Gestión Integral en Colombia*. Colombia:Instituto de Investigación de Recursos Biológicos Alexander von Humboldt, 64–87.

Velho, N., & Laurance, W. F. (2013). Hunting practices of an Indo-Tibetan Buddhist tribe in Arunachal Pradesh, north-east India. *Oryx*, **47**(3), 389–392.

Verdu, P., Austerlitz, F., Estoup, A., *et al.* (2009). Origins and genetic diversity of Pygmy hunter-gatherers from Western Central Africa. *Current Biology*, **19**(4), 312–318.

Vermeulen, C., Julve, C., Doucet, J.-L., & Monticelli, D. (2009). Community hunting in logging concessions: Towards a management model for Cameroon's dense forests. *Biodiversity and Conservation*, **18**(10), 2705–2718.

Vickers, W. T. (1980). An analysis of Amazonian hunting yields as a function of settlement age. In W. T. Vickers, & K. M. Kensinger, eds., *Working Papers on South American Indians*, Bermington College, Vermont, 7–29.

(1984). The faunal components of lowland South American hunting kills. *Interciencia*, **9**, 366–376.

(1994). From opportunism to nascent conservation: The case of the Siona-Secoya. *Human Nature*, **5**(4), 307–337.

Villén-Pérez, S., Moutinho, P., Nóbrega, C. C., & De Marco, P. (2020). Brazilian Amazon gold: Indigenous land rights under risk. *Elementa: Science of the Anthropocene*, **8**, 31. https://online.ucpress.edu/elementa/article/doi/10.1525/elementa.427/114461/Brazilian-Amazon-gold-indigenous-land-rights-under

Visconti, P., Bakkenes, M., Baisero, D., *et al.* (2016). Projecting global biodiversity indicators under future development scenarios: Projecting biodiversity indicators. *Conservation Letters*, **9**(1), 5–13.

Volpato, G., Fontefrancesco, M. F., Gruppuso, P., Zocchi, D. M., & Pieroni, A. (2020). Baby pangolins on my plate: Possible lessons to learn from the COVID-19 pandemic. *Journal of Ethnobiology and Ethnomedicine*, **16**(1), art. 19.

von Carlowitz, H. C. (1713). *Sylvicultura Oekonomica oder haußwirthliche Nachricht und naturmäßige Anweisung zur Wilden Baum-Zucht*. Leipzig: Braun.

Voss, R. S., & Emmons, L. H. (1996). Mammalian diversity in Neotropical lowland rainforests: A preliminary assessment. *Bulletin of the American Museum of Natural History*, **230**, 3–115.

Wade, P. R. (1998). Calculating limits to the allowable human-caused mortality of cetaceans and pinnipeds. *Marine Mammal Science*, **14**(1), 1–37.

Wadley, L. (2010). Were snares and traps used in the Middle Stone Age and does it matter? A review and a case study from Sibudu, South Africa. *Journal of Human Evolution*, **58**(2), 179–192.

Wadley, L., & Mohapi, M. (2008). A segment is not a monolith: Evidence from the Howiesons Poort of Sibudu, South Africa. *Journal of Archaeological Science*, **35**(9), 2594–2605.

Walker, A., & Shipman, P. (1996). *The Wisdom of Bones: In Search of Human Origins*, New York: Alfred A Knopf.

Walker, B., Carpenter, S., Anderies, J., *et al.* (2002). Resilience management in social-ecological systems: A working hypothesis for a participatory approach. *Conservation Ecology*, **6**(1), 14.

Walsh, P. D., Abernethy, K. A., Bermejo, M., *et al.* (2003). Catastrophic ape decline in western equatorial Africa. *Nature*, **422**(6932), 611–614.

Walters, G., Schleicher, J., Hymas, O., & Coad, L. (2015). Evolving hunting practices in Gabon: Lessons for community-based conservation interventions. *Ecology and Society*, **20**(4), 31. http://dx.doi.org/10.5751/ES-08047-200431

Walz, E., Wilson, D., Stauffer, J. C., *et al.* (2017). Incentives for bushmeat consumption and importation among West African Immigrants, Minnesota, USA. *Emerging Infectious Diseases*. **23**(12), 2095–2097.

Wang, T., Feng, L., Yang, H., *et al.* (2017). A science-based approach to guide Amur leopard recovery in China. *Biological Conservation*, **210** (2017), 47–55.

Ward, D. (1992). The role of satisficing in foraging theory. *Oikos*, **63**(2), 312–317. (1993). Foraging theory, like all other fields of science, needs multiple working hypotheses. *Oikos*, **67**(2), 376–378.

Waterman, P. G., & McKey, D. (1989). Herbivory and secondary compounds in rain-forest plants. *Ecosystems of the World*, **14**, 513–536.

Waterman, P. G., Ross, J. A., Bennett, E. L., & Davies, A. G. (1988). A comparison of the floristics and leaf chemistry of the tree flora in two Malaysian rain forests and the influence of leaf chemistry on populations of colobine monkeys in the Old World. *Biological Journal of the Linnean Society*, **34**(1), 1–32.

Watson, J. E. M., Shanahan, D. F., Di Marco, M., *et al.* (2016). Catastrophic declines in wilderness areas undermine global environment targets. *Current Biology*, **26**(21), 2929–2934.

Watts, D. P. (2008). Scavenging by chimpanzees at Ngogo and the relevance of chimpanzee scavenging to early hominin behavioral ecology. *Journal of Human Evolution*, **54**(1), 125–133.

WCS (Wildlife Conservation Society). (2020). WCS Statement and Analysis on the Chinese Government's Decision Prohibiting Some Trade and Consumption of Wild Animals. New York: WCS. https://newsroom.wcs.org/News-Releases/articleType/ArticleView/articleId/13855/WCS-Statement-and-Analysis-On-the-Chinese-Governments-Decision-Prohibiting-Some-Trade-and-Consumption-of-Wild-Animals.aspx

Wearn, O. R., Reuman, D. C., & Ewers, R. M. (2012). Extinction debt and windows of conservation opportunity in the Brazilian Amazon. *Science*, **337**(6091), 228–232.

Weinbaum, K. Z., Brashares, J. S., Golden, C. D., & Getz, W. M. (2013). Searching for sustainability: Are assessments of wildlife harvests behind the times? *Ecology Letters*, **16**(1), 99–111.

Weiss, R. A. (2001). Animal origins of human infectious disease (The Leeuwenhoek Lecture 2001). *Philosophical Transactions of the Royal Society B: Biological Sciences*, **356**(1410), 957–977.

(2003). HIV and AIDS in relation to other pandemics: Among the viruses plaguing humans, HIV is a recent acquisition. Its outstanding success as an infection poses immense scientific challenges to human health and raises the question 'What comes next?' *EMBO Reports*, **4**(S1), S10–S14.

Weiss, S., Nowak, K., Fahr, J., *et al.* (2012). Henipavirus-related sequences in fruit bat bushmeat, Republic of Congo. *Emerging Infectious Diseases*, **18**(9), 1535–1536.

Welch, J. R. (2014). Xavante ritual hunting: Anthropogenic fire, reciprocity, and collective landscape management in the Brazilian cerrado. *Human Ecology*, **42**(1), 47–59.

Wells, M. P., & McShane, T. O. (2004). Integrating protected area management with local needs and aspirations. *AMBIO: A Journal of the Human Environment*, **33**(8), 513–519.

Wemmer, C., & Sunquist, M. (2005). John Frederick Eisenberg: 1935–2003. *Journal of Mammalogy*, **86**, 429–437.

Wenzel, G. W. (2019). Canadian Inuit subsistence: Antinomies of the mixed economy. *Hunter Gatherer Research*, **3**(4), 567–581.

Western, D. (1989). The ecological value of elephants: A keystone role in African ecosystems. In S. Cobb, ed., *The Ivory Trade and the Future of the African Elephant*, Vol. 2, Gland: IUCN.

White, L. J. (1994). Biomass of rain forest mammals in the Lopé Reserve, Gabon. *Journal of Animal Ecology*, **63**, 499–512.

Whitman, K., Starfield, A. M., Quadling, H. S., & Packer, C. (2004). Sustainable trophy hunting of African lions. *Nature*, **428**(6979), 175–178.

Whittington, S. L., & Dyke, B. (1984). Simulating overkill: Experiments with the Mosimann and Martin Model. In P. S. Martin, & R. G. Klein, eds., *Quaternary Extinctions: A Prehistoric Revolution*, Tucson: University of Arizona Press, 451–465.

WHO. (2003). Outbreak news: Severe acute respiratory syndrome (SARS). *Weekly Epidemiological Record*, **78**(12), 81–83.

(2004a). Human plague in 2002 and 2003. *Weekly Epidemiological Record*, **79**(301), 6.

(2004b). Report of the WHO/FAO/OIE joint consultation on emerging zoonotic diseases, World Health Organization.

(2016a). Ebola outbreak. www.who.int/csr/disease/ebola/en/

(2016b). Ebola Situation Report - 30 March 2016, WHO. https://apps.who.int/ebola/current-situation/ebola-situation-report-30-march-2016

(2020). WHO-convened Global Study of the Origins of SARS-CoV-2. www.who.int/publications/m/item/who-convened-global-study-of-the-origins-of-sars-cov-2

Whytock, R. C., Buij, R., Virani, M. Z., & Morgan, B. J. (2016). Do large birds experience previously undetected levels of hunting pressure in the forests of Central and West Africa? *Oryx*, **50**(1), 76–83.

Wicander, S., & Coad, L. (2018). Can the provision of alternative livelihoods reduce the impact of wild meat hunting in West and Central Africa? *Conservation and Society*, **16**(4), 441.

Wielinga, P. R., & Schlundt, J. (2013). Food safety: At the center of a One Health approach for combating zoonoses. In J. S. Mackenzie, M. Jeggo, P. Daszak, & J. A. Richt, eds., *One Health: The Human-Animal-Environment Interfaces in Emerging Infectious Diseases*, Heidelberg: Springer, 3–18.

Wiessner, P. W., Wiessner, P., & Schiefenhövel, W. (1996). *Food and the Status Quest: An Interdisciplinary Perspective*, Providence: Berghahn Books.

Wilcove, D. S., Giam, X., Edwards, D. P., Fisher, B., & Koh, L. P. (2013). Navjot's nightmare revisited: Logging, agriculture, and biodiversity in Southeast Asia. *Trends in Ecology & Evolution*, **28**(9), 531–540.

Wilcox, B. A., & Ellis, B. (2006). Forests and emerging infectious diseases of humans. *Unasylva*, **57**(2), 11–18.

Wilkie, D. (2006). Bushmeat: A disease risk worth taking to put food on the table? *Animal Conservation*, **9**(4), 370–371.

Wilkie, D. S. (1987). Impact of swidden agriculture and subsistence hunting on diversity and abundance of exploited fauna in the Ituri Forest of Northeastern Zaire. (PhD dissertation), University of Massachusetts.

(1989). Impact of roadside agriculture on subsistence hunting in the Ituri forest of northeastern Zaire. *American Journal of Physical Anthropology*, **78**(4), 485–494.

Wilkie, D. S., & Carpenter, J. F. (1999). Bushmeat hunting in the Congo Basin: An assessment of impacts and options for mitigation. *Biodiversity and Conservation*, **8**, 927–955.

Wilkie, D. S., & Godoy, R. A. (2001). Income and price elasticities of bushmeat demand in Lowland Amerindian Societies. *Conservation Biology*, **15**(3), 761–769.

Wilkie, D. S., Starkey, M., Abernethy, K., Effa, E. N., Telfer, P., & Godoy, R. (2005). Role of prices and wealth in consumer demand for bushmeat in Gabon, Central Africa. *Conservation Biology*, **19**(1), 268–274.

Wilkie, D. S., Wieland, M., Boulet, H., et al. (2016). Eating and conserving bushmeat in Africa. *African Journal of Ecology*, **54**(4), 402–414.

Wilkie, D., Shaw, E., Rotberg, F., Morelli, G., & Auzel, P. (2000). Roads, development, and conservation in the Congo Basin. *Conservation Biology*, **14**(6), 9.

Wilkinson, N. M. (2016). Conserving the unknown: Decision-making for the Critically Endangered saola Pseudoryx nghetinhensis in Vietnam (PhD thesis), Department of Geography, University of Cambridge.

Willcox, A. S., & Nambu, D. M. (2007). Wildlife hunting practices and bushmeat dynamics of the Banyangi and Mbo people of Southwestern Cameroon. *Biological Conservation*, **134**(2), 251–261.

Willig, M. R., Kaufman, D. M., & Stevens, R. D. (2003). Latitudinal gradients of biodiversity: Pattern, process, scale, and synthesis. *Annual Review of Ecology, Evolution, and Systematics*, **34**(1), 273–309.

Willig, M. R., Presley, S. J., Plante, J.-L., et al. (2019). Guild-level responses of bats to habitat conversion in a lowland Amazonian rainforest: Species composition and biodiversity. *Journal of Mammalogy*, **100**(1), 223–238.

Wilmers, C. C., Estes, J. A., Edwards, M., Laidre, K. L., & Konar, B. (2012). Do trophic cascades affect the storage and flux of atmospheric carbon? An analysis of sea otters and kelp forests. *Frontiers in Ecology and the Environment*, **10**(8), 409–415.

Winterhalder, B. (1981). Foraging strategies in the boreal forest: An analysis of Cree hunting and gathering. In B. Winterhalder, & E. Alden Smith, eds., *Hunter-Gatherer Foraging Strategies: Ethnographic and Archeological Analyses*, Chicago, IL: University of Chicago Press, 66–98.

(1986a). Diet choice, risk, and food sharing in a stochastic environment. *Journal of Anthropological Archaeology*, **5**(4), 369–392.

(1986b). Optimal foraging: Simulation studies of diet choice in a stochastic environment. *Journal of Ethnobiology*, **6**(1), 205–223.

Wojtal, P., & Wilczyński, J. (2015). Hunters of the giants: Woolly mammoth hunting during the Gravettian in Central Europe. *Quaternary International*, **379**, 71–81.

Wolfe, N. D., Daszak, P., Kilpatrick, A. M., & Burke, D. S. (2005a). Bushmeat hunting, deforestation, and prediction of zoonotic disease emergence. *Emerging Infectious Diseases*, **11**(12), 1822–1827..

Wolfe, N. D., Escalante, A. A., Karesh, W. B., Kilbourn, A., Spielman, A., & Lal, A. A. (1998). Wild primate populations in emerging infectious disease research: The missing link? *Emerging Infectious Diseases*, **4**(2), 149–158.

Wolfe, N. D., Heneine, W., Carr, J. K., *et al.* (2005b). Emergence of unique primate T-lymphotropic viruses among central African bushmeat hunters. *Proceedings of the National Academy of Sciences of the United States of America*, **102**(22), 7994–7999.

Wolfe, N. D., Switzer, W. M., Carr, J. K., *et al.* (2004). Naturally acquired simian retrovirus infections in central African hunters. *The Lancet*, **363**(9413), 932–937.

Wood, C. L., & Lafferty, K. D. (2013). Biodiversity and disease: A synthesis of ecological perspectives on Lyme disease transmission. *Trends in Ecology & Evolution*, **28**(4), 239–247.

Woodburn, J. (1980). Hunters and gatherers today and reconstruction of the past. In E. Gellner, ed., *Soviet and Western Anthropology*, London: Duckworth.

(1998). Sharing is not a form of exchange: An analysis of property-sharing in immediate-return hunter-gatherer societies. In C. M. Hann, ed., *Property Relations: Renewing the Anthropological Tradition*, Cambridge: Cambridge University Press, 48–63.

Woolhouse, M. E. J. (2002). Population biology of emerging and re-emerging pathogens. *Trends in Microbiology*, **10**(10), s3–s7.

Woolhouse, M. E. J., & Dye, C. (2001). Population biology of emerging and re-emerging pathogens. Preface. *Philosophical Transactions: Biological Sciences*, **356**(1411), 981–982.

World Bank. (2016). 2014–2015 West Africa Ebola Crisis: Impact Update. www .worldbank.org/en/topic/macroeconomics/publication/2014-2015-west-africa-ebola-crisis-impact-update

Worobey, M., Gemmel, M., Teuwen, D. E., *et al.* (2008). Direct evidence of extensive diversity of HIV-1 in Kinshasa by 1960. *Nature*, **455**(7213), 661–664.

Worobey, M., Levy, J. I., Serrano, L. M. M. (2022). The Huanan market was the epicenter of SARS-CoV-2 emergence. *Zenodo*, https://doi.org/10.5281/zenodo.6299115

Wright, J. H., & Priston, N. E. C. (2010). Hunting and trapping in Lebialem Division, Cameroon: Bushmeat harvesting practices and human reliance. *Endangered Species Research*, **11**, 1–12.

Wright, S. J., & Muller-Landau, H. C. (2006). The future of tropical forest species. *Biotropica*, **38**(3), 287–301.

Wright, S. J., Stoner, K. E., Beckman, N., *et al.* (2007). The plight of large animals in tropical forests and the consequences for plant regeneration. *Biotropica*, **39**(3), 289–291.

Wright, S. J., Zeballos, H., Domínguez, I., Gallardo, M. M., Moreno, M. C., & Ibáñez, R. (2000). Poachers alter mammal abundance, seed dispersal, and seed predation in a Neotropical forest. *Conservation Biology*, **14**(1), 227–239.

Wroe, S., & Field, J. (2006). A review of the evidence for a human role in the extinction of Australian megafauna and an alternative interpretation. *Quaternary Science Reviews*, **25**(21–22), 2692–2703.

Wroe, S., Field, J., Fullagar, R., & Jermin, L. S. (2004). Megafaunal extinction in the late Quaternary and the global overkill hypothesis. *Alcheringa: An Australasian Journal of Palaeontology*, **28**(1), 291–331.

Wynn, T., & Coolidge, F. (2003). The role of working memory in the evolution of managed foraging. *Before Farming*, **2003**(2), 1–16.

Wynne-Edwards, V. C. (1962). *Animal Dispersion in Relation to Social Behaviour*, New York: Hafner.

(1965). Self-regulating systems in populations of animals. *Science*, **147**(3665), 1543–1548.

Yang, N., Liu, P., Li, W., & Zhang, L. (2020). Permanently ban wildlife consumption. *Science*, **367**(6485), 1434–1434.

Yao, K. A., Bitty, E. A., Kassé, K. B., *et al.* (2017). Distribution and relative abundance of forest duikers in Dassioko Sud Forest Reserve (coastal Côte d'Ivoire). *Wildlife Research*, **44**, 660–668.

Yasuoka, H. (2006a). Long-term foraging expeditions (molongo) among the Baka hunter-gatherers in the northwestern Congo Basin, with special reference to the 'wild yam question.' *Human Ecology*, **34**(2), 275–296.

(2006b). The sustainability of duiker (*Cephalophus* spp.) hunting for the Baka hunter-gatherers in southeastern Cameroon. *African Study Monographs, Suppl.* **33**, 95–120.

(2009). Concentrated distribution of wild yam patches: Historical ecology and the subsistence of African rainforest hunter-gatherers. *Human Ecology*, **37**(5), 577–587.

(2012). Fledging agriculturalists? Rethinking the adoption of cultivation by the Baka hunter-gatherers. *African Study Monographs*, **43**(Suppl.), 85–114.

(2014). Snare hunting among Baka hunter-gatherers: Implications for sustainable wildlife management. *African Study Monographs*, **49**(Suppl.), 115–136.

Yasuoka, H., Hirai, M., Kamgaing, T. O. W., Dzefack, Z. C. B., Kamdoum, E. C., & Bobo, K. S. (2015). Changes in the composition of hunting catches in southeastern Cameroon: A promising approach for collaborative wildlife management between ecologists and local hunters. *Ecology and Society*, **20**(4), 25. http://dx.doi.org/10.5751/ES-08041-200425

Yeatter, R. E., & Thompson, D. H. (1952). Tularemia, weather, and rabbit populations. *Illinois Natural History Survey Bulletin*, **25**(1–6), 351–382.

Yellen, J. E., & Lee, R. B. (1976). The Dobe-/Du/da environment: Background to a hunting and gathering way of life. In R. B. Lee, & I. DeVore, eds., *Kalahari Hunter Gatherers: Studies of the!Kung San and their Neighbors*, Cambridge: Cambridge University Press, 27–46.

Yost, J. A., & Kelley, P. M. (1983). Shotguns, blowguns, and spears: The analysis of technological efficiency. In R. B. Hames, & W. T. Vickers, eds., *Adaptive Responses of Native Amazonians*, New York: Academic Press, 189–224.

Young, H. S., Dirzo, R., Helgen, K. M., *et al.* (2014). Declines in large wildlife increase landscape-level prevalence of rodent-borne disease in Africa. *Proceedings of the National Academy of Sciences of the United States of America*, **111**(19), 7036–7041.

Young, H. S., McCauley, D. J., Galetti, M., & Dirzo, R. (2016). Patterns, causes, and consequences of Anthropocene defaunation. *Annual Review of Ecology, Evolution, and Systematics*, **47**(1), 333–358.

Yu, H., Wu, J. T., Cowling, B. J., *et al.* (2014). Effect of closure of live poultry markets on poultry-to-person transmission of avian influenza A H7N9 virus: An ecological study. *The Lancet*, **383**(9916), 541–548.

Zapata-Ríos, G., Urgilés, C., & Suárez, E. (2009). Mammal hunting by the Shuar of the Ecuadorian Amazon: Is it sustainable? *Oryx*, **43**(03), 375.

Zeder, M. A. (2012). The Broad Spectrum Revolution at 40: Resource diversity, intensification, and an alternative to optimal foraging explanations. *Journal of Anthropological Archaeology*, **31**(3), 241–264.

Zhang, X., Zhu, C., Lin, H., *et al.* (2007). Wild fulvous fruit bats (*Rousettus leschenaulti*) exhibit human-like menstrual cycle 1. *Biology of Reproduction*, **77**(2), 358–364.

Zhou, P., Yang, X.-L., Wang, X.-G., *et al.* (2020). A pneumonia outbreak associated with a new coronavirus of probable bat origin. *Nature*, **579**(7798), 270–273.

Ziegler, S. (2010). Application of food balance sheets to assess the scale of the bushmeat trade in Central Africa. *TRAFFIC Bulletin*, **22**(3), 105–116.

Ziegler, S., Fa, J. E., Wohlfart, C., Streit, B., Jacob, S., & Wegmann, M. (2016). Mapping bushmeat hunting pressure in Central Africa. *Biotropica*, **48**(3), 405–412.

Zohdy, S., Schwartz, T. S., & Oaks, J. R. (2019). The coevolution effect as a driver of spillover. *Trends in Parasitology*, **35**(6), 399–408.

Index

CPSIA information can be obtained
at www.ICGtesting.com
Printed in the USA
LVHW081642240822
726743LV00008B/303